JN413202

반석

TOEFL 급상승

Reading 스타트

기영석(Mike Ki)

- 미국 캘리포니아 주립대학원 정치학과 졸업
- 민병철 어학원 TOEFL(유학준비반) 강의
- 종로엘리트 학원 TOEFL(대입영어 특차전형반) 강의
- 가천대, 한성대 영어강의
- (현) MK영어교육 대표

Kevin Were

- 호주 뉴잉글랜드 대학원 응용언어학과 졸업
- 이지어학원 TOEFL(외고대비반) 강의
- 한성대학교 TOEFL(고급과정) 강의
- 건국대, 홍익대 영어강의
- (현) 국민대학원 영문과 조교수

반석

TOEFL 급상승 Reading 스타트 [기본강의서]

저 자 기영석 · Kevin Were
발행인 고본화
발 행 반석출판사
2016년 2월 10일 초판 1쇄 인쇄
2016년 2월 15일 초판 1쇄 발행
홈페이지 www.bansok.co.kr
이메일 bansok@bansok.co.kr
블로그 blog.naver.com/bansokbooks

157-779 서울시 강서구 양천로 583번지 B동 904호
　　　(서울시 강서구 염창동 240-21번지 우림블루나인 비즈니스센터 B동 904호)
대표전화 02) 2093-3399 **팩 스** 02) 2093-3393
출 판 부 02) 2093-3395 **영업부** 02) 2093-3396
등록번호 제315-2008-000033호

Copyright ⓒ 기영석 · Kevin Were

ISBN 978-89-7172-789-8 (13740)

- 교재 관련 문의: bansok@bansok.co.kr을 이용해 주시기 바랍니다.
- 이 책에 게재된 내용의 일부 또는 전체를 무단으로 복제 및 발췌하는 것을 금합니다.
- 파본 및 잘못된 제품은 구입처에서 교환해 드립니다.

반석 TOEFL Reading 스타트

Bansok

iBT 토플 Reading을 포함하여 모든 독해는 정확하고 빠른 이해력을 요구합니다. 정확하고 빠른 독해를 위해서 무엇이 중요할까요? 우선 많은 어휘를 문맥에 맞게 알아야 합니다. 어휘는 전투에서의 총탄이라고 할 수 있습니다. 하지만 개별 어휘만으로는 해석이나 독해가 가능하지 않습니다.

총탄만으로 전투를 치를 수 없듯, 어휘와 함께 무기가 될 수 있는 문법이 필요합니다. 독해를 위한 문법은 연관된 어휘, 구, 절 사이에서 핵심어와 세부어를 구분하는 데 주로 활용할 수 있습니다. 의미 단위의 끊어읽기, 긴 주어와 목적어, 본동사를 찾는 훈련, 핵심어와 세부어의 수식관계의 연관성 파악이 필요합니다. 그래서 이 책에서는 끊어읽기와 그려읽기를 강조하였습니다.

다음으로 총을 다루는 기술을 알아야겠죠. 어휘와 문법이 갖추어졌다면 Skimming(스키밍), Scanning(스캐닝), Paraphrasing(패러프레이징)이 바로 총을 다루는 기술에 해당합니다.

저자는 위의 방법으로 정확하고 빠른 독해를 위한 체력을 키우는 데 이 책의 초점을 두었습니다. 단순히 눈으로 문제만 풀어서는 독해력 향상을 기대할 수 없습니다. 우선 어휘를 여러 번 써서 암기하고, 토플 실전유형의 문제에 대해 끊어읽기와 그려읽기, Skimming, Scanning, Paraphrasing을 하는 습관을 들여야 합니다. 그리고 힘들고 귀찮더라도 본문의 한역과 영역을 반복 대조하는 노력이 필요합니다.

이 책의 단계별 훈련을 통해 체계적이고 효과적인 독해력 향상이 이루어지기 기원합니다.

2016년 2월
어머니를 그리며, 기영석 · Kevin Were 드림

CONTENTS

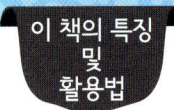
Section 01 Powerful Reading Skills

토플 초급자들에게 반드시 필요한 빠른 독해를 위한 기본기를 다질 수 있다. 매 유닛(끊어읽기 / 그려읽기 / **Skimming** / **Scanning** / **Paraphrasing**)마다 문장의 정확한 분석을 위한 **Quick Check**과 30여 개의 연습문제를 실었다. 특히 지문의 속독능력과 신속한 정보 찾기 능력을 향상시키는 데 많은 도움이 되게 구성했다.

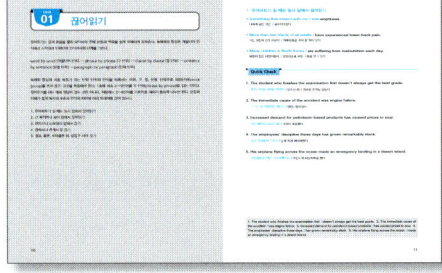

Section 02 Types of Questions

섹션 1을 토대로 하여 실전에서 출제되는 여러 문제 유형을 자세하게 접할 수 있다. 여기서는 문제를 **Sentence Simplification** / **Fact** & **Negative Fact** / **Vocabulary** / **Reference** / **Rhetorical Purpose** / **Inference** / **Insertion** / **Summary** / **Category Chart** 등의 9개의 유형으로 분류했다.

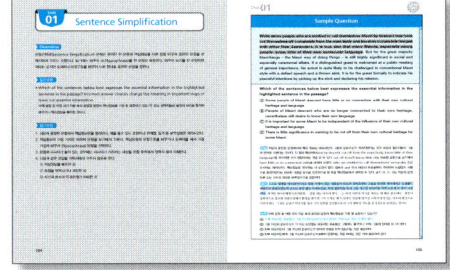

매 유닛마다 문제유형에 맞춘 샘플문제를 제시했고, 연습문제 2개와 실전문제 2개를 실었다.

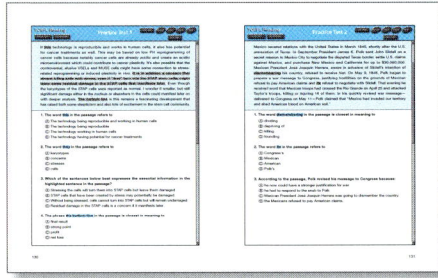

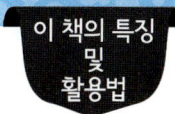

Section 03 Themes

10개의 주제 History / Environment / Economy /
Society / Computer / Nature / Education /
Culture / Science & Technology /
Art & Literature를 통해 실전감각을 길러보자.

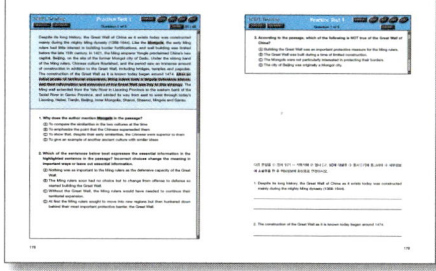

매 유닛마다 다양한 유형의 실전문제가 5개씩
실려 있고, Vocabulary & Paraphrasing란에는
주제별 필수어휘와 바꿔쓰기를 할 수 있는
연습문제를 담았다.

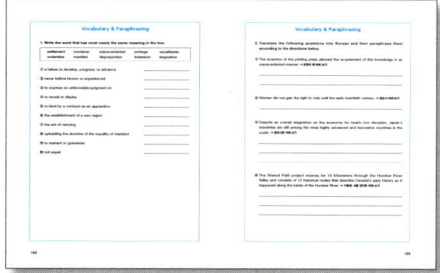

Powerful Reading Skills

독해의 목적은 읽은 내용을 빨리 정확하게 이해하는 것이다. 이를 위해서 두 가지 방법으로 읽기훈련을 할 수 있다. 하나는 문장을 의미단위(sense group)로 끊어 읽는 것이며, 다른 하나는 의미단위의 관계를 그리며 읽는 것이다. 끊어읽기는 빠른 독해에, 그려읽기는 특히 내용의 정확한 이해에 도움이 된다.

끊어읽기

끊어읽기는 글의 흐름을 빨리 파악하여 전체 문장의 맥락을 쉽게 이해하게 도와준다. 독해력의 향상은 개별단어 인식에서 시작하여 단락단위 인식까지의 단계를 거친다.

word by word (개별단어 단위) → phrase by phrase (구 단위) → clause by clause (절 단위) → sentence by sentence (문장 단위) → paragraph by paragraph (단락 단위)

독해력 향상의 최종 목표가 되는 단락 단위의 인식을 위해서는 어휘, 구, 절, 문장, 단락으로 의미단위(sense group)를 먼저 끊고, 그것을 확장해야 한다. 1초에 최소 4~5단어를 구 단위(phrase by phrase)로 읽는 것이다. 끊어읽기를 하는 데에 정답이 있는 것은 아니다. 처음에는 3~4단어를 기본으로 의미가 통하게 나누면 된다. 문장의 이해가 쉽게 독자의 수준과 인식의 차이에 따라 아래처럼 끊어 읽는다.

1. 주어파트가 길 때는 동사 앞에서 끊어읽기
2. 긴 목적어나 보어 앞에서 끊어읽기
3. 전치사나 to부정사 앞에서 끊어읽기
4. 접속사나 관계사 앞 끊어읽기
5. 쉼표, 콜론, 세미콜론 뒤, 삽입구 사이 끊어읽기

1. 주어파트가 길 때는 동사 앞에서 끊어읽기

• **Something that stayed with me / was emptiness.**
나에게 남은 것은 / 공허감이었다.

• **More than two-thirds of all adults / have experienced lower-back pain.**
모든 성인의 2/3 이상이 / 하부요통을 겪어 본 적이 있다.

• **Many children in North Korea / suffer from malnutrition each day.**
북한의 많은 어린이들이 / 영양실조로 매일 고통을 받고 있다.

Quick Check

1. **The student who finishes the examination first doesn't always get the best grade.**
먼저 시험을 마치는 학생이 / 반드시 최고 점수를 받지는 않는다.

2. **The immediate cause of the accident was engine failure.**
그 사고의 직접적인 원인은 / 엔진고장이었다.

3. **Increased demand for petroleum-based products has caused prices to soar.**
석유제품의 수요증가로 / 가격이 폭등했다.

4. **The employees' discipline these days has grown remarkably slack.**
요즘 직원들의 기강이 / 눈에 띄게 해이해졌다.

5. **His airplane flying across the ocean made an emergency landing in a deserted island.**
대양횡단을 하던 그의 비행기는 / 무인도에 비상착륙을 했다.

1. The student who finishes the examination first / doesn't always get the best grade. 2. The immediate cause of the accident / was engine failure. 3. Increased demand for petroleum-based products / has caused prices to soar. 4. The employees' discipline these days / has grown remarkably slack. 5. His airplane flying across the ocean / made an emergency landing in a desert island.

01. The art form of the opera was first developed in Italy.

_____

02. Hundreds of children in African villages are infected by malaria each day.

_____

03. The instabilities in the Earth's magnetic field are caused by solar wind.

_____

04. The best way to improve your performance is always to practice.

_____

05. A child that always receives sympathy often cries over little troubles.

_____

06. Finding financial partners to defray the expenses is very important for some studios.

_____

07. Steve Jobs' most important contribution to American IT business was his introduction of the iPhone.

_____

08. The increasing importance of the media is particularly observed in election campaigns.

_____

09. The collapse of Soviet Union in the 1990s provided an important lesson for communist China.

_____

10. The idea of the death penalty in that situation doesn't make sense to me at all.

_____

11. One way of satisfying this curiosity is through travel.

_____

12. People all around the world spend an average of 1.1 hours on the road each day.

_____

13. The instabilities in the Earth's ozone layer are being caused by global warming.

_____

14. The number of hunting accidents has increased sharply these days.

_____

15. Ignoring other people and their advice has eventually made me more popular.

_____

16. People who ask you for money will ask for more if you do them a favor.

_____

17. The student who finishes the test last often receives a perfect grade.

_____

18. The deeply philosophical question of "why God created us" was put to some students.

_____

19. Bill Gates' most precious contribution to mankind is his development of the Windows platform.

_____

20. The jobs that most companies provide in information and technology today would have not been available several decades ago.

_____

21. Much of the scholarship of early women's studies went into documenting the invidious nature of sexual differences.

_____

22. A list of authorized service depots is packaged with the appliance.

_____

23. Significant numbers of youngsters are growing up in poverty.

_____

24. The rights of the individual are the most important rights in a free society.

_____

25. The quick recognition of disease is important to identify effective treatment.

_____

26. The first indication of an anomaly occurred three minutes before the plane crash.

_____

27. The first semester of freshman year was the hardest year in dealing with organization.

_____

28. Accurate oven temperature and baking times are critical.

_____

29. Her hesitation about signing the contract was based on financial concerns.

_____

30. A company representative from the oil company talked about the oil spill.

_____

2. 긴 목적어나 보어 앞에서 끊어읽기

• **Many people complain** / that they don't have enough time to read cultural books.
많은 사람들은 ~에 대해 불평한다 / 교양도서를 읽을 시간이 없다는 것

• **A cup of coffee in the morning has become** / a part of my daily life since I got married.
아침에 마시는 커피 한 잔은 ~가 되었다 / 결혼 한 후 나의 일상생활의 일부

• **The Crusades were** / a series of religious wars between European Christians and Muslims of the Middle East.
십자군 전쟁은 ~이었다 / 유럽의 기독교와 중동의 이슬람교 사이에 연속된 종교전쟁

Quick Check

1. The period before the Renaissance was the Middle Ages, which lasted for about 1000 years.
르네상스 이전의 시기는 ~이었다 / 약 1,000년간 지속된 중세시대

2. The good news for her children is their symptoms are not serious and can be easily treated with medicine.
그녀의 아이들에게 좋은 소식은 ~이다 / 그들의 증상이 심각하지 않고 약으로 쉽게 치료될 수 있다는 것

3. People tend to form their first impressions on the basis of how you look.
사람들은 ~을 형성하는 경향이 있다 / 보이는 외모에 근거를 두어 첫 인상

4. Keeping discipline is a key part of a teacher's responsibilities.
훈육을 하는 일은 ~이다 / 선생님의 책임중의 중요한 부분

5. They insist on the right of Palestinians to return to their land.
그들은 ~를 주장한다 / 팔레스타인 주민들이 그들의 영토로 돌아갈 수 있는 권리

1. The period before the Renaissance was / the Middle Ages, which lasted for about 1000 years. 2. The good news for her children is / their symptoms are not serious and can be easily treated with medicine. 3. People tend to form / their first impressions on the basis of how you look. 4. Keeping discipline is / a key part of a teacher's responsibilities. 5. They insist on / the right of Palestinians to return to their land.

01. Some people don't believe that well begun is half done.

_____

02. Vincent refused to accept my invitation to the garden party tonight.

_____

03. You see now how foolish you are to say so.

_____

04. The desire for profit motivates employers to operate their shops efficiently.

_____

05. The speaker showed his knowledge of the subject by his excellent lecture.

_____

06. Our staff members are people who take pride in their work and support each other.

_____

07. The US government has decided to make a shift in its Asia-conscious foreign policy.

_____

08. My father has a miscellaneous collection of coins, stamps, and many other things.

_____

09. Some of the neutral countries tried to get the warlike nations to discuss the terms of peace.

_____

10. The President of the United States found out that maintaining security on the Korean Peninsular is not an easy task.

_____

11. That is why I appreciate coming across poetry in everyday life.

_____

12. Columbia is one of the most dangerous countries in the world for journalists.

_____

13. Few people are aware that our government is suffering from budget shortages.

_____

14. The essential role of hand gestures is to mark the points of emphasis in our speech.

_____

15. The most important issue facing these Muslim countries is understanding the differences among cultures.

_____

16. The best policy in the present situation is that we should be honest enough to tell the truth.

_____

17. The two Koreas should learn the lesson of peaceful reunification from East and West Germany.

_____

18. The American Revolution was a war between England and the American colonies of England.

_____

19. Some hand gestures are used when we want to express ourselves with great emphasis.

_____

20. One of the most challenging experiences in my life was climbing to the top of Mount Everest in Nepal last summer.

_____

21. I think the key thing is that both of the parties work together.

_____

22. These giant jigsaws contain air-filled cavities not easily penetrated by sound.

_____

23. People don't know much about the history of the Vatican.

_____

24. The computer is one of the most widely used scientific tools.

_____

25. They insist that the rights of animals be acknowledged and respected.

_____

26. The Renaissance was a rebirth of ideas and morality.

_____

27. The good news is that most cases are not serious and can be easily treated with medicine.

_____

28. The research shows that pre-school children are capable of thinking in abstract terms.

_____

29. She commended the steadfast courage of families caring for handicapped children.

_____

30. The Mayan civilization is one of the best-known civilizations that existed in the Americas.

_____

3. 전치사나 to부정사 앞에서 끊어읽기

- **This monument was built /** (in) **memory of the first principal of the school.**
  이 기념비는 만들어졌다 / 초대 교장을 기념하여

- ***There* are no clothing shops /** (near) **the university that I graduated from.**
  옷가게가 없다 / 내가 졸업한 대학교 근처에는

- **Mom sent her son to the door /** (to tell) **the salesperson that she is not at home.**
  어머니는 아들을 문간으로 보냈다 / 외판원에게 엄마가 집에 없다고 말을 하라고

Quick Check

1. **My father has provided me with whatever is needed in order to achieve my academic goals.**
   아버지는 필요한 것은 무엇이든 해주셨다 / 나의 학구적인 목표를 성취하기 위해

2. **I'd like to congratulate you on your remarkable achievements in college.**
   나는 축하하고 싶다 / 대학에서 이룬 탁월한 성과에 대해

3. **This information is used to determine how weight is distributed when a patient walks.**
   이 정보는 사용된다 / 환자가 걸을 때 무게가 어떻게 분산되는지를 측정하는데

4. **The best way to build up your stamina is to work out everyday.**
   체력을 강화하는 가장 좋은 방법은 ~이다 / 매일같이 운동 하는 것

5. **'Kidfluence' describes the secondary influence of children on their parents spending.**
   '키드플루언스'는 간접적인 영향을 설명한다 / 자녀들이 그들의 부모의 소비에 미치는

---

1. My father has provided me with whatever is needed / in order to achieve my academic goals. 2. I'd like to congratulate you / on your remarkable achievements in college. 3. This information is used / to determine how weight is distributed when a patient walks. 4. The best way to build up your stamina is / to work out everyday. 5. "Kidfluence" describes the secondary influence / of children on their parents spending.

01. We had to go to the airport by taxi in order not to miss the flight to Vancouver.

_____

02. He inspired people to make peaceful protests and disobey the British laws.

_____

03. We are looking for opportunities to improve organizational and operational efficiencies.

_____

04. The authors are to be congratulated on producing such a clear and authoritative work.

_____

05. The earth was entirely covered by a warm water ocean, and pelted by ceaseless rain.

_____

06. Most American voters are divided into two camps, Republicans and Democrats.

_____

07. Major changes in tax and spending policies are in the offing for the first time in 11 years.

_____

08. We should carefully think about the reason for someone's behavior to avoid coming to a hasty conclusion about it.

_____

09. The federal government had control over the states, industry, trade and slavery.

_____

10. The fireman rescued the baby within a measurable distance of the building collapse.

_____

11. I had a hard time convincing him to turn himself in to the police.

_____

12. A large dose of poison was detected in the dead man's stomach.

_____

13. Plenty of exercise is the best way to lose weight without any side effects.

_____

14. Mexican immigration to the U.S. has increased greatly in recent decades.

_____

15. Most Americans make it a rule to make an appointment before their visit.

_____

16. It was not that easy for Monica to forget the past and make a fresh start.

_____

17. You must be out of your mind to believe such nonsense and act in that way.

_____

18. The depression in the United States lasted until the beginning of the Second World War.

_____

19. The spider-monkey's tail can be used to pick up fruit or grab the branches of trees.

_____

20. The commuting time is usually longer for suburban residents than for those living in the city.

_____

21. The personal computer was first developed by Steve Jobs in the United States.

_____

22. You must always work hard in anything and everything to survive to the end.

_____

23. The media plays a very important role in election campaigns across the world.

_____

24. Don't come up with the evil intention of using the Internet during the exams.

_____

25. I'd like to congratulate you on your remarkable achievements in college.

_____

26. A father wanted to show his son how to farm without agricultural chemicals.

_____

27. The senator is accused of accepting bribes in exchange for using his political influence.

_____

28. A recent survey shows that there is a gap between the labor supply and demand in the e-business industry.

_____

29. It is vital to find investment partners to pay for the cost of film production.

_____

30. His articles are thoroughly enjoyable for readers.

_____

4. 접속사나 관계사 앞 끊어읽기

- I can't tolerate my brother's whistling / (while) I am studying.

  동생이 휘파람 부는 것을 참을 수 없다 / 내가 공부할 때

- We can't meet in the conference room tomorrow / (because) another department has taken it.

  우리는 내일 회의실에서 만날 수 없다 / 다른 부서가 그곳을 차지했기 때문에

- I had never expected to see a girl / (as) attractive as Monica in my life.

  모니카는 가장 매력적인 여자였다 / 내가 일생에서 결코 만나리라 기대하지 못했던

Quick Check

1. Predatory lenders prey on those who have a low-level of education.

   악덕 고리업자들은 사람들을 먹잇감으로 삼는다 / 교육수준이 낮은

2. We had a debate during the meeting but eventually came to an agreement.

   우리는 회의에서 논쟁이 있었다 / 하지만 결국 합의를 보았다.

3. It is our illusion that the economy will develop and remain strong for a few decades.

   우리의 착각이다 / 경제가 발전하고 / 수십 년간 견고하게 유지될 것이라는 것은

4. My puppy always was waiting for me all day long at the door, which made me feel sorry for him.

   나의 강아지는 하루 종일 문 앞에서 나를 기다리고 있는데, / 그것이 강아지에게 미안함을 느끼게 했다.

5. You can make a contribution to help the African children who have suffered from malaria attacks.

   당신은 아프리카 아이들을 돕기 위해 기부할 수 있다 / 학질로 시달리는

---

1. Predatory lenders prey on those / who have a low-level of education. 2. We had a debate during the meeting / but eventually came to an agreement. 3. It is our illusion / that the economy will develop / and remain strong for a few decades. 4. My puppy always was waiting for me all day long at the door, / which made me feel sorry for him. 5. You can make a contribution to help the African children / who have suffered from malaria attacks.

영어문장을 끊어읽기 한 후 해석하시오.

01. Choosing a career is a matter which calls for reflection.

_____

02. I know in my bones that I will never break up with Monica.

_____

03. Mike called his girlfriend whose hobby is going to the movies.

_____

04. We started with an argument, but our talks ended with an agreement.

_____

05. She felt very strongly that I should be adopted by college graduates.

_____

06. The number of alligators which they caught each time went down sharply.

_____

07. Amusement parks are packed with people when the weather is nice.

_____

08. The stock market had reached 2700 points but nose-dived to 1900 points in a week.

_____

09. Rumor says that there is a special chemical in this liquid which prevents cancer.

_____

10. Some of the students arrived early and gathered near the main entrance, even though they were not supposed to stay there.

_____

11. The bank acknowledged its error but refused to compensate the customers for their losses.

_____

12. People have lost interest in modern arts and have turned to sports stars and other popular figures to find their role models.

_____

13. His lecture made me focus on what is more important in life.

_____

14. Advertisers change people's thinking by using language which appeals to emotions.

_____

15. Our store has a wide selection of cameras at reasonable prices so you don't have to shop around.

_____

16. A meteorologist is a person who studies the earth's atmosphere to predict weather conditions.

_____

17. The software filters out Internet sites whose content is not suitable for children.

_____

18. The child had suffered what has become known as "battered baby syndrome."

_____

19. At Taiji in Central Japan, they force the dolphins into a small inlet, where the water turns red with their blood.

_____

20. The whole team has autographed the football, which will be used as a prize.

_____

21. They deserve your attention and care, even if all you do is smile and say hello.

_____

22. African slaves began to have the right to claim suffrage and citizenship after the Civil War ended in 1866.

_____

23. Audiences rarely find the speaker interesting and don't try to listen carefully to what he says.

_____

24. There is also a quantity discount, which is offered to individuals who order large quantities of a product.

_____

25. It's quite important for businessmen who are engaged in international trade to learn about different cultures and to learn languages.

_____

26. We were amazed at a magical sunrise, which made me understand why Korea is often called "Land of the Morning Calm."

_____

27. All I ask in return is that you take good enough care of yourself so that someday you can do the same thing for someone else.

_____

28. Most foreign workers are being taught by Korean coworkers or volunteers who have no or little teaching experience.

_____

29. James II soon changed his mind when he found out how attractive the game was, and it immediately became popular again.

_____

30. Place your watch on the table in front of you or keep your eyes on the clock in the back of the room if you don't want to go over the allotted time.

_____

5. 쉼표, 콜론, 세미콜론 뒤, 삽입구 사이 끊어읽기

- I have read the first math problem, / which I can't understand, several times.

  나는 수학 첫 번째 문제를 여러 번 읽었다, / 하지만 이해할 수 없다.

- Everyone makes a mistake once in a while; / no one in this world is infallible.

  누구나 가끔씩 실수를 한다: / 세상에 완벽한 사람은 없다.

- Monica, / who has come late to every meeting we have held, / surprised us today by being punctual.

  모니카가, / 우리가 여는 모임에는 모두 늦게 왔지만, / 오늘은 제시간에 도착해서 우리를 놀라게 했다.

Quick Check

1. The best way to lose weight, without side effects, is plenty of exercise and a balanced diet.

   살을 빼는 가장 좋은 방법은 / 부작용 없이 / 많은 운동과 균형 잡힌 식사이다

2. The truth is, life is rarely exactly the way we want it to be, and other people often don't act as we would like them to.

   진실은 ~이다 / 삶은 좀처럼 우리가 원하는 방식대로 되지 않으며 / 다른 사람들은 종종 우리가 그들이 해주었으며 하는 대로 행동하지는 않는다는 것

3. Pusan, the second largest city in Korea, is famous for its beautiful beaches and the international film festival.

   부산은 / 한국에서 두 번째로 큰 도시인 / 아름다운 해변과 국제영화제로 유명하다

4. In Thailand and other Asian countries, "white elephant" today is a phrase, meaning something that is very expensive and of little use.

   태국과 다른 아시아 국가에서 / 오늘날 '흰색코끼리'는 관용어가 되었다 / 비용이 많이 들면서도 거의 쓸모가 없는 것이라는 의미의

---

1. The best way to lose weight, / without side effects, / is plenty of exercise and a balanced diet. 2. The truth is, / life is rarely exactly the way we want it to be, / and other people often don't act as we would like them to. 3. Pusan, / the second largest city in Korea, / is famous for its beautiful beaches and the international film festival. 4. In Thailand and other Asian countries, / "white elephant" today is a phrase, / meaning something that is very expensive and of little use.

01. The tango, the traditional Argentine dance, has a fascinating history.

_____

02. When the civil war ended in 1866, blacks could receive citizenship and the right to vote.

_____

03. I remember the story of the child, who was adopted and raised by a chimpanzee.

_____

04. As a result, the responsibilities and the discretion of the police have changed.

_____

05. Snake bites, bee stings, and hedgehog spines give their victims a sharp pain.

_____

06. After you hear a question, read the four choices on your test paper, and decide which one is correct.

_____

07. Five young women in the Chinese village, who were waiting for the matchmaker to look them over, were gathered together.

_____

08. It's extremely important to learn different languages and learn about different cultures, especially for those who are in the student exchange programs.

_____

09. Many animals adjust to changes in their environment in ways of finding food, protecting themselves from their enemies, and reproducing.

_____

10. Each year, Brazilians all over the country celebrate Carnival, a month long holiday, with dancing, parades, extravagant costumes, and traditional food.

_____

11. I say follow your bliss and don't be afraid, and doors will open when you don't expect them to.

_____

12. Alberto Giacometti, known as a sculptor of tall, haunting, stick-like figures, was born in 1901 in Borgonovo.

_____

13. The consonant "C" was left off; but I realized that the tears that flowed with Tiffany's declaration made me the wealthiest woman in the world.

_____

14. Sir Francis Drake, who was an English explorer, privateer, and pirate, was the first English man to sail around the world.

_____

15. Buying packs of cigarettes everyday costs a lot of money in the long run; moreover, smoking causes various diseases including cancer.

_____

16. A rich man once asked a friend, "Why am I criticized for being miserly?"

_____

17. The issues that were brought up included air pollution, ozone depletion, and global warming.

_____

18. He kept persuading juries, under disadvantages, and finally proved his innocence.

_____

19. Grayson Bank is expected to announce, as early as tomorrow, that it is pulling its merger offer.

_____

20. Warning: You are about to change your Internet settings. If you wish to continue click "OK," otherwise click "Cancel."

_____

21. Having watched the news on TV, I know about the suicide bombing in Iraq.

_____

22. I used to be very active when I was in college – going hiking, horseback riding, canoeing – but I haven't done any of those things in years.

_____

23. The Great Depression, which started in 1929 in the United States, was a severe economic crisis.

_____

24. If you have finished selecting a topic for your assignment, please begin the research project with your group members.

_____

25. The work of the housewife is varied; she cleans, washes, cooks, and takes care of the children.

_____

26. The purpose of our business is to sell products, to offer the best follow-up service, and to make profits.

_____

27. After you fill out a brief online subscription form, your free publications will start arriving at your door.

_____

28. While he was in Mongolia, the archaeologist found fossils, which turned out to be dinosaur fossils.

_____

29. I had easily answered all the questions until I read the last one: "What is the name of the woman who manages the school?"

_____

30. Over 10 million people all over the world enjoy celebrating the Rio Carnival every year, which is also called the Samba Festival, a month long holiday of dancing Samba.

_____

그려읽기

그려읽기는 구문의 이해를 높여 정확하게 이해할 수 있도록 해주며, 단어와 구의 관계를 파악하는 것이다. 그려읽기를 하는 방법은 다음과 같다.

첫째, 먼저 본동사 [구](조동사와 to부정사, 현재분사, 과거분사, 동명사 등의 준동사 포함)를 찾아 동그라미를 그린다. 주절에 핵심정보(key information)가 들어 있기 때문에 문장을 이끄는 주절(main clause)의 본동사 [구]를 찾는다. 동사는 주부와 술부를 구분하고 연결시켜준다. 사람으로 보면 뇌와 신체 부위를 연결시켜주는 신경세포의 역할을 하므로 중요하다. 동사구를 찾으면 주어를 파악하고 동사에 따라 그 뒤에 무슨 내용이 올 수 있을지 예측이 가능하다. 또한 동사는 문장의 밑그림(내용)을 그려주는 역할을 한다.

둘째, 명사를 뒤에서 수식하는 긴 형용사 [구와 절]에 소괄호를 치고 명사로 화살표를 한다. 영어는 결론(핵심정보)이 먼저 나오고 세부적인 정보가 뒤에 나오는 구조이다. 따라서 수식어가 주로 핵심어를 뒤에서 꾸며준다. 긴 형용사가 명사의 뒤에서 꾸며준다는 것이다. 긴 수식어는 앞의 명사를 설명하는 세부정보이므로 결론(핵심정보)을 찾기 위해 소괄호를 친다.

셋째, 동사 뒤에서 수식하는 긴 부사 [구와 절]에 소괄호를 치고 동사로 화살표를 한다. 부사는 동사를 주로 꾸며준다. 긴 형용사(형용사구와 절)가 뒤에서 명사를 수식하는 것처럼 긴 부사도 주로 동사를 뒤에서 꾸며 준다. 동사 역시 결론(핵심정보)이 먼저 나오고 세부적인 정보가 뒤에 나오는 구조이다. 긴 수식어는 앞의 동사에 속하는 세부정보이므로 결론(핵심정보)을 찾기 위해 소괄호를 치는 것이 필요하다.

넷째, 긴 명사 [구와 절]는 대괄호를 친다. 명사는 문장에서 주어와 목적어와 보어로 중요하게 쓰인다. 그런데 단어가 아닌 구나 절로 나오는 경우가 적지 않다. 이런 명사구나 명사절 등의 긴 명사를 하나로 묶어 이해하여야 문장의 구조가 보이므로 대괄호를 치도록 한다.

다섯째, 연결어에 세모를 친다. 연결어는 독해의 흐름과 주장을 이어주거나 바꾸어 준다. 따라서 글의 결론을 다르게 만들기도 하므로 확인한다. 예를 들어 Such as나 For example, For instance 뒤에는 부가정보가 나오므로 가볍게 넘어갈 수 있다. 하지만 Although, While, But, In spite of, Despite, Nevertheless, Actually, However, On the other hand나 Therefore, Consequently, As a result, Thus, Hence, Accordingly 같은 연결어 뒤에는 흐름이 바뀌거나 결론이 주로 나오므로 주의해야 한다.

1. 본동사구에 동그라미

- Some teenagers (work for) their money rather than wait for their parents to hand it to them.

  어떤 10대들은 부모님이 그들에게 돈을 건네주는 것을 기다리기보다 스스로 돈을 벌려고 (일을 한다).

- The psychology of dying and death (is fascinating) but (not well understood)

  죽음과 죽음의 심리학은 (매력적이지만 쉽게 이해가 되지 않는다).

- The "cumbia" (was created) by African slaves who were brought to the hot regions of the country to work in the gold mines.

  '쿰비아 음악'은 금광에서 일하기 위해 더운 지역으로 이송된 아프리카 노예에 의해 (만들어졌다)

Quick Check

1. Compared to the past, the international meeting that some companies used to have is now possible with computer-based video conferencing.

   과거와 비교하여, 몇몇 회사들이 했던 국제회의는 이제 컴퓨터로 하는 화상회의로 가능(하다).

2. I answered hesitatingly that I would never miss such an easy ball again at the World Series.

   나는 주저하며 다시는 월드시리즈에서 그런 쉬운 공을 놓치지 않겠다고 (대답했다).

3. The computer can figure out the most logical order for cutting materials, and so on.

   컴퓨터가 자재 절단 등의 작업에 가장 적합한 논리적인 순서를 (알아낼 수 있다).

4. Solar cells generate electricity directly when struck by sunlight.

   태양 전지들은 햇빛을 받으면 곧 전기를 (발생시킨다)

---

1. Compared to the past, the international meeting that some companies used to have (is) now possible with computer-based video conferencing. 2. I (answered) hesitatingly that I would never miss such an easy ball again at the World Series. 3. The computer (can figure out) the most logical order for cutting materials, and so on. 4. Solar cells (generate) electricity directly when struck by sunlight.

01. Any question seems easier after you get your paper back.

_____

02. In situations like this, I used to lose my temper when I was much younger.

_____

03. When my two daughters went to visit their grandparents, I could be absorbed in reading.

_____

04. Animals ultimately depend on other living things, a supply of plants, to live.

_____

05. Scientists have found a way to extend the life of the fruit fly by as much as one month.

_____

06. This discovery might someday help humans' live longer and without disease.

_____

07. As a consultant, I was supposed to spend about an hour with the department heads discussing their thoughts.

_____

08. Poetry provides us with what is missing in our own lives — the experience of imaginative pleasure.

_____

09. My teacher said that the United States was a colony of Great Britain for about 170 years from the beginning of the 17th century.

_____

10. Microsoft chairman Bill Gates has promised to donate $ 200 million to help libraries in low-income areas throughout America.

_____

11. Many people form their first impression according to how you look.

_____

12. The official unemployment rate has declined modestly over the past year.

_____

13. The leading candidate for President said that America was born in the 18th century out of the bold conviction that we are all created equal.

_____

14. In a study conducted at the university laboratory, the growth of some plants was affected by playing music to them.

_____

15. Developing connections between commerce and culture gives us a chance to lift the fortunes and spirit of people all over the world.

_____

16. A clear introduction should be made, therefore, if you want to build good social relationships with others.

_____

17. Nigeria, a former British colony, is one of the world's largest oil producers, but the oil industry has produced unwanted side effects.

_____

18. It seems that English-speaking people are pretty good at inventing new words by clipping the longer forms or by putting the initials of some words together.

_____

19. Veterans from other countries who had fought in the Korean War were impressed by the Seoul World Cup Stadium and the panoramic views of Seoul from the 63 Building.

_____

20. For many years men caught and killed the blue whales in huge factory ships, so that the number of blue whales decreased from hundreds of thousands to fewer than one thousand.

_____

_____

21. They involve physical skill, strength and endurance.

_____

22. This art and craft with a difference inspires me with a new idea.

_____

23. She realized that her youth and inexperience were being exploited.

_____

24. The programs would provide workers with information about the risk of injuries.

_____

25. Do not experiment with wild flowers unless you are certain they are edible.

_____

26. Sam wanted to stop watching the movie because he found it very boring.

_____

27. They estimate that the trip from downtown to the airport will take less than half an hour.

_____

28. Some cars on the KTX are designated as no smoking areas.

_____

29. I fully acknowledge that there is more than one way to approach an issue.

_____

30. It was so dark that I couldn't distinguish the faces of people right in front of me.

_____

2. 명사 뒤에서 수식하는 긴 형용사 [구와 절]에 소괄호 치고 화살표

- Many bacteria (that live in your body) are actually good for you, while some cause diseases.

  몇몇 박테리아가 질병을 일으키지만 (몸에 사는) 많은 박테리아는 사실 당신에게 도움이 된다.

- The most preposterous fact in this case is the evidence (that suggests he could be a suspect).

  이 사건에서 가장 터무니없는 사실은 (그가 용의자일 수 있다고 말해주는) 증거이다.

- Columbus' belief (which was peculiar to the people in the 16th century) was that the world is round.

  (16세기 사람들에게 이상했던) 콜럼버스의 믿음은 지구가 둥글다는 것이었다.

Quick Check

1. In making a successful school, we must consider the relationships among the people involved in the school community.

   성공적인 학교를 만들고자 할 때 우리는 (학교 공동체에 관련된) 사람들 간의 관계를 고려해야 한다.

2. The wind, which had traveled from the North Pole, where I was going, gave me a taste of the icy climate.

   (내가 향해가고 있던 북극에서 불어온) 바람은 (얼음같이 차가운 기후의) 맛을 보게 했다.

3. A child spoiled too much in his youth will not learn how to be considerate of others' feelings.

   (어렸을 때 너무 응석받이로 키워진) 아이는 남의 감정을 배려하는 방법을 배우지 못 할 것이다.

4. There is serious concern about the amount of herbicides and pesticides used in farming.

   (농업에 이용되는 제초제 및 살충제의 양에 대한) 심각한 우려가 있다.

---

1. In making a successful school, we must consider the relationships among the people (involved in the school community). 2. The wind, (which had traveled from the North Pole, where I was going), gave me a taste (of the icy climate). 3. A child (spoiled too much in his youth) will not learn how to be considerate of others' feelings. 4. There is serious concern (about the amount of herbicides and pesticides used in farming).

Exercise

형용사 [구, 절]에 소괄호를 치고 앞의 명사까지 화살표 하시오.(한글 해석포함)

01. The butterflies which the entomologist found in Africa turned out to be bats.

_____

02. The first emotions surging in Ann's mind were curiosity and jealousy.

_____

03. My father took us to see a naughty bear that caught our attention.

_____

04. The number of deaths caused by traffic accidents has sharply increased since last year.

_____

05. His airplane which was expected to fly across the Atlantic ocean to New York made an emergency landing on a deserted island.

_____

06. The jobs that most companies are doing with information these days were not available.

_____

07. In a laboratory study conducted at the university, some changes in plant growth patterns were brought about by playing music to the plants.

_____

08. The women wearing black and white uniforms are walking down the main street.

_____

09. The importance of chocolate as a food is overshadowed by its universal use as a snack.

_____

10. One of the best ways to lose weight without side effects is a balanced diet with enough exercise.

_____

11. I have a boy who watches commercials on television and then tries to get me to buy every item he has seen.

_____

12. I learned later that we had hit a car coming from the other direction.

_____

13. He doesn't seem like the kind of person that would do something like that.

_____

14. Growing as a person is to travel to places where there are new challenges.

_____

15. People walking down the street street are wearing leather jackets as if they just arrived in a time machine.

_____

16. Peter Thompson, with whom I have a close working relationship, mentioned your name to me and strongly suggested I contact you.

_____

17. The odd thing about our communication is we're more likely to talk about something that is nothing.

_____

18. We conducted a survey of the people who lived near the airport and had complained for years about the noise.

_____

19. I was able for the first time in my life to say the exact thing I wanted to say at the exact moment I wanted to say it.

_____

20. The astronauts will meet the rest of the other Russian crew who have been working at the International Space Station since mid May.

_____

21. Their launch was watched by their families from an observation platform in the cosmodrome located in the steppes of the Central Asian country.

_____

22. The information conveyed in this high-tech manner somehow adds authority to what is conveyed, when in fact the Internet is a global conveyer of unfiltered, unedited, untreated information.

_____

_____

23. One reason most dogs are much happier than most people is that dogs aren't affected by external circumstances the way we are.

_____

24. This asymmetry means females who warn close kin by emitting alarm calls, while males generally do not emit calls.

_____

_____

25. Recent evidence suggests that the common ancestor of Neanderthals and modern people, living about 350,000 years ago, may have already been using pretty sophisticated language.

_____

_____

26. The number of cars exported in 2012 is greater than in 2011, but the average price is not much higher.

_____

27. Gregorio Dati was a successful merchant of Florence, who entered into many profitable partnerships dealing in wool, silk, and other merchandise.

_____

28. This is particularly true among people who might not themselves have access to the Internet but hear a piece of news or gossip from the people around them who do have access.

_____

_____

29. It appears that measures that protect drivers from the consequences of bad driving encourage bad driving.

_____

30. Fast muscle fibers are cells that can contract more quickly and powerfully than slow muscle fibers but fatigue much more easily; they function best for short bursts of intense activity, like weight lifting or sprinting.

_____

_____

3. 동사(준동사) 뒤에서 수식하는 긴 부사 [구와 절]에 소괄호 치고 화살표

- We must ensure that our buildings <u>face</u> south (so that they admit plenty of light).
  우리는 (빛이 많이 들어오도록) 건물이 남쪽으로 <u>향하게 하는</u> 것을 확실히 해야 한다.

- You <u>need to make sure</u> that your passport and visa are valid (before traveling out of the country).
  너는 (해외여행을 떠나기 전에) 여권과 비자가 유효한지 <u>확인해야 한다</u>.

- The Department of transportation <u>banned</u> private cars from entering the bus-only lanes during the morning and evening hours (to promote using public transportation.)
  교통부는 (대중교통이용을 장려하기 위해) 아침과 저녁시간에 자가용들이 버스전용차선에 들어가는 것을 <u>금지했다</u>.

Quick Check

1. Several wealthy businessmen have donated 250 million dollars to charity in the past few years to help those children with heart disease.
   몇몇 부유한 사업가들이 (심장병 어린이들을 돕기 위해) 지난 몇 년간 250만 달러를 자선단체에 <u>기부해왔다</u>.

2. The traces of dissolved salts were gradually concentrated in the shrinking lake as the water evaporated.
   (물이 증발하면서) 미량의 용해된 소금이 줄어드는 호수에 서서히 <u>농축되었다</u>.

3. Most parents don't want their children influenced by TV advertisements or violence.
   대부분의 부모는 그들의 아이들이 (TV 광고나 폭력에 의해) <u>영향 받는</u> 것을 원치 않는다.

4. Busy families use robots to clean their floors so that they can get on with other more interesting things.
   바쁜 가정에서는 (다른 흥미로운 일을 더 많이 할 수 있도록) 바닥을 청소하는 데 로봇을 <u>사용한다</u>.

---

1. Several wealthy businessmen <u>have donated</u> 250 million dollars to charity in the past few years (to help those children with heart disease). 2. The traces of dissolved salts <u>were</u> gradually <u>concentrated</u> in the shrinking lake (as the water evaporated). 3. Most parents don't want their children <u>influenced</u> (by TV advertisements or violence). 4. Busy families <u>use</u> robots to clean their floors (so that they can get on with other more interesting things).

부사 [구, 절]에 소괄호를 치고 앞의 동사(준동사)까지 화살표 하시오.(한글 해석 포함).

01. It is generally accepted that people are motivated by success.

_____

02. You should keep eating fresh fruit and vegetables to prevent diabetes.

_____

03. Employers run their businesses efficiently to get more profits.

_____

04. He spent the whole weekend studying in order to do well on his mid-term exam.

_____

05. They spoke in Korean in the interview after the concert although the team members conducted the concert in Japanese.

_____

06. The Korean government has spent a lot of money and time recently trying to increase the birth rate.

_____

07. The amusement parks in America were always crowded with tourists from Korea when I visited there in 2012.

_____

08. Many housewives feel stressed whenever they think of the upcoming holidays.

_____

09. All the new buildings were built in a modern style so as to accommodate the airport around them.

_____

10. The Vietnamese found themselves continuously fighting against corruption and poverty at the turn of the century.

_____

11. Alex liked sports and loud music a lot like most other kids.

_____

12. I called him several times last night to borrow some money from him.

_____

13. I started teaching English in China as soon as I graduated from university in 1997.

_____

14. King Harold was killed at the Battle of Hastings and his Anglo-Saxon army was defeated.

_____

15. The farmer should change the cow's food slowly so that the cow can adapt to the new food.

_____

16. He could become a major league player quickly as he is determined to create a role for himself and practices very hard.

_____

17. England has not been isolated from Europe throughout its history although it was an island nation.

_____

18. Many animals adapt to their surroundings by scavenging for food, reproducing, and protecting themselves from predators.

_____

19. The pedestrian was lying in the back of the ambulance in agony after a hit-and-run driver knocked him down and drove away.

_____

20. Jeffrey Newell, president of Hartley Hotels, will come this week to speak to local business people about ways to develop international tourism.

_____

21. Elementary biology textbooks help to produce a misleading impression of what perception entails by likening the eye to a camera.

_____

22. Drivers feel less vulnerable and tend to take more chances as safety features are added to vehicles and roads.

_____

23. Scientists can lessen bias by running as many trials as possible and by keeping accurate notes of each observation made.

_____

24. According to recent studies, although praise may encourage children to continue an activity while an adult is watching, they are less likely to continue the activity when the adult leaves or to repeat the activity in the future.

_____

_____

25. However, the disadvantage is shared among all the cattle-owners using the pasture, so that the individual owner suffers only a fraction of the disadvantage.

_____

26. Children who wear protective gear during their games have a tendency to take more physical risks.

_____

27. A black and white cat was sitting in silence at the top of the steps as soon as I opened the front door to look outside.

_____

28. We stood back there in order to see what was going on in the ice cube.

_____

29. Body weight is usually normal or low although people may perceive themselves as being overweight.

_____

30. Henry was convicted of murder and sentenced to life in prison at Ken Wood Court at the beginning of the month.

_____

4. 긴 명사 [구와 절]에 대괄호 치기

• [Whichever one the baby picks up first] is said to show his or her future.
  [아기가 처음으로 집는 것이 무엇이든지, 그것이] 아이의 장래를 보여주는 것이라고 한다.

• This suit has [the perfect combination of stylish good looks and sturdy details].
  이 양복은 [세련되고 멋진 디자인과 견고한 세부마감의 완벽한 조화] 를 이루고 있습니다.

• For parents with teenagers, [having them do well on the university entrance exam] is their biggest concern.
  십대의 자녀를 둔 부모들에게는 [자녀가 대학 입학시험에서 좋은 성적을 거둘 수 있도록 하는 게] 가장 큰 관심사이다.

Quick Check

1. Inspectors from the International Atomic Energy Agency (IAEA) arrived in Korea on September 19 to carry out an investigation into South Korea's nuclear activities.
   [국제원자력기구(IAEA) 사찰단원들]이 9월 19일 [한국의 핵 이용 활동 조사]를 하기 위해 한국에 도착했다.

2. To express feelings when you get stressed is good for your mental health.
   [스트레스를 받을 때 자신의 감정을 표현하는 것]은 정신 건강에 좋습니다.

3. Trying to see the other person's point of view is a good rule in friendship.
   [상대의 견해를 파악하려 노력하는 것]은 우정에 있어 좋은 방법이다.

4. To see the faults of others is easy but to find those of your own is quite hard.
   [남의 잘못을 찾기]는 쉬우나 정작 [자신의 잘못을 찾기]는 어렵다.

---

1. [Inspectors from the International Atomic Energy Agency (IAEA)] arrived in Korea on September 19 to carry out [an investigation into South Korea's nuclear activities.] 2. [To express feelings when you get stressed] is good for your mental health. 3. [Trying to see the other person's point of view] is a good rule in friendship. 4. [To see the faults of others] is easy but [to find those of your own] is quite hard.

01. What makes the neuron so special is its ability to communicate.

_____

02. Restrictions on trade with a country influences its political development.

_____

03. Many people make it a rule not to call on others without an appointment.

_____

04. It's essential for an exchange student to learn different languages and learn about other cultures.

_____

05. You must find what you think is right and do something to achieve it.

_____

06. It is certainly true that the sculpture is grotesque and doesn't match well with the buildings on the street.

_____

07. Isn't it interesting that the Industrial Revolution relied on the ability to transport materials and goods?

_____

08. When you open a bank account here, you will get what is called a "student account" with special concessions for students.

_____

09. The power struggle between the rich and the poor has increased in strength and become more violent since the beginning of the 21st century.

_____

10. Describing the dimensions of a "typical" neuron is not easy at all because these cells come in hundreds of different shapes and sizes - depending on their specific function.

_____

_____

11. Giving up bad habits is not easy, especially when people get older.

_____

12. It seemed obvious until the 15th century that the earth must be flat.

_____

13. Many office workers complain that they don't have enough time for their family.

_____

14. Fifteen minutes in warm water before going to bed helps those who suffer from sleeplessness.

_____

15. Maria didn't know how to express her feelings because it was the first time she had taken the top spot since her debut.

_____

16. Some teenagers earn money by working themselves instead of waiting for an allowance from their parents.

_____

17. The increasing amount of information available to children is hastening the beginning of adulthood for many children these days.

_____

18. Providing up-to-date information about your products will increase your chances of doing better business as more people will visit your site.

_____

19. U.N. Secretary-General Ban Ki-moon realized that encouraging developing countries to join international efforts to fight global warming is not easy.

_____

_____

20. Being with her is as refreshing as a colorful rainbow, a fresh box of crayons or a cool shower on a hot day.

_____

21. Making a good impression during the first meeting is very important.

_____

22. Of course one reason for the decline in newspaper readership is due to the fact we are doing more of our newspaper reading online.

_____

23. China's state-owned media report that the new law, "Law on Penalties for Offenses against Public Order," provides guidelines on how to punish violators for 128 different offenses.

_____

_____

24. Using a computer for long periods can also cause damage to our neck.

_____

25. Making better decisions when picking out jars of jam or bottles of wine is best done with the emotional brain, which generates its verdict automatically.

_____

26. The advantage is that the cattle-owner receives all of the profit from the sale of the additional animal.

_____

27. The appeal to a genetic change driving evolution gets gene-culture co-evolution backwards.

_____

28. In a complex, intellectually demanding and high-pressure task such as that of air traffic controllers, for example, having chronically high anxiety is an almost sure predictor that a person will eventually fail in training or in the field.

_____

_____

5. 연결어에 세모 치기

- The materials are available in limited areas. In addition, they are quite expensive.
  이 물질들은 제한된 지역에서 사용 가능하다. 게다가 이 물질들은 상당히 비싸다.

- The number of animals processed annually has continued to increase, despite the downward trend in meat prices since 2001.
  2001년 이후 고기 가격의 하락 추세에도 불구하고 가공 처리되는 동물의 수는 매년 늘어왔다.

- Poor nutrition is one of the key factors in the symptoms of depression. On the other hand, good nutritional practices dramatically help eliminate the depression symptoms.
  부실한 영양 섭취는 우울증 증세에 있어서 중요한 요소 중 하나이다. 이와는 반대로, 좋은 영양 섭취 습관은 우울증 증세를 제거하는데 상당히 도움을 준다.

Quick Check

1. The theory that color can affect the nervous system in some way seems proven by the results of an experiment. Following this, more people became interested in color therapy, believing that color therapy has positive effects on both their mental and physical wellbeing.
   색이 신경조직에 어떻게든 영향을 끼친다는 이론이 실험결과에 의해 증명되는 듯하다. 그 결과 더 많은 사람들이 색채요법에 관심을 갖게 되었다. 그들은 색채요법이 그들의 정신과 신체건강에 긍정적인 효과를 미친다고 믿는다.

2. The world-wide economic slump is hurting everyone. Despite the downward spiral of the auto industry, people continue to look for new ways to lower gas consumption in cars.
   전 세계적인 불황으로 모든 사람들이 어려움을 겪고 있다. 자동차산업의 급락에도 불구하고 사람들은 자동차 연료소모를 줄이기 위한 새로운 방법들을 찾고 있다.

1. As a result 2. Despite

58

연결어에 세모를 치고 해석하시오.

01. The result is a wide range of regulations for maintaining the Thames as a public amenity. For example, Transport for London plays a role in regulating river use and river users.

_____

_____

02. By 1857, Elizabeth opened a new hospital with her sister who is also a doctor. In addition to this, she also founded the first medical school for women.

_____

_____

03. According to marketing research, there will be 138 million smart TV sets in use in 2015, taking up 47 percent of the TV market. Nevertheless, some analysts, point out that there exist hurdles for the penetration of smart TVs.

_____

_____

04. The Industrial Revolution relied on the ability to transport materials and goods. Hence, the story of the Industrial Revolution is also the story of a revolution in transportation.

_____

_____

05. A recent consumer report said that heavy metals were found in herbal medicines in markets. As a result, sales of herbal medicines have declined for the last three quarters since 2010.

_____

_____

06. No written records were made in prehistoric times by definition. However, we can get some insight into how the world and its mechanisms were understood or interpreted by prehistoric men by direct and indirect evidence.

---

07. The Fisheries Department has reported that the river has again become home to plenty of species of fish including sea bass, flounder, and salmon. Despite the good news, things were not always rosy.

---

08. Clinton saw Gore's election as ratification of his own leadership. For this reason, he did more to help his protege's political fortunes than any president since Theodore Roosevelt.

---

09. Germany's national humiliation after the loss of World War I and the economic depression of the 1930s has received most of the blame for Hitler's popularity. Yet it is more alarming that he polled more voters in a free election than any other German before him.

---

10. Popular belief holds that a rattle snake's age can be told by counting its rings, but this is a fallacy. Actually, the snake may lose its old skin as often as four times a year.

_____

_____

11. The company is currently being challenged by the disqualification of the CEO. On top of the CEO's criminal charges, the company is facing a couple of law suits pending against it.

_____

_____

12. The health plans in turn raise premiums to cover the more expensive costs. In short, the problem with the health insurance structure is that it is too market oriented.

_____

_____

13. According to psychologists, your physical appearance makes up 55% of a first impression. The physical appearance includes facial expression, eye contact, and general appearance.

_____

_____

14. Regarding their marriages, you should know that the only way to have a wife there is to purchase her. For this reason, the girls are often mature when they are married, for the parents always keep them until they sell them.

_____

_____

15. Health care premiums are generally too expensive because of the potential for expensive treatments. On the other hand we are forced to pay all the medical insurance premiums the government has set.

_____

_____

16. Primitive man did not know what time meant. For instance, he kept no records of birthdays or wedding anniversaries or the hour of death. He had no idea of days or weeks or even years either.

_____

_____

17. I can't learn how to use a computer just by reading an instruction manual. However many people seem to learn how to use a computer just by reading the manual. Therefore people learn things in different ways.

_____

_____

18. Some parents only control how long their kids watch television or play computer games while other parents decide what entertainment is appropriate for their children in the age of video cassettes, DVD's, computer games and cable television.

_____

_____

_____

19. Books, clothing, and buildings are some examples of material culture. We have a shared understanding of their purposes and meanings. In contrast, nonmaterial culture consists of human creations that are not physical. Examples of nonmaterial culture are values and customs.

_____

_____

_____

20. In recent years, Colombia has not received much money from its exports. Its major export crop is coffee. But the demand for coffee in the world has dropped. Also, other countries have begun to export more coffee, so the price has fallen. Finally, the Colombian government has encouraged the farmers to produce more food so that the country can become self-sufficient in food; as a result, the farmers have produced less coffee. Because of these factors, Colombia now gets much less cash from its coffee exports than it did ten years ago.

_____

_____

_____

_____

21. His career, however, especially early on, knew the vicissitudes characteristic of Renaissance business. For example, while he was en route to Spain as his enterprise's traveling partner, a role typical for young men, pirates robbed him of all his goods, including a consignment of pearls, and of his own clothes.

_____

_____

_____

22. Getting on a radio playlist was difficult, but once a song was in heavy rotation on the radio, it had a high probability of selling. Then, in the 1980s, came MTV, which became the second way to create a hit.

_____

_____

23. Each person has his or her own truth, and there is distortion on both sides. Therefore, to apologize sincerely we must first listen attentively to how the other person really feels about what happened, not simply assert what we think happened.

_____

_____

_____

24. There is, however, a limit to their benefit. Until recently, even "successful" agriculture failed to guarantee unlimited animal products to the masses. But industrial agriculture changed that, and since 1950, almost anyone in a developed country who could afford a car could also afford to eat meat, dairy products and / or eggs as often as he or she liked.

_____

_____

_____

25. In the mid-1980s, the total aid flow to Egypt from the United States was equivalent to about seven percent of Egypt's economy. Today, it's about point-seven percent. So it's a 10-fold drop as compared to the size of the Egyptian economy. Thus, you don't get much leverage when you're looking at aid flows of point-seven percent the size of the Egyptian economy.

_____

_____

_____

26. A summer of drought in the United States and Russia has reduced expectations of corn and wheat supplies. As a result, the measure of food prices by the U. N Food and Agriculture Organization rose six percent in July. But FAO economist Conception Calpe says the expected reductions did not get any worse in August.

_____

_____

_____

27. The Study has raised new questions about "body mass index", or BMI. Namely, this is a measurement of body fat as a ratio of height to weight. BMI guidelines were used as a basis for the study. Recently, many public health experts have promoted BMI as a way to predict the risk of health problems. However, a person's BMI can be misleading in some cases.

_____

_____

_____

28. Children with parents who didn't read to them were somewhat slow to learn at preschools. Conversely, preschoolers whose parents read to them were better prepared to begin school and performed at higher rates than those not exposed to reading.

_____

_____

_____

29. Nonetheless, some observers say China needs to take steps before it can become the world's biggest economy. Also Patrick believes that several things could affect the country's economic growth. Therefore, China's growth is extremely resource dependent and those resources are becoming scarcer and scarcer. In particular, in northern China, there is a growing scarcity of water which, along with other resource constraints might limit China's prospects of going forward.

_____

_____

_____

_____

30. Some consequences of this unconscious assumption that "good-looking equals good" scare me. For example, a study of the 1974 Canadian federal elections found that attractive candidates received more than two and a half times as many votes as unattractive candidates. Despite such evidence of favoritism toward handsome politicians, follow-up research demonstrated that voters did not realize their bias. In fact, 73 percent of Canadian voters surveyed denied in the strongest possible terms that their votes had been influenced by physical appearance; only 14 percent even allowed for the possibility of such an influence.

_____

_____

_____

_____

스키밍(Skimming)

Skimming은 글의 주제(main idea)를 파악하기 위해 지문을 빨리 훑어보는 것이다. 글의 주제를 찾는다는 점이 세부사항을 찾아 빨리 읽는 Scanning과 구별된다. 대부분의 Reading 문제는 글의 포괄적인 요지 파악 능력이 우선되어야 풀 수 있다. 따라서 Skimming은 Reading에서 대단히 중요하다. 주제를 찾기 위해서는 글을 훑어 읽으면서 주제문(topic sentence)과 반복되는 핵심어(keyword)를 찾는 것이 중요하다. Skimming을 요구하는 TOEFL의 문제유형은 주로 문장간단화(Sentence Simplification), 추론(Inference), 수사적 의도파악(Rhetorical Purpose), 요약표 완성(Summary) 등이다. Skimming이 필요한 문제들은 지문의 속독능력을 요구하는 데, 다음과 같은 글의 구조를 파악하면 Skimming을 더욱 빨리 할 수 있다.

Sentence Structure

Topic sentence Supporting sentences **main idea at the beginning**	Introduction or General statement **Topic sentence** Supporting sentences **main idea in the middle**
Introduction or General statement Supporting sentences **Topic sentence** **main idea at the end**	**Topic sentence** Supporting sentences **Topic sentence** **main idea at the beginning & at the end**

1. In the old societies where courts and judges simply didn't exist, self-help was necessary and socially acceptable in disputes. For instance, when a cow was stolen, the owner's friends and relatives got together and helped him get the animal back. In small villages, everyone, in a sense, became a judge; in such societies, where people's neighbors were also friends, members of their families, or co-workers, the opinions of the villagers were very important. For this, social disapproval of people's activities could serve both as powerful punishment for and as strong deterrent to crime.

Topic Sentence In the old societies where courts and judges simply didn't exist, self-help was necessary and socially acceptable in disputes.

Sentence Structure T(Topic sentence) → S(Supporting sentences)

해석 법원이나 재판관이 존재하지 않는 오래된 사회에서 분쟁이 발생했을 때 자구행위는 필요했으며 사회적으로 받아들여졌다. 예를 들어 소 한 마리를 도난당했을 때, 그 소의 주인과 친구들과 친척들이 함께 모여 그 소를 찾는 일을 도와줬다. 어떤 의미에서 작은 마을 사람들 모두는 재판관이 되었다. 즉, 이웃들이 친구들이거나 가족의 일원이고 협력자들인 사회에서 마을 사람들의 의견은 매우 중요했다. 그래서 사람들의 행동에 대한 그 사회의 불인정은 범죄에 대한 강력한 처벌과 강한 억지책의 역할을 할 수 있었다.

2. One of the most cutting-edge technologies used to control prosthetic limbs is called targeted muscle reinnervation (TMR). In the procedure, the amputated nerves are redirected to control a substitute healthy muscle elsewhere in the body. For example, the surgeon might attach the same nerves that once controlled an arm to a portion of the chest muscles. After this procedure, when the patient attempts to move his or her amputated arm, the control signals traveling through the original arm nerve will now cause a portion of chest muscles to contract instead. This is valuable, because the electrical activity of these muscles can be sensed with electrodes and used to provide control signals to a prosthetic limb. The end result is that just by thinking of moving the amputated arm, a patient causes the prosthetic arm to move instead. This is a ground-breaking technology that gives hope to disabled patients.

Topic Sentence One of the most cutting-edge technologies used to control prosthetic limbs is called targeted muscle reinnervation (TMR). This is a ground-breaking technology that gives hope to disabled patients.

Sentence Structure T(Topic sentence) → S(Supporting sentences) → T(Topic sentence)

해석 팔 보철을 통제하기 위해 사용된 가장 최첨단 기술 중 하나는 선별근육재생(TMR)이라고 불려진다. 수술과정 동안에 절단된 신경들이 몸 전체에 있는 대체된 건강한 근육을 조절하기 위해 전용된다. 예를 들면, 한때 팔을 조절했던 같은 신경들을 가슴 근육에 붙일 수도 있다. 이 과정 후에 환자가 그 또는 그녀의 절단된 팔을 사용하려고 시도했을 때 원래의 팔 신경을 통해 움직이는 조절 시그널은 이제 가슴 근육 부분에 대신 수축을 일으킬 것이다. 이것은 이 근육들의 전기적인 활동이 전극판으로 분별될 수 있고, 팔 보철에 조절 시그널을 제공하는 데 사용되기 때문에 가치가 있다. 최종 결과는 절단된 팔을 움직인다고 생각하는 것만으로 환자들은 대신 팔 보철을 움직이게 하는 원인이 된다. 이것은 장애가 있는 환자들에게 희망을 주는 획기적인 기술이다.

01. The worst thing about society silencing the expression of an opinion is that it is robbing the human race. This harms people in the future as well as the existing generation. It harms those who disagree with the opinion, as well as those who believe in it. If the opinion is right, we all miss the chance to learn the true idea. If it is wrong, we all lose because we can not gain a better idea of the truth, which we could learn from having a debate about the idea.

Topic Sentence

_____

_____

Sentence Structure

_____

_____

02. Economists cling to the idea that human labor and machinery create only value, because they believe in the paradigm of permanent and unlimited material progress. But we know from the 2nd Law of Thermodynamics that every time energy of any sort is used to make something of value, it is done at the expense of creating even greater disorder and waste. We also know that even the things of value that we make eventually end up as waste or dissipated energy. Thus, there is no such thing as "material" progress in the sense of accumulating a "permanent" store of usable goods, for everything we make in the world eventually ends up as dust in the wind.

Topic Sentence

_____

_____

Sentence Structure

_____

03. It was chiefly in the eighteenth century that a very different conception of history grew up. Historians then came to believe that their task was not so much to paint a picture as to solve a problem; to explain or illustrate the successive phases of national growth, prosperity, and adversity. The history of morals, of industry, of intellect, and of art; the changes that take place in manners or beliefs; the dominant ideas that prevailed in successive periods; the rise, fall, and modification of political constitutions; in a word, all the conceptions of national well-being became the subjects of their work. They sought to write more a history of peoples than a history of kings. They looked especially in history for the chain of causes and effect. This change by the historians in the eighteenth century contributed to developing the welfare of the society in their states.

Topic Sentence

_____

Sentence Structure

_____

04. A technology revolution is fast replacing human beings with machines in virtually every sector and industry in the global economy. Already, millions of workers have been permanently eliminated from the economic process, and whole work categories and job assignments have shrunk, been restructured, or disappeared. Global unemployment has now reached its highest level since the great depression of the 1930s. More than 800 million human beings are now unemployed or underemployed in the world. That figure is likely to rise sharply between now and the turn of the century as millions of new entrants into the workforce find themselves without jobs.

Topic Sentence

_____

_____

Sentence Structure

_____

05. Space is a frontier that mankind has sought to conquer for many years, but up until now if the average person entertained the idea of venturing into space within their lifetime they would not have been taken seriously by most, if not all, reasonable people. However, within the last few months several events have taken place that may lead that reasonable person to rethink his position on the matter of privately funded civilian space travel. All this is now possible because a few people who shared a common goal gathered together and decided to further their cause for the benefit of all mankind. The X PRIZE Foundation was established in 1994 as an educational nonprofit organization dedicated to inspiring private, entrepreneurial advancements in space travel, and the sole purpose of its founders was to realize the dream of spaceflight for the general public. What a great place the world would be if men like these were more common.

Topic Sentence

_____

Sentence Structure

_____

06. We should further reduce our excessive reliance on prisons by making extensive use of alternatives to imprisonment, such as fines, restitution, and other probationary methods, which could at least as effectively meet society's need for legal sanctions. However, such alternatives must be made available to all people who have committed similar offenses, so as not to become a means for the more affluent to buy their way out of prison. And where some kind of confinement seems necessary, halfway houses, community centers, group homes, and other methods of keeping offenders within the community should be preferred to prison.

Topic Sentence

_____

_____

Sentence Structure

_____

Unit 04 스캐닝(Scanning)

Scanning은 질문과 관련된 필요한 내용만을 찾아 정확하고 빠른 속도로 읽는 것을 말한다. 우리가 인터넷 검색을 할 때 키워드로 정보를 찾거나 식당 메뉴에서 원하는 메뉴를 빠르게 선택하는 것과 비슷하다. Scanning에서는 특정정보를 찾기 위해 필요 없는 정보를 빨리 훑어 지나가야 한다. 빗자루로 쓸어 내듯이 최대한 빨리 읽어 나가며 필요한 정보를 찾기 때문에 집중도와 이해도를 향상시킬 수 있다.

Scanning이 적용되는 TOEFL의 문제 중에는 특정정보(specific information)나 사실(facts)을 명시하고, 그 정보나 사실의 지문 속 위치를 찾는 유형들이 많다. 세부사항(Facts), 범주표 완성(Category Chart), 지시어(Reference), 문장삽입(Insertion), Vocabulary(어휘) 등이 이런 유형에 속한다. 이런 문제를 해결하기 위해서는 지문의 글을 읽기 전에 문제의 조건과 관련되는 단어와 표현을 파악해야 한다. 그리고 필요한 정보를 신속히 찾아서 선택지와 비교해야 한다. 문제의 핵심어는 주로 T / F(True, False) 또는 5W1H(Who, What, When, Where, Why, How)와 관련된다.

종종 지문에서는 주로 문제와 선택지와 같은 단어가 함정으로 등장한다. 따라서 Scanning을 할 때에는 유사한 의미를 가진 다른 단어와 표현을 반드시 포함시켜 검색해야 한다.

1. There is no clear or accepted origin of the indigenous people of Australia. Although they migrated to Australia through Southeast Asia they are not demonstrably related to any known Asian or Polynesian population. There is evidence of genetic and linguistic interchange between Australians in the far north and the Austronesian peoples of modern-day New Guinea and the islands, but this may be the result of recent trade and intermarriage. Historians believe that first human migration to Australia was achieved when this landmass formed part of the Sahul continent, connected to the island of New Guinea via a land bridge. It is also possible that they came by boat across the Timor Sea. The exact timing of the arrival of the ancestors of the Indigenous Australians has been a matter of dispute among archaeologists. The most generally accepted date for the first arrival is between 40,000-80,000 years BC.

Q. 호주 토착민 조상의 정확한 도착 시점은 누구에게 논쟁거리인가?

ⓐ 원주민 ⓑ 호주인 ⓒ 역사학자 ⓓ 고고학자

Key Word in Question 도착시점, 누구에게

Key Word & Sentence The exact timing of the arrival of the ancestors of the Indigenous Australians has been a matter of dispute among archaeologists.

해석 호주 토착민의 기원은 불분명하다. 그들이 동남아시아를 통해 호주로 이주해 갔다고 하더라도 지금까지 알려진 어떤 아시아나 폴리네시아 주민과 명백히 연관되지 않는다. 호주 북부 사람들과 현재 뉴기니의 오스트로네시아인들 사이에 유전적, 언어적 교환의 증거가 있지만 이것은 최근의 무역과 서로간의 결혼의 결과일 수 있다. 역사학자들은 이 거대한 땅 덩어리가 다리가 되어진 땅을 통해 뉴기니 섬과 연결되어 서훌대륙의 일부가 되었다고 믿는다. 또한 그들이 티모르 바다를 보트로 건너왔다는 것도 가능하다. 호주 토착민 조상의 정확한 도착 시점은 고고학자들의 논쟁거리가 되어왔다. 가장 일반적으로 받아들여지는 호주 토착민의 첫 도착 시기는 기원전 4만년에서 8만년 사이이다.

2. In the year 2012, the City Council made a goal to reduce the number of inactive people in our city by 20% by the year 2015. This plan is called "the well-being project for healthy citizens." Though it's well known that an inactive lifestyle can lead to serious health risks, less than 30% of the citizens include enough physical activity in their lives. It's time for change. In the future, we will continue to ensure that our citizens have access to the finest recreational facilities and fitness programs. We encourage you to make physical activity part of your everyday life. Your participation in this plan will provide a healthy lifestyle for your family. Take part in "the well-being project for healthy citizens."

Q. 시민들이 하도록 시의회가 제안하는 것은?

    ⓐ 비활동적인 인구를 줄여라.   ⓑ 행복 프로젝트에 참가하라.

    ⓒ 주말에 운동을 해라.   ⓓ 가족의 건강을 챙겨라.

`Key Word in Question` 제안

`Key Word & Sentence` Take part in "the well-being project for healthy citizens."

해석 2012년도에 시의회는 2015년까지 우리 시의 비활동적인 인구를 20% 줄이는 목표를 세웠습니다. 이 계획은 '건강한 시민을 위한 프로젝트' 라고 합니다. 생활 속에서 비활동적인 생활방식이 심각한 건강상의 위험을 가져올 수 있다는 사실이 잘 알려져 있지만 생활 속에서 충분한 신체활동을 하는 시민은 30% 미만입니다. 이제 변화할 때입니다. 앞으로는 시민들이 최고의 여가활동과 운동 프로그램을 이용할 수 있도록 하겠습니다. 저희는 여러분이 신체운동을 일상생활화하도록 권합니다. 이 계획에 참여하시면 여러분의 가족이 건강한 생활을 하게 될 것입니다. '건강한 시민을 위한 프로젝트'에 참여하세요.

01. In 1829 Mendelssohn paid his first visit to Britain. He took a vacation in Scotland during the summer. The excursion, including a visit to Edinburgh and a trip through the Highlands, lasted less than three weeks. He met the composer John Thomson when he visited Edinburgh. The trip produced many pleasant memories as witnessed in his letters and a few drawings he made of scenery. But except for that, the trip didn't mean much to him in his career. One of the most significant in terms of his success in Britain was his eighth visit in the Summer of 1844. He conducted five of the Philharmonic concerts in London.

Q. 지문의 내용과 일치하는 것은?

ⓐ 멘델스존의 영국여행의 첫 방문지는 런던이었다.

ⓑ 스코틀랜드의 휴가는 그의 성공과 관련이 적었다.

ⓒ 멘델스존의 스코틀랜드에서의 휴가는 지루했다.

ⓓ 멘델스존은 필하모니 음악회의 곡을 작곡했다.

Key Word in Question

_____

Key Word & Sentence

_____

_____

_____

02. Computers use a language called Binary to communicate information to and from the parts of a computer. Binary language is a system of code that translates information like "yes" and "no" into series of "ones" and "zeroes." This language forms the basis for all other computer languages, such as Bertrand, C++, and Fortran. Each one or zero is called a "bit," and it represents the smallest piece of information. The word bit comes from the combination of "B" from binary and "it" from digit. And 8 bits are strung to make one byte. One thousand bites is a kilobyte; a million bytes is a megabyte; and a billion byte is a gigabyte. And a unit of information equal to 1000 gigabytes is called a terabyte.

Q. 지문의 내용과 일치하지 않는 것은?

ⓐ 컴퓨터는 2진수를 사용한다.

ⓑ 2진수는 버트란, C++, 또는 포트란과 같은 모든 컴퓨터 언어의 가장 기본적인 형식이다.

ⓒ byte라는 단어는 binary의 B와 digit의 it에서 왔다.

ⓓ 테라바이트는 기가바이트보다 천배 정도 크다.

Key Word in Question

_____

Key Word & Sentence

_____

_____

_____

03. In her job as a beautician, my wife is a Sunday driver. One day she was frightened to see the red flasher of a highway-patrol car behind her. Soon she was confronted by a young police officer, who gave her a speeding ticket. The next day when ① she answered the phone, a woman's voice reluctantly inquired whether this was the woman ticketed for speeding on Park Avenue the day before. Told that it was, ②she confessed that her husband was the traffic officer, and that he several times mentioned that the lady was wearing the loveliest perfume he had ever smelled. ③She decided to find out what it was. ④She is now one of my wife's best clients, and the cost of the speeding ticket has been compensated many times over.

Q. 지문에서 밑줄 친 대상이 나머지 셋과 다른 것은?

Key Word in Question

_____

Key Word & Sentence

_____

_____

_____

04. Should the U.S. place limits on the development of space weapons? What should go in the category of space weapon? What challenges will be faced in the development of space weapons? How will these developments tie into furthering technology for space travel? How will these advances affect life here on earth? Currently the United States does not have weapons of mass destruction in space. The United States does have tactical devices in space providing defense and supporting campaigns that take place here on earth. The United States can jam or destroy enemy satellite ground control stations with aircraft or special operations forces. Using surveillance satellites U.S. military forces are able to utilize the most up to date intelligence available giving the U.S. military a distinct tactical advantage. Weather reports everywhere on the planet are available at any given moment. The weaponization of space is the next logical step for the U.S. military.

Q. 지문의 내용과 일치하는 것은?

ⓐ 미국은 우주 무기의 개발에 제한을 두어야 한다.

ⓑ 미국은 전술 장치를 우주에 보유하고 있다.

ⓒ 미국은 대량 파괴 무기를 보유하고 있지 않다.

ⓓ 지구 어디에서나 정찰 위성을 통해 일기 예보가 가능한 것은 아니다.

Key Word in Question

_____

Key Word & Sentence

_____

_____

_____

05. This is how to open a can. Please follow the steps below.

1. Lift the piercing lever.
2. Lean the can so that the rim is under the locating post, then push down on the piercing lever, making sure the cutter blade is inside the rim of the can. Note: Because of the hands-free feature, it is not necessary to hold the lever down or hold the can during cutting. However, you may have to support very tall or heavy cans.
3. To remove the can, hold it with one hand and raise the lever with the other. Caution: Avoid contact with the cut edges of the can or lids — they are sharp. During opening process, the design of your can opener will roll the rim of the can to prevent sharp edges; however, handle with caution and always handle the lid with caution, as these edges are not rolled.
4. Carefully discard the lid from the magnet.
   Important Tips:
   • Do not use this can opener to open cans with a pull tab, peel-off foil seal, or rolling key or rimless cans.
   • Open frozen juices or foods in cardboard cans right from the freezer, while they are frozen.
   • Aluminum lids will not stick to the magnet.

Q. 지문의 내용과 일치하지 않는 것은?

ⓐ 핸즈프리 기능이 있지만, 일부 캔은 절단하는 동안에 붙잡고 있어야 한다.

ⓑ 알루미늄 캔은 이 캔 오프너에 부적절하다.

ⓒ 이 오프너는 테두리가 있는 캔만 열 수 있다.

ⓓ 이 오프너는 날카로운 가장자리에 손이 베이는 것을 막기 위해 자동으로 작동된다.

Key Word in Question

_____

Key Word & Sentence

_____

_____

_____

06. Embryonic stem cell transplantation is a related course of cells that are in charge of certain functions and systems of the body. The cells used in the transplantation process are contrived from "cryopreserved suspensions" from the fetal liver, thymus, bone marrow, spleen, brain, and the pancreas. Introducing ① <u>them</u> to the body can be approached in different ways.

One of ② <u>them</u> is engrafting or multiplying cells in the affected area.

(A) Production then commences with considerable amounts of biologically active substances such as nerve growth factor, tumor necrosis factor and interleukins etc.

(B) These cells will then supplement missing or declining cells and replace [repair] missing functions of the body.

(C) When ③ <u>they</u> have been transplanted, they are capable of migrating, establishing intercellular links and responding to various effects.

However, because of their immature transplantation to the human body, ④ <u>they</u> cause a weaker immune response than mature cells.

Q. 지문에서 밑줄 친 대상이 나머지 셋과 다른 것은?

Key Word in Question

_____

Key Word & Sentence

_____

_____

_____

Unit 05 패러프레이징(Paraphrasing)

1. 동의어 찾기

- **consist of** = be composed of = be made up of ~로 구성되어 있다
- **take after** = resemble = look like ~와 닮다
- **be on good terms with** = get along with = be friendly with ~와 사이좋게 지내다
- **be liable to** = tend to = be inclined to ~하는 경향이 있다
- **anything but** = by no means = never 결코 ~ 아니다
- **hit the nail on the head** = come to the point = say or do exactly the right thing 핵심을 찌르다

Exercise 동의어를 써 보시오.

01. **count on** = _____ = _____ = _____ ~을 의존하다, 기대하다

02. **answer for** = _____ = _____ = _____ ~에 대해 책임지다

03. **furnish A with B** = _____ = _____ = _____ A에게 B를 제공하다

04. **as to** = _____ = _____ = _____ ~에 관해서

05. **at once** = _____ = _____ = _____ 즉시

06. **put up with** = _____ = _____ = _____ 참다, 견디다

07. **carry out** = _____ = _____ = _____ ~을 수행하다, 성취하다

08. **apply oneself to** = _____ = _____ = _____ ~에 몰두하다

09. **be liable to** = _____ = _____ = _____ ~ 하는 경향이 있다

10. **pass over** = _____ = _____ = _____ 무시하다

11. **as good as** = _____ = _____ = _____ ~ 와 다름없는

12. **be anxious about** = _____ = _____ = _____ ~을 걱정하는

13. **as a rule** = _____ = _____ = _____ 대체로

14. **be at a loss** = _____ = _____ = _____ 당황하다

15. **be accountable for** = _____ = _____ = _____ 을 책임지다

16. **break away** = _____ = _____ = _____ 도망가다

17. **abide by** = _____ = _____ = _____ 따르다

18. **be at home in** = _____ = _____ = _____ ~에 정통하다

19. **all thumbs** = _____ = _____ = _____ 서투른

20. **nothing but** = _____ = _____ = _____ 단지 ~에 불과한

2. 쉬운 단어로 바꿔 쓰기

- <u>Bear in mind</u> that practice makes perfect.
  → <u>Remember</u> that practice makes perfect.
  자꾸 연습하다 보면 잘하게 된다는 것을 명심해라.

- The student <u>was at a loss for words</u>.
  → The student <u>was confused</u>.
  그 학생은 당황해서 어찌할 바를 몰랐다.

- The landing of our airplane on time seemed to be <u>out of the question.</u>
  → The landing of our airplane on time seemed to be <u>impossible</u>.
  우리 비행기가 제시간에 착륙하는 것은 불가능해 보였다.

Exercise   쉬운 단어로 바꿔 쓰고 해석하시오.

01. Badly-fitting shoes can <u>deform</u> your feet.
  → Badly-fitting shoes can m_____ your feet u_____.

_____

02. "A dude" is a <u>colloquial</u> expression for "a guy."
  → "A dude" is an i_____ e_____ u_____ in c_____ for a "guy."

_____

03. Monica is an <u>eloquent</u> speaker because her arguments are always pretty convincing.
  → Monica i_____ g_____ at s_____ because her arguments are always pretty convincing.

_____

04. Knowledge without common sense <u>counts for nothing</u>.
  → Knowledge without common sense is u_____.

_____

05. Among Korean soccer players, Park Ji-sung is <u>second to none</u>.
  → Among Korean soccer players, Park Ji-sung is the b_____.

_____

06. The peace conferences have been held in various venues <u>biannually</u> since 1985 but they have often failed to produce a settlement.

→ The peace conferences have been held in various venues t_____ a y_____ since 2001 but they have often failed to produce a settlement.

07. You were <u>the last person</u> I would expect to see in New York.

→ I h_____ n_____ expected to see you in New York.

08. I need to catch a bus <u>bound for</u> Denver, Colorado.

→ I need to catch a bus that g_____ t_____ Denver, Colorado.

3. 부정문 바꿔 쓰기

- The results of the survey were <u>not as astonishing as</u> they had expected.
  → The results of the survey were <u>less astonishing than</u> they expected.
  그 조사의 결과는 그들이 예상했던 것만큼 놀랍지는 않았다.

- <u>No sooner</u> had the rescue team set out running a risk of the storm <u>than</u> they were attacked by a pirate ship.
  → <u>As soon as</u> the rescue team set out running a risk of the storm, they were attacked by a pirate ship.
  폭풍우를 무릅쓰고 구조대가 출발하자마자 그들은 해적선의 공격을 받았다.

- It <u>makes no difference</u> whether you're black or white, but age makes some difference to your eligibility to enlist as a soldier.
  → It <u>matters little</u> whether you're black or white, but age makes some difference to your eligibility to enlist as a soldier.
  당신이 흑인이건 백인이건 상관이 없지만, 나이는 군에 지원할 때 어느 정도 문제가 된다.

Exercise   부정문을 바꿔 쓰고 해석하시오.

01. My laptop is much slower than it used to be, so I have <u>almost never</u> used it for several months.
  → My laptop is much slower than it used to be, so I have <u>h_____ e_____</u> used it for several months.

_____

02. I did <u>not</u> realize that I had left my notebook on the train <u>until</u> I got off the subway.
  → I realized I had left my notebook on the train <u>w_____</u> I got off the subway.

_____

03. While I was doing research on many religions and their historic events, <u>I couldn't help being confused</u> because the Bible says there's only one truth, one God.
  → While I was doing research on many religions and their historic events, I <u>w_____ o_____ c_____</u> because the Bible says there's only one truth, one God.

_____

04. Mike has <u>never</u> <u>failed</u> to get a score of 90 or above on any English exam.

→ Mike has a_____ g_____ a score of 90 or above on any English exam.

_____

05. Under the white apartheid regime, blacks were <u>not</u> allowed to pass through white areas <u>without</u> permission.

→ Under the white apartheid regime, blacks were allowed to pass through white areas o_____ w_____ permission.

_____

06. <u>Unless</u> <u>you</u> <u>spend</u> a reasonable amount of time together, talking on the phone, writing letters, and being together, friendship will go away.

→ W_____ y_____ s_____ a reasonable amount of time together, talking on the phone, writing letters, and being together, friendship will go away.

_____

07. <u>No</u> <u>one</u> <u>has</u> <u>to</u> let errors of the past destroy their present or cloud their future.

→ A_____ s_____ n_____ let errors of the past destroy their present or cloud their future.

_____

08. Discussion <u>rarely</u> changed his mind, and disagreement was not tolerated.

→ Discussion d_____ o_____ change his mind, and disagreement was not tolerated.

_____

4. 문장의 태 바꿔 쓰기

- We do not often <u>see</u> many adults commuting to work by bicycles, but in some foreign countries it is common.

  → Many adults <u>are</u> not often <u>seen</u> commuting to work by bicycles, but in some foreign countries it is common.

  우리는 많은 어른들이 자전거로 출근하는 걸 자주 볼 수 없지만 몇몇 나라에서는 흔한 일이다.

- Curiosity and jealousy <u>were discovered</u> in Jessica's mind by the doctor.

  → What the doctor <u>discovered</u> in Jessica's mind was curiosity and jealousness.

  호기심과 질투심이 Jessica의 마음속에서 발견되었다.

- The Wright brothers <u>made</u> the crude aircraft in 1903, and it became the prototype of the modern airplane.

  → The crude aircraft <u>was made</u> in 1903 <u>by</u> the Wright brothers, and it became the prototype of the modern airplane.

  라이트형제는 1903년에 투박한 비행기를 만들었고 그것이 현대 비행기의 원형이 되었다.

Exercise 문장의 태를 바꿔 쓰고 해석하시오.

01. Our defeat in the final game <u>was</u> somewhat <u>predicted</u> by the injury to Jason, who is our star player, in a previous game.

    → The injury to Jason, who is our star player, in a previous game somewhat p_____ our defeat in the final game.

    _____

02. My adviser <u>told</u> me that I should take Dr. Green's class because he is an expert in international politics.

    → I w_____ t_____ t_____ take Dr. Green's class by my adviser because he is an expert in international politics.

    _____

03. <u>No one has fully solved</u> the problem of the space shuttle exactly yet because the NASA scientists found it more difficult than they expected.

    → The problem of the space shuttle h_____ n_____ b_____ s_____ fully by a_____ yet because it was found to be more difficult than the NASA scientists expected.

    _____

04. The trip <u>had</u> completely <u>defeated</u> the father's purpose.

→ The father's purpose h_____ b_____ completely d_____ on the trip.

_____

05. Teachers <u>should</u> <u>encourage</u> students to develop their imaginations.

→ Students s_____ b_____ e_____ to develop their imaginations by teachers.

_____

06. The rule <u>was</u> <u>changed</u> shortly after by Alex, when he found out how dangerous the game was.

→ Sam <u>c</u>_____ the rule shortly after, when he found out how dangerous the game was.

_____

07. You <u>should</u> <u>make</u> a clear introduction, if you want to build good social relationships with others.

→ A clear introduction s_____ b_____ m_____ , if you want to build good social relationships with others.

_____

08. Most foreign workers <u>are</u> <u>being</u> <u>taught</u> by Korean coworkers or volunteers who have no or little teaching experience.

→ Korean coworkers or volunteers who have no or little teaching experience <u>a</u>_____ t_____ most foreign workers.

_____

5. 비교구문 바꿔 쓰기

- Not taking a difficult exam is worse than failing it.
  - → It is better to fail a difficult exam than not to take it.

  어려운 시험을 치르지 않는 것은 그 시험에 실패하는 것보다 나쁘다.

- My father's company takes small jobs as well as large ones.
  - → My father's company takes not only small jobs but also large ones.

  아버지 회사는 큰 일뿐 아니라 작은 일도 맡는다.

- More than half of South Korea's leading conglomerates do business with their sons.
  - → The majority of South Korea's leading conglomerates do business with their sons.

  절반이 넘는 대한민국의 대표적인 재벌들은 그들의 아들과 함께 경영을 한다.

Exercise 비교구문으로 바꿔 쓰고 해석하시오.

01. Let's figure out why Pluto is no longer considered a planet.
→ Let's figure out why Pluto is n_____ considered a planet a_____ l_____

_____

02. According to the Johns Hopkins Medical School report, the health problems caused by caffeine are usually less serious than we know.
→ According to the Johns Hopkins Medical School report, the health problems caused by caffeine are usually n_____ a_____ s_____ a_____ we know.

_____

03. We looked at the total costs of wireless mobile products, and found that the more functions the device has, the higher the cost becomes.
→ We looked at the total costs of wireless mobile products, and found that w_____ the device has m_____ functions, the cost becomes h_____.

_____

04. Today our spaceships are no faster than one percent the speed of light.
→ Today our spaceships are n_____ a_____ f_____ a_____ one percent the speed of light.

_____

05. <u>Nothing</u> was <u>worse</u> <u>than</u> his father's sudden death because he was forced to give up school.
→ His father's sudden death was t_____ w_____ t_____ because he was forced to give up school.

06. This program can be a good guide to use for speaking purposes since we speak <u>more</u> <u>informally</u> than we write.
→ This program can be a good guide to use for speaking purposes since we speak l_____ f_____ than we write.

07. Conventional MP3 players used to be <u>no</u> <u>more</u> <u>than</u> a devices with audio functions.
→ Conventional MP3 players used to be <u>o</u>_____ a devices with audio functions.

08. <u>Less</u> <u>than</u> ten percent of the subscribers chose not to renew their daily newspaper.
→ M_____ t_____ ninety percent of the subscribers chose to renew their daily newspaper.

6. 강조 [도치]구문으로 바꿔 쓰기

- Highly elaborate forms of communication happen <u>among such animals as bats and whales</u>.

  → <u>Among such animals as bats and whales</u> happen highly elaborate forms of communication are found.

  매우 정교한 형태의 의사소통이 박쥐와 고래 같은 동물 간에 일어난다.

- Scientists learned about the existence of dinosaurs <u>only</u> two hundred years ago.

  → <u>Not until</u> two hundred years ago did scientists learn about the existence of dinosaurs.

  과학자들은 공룡의 존재를 200년 전에야 알았다.

- Alex realized that he had forgotten to turn off the heater <u>as soon as</u> he had left his office.

  → <u>No sooner</u> had Alex left his office <u>than</u> he realized he had forgotten to turn off the heater.

  알렉스는 그의 사무실을 나서자마자 히터 끄는 것을 잊고 나왔다는 것을 깨달았다.

Exercise   강조 [도치]구문으로 바꿔 쓰고 해석하시오.

01. A justice of the Supreme Court is known as <u>the</u> <u>last</u> man to be influenced by power.

→ A justice of the Supreme Court is know as the man who will n_____ be influenced by power.

_____

02. <u>It</u> <u>is</u> <u>only</u> <u>when</u> <u>they</u> <u>are</u> <u>gone</u> <u>and</u> <u>we</u> <u>never</u> <u>see</u> <u>them</u> <u>that</u> we find they are Indivisible from us.

→ We find we are indivisible from them o_____ w_____ t_____ a_____ g_____ a_____ w_____ n_____ s_____ t_____.

_____

03. <u>No</u> <u>matter</u> <u>what</u> our goals are, there are always obstacles that can prevent us from attaining them.

→ E_____ i_____ w_____ our goals are, there are always obstacles that can prevent us from attaining them.

_____

04. Neither Alex nor other most skilled system engineers could retrieve the password.

→ N_____ o_____ Alex and other most skilled system engineers could retrieve the password either.

_____

05, I little dreamed that I would be such an influential man in the world as U.N. Secretary General.

→ Little d_____ I d_____ that I would be such an influential man in the world as U.N. Secretary General.

_____

06. Famous golfer Jack Nicklaus, for example, never took a golf shot without first thinking out the shot and practicing it in his imagination.

→ Famous golfer Jack Nicklaus, for example, a_____ takes a golf shot with first thinking out the shot and practicing it in his imagination.

_____

07. No longer were the shores densely wooded, nor could I see any wildlife.

→ I c_____ n_____ l_____ s_____ the shores densely wooded, nor any wildlife.

_____

08. Only with great difficulty could the coalition cabinet be created in continental European countries after overthrowing the Monarchy.

→ The c_____ c_____ c_____ be c_____ only with great difficulty in continental European countries after overthrowing the Monarchy.

_____

7. 전치사 [구]를 접속사 [절]로 바꿔 쓰기

- <u>On returning</u> from space, the astronauts were greeted like conquering heroes with thundering applause.

  → <u>As soon as the astronauts returned</u> from space, they were greeted like conquering heroes with thundering applause.

  → 우주 비행사들은 돌아오자마자 정복하고 돌아온 영웅같이 우레와 같은 갈채와 환영을 받았다.

- <u>In warmer weather</u>, the ice began to break and melt, and the mallard ducks managed to find their way to the water.

  → <u>As the weather became warmer</u>, the ice began to break and melt, and the mallard ducks managed to find their way to the water.

  따뜻해진 날씨에 얼음이 깨져 녹기 시작하고 청둥오리들은 물가로 가는 길을 찾아냈다.

- <u>Without Mr. Johnson's help</u>, it would have been impossible for me to complete the team project on time and write my doctoral thesis.

  → <u>If Mr. Johnson had not helped me</u>, it would have been impossible for me to complete the team project on time and write my doctoral thesis.

  존슨 씨의 도움이 아니었다면 내가 제시간에 팀 프로젝트를 마치고 박사 논문을 쓰는 게 불가능했을 것이다.

Exercise 전치사 [구]를 접속사 [절]로 바꿔 쓰고 해석하시오.

01. China will be unable to produce enough biodiesel domestically in the near future <u>due to</u> the absence of a proper industrial structure.

    → China will be unable to produce enough biodiesel domestically in the near future b_____ o_____ the absence of a proper industrial structure.

    _____

02. <u>In spite of</u> his tremendous physical disabilities, Stephen Hawking has already made some very important discoveries about the origin of the universe.

    → A_____ h_____ h_____ tremendous physical disabilities, Stephen Hawking has already made some very important discoveries about the origin of the universe.

    _____

03. Citizens' groups <u>raised</u> <u>their</u> <u>voices</u> <u>in</u> <u>criticism</u> <u>of</u> the government's policies on environmental issues based upon their case study of a large-scale land reclamation.

→ Citizens' groups h_____ c_____ the government's policies on environmental issues based upon their case study of a large-scale land reclamation.

_____

04. <u>Due</u> <u>to</u> keen competition with Apple, we are anxious to get our products into the market as soon as possible.

→ O_____ t_____ keen competition with Apple, we are anxious to get our products into the market as soon as possible.

_____

05. They gave him a standing ovation <u>as</u> <u>soon</u> <u>as</u> the President had finished his speech before Congress.

→ N_____ s_____ had the President finished his speech before Congress t_____ they gave him a standing ovation.

_____

06. <u>Although</u> he wrote many beautiful pieces of music, he dressed badly and hardly ever cleaned his room.

→ I_____ s_____ o_____ his writing many beautiful pieces of music, he dressed badly and hardly ever cleaned his room.

_____

07. The increased population brought more demand for food, <u>so</u> more money went into farming.

→ More money went into farming b_____ the increased population brought more demand for food.

_____

08. A consultant should more objectively analyze <u>not</u> <u>only</u> the opportunities and threats that face the company <u>but</u> <u>also</u> its strengths and weaknesses

→ A consultant should more objectively analyze the company's strengths and weaknesses a_____ w_____ a_____ the opportunities and threats that face it.

_____

94

8. 주어 바꿔 쓰기

- **5 minutes' walk brought** me to the park.
  - → **It took 5 minutes** for me to get to the park.

  5분을 걸어서 공원에 도착했다.

- **The stomachache kept** me awake all night and **brought** me to the hospital.
  - → I woke up all night **because of** a **stomachache** and **went** to the hospital.

  복통 때문에 밤새 깨어 있다가 병원에 갔다.

- **The article says** that this finding could lead to more effective therapies for people with rare kinds of liver diseases.
  - → **According to** the article, this finding could lead to more effective therapies for people with rare kinds of liver diseases.

  이 글에 따르면 이번 실험 결과가 희귀한 종류의 간 질환을 앓고 있는 환자들에게 보다 효과적인 치료법을 제공하게 될 것이라고 한다.

Exercise
주어를 바꿔 쓰고 해석하시오.

01. His laziness prevented him from going to work.
  → He had to stop going to work b_____ o_____ h_____ l_____

_____

02. Despite their hard practice they gave a poor performance in the concert .
  → A_____ t_____ p_____ h_____, their concert performance was poor.

_____

03. The Internet enables us immediately to find out what's going on the other side of the world, to understand the problems there, and to fight evil people by convincing others to promote peace.
  → T_____ t_____ t_____ I_____ we can immediately find out what's going on the other side of the world, to understand the problems there, and to fight evil people by convincing others to promote peace.

_____

04. The bad weather prevented us from continuing our journey .
  → W_____ couldn't continue our journey as the weather was bad.

_____

05. If <u>you</u> compare these items carefully, you will tell the difference easily.

→ A c_____ c_____ of t_____ i_____ will help you tell the difference easily.

_____

06. <u>Hard</u> <u>work</u> <u>and</u> <u>determination</u> helped her make it on a professional volleyball team.

→ S_____ made it on a professional volleyball team because of her hard work and determination.

_____

07. <u>His</u> <u>youth</u> enabled him to work.

→ H_____ was able to work, thanks to his youth.

_____

08. <u>His</u> <u>never</u> <u>failing</u> <u>love</u> <u>and</u> <u>his</u> <u>sense</u> <u>of</u> <u>humor</u> made Lincoln a leader in any society he entered.

→ L_____ could become a leader in any society he entered because of his never failing love and his sense of humor.

_____

9. 분사구문 바꿔 쓰기

- <u>Having</u> no telephone, I can still keep in touch with my friends by instant message, email, and through our blogs.

  ➡ <u>Even if I have</u> no telephone, I can still keep in touch with my friends by instant message, email, and through our blogs.

  전화가 없어도 나는 메신저, 이메일, 블로그를 통해 친구들과 연락할 수 있다.

- <u>The avalanche having stopped</u>, the survivors started looking for their friends who might have been buried under 3 meters of snow.

  ➡ <u>After the avalanche had stopped</u>, the survivors started looking for their friends who might have been buried under 3 meters of snow.

  눈사태가 멈춘 후 생존자들은 눈 3m 아래 묻혔을지 모를 그들의 친구를 찾기 시작했다.

- My mom was sitting on the sofa <u>folding</u> her arms and <u>closing</u> her eyes while watching a daily soap opera.

  ➡ My mom was sitting on the sofa <u>with</u> her arms <u>folded</u> and her eyes <u>closed</u> while watching a daily soap opera.

  엄마는 일일 연속극을 보면서 팔을 접고 눈을 감은 채 소파에 앉아 있었다.

Exercise   분사구문 바꿔 쓰고 해석하시오.

01. <u>Having kept</u> the secret to himself for forty years until he died of cancer, he helped the case remain one of the greatest unsolved mysteries in Korean modern history.

➡ A_____ h_____ h_____ k_____ the secret to himself for forty years until he died of cancer, he helped the case remain one of the greatest unsolved mysteries in Korean modern history.

_____

02. <u>Suffering</u> from Alzheimer's disease, more than 4 million Americans have lost their memories making it difficult for them to take care of themselves.

➡ W_____ t_____ w_____ s_____ from Alzheimer's disease, more than 4 million Americans have lost their memories making it difficult for them to take care of themselves.

_____

03. Although I have known many kinds of people, I would like to place him above any of the corporate executives and celebrities in my country, for companionship and good conversation and power of stimulating the minds of others.

→ H_____ k_____ many kinds of people, I would like to place him above any of the corporate executives and celebrities in my country, for companionship and good conversation, intelligence, and power of stimulating the minds of others.

_____

04. As I had lots of work to do for the new project, I had to stay up all night in the office.

→ H_____ lots of work to do, I had to stay up all night in the office.

_____

05. After recognizing the healing power of humor, many hospitals started to take laughing matters seriously.

→ A_____ m_____ h_____ r_____ the healing power of humor, they started to take laughing matters seriously.

_____

06. Looking through his telescope at the sun, Galileo found something surprising, but he could never explain what it was.

→ W_____ G_____ l_____ t_____ his telescope at the sun, he found something surprising, but he could never explain what it was.

_____

07. While we were playing cards last night, we heard someone knocking on the door.

→ P_____ c_____ last night, we heard someone knocking on the door.

_____

08. Although his patients didn't know what had happened inside their bodies the whole time under hypnosis, most of them were cured.

→ N_____ k_____ what had happened inside their bodies the whole time under hypnosis, most of his patients were cured.

_____

10. 관계사구문 바꿔 쓰기

- Indeed, <u>everything</u> <u>that</u> <u>we</u> <u>do</u> depends on the transfer of signals from one neuron to another.
  → Indeed, <u>all of our actions</u> depend on the transfer of signals from one neuron to another.
  사실 우리가 하는 모든 행동은 뉴런에서 다른 뉴런으로의 신호 전달에 달려있다.

- <u>All</u> the delegates <u>that</u> were present at the meeting agreed to pass the controversial laws about religion.
  → <u>As</u> many delegates <u>as</u> were present at the meeting agreed to pass the controversial laws about religion.
  그 모임에 참석한 모든 대표자들은 논란이 되는 종교관련 법안 통과에 동의했다.

- General MacArthur was a famous American soldier <u>who</u> molded the destiny of Korea through the Incheon landing operation during the Korean war in the 1950s.
  → General MacArthur was a famous American soldier. <u>He</u> molded the destiny of Korea through the Incheon landing operation during the Korean war in the 1950s.
  맥아더장군은 1950년대 한국 전쟁 중에 인천 상륙 작전으로 한국의 운명을 좌우한 유명한 미군이다.

Exercise   관계사구문 바꿔 쓰고 해석하시오.

01. We know that there is no rule <u>but</u> <u>it</u> has some exceptions in the world.
  → We know that there is no rule t_____ d_____ have some exceptions in the world.

_____

02. I think <u>whoever</u> is in power would end up with political suicide.
  → I think n_____ m_____ w_____ is in power, they would end up with political suicide.

_____

03. The source of national stability in many ancient countries was from farmers <u>who</u> owned land, cherished it, and worked it well.
  → The source of national stability in many ancient countries was from farmers. T_____ owned land, cherished it, and worked it well.

_____

04. <u>Whatever</u> my parents may say, I will not change my decision to marry her.

➔ N_____ m_____ w_____ my parents may say, I will not change my decision to marry her.

_____

05. One of the major embarrassments is the audience's looking at their watches. Most lecturers feel <u>it</u>.

➔ One of the major embarrassments w_____ most lecturers feel is the audience's looking at their watches.

_____

06. The baseball game <u>which</u> was scheduled for Saturday was canceled because of heavy rain.

➔ The baseball game was canceled because of heavy rain. I_____ was scheduled for Sunday.

_____

07. Such books <u>as</u> I enjoyed when I was a kid no longer interest me but I find some of them still instructive.

➔ Such books no longer interest me but I find some of them still instructive. I enjoyed t_____ when I was a kid.

_____

Types of Questions

섹션 1을 토대로 하여 실전에서 출제되는 여러 문제 유형을 자세하게 접할 수 있다. 여기서는 문제를 Sentence Simplification / Fact & Negative Fact / Vocabulary / Reference / Rhetorical Purpose / Inference / Insertion / Summary / Category Chart 등의 9개의 유형으로 분류했다. 매 유닛마다 문제유형에 맞춘 샘플문제를 제시했고, 연습문제 2개와 실전문제 2개를 실었다.

Unit 01. Sentence Simplification

Unit 02. Fact & Negative Fact

Unit 03. Vocabulary

Unit 04. Reference

Unit 05. Rhetorical Purpose

Unit 06. Inference

Unit 07. Insertion

Unit 08. Summury

Unit 09. Category Chart

Sentence Simplification

Overview

문장간략화(Sentence Simplification) 문제는 주어진 한 문장의 핵심정보를 다른 말로 바꿔 표현한 문장을 선택지에서 고르는 유형이다. 보기에는 바꿔 쓰기(paraphrase)를 한 문장이 등장한다. 바꿔 쓰기를 한 문장이란 의미는 같지만 동의어나 문장구조를 바꿔 다른 형태로 표현한 문장을 말한다.

질문유형

• Which of the sentences below best expresses the essential information in the highlighted sentence in the passage? Incorrect answer choices change the meaning in important ways or leave out essential information.

아래 문장 중 어떤 것이 지문 속의 음영된 문장의 핵심정보를 가장 잘 표현하고 있는가? 오답 선택지들은 문장의 의미를 현저히 바꾸거나 핵심정보를 빠뜨린 것이다.

접근방법

1. 지문의 음영된 문장에서 핵심정보만을 골라낸다. 예를 들고 있는 표현이나 관계절, 동격 등 부연설명은 제외시킨다.
2. 핵심정보와 가장 가까운 의미의 문장을 보기에서 고른다. 핵심문장의 문장구조를 바꾸거나 동의어를 써서 가장 가깝게 바꿔 쓴(paraphrase) 문장을 선택한다.
3. 문장에 지시어가 들어 있는 경우에는 지시어가 가리키는 대상을 문장 주위에서 정확히 찾아 이해한다.
4. 다음과 같은 오답을 선택지에서 고르지 않도록 한다.
   ① 핵심정보를 빠뜨린 것
   ② 초점을 벗어나거나 과장된 것
   ③ 사건의 순서와 인과관계가 뒤바뀐 것

Sample Question

While some people who are entitled to call themselves Maori by descent may have cut themselves off completely from the main body and become completely merged with other New Zealanders, it is true also that many Maoris, especially young people, know little of their own vernacular language. But for the great majority Maoritanga – the Maori way of doing things – is still highly significant in social and especially ceremonial affairs. If a distinguished guest is welcomed at a public meeting of general importance, his arrival is quite likely to be challenged in conventional Maori style with a defiant speech and a thrown stick. It is for the guest formally to indicate his peaceful intentions by picking up the stick and declaring his mission.

Which of the sentences below best expresses the essential information in the highlighted sentence in the passage?

Ⓐ Some people of Maori descent have little or no connection with their own cultural heritage and language.

Ⓑ People of Maori descent who are no longer connected to their own heritage, nevertheless still desire to know their own language.

Ⓒ It is important for some Maori to be independent of the influence of their own cultural heritage and language.

Ⓓ There is little significance in wanting to be cut off from their own cultural heritage for some Maori.

해설 지문의 음영된 문장에서의 핵심 정보는 마오리인이 그들의 문화유산과 격리되었다는 것과 마오리 젊은이들이 그들의 언어를 모른다는 것이다. 각 절의 핵심어(Maori by descent, cut off from the main body, know little of their language)를 파악하면 Ⓐ가 정답이라는 것을 알 수 있다. cut off from과 know little of는 비슷한 표현으로 보기에서 have little or no connection with로 바뀌어 쓰였다. who are entitled to call themselves나 vernacular 같은 수식어는 제외시켜도 핵심정보를 파악하는 데 상관이 없다. 접속사 and 역시 마오리 주류로부터 격리되어 뉴질랜드 사람으로 통합되었다는 비슷한 내용을 앞뒤로 연결하므로 한 쪽을 핵심정보에서 생략할 수 있다. 보기 Ⓑ, Ⓒ, Ⓓ는 지문의 문장 일부 또는 모두의 의미를 바꾸었으므로 오답이다.

해석 스스로 태생을 마오리인이라고 부를 자격이 있는 사람들이 마오리 주류로부터 그들을 완전히 격리시키고 뉴질랜드 사람으로 융합되었을지 모르는 동안 많은 마리오인들, 특히 젊은이들 역시 그들 자신의 토착어를 거의 모르게 된 것이 사실이다. 하지만 대다수에게 마오리문화 – 일을 하는 마오리 방식 – 는 아직 사회적 의식을 치르는 데 매우 중요하다. 귀빈이 일반적으로 중요한 대중모임에서 환영을 받으면 그의 도착은 꽤 도전적인 연설과 던져진 나뭇가지가 있는 마오리 방식으로 이루어진다. 그것은 손님이 막대기를 집고 그의 임무를 선언함으로서 그의 평화적 의도를 공식적으로 보여주는 것이다.

문제 아래 문장 중 어떤 것이 지문 속의 음영된 문장의 핵심정보를 가장 잘 표현하고 있는가?
Ⓐ 일부 마오리인 후손들은 그들 자신의 문화유산이나 언어와 거의 또는 전혀 관계가 없다.
Ⓑ 그들 자신의 문화유산과 더 이상 상관없는 마오리인 후손들은 그럼에도 불구하고 아직 그들의 언어를 알고자 한다.
Ⓒ 일부 마오리인이 그들 자신의 문화유산과 언어의 영향을 받지 않는다는 것은 중요하다.
Ⓓ 일부 마오리인에게 그들 자신의 문화유산으로부터 단절되는 것을 바라는 것은 거의 중요하지 않다.

Exercise 1

Political power within India has become increasingly centralized at a time when India's civil society has become mobilized along lines that reflect the country's social diversity. **The unresponsiveness of India's political parties and government has encouraged the Indian public to mobilize through NGOs and social movements**. The consequent development of India's civil society has made Indians less confident of the transformative power of the state and more confident of the power of the individual and local community. The development is shifting a larger share of the initiative for resolving India's social problems from the state to the society. State institutions that will accommodate the diverse interests that are now mobilized in Indian Society are the major challenge confronting the Indian polity in the new millennium.

Which of the sentences below best expresses the essential information in the highlighted sentence in the passage?

(A) The development of NGOs and social movements is a direct consequence of the failure of the Indian government to address social problems.

(B) NGOs and social movements reflect new avenues for public political involvement in the face of entrenched official indifference.

(C) Public mobilization through the state has made Indians aware of the lack of effectiveness of their political parties.

(D) Without NGOs and social movements, Indians would have no voice in the political process.

Last Wednesday was a very good day to be a fourth grader at Rutherford Elementary School in Mesquite, Texas. pairs of eager eyes followed the motions of school principal Holly Grubbs as she fiddled with the lock of the computer cart that contained the most eagerly anticipated learning tools in the school's history: brand new Apple iPads. This is not Rutherford's first experience with the popular tablet devices. All the school's fifth graders have been using the gadgets with great success already. According to The Dallas Morning News, since the device has been put in constant use, student engagement has gone up while discipline problems have been on a steady decline. Still, some might consider putting such expensive – and fragile –pieces of equipment into the hands of 9-year-olds to be both fiscally irresponsible and risky. **This is not a point of view, however, that is very popular in Rutherford halls**. Here, the goal is, as it has been since the first set of iPads were distributed, to integrate the iPads fully into the academic programs and use them extensively to help each child learn.

Which of the sentences below best expresses the essential information in the highlighted sentence in the passage?

Ⓐ Students are not very happy to hear this.

Ⓑ It is a view that goes against popular opinion of the teachers.

Ⓒ Students don't want to lose their iPads.

Ⓓ Without the iPads the school would become too noisy again.

1. **지문**
인도 내에서 정치권력은 인도의 시민 사회가 국가의 사회적 다양성을 반영하는 방식으로 동원될 때마다 점점 더 중앙 집중화되고 있다. **인도의 정당과 정부의 무반응은 시민 단체와 사회 운동을 통해 인도 대중이 결집하도록 조장했다.** 인도 시민 사회의 발전은 결과적으로 인도인들이 국가로의 권력 이전을 덜 확신하고 개인과 지역 사회의 권력을 더 확신하게 했다. 개발은 인도의 사회 문제를 해결하기 위한 주도권의 더 큰 몫을 국가에서 시민 사회로 이동시키고 있다. 현재 인도 사회에 동원되는 다양한 관심사를 수용할 국가 기관은 새 천년에 인도의 정치가 직면한 주요 과제이다.

어휘
at a time 따로따로, 한번에 unresponsiveness 불감응성, 반응 없음 consequent ~의 결과로 일어나는 initiative 계획, 진취성, 추진력 state institutions 국가 기관

문제
아래 문장 중 어떤 것이 지문 속의 음영된 문장의 핵심정보를 가장 잘 표현하고 있는가?
Ⓐ 시민 단체와 사회 운동의 발전은 인도 정부가 사회 문제를 다루는데 실패한 직접적인 결과이다.
Ⓑ 시민 단체와 사회 운동은 뿌리 깊은 공무원의 무관심에 대응하는 대중의 정치 참여의 새로운 길을 가져온다.
Ⓒ 국가적인 대중 동원은 인도인이 그들 정당의 효율성이 부족하다는 점을 깨닫게 하였다.
Ⓓ 시민 단체와 사회 운동 없이 인도인들은 정치 과정에 어떤 목소리도 낼 수 없을 것이다.

해설
인도 정당과 정부의 무반응이 시민 단체와 사회 운동을 통해 대중을 동원하였다고 하였으므로 the unresponsiveness of India's political parties and government를 official indifference로 바꿔 표현한 Ⓑ가 정답이다. 나머지 보기는 초점을 벗어나거나 논리의 비약 또는 사건의 순서와 인과 관계가 뒤바뀐 오답이다.

정답
Ⓑ

---

2. **지문**
지난 수요일은 텍사스 메스키트에 있는 루더퍼드 초등학교의 4학년에게 아주 좋은 날이었다. 열정적인 눈망울들이 학교 총장인 홀리 그럽스가 학교 개교 이래 가장 기대했던 학습 도구: 완전 신제품인 애플 아이패드가 담겨있는 컴퓨터 카트의 고정 장치를 만지작거리는 대로 따라갔다. 이것은 루더포드가 처음으로 인기 있는 태블릿 장비를 경험한 것이 아니다. 모든 학교의 5학년 학생들이 이미 훌륭한 성과를 거두며 그 장치를 사용해오고 있다. 달라스 모닝 뉴스에 따르면 그 장치는 언제든 사용이 가능하기 때문에 규율의 문제가 꾸준히 감소하는 반면 학생들의 참여는 증가하였다. 아직도 몇몇은 그런 비싸고 부서지기 쉬운 장비를 9세 된 아이 손에 들어가도록 하는 것이 재정상 무책임하고 위험하다고 생각할지도 모른다. **그러나 이것이 루더포드 회관에서 대부분의 일반적인 의견은 아니다.** 여기 첫 번째 아이패드가 배포된 이래로 그래왔듯이 그 목표는 아이패드를 학업 프로그램들과 완전히 통합시키고 아이들이 각자 배우는데 도움이 되도록 그것들을 널리 사용하도록 하는 것이다.

어휘
pairs of ~의 쌍 gadgets 도구, 장치 gone up 올라가다, 들어서다 irresponsible 무책임한, 비양심적인

문제
아래 문장 중 어떤 것이 지문 속의 음영된 문장의 핵심정보를 가장 잘 표현하고 있는가?
Ⓐ 학생들은 이 말을 듣는 것을 좋아하지 않는다.
Ⓑ 선생님들의 일반적인 견해와 반대되는 입장이다.
Ⓒ 학생들은 그들의 아이패드를 잃어버리지 않기 원한다.
Ⓓ 아이패드 없이 학교는 다시 너무 시끄러워질 것이다.

해설
주어진 지문에서 this는 앞의 의견(비싸고 부서지기 쉬운 장비를 9세 된 아이 손에 들어가도록 하는 것이 재정상 무책임하고 위험하다고 생각하는)이다. 그리고 루더포드 회관에 있는 이들은 학생이므로 정답은 Ⓐ이다. 문장에 지시어가 들어 있는 경우에는 지시어가 가리키는 대상을 정확히 파악하여야 한다.

정답
Ⓐ

Sparta was a warrior society in ancient Greece that reached the height of its power after defeating rival city-state Athens in the Peloponnesian War (431-404 B.C.). Spartan culture was centered on loyalty to the state and military service. At age 7, Spartan boys entered a **rigorous** state-sponsored education, military training and socialization program. Known as the Agoge, the system emphasized duty, discipline and endurance. Although Spartan women were not active in the military, they were educated and enjoyed more status and freedom than other Greek women. Because Spartan men were professional soldiers, all manual labor was done by a slave class, the Helots. **Despite their military bravery, the Spartans' dominance was short-lived: In 371 B.C., they were defeated by Thebes at the Battle of Leuctra, and their empire went into a long period of decline.**

1. The word rigorous in the passage is closest in meaning to

(A) precise

(B) harsh

(C) indulgent

(D) stimulating

2. Which of the sentences below best expresses the essential information in the highlighted sentence in the passage?

(A) Without Thebes, Sparta would have enjoyed a long period of military dominance.

(B) The Spartans were defeated by Thebes because they lacked military mastery.

(C) Thebes was undeterred by Sparta's military might and pressed their attack to their advantage.

(D) Great military power was not enough for the Spartans to maintain military dominance for long.

3. According to the passage, which of the following is true?

(A) Spartan women enjoyed benefits denied to other Greek women.

(B) The Spartan's military strength meant they were a dominant power for a long time.

(C) Boys whose families could not afford for them to enter the military became slaves doing manual labor.

(D) Warrior societies maintained their discipline through the status of their women.

Ulysses Grant (1822-1885) commanded the victorious Union army during the American Civil War (1861-1865) and served as the 18th U.S. president from 1869 to 1877. An Ohio native, Grant graduated from West Point and fought in the Mexican-American War (1846-1848). During the Civil War, Grant, an aggressive and determined leader, was given command of all the U.S. armies. After the war he became a national hero, and was nominated for president in 1868. **A primary focus of Grant's administration was Reconstruction, and he worked to reconcile the North and South while also attempting to protect the civil rights of newly freed black slaves**. While Grant was personally honest, **some of his associates were corrupt** and his administration was tarnished by various scandals. After retiring, Grant invested in a brokerage firm that went bankrupt, costing him his life savings. He spent his final days penning his memoirs, which were published the year he died and proved a **critical** and financial success.

1. **Which of the sentences below best expresses the essential information in the highlighted sentence in the passage?**

   Ⓐ It was important for Grant to have reconciliation between blacks and whites during Reconstruction.
   Ⓑ It was necessary to protect the rights of the newly freed black slaves for Reconstruction.
   Ⓒ By focusing on reconciliation between North and South, it was possible to assure the rights of blacks.
   Ⓓ Grant's administration tried to make reconciliation and overcoming injustice a priority.

2. **Why does the author mention that some of Ulysses Grant's associates were corrupt?**

   Ⓐ To contrast Ulysses Grant's honesty and integrity with that of his associates.
   Ⓑ To show that they were responsible for scandals that tarnished Grant's administration.
   Ⓒ To give an example of how it is difficult to control administrations.
   Ⓓ To emphasize the lack of morality of the administration at the time.

3. **The word critical in the passage is closest in meaning to**

   Ⓐ unfavorable
   Ⓑ indispensable
   Ⓒ evaluative
   Ⓓ serious

Fact & Negative Fact

Overview

일치(Fact & Negative Fact)문제는 지문에서 언급된 내용을 재진술(Restate)한 선택지 중에서 일치 또는 불일치한 것을 고르는 유형이다. 일치문제는 두 부류로 나뉜다. 지문의 일부에서 언급된 정보가 선택지와 일치하는지 묻는 문제와 지문의 전반적인 내용이 일치하는지를 묻는 문제이다.

질문유형

1. 지문 일부의 특정정보나 일치를 묻는 문제

- According to the passage, why [what, when, where, how] _____?

  지문에 의하면 왜 [무엇이, 언제, 어디서, 어떻게] _____했는가?

- According to paragraph #, which of the following is (NOT) true of _____?

  단락 #에 의하면 다음 중 _____에 관해 사실인(사실이 아닌) 것은?

2. 지문 전반적인 내용과의 일치를 묻는 문제

- According to passage, which of the following is (NOT) true of _____?

  지문에 의하면 다음 중 _____에 관해 사실인(사실이 아닌) 것은?

- According to the passage, all of the following are mentioned as EXCEPT _____.

  지문에 따르면 _____를 제외하고 다음의 모든 것이 언급되어 있다.

- According to the passage, the author states that _____.

  지문에 의하면 저자는 _____라고 말한다.

접근방법

1. 먼저 질문이 요구하는 것이 일치인지, 불일치인지, 특정정보를 찾는 것인지 주의한다.

2. 주어진 문제와 선택지에 포함된 핵심어(keyword)를 지문에서 빠르게 찾아(scan) 주변 문장을 세심하게 읽는다.

3. 지문에서 답의 근거가 되는 부분을 선택지와 비교하여 올바르게 바꿔 쓴(paraphrase) 선택지를 고른다.

4. 자신의 경험이나 상식이 아닌 지문에 나오는 정보에만 근거하여 답을 고른다.

5. 다음과 같은 오답을 선택지에서 고르지 않도록 한다.

   ① 지문에 언급되지 않은 것   ② 초점을 벗어나거나 과장된 것

   ③ 주어, 서술어, 목적어 등 일부 내용만 일치하는 것   ④ 사건의 순서와 인과 관계가 뒤바뀐 것

   ⑤ 시제가 불일치하는 것

Sample Question

High-level programming languages, while simple compared to human languages, are more complex than the languages the computer actually understands, called machine languages. Each different type of CPU has its own unique machine language. Lying between machine languages and high-level languages are languages called assembly languages. Assembly languages are similar to machine languages, but they are much easier to program in because they allow a programmer to substitute names for numbers. Machine languages consist of numbers only. Lying above high-level languages are languages called fourth-generation languages (usually abbreviated 4GL). 4GLs are far removed from machine languages and represent the class of computer languages closest to human languages. Regardless of what language you use, you eventually need to convert your program into machine language so that the computer can understand it. There are two ways to do this: compile the program and interpret the program.

According to the passage, which of the following is true?

Ⓐ Computers can only understand machine languages.

Ⓑ Computer languages are more complex than human languages.

Ⓒ You cannot program a computer without using a machine language.

Ⓓ Machine languages can be rewritten using names for numbers.

해설 주어진 문제와 선택지에 포함된 핵심어(keyword)를 지문에서 빠르게 찾아(scan)본다. 보기 Ⓐ에 Computers can only understand machine languages의 핵심어(computer, understand, machine languages)가 지문의 열 번째(아래에서 세 번째) 문장 you eventually need to convert your program into machine language so that the computer can understand it.에 언급되어 있다. 그리고 본문의 need to를 only로 바꿔 썼다. Ⓑ는 첫 번째 문장에서 비교의 순서가 바뀌었으며 Ⓒ는 네 번째 문장에서 어셈블리어가 기계어보다 프로그램을 하기 쉽다고 하였으므로 답이 아니다. 마찬가지로 기계어가 아닌 어셈블리어가 숫자를 이름으로 대체하기(다시 쓰여 지기) 때문에 Ⓓ도 답이 아니다.

해석 높은 수준의 프로그래밍 언어는 인간의 언어에 비해 간단하지만 기계어라는 컴퓨터가 실제로 이해하는 언어보다 더 복잡하다. 서로 다른 종류의 CPU는 고유의 기계어를 갖고 있다. 어셈블리어라는 언어는 기계어와 고급어 사이에 있다. 어셈블리어는 기계어와 유사하지만 숫자를 이름으로 대체할 수 있게 해주기 때문에 프로그래머가 프로그래밍하기에 훨씬 쉽다. 기계어는 숫자로만 구성된다. 4세대 언어(보통 4GL로 축약)라는 언어가 고급어 위에 있다. 4GL은 기계어와 전혀 다르고 인간의 언어에 가장 가까운 컴퓨터 언어 등급을 나타낸다. 당신이 사용하는 언어에 관계없이 당신은 결국 컴퓨터가 이해할 수 있도록 프로그램을 기계어로 변환해야 한다. 이 작업을 수행하기 위한 두 가지 방법이 있다: 프로그램 명령어를 번역하고 해석하는 것이다.

문제 지문에 따르면 다음 중에 어느 것이 사실인가?

Ⓐ 컴퓨터는 기계어만 이해할 수 있다.

Ⓑ 컴퓨터 언어는 인간의 언어보다 더 복잡하다.

Ⓒ 기계어의 사용 없이는 컴퓨터 프로그램을 할 수 없다.

Ⓓ 기계어는 숫자를 사용하여 다시 쓰여질 수 있다.

Exercise 1

In mid-2011, the world's worst food crisis was felt in East Africa, in Ethiopia, Somalia and Kenya. Despite successive failed rains, the crisis has been criticized as avoidable and man-made. This is because the situation had been predicted many months before by an international early warning system. Both the international community and governments in the region had been accused of doing very little in the lead up to this crisis. In addition, high food prices forced food out of the reach of many people, while local conflicts exacerbated the situation. International organizations maintained that 12 million people were in dire need of food, clean water, and basic sanitation. Loss of life on a massive scale was a very real risk, and the crisis was set to worsen over the later months of the year, particularly for pastoralist communities.

According to the passage, which of the following is true?

Ⓐ The crisis could not have been prevented with failed rains.

Ⓑ The early warning system was inadequate.

Ⓒ The government was unable to do anything before the crisis.

Ⓓ If it had rained, the crisis could probably have been averted.

Exercise 2

They came to Canada for a better life, a young couple who left behind relatives in the western Indian state of Gujarat in search of a corner of their own to start a family. But the journey has been anything but easy for Jatin Bhatt and Hetal Rajgor since moving into their Scarborough apartment. Both university educated, the pair has struggled to find enough work to pay rent and give their two-year-old son Aarav the life they hoped they would find in Canada. "It makes you frustrated wondering what is going to happen to your child. It's a frustration familiar to newcomer families across the region, many of whom must overcome cultural and language barriers to find work and integrate into their new communities." "You have this big dream for them to become a doctor or an engineer, but with no money..." said Rajgor, 30, trailing off as her toddler flew into the sparsely-furnished room atop a brightly-colored tricycle."It's his favorite. We borrowed it from a friend," she said. "Sometimes I feel so bad I cannot buy him things I think he has a right to have... it's hard."

According to the passage, which of the following is true of immigrants in Canada?

(A) They can afford to buy new things for their children that they couldn't buy in their home country.

(B) Life is much more difficult than they expected.

(C) They will be able to realize their dreams if they work hard.

(D) They can earn more money compared to their home country.

1. 지문

2011년 중반 세계 최악의 식량 위기가 동아프리카, 에티오피아, 소말리아와 케냐에서 감지되었다. 비가 계속적으로 오지 않았음에도 불구하고 위기는 피할 수 있었고, 인재였다고 비판을 받아왔다. 그 위기 상황이 국제 조기경보 시스템에 의해 여러 달 전에 예측되었기 때문이다. 국제 사회와 이 지역의 정부 모두가 이 위기를 불러일으킨 데 대해 거의 아무 일도 안했다고 비난을 받아 왔다. 더불어 지역의 갈등이 상황을 악화시키면서 높은 식량 가격은 많은 사람들이 음식을 구하기 힘들게 만들었다. 국제기구들은 1,200만 명의 사람들이 음식과 깨끗한 물 그리고 기본적인 위생이 절실히 필요하다고 주장했다. 거대한 규모의 인명 피해는 매우 실질적인 위험이었다. 그리고 식량 위기는 그해 하반기에 걸쳐 특히 목축업 지역 사회를 악화시켰다.

어휘

food crisis 식량 위기 predicted 예상되는 be accused of ~로 비난을 받다 sanitation 위생시설 [관리] pastoralist community 목축업 지역 사회

문제

지문에 따르면 다음 중에 어느 것이 사실인가?
Ⓐ 그 위기(식량 위기)는 비가 적게 오면 막을 수 없었을 것이다.
Ⓑ 조기 경보 시스템은 부적절하였다.
Ⓒ 정부는 위기 전에 어떤 것도 할 수 없었다.
Ⓓ 비가 내렸더라면 아마도 그 위기를 비켜갈 수 있었을 것이다.

해설

위기는 비가 내리지 않아 발생하였으므로 비가 내렸더라면 위기를 비켜갈 수 있었을 것이라고 가정한 Ⓓ가 답이다. 나머지 보기는 주어, 서술어, 목적어 등의 일부 내용만 일치하거나 인과 관계가 적절하지 않으므로 오답이다.

정답

Ⓓ

---

2. 지문

가정을 꾸릴 그들만의 공간을 찾아 구자르트의 인도 서부에 있는 친척들을 뒤로한 채 그들은 더 나은 삶을 위해서 캐나다로 왔다. 그러나 그들이 스카보로 아파트로 이사한 이후로 재틴 바트와 헤탈레이거에게 그 여정은 결코 쉽지 않았다. 두 사람 모두 대학을 졸업한 이 커플은 월세를 지불할 충분한 일을 찾고 캐나다에서 그들이 찾길 희망했던 삶을 그들의 2세 된 아들 어레브에게 주기 위해 힘든 시간을 보내 왔다. '당신의 아이에게 무슨 일이 일어날까 하는 생각이 당신을 좌절하도록 만들어요. 그것은 지역을 건너 새로 온 가족이 겪는 것과 유사한 좌절인데 그들의 대부분은 일을 찾고 그들의 새로운 지역과 흡수되기 위해 문화적 언어적 장벽을 극복해야 합니다.' '당신은 그들이 의사나 엔지니어가 되기를 바라는 그런 꿈을 가지고 있지만 돈이 없이는...' 그녀의 아이가 가구가 간소하게 갖춰진 방으로 밝게 칠해진 세발자전거를 타고 들어갈 때 30세인 레이저가 목소리가 잦아들면서 말했다. '이것은 그가 가장 좋아하는 것이에요. 우리는 친구에게서 그것을 빌렸어요..'라고 그녀는 말했다. '가끔 저는 제 아들이 가질 수 있다고 생각하는 것들을 사 줄 수 없을 때 기분이 너무 안 좋아요... 그게 힘들어요.'

어휘

frustrated 좌절감을 느끼는. 불만스러운 barrier 장벽. 차단막 integrate into ~에 통합 [흡수]되다 trail off 차츰 잦아들다 fly into ~로 날아들다

문제

지문에 의하면 다음 중 캐나다 이민자들에 관해 사실인 것은?
Ⓐ 그들은 그들의 고국에서 아이들을 위해 살 수 없었던 새로운 것들을 사 줄 수 있다.
Ⓑ 삶이 그들이 기대했던 것보다 훨씬 더 힘들다.
Ⓒ 열심히 일하면 그들의 꿈을 이룰 수 있을 것이다.
Ⓓ 그들의 고국에서와 비교하면 더 많은 돈을 벌 수 있다.

해설

지문 전반에 걸친 내용의 일치문제이다. 지문 전체에 걸쳐 캐나다로 이민 온 가족의 힘든 모습들이 파악되므로 답은 Ⓑ이다. 나머지 보기는 본문에 언급이 안 되었거나 반대의 내용이므로 오답이다.

정답

Ⓑ

It is important that burns are cared for as they can cause infection, leave scars, and predispose you to cancer. First-degree burns are the mildest of all burns. They tend to be thin, not reaching far below the skin's surface. **First-degree burns** are usually pink or red and very sore. Often, they will turn white when you apply pressure. Depending on the person, first-degree burns may swell a bit. These superficial burns usually heal within 3 to 6 days. Most frequently, the top layer of skin over the burn will peel off in 1 or 2 days, makin g way for **new and healthy skin**. Immediately following the incident, soak the burn in cool water to reduce the temperature of the area. When the sting begins to lessen, treat the burn with a healing gel such as aloe vera or an antibiotic ointment. Cover the burned area with a dry gauze bandage, and take something to ease the pain.

1. **According to the passage, which of the following can be inferred about first degree burns?**

   Ⓐ They are more serious than people think.

   Ⓑ They are difficult to treat effectively.

   Ⓒ They do not require hospitalization.

   Ⓓ They are the most common type of burn.

2. **Why does the author mention new and healthy skin?**

   Ⓐ To emphasize that burning is temporary

   Ⓑ To show that the skin will repair itself

   Ⓒ To compare the difference with pink and red burns

   Ⓓ To give evidence that first-degree burns are only superficial

3. **According to the passage, which of the following is true?**

   Ⓐ You should not touch first-degree burns for 3 to 6 days.

   Ⓑ A burn should be kept dry until the swelling has gone down.

   Ⓒ Burns below the layer of the skin are not first-degree burns.

   Ⓓ It's important to apply pressure to a burn if the skin is white.

The heater uses engine coolant to warm the air. If the engine is cold, it will be several minutes before you feel warm air coming from the system. Set the temperature to maximum. Make sure the A/C is off. Select fresh air mode. Set the fan to the desired speed. You can set the temperatures and modes for the driver's side and the passenger's side separately when **this button** is pressed. When the indicator in the dual button is off, you can adjust both sides to the same temperature and mode with the driver's side temperature control buttons and mode control button. The driver's side mode and passenger's side mode can be selected separately when the dual button is pressed. However, when selected on the driver's side, mode selection on the passenger's side is not possible. The flow-through ventilation system draws in outside air, circulates it through the interior, and then **exhausts** it through the vents near the rear window.

1. **The phrase this button in the passage refers to**

Ⓐ the fan speed button

Ⓑ the temperature button

Ⓒ the driver's side button

Ⓓ the passenger's side button

2. **The word exhausts in the passage is closest in meaning to**

Ⓐ wears out

Ⓑ lets out

Ⓒ deprives

Ⓓ destroys

3. **According to the passage, which of the following is NOT true when the dual button is on?**

Ⓐ The driver has priority over the passenger controling the mode selection.

Ⓑ The passenger's temperature can be set separately from the driver's.

Ⓒ Mode selection on the passenger's side is possible.

Ⓓ The driver can't adjust both sides to the same temperature and mode.

Vocabulary

Overview

어휘(Vocabulary) 문제는 지문에 음영 처리되어 있는 단어 또는 구의 동의어를 선택지 중에서 고르는 유형이다. 어휘는 문맥에서 의미가 달라질 수 있으므로 문맥을 파악하는 것이 어휘 못지않게 중요하다. 한 지문에 3~4문항이 출제될 정도로 높은 빈도수를 보인다.

질문유형

• The word "   " in the passage is closest in meaning to
  지문의 단어 '   '와 의미상 가장 가까운 것은?

• The phrase "   " in the passage is closest in meaning to
  지문의 구 '   '와 의미상 가장 가까운 것은?

접근방법

1. 토플에 자주 나오는 어휘를 최대한 많이 암기한다. 빈출 어휘를 동의어와 반의어, 파생어 등으로 묶어 외운다.

2. 주어진 단어의 사전적 의미가 우선이지만 여러 의미를 가진 단어가 출제되었을 때에는 반드시 문맥에 적절한 어휘를 고른다.

3. 모르는 어휘 주변의 동격 또는 대조 어구를 바탕으로 의미를 유추한다.
   ① 관계 대명사 뒤의 be동사
   ② or, and 등 접속사
   ③ 예를 보여주는 표현(such as, like, including)
   ④ 비교 / 대조 표현(but, however, on the other hand, in comparison, similarly, likewise 등)
   ⑤ 반복을 피하기 위해 사용된 동의어

4. 선택지의 어휘는 문법과 관련이 없다. 토플 어휘 문제의 보기는 주어진 단어와 품사가 같고 수가 일치하므로 수 일치나 품사 일치로 문제를 풀 수 없다.

Sample Question

The hosting of any major sporting event can both be seen as an opportunity for great development, or an **impending** disaster. The World Cup in Brazil is no different, and opposing groups have already been debating the cost benefit of hosting the competition for some time. Somewhat unsurprisingly, they come up with very different figures. The hosting of the World Cup can be twisted to suit the agenda of any political group. However, for all the potential economic benefits, will it actually be the Brazilian public who benefit? That much is open to very serious questions. While bidding for the tournament, the emphasis had been on the social benefit that hosting the World Cup would bring. Those benefits—largely based around the sizable issue of urban mobility— have now been swiftly forgotten about.

The word impending in the passage is closest in meaning to

Ⓐ forthcoming

Ⓑ damaging

Ⓒ closing

Ⓓ judging

해설 Impending은 주로 불쾌한 일이 '곧 닥칠'의 의미를 갖는다. impending의 뒤에 나오는 단어가 disaster(재난)이고 다가오는 브라질 월드컵에 대한 반대 그룹에 대한 문장이 나오므로 Ⓐ forthcoming이 답이다. 접속사 임박한 재난 앞의 or는 발전의 기회와 대조하는 역할을 한다. 일반적으로 or는 앞의 말과 유사한 내용을 설명하지만 대조하는 경우도 있으므로 주의한다.

해석 주요 스포츠 이벤트의 개최는 모두 커다란 발전의 기회 또는 임박한 재난으로 볼 수 있다. 브라질 월드컵도 예외는 아니며 반대 그룹은 이미 얼마 동안 시합 개최에 드는 비용 대비 이익을 논의하고 있다. 어느 정도 예상한대로 그들은 매우 다른 그림을 제시했다. 월드컵 개최는 어떠한 정치 단체의 의제에 맞추어 휘둘릴 수 있다. 하지만 모든 잠재적인 경제적 이익이 실제로 브라질 대중에게 혜택으로 돌아갈까? 그것은 매우 심각한 문제로 남아 있다. 대회를 위해 입찰하면서 주안점은 월드컵 개최가 가져다 줄 사회적 이익에 있었다. 이러한 이익은 – 주로 도시 유동성에 꽤 큰 비중을 둔 – 지금 빠르게 잊혀져가고 있다.

문제 지문의 임박한과 의미가 가장 가까운 것은?

Ⓐ 다가오는

Ⓑ 손해를 입히는

Ⓒ 마무리 짓는

Ⓓ 판단하는

Exercise 1

Whether capturing a U.S. president, a willowy super model for a fashion magazine or a costumed actor destined to grace a movie poster, noted photographer Albert Watson maintains the same philosophy. "I treat everybody the same. It doesn't matter who is in front of the camera," he told CBC News, during a recent Toronto visit to unveil Albert Watson: Archive, his first photography show in Canada. "I can usually find something there. The human race is very interesting." The award-winning Scottish-born photographer and director is known for his evocative art, fashion and commercial imagery as well as his **striking** portraits of icons and celebrities. He has travelled the world and his work appears in galleries and museums around the globe. He's particularly adept at shooting cover images: from the more than 100 magazine covers he's shot for Vogue to the posters for movies such as Kill Bill and Memoirs of a Geisha. His lens captured the iconic portrait of Steve Jobs that fronted the recent Jobs biography and which Apple also displayed on its website the week its innovative founder died.

The word striking in the passage is closest in meaning to

Ⓐ conspicuous
Ⓑ natural
Ⓒ hitting
Ⓓ touching

Exercise 2

Shaquille O'Neal knows that being rich and buying houses is fun, so despite living in a 70,000-square-foot mansion he dropped $235k on a second, regular person house 30 miles away. Shaq, who is reportedly worth around $250 million, currently lives in an 11-bedroom, 13-bath palace outside Orlando, Florida, which includes a 20,000-square-foot basketball court and garage filled with dozens of sports cars. But that just wasn't enough because in July the former NBA superstar laid down $235k on a very normal 3,900-square-foot **abode** in Mount Dora, Florida. It's unclear why he bought the spare pad. Investment? Gift? Kicks and giggles? But we do know the house is pretty nice, for those of us not sitting on fat bank accounts. The new pad is rocking 5 bedrooms, 4 baths, granite counter tops, wet bar, entertainment room, and cherry cabinets. This would all be really awesome if his other house wasn't way more awesome. We reached out to Shaq's people to ask him about the new purchase but so far there's been no word back.

The word abode in the passage is closest in meaning to

- (A) structure
- (B) building
- (C) real estate
- (D) home

1. 지문

미국 대통령이든지, 패션 잡지의 호리호리한 슈퍼 모델이나 영화 포스터를 장식할 잘 차려입은 영화배우든지간에 유명한 사진작가인 앨버트 왓슨은 같은 철학을 지킨다. '저는 모든 사람을 똑같이 대합니다. 누가 카메라 앞에 있는지는 중요하지 않습니다.' 그는 캐나다에서 그의 첫 번째 사진전이 열리는 앨버트 왓슨 기록 보관소를 개막하기 위해 최근 토론토를 방문하는 동안 CBC 뉴스에서 말했다. '저는 대개 거기서 뭔가를 찾아냅니다. 인류는 참 흥미롭습니다.' 상을 받은 스코틀랜드 태생 사진작가이자 감독으로 그는 상징적 인물들과 유명 인사들의 <mark>눈에 띄는</mark> 인물 사진뿐만 아니라 훌륭한 예술, 패션 그리고 상업적 형상화로 잘 알려져 있다. 그는 세계 여행을 해왔고 그의 작품은 전 세계의 갤러리와 박물관에서 전시되고 있다. 그는 특히 표지 이미지를 찍는 데 능숙하다: 그가 보그를 위해 찍은 100장이 넘는 잡지 표지부터 킬빌 같은 영화 포스터 그리고 게이사의 회고록까지. 그의 렌즈는 최근 잡스 전기의 앞면을 장식했고 또한 혁신적인 창립자가 세상을 떠난 주에 애플이 웹사이트에 올린 스티브 잡스의 상징적인 사진을 담아냈다.

어휘

unveil 덮개를 벗기다 evocative 연상시키는, 상기시키는 portrait 초상화, 인물 사진 be adept at ~에 능숙하다 iconic ~의 상징이 되는, 우상의 innovative 획기적인

문제

지문의 <mark>눈에 띄는</mark>이라는 어휘와 의미가 가장 비슷한 것은?

Ⓐ 두드러진
Ⓑ 자연스런
Ⓒ 때리는
Ⓓ 감동적인

해설

Striking은 <mark>눈에 띄는</mark>의 의미를 갖는다. 문맥에서도 상징적 인물들과 유명 인사들의 사진이 눈에 띄는 것이 자연스러우므로 Ⓐ conspicuous(두드러진)가 답이다. 보기 Ⓒ hitting이나 Ⓓ touching은 strike(때리다)를 연상하게 하는 오답이다. striking(눈에 띄는), touching(감동적인)처럼 현재분사가 되어 문맥에서 다른 뜻을 갖는 어휘에 주의한다.

정답

Ⓐ

2. 지문

샤킬 오닐은 부자이면서 집을 사들이는 것이 재미있다는 것을 안다. 그래서 7만 평방피트 맨션에 살고 있음에도 불구하고 30마일이 떨어진 곳에 두 번째 집을 23만 5천 달러에 싸게 샀다. 소문에 의하면 2억 5천만 달러 정도 가치가 있는 샤크는 현재 플로리다 올란도 외곽에 11개의 방과 13개의 욕실이 있는 궁전에 살고 있는데 이는 2만 평방피트의 농구장과 십여 개의 스포츠 차를 가진 차고를 포함한다. 그러나 그 정도로 그치지 않았는데 그 이유는 왕년의 NBA 수퍼스타는 7월에 플로리다 마운트 도라 지역에 3천 9백 평방피트의 <mark>거주지</mark>를 사들였기 때문이다. 왜 그가 여분의 거주지를 구입했는지는 확실하지 않다. 투자? 선물? 재미로? 그러나 돈 많은 은행 계좌를 가지고 있지 않은 우리는 그 집이 꽤 좋다는 것을 분명히 안다. 그 새로운 거주지는 방이 5개, 욕실이 4개, 화강암 작업대 갑판, 집안에 설치된 바, 실내 놀이방 그리고 체리나무 캐빗으로 훌륭하다. 만약 그의 다른 집이 훨씬 더 으리으리하지 않았다면 이번 집에 정말 경탄할 만했을 것이다. 우리는 그 집을 새로 구입한 것에 대해 그에게 물어보려고 샤크 주위 사람들에게 접근하였지만 아직까지 아무런 말이 없다.

어휘

square-foot 평방피트, 제곱피트 reportedly 전언에 따르면, 소문에 의하면 be filled with ~로 가득 차다 dozens of 수십의, 많은 ~ granite 화강암 awesome 경탄할 만한 reach out ~에 닿다, 접근하다

문제

지문의 <mark>거주지</mark>라는 단어의 의미가 가장 비슷한 것은

Ⓐ 구조물
Ⓑ 건물
Ⓒ 부동산
Ⓓ 집

해설

Abode는 거주지를 의미하고 문맥에서 뒤에 그 집이 꽤 좋다고 하였으므로 Ⓒ home이 답이다. 보기 Ⓐ, Ⓑ, Ⓒ는 거주지만을 가리키는 단어가 아니므로 오답이다.

정답

Ⓓ

India's Chandrayaan-1 satellite confirmed the presence of water on the moon in September 2009, building on observations by other probes that were on their way to other planets. Although the surface of the moon is still drier than Earth's driest desert, evidence of water is there, suggesting there could be an interaction between the solar wind and the moon's surface that produces water and hydroxyl molecules. It doesn't mean there are abundant lakes and oceans, but future moon colonists could extract and purify the traces of water from the surface to use for drinking, food **cultivation**, oxygen and fuel. Alternatively, **colonists** of the moon could go to the moon's poles to mine water from the deepest craters. On Oct. 9, 2009, NASA dropped a spent rocket into a crater that created a 100-foot-wide hole. They found water there too. The plume of dust from that rocket was analyzed and it was found that there was at least 25 gallons of water ice in the plume.

1. The word cultivation in the passage is closest in meaning to

Ⓐ refinement

Ⓑ production

Ⓒ development

Ⓓ growing

2. The word colonists in the passage is closest in meaning to

Ⓐ imposters

Ⓑ inhabitants

Ⓒ settlers

Ⓓ workers

3. According to the passage, which of the following can be inferred about the moon?

Ⓐ Without the solar wind there probably would be no water on the moon.

Ⓑ Moon colonists could easily extract water on the moon.

Ⓒ The existence of dust confirmed the dryness of the moon.

Ⓓ There could be various ways to get water on the moon in the future.

I still remember my high school photography teacher instructing our class with this rule. He drummed it into us week after week and his words have echoed in my ears ever since – 20-something years –almost every time I raise my camera to take a portrait. The rule was well intentioned and good advice. As I think back to the portraits my classmates and I took back then – many of them were of subjects that could have done well to have the subjects filling the frame more. Many of my early shots had my subject well back from the lens and the result was that they were small in the frame – **lacking** detail and getting lost in the image. Filling the frame with your subject helps those viewing the image to know where to look without distraction and in many cases will leave you with a portrait that is **intimate** and impactful.

1. **The word lacking in the passage is closest in meaning to**

   Ⓐ deficient
   Ⓑ disturbing
   Ⓒ emphasizing
   Ⓓ efficient

2. **The word intimate in the passage is closest in meaning to**

   Ⓐ confidential
   Ⓑ special
   Ⓒ cozy
   Ⓓ immediate

3. **According to the passage, which of the following is true?**

   Ⓐ His high school photography teacher was a drummer.
   Ⓑ In his early portraits, the subjects were too far away.
   Ⓒ You cannot have an intimate portrait if the subject is too large.
   Ⓓ Without having good intentions, you cannot give good advice.

4. **According to the passage, which of the following can be inferred about his high school photography teacher?**

   Ⓐ He was methodical and well organized in his teaching.
   Ⓑ His portraits had won many prizes.
   Ⓒ Some students did not like his teaching because it was boring.
   Ⓓ He was insistent and vocal about a particular rule.

Unit 04 Reference

Overview

지시어(Reference) 문제는 지문에 음영 처리되어 있는 지시어가 가리키는 지시 대상을 선택지 중에서 고르는 유형이다. 지시어는 글에서 같은 표현의 반복적 사용을 피하여 글의 간결성과 일관성을 높이기 위해 사용된다. 출제되는 지시어는 주로 인칭 대명사나 지시 대명사이다. 하지만 부정 대명사나 관계 대명사 또는 명사어구가 제시되기도 한다. 한 지문에 1문항 정도 출제된다.

질문유형

· The word "＿＿＿＿" in the passage refers to
  지문의 단어 '＿＿＿＿'가 가리키는 것은?

· The phrase "＿＿＿＿" in the passage refers to
  지문의 구 '＿＿＿＿'가 가리키는 것은?

접근방법

1. 지시어가 가리키는 지시 대상은 대부분 지시어보다 앞에 언급되어 있다.
2. 문제에 주로 출제되는 지시어는 다음과 같다.
    ① 인칭 대명사: it, its, they, their, them
    ② 지시 대명사: this, these, that, those
    ③ 부정 대명사: one, another, the other, some, others, any, none, many, most
    ④ 관계 대명사: who, whose, whom, which, that
    ⑤ 명사어구: this + 단수명사, these + 복수명사, that + 단수명사, those + 복수명사, the + 명사
3. 지시어가 있는 문장에서 지시어와 지시 대상의 자리(주어, 목적어)는 일치하는 경우가 많으므로 문장 구조를 확인한다.
4. 예상되는 답을 고른 후에는 지문의 지시어 자리에 넣고 해석을 해본다. 이때 해석이 문맥상 자연스러운지 확인한다. 문맥상 연결이 되지 않으면 오답이다.
5. 선택지의 어휘는 문법과 관련이 없다. 토플 지시어 문제의 선택지는 지시어 앞뒤의 명사들이며 주어진 단어와 품사가 같고 수가 일치하므로 수 일치나 품사 일치로 문제를 풀 수 없다.

Almost any type of restaurant food is a discretionary purchase: if the price is too high, people can and will refuse to buy. **That** presents a real problem if businesses are seeing significant increases in the price of the food commodities they must purchase. For a business that is squeezed between rising input prices and tepid demand, investment in labor-saving technology can represent one of the few viable paths to continued profitability. Increased automation in fast food and beverage providers is likely to someday offer increased convenience, speed, and ordering accuracy. Robotic food preparation could also be viewed as more hygienic as fewer workers come into contact with food. And of course, price will ultimately be the determining factor.

The word That in the passage refers to

Ⓐ discretionary purchasing of food commodities

Ⓑ restaurant food having too high a price

Ⓒ refusing to buy restaurant food

Ⓓ having discretionary choice about purchases

해설 앞 문장에서 가격이 너무 높으면 사람들이 구매를 거부할 것이라고 하였고 그 다음 문장에서 그것이 현실적인 문제로 나타난다고 하였으므로 Ⓒ가 답이다. 지시어가 가리키는 지시 대상은 대부분 지시어보다 앞에 언급되어 있다. 지시어 앞의 문장에서 사람들이 자유재량에 따라 구매를 거부하는 것은 restaurant food(식당 음식)이지 food commodities(식료품)가 아니다. 따라서 비슷한 단어라도 지시어가 가리키는 대상이 다를 수 있으므로 답을 지시어 자리에 넣고 문맥상 자연스러운지 확인한다.

해석 대부분의 모든 식당 음식 유형은 자유재량에 의한 구매이다: 가격이 너무 높으면 사람들은 구매를 거부할 것이다. 그것은 기업이 구입해야 할 식료품의 가격이 상당히 오른 것을 볼 때 현실적인 문제로 나타난다. 상승하는 공급가격과 미지근한 수요사이에 압박받는 사업의 경우 노동 절약 기술에 대한 투자는 지속적인 수익성을 위한 몇 가지 가능한 방향 중 하나를 제시할 수 있다. 늘어나는 패스트푸드와 음료 제공업체의 자동화는 언젠가 편의, 속도 및 주문의 정확도 증진을 제공할 가능성이 높다. 더 적은 노동자가 식품과 접촉함으로 로봇의 음식조리가 더 위생적으로 보여질 수 있다. 그리고 물론 가격이 궁극적인 결정 요인이 될 것이다.

문제 지문의 단어 that이 가리키는 것은?

Ⓐ 식료품의 자유재량에 의한 구입

Ⓑ 너무 비싼 물가를 지닌 식당 음식

Ⓒ 사람들의 식당 음식 구매 거절

Ⓓ 자유재량에 의한 구매 선택

Exercise 1

Golf remains largely an elitist sport in China, though it is growing; the number of courses there has increased from 170 to nearly600 in the last eight years, according to a story by China Daily. We asked Dan Washburn, an expert on golf in China and a contributor to Golf Digest and Golf World for his thoughts on what impact Guan might have on Chinese golf. His email response: "Guan's historic achievement certainly can't hurt golf's prospects for growth in China, but the obstacles **it** faces in the country are real. It will be interesting to see how much coverage Guan's Masters adventure attracts in China beyond the niche golf publications. Even Feng Shanshan, winner of China's first major, struggles for recognition in her home country" "Golf is going to grow in China - there is no doubt about that. Trying to predict how fast or to what heights, however, is a fool's errand. But if this drumbeat continues - Feng, Zhang, and now Guan - Chinese golf is soon going to be hard for the world to ignore, no matter how far from the mainstream the sport continues to be in China."

The word it in the passage refers to

Ⓐ Guan's historic achievement

Ⓑ Golf World

Ⓒ golf's prospects for growth in China

Ⓓ the impact of Guan on Chinese golf

Exercise 2

During adverse weather conditions, accurate weather-related campus information including delayed openings, class cancellations, or closings will be disseminated on the Rutgers website and New Brunswick website with links to the Campus Operating Status page. Additionally, information will be distributed via email and will be available on RU-tv Channel 3 and via RU-info at 732-445-INFO (including 24-hour voice mail). Please refrain from calling the Rutgers University Police Department with weather status questions as **this** overloads the phone system during a critical time. For additional details, including links to University Policies and Procedures, visit the New Brunswick Campus Adverse Weather Information web site at http://emergency.rutgers.edu/weather.shtml.

The word this in the passage refers to

Ⓐ adverse weather conditions

Ⓑ class cancellations

Ⓒ calling with weather status questions

Ⓓ information disseminated on the Rutgers website

1. **지문**

비록 골프장이 늘어나고 있지만, 중국에서 골프는 여전히 엘리트 스포츠이다; 차이나 데일리 기사에 따르면 지난 8년 동안에 코스의 수가 170개에서 거의 600개로 늘었다. 우리는 중국에서 골프에 대해 전문가이며 골프 다이제스트와 골프 월드의 기고자인 댄 와쉬번에게 관 씨가 중국 골프에 어떤 영향을 미칠 것인가에 대한 그의 생각을 물어 보았다. 그는 이메일에서 답한다: '관 씨의 역사적인 성과가 분명히 중국의 골프 성장의 전망에 해를 끼치지는 않겠지만 그 나라에서 그것이 직면하는 장애물이 존재한다. 틈새 골프 출판 간행물을 넘어 중국에서 관의 마스터스 시도가 얼마나 많은 방송 보도로 주목받을지 보는 것은 흥미로울 것이다. 심지어 중국의 최초 메이저의 승리자인 펑산산도 그녀의 모국에서 인정받기 위하여 분투한다.' '중국에서 골프는 성장할 것이다 – 그것에 대해 의심의 여지는 없다. 그러나 얼마나 빠르게 어느 정도 높게 성장할지 예상하려는 노력은 헛고생이다. 하지만 만약 이렇게 반복되는 뉴스가 계속된다면 – 펑 씨, 장 씨 그리고 이제 관 씨 – 주류에서 얼마나 떨어져 있든 그 스포츠는 중국에서 계속될 것이고 곧 세계가 무시하기 어렵게 될 것이다.'

어휘

contributor 기고자, 토론자, 기부자 prospect for ~의 전망 obstacle 장애물 niche 아주 편한 자리 [역할] mainstream 주류, 대세

문제

지문의 단어 it이 가리키는 것은?
Ⓐ 관 씨의 역사적인 성과
Ⓑ 골프 세상(골프 잡지)
Ⓒ 중국의 골프 성장의 전망
Ⓓ 중국 골프에 끼치는 관의 영향

해설

It을 포함한 절의 앞에 관의 역사적 성과와 중국의 골프 성장의 전망에 대해 긍정적으로 말한다. 문맥에서 장애물이 존재할 수 있는 것은 성장과 관련되므로 Ⓒ가 답이다.

정답

Ⓒ

2. **지문**

악천후 상황 동안에 지연된 개강, 수업 취소나 종강을 포함하여 기상과 관련이 있는 정확한 캠퍼스 정보가 캠퍼스 운영 정보 페이지와 링크되어 러트거즈 웹사이트와 뉴 브런즈윅 웹사이트에서 전해질 것이다. 추가적으로 정보는 이메일을 통해 배포되거나 RU 텔레비전 채널 3과 732-445-인포의 RU-인포(24시간 음성 메일도 포함하여)로 얻을 수 있을 것이다. 응급 시간대에는 이것이 전화 시스템에 과부하를 걸기 때문에 기상 상황의 전화질문은 러트거즈 대학의 구내 경찰부서에 삼가 바란다. 추가적인 정보를 위해 구내 경찰 처리과에 연결되어 있는 링크를 포함하여 http://emergency.rutgers.edu/weather.shtml의 뉴브런즈윅 캠퍼스 악천후 기상 정보 사이트를 방문하길 바란다.

어휘

be disseminated 전파되다 refrain from ~을 삼가다 overload 과적하다 critical 비판적인, 비난의

문제

지문의 단어 this가 가리키는 것은?
Ⓐ 악천후 상황
Ⓑ 수업 취소
Ⓒ 기상 상황의 질문 전화
Ⓓ 러트거즈 웹사이트에서 보도되는 정보

해설

this가 있는 절의 앞에 기상 상황의 전화 질문을 삼가하라고 하고 this가 과부하가 걸리는 이유를 설명하므로 Ⓒ가 답이다.

정답

Ⓒ

If this technology is reproducible and works in human cells, it also has potential for cancer treatments as well. **This** may be based on low PH reprogramming of cancer cells because notably cancer cells are already acidic and create an acidic microenvironment which could contribute to cancer plasticity. It's also possible that the controversial, elusive VSELs and MUSE cells might have some connection to stress-related reprogramming or induced plasticity in vivo. **It is in addition a concern that almost killing cells with stress, even if "they" turn into the STAP stem cells, might leave some residual damage in the STAP cells that manifests later**. Even though the karyotypes of the STAP cells were reported as normal, I wonder if smaller, but still significant damage either in the nucleus or elsewhere in the cells could manifest later on with deeper analysis. **The bottom line** is this remains a fascinating development that has raised both some skepticism and also lots of excitement in the stem cell community.

1. The word **this** in the passage refers to

   (A) the technology being reproducible and working in human cells
   (B) the technology being reproducible
   (C) the technology working in human cells
   (D) the technology having potential for cancer treatments

2. The word **they** in the passage refers to

   (A) karyotypes
   (B) concerns
   (C) stresses
   (D) cells

3. Which of the sentences below best expresses the essential information in the highlighted sentence in the passage?

   (A) Stressing the cells will turn them into STAP cells but leave them damaged.
   (B) STAP cells that have been created by stress may potentially be damaged.
   (C) Without being stressed, cells cannot turn into STAP cells but will remain undamaged.
   (D) Residual stress in the STAP cells is a concern if it manifests later.

4. The phrase **the bottom line** in the passage is closest in meaning to

   (A) main point
   (B) strong point
   (C) profit
   (D) net loss

Mexico severed relations with the United States in March 1845, shortly after the U.S. annexation of Texas. In September President James K. Polk sent John Slidell on a secret mission to Mexico City to negotiate the disputed Texas border, settle U.S. claims against Mexico, and purchase New Mexico and California for up to $ 30,000,000. Mexican President José Joaquín Herrera, aware in advance of Slidell's intention of **dismembering** his country, refused to receive him. On May 9, 1846, Polk began to prepare a war message to Congress, justifying hostilities on the grounds of Mexican refusal to pay American claims and **its** refusal to negotiate with Slidell. That evening he received word that Mexican troops had crossed the Rio Grande on April 25 and attacked Taylor's troops, killing or injuring 16 of them. In his quickly revised war message— delivered to Congress on May 11—Polk claimed that "Mexico had invaded our territory and shed American blood on American soil."

1. The word dismembering in the passage is closest in meaning to

   Ⓐ dividing

   Ⓑ depriving of

   Ⓒ killing

   Ⓓ founding

2. The word its in the passage refers to

   Ⓐ Congress's

   Ⓑ Mexican

   Ⓒ American

   Ⓓ Polk's

3. According to the passage, Polk revised his message to Congress because:

   Ⓐ he now could have a stronger justification for war.

   Ⓑ he had to respond to the snub to Polk.

   Ⓒ Mexican President José Joaquín Herrera was going to dismember the country.

   Ⓓ the Mexicans refused to pay American claims.

Rhetorical Purpose

Overview

수사적 의도파악(Rhetorical Purpose) 문제는 지문에서 저자가 특정효과를 거두기 위해 사용하는 다양한 수사법 (rhetoric)의 의도를 선택지 중에서 고르는 유형이다. 수사법은 글의 효과적인 표현과 전달을 위한 기법이다. 이 유형의 문제는 특정한 단어나 구에 대한 저자의 의도를 묻거나 특정한 단락이 지문에서 어떤 목적이나 방식으로 사용되는지를 묻는다.

질문유형

1. 특정 단어 / 구를 언급한 목적을 물을 때

   • Why does the author mention _____ in the passage?

   왜 저자는 지문에서 _____ 를 언급하고 있는가?

   • The author mentions _____ in paragraph # in order to

   저자는 단락의 #에서 ~를 하기 위해 _____ 를 언급하고 있다.

2. 특정 단락의 기능이나 전개 방식을 물을 때

   • What is the purpose of paragraph # in the overall discussion?

   전체적인 맥락에서 단락 #의 기능은 무엇인가?

   • In paragraph #, how does the author explain _____ ?

   단락 #에서 저자는 _____ 를 어떤 방식으로 설명하고 있는가?

접근방법

1. 수사적 의도를 묻는 문제의 답은 문제에 제시된 단어나 구가 있는 문장의 주변에 있다. 따라서 그 앞뒤 문장을 읽으면서 내용 관계를 파악한다.

2. 저자의 의도를 제대로 알기 위해서는 글의 흐름을 이해하는 것이 중요하며 글의 전개 방식을 파악하기 위해 자주 사용되는 표현을 확인한다. 해당 표현은 다음과 같다. 참고로 compare는 비교로서 공통점과 차이점 모두에 사용하며 contrast는 대조로서 차이점에만 사용한다.

   ① 예를 들어주기 위해: to give an example, to describe, to explain, to illustrate...

   ② 비교 / 대조하기 위해: to compare, to contrast...

   ③ 분류 / 나열하기 위해: to classify, to list...

   ④ 지지 / 반박하기 위해: to support, to contradict, to criticize...

   ⑤ 제안 / 증명하기 위해: to suggest, to demonstrate, to show...

   ⑥ 부연 / 강조하기 위해: to emphasize, to highlight, to further develop the idea...

3. 특정 단락의 기능이나 전개 방식을 이해하기 위해 사용되는 표현들(부사, 접속사)을 지문에서 찾아본다.
    ① 비교 / 대조함으로써: similar to, similarly, akin to, in comparison, while, whereas, in contrast, on the other hand...
    ② 과정을 보여줌으로써: first, second, next, last...
4. 다음과 같은 오답을 선택지에서 고르지 않도록 한다.
    ① 글의 기능이나 전개방식을 잘못 말한 것
    ② 지문의 내용을 잘못 말한 것
    ③ 지문의 일부만 언급한 것

Sample Question

In a career spanning more than 70 years, Sci-fi legend Ray Bradbury, the author of "The Martian Chronicles" and "Something Wicked This Way Comes," has inspired generations of readers to dream, think and create. A prolific author of hundreds of short stories and close to 50 books as well as numerous poems, essays, operas, plays, teleplays and screenplays, Bradbury was one of the most celebrated writers of our time. Bradbury wrote the screenplay for John Huston's classic film adaptation of "Moby Dick." He adapted 65 of his stories for television's "The Ray Bradbury Theater" and won an Emmy for his teleplay of "The Halloween Tree." "In my later years I have looked in the mirror each day and found a happy person staring back." He wrote in a book of essays published in 2005. "Occasionally I wonder why I can be so happy. The answer is that every day of my life I've worked only for myself and for the joy that comes from writing and creating. The image in my **mirror** is not optimistic, but the result of optimal behavior."

Why does the author mention a mirror in the passage?

Ⓐ To compare his life situation with that of looking at himself

Ⓑ To emphasize the value of reflection in being able to have a happy life

Ⓒ To suggest that he loved to look at himself in a mirror

Ⓓ To underline his point that he has done what he wanted to do in life

해설 지문은 작가 브래드버리의 수상 소감에 대한 글이다. 작가는 다섯 번째 문장에서 거울을 바라보고 행복하다고 한 후 뒤에 자신만을 위해 일해 기뻤다고 하므로 답은 Ⓓ이다. 일정 단어나 구, 절이 지정되어 있으면 대개 질문지의 핵심어 주변에서 답의 근거를 찾을 수 있다. 답을 고른 후에는 지문 전체에서 제시되는 결론, 주제, 작가의 생각과 입장을 고려하여 어떤 의미나 의도로 사용되었는지 파악한다.

해석 70년 이상 일이 계속되는 동안 '마틴 연대기'와 '이상한 실종'의 저자인 SF 전설 레이 브래드버리는 여러 세대의 독자들을 꿈꾸고 생각하고 창조하도록 영감을 주어 왔다. 셀 수 없는 시, 에세이, 오페라, 연극, 텔레비전 드라마 그리고 영화 대본뿐만 아니라 수백 개의 짧은 이야기들과 50여 권의 책들을 다작하는 저자인 브래드버리는 우리 시대의 가장 유명한 작가들 중에 하나이다. 브래드버리는 존 휴스턴의 명작 '모비딕'의 영화 각색의 대본을 썼다. 그는 텔레비전의 '브래드버리 극장'을 위해 65개의 그의 이야기를 각색하였고 '할로윈 나무'의 텔레비전 드라마로 에미상을 수상하였다. '저는 말년에 매일 거울을 바라보았고 행복한 사람이 저를 바라보는 것을 알 수 있었습니다.' 2005년에 출판된 수필집에는 이렇게 적었다. '가끔 저는 제가 왜 이렇게 행복한지 궁금합니다. 정답은 저의 삶의 매일을 저 자신만을 위해 그리고 글쓰기와 창조하기에서 생기는 기쁨을 위해 일하였습니다. 저의 거울 속 이미지는 낙관적이지는 않지만 최선을 다한 행동의 결과입니다.'

문제 작가는 왜 지문에서 거울을 언급하고 있는가?

Ⓐ 사회에서의 자신의 입장을 자신을 스스로 볼 때의 입장과 비교하기 위해

Ⓑ 행복한 삶을 사는 데에 비친 모습의 가치를 강조하기 위해

Ⓒ 그가 거울을 보기 좋아한다는 것을 말하기 위해

Ⓓ 그가 삶에서 하고 싶었던 것을 해 냈다는 점을 강조하기 위해

The chocolate company is hiring a Senior Manager in Foresight Activation, someone with experience converting existing foresight (trends, forecasts, scenarios) into strategic opportunities(SOs). The company's posting never breaks down just what "foresight" means, though it does specify applicants should be "collaborate with and align multi-functional stake holders." Foresight means trying to understand the future. In other words, it is hiring a chocolate futurist. Of course, this is not an outlandish position. Companies everywhere analyze trends, try to figure out what threatens their business, and make plans accordingly. If they depend on products of the land, they specifically try to plan for the big, future risk of climate change. Little wonder: a study found that even small amounts of climate change could ravage the cocoa market, sending yields crashing and prices soaring. It has even been insisted that climate change, more than anything else, threatens the global supply chain of coffee, and, thus, the **coffee business** as well.

Why does the author mention coffee business?

Ⓐ To emphasize the need to be aware of threats in global supply chains

Ⓑ To contrast the situation with the future of chocolate

Ⓒ To give support for the idea that companies are taking climate change seriously

Ⓓ To give an example of why climate change will be a serious issue in the future

China may not hold the best human rights record, but one has to recognize true progress and intention regarding their workaholic efforts in changing the planet. China has for over a decade been the leading clean energy proponent, with action and visible deliverables as opposed to the hot-air paper-promises being emitted by western powers. Not only has the Chinese's government injected billions into subsidizing the production of solar panels, they have made green energy and the associated infrastructure affordable, one of the greatest problems holding back the conversion of ordinary people from dirty technology such as coal and fossil fuel to cleaner technologies. So the big oil bullies, the United States (US) and the European Union (EU), are trying to clamp down on China with tariffs. Economic bullies hate anyone usurping their oil-dominant economies and are not committed at grassroots level to cleaner technology. Why is that? Cleaner energy, the real one, not **the green-washing farces**, means less dependency on toxic industries making them billions. If anything, the EU and the US's unethical attack on China reflects their true non-commitment to a new energy equitable planet. A twenty percent replacement of dirty energy with clean, green energy has been achieved globally, not enough to turn the tide on climate change, but if the EU and the US are successful in suppressing China's affordable solar panel move with tariffs, this will result in a collapse of China's successful climate change campaign.

The author mentions the green-washing farces in the passage in order to

Ⓐ prove that the EU and the US don't realize the importance of clean energy

Ⓑ describe that China needs to reduce its tariffs to lead clean energy business

Ⓒ suggest that the success of China's economy relies on developing clean energy

Ⓓ show that the US and the EU are hypocritical about their interest in green energy

1. 지문

초콜릿 회사는 기존의 선견지명(동향, 예측, 시나리오)을 전략적 기회(SOs)로 바꾸는 경험을 갖고 있는 자를 포사이트 액티베이션의 수석 관리자로 채용하고자 한다. 이 회사의 공고는 지원자가 '다중 역할의 당사 주주와 협력하고 이해 관계를 맞추도록' 명시되어 있지만 '선견지명'의 본래 의미를 퇴색시키는 것은 아니다. 선견지명은 미래에 대해 이해하는 것이다. 다시 말해 미래의 초콜릿 전문가를 고용하려는 것이다. 물론 이것은 기이한 자리가 아니다. 어느 회사든지 동향을 분석하고 자신의 사업을 위협하는 것을 알아내기 위해 노력하며 그에 따라 계획을 세운다. 그들이 땅에서 생산되는 제품에 의존하는 경우 특히 기후 변화 등 미래의 커다란 위험에 대비한 계획을 수립하려고 한다. 당연하다: 한 연구는 아주 작은 기후 변화가 농작물의 생산을 급락시켜 가격이 급등하고 코코아 시장을 황폐화시킬 수 있다는 사실을 발견했다. 심지어 무엇보다도 기후 변화는 커피의 글로벌 공급망을 위협하고 따라서 커피 사업도 위협하고 있다고 주장되어 왔다.

어휘

foresight 예지력, 산견지명 strategic 전략적인 break down 부수다, 고장 나다 in other words 다시 말해서 figure out ~을 이해하다, 산출하다 ravage 황폐하게 하다, 유린하다

문제

왜 작가는 지문에서 커피 사업을 언급하고 있는가?
Ⓐ 글로벌 공급 체인의 위협에 대한 인식의 필요성을 강조하기 위해
Ⓑ 미래의 초콜릿 상황과 대조하기 위해
Ⓒ 기업들이 기후 변화를 심각하게 받아들이고 있다는 생각을 지지하기 위해
Ⓓ 왜 기후 변화가 미래의 심각한 안건이 될지 예를 들기 위해

해설

커피 사업은 초콜릿 회사와 마찬가지로 기후 변화에 기업들이 영향을 받는다는 사례를 보여주기 위해 언급하고 있으므로 Ⓒ가 답이다. 작가는 기후 변화와 커피 사업의 연관 관계를 설명하고 있으므로 한 쪽만 언급된 나머지는 오답이다.

정답

Ⓒ

---

2. 지문

중국이 아마 가장 훌륭한 인권 기록을 지니고 있지 않을 수 있지만 지구를 변화시키는 그들의 일 중독적인 노력에 관한 진정한 진전과 의도를 인식해야만 한다. 중국은 10년이 넘는 동안에 서양의 권력들로부터 제시되고 있는 말로만인 형식적인 약속들과는 대조적으로 행동과 눈에 보이는 실천으로 선두적인 청정에너지 지지자였다. 중국의 정부는 태양 전지판의 생산을 지원하는 데 수십 억을 투자해왔을 뿐만 아니라 청정에너지와 서민들이 석탄과 화석 연료 같은 지저분한 기술로부터 더욱 깨끗한 기술로의 전환을 방해하고 있는 가장 큰 문제들 중의 하나인 관련 기반 시설의 비용을 감당할 수 있도록 만들어 왔다. 그래서 석유 시장의 골목대장인 미국과 유럽 연합들은 관세로 중국을 엄하게 단속하려 하고 있다. 경제적 강자들은 그들의 석유 지배 경제를 강탈하려는 누구든 증오하며, 기초 수준의 청정 기술에 전념하지 않는다. 왜 그럴까? 청정에너지는 진짜 에너지이며 위장 환경주의의 웃음거리가 아닌 그들에게 수십억 달러를 벌어주는 유독성 산업에 덜 의존한다는 것을 의미한다. 오히려 중국에 대한 유럽 연합이나 미국의 비윤리적인 공격은 새로운 에너지 공정 세상에 대하여 사실상 그들의 애매한 입장을 반영한다. 20퍼센트의 환경 오염을 일으키는 에너지의 깨끗한 청정에너지로의 대체는 기후 변화의 조수를 되돌리는 데 충분하지 않았지만 세계적으로 성공을 거두어 왔다. 하지만 만약 유럽 연합과 미국이 중국의 적당한 태양 전지판 조치를 관세와 함께 억압하는 데 성공한다면 이것은 중국의 성공적인 기후 변화 캠페인의 실패를 야기할 것이다.

어휘

infrastructure 사회 기반시설 affordable 알맞은, 줄 수 있는 usurping 빼앗다, 찬탈하다 non-commitment 언질을 주지 않음 tide 조수, 일어나다, 생기다 collapse 붕괴되다, 무너지다

문제

지문에서 작가는 _____ 위해 위장 환경주의의 웃음거리를 언급하고 있다.
Ⓐ 유럽 연합과 미국이 청정에너지의 중요성을 인식하지 못한다는 것을 입증하기
Ⓑ 청정에너지 산업을 선도하기 위해서는 중국이 관세를 줄여야 한다는 것을 설명하기
Ⓒ 중국 경제의 성공은 청정에너지의 개발에 의존한다는 것을 제안하기
Ⓓ 미국과 유럽 연합은 청정에너지에 대한 그들의 관심에 위선적이라는 것을 보여주기

해설

작가는 미국이나 유럽 연합이 석유 지배 경제를 지키려고 청정에너지에 대해 적극적이지 않다는 점을 비난하고 있기 때문에 답은 Ⓓ이다. 나머지 보기는 지문의 내용에 언급되어 있지 않거나 다르므로 오답이다.

정답

Ⓓ

In the 1940s and 1950s, astronomer Rupert Wildt used all the available data to derive a picture of Jupiter that is still generally accepted. He noted that both the low total density and the observed presence of **hydrogen-rich compounds** in the atmosphere were consistent with a bulk composition similar to that of the Sun and stars. This "cosmic composition" is dominated by the two simplest elements, hydrogen and helium, which together make up nearly 99 percent of all the universe's material. Wildt **hypothesized** that Jupiter, because of its large size, had succeeded in retaining this primordial composition. He also used his knowledge of the properties of hydrogen and helium to calculate what the interior structure of Jupiter might be like, concluding that the planet is mostly liquid or gas. Wildt suggested that there probably was a core of solid material deep in the interior, but that much of Jupiter is fluid, extremely viscous and compressed deep below the visible atmosphere, but still not solid. The atmosphere seen from above is just the thin, topmost layer of an ocean of gases thousands of kilometers thick.

1. **The author mentions hydrogen-rich compounds in the passage in order to emphasize**

    Ⓐ the fact that Jupiter is mostly liquid or gas
    Ⓑ that Jupiter's composition was not similar to that of the Sun and stars
    Ⓒ Jupiter's primordial composition.
    Ⓓ the cosmic composition of Jupiter's atmosphere.

2. **According to the passage, which of the following is true?**

    Ⓐ New data has now significantly changed our understanding of Jupiter.
    Ⓑ The properties of hydrogen and helium preclude the interior of Jupiter from being mostly liquid or gas.
    Ⓒ Without his knowledge of the interior structure of Jupiter, Wildt would have arrived at different conclusions.
    Ⓓ Retaining the primordial composition is affected by the size of Jupiter.

3. **The word hypothesized in the passage is closest in meaning to**

    Ⓐ accepted
    Ⓑ supposed
    Ⓒ investigated
    Ⓓ explained

On January 22, 2013 debris from the Chinese FENGYUN 1C collided with Russia's BLITS satellite. The FENGYUAN 1C is the satellite that was destroyed by China on January 11, 2007 in a test of an anti-satellite missile. The collision changed the orbit of the Russian satellite, along with **its** spin velocity and attitude. The collision wasn't reported until February 4, 2013 when engineers at the Institute for Precision Instrument Engineering (IPIE) in Moscow reported to CSSI a significant change in the orbit for their BLITS satellite. BLITS is tracked to high precision by the International Laser Ranging Service (ILRS), and IPIE had detected a sudden decrease of 120 meters in the semi-major axis of its orbit and a change in its spin velocity and attitude. Teams looking at the event had to **work backwards** to review archival satellite data and determine what piece of space debris could be large enough to cause a change in orbit in the BLITS satellite. They found a close approach between debris from FENGYUN 1C and the BLITS satellite. Although the predicted distance would seem to preclude a collision, the fact that the close approach occurred within 10 seconds of the estimated change in orbit made it appear likely that this piece of FENGYUN 1C debris actually collided with BLITS.

1. The word its in the passage refers to

Ⓐ IPIE

Ⓑ BLITS

Ⓒ CSSI

Ⓓ FENGYUN 1C

2. The author mentions that the teams had to work backwards in the passage in order to

Ⓐ discover what happened in the 10 seconds after the BLITS satellite changed orbit

Ⓑ measure the high precision required to track the satellite movements

Ⓒ figure out the sequence of events leading up to the collision

Ⓓ conclude which piece of debris caused the BLITS satellite to change in orbit

3. According to the passage, which of the following can be inferred about the predicted distance of the debris?

Ⓐ It seemed to indicate that a collision would occur.

Ⓑ It was not accurate.

Ⓒ It did not allow for random factors.

Ⓓ It was not enough for the teams to reach their conclusion.

Overview

추론(Inference) 문제는 지문에 나오는 정보를 바탕으로 추론해낼 수 있는 내용을 선택지 중에서 고르는 유형이다. 저자의 함축적인 생각을 파악해야하기 때문에 선택지가 지문에 명백하게 드러나지 않는다. 하나의 문장이나 단락 또는 전체 지문을 통해 유추하는 문제가 출제된다. 지문의 내용을 근거로 논리적이고 객관적인 정보를 찾아야 하기 때문에 토플문제 중 까다로운 유형이다.

질문유형

• According to the passage, which of the following can be inferred about _____?
   지문에 따르면 다음 중 어느 것이 _____에 관해 추론될 수 있는가?

• It can be inferred from the passage # that _____.
   단락 #의 내용에서 _____를 유추할 수 있다.

• Which of the following can be concluded from the passage?
   다음 중 어느 것이 지문의 내용으로부터 결론 내려질 수 있는가?

• What does the author imply about _____ in paragraph #?
   단락 #에서 작가는 _____에 관해 무엇을 암시하고 있는가?

• Which of the following would the author most likely support about _____?
   _____에 관해서 작가는 다음 중 어느 것을 가장 지지할 것 같은가?

접근방법

1. 반드시 글에서 주어진 내용으로만 추론한다. 상식이나 선입견을 갖고 답을 고르면 안된다.

2. 문장을 추론하는 경우 문제에 제시된 문장의 주변에 단서가 있으므로 앞뒤 문장을 자세히 읽는다.

3. 지문 전체에 관한 결론이나 저자의 의견을 묻는 경우에는 일부 단락만 보아서는 안된다. 단락의 소주제를 종합하여 전체 주제에 알맞은 선택지를 골라야 한다.

4. 비교 구문과 수동태 등 선택 지문에 자주 나오는 문법 구문을 알아둔다. 해석에 필요한 문제 풀이 시간을 줄일 수 있다.

5. 다음과 같은 오답을 선택지에서 고르지 않도록 한다.
   ① 지문의 내용과 다른 것
   ② 지문에서 보여주지 않은 것
   ③ 지문 내용보다 비약이 심한 것

Sample Question

Many business travelers face a culinary and social dilemma in foreign countries. They don't want to insult their hosts or lose a business deal, but what's being served appears difficult to consume or downright unpalatable. Experts in business etiquette say there's no easy answer, and their suggestions about what to do are mixed. Many travelers don't have the stomach of Andrew Zimmern, who has put foods strange to Americans in vogue with his long-running Bizarre Foods television program on the Travel Channel. "I have always tried everything put in front of me," says Zimmern, who has visited 32 countries to eat bizarre foods for more than 100 episodes during the past six years. "I would tell diners to be adventurous and remember that commercially processed supermarket hot dogs contain foods you don't want to know about —none of which are fresh or of good quality — and everyone loves them."

According to the passage, which of the following can be inferred about business travelers?

Ⓐ They need to learn more about etiquette in foreign countries.

Ⓑ Their taste in food leaves a lot to be desired.

Ⓒ They tend to be conservative in their taste for food.

Ⓓ Their stomachs are more sensitive than Andrew Zimmern's.

해설 첫 번째와 두 번째 문장에서 업무상 해외여행을 하는 사람들이 직면하는 음식 문제를 다루고 있다. 그들은 접대하는 외국인의 식탁에 오른 것이 먹기에 힘들거나 전혀 입에 안맞는 것 같다고 하였으므로 음식 맛에 보수적이라고 한 Ⓒ가 답이다. 그들에게 문제가 되는 것은 음식이고 세 번째 문장에서 비즈니스 에티켓 전문가들도 쉬운 답이 없다고 하였으므로 Ⓐ는 답이 아니다. Ⓑ나 Ⓓ도 지문에 제시되지 않았거나 비약된 내용이므로 오답이다.

해석 많은 사업가들은 외국에서 음식과 사회적 딜레마에 직면한다. 그들은 초대한 주인을 모욕하거나 사업상 거래를 잃고 싶어하지 않지만 식탁에 오른 것은 먹기에 힘들거나 완전히 입에 안 맞는 것 같다. 비즈니스 에티켓 전문가들은 쉬운 답이 없다고 말하며 어떻게 해야 할지에 대한 그들의 제안은 엇갈린다. 많은 여행객들은 여행 채널의 인기 장수 TV 프로그램인 Bizzare Foods에서 미국 사람들에게 기이한 음식을 소개한 앤드류 짐먼의 위장을 가지고 있지 않다. '저는 항상 제 앞에 놓인 모든 것을 시도합니다.' 지난 6년 동안 100편이 넘는 에피소드를 위한 기이한 음식을 먹기 위해 32개국을 방문한 짐먼이 말했다. '저는 식사하는 분들에게 용기를 내서 먹어보고 상업적으로 가공된 슈퍼마켓 핫도그는 당신이 알기 원치 않는 성분을 함유하고 있다는 것을 기억하라고 말하고 싶습니다. – 그것들 중 어느 것도 신선하거나 좋은 질을 가지고 있지 않습니다. – 그리고 모두가 그것들을 아주 좋아합니다.'

문제 지문에 따르면 다음 중 어느 것이 업무상 해외여행을 하는 사람에 관해 추론될 수 있는가?

Ⓐ 그들은 외국에서의 에티켓에 대해 더 배울 필요가 있다.

Ⓑ 그들은 음식을 맛보는 데 감각이 뛰어나다.

Ⓒ 그들은 음식을 맛보는 데 보수적이다.

Ⓓ 그들의 위장은 앤드류 짐먼보다 덜 민감하다.

Exercise 1

Once a boisterous center for congregation, coffee houses have become places where we go to be alone together. Sure, we may occasionally meet a friend for coffee, but in most cases, the coffee house is populated by workers, writers, and observers—people who are otherwise absorbed in their tasks but draw energy from the busy-ness of those around them. It is a space where we are publicly anonymous, and as such, we are not bound by the regulations that govern official workspaces, waiting rooms, and even our own homes. We are physically present, but can choose to be elsewhere, without repercussions. There is a coffeehouse "community" that arises: you frequent the same place, the Baristas come to know your name (and possibly your order), you sit in the same place, and see the same people. But you aren't required to perform any particular role in this space, and what's more, you could visit any space like it, and find that this is essentially the case.

According to the passage, which of the following can be inferred about coffee houses?

Ⓐ There are no social rules to restrict what people can do.

Ⓑ The people make it possible to cast off your worries and relieve all your stress.

Ⓒ Most people like the atmosphere but prefer to do their own thing.

Ⓓ They are usually too boisterous for someone who wants a peaceful place.

"If you trade frequently you're almost guaranteed to lose money." Stein says in the attached video. "Unless you're a high frequency trader with access to incredibly powerful computers, a limitless base of capital and access to inside information" the only road to success is to "buy and hold big, broad indexes forever." The second financial landmine that Stein brings up is trading foreign currencies, a racket he describes as "so treacherous and so difficult" that the top dogs at the top firms can barely make a go of it with the very best resources and technology. He says ordinary investors should stay away from for ex markets, and instead seek out what Warren Buffett urged him to invest in. "Just buy productive assets, in the form of stocks, and then buy the indexes and hold on for dear life," he says. And finally, Stein adds to his financial disaster list the doomed notion of believing in your heart that you can pick stocks. "If you're Buffett and you have incredible opportunities and if you are an incredible genius beyond reasoning" then sure, go be a stock picker. "But for anyone else, no!" Stein advises.

According to the passage, which of the following can be inferred about Warren Buffet?

Ⓐ He has a limitless base of capital and access to inside information.

Ⓑ His investment advice is generally reliable.

Ⓒ He doesn't think ordinary investors should be involved in ex markets.

Ⓓ It is not advisable to do the same things that he does.

1. **지문** 한때 모임으로 북적이던 커피숍이 우리만 함께하기 위해 가는 곳이 되었다. 물론 때때로 커피 마시러 친구를 만날 수 있지만 대부분의 경우에 커피숍은 노동자, 작가와 옵서버 — 주변 사람들이 바쁜 데서 힘을 얻어가거나 그렇지 않으면 자신의 작업에 몰두하는 사람들로 붐빈다. 그곳은 우리가 공식적으로 익명인 공간이며 직장이나 대합실 그리고 집에서조차 통제하는 규제에 구속받지 않는 공간이다. 우리는 실제로 거기에 있지만 아무 영향 없이 다른 곳을 선택할 수 있다. 뜨고 있는 커피숍 '커뮤니티'가 있다: 당신은 그곳을 자주 방문하고 바리스타는 당신의 이름 (그리고 아마도 당신의 주문)을 알게 되고 같은 장소에 앉아 같은 사람을 보게 된다. 하지만 당신은 이 공간에서 특정 역할을 수행할 필요가 없고 무엇보다 당신은 원하는 공간을 방문할 수 있고 이것이 중요한 사실이라는 것을 알게 될 것이다.

   어휘 boisterous 활기가 넘치는 anonymous 익명의 be not bound by ~에 의해 구속되지 않다 repercussion 영향

   문제 지문에 따르면 다음 중 어느 것이 커피숍에 관해 추론될 수 있는가?
   Ⓐ 사람들이 무엇을 할 수 있는지 제한하는 사회 규범이 없다.
   Ⓑ 그(커피숍의) 사람들이 당신의 걱정을 쫓아버리고 모든 스트레스를 덜 수 있도록 해준다.
   Ⓒ 대부분의 사람들은 분위기를 즐기지만 자신의 일을 한다.
   Ⓓ 그것들(커피숍)은 평온한 장소를 원하는 사람에게는 너무 북적인다.

   해설 지문 전체와 두 번째 문장에 커피숍이 작업에 몰두하는 사람과 주변 사람들이 바쁜 데서 힘을 얻어가는 사람으로 나뉜다고 하였으므로 Ⓒ가 답이다. 나머지 보기는 지문 내용의 일부를 비약하였으므로 오답이다.

   정답 Ⓒ

2. **지문** '만약 당신이 자주 거래를 한다면 당신은 돈을 잃는 것이 거의 확실하다.' 스타인은 첨부된 비디오에서 말한다. '당신이 엄청나게 강력한 컴퓨터에 접속이 가능하고 자본이 무제한이며 내부 정보에 접근이 가능한 초단타 거래자라면' 성공을 위한 유일한 길은 '사서 크고 광범위한 지수 때까지 영원히 소유하라.' 스타인이 꺼낸 두 번째 재정 지뢰는 외화를 거래하는 것인데 그가 묘사하기를 최고의 회사 정상에 있는 자들이 최고급 정보와 기술로 가까스로 성공할 수 있는 '정말 신뢰할 수 없고 너무 어렵다'고 하는 부적절한 돈벌이이다. 그는 일반 투자자들은 외환 시장에서 멀리 떨어져 있어야 하며 대신 워런 버핏이 그에게 투자하라고 충고한 것을 찾으라고 한다. '그냥 주식으로 생산적인 자산을 사라. 그런 다음에 지수를 얻어서 평생 보유하라.'라고 그는 말한다. 그리고 마지막으로 스타인은 당신 마음속에 당신이 주식을 고를 수 있다고 믿는 그 불운한 생각을 그의 재정재난 목록에 더했다. '만약 당신이 버핏이고 당신이 아주 좋은 기회를 갖고 있으며 논리를 벗어나 굉장한 천재라면' 물론 증권 컨설턴트가 되라. '하지만 다른 사람들은 안된다!'라고 스타인은 충고한다.

   어휘 high frequency 고주파 treacherous 신뢰할 수 없는 barely 간신히, 가까스로
   seek out ~을 찾아내다, ~을 구하다 asset 자산 financial disaster 재정적 재앙
   doomed notion 불운한 개념 stock picker 증권 컨설턴트

   문제 지문에 따르면 다음 중 어느 것이 워런 버핏에 관해 추론될 수 있는가?
   Ⓐ 무한한 자본을 갖고 내부 정보에 접속할 수 있다.
   Ⓑ 그의 투자 조언은 일반적으로 믿을 만하다.
   Ⓒ 일반 투자자들이 외환 시장에 몰두해야 한다고 생각하지 않는다.
   Ⓓ 그가 하는 것과 똑같이 하는 것은 바람직하지 않다.

   해설 스타인은 일반 투자자들의 외환 투자에 대한 위험성을 알리며 네 번째 문장에서 워런 버핏이 투자하라고 충고한 것을 찾으라고 하므로 워런 버핏의 조언이 믿을 만하다는 Ⓑ가 답이다. Ⓒ는 스타인의 의견이므로 오답이다.

   정답 Ⓑ

The announcement of the first evidence of a new particle, most probably the long-awaited Higgs boson, has a lot to teach us — and not all of it is about science. It took an international team funded by the global community of taxpayers to bring it about. Obviously the science is extremely exciting. The Higgis was first proposed in the 1960s and is thought to be the remnant of an interaction common to all objects with mass. It took a colossal new scientific instrument, the Large Hadron Collider, or LHC, at CERN — the European Organization for Nuclear Research in Switzerland — to produce the few hundred examples of this new object thought to be the Higgs. This much-anticipated discovery is in one sense the culmination of a huge intellectual effort, and in another sense the beginning of a new field of research. It is also the result of a worldwide effort. The Higgs could well be the first science discovery brought about by all of us in the broadest sense, the planet-wide human community. It seems appropriate that nature's secrets are unwrapped by all of us; that we own and enjoy the discovery corporately. Let us hope that this is the first of many such endeavors.

Which of the following can be concluded from the passage?

Ⓐ The Higgs boson would not have been found without worldwide collaboration between scientists.

Ⓑ The author cannot believe that this discovery has been made.

Ⓒ The discovery of the Higgs boson will revolutionize the field of science.

Ⓓ The magnitude of the effort involved to make this discovery was on a huge scale.

Herb's face hardened, making him look old and senatorial. I had always made the less conventional choices: I played in garage bands while he went to college; taught exotic martial arts while he made a grown-up income in suits and ties. My wife, Carolyn and I spoiled a parade of cats while Herb and his wife had two brilliant boys. I was the artsy, bohemian, quasi-monk; he was the affable, solid, business executive and family man. But, however different we were, we'd grown to respect each other through thirty years of friendship. We'd gone through the baffling shame of an adolescence without girlfriends, the tacky iniquities of pot smoking in high school, and the discovery of then-new music like Devo and Elvis Costello. In our twenties, we'd spent long hours talking excitedly about philosophy — in those days, my man was the Indian iconoclast J. Krishnamurti and Herb was into Trappist monk Thomas Merton. We'd each been the other's best man at our weddings (his, resplendent, something out of Jane Austen; mine, a dozen people in a park, more like something out of The Beverly Hillbillies). And as we stumbled into our late-thirties, we tussled with the usual existential crises of middleclass, middle-aged men. **Now all of that history seemed to be evaporating.**

What can be inferred from the highlighted sentence in the passage?

Ⓐ They had lost their interest in history.

Ⓑ Their relationship seemed to have changed.

Ⓒ They could no longer remember all the things they had done together.

Ⓓ Despite their differences they still remained best friends.

Insertion

Overview

삽입(Insertion) 문제는 출제 문장을 지문에 표시된 4개의 네모 박스 중 한 곳에 클릭하여 삽입하는 유형이다. 삽입 문제에서는 각 문장이 논리적으로 자연스럽게 전개되는지를 확인한다. 각 문장이 적절히 연결되기 위해서는 연결어와 지시어 그리고 동일(유사)어구 등을 잘 살펴보아야 한다.

질문유형

지문에 4개의 네모 박스 [■]가 보여지고 하나를 클릭하면 그 자리에 출제 문장이 볼드체로 보여진다.

Look at the four squares [■] that indicate where the following sentence could be added to the passage? 다음의 문장이 지문에 추가될 수 있는 곳을 표시하는 네모 박스 [■]를 보시오.

출제문장

Where would the sentence best fit? 문장이 어느 곳에 가장 적합한가?

Click on a square [■] to add the sentence to the passage. 문장을 지문에 추가하도록 한 개의 네모 박스 [■]를 클릭하시오.

접근방법

1. 삽입을 위해 제시된 문장에 반드시 단서가 있다.
2. 다음과 같은 연결어를 확인한다.
   ① 비교 / 대조 → 비교 / 대조 대상이 바로 뒤에 삽입된다.
   however, yet, but, on the other hand, in contrast, on the contrary, similarly, wherease, likewise
   ② 부연 / 첨가 → 정의 뒤에 예를 든 문장이 삽입된다.
   also, besides, in addition, moreover, and, for example, for instance, furthermore
   ③ 나열 / 순서 → 시간 순서에 맞춘 문장이 삽입된다.
   first, second, next, later, then, last, finally, after, afterwards, meanwhile, at the same time
   ④ 인과 관계 → 원인과 결과 혹은 결과와 원인의 문장이 삽입된다.
   therefore, as a result, consequently, then, for this reason, thus, in conclusion, hence, so
3. 삽입 문장에 지시어 또는 동일(유사)어구의 단서가 있다. 그 지시어가 가리키거나 동일(유사)어구가 반복되는 주위에 삽입한다.
4. 삽입 문장의 〈정관사(the) + 명사〉에 주의한다. 〈정관사(the) + 명사〉는 〈부정관사(a, an) + 명사〉 뒤에 삽입한다.
5. 삽입 문장을 넣은 후 앞뒤 해석과 연결이 자연스러운지 확인한다.

The two faintest star-like objects ever found, a pair of twin brown dwarfs each just a millionth as bright as the Sun, have been spotted. Both of these objects are the first to break the barrier of one millionth the total light-emitting power of the sun. Ⓐ ■ Astronomers had thought the pair of dim bulbs was just a single typical, faint brown dwarf with no record-smashing titles. Ⓑ ■ The brightness of the object was twice what would be expected for a brown dwarf with its particular temperature suggesting the object must have twice the surface area. Ⓒ ■ In other words, it is twins, with each body shining only half as bright, and each with a mass of 30 to 40 times that of Jupiter. Ⓓ ■ Both bodies are one million times fainter than the sun in total light, and at least one billion times fainter in visible light alone.

Look at the four squares [■] that indicate where the following sentence could be added to the passage.

However the Spitzer Space Telescope revealed that what seemed to be a single brown dwarf is in fact twins.

Where would the sentence best fit?
Click on a square [■] to add the sentence to the passage.

해설 출제 문장에 들어있는 연결사 however가 문제를 푸는 단서이다. 출제 문장에서 하나라고 여겼던 갈색 왜성이 쌍둥이라는 것을 밝혀내었다고 하였으므로 그 앞에는 갈색 왜성이 하나라고 여겨졌다는 문장이 와야 한다. 따라서 Ⓑ가 답이다. 출제 문장을 Ⓑ의 자리에 넣어 보면 우주 망원경이 발견한 갈색 왜성에 대한 세부 정보가 뒤따라 나오므로 내용이 자연스럽게 이어진다.

해석 우주에서 지금까지 발견된 가장 희미한 별과 같은 두 개의 물체가 관측되었다. 쌍둥이 갈색 왜성으로서 밝기는 겨우 태양의 100만분의 1 정도이다. 이 두 물체는 태양의 총 발광력의 100만 분의 1 장벽을 처음으로 깨뜨렸다. Ⓐ 천문학자들은 이 흐린 두 개의 전구 같은 물체는 두 개가 아닌 한 개라고 생각했으며 희미한 갈색 왜성으로 기록된 이름을 다르게 부를 수 없었다. 하지만 스피처 우주 망원경은 하나라고 여겼던 갈색 왜성이 사실은 쌍둥이라는 것을 밝혀냈다. Ⓑ 이 물체의 밝기는 예상했던 갈색 왜성의 특정 온도보다 2배가 되어 표면적이 2배가 될 것으로 추정하였다. Ⓒ 다시 말해서 그것은 쌍둥이 물체로서 자체 밝기의 반만 빛을 발하며 각각의 질량은 목성보다 약 30배에서 40배에 달한다. Ⓓ 두 물체의 총 빛은 태양보다 100만 배 정도 흐리며 적어도 가시광선보다 최소 10억 배 정도 흐리다.

문제 다음 문장이 지문의 어느 곳에 추가될 수 있는지를 나타내는 네 개의 네모를 살펴보시오.
하지만 스피처 우주 망원경은 하나라고 여겼던 갈색 왜성이 사실은 쌍둥이라는 것을 밝혀냈다.
문장이 어느 곳에 가장 적합한가?
문장을 지문에 추가하도록 한 개의 네모 박스 [■]를 클릭하시오.

정답 Ⓑ

Exercise 1

Hurricane Sandy tore through the northeast this week, causing billions of dollars in damage and leaving 7 to 8 million people without power. It also damaged 25 percent of the nation's wireless companies' cell sites to the point that the towers are not operational. Ⓐ ■ It may take a considerable amount of time to have those sites, spread out across 158 counties in 10 states, fully functional. Ⓑ ■ While the work to fix the towers could take several days, it may take even longer because of other complications related to the storm. Ⓒ ■ Wireless companies may also have to wait until utility companies manage to restore power in affected areas. Ⓓ ■ Things may actually get worse. Customers who have mobile phone service now may lose service if backup batteries run out of power, and increased activity on fewer towers might further strain networks.

Look at the four squares [■] that indicate where the following sentence could be added to the passage.

Power outages and roadways inaccessible because of debris may make it difficult to reach cell sites to provide necessary repairs.

Where would the sentence best fit?
Click on a square [■] to add the sentence to the passage.

147

Exercise 2

One interviewer had to ask the president about the amazingly ubiquitous Gangnam Style song, video, and dance craze by South Korean rapper, pop star, Psy. "I just saw that video for the first time," Obama said in a radio interview with WZID in New Hampshire. Ⓐ ■ "I think I can do that move. But I'm not sure that the inauguration ball is the appropriate time to break that out." Ⓑ ■ Both Obama and his GOP challenger Mitt Romney like to sing in public, but so far no one's seen either of them bopping around a stage like a guy on a horse, with sunglasses. Ⓒ ■ But stranger things have been happened with this craze; after all, everybody's doing it, from sports stars and race-car drivers to robots and Philippine convicts. Psy, whose real name is Park Jae-sang, even tried to teach the goofy dance to UN General Secretary Ban Ki-moon at the UN in New York last month. Ⓓ ■ It's a Gangnam Style world these days.

Look at the four squares [■] that indicate where the following sentence could be added to the passage.

"Maybe," he concluded, "do it privately for Michelle."

Where would the sentence best fit?
Click on a square [■] to add the sentence to the passage.

1. 지문

허리케인 샌디는 이번 주 수 십 억의 손해를 입히고 700만에서 800만의 사람들을 전기 공급이 끊기게 하며 북부지역을 강타했다. 이는 또한 지역의 무선 통신 회사 기지국들의 25%의 송신탑들이 작동되지 않을 정도로 손상을 입혔다. Ⓐ 10개 주의 158개 지역을 가로질러 퍼져 있는 이 기지국들이 완전히 제 기능을 하는 데는 상당한 시간이 걸릴 수 있다. Ⓑ 탑들을 고치는 작업은 며칠이 걸리지만 폭풍과 관련된 다른 문제들 때문에 심지어 더 오래 걸릴 수도 있다. 정전과 잔해로 인하여 접근이 어려운 철도가 필요한 수리를 제공하기 위해 기지국에 도달하기 어려울 수 있다. Ⓒ 무선 통신 회사들은 또한 공익 기업들이 영향을 받은 지역에 전력을 복구할 때까지 기다려야만 할 것이다. Ⓓ 사실 상황은 더 나빠질 수 있다. 휴대폰 서비스를 지금 사용하고 있는 소비자들은 만약 여분의 배터리가 다 떨어지면 서비스가 끊길 수 있으며 소수의 탑에 증가된 활동은 네트워크에 더욱 부담이 될 수 있다.

어휘

complication 합병증 utility 공익사업. 유용성 run out of ~을 다 써버리다

문제

다음 문장이 지문의 어느 곳에 추가될 수 있는지를 나타내는 네 개의 네모를 살펴보시오.

정전과 잔해로 인하여 접근이 어려운 철도가 필요한 수리를 제공하기 위해 기지국에 도달하기 어려울 수 있다.

문장이 어느 곳에 가장 적합한가?

문장을 지문에 추가하도록 한 개의 네모 박스 [■]를 클릭하시오.

해설

출제 문장은 지문에서 복구 작업이 지연되는 데에 대한 이유를 부가설명 해주고 있으므로 Ⓒ가 답이다. 뒤에 복구 작업의 지연으로 무선 통신 회사들이 기다려야 한다는 결과가 나오므로 Ⓒ에 삽입해야 글의 흐름이 자연스럽다.

정답

Ⓒ

---

2. 지문

한 인터뷰 기자는 대한민국 랩 가수이며 팝 스타인 싸이의 어디에서나 흘러나오는 강남 스타일의 노래, 비디오, 춤 열풍에 대해 대통령에게 물어봐야만 했다. '저는 막 그 비디오를 처음으로 봤습니다.' 뉴 햄프셔에서 WZID(라디오 방송사)와의 인터뷰에서 오바마가 말했다. Ⓐ '저는 제가 그 춤 동작을 할 수 있을 것이라고 생각합니다. 하지만 취임식이 그것을 보여줄 적절한 때인지는 확신할 수 없습니다. 그는 아마도 미셸을 위해 사적으로 할 수 있겠죠.'라며 마무리했다. Ⓑ 오바마와 그의 공화당 도전자인 미트 롬니는 모두 공개적으로 노래하는 것을 좋아하지만 아직 그들 어느 누구도 선글라스를 쓰고 말을 탄 남자처럼 무대에서 춤을 추는 게 목격되지는 않았다. Ⓒ 하지만 이 열풍으로 더 이상의 일들이 일어났다; 결국 스포츠 스타들과 자동차 경주 선수부터 로봇과 필리핀 죄수들까지 모든 사람들이 그것을 한다. 진짜 이름이 박재상인 싸이는 심지어 지난달 뉴욕 UN에서 그 우스꽝스러운 춤을 UN 사무총장인 반기문에게 가르쳤다. Ⓓ 요즘은 강남 스타일 세상이다.

어휘

ubiquitous 아주 흔한, 어디에나 있는 inauguration ball 취임식 무도회 appropriate time 적절한 시기 after all 결국에는, 어쨌든 convict 유죄를 선고하다

문제

다음 문장이 지문의 어느 곳에 추가될 수 있는지를 나타내는 네 개의 네모를 살펴보시오.

그는 '아마도 미셸을 위해 사적으로 할 수 있겠죠.'라며 마무리 했다.

문장이 어느 곳에 가장 적합한가?

문장을 지문에 추가하도록 한 개의 네모 박스 [■]를 클릭하시오.

해설

주어진 문장의 지시어 it(그것)은 앞의 that move(그 동작)를 가리키므로 Ⓑ가 답이다. 출제 문장에 concluded(마무리 했다)라는 말이 나오므로 주어진 문장은 인터뷰를 마무리한 위치에 와야 한다.

정답

Ⓑ

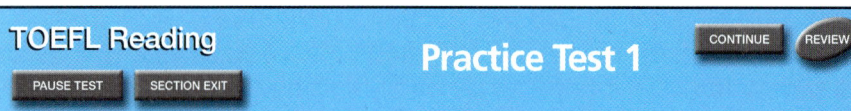
The great majority of songbirds learn and memorize their songs from a mentor, either their own father or another singing male. Ⓐ ■ Mockingbirds, however, take most of their sounds from the environment, sometimes from other mockingbirds, and always including a range of other bird vocalizations. Ⓑ ■ Mockingbird songs may also include the vocalizations of non-avian species, such as mammals or frogs, and even electronic **sounds**, like car alarms and cell phones. Ⓒ ■ From one spring to the next, an individual male mockingbird repeats a minimum of 35 to 63 percent of his previously heard song types, while at the same time adding more songs to his delivery. Ⓓ ■ As a result, his vocal repertoire eventually grows to as many as 200 at old age.

Look at the four squares [■] that indicate where the following sentence could be added to the passage.

These sounds are learned, memorized, and incorporated into the mockingbird's ever-expanding repertoire.

Where would the sentence best fit?

Click on a square [■] to add the sentence to the passage.

Universal health care is health coverage for all citizens of a nation. Ⓐ ■ Some argue that a universal system requires some level of transfer of wealth from those who have to support those who have not. Ⓑ ■ Any such transfer infringes on the freedom of the individual being taxed. Others argue that providing access to health care enables one to enjoy freedom, and as a society it is a shared responsibility (much like sharing the burden of funding a military or providing education for all). Ⓒ ■ However, as such, social equity and individual freedom do not necessarily have to conflict. Ⓓ ■ At some point the debate becomes ideological rather than practical, and most nations that attempt universal health care, while often supporting individual freedoms see value in a society generally being healthy.

Look at the four squares [■] that indicate where the following sentence could be added to the passage.

Does provision of universal health care infringe on individual human rights?

Where would the sentence best fit?

Click on a square [■] to add the sentence to the passage.

Overview

요약(Summary) 문제는 선택지에서 지문을 골라 요약표를 완성시키는 것이다. 각 지문의 마지막 문제로 Category Chart문제와 번갈아 출제된다. 문제에는 도입문장(introductory sentence)이 제시되어 있는데 도입문장은 지문 전체의 주제문일 수도 있고 단순히 지문 요약의 도입 역할을 하는 경우도 있다. 요약 문제는 저자가 글을 통해 무엇에 관하여 어떤 생각을 전달하고자 하였는지 파악하는 것이 중요하다.

질문유형

6개의 선택지 중 3개를 골라 요약표 안으로 끌어당겨 넣는다. 2점짜리 문제로 정답 3개를 모두 맞추면 2점, 2개를 맞추면 1점이 주어진다.

Directions: An introductory sentence for a brief summary of the passage is provided below. Complete the summary by selecting the THREE answer choices that express the most important ideas in the passage. Some sentences do not belong in the summary because they express ideas that are not presented in the passage or are minor ideas in the passage. **This question is worth 2 points**.

Drag your answer choices to the spaces where they belong. To remove an answer choice, click on it. To review the passage, click on **View Text**.

An introductory sentence

-
-
-

Answer Choices

지시사항: 지문을 간략하게 요약하기 위한 도입문장이 아래에 제시되어 있다. 지문에서 가장 중요한 정보를 담고 있는 3개의 선택지를 선택하여 요약을 완성한다. 지문에 제시되지 않은 정보나 세부정보를 담고 있는 일부 문장은 요약에 들어가지 않는다. **이 문제는 2점이 주어진다.**

선택지를 관련있는 곳으로 끌어당기시오. 끌어당긴 선택지를 삭제하려면 그 위에 대고 클릭하시오. 지문을 다시 보려면 **View Text** 아이콘을 클릭하시오.

도입문장

-
-
-

선택지

접근방법

1. 처음 지문을 읽을 때 각 단락의 중심정보를 간략하게 note-taking한다. 각 단락의 주제문은 주로 앞에 있지만 뒤나 중간에 위치하는 경우도 있다.
2. 선택지의 핵심정보(key word)가 글의 중심정보인지 사소한 정보인지 확인한다. 오답의 선택지는 지문의 내용과 일치하지만 사소한 세부정보이다.
3. 선택지의 표현은 지문 그대로가 아니고 바꿔 쓰기(paraphrase)되어 있으므로 꼼꼼히 비교한다.

French is not dying but it is in decline, and for many Americans, that's as good a reason as any to retain it. When Jaclyn Davis answers the phone at La Gourmandine bakery in Lawrenceville, her accent is as authentically French as the tarte aux fraises sold there. The 22-year old cashier at the new bakery is also a student at the University of Akron, working towards a teaching certificate in French, a culture she adores but a career choice she has to defend to her fellow Americans nearly every day. "When I was working at Home Depot, I'd get wisecracks all the time," Ms. Davis said, "mostly from people who couldn't understand why she'd want to learn French."

Likewise for Megan Leinbach, a German major at the University of Pittsburgh. "My classes are full," said Ms. Leinbach, "But some of my friends say German's a dying language, and I have to remind them that Germany is an economic powerhouse, so I don't think it's dying, exactly."Once upon a time, they were known as The Big Three: Spanish, French and German, and they are still the top three languages taught in colleges across America—although Spanish leads the other two by a mile. Alas! Is French passe? Is German kaput? Not exactly, but signs of decline are there, locally and nationally as some universities are seriously debating whether to offer French and German majors after current students graduate

Directions: An introductory sentence for a brief summary of the passage is provided below. Complete the summary by selecting the THREE answer choices that express the most important ideas in the passage. Some sentences do not belong in the summary because they express ideas that are not presented in the passage or are minor ideas in the passage. **This question is worth 2 points**.

Drag your answer choices to the spaces where they belong. To remove an answer choice, click on it. To review the passage, click on **View Text**.

Americans now think that there is little point in studying French and German.

-
-
-

Answer Choices

Ⓐ Jaclyn has to defend her career choice.

Ⓑ Nearly half a billion people speak Spanish.

Ⓒ Jaclyn would respond to the jokes about studying French.

Ⓓ Leinbach argues that Germany is an economic powerhouse.

Ⓔ Spanish, French and German are still taught in American colleges.

Ⓕ Some universities debate whether to offer French and German majors.

Sample Question

해설 도입문장에서 '미국인들은 프랑스어와 독일어를 배우는 게 무의미하다고 생각한다.'라고 하였다. 대부분 도입문장이 주제이므로 그에 관련된 3개의 선택지를 고르면 된다. Ⓐ와 Ⓒ, Ⓕ는 재클린이 프랑스어를 배우는 것을 다른 미국인들이 이해 못한다거나 대학에서 프랑스어와 독일어 전공을 제공해야 할지 논의하고 있다고 했으므로 지문의 내용과 일치한다. 나머지 선택지는 지문의 내용과 일치하지만 스페인어나 독일어, 프랑스어가 중요하다는 것이므로 도입문장의 내용과 다른 오답이다.

해석 프랑스어는 사라지지 않고 쇠퇴하고 있으며 많은 미국인들에게 그것은 프랑스어를 보유해야 하는 타당한 이유가 된다. 재클린 데이비스가 로렌스빌에 있는 라과만딘 제과점에서 전화를 받을 때 그녀의 억양은 그곳에서 팔리는 타르토프레즈만큼이나 진짜 프랑스적이다. 그 새로운 제과점의 22세 계산원은 또한 애크론 대학교에서 프랑스어 교사 자격증을 위해 노력하고 있는 학생이며 그녀가 아주 좋아하는 문화이기는 하지만 거의 매일 그녀의 미국인 동료들에게 자신의 직업선택에 대한 변호를 해야 한다. '제가 홈디포에서 일하고 있었을 때 저는 항상 농담을 듣곤 했습니다.' '대부분은 그녀가 왜 프랑스어를 공부하는지 이해하지 못하는 사람들로부터'라고 데이비스는 말했다.

피츠버그 대학교에서 독일어를 전공하고 있는 메간 레인바크도 마찬가지다. '제가 듣는 수업은 꽉 찹니다.' 레인바크가 말했다. '하지만 제 친구 몇 명은 독일어가 사라지고 있는 언어라고 말합니다. 그러면 저는 독일이 경제 강국이라는 것을 그들에게 다시 상기시켜야 하고 그래서 저는 확실하게 독일어가 사라지고 있다고 생각하지 않습니다.' 예전에는 그것들이 3대 언어로 알려져 있었다: 스페인어, 프랑스어 그리고 독일어 그리고 그것들은 아직도 미국 전체에 걸친 대학교에서 가르치는 상위 3개 언어이다. ─ 비록 스페인어가 다른 두 개의 언어보다 훨씬 선두이지만. 아! 프랑스어 유행이 지났는가? 독일어는 끝났는가? 꼭 그런 것은 아니지만 몇몇 대학들이 현 학생들이 졸업한 후에 프랑스어와 독일어 전공을 제공해야 할지에 대해 심각하게 논의하는 것 같은 하락의 조짐은 지역적으로 그리고 국가적으로 존재한다.

문제 지시사항: 지문을 간략하게 요약하기 위한 도입문장이 아래에 제시되어 있다. 지문에서 가장 중요한 정보를 담고 있는 3개의 선택지를 선택하여 요약을 완성한다. 지문에 제시되지 않은 정보나 세부정보를 담고 있는 일부 문장은 요약에 들어가지 않는다. **이 문제는 2점이 주어진다.**

선택지를 관련있는 곳으로 끌어당기시오. 끌어당긴 선택지를 삭제하려면 그 위에 대고 클릭하시오. 지문을 다시 보려면 **View Text** 아이콘을 클릭하시오.

미국인들은 프랑스어와 독일어를 배우는 게 무의미하다고 생각한다.

-
-
-

선택지

Ⓐ 재클린은 그녀의 직업선택에 대해 변호를 해야 한다.

Ⓑ 거의 5억 명의 사람들이 스페인어를 한다.

Ⓒ 재클린이 프랑스어를 공부하는 것에 대한 농담에 응하곤 했다.

Ⓓ 레인바크는 독일이 경제 강국이라고 주장한다.

Ⓔ 스페인어, 프랑스어 그리고 독일어는 아직도 미국 대학교에서 가르쳐지고 있다.

Ⓕ 몇몇 대학들이 프랑스어와 독일어 전공을 제공해야 할지에 대해 논의한다.

정답 Ⓐ, Ⓒ, Ⓕ

Films like De Sica's The Bicycle Thief, Rossellini's Rome, Open City, and Visconti's Ossessione presented a new and dynamic way of presenting the world, which went on to influence movements such as Nouvelle Vague and directors as different as Martin Scorsese and Derek Jarman. Neo Realist films dealt with difficulties faced everyday by the working class; stories were rooted in the reality of a war ruined Italy; there were no simplistic morality tales, issues were complex, and often open-ended; actors mixed with non-actors; stylistically the films were loose, fluid, often documentary-like. However, their content did not please some Italians, who thought Neo-Realism only highlighted the bad things about Italy, which they feared might make Italians seem to be just thieves and bums.

Directions: An introductory sentence for a brief summary of the passage is provided below. Complete the summary by selecting the THREE answer choices that express the most important ideas in the passage. Some sentences do not belong in the summary because they express ideas that are not presented in the passage or are minor ideas in the passage. **This question is worth 2 points**.

Drag your answer choices to the spaces where they belong. To remove an answer choice, click on it. To review the passage, click on **View Text**.

The Neo-Realism of Italian film-makers brought a new and dynamic style to films.

-
-
-

Answer Choices

Ⓐ Nouvelle Vague, Martin Scorsese, and Derek Jarman influenced such movies as De Sica's The Bicycle Thief, Rosselini's Rome, and Open City.

Ⓑ The movie stories were rooted in the reality of a war ruined Italy.

Ⓒ The movies dealt with complex moral issues.

Ⓓ The Neo-Realism of Italian film-makers highlighted the bad things about Italy.

Ⓔ The films were loose, fluid, often documentary-like.

Ⓕ The movie characters were mostly thieves and bums.

Exercise 2

In many ways the public art projects scattered across this city exist as failed utopias. Since 2000 the Tate Modern's Turbine Hall has housed a series of blockbuster art pieces. This afternoon TinoSehgal's "These Associations" is being rehearsed in the cavernous expanse. Performers form a circle in the darkened hall, murmuring and half singing. They break into clusters, coiling across the space. It does seem removed from the weight of previous, rather precarious Turbine Hall spectacles. Chinese dissident artist Ai Weiwei previously flooded the hall with 100 million porcelain sunflower seeds, but the dust kicked up when visitors waded through was soon deemed a safety hazard. By the end, "Sunflower Seeds" was stripped of its central experience - only to be viewed from behind security ropes. In any case Sehgal's "constructed situation" has now gathered near universal adoration since its opening.

Directions: An introductory sentence for a brief summary of the passage is provided below. Complete the summary by selecting the THREE answer choices that express the most important ideas in the passage. Some sentences do not belong in the summary because they express ideas that are not presented in the passage or are minor ideas in the passage. **This question is worth 2 points**.

Drag your answer choices to the spaces where they belong. To remove an answer choice, click on it. To review the passage, click on **View Text**.

Tate Modern's Turbine Hall has showcased several blockbuster art pieces.

-
-
-

Answer Choices

Ⓐ TinoSehgal's "These Associations" is being rehearsed.

Ⓑ Performers break into clusters across the space.

Ⓒ Tate Modern's Turbine Hall has a big empty space.

Ⓓ A Chinese dissident artist previously flooded the hall with porcelain sunflower seeds.

Ⓔ The dust generated by visitors wading through seemed to be a safety hazard.

Ⓕ Sehgal's "constructed situation" has attracted a large number of viewers.

1. 지문

데시타의 자전거 도둑, 로셀리니의 로마, 오픈시티와 비스콘티의 오세시온 같은 영화들은 누벨바그나 마틴 스콜세스와 데릭저먼 같은 서로 다른 감독들에게 영향을 주며 세계를 표현하는데 새롭고 역동적인 방법을 보여주었다. 신사실주의 영화들은 노동자 계급의 일상에서 직면하는 어려움들을 다루었다; 이야기들은 이탈리아를 황폐하게 한 전쟁의 현실에 바탕이 되었다; 지나치게 단순화한 도덕적인 이야기가 없고 이슈들은 복잡하며 종종 넓은 해석이 가능했다; 배우가 아닌 사람들과 섞여 있는 배우들; 스타일적으로 영화는 자유롭고 유동적이며 다큐멘터리 같았다. 그러나 그것들의 내용은 신사실주의가 이탈리아의 나쁜 점만을 부각한다고 생각하는 몇몇 이탈리아 사람들을 언짢게 했다. 그들은 이탈리아인들이 그저 도둑이나 부랑자들로 보이게 할 것을 우려했다.

어휘

Neo-Realist 신사실주의(자) morality 도덕, 도덕률 open-ended 제약을 두지 않은 highlight 강조하다. 클로즈업하다 feared 무서워하는, 두려워하는 bum 부랑자

문제

지시사항: 지문을 간략하게 요약하기 위한 도입문장이 아래에 제시되어 있다. 지문에서 가장 중요한 정보를 담고 있는 3개의 선택자를 선택하여 요약을 완성한다. 지문에 제시되지 않은 정보나 세부정보를 담고 있는 일부 문장은 요약에 들어가지 않는다. **이 문제는 2점이 주어진다.**

> 선택지를 관련 있는 곳으로 끌어당기시오. 끌어당긴 선택지를 삭제하려면 그 위에 대고 클릭하시오. 지문을 다시 보려면 **View Text** 아이콘을 클릭하시오.

이탈리아 영화 제작자의 신사실주의는 새롭고 역동적인 방법을 영화에 가져왔다.

-
-
-

선택지

Ⓐ 누벨바그나 마틴 스콜세스와 데릭저먼은 자전거 도둑, 로셀리니의 로마, 오픈시티 같은 영화에 영향을 미쳤다.
Ⓑ 이야기들은 이탈리아를 황폐하게 한 전쟁의 현실에 바탕이 되었다.
Ⓒ 영화는 복잡한 도덕적인 이슈를 다루었다.
Ⓓ 이탈리아 영화 제작자의 신사실주의는 이탈리아의 나쁜 것들을 강조했다.
Ⓔ 영화는 자유롭고 유동적이며 다큐멘터리 같았다.
Ⓕ 영화의 등장인물은 대개 도둑과 부랑자들이었다.

해설

도입지문은 '이탈리아 영화 제작자의 신사실주의는 새롭고 역동적인 방법을 영화에 가져왔다.'는 것이다. 지문에서 신사실주의 영화에 관한 가장 중요한 정보를 찾으면 Ⓑ, Ⓒ, Ⓔ가 답이다. Ⓐ는 인과 관계가 잘못되어 있으며 Ⓓ와 Ⓕ는 일부 이탈리아인들의 의견이거나 지문과 다른 정보이므로 오답이다.

정답

Ⓑ, Ⓒ, Ⓔ

---

2. 지문

여러 면에서 도시 전체에 널리 퍼져 있는 공공 예술 프로젝트는 실패한 이상향의 형태로 존재한다. 2000년 이후 테이트 현대 미술관 터빈 홀은 블록버스터 예술품 시리즈를 전시해오고 있다. 오늘 오후 텅 빈 전시장 공간에서 티노 세갈의 '디즈 어소셰이션즈'가 예행 연습되고 있다. 공연자들은 어두운 홀에서 원을 그리며 중얼거리거나 노래를 부르기도 한다. 그들은 텅 빈 공간에 코일처럼 여러 무리로 모여 든다. 터빈 홀의 이전의 차라리 위태로운 광경의 무게감이 정말로 사라지는 것 같다. 중국의 반체제 예술가 아이웨이웨이는 전에 1억 개의 자기로 만든 해바라기 씨로 홀을 가득 채운 적이 있다. 그러나 관람객들이 걸어 들어오자 먼지가 일어났고 이 장면은 안전상 해로운 듯 보였다. 마침내 '해바라기 씨'는 핵심적인 경험의 모습을 드러내었다. – 관객들에게 안전 로프 뒤에서만 보여지며. 어쨌든 세갈의 '상황 구축'은 개막 이래 지금까지 거의 모든 사람들의 존경을 받고 있다.

어휘

cavernous 휑뎅그렁한, 동굴 같은 break into 침입하다 dissident 반체제 인사 porcelain 자기(磁器) kick up 소란을 피우다, ~을 일으키다 adoration 경배, 흠모

문제**지시사항**: 지문을 간략하게 요약하기 위한 도입문장이 아래에 제시되어 있다. 지문에서 가장 중요한 정보를 담고 있는 3개의 선택지를 선택하여 요약을 완성한다. 지문에 제시되지 않은 정보나 세부정보를 담고 있는 일부 문장은 요약에 들어가지 않는다. **이 문제는 2점이 주어진다.**

> 선택지를 관련 있는 곳으로 끌어당기시오. 끌어당긴 선택지를 삭제하려면 그 위에 대고 클릭하시오. 지문을 다시 보려면 **View Text** 아이콘을 클릭하시오.

테이트 현대 미술관 터빈 홀은 초대형 예술품 시리즈를 전시해오고 있다.

-
-
-

선택지

Ⓐ 티노 세갈의 '디즈 어소셰이션즈'가 예행 연습 되고 있다.

Ⓑ 공연자들은 텅 빈 공간에 여러 무리로 모여 든다.

Ⓒ 테이트 현대 미술관 터빈 홀에는 커다란 빈 공간이 있다.

Ⓓ 중국의 반체제 예술가가 전에 자기로 만든 해바라기 씨로 홀을 가득 채운 적이 있다.

Ⓔ 방문객이 헤치며 걸으면서 발생된 먼지는 안전상 해로운 듯 보였다.

Ⓕ 세갈의 '상황 구축'은 많은 관람객을 끌고 있다.

해설도입문장에서 '테이트 현대 미술관 터빈 홀은 초대형 예술품 시리즈를 전시해오고 있다.'라고 하였다. 여기서는 도입 문장이 주제이므로 그에 관련된 3개의 보기를 고르면 된다. Ⓐ와 Ⓓ, Ⓕ는 테이트 현대 미술관 터빈 홀에서 전시하는 블록버스터 예술품에 관한 주요 정보로서 도입문장과 일치한다. 나머지 보기는 지문의 내용과 일치하지만 공연 연습, 테이트 현대 미술관 터빈 홀의 크기 또는 전시 에피소드 등의 사소한 세부정보이므로 오답이다.

정답Ⓐ, Ⓓ, Ⓕ

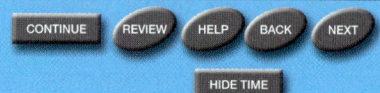
Compared to North America, there seems to be more history in Peru: more pre-Columbian history, more colonial history and quite a lot of recent history. There are more birds in Peru, and they have more colors in their bright wings. More foods come originally from Peru — including both potatoes and tomatoes — than from anywhere else. There are more languages spoken in Peru, even if some are spoken by very few people. There are more different climates there, packed in tight next to one another, with most of the world's ecosystems co-existing in long, thin lines. When it rains, it pours; and when the sun is overhead, it is scorching hot. The rivers are bigger and wider and faster, the earthquakes stronger. Peru has the Americas' deepest canyon and the world's driest desert. There are definitely more holidays in Peru, because there is more religious faith there, and from the wilds of the country on moonless nights, there seem to be more stars in the sky.

Directions: An introductory sentence for a brief summary of the passage is provided below. Complete the summary by selecting the THREE answer choices that express the most important ideas in the passage. Some sentences do not belong in the summary because they express ideas that are not presented in the passage or are minor ideas in the passage. **This question is worth 2 points**.

Drag your answer choices to the spaces where they belong. To remove an answer choice, click on it. To review the passage, click on **View Text**.

Peru is a land of extremes.

-
-
-

Answer Choices

Ⓐ Compared to Asia, there seems to be more history in Peru.

Ⓑ Some languages are spoken by very few people.

Ⓒ Most of the world's ecosystems co-exist in Peru.

Ⓓ When it rains, it pours.

Ⓔ Peru has the Americas' deepest canyon.

Ⓕ Peruvians have more holidays.

The most important characteristic, and the most important innovation, of what is called neorealism is to have realized that the necessity of the story was only an unconscious way of disguising a human defeat, and that the kind of imagination it involved was simply a technique of superimposing dead formulas over living social facts. Now it has been perceived that reality is hugely rich, that to be able to look directly at it is enough; and that the artist's task is not to make people moved or indignant at metaphorical situations, but to make them reflect on what they and others are doing, on the real things, exactly as they are. It stood for the first act of critical, political consciousness that Italy had experienced. Italy up to that point had no history, no unified history as a nation, only a history as many divided little peoples, divided little countries, and with a great gap between north and south.

Directions: An introductory sentence for a brief summary of the passage is provided below. Complete the summary by selecting the THREE answer choices that express the most important ideas in the passage. Some sentences do not belong in the summary because they express ideas that are not presented in the passage or are minor ideas in the passage. **This question is worth 2 points**.

Drag your answer choices to the spaces where they belong. To remove an answer choice, click on it. To review the passage, click on **View Text**.

Neorealism Italian history brought a critical, political consciousness to the vision of the artist in Italy.

-
-
-

Answer Choices

Ⓐ They looked upon the story as only an unconscious way of disguising a human defeat.

Ⓑ They superimposed simple techniques over living social facts.

Ⓒ Their task was to make people reflect on real things.

Ⓓ They up to that point had no unified history as a nation.

Ⓔ There was a great gap between north and south in Italy.

Ⓕ Italy had many divided little peoples and little countries.

Category Chart

Overview

정보 분류표(Category Chart) 문제는 선택지의 항목을 지문에서 설명하고 있는 범주에 맞게 분류하여 표를 완성하는 유형이다. 정보 분류표 문제는 각 지문의 마지막 문제로 요약(Summary) 문제가 나오지 않는 지문에 대해 1개가 출제된다. 지문을 읽을 때 두 개 이상의 비교 / 대조가 나오면 정보 분류표 문제가 출제될 확률이 높다.

질문유형

선택지 개수는 표에 정답으로 들어가는 것보다 많이 주어진다. 7개의 선택지 중 5개 또는 9개의 선택지 중 7개를 골라 표의 각 범주 아래로 끌어다 놓는다. 선택지가 7개면 3점, 선택지가 9개면 4점이며 부분 점수도 주어진다. 선택지가 7개인 경우 5개를 모두 맞히면 3점, 4개는 2점, 3개를 맞히면 1점을 얻게 된다. 선택지가 9개인 경우 7개를 모두 맞히면 4점, 6개는 3점, 5개는 2점, 4개를 맞히면 1점이 주어진다.

Directions: Select the appropriate phrases from the answer choices and match them to the types to which they relate. **This question is worth 3 points.**

Drag your answer choices to the spaces where they belong. To remove an answer choice, click on it. To review the passage, click on **View Text**.

Answer Choices	Category1
	•
	•
	Category2
	•
	•
	•

지시사항: 선택지에서 알맞은 구를 선택하여 그것과 관련된 항목에 맞게 연결하시오. **이 문제는 3점이 주어진다.**

선택지를 관련 있는 곳으로 끌어당기시오. 끌어당긴 선택지를 삭제하려면 그 위에 대고 클릭하시오. 지문을 다시 보려면 **View Text** 아이콘을 클릭하시오.

선택지	범주 1
	•
	•
	범주 2
	•
	•
	•

접근방법

1. 문제에 제시된 표에 나온 범주를 확인한 후 지문을 읽는다.

2. 선택지의 핵심 내용(key word)을 골라 각 범주를 뒷받침하는 세부사항을 분류한다.

3. 선택지의 표현은 지문 그대로가 아니고 바꿔 쓰기(paraphrase)되어 있으므로 꼼꼼히 비교한다.

4. 다음과 같은 오답을 선택지에서 고르지 않도록 한다.

　① 지문의 내용과 상반되는 것

　② 지문에서 보여주지 않은 것

　③ 지문에 쓰인 단어나, 비슷한 단어인데 내용이 왜곡된 것

Since 1999, the number of children who are being homeschooled has increased by 75%. Although currently only 4% of all school children nationwide are educated at home, the number of primary school kids whose parents choose to forgo traditional education is growing seven times faster than the number of kids enrolling in K-12 every year. As the dissatisfaction with the U.S. education system among parents grows, so does the appeal of homeschooling. Any concerns expressed about the quality of education offered to the kids by their parents can surely be put to rest by the consistently high placement of homeschooled kids on standardized assessment exams. Data shows that those who are independently educated typically score between 65th and 89th percentile on such exams, while those attending traditional schools average on the 50th percentile. Furthermore, the achievement gaps, long plaguing school systems around the country, aren't present in homeschooling environments. There's no difference in achievement between sexes, income levels or race, ethnicity as well. Recent studies laud homeschoolers' academic success, noting their significantly higher ACT-Composite scores as high schoolers and higher grade point averages as college students.

Directions: Select the appropriate phrases from the answer choices and match them to the types of education to which they relate. **This question is worth 3 points.**

Drag your answer choices to the spaces where they belong. To remove an answer choice, click on it. To review the passage, click on **View Text**.

Answer Choices	Homeschooling
Ⓐ dissatisfaction of students' parents	•
Ⓑ growing seven times faster	•
Ⓒ students' physical condition	•
Ⓓ score between 65th and 89th percentile on standardized assessment exams	**Traditional Education**
Ⓔ achievement gaps between ethnic groups	•
Ⓕ satisfaction with the U. S. education system	•
Ⓖ higher ACT-Composite scores	

Sample Question

해설 홈스쿨 교육의 특징인 ⑧는 지문의 네 번째, ⑩는 아홉 번째, ⑥는 마지막 문장을 통해 알 수 있다. 전통적인 교육의 특징인 보기 ⑧는 지문의 5번째, ⑥의 인종 집단간의 성취도 격차는 홈스쿨 교육과 전통적 교육을 비교하는 열한 번째 문장에서 홈스쿨 교육에 없다고 하므로 전통적 교육에 있다고 할 수 있다. ⓒ는 지문에 전혀 언급되지 않았고 ⑤는 지문의 내용과 상반되므로 오답이다.

지시사항: 선택지에서 알맞은 구를 선택하여 그것과 관련된 교육 유형에 맞게 연결하시오. **이 문제는 3점이 주어진다.**

선택지를 관련있는 곳으로 끌어당기시오. 끌어당긴 선택지를 삭제하려면 그 위에 대고 클릭하시오. 지문을 다시 보려면 **View Text** 아이콘을 클릭하시오.

선택지	홈스쿨 교육
⒜ 학부모의 불만족	•
⒝ 일곱 배 빠른 성장	•
⒞ 학생 건강 상태	•
⒟ 65점에서 89점의 표준화된 평가 테스트의 백분위 점수	**전통적 교육**
⒠ 인종 집단간의 성취도 격차	
⒡ 미국 교육시스템에 대한 만족	•
⒢ 더 높은 ACT–복합(미국 대학 입학 고사) 점수	•

해석 1999년 이래로 홈스쿨을 받는 아이들의 수가 75% 증가했다. 비록 현재 전국적으로 모든 학생의 4%만이 집에서 교육을 받고 있지만 전통적 교육을 포기하기를 결정한 부모의 초등학교 학생들의 수는 매년 K-12(미국 초등 교육 과정)에 등록하는 아이들의 수보다 7배나 더 빠르게 증가하고 있다. 부모들 사이의 미국 교육 시스템에 대한 불만족이 증가함에 따라 홈스쿨 교육의 인기도 커지고 있다. 그들의 부모들에 의해 아이들에게 제공되는 교육의 질에 대해 나타나는 일부의 염려는 홈스쿨을 받는 아이들이 지속적으로 표준화된 평가 테스트에서 최고 수준의 배치 고사 점수를 받으므로 확실히 잠재워질 수 있다. 한 자료는 전통적인 학교에 출석하는 아이들이 평균 50점의 백분위 점수를 얻는 반면에 독립적으로 교육을 받은 학생들은 그런 시험에서 전형적으로 65점에서 89점의 백분위 점수를 얻는다는 것을 보여준다. 더군다나 나라 전반에 걸쳐 성가신 학교 시스템인 성취도 격차는 홈스쿨 환경에 존재하지 않는다. 성별, 수입 수준이나 인종, 민족 사이의 성취도 차이도 없다. 최근 연구는 홈스쿨 받는 학생들의 고등학생처럼 상당히 높은 ACT–복합(미국 대학 입학 고사) 점수와 대학생들만큼 높은 평점에 주목하면서 홈스쿨 받는 학생들의 학업 성공을 극찬한다.

정답 Homeschooling – ⑧, ⑩, ⑥
Traditional Education – ⒜, ⑥

Heat kills thousands of people every year by pushing the human body beyond its limits. In extreme heat and high humidity, evaporation is slowed and the body must work extra hard to maintain a normal temperature. Most heat disorders occur because the victim has been overexposed to heat or has over-exercised for his or her age and physical condition. Older adults, young children and those who are sick or overweight are more likely to succumb to extreme heat. Conditions that can induce the heat-related illnesses include stagnant atmospheric conditions and poor air quality. Consequently, people living in urban areas may be at greater risk from the effects of a prolonged heat wave than those living in rural areas. Also, asphalt and concrete store heat longer and gradually release heat at night, which can produce higher nighttime temperatures known as the "urban heat island effect."

Directions: Select the appropriate phrases from the answer choices and match them to the heat disorders to which they relate. **This question is worth 3 points.**

Drag your answer choices to the spaces where they belong. To remove an answer choice, click on it. To review the passage, click on **View Text**.

Answer Choices	Conditions
Ⓐ high humidity	•
Ⓑ overweight	•
Ⓒ stagnant atmosphere	•
Ⓓ overexposure to heat	**Causes**
Ⓔ poor air quality	•
Ⓕ over-exercise	•
Ⓖ rural areas	

Microsoft is secretly working on a 7-inch Xbox Surface tablet, according to a report from tech blog The Verge. The site reported Tuesday that the tablet will be gaming focused and is expected to launch ahead of the next version of the Xbox home console, which is rumored to be coming sometime next year. The Verge said it had confirmed with multiple sources that the Xbox Surface will likely include a custom ARM processor and high-bandwidth RAM designed specifically for gaming tasks. This isn't the first time this gaming tablet rumor has made the rounds. Right before Microsoft revealed its new Surface RT and Surface Pro tablets a document supposedly outlining the specifications for a gaming-specific, Xbox-branded Surface tablet was leaked. That document revealed a tablet with a 7-inch screen with 1280 x 720 resolution, SD card support and support of up to four wireless game controllers. The Verge reported Tuesday that their sources say those initial specs are accurate and, additionally, that Microsoft's Xbox Surface won't run a full version of Windows, but a Windows kernel instead. An Xbox-tied, gaming-centric tablet certainly makes sense, especially as "second-screens" are already being integrated into gaming by Microsoft's competitors. Meanwhile, Sony has been bringing its handheld Vita game machine (with its 5-inch touchscreen) into play with some of its PlayStation 3 games. Microsoft has already made steps in this direction as well, launching its SmartGlass app last month alongside Windows 8 and its Surface tablets (which have 10.6-inch displays). The app connects phones and tablets with the Xbox 360 so the portable devices can act like a kind of remote control for the game machine. But if the specs for the rumored Xbox Surface tablet turn out to be true, it's the device's support of up to four traditional gaming controllers that is perhaps most interesting to video game fans. Tablets have become a popular destination for gaming — but mostly for playing more casual games "AngryBirds," "Plants vs. Zombies," etc. That's because the tablet's touch-screen controls are less-than-ideal when it comes to playing the more hard-core oriented games and certainly first-person shooting games. An Xbox Surface tablet paired with traditional Xbox controllers could bring core gaming to tablets in a much bigger, better way.

Directions: Select the appropriate phrases from the answer choices and match them to the game devices to which they relate. **This question is worth 3 points.**

Drag your answer choices to the spaces where they belong. To remove an answer choice, click on it. To review the passage, click on **View Text**.

Answer Choices	Xbox Surface Tablet
Ⓐ Windows kernel	•
Ⓑ Windows full version	•
Ⓒ PlayStation 3 games	•
Ⓓ supporting four wireless game controllers	**Vita Game Machine**
Ⓔ 5-inch touchscreen	•
Ⓕ supporting traditional gaming controllers	•
Ⓖ playing more casual games	

1.

지문

몸이 열을 견딜 수 있는 한도를 넘게 되어 매년 수천 명의 사람들이 목숨을 잃는다. 높은 열과 습도에서는 열의 발산이 늦어지고 신체는 정상 온도를 유지하기 위해 무리하게 노력한다. 대부분의 열 관련 신체장애는 희생자가 열에 과도하게 노출되거나 자신의 연령 및 신체 조건에 비해 심하게 운동을 해서 일어난다. 노인이나 어린이 그리고 질병을 앓거나 과체중인 사람들은 고열에 더 취약할 수 있다. 열 관련 질병을 유발할 수 있는 조건에는 순환이 안되고 질이 나쁜 공기가 포함된다. 따라서 도시 지역에 사는 사람들이 시골 지역에 사는 사람들보다 계속되는 복사열의 영향으로 더 위험할 수 있다. 또한 아스팔트와 콘크리트는 열을 더 오래 저장하고 밤에 서서히 내보내는데, 이는 '도시 열 섬 효과'로서 야간의 온도를 더 높게 만든다.

어휘

humidity 습도, 습기 evaporation 증발, 발산 disorder 난동, 무질서 victim 희생자, 피해자 succumb to ~에 굴복하다 prolonged 오래 계속되는 heat wave 열파

문제

지시사항: 선택지에서 알맞은 구를 선택하여 그것과 관련된 열 관련 신체장애에 맞게 연결하시오. **이 문제는 3점이 주어진다.**

> 선택지를 관련있는 곳으로 끌어당기시오. 끌어당긴 선택지를 삭제하려면 그 위에 대고 클릭하시오. 지문을 다시 보려면 **View Text** 아이콘을 클릭하시오.

선택지	조건
Ⓐ 높은 습도	•
Ⓑ 과체중	•
Ⓒ 순환이 안되는 대기	•
Ⓓ 열에 과도 노출	이유
Ⓔ 질이 나쁜 공기	
Ⓕ 과도한 운동	•
Ⓖ 시골 지역	•

해설

열 관련 신체장애의 조건 Ⓐ는 지문의 두 번째, Ⓒ와 Ⓔ은 다섯 번째 문장을 통해 알 수 있다. 세 번째 문장에서 대부분의 열 관련 신체장애가 열에 과도하게 노출되거나 심하게 운동을 해서 일어난다고 하였으므로 Ⓓ와 Ⓕ가 열 관련 신체장애의 이유가 된다. Ⓑ의 과체중인 사람들은 고열에 더 취약할 수 있지만 직접적인 이유가 아니므로 오답이다.

정답

Conditions— Ⓐ, Ⓒ, Ⓔ
Causes — Ⓓ, Ⓕ

2.

지문

기술 블로그 더 버지(컴퓨터 잡지)의 보고서에 따르면 마이크로 소프트는 7인치 엑스박스 서피스 태블릿에 공을 들이고 있다. 그 사이트는 그 태블릿이 게임용이고 내년 쯤에 출시될 것으로 소문이 도는 엑스박스 가정용 오락기 다음 버전 전에 출시될 것으로 기대되고 있다고 화요일에 발표하였다. 더 버지(컴퓨터 잡지)는 엑스박스 서피스가 특별히 게임용을 위해 디자인된 주문제작 ARM 프로세스와 고대역 RAM을 포함할 것으로 예상된다는 것을 여러 출처에서 확인했다고 말했다. 이 게임 태블릿 루머가 도는 것은 처음이 아니다. 마이크로소프트가 새로운 서피스 RT와 서피스 프로에 대해 밝히기 바로 전에 게임 중심 사양에 대한 윤곽이 그려진 것으로 추정되는 엑스박스 브랜드 서피스 태블릿 서류가 유출되었다. 그 서류는 1280 x 720해상도와 SD카드 지원인 7인치 스크린이 탑재되고 무선 게임 조종기를 4개까지 지원하는 태블릿에 관해 폭로했다. 더 버지는 그들의 출처가 그 초기 사양이 정확하다고 말하며 게다가 마이크로 소프트의 엑스박스 서피스는 윈도우의 풀 버전이 아닌 윈도우 커널(핵심)을 대신 운영한다고 전했다. 특히 '두 번째 스크린'이 이미 마이크로 소프트의 경쟁사들에 의해 통합되고 있기 때문에 엑스박스로 연결된 게임 중심 태블릿은 확실히 이해가 된다. 그 사이에 소니는 플레이스테이션 3게임들 중에 몇 가지를 할 수 있는 손바닥 크기의 비타 게임 기계를(5인치 터치스크린을 갖는) 도입하고 있다. 마이크로소프트는 윈도우 8과 서피스 태블릿(10.6 인치 디스플레이를 갖는)과 나란히 스마트글라스앱을 저번 달에 출시하면서 이미 이 방향으로 또 한걸음 내디뎠다. 그 앱은 전화기와 태블릿을 엑스박스 360과 연결하여 휴대용 장치들

이 게임 기계의 원격 조종의 한 유형으로 행동할 수 있다. 그러나 만약 그 소문에 의한 엑스박스 서피스 태블릿의 사양이 사실이라고 밝혀지고 예전 게임 조정기를 4개까지 지원하는 장치라면 그것은 아마도 비디오 게임 팬들에게는 가장 흥미가 있을 것이다. 그러나 대부분 '앵그리 버드', '플랜트 대 좀비' 등등과 같은 캐주얼 게임만 태블릿에서 인기를 끌었다. 그것은 태블릿의 터치스크린 제어가 더 하드코어 위주나 개인용 슈팅 게임을 할 때는 확실히 결코 이상적이지 않기 때문이다. 예전 엑스박스 조종기와 연결된 엑스박스 서피스 태블릿은 훨씬 뛰어나고 나은 방법으로 코어 게임을 태블릿으로 제공할 수 있을 것이다.

어휘

ahead of ~앞에, ~보다 앞서 high-bandwidth 고대역 reveal 누설하다, 밝히다 specifications 명세서, 설명서 resolution 해상도 해결 integrated 통합된 alongside ~옆에, 나란히 turn out ~을 판명하다, 드러내다 paired with ~와 병행된

문제

지시사항: 선택지에서 알맞은 구를 선택하여 그것과 관련된 게임 기기에 맞게 연결하시오. **이 문제는 3점이 주어진다.**

선택지를 관련있는 곳으로 끌어당기시오. 끌어당긴 선택지를 삭제하려면 그 위에 대고 클릭하시오. 지문을 다시 보려면 **View Text** 아이콘을 클릭하시오.

선택지	엑스박스 서피스 태블릿
Ⓐ 윈도우 커널	•
Ⓑ 윈도우 풀버전	•
Ⓒ 플레이스테이션 3게임	•
Ⓓ 4개의 무선 게임 조정기 지원	**비타 게임 기계**
Ⓔ 5인치 터치스크린	•
Ⓕ 이전 게임 조정기 지원	•
Ⓖ 캐주얼 게임 더 하기	

해설

게임 기기 엑스박스 서피스 태블릿에 관한 내용은 지문의 여섯 번째(4개의 무선 게임 조정기 지원), 일곱 번째(윈도우 커널), 열두 번째(이전 게임 조정기 지원)문장에서 Ⓐ, Ⓓ, Ⓕ임을 찾을 수 있다. 비타 게임 기계와 관련된 내용은 지문의 아홉 번째(5인치 터치스크린, 플레이스테이션 3게임)에 나와 있으므로 Ⓒ와 Ⓔ가 답이다. 캐주얼 게임을 더 하는 것은 구형 태블릿 게임의 한계를 설명한 것이므로 Ⓖ는 오답이다.

정답

Xbox Surface Tablet - Ⓐ, Ⓓ, Ⓕ
Vita Game Machine - Ⓒ, Ⓔ

In situations where some land is available for different farmers to graze their animals, it's likely to become overused and degraded. Similarly, common fishing areas are likely to be overfished, perhaps to the point where fish disappear. Common logging forests will be over logged and laid waste. This is an ancient problem that was used to justify Britain's "enclosure movement" many centuries ago, when economists decided it was clearly a problem of property rights. Because no one owned the common area, no one had an economic incentive to look after it. Indeed, each individual had an incentive to get in and use as much of it as possible, as quickly as possible, before other individuals used it up. So what was everyone's property was actually no one's property – and many economists thought it obvious that the solution was to allocate private property rights over the commons. Who they were allocated to, and how they were allocated, didn't matter much. What mattered was that once someone owned the asset, they would have the economic incentive to look after it and prevent its degradation.

Directions: Select the appropriate phrases from the answer choices and match them to the property rights to which they relate. **This question is worth 3 points.**

Drag your answer choices to the spaces where they belong. To remove an answer choice, click on it. To review the passage, click on **View Text**.

Answer Choices	Common Areas
Ⓐ degradation prevented	•
Ⓑ enclosure movement	•
Ⓒ overused and degraded	•
Ⓓ looked after	**Private Property**
Ⓔ a problem of property rights	•
Ⓕ no economic incentive to care for	•
Ⓖ using as much as possible before others	

Human-generated stress can be damaging for coral reefs. Pollution from pesticides and soil runoff is smothering sections of the small reef that fringes Costa Rica in the Caribbean. Reefs off Jakarta, the capital of Indonesia and a city of 9.5 million, were slowly killed by untreated sewage, reef mining, and soil runoff. Dynamite fishing and large-scale, illegal harvesting of coral for the aquarium trade have devastated reef communities ringing the Philippines. Even ecotourism - hoped by many to be the saving grace for the world's wild places - scars reefs, as inexperienced divers inadvertently mar the very places they treasure. Just one touch can be fatal to sensitive reef builders. "Reefs are among the oldest ecosystems on earth," says a marine biologist with the Smithsonian Institution in Washington, D.C. "Yet we are rapidly destroying an ecosystem we are only just starting to understand."

Directions: Select the appropriate phrases from the answer choices and the places of the pollutants to which they relate. **This question is worth 3 points.**

Drag your answer choices to the spaces where they belong. To remove an answer choice, click on it. To review the passage, click on **View Text**.

Answer Choices	Jakarta & Costa Rica
Ⓐ pollution from pesticides	•
Ⓑ untreated sewage	•
Ⓒ dynamite fishing	•
Ⓓ illegal harvesting of coral	**The Philippines**
Ⓔ experienced divers	•
Ⓕ soil runoff	•
Ⓖ sensitive reef builders	

Themes

10개의 주제 **History** / **Environment** / **Economy** / **Society** / **Computer** / **Nature** / **Education** / **Culture** / **Science** & **Technology** / **Art** & **Literature**를 통해 실전감각을 길러보자. 매 유닛마다 다양한 유형의 실전문제가 **5**개씩 실려 있고, **Vocabulary** & **Paraphrasing**란에는 주제별 필수어휘와 바꿔쓰기를 할 수 있는 연습문제를 담았다.

History

 TOEFL Reading
PAUSE TEST   SECTION EXIT

Practice Test 1
Question 1 of 5

 CONTINUE REVIEW HELP BACK NEXT

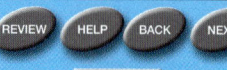 HIDE TIME 01 : 40

Despite its long history, the Great Wall of China as it exists today was constructed mainly during the mighty Ming dynasty (1368-1644). Like the **Mongols**, the early Ming rulers had little interest in building border fortifications, and wall building was limited before the late 15th century. In 1421, the Ming emperor Yongle proclaimed China's new capital, Beijing, on the site of the former Mongol city of Dadu. Under the strong hand of the Ming rulers, Chinese culture flourished, and the period saw an immense amount of construction in addition to the Great Wall, including bridges, temples and pagodas. The construction of the Great Wall as it is known today began around 1474. **After an initial phase of territorial expansion, Ming rulers took a largely defensive stance, and their reformation and extension of the Great Wall was key to this strategy.** The Ming wall extended from the Yalu River in Liaoning Province to the eastern bank of the Taolai River in Gansu Province, and winded its way from east to west through today's Liaoning, Hebei, Tianjin, Beijing, Inner Mongolia, Shanxi, Shaanxi, Ningxia and Gansu.

1. **Why does the author mention Mongols in the passage?**

   Ⓐ To compare the similarities in the two cultures at the time

   Ⓑ To emphasize the point that the Chinese superseded them

   Ⓒ To show that, despite their early similarities, the Chinese were superior to them

   Ⓓ To give an example of another ancient culture with similar ideas

2. **Which of the sentences below best expresses the essential information in the highlighted sentence in the passage? Incorrect choices change the meaning in important ways or leave out essential information.**

   Ⓐ Nothing was as important to the Ming rulers as the defensive capacity of the Great Wall.

   Ⓑ The Ming rulers soon had no choice but to change from offense to defense so started building the Great Wall.

   Ⓒ Without the Great Wall, the Ming rulers would have needed to continue their territorial expansion.

   Ⓓ At first the Ming rulers sought to move into new regions but then hunkered down behind their most important protective barrier, the Great Wall.

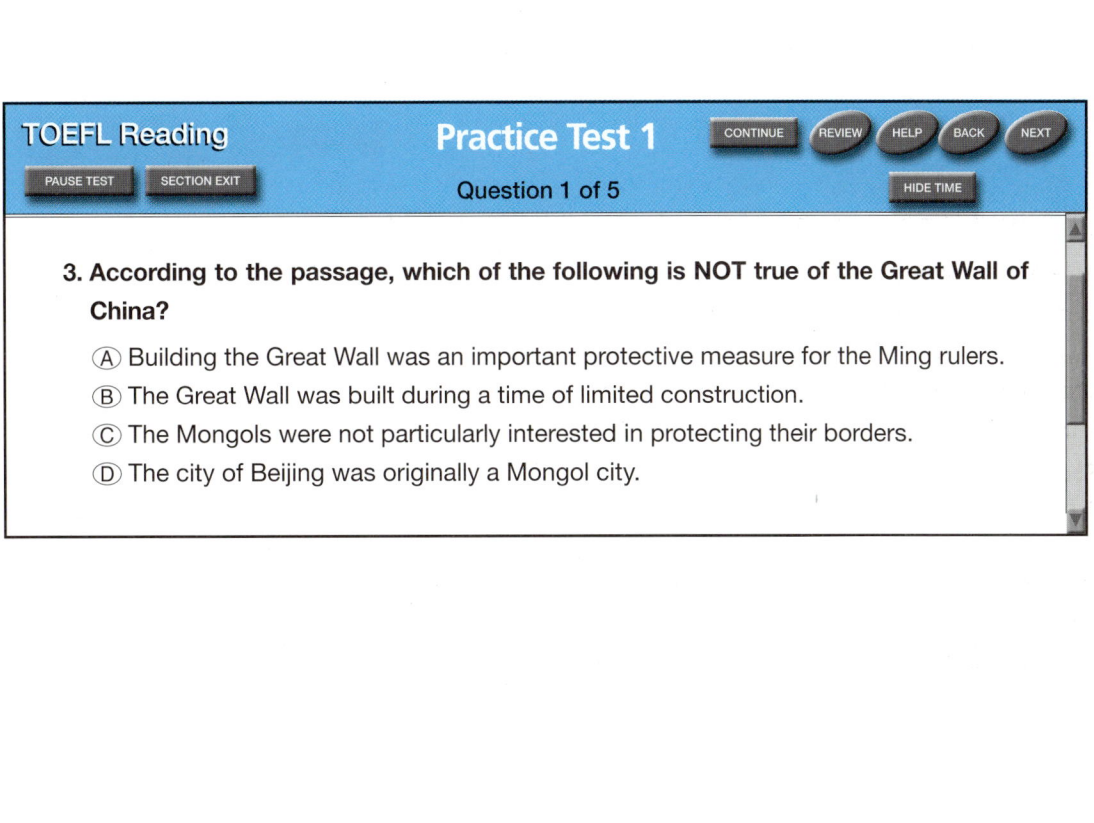

3. **According to the passage, which of the following is NOT true of the Great Wall of China?**

   Ⓐ Building the Great Wall was an important protective measure for the Ming rulers.

   Ⓑ The Great Wall was built during a time of limited construction.

   Ⓒ The Mongols were not particularly interested in protecting their borders.

   Ⓓ The city of Beijing was originally a Mongol city.

다음 문장을 ① 끊어 읽기 → 직독직해 ② 명사 [구, 절]에 대괄호 ③ 동사 [구]에 동그라미 ④ 세부정보에 소괄호를 한 후 핵심정보에 화살표로 연결하시오.

1. Despite its long history, the Great Wall of China as it exists today was constructed mainly during the mighty Ming dynasty (1368-1644).

   _____

   _____

2. The construction of the Great Wall as it is known today began around 1474.

   _____

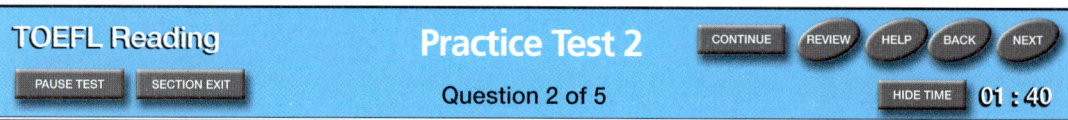
When the Germanic tribes entered the lands of the Western Roman Empire, they brought many of their customs and traditions with them, among them being those customs and traditions that comprised their system of justice. The **operative** unit of society was the kindred, the clan or extended family. When a member of one kindred harmed a member of another in person or in property, the aggrieved person's relatives sought retribution in what is now termed a vendetta or feud. Given the collective nature in which people operated, it should come as no surprise to find that retribution was not sought specifically from the person at fault, but from him or any member of his kindred. In addition, there was always the danger that a kindred would consider that their opponents had been excessive in their retribution and would seek their own retribution as a means of striking a suitable balance. Such games of tit for tat could go on for years with men being killed long after the original basis of complaint had been forgotten.

1. The word operative in the passage is closest in meaning to

Ⓐ being used

Ⓑ functioning effectively

Ⓒ producing a desired effect

Ⓓ fruitful

2. Which of the following can be concluded from the passage?

Ⓐ The Germanic tribes had good memories.

Ⓑ These tribes didn't expect to seek revenge for any harm that was done to their clan.

Ⓒ It was not easy to agree on a suitable level of retribution for a wrong.

Ⓓ Clans were extremely bloodthirsty and always looking for a way to attack others.

3. Directions: An introductory sentence for a brief summary of the passage is provided below. Complete the summary by selecting the THREE answer choices that express the most important ideas in the passage. Some sentences do not belong in the summary because they express ideas that are not presented in the passage or are minor ideas in the passage. **This question is worth 2 points**.

Drag your answer choices to the spaces where they belong. To remove an answer choice, click on it. To review the passage, click on **View Text**.

TOEFL Reading

PAUSE TEST   SECTION EXIT

Practice Test 2

Question 2 of 5

CONTINUE   REVIEW   HELP   BACK   NEXT

HIDE TIME

There were ways of resolving grievances in collective societies.

-
-
-

Answer Choices

Ⓐ The operative unit of society was the kindred, the clan or extended family.

Ⓑ The aggrieved person's relatives sought retribution in a vendetta or feud.

Ⓒ Retribution was not sought specifically from the person at fault.

Ⓓ Opponents had been excessive in their retribution.

Ⓔ Games of tit for tat could go on for a long time.

Ⓕ The original basis of complaint had been forgotten.

다음 문장을 ① 끊어 읽기 → 직독직해 ② 명사 [구, 절]에 대괄호 ③ 동사 [구]에 동그라미 ④ 세부정보에 소괄호를 한 후 핵심정보에 화살표로 연결하시오.

1. Such games of tit for tat could go on for years with men being killed long after the original basis of complaint had been forgotten.

_____

_____

2. In addition, there was always the danger that a kindred would consider that their opponents had been excessive in their retribution and would seek their own retribution as a means of striking a suitable balance.

_____

_____

_____

On September 2, 1945, the two most powerful nations in the world broke into a war of pride and power, known as the Cold War. The Soviet Union and the United States battled fiercely for a reputation that would be venerated for ages to come. Aggressively, these two nations pushed to be the greatest in the world through politics, weapons, and science. These actions and attitudes significantly promoted the need for space exploration, and soon fueled a pursuit that altered history forever. **The space race** had many motivations and many things that kept the competition going. One of the main motivations was for military security. To have power in the world these countries needed to have missiles and rockets that could go higher, faster, and farther than the other country. These rivals needed to place themselves in space to have dominance over one another. They could potentially have orbital weapon systems, be able to intercept and inspect communications of their enemies, and also have a possible military use for the moon. **These things** motivated the military part of the space race.

1. Why does the author mention the space race in the passage?

   Ⓐ To urge for restraint in the buildup of military weaponry

   Ⓑ To celebrate the power and possibilities of orbital weapon systems

   Ⓒ To condemn the dangerous escalation of power fueled by pride

   Ⓓ To illustrate one outcome of the rivalry between the two countries.

2. The phrase these things in the passage refers to

   Ⓐ have orbital weapon systems, be able to intercept and inspect communications of their enemies, and also have a possible military use for the moon

   Ⓑ have missiles and rockets that could go higher, faster, and farther than the other country

   Ⓒ placing themselves in space to have dominance over one another

   Ⓓ actions and attitudes

3. Directions: Select the appropriate phrases from the answer choices and match them to the motivations of the competition to which they relate. **This question is worth 3 points.**

Drag your answer choices to the spaces where they belong. To remove an answer choice, click on it. To review the passage, click on **View Text.**

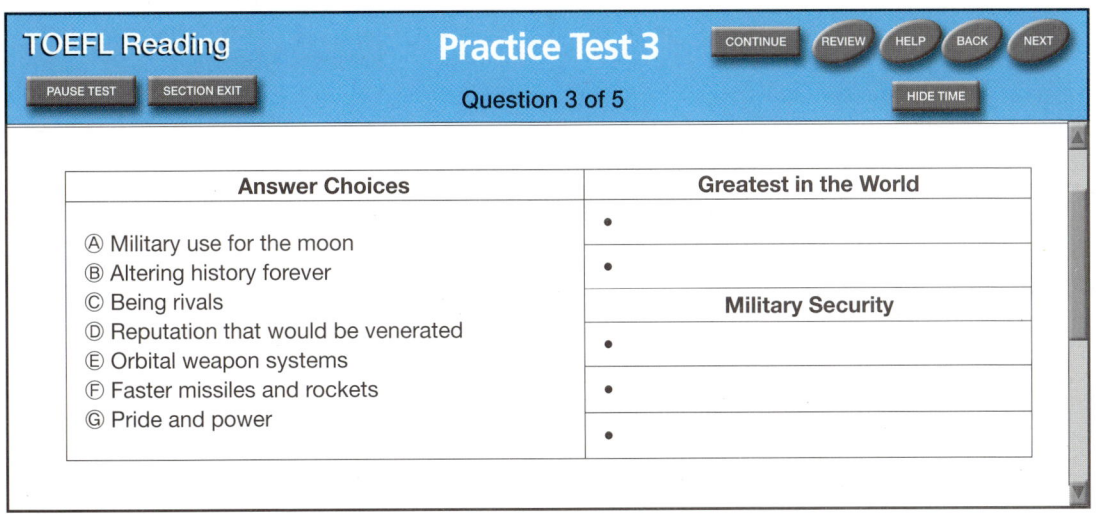

Answer Choices	Greatest in the World
Ⓐ Military use for the moon	•
Ⓑ Altering history forever	•
Ⓒ Being rivals	**Military Security**
Ⓓ Reputation that would be venerated	•
Ⓔ Orbital weapon systems	•
Ⓕ Faster missiles and rockets	•
Ⓖ Pride and power	

다음 문장을 ① 끊어 읽기 → 직독직해 ② 명사 [구, 절]에 대괄호 ③ 동사 [구]에 동그라미 ④ 세부정보에 소괄호를 한 후 핵심정보에 화살표로 연결하시오.

1. To have power in the world these countries needed to have missiles and rockets that could go higher, faster, and farther than the other country.

_____

_____

2. On September 2, 1945, the two most powerful nations in the world broke into a war of pride and power, known as the Cold War.

_____

_____

181

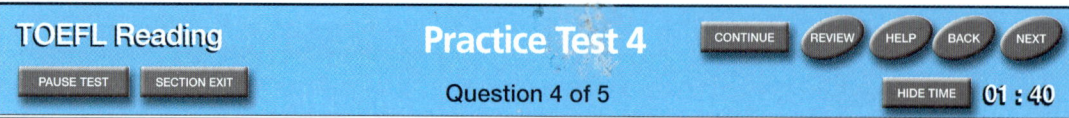
The first European settlements date from the early sixteenth century and included Spanish towns in Florida and California, French outposts in Louisiana, and British settlements in New England. The United States of America was declared in 1776 by colonists from England who wanted independence from that country and its elite representatives in the colonies. Ⓐ ▪ The class, racial, ethnic, and gender relationships of the contemporary nation have their roots in the colonial period. Unsuccessful efforts by British settlers to enslave Native Americans were followed by the importation of African slaves to work on cotton plantations in the South and of white indentured servants to work in the emerging industries in the North. Ⓑ ▪ British taxation fell disproportionately on poor white laborers and indentured servants. Ⓒ ▪ Women participated in the Revolution by running farms and businesses during the war. Ⓓ ▪ **The equalitarian rhetoric of the Revolution did not extend to slaves, and after independence, full citizenship rights did not extend to all whites.** Men and women who did not own property had no voting rights. Women did not gain the right to vote until the early twentieth century. The area west of the Appalachians was settled by poor whites seeking land and autonomy from wage labor.

1. **Look at the four squares [▪] that indicate where the following sentence could be added to the passage.**

   This sector was instrumental in organizing the protests and boycotts of British goods that culminated in the American Revolution.

   Where would the sentence best fit?
   Click on a square [▪] to add the sentence to the passage.

2. **Which of the sentences below best expresses the essential information in the highlighted sentence in the passage? Incorrect choices change the meaning in important ways or leave out essential information.**

   Ⓐ There was a disjunct between the ideals and reality of the Revolution regarding equal rights.
   Ⓑ Despite their claims, supporters of the Revolution were able to implement their high ideals.
   Ⓒ The Revolution was thwarted in its efforts to bring equal rights to everyone.
   Ⓓ It was unrealistic of the Revolution to expect that equal rights could be extended to everyone.

TOEFL Reading

PAUSE TEST   SECTION EXIT

Practice Test 4

Question 4 of 5

CONTINUE   REVIEW   HELP   BACK   NEXT

HIDE TIME

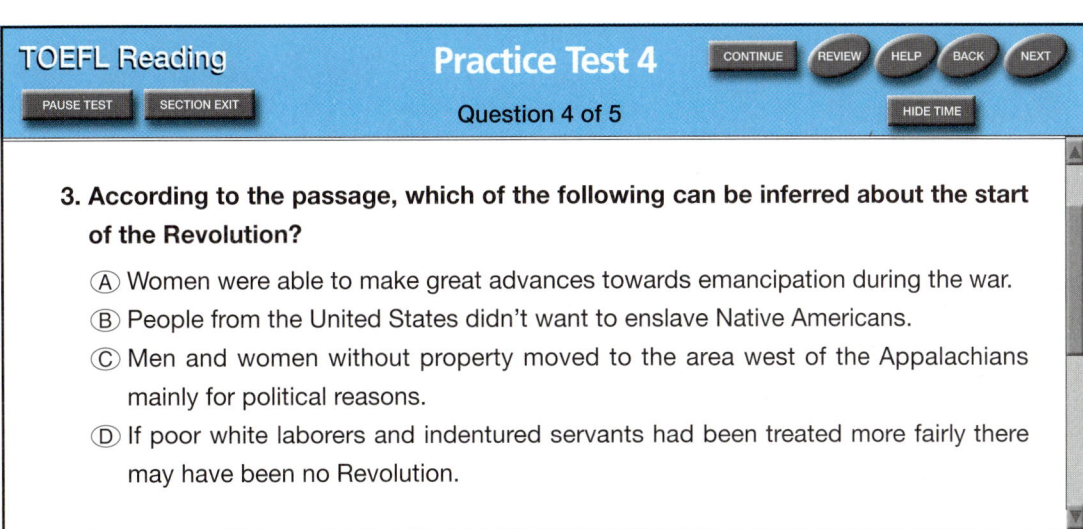

3. According to the passage, which of the following can be inferred about the start of the Revolution?

Ⓐ Women were able to make great advances towards emancipation during the war.

Ⓑ People from the United States didn't want to enslave Native Americans.

Ⓒ Men and women without property moved to the area west of the Appalachians mainly for political reasons.

Ⓓ If poor white laborers and indentured servants had been treated more fairly there may have been no Revolution.

다음 문장을 ① 끊어 읽기 → 직독직해 ② 명사 [구, 절]에 대괄호 ③ 동사 [구]에 동그라미 ④ 세부정보에 소괄호를 한 후 핵심정보에 화살표로 연결하시오.

1. Unsuccessful efforts by British settlers to enslave Native Americans were followed by the importation of African slaves to work on cotton plantations in the South and of white indentured servants to work in the emerging industries in the North.

_____

_____

_____

2. The first European settlements date from the early sixteenth century and included Spanish towns in Florida and California, French outposts in Louisiana,and British settlements in New England.

_____

_____

_____

TOEFL Reading

PAUSE TEST   SECTION EXIT

Practice Test 5

Question 5 of 5

CONTINUE   REVIEW   HELP   BACK   NEXT

HIDE TIME   01 : 40

Why did the forces of globalization, nationalism, interlocking alliances, and power transition combine to produce war in 1914 specifically? The factors may all be thought of as **conditions for permission** to conflict: these forces may have helped to pave the way to the Great War's onset, but none alone was the immediate cause of war in 1914. Moreover, these forces were almost certainly present in Europe prior to that fateful year. Why, then, did they not combine to produce a major war when Austria annexed Bosnia in 1908? Why did they not stoke the Balkan Wars of 1912 and 1913 and produce global conflagration then? If we are to accept that any specific set of conditions caused the First World War in 1914, we must also be able to explain why those forces did not produce war earlier or later, or why conflict could not have been avoided altogether despite their prevalence. Indeed, in the copious literature on World War I, scholars have attempted to dissect these important counterfactuals. Some argue that the structural conditions really did make a European conflict inevitable — interlocking alliances, the Anglo-German power transition, nationalism, and other factors meant that war would have occurred in 1915 or 1916 if it did not in 1914. But other analysts insist that the Great War was the immediate result of assassination of the Austrian Archduke Franz Ferdinand. If he had not been killed in Sarajevo on June 28, 1914 — or if he had been shot and lived — the great powers might have avoided war, not just in that year, but in perpetuity. **If an idiosyncratic event like the Archduke's assassination is the key to explaining the war, however, it is not clear how much credence we should give to other underlying factors.**

1. Which of the following can be concluded from the passage?

Ⓐ Scholars will never completely agree about the cause of the war.

Ⓑ The war could not have started at any time.

Ⓒ The time was ripe for war and one small incident was enough to start it.

Ⓓ Wars were unavoidable in the past.

2. The phrase conditions for permission in the passage is closest in meaning to

Ⓐ conditions that are free

Ⓑ conditions that are restricted

Ⓒ conditions that are optional

Ⓓ conditions that are approved

TOEFL Reading

Practice Test 5

CONTINUE REVIEW HELP BACK NEXT

PAUSE TEST SECTION EXIT

Question 5 of 5

HIDE TIME

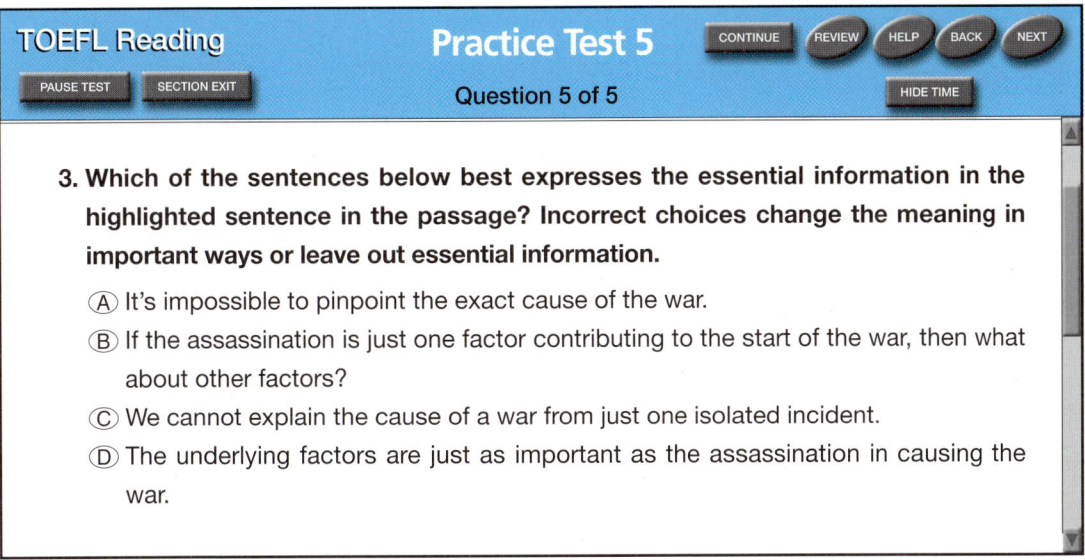

3. **Which of the sentences below best expresses the essential information in the highlighted sentence in the passage? Incorrect choices change the meaning in important ways or leave out essential information.**

(A) It's impossible to pinpoint the exact cause of the war.

(B) If the assassination is just one factor contributing to the start of the war, then what about other factors?

(C) We cannot explain the cause of a war from just one isolated incident.

(D) The underlying factors are just as important as the assassination in causing the war.

다음 문장을 ① 끊어 읽기 → 직독직해 ② 명사 [구, 절]에 대괄호 ③ 동사 [구]에 동그라미 ④ 세부정보에 소괄호를 한 후 핵심정보에 화살표로 연결하시오.

1. If we are to accept that any specific set of conditions caused the First World War in 1914, we must also be able to explain why those forces did not produce war earlier or later, or why conflict could not have been avoided altogether despite their prevalence.

_____

_____

_____

2. If an idiosyncratic event like the Archduke's assassination is the key to explaining the war, however, it is not clear how much credence we should give to other underlying factors.

_____

_____

_____

185

Vocabulary & Paraphrasing

1. Write the word from the box that matches each meaning below.

settlement	condemn	unprecedented	portage	equalitarian
undertake	manifest	disproportion	indenture	stagnation

① a failure to develop, progress, or advance _____

② never before known or experienced _____

③ to express an unfavorable judgment on _____

④ to reveal or display _____

⑤ to bind by a contract as an apprentice _____

⑥ the establishment of a new region _____

⑦ the act of carrying _____

⑧ upholding the doctrine of the equality of mankind _____

⑨ to warrant or guarantee _____

⑩ not equal _____

Vocabulary & Paraphrasing

2. Translate the following questions into Korean and then paraphrase them according to the directions below.

① The invention of the printing press allowed the acquisition of this knowledge in an unprecedented manner. → 문장의 태 바꿔 쓰기

_____

_____

② Women did not gain the right to vote until the early twentieth century. → 접속사 바꿔 쓰기

_____

③ Despite an overall stagnation in the economy for nearly two decades, Japan's industries are still among the most highly advanced and innovative in the world. → 접속사로 바꿔 쓰기

_____

_____

_____

④ The Shared Path project weaves for 10 kilometers through the Humber River Valley and consists of 13 historical nodes that describe Canada's early history as it happened along the banks of the Humber River. → 수동태, 쉬운 단어로 바꿔 쓰기

_____

_____

_____

Practice Test 1

1. Despite its long history, / the Great Wall of China / (as it exists today) (was constructed) mainly / during the mighty Ming dynasty (1368-1644).

   긴 역사에도 불구하고 오늘날 존재하는 중국의 만리장성은 대부분 강력한 명나라 시대(1368-1644)에 건설되었다.

2. [The construction of the Great Wall] (as it is known today) (began) around 1474.

   오늘날 알려져 있는 만리장성의 건설은 1474년 무렵 시작되었다.

Practice Test 2

1. [Such games of tit for tat] (could go on) for years / (with men being killed) / long after [the original basis of complaint] / had been forgotten.

   이런 '눈에는 눈, 이에는 이'의 보복게임들은 불평의 원인이 잊힌 후에도 수년간 사람들이 살해되는 등 계속될 수 있었다.

2. In addition, / there (was) always the danger / (that a kindred would consider,) [that their opponents had been excessive in their retribution / and would seek their own retribution / as a means of striking a suitable balance].

   더불어 친족은 적들이 보복의 도를 넘어섰다고 여기고 응징의 적절한 균형 유지 수단으로써 그들만의 보복을 추구하고자 할 위험이 항상 있었다.

Practice Test 3

1. To have power in the world / these countries (needed to have) missiles and rockets / (that could go higher, faster, and farther than the other country).

   세계를 지배하는 힘을 갖기 위해 두 나라는 다른 나라보다 더 높이, 더 빨리, 그리고 더 멀리 갈 수 있는 미사일과 로켓을 만드는 게 필요했다.

2. On September 2, 1945, / [the two most powerful nations in the world] / (broke into) a war of pride and power, / (known as the Cold War).

   1945년 9월 2일 세계에서 가장 강대국인 두 나라가 냉전으로 알려진 자존심과 권력의 전쟁으로 치닫기 시작했다.

Practice Test 4

1. Unsuccessful efforts (by British settlers) / (to enslave Native Americans) / (were followed) (by the importation of African slaves) / (to work on cotton plantations in the South) / and of white indentured servants / (to work in the emerging industries in the North).

   영국 정착민들은 미 대륙 원주민을 노예로 만들고자 하는 노력이 실패하면서 남부에서 목화 농장에서 일을 시키거나 북부의 신흥 산업에서 일을 시키기 위한 백인들의 계약 하인으로 아프리카 노예를 수입하게 되었다.

2. [The first European settlements] / (date from) [the early sixteenth century] / and (included) Spanish towns (in Florida and California,) / French outposts (in Louisiana,) / and British settlements (in New England).

   최초의 유럽인 정착지는 16세기 초로 거슬러 올라가며, 플로리다와 캘리포니아에 있는 스페인 마을과 루이지애나에 있는 프랑스인들의 전초기지와 뉴잉글랜드의 영국인 임시거주지가 여기에 속한다.

Practice Test 5

1. If we are to accept / [that any specific set of conditions / caused the First World War in 1914,] / we (must also be able to explain) [why those forces did not produce war earlier or later,] / or [why conflict could not have been avoided altogether / despite their prevalence].

   우리가 여러 조건의 조합 중 하나의 특정 조합이 1914년에 제1차 세계대전을 일으켰다고 받아들인다면 왜 이러한 요인들이 더 일찍 또는 더 늦게 전쟁을 일으키지 못했는지 또는 그것들이 만연했음에도 불구하고 물리적 충돌을 왜 함께 피할 수 없었는지 또한 설명할 수 있어야 한다.

2. If an idiosyncratic event / (like the Archduke's assassination) / is the key to explaining the war, / however, / it (is) not clear / [how much credence we should give / to other underlying factors].

   하지만, 대공의 암살과 같은 특이한 사건이 전쟁을 설명하는 열쇠라면 우리가 다른 근본적인 요인에 얼마나 많은 신빙성을 부여해야 할지 명확하지 않다.

Unit 02

Environment

TOEFL Reading

PAUSE TEST   SECTION EXIT

Practice Test 1

CONTINUE   REVIEW   HELP   BACK   NEXT

Question 1 of 5

HIDE TIME   01 : 40

Across the vast Pacific, the mighty bluefin tuna carried radioactive contamination that leaked from Japan's crippled nuclear plant to the shores of the United States 6,000 miles away – the first time a huge migrating fish has been shown to carry radioactivity such a distance. Ⓐ ■ But even so, that's still far below safe-to-eat limits set by the U.S. and Japanese governments. Ⓑ ■ Previously, smaller fish and plankton were found with **elevated** levels of radiation in Japanese waters after a magnitude-9 earthquake in March 2011 triggered a tsunami that badly damaged the Fukushima Dai-ichi reactors. Ⓒ ■ But scientists did not expect the nuclear fall out to linger in huge fish that sail the world because such fish can metabolize and shed radioactive substances. One of the large stand speediest fish, Pacific bluefin tuna can grow to 10 feet and weigh more than 1,000pounds. Ⓓ ■ They spawn off the Japan coast and swim east at breakneck speed to school in waters off California and the tip of Baja California, Mexico. Five months after the Fukushima disaster, a team decided to test Pacific bluefin that were caught off the coast of San Diego. To their surprise, tissue samples from all 15 tuna captured contained levels of two radioactive substances – cesium-134 and cesium-137 – that were higher than in previous catches.

1. **Look at the four squares [■] that indicate where the following sentence could be added to the passage.**

The levels of radioactive cesium were 10 times higher than the amount measured in tuna off the California coast in previous years.

Where would the sentence best fit?
Click on a square [■] to add the sentence to the passage.

2. **The word elevated in the passage is closest in meaning to**

Ⓐ high-minded
Ⓑ increased
Ⓒ produced
Ⓓ above the ground

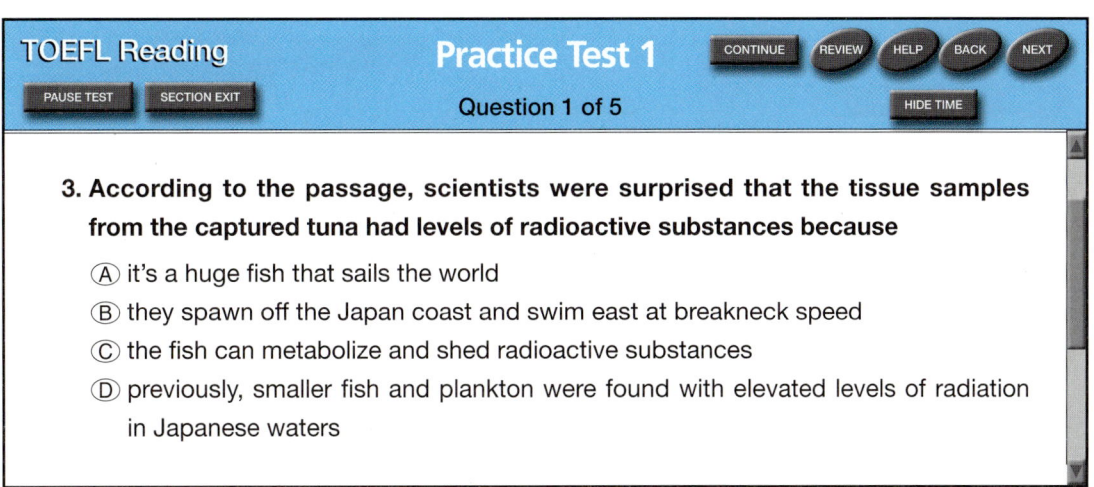

3. According to the passage, scientists were surprised that the tissue samples from the captured tuna had levels of radioactive substances because

Ⓐ it's a huge fish that sails the world

Ⓑ they spawn off the Japan coast and swim east at breakneck speed

Ⓒ the fish can metabolize and shed radioactive substances

Ⓓ previously, smaller fish and plankton were found with elevated levels of radiation in Japanese waters

다음 문장을 ① 끊어 읽기 → 직독직해 ② 명사 [구, 절]에 대괄호 ③ 동사 [구]에 동그라미 ④ 세부정보에 소괄호를 한 후 핵심정보에 화살표로 연결하시오.

1. Across the vast Pacific, the mighty bluefin tuna carried radioactive contamination that leaked from Japan's crippled nuclear plant to the shores of the United States 6,000 miles away – the first time a huge migrating fish has been shown to carry radioactivity such a distance.

_____

_____

_____

2. But scientists did not expect the nuclear fall out to linger in huge fish that sail the world because such fish can metabolize and shed radioactive substances.

_____

_____

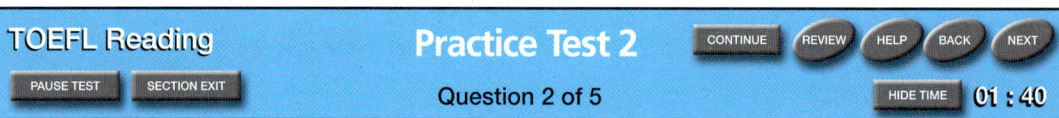

TOEFL Reading

PAUSE TEST   SECTION EXIT

Practice Test 2

CONTINUE   REVIEW   HELP   BACK   NEXT

Question 2 of 5

HIDE TIME   01 : 40

Water depletion from afforestation — the establishment of trees or tree stands on the land where none previously were — is the unintended consequence of a widely popular federal policy. For millenniums, fires set by lightning or Native Americans limited forest stocks to roughly a few dozen trees per acre. All that changed after the wildfires of 1910, which led to a war on wildfire with security watchtowers, propaganda, aerial bombing and color-coded threat alerts. Elite crews were trained to put out enemy flames. Congress annually funded the war effort but decades of heroic victories against fire led to gradual defeat in the larger war. Fuel builds up, and when it ignites, the fires burn hotter, faster and more destructively. More new trees compete for less sunlight, thinner soil nutrients and scarcer water resources. Native wildlife suffers. Insects and diseases spread faster. Public subsidies protect private properties at the wildland-urban interface by planting trees. These kinds of acts to prevent erosion and secure downstream navigable rivers made sense in damp Eastern states, but **it** had the opposite effect in the semiarid West.

1. Which of the following can be concluded from the passage?

   Ⓐ The war on wildfires was finally won.

   Ⓑ There were unintended side effects from afforestation.

   Ⓒ Improving forest stocks by afforestation was successful.

   Ⓓ The war on wildfires eventually spread to the West.

2. The word it in the passage refers to

   Ⓐ protecting trees

   Ⓑ making rivers navigable

   Ⓒ planting trees

   Ⓓ preventing erosion

3. Directions: An introductory sentence for a brief summary of the passage is provided below. Complete the summary by selecting the THREE answer choices that express the most important ideas in the passage. Some sentences do not belong in the summary because they express ideas that are not presented in the passage or are minor ideas in the passage. **This question is worth 2 points**.

Drag your answer choices to the spaces where they belong. To remove an answer choice, click on it. To review the passage, click on **View Text**.

TOEFL Reading

PAUSE TEST   SECTION EXIT

Practice Test 2

Question 2 of 5

CONTINUE   REVIEW   HELP   BACK   NEXT

HIDE TIME

The wildfires of 1910 led to a war on wildfire.

-
-
-

Answer Choices

Ⓐ Acts to prevent erosion and secure downstream navigable rivers had the opposite effect in the semiarid West.

Ⓑ Congress annually funded the war effort.

Ⓒ Native wildlife suffers.

Ⓓ The government became concerned about fire alarm facilities.

Ⓔ Fires set by lightning or Native Americans limited forest stocks to roughly a few dozen trees per acre.

Ⓕ Elite crews were trained to put out enemy flames.

다음 문장을 ① 끊어 읽기 → 직독직해 ② 명사 [구, 절]에 대괄호 ③ 동사 [구]에 동그라미 ④ 세부정보에 소괄호를 한 후 핵심정보에 화살표로 연결하시오.

1. Water depletion from afforestation — the establishment of trees or tree stands on the land where none previously were — is the unintended consequence of a widely popular federal policy.

_____

_____

_____

2. These kinds of acts to prevent erosion and secure downstream navigable rivers made sense in damp Eastern states, but it had the opposite effect in the semiarid West.

_____

_____

The aim of Clean Space is to transmit the space environment to future generations as we have found it, that is, pristine. It will impact regulations regarding substances such as **hydrazine** which is used widely as a propellant in space programs and the development of Green Propulsion with propellants that have a reduced toxicity. Environmental friendliness and sustainability often mean increased efficiency, which hopes to give the industry a competitive advantage, so they are looking at technologies which will consume less energy and produce less waste, therefore cutting costs. Finally they looked at debris mitigation to minimize the impact to the space environment as well as the debris footprint on Earth using controlled and uncontrolled re-entry events and passive de-orbiting systems along with active de-orbiting and re-orbiting systems. They are even considering ropes or sails to help drag abandoned satellites out of low orbit within 25 years. New 'design for demise' concepts hope to prevent chunks of satellites surviving re-entry and hitting the ground intact. Active removal of existing debris is also needed, including robotic missions to repair or de-orbit satellites.

1. The author mentions hydrazine in the passage in order to

Ⓐ emphasize the need for environmentally friendly propellants

Ⓑ give an example of a toxic propellant

Ⓒ list which substances will be regulated

Ⓓ classify a toxic substance which has reduced toxicity

2. Which of the following is true according to the passage?

Ⓐ Environmentally friendly technologies are more efficient but cost more.

Ⓑ Robots will have a role in the Clean Space program.

Ⓒ After 25 years, satellites cannot be removed from low orbit.

Ⓓ Propellants are the major cause of space toxicity.

3. Directions: Select the appropriate phrases from the answer choices and match them to the response to the type of pollution to which they relate. Two of the answer choices will NOT be used. **This question is worth 3 points**.

Drag your answer choices to the spaces where they belong. To remove an answer choice, click on it. To review the passage, click on **View Text**.

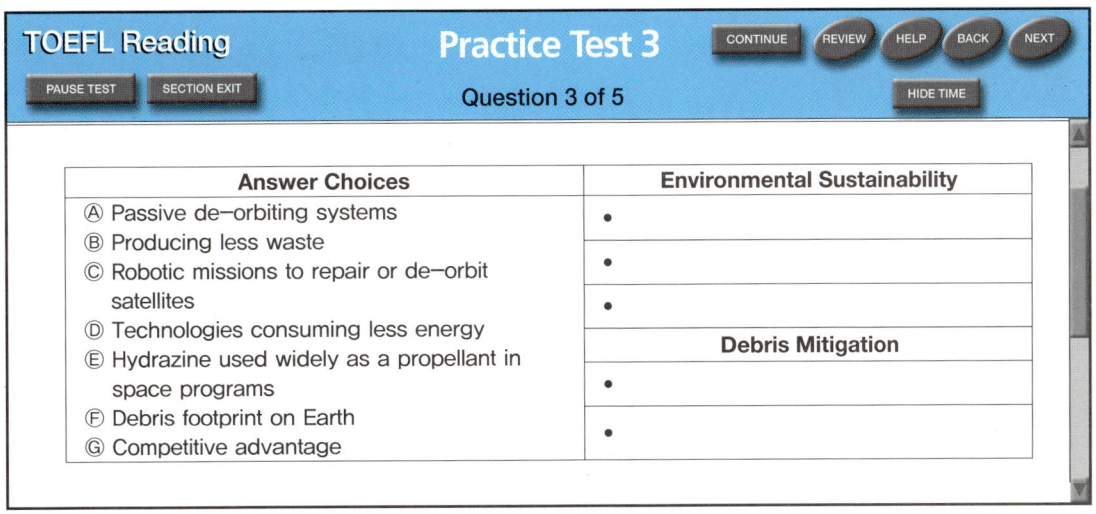

Answer Choices	Environmental Sustainability
Ⓐ Passive de-orbiting systems	•
Ⓑ Producing less waste	•
Ⓒ Robotic missions to repair or de-orbit satellites	•
Ⓓ Technologies consuming less energy	**Debris Mitigation**
Ⓔ Hydrazine used widely as a propellant in space programs	•
Ⓕ Debris footprint on Earth	•
Ⓖ Competitive advantage	

다음 문장을 ① 끊어 읽기 → 직독직해 ② 명사 [구, 절]에 대괄호 ③ 동사 [구]에 동그라미 ④ 세부정보에 소괄호를 한 후 핵심정보에 화살표로 연결하시오.

1. It will impact regulations regarding substances such as hydrazine which is used widely as a propellant in space programs and the development of Green Propulsion with propellants that have a reduced toxicity.

_____

_____

_____

2. The aim of Clean Space is to transmit the space environment to future generations as we have found it, that is, pristine.

_____

_____

TOEFL Reading

PAUSE TEST   SECTION EXIT

Practice Test 4

Question 4 of 5

CONTINUE   REVIEW   HELP   BACK   NEXT

HIDE TIME   01 : 40

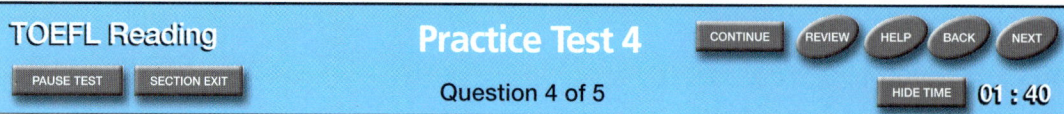

Antarctica and its surrounding waters are under pressure from a variety of forces that are already transforming the area, scientists warn. Ⓐ ■ The most immediate threats are regional warming, ocean acidification and loss of sea ice, all linked to global levels of carbon dioxide. Sea ice cover, crucial to the survival of virtually every animal that lives on and near the continent, already has been reduced by warming, according to a new study. Ⓑ ■ Visits by tourists, researchers and other people also threaten to change Antarctica, as does the harvesting of animals like krill that are key to the Antarctic food chain. Ⓒ ■ The continent is governed by the Antarctic Treaty System, a series of international agreements that regulates research and tourism. So far the treaty has done a good job of conserving Antarctica's environment and resources. Ⓓ ■ The Antarctic Peninsula, only a few days' sea voyage from South America, is changing particularly quickly. The area surrounding the peninsula's Palmer Station is experiencing the fastest winter warming of any place on Earth, and 87 percent of the peninsula's land-bound glaciers are in retreat. In some areas of the Antarctic Ocean, sea ice is absent three months longer than it was a few decades ago. The foundation of the ecosystem is melting away. For example, loss of sea ice has hurt the Adelie penguin, which lives on the ice; its populations have decreased by 80 percent since 1975. Krill in the area (a primary food source for Adelies) also have decreased by 80 percent since 1991.

1. The word its in the passage refers to

Ⓐ sea ice

Ⓑ the foundation of the ecosystem

Ⓒ the Adelie penguin

Ⓓ the land-bound glacier

2. Which of the following can be concluded from the passage?

Ⓐ Tourism is more beneficial than harmful for Antarctica.

Ⓑ The Antarctic Treaty System needs to be reappraised.

Ⓒ It's not as cold in Antarctica as it was in the past.

Ⓓ The sea ice cover will eventually disappear completely.

3. Look at the four squares [■] that indicate where the following sentence could be added to the passage.

But changes are happening so fast that they need extra attention.

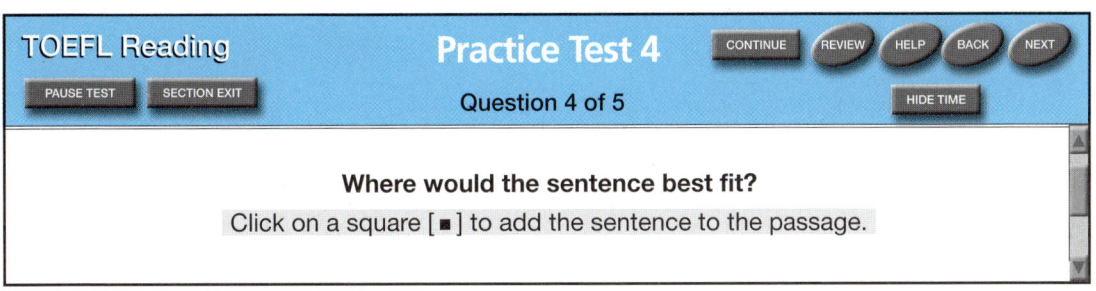

TOEFL Reading | Practice Test 4 | CONTINUE | REVIEW | HELP | BACK | NEXT

PAUSE TEST | SECTION EXIT

Question 4 of 5

HIDE TIME

Where would the sentence best fit?

Click on a square [■] to add the sentence to the passage.

다음 문장을 ① 끊어 읽기 → 직독직해 ② 명사 [구, 절]에 대괄호 ③ 동사 [구]에 동그라미 ④ 세부정보에 소괄호를 한 후 핵심정보에 화살표로 연결하시오.

1. Sea ice cover, crucial to the survival of virtually every animal that lives on and near the continent, already has been reduced by warming, according to a new study.

_____

_____

2. The area surrounding the peninsula's Palmer Station is experiencing the fastest winter warming of any place on Earth, and 87 percent of the peninsula's land-bound glaciers are in retreat.

_____

_____

3. Antarctica and its surrounding waters are under pressure from a variety of forces that are already transforming the area, scientists warn.

_____

_____

4. The continent is governed by the Antarctic Treaty System, a series of international agreements that regulates research and tourism.

_____

_____

Millions of trees are being destroyed every year to produce paper, and for housing projects. New programs are being set up to plant trees in place of the destroyed ones. Little do people realize how much damage could be done when dealing with nature. These housing projects are built where beautiful trees are to sit letting cool breeze pass through their leaves. Now, the Recycling Foundation has set up a program for young kids to plant trees in their neighborhood to save "Mother Earth." These trees are being planted at almost every street corner. Although the kids don't know what's likely to happen, they think they are doing good for their community. Trees creep up underneath the sidewalk all over town. No one really pays attention to a tree growing in front of their house until at some point of growth it's finally noticeable. **Many people in the United States don't think that what they don't know can hurt them.** But it can. Trees have cost many people their lives. Either the trees grew over their houses or a heavy thunderstorm blew it off its roots onto a house. Last year, in a town near where I live, a father was taking his kids to school. The wind that day was so powerful that it picked a tree off its roots and the tree landed right on the jeep killing all three kids in the back seat. Statistics on Channel Seven show that last year New Jersey had the highest death rates from trees.

1. **Which of the sentences below best expresses the essential information in the highlighted sentence in the passage? Incorrect choices change the meaning in important ways or leave out essential information.**

   Ⓐ You can't always know what is going to happen.
   Ⓑ Nothing will hurt them if they don't know about it.
   Ⓒ Even if the people are not conscious of something, it can have an impact on their lives.
   Ⓓ If something doesn't hurt you, then you don't know about it.

2. **Which of the following would the author most likely support about planting neighborhood trees?**

   Ⓐ It should be stopped.
   Ⓑ People should keep planting trees.
   Ⓒ People should pay more attention to it.
   Ⓓ It should be thought through more carefully.

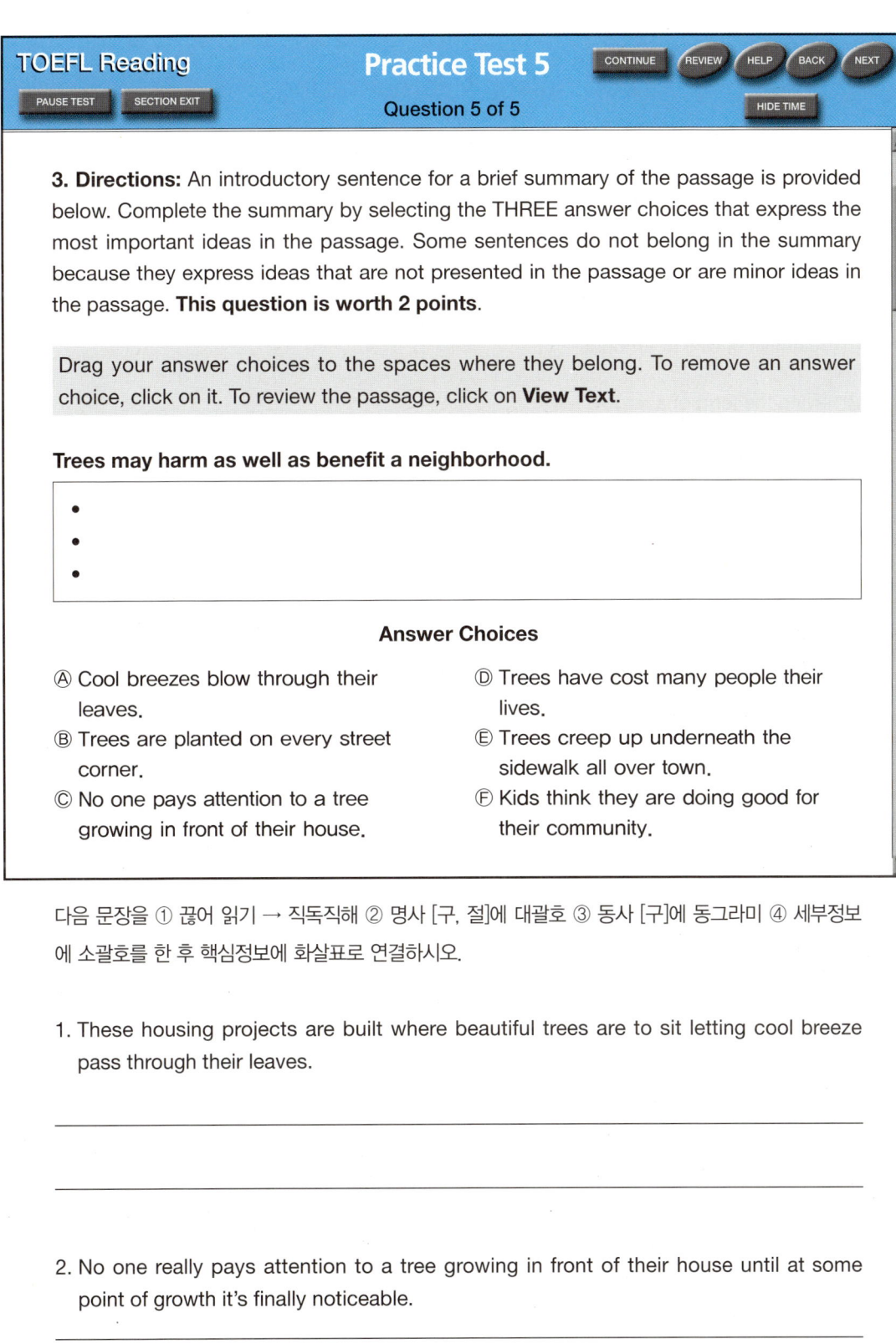

3. Directions: An introductory sentence for a brief summary of the passage is provided below. Complete the summary by selecting the THREE answer choices that express the most important ideas in the passage. Some sentences do not belong in the summary because they express ideas that are not presented in the passage or are minor ideas in the passage. **This question is worth 2 points.**

Drag your answer choices to the spaces where they belong. To remove an answer choice, click on it. To review the passage, click on **View Text**.

Trees may harm as well as benefit a neighborhood.

-
-
-

Answer Choices

Ⓐ Cool breezes blow through their leaves.

Ⓑ Trees are planted on every street corner.

Ⓒ No one pays attention to a tree growing in front of their house.

Ⓓ Trees have cost many people their lives.

Ⓔ Trees creep up underneath the sidewalk all over town.

Ⓕ Kids think they are doing good for their community.

다음 문장을 ① 끊어 읽기 → 직독직해 ② 명사 [구, 절]에 대괄호 ③ 동사 [구]에 동그라미 ④ 세부정보에 소괄호를 한 후 핵심정보에 화살표로 연결하시오.

1. These housing projects are built where beautiful trees are to sit letting cool breeze pass through their leaves.

_____

_____

2. No one really pays attention to a tree growing in front of their house until at some point of growth it's finally noticeable.

_____

_____

Vocabulary & Paraphrasing

1. Write the word from the box that matches each meaning below.

picturesque	tweak	magnitude	gauge	forage
spawn	catalyst	symmetric	annular	futile

① greatness of size or amount _____

② having the form of a ring _____

③ not successful _____

④ to search for food _____

⑤ visually pleasing _____

⑥ a person or thing that causes a change _____

⑦ to measure or determine the amount, quantity, or size _____

⑧ well-proportioned, as a body or whole _____

⑨ to deposit eggs or sperm into the water, as fishes _____

⑩ to make a minor adjustment to _____

Vocabulary & Paraphrasing

2. Translate the following questions into Korean and then paraphrase them according to the directions below.

① But scientists did not expect the nuclear fall out to linger in huge fish that sail the world because such fish can metabolize and shed radioactive substances.
→ 접속사, 동의어 바꿔 쓰기

_____

_____

② Sunspots are linked to eruptions of intense electromagnetic radiation called solar flares, which can cause disturbances to radio communications on Earth and also hinder radio astronomers' views of the universe. → 관계사, 문장의 태 바꿔 쓰기

_____

_____

_____

③ To test the relevance of body weight and experience in foraging, researchers saddled ants with electronic tags smaller than a pinhead and installed a mini automatic door in the colony's nest to control who could leave. → 접속사, 쉬운 단어로 바꿔 쓰기

_____

_____

_____

④ It has been found that the intermediate molecules bond too tightly or too loosely to the cathode surface, slowing the reaction and causing a drop in voltage.
→ 문장의 태, 전치사구 바꿔 쓰기

_____

_____

Practice Test 1

1. Across the vast Pacific, / the mighty bluefin tuna carried radioactive **contamination** / (that leaked from Japan's crippled nuclear plant) / to **the shores** (of the United States 6,000 miles away) / – the first **time** (a huge migrating fish has been shown / to carry radioactivity such a distance).

   방대한 태평양을 건너, 힘이 센 다랑어는 일본의 손상된 핵발전소에서 새어 나온 방사능 오염을 6,000마일 떨어져 있는 미국 해안까지 옮겨 왔다. – 이동하는 거대한 물고기는 처음으로 방사능을 그런 거리까지 옮겨 왔다고 보인다.

2. But scientists did not expect / [the nuclear fall out to linger in huge **fish**] / (that sail the world) / because such fish can metabolize / and shed radioactive substances.

   그러나 거대한 물고기들은 대사 작용을 할 수 있고 방사능 물질을 저절로 흘려버릴 수 있기 때문에 세계를 항해한 큰 물고기에 핵 낙진이 남아 있을 것이라고 과학자들은 기대하지 않았다.

Practice Test 2

1. [Water depletion from afforestation] / [— the establishment of trees or tree stands on **the land** / (where none previously were) —] / is the unintended **consequence** / (of a widely popular federal policy).

   아무것도 없던 땅에 나무를 심거나 부지를 만드는 조림 사업을 실시하면서 생기는 수분 고갈은 널리 시행되고 있는 연방 정책에 따른 의도하지 않던 결과이다.

2. [These kinds of **acts** / (to prevent erosion and secure downstream navigable rivers)] / made sense (in damp Eastern states,) / but it had the opposite effect / (in the semiarid West).

   습한 동부 주에서는 침식을 막고 하류로 배가 다닐 수 있는 강을 확보하기 위한 이런 조치가 적합했지만 그것은 비가 거의 오지 않는 서부에서는 역효과를 낳았다.

Practice Test 3

1. It will impact **regulations** / (regarding substances such as **hydrazine**) / (which is used widely as a propellant in space programs) / and **the development** (of Green Propulsion with **propellants**) / (that have a reduced toxicity).

   이 목적은 우주 프로그램에서 추진제로 널리 사용되는 히드라진과 같은 물질과 독성이 감소된 추진제와 함께 녹색 추진 정책의 개발에 관한 규정에 영향을 미칠 것이다.

2. The aim of Clean Space is / [to **transmit** the space environment to future generations] / (as we have found **it**,) / (that is, pristine).

   청정 우주의 목적은 우리가 처음 우주를 발견하였을 때처럼 깨끗한 환경을 다음 세대에 전해주는 것이다.

Practice Test 4

1. Sea ice **cover**, / (crucial to the survival of virtually every **animal**) / (that lives on and near the continent,) / already has been reduced by warming, / according to a new study.

   새로운 연구에 따르면 그 대륙이나 가까이 살고 있는 사실상 모든 동물들의 생존에 중요한 해빙 덮개는 이미 온난화로 줄어들고 있다.

2. **The area** (surrounding the peninsula's Palmer Station) / is experiencing the fastest winter **warming** / (of any place on Earth,) / and 87 **percent** (of the peninsula's land-bound glaciers) / are in retreat.

   반도의 파머기지를 둘러싸고 있는 지역은 지구 어느 지역보다 가장 빠른 겨울 온난화를 경험하고 있으며 땅과 이어진 87%의 빙하도 줄어들고 있다.

3. [Antarctica and its surrounding waters are / under pressure from a variety of **forces**] / (that are already transforming the area,) / scientists warn.

   과학자들은 남극과 그 주변의 바다가 그 지역을 이미 변화시키고 있는 다양한 물리적 영향력의 압력을 받고 있다고 경고한다.

4. The continent is governed / (by the Antarctic Treaty System,) / [a series of international **agreements**] / (that regulates research and tourism).

   남극 대륙은 연구와 관광을 규제하는 국제법인 남극 조약 체제에 의해 관리되고 있다.

Practice Test 5

1. These housing projects are built / (where beautiful trees are to sit) / (letting cool breeze pass through their leaves).

   이러한 주택을 짓는 계획은 시원한 바람이 나뭇잎 사이로 통과할 수 있도록 두면서 아름다운 나무들이 있는 곳에 만들어진다.

2. No one really pays attention to **a tree** / (growing in front of their house) / (until at some **point** of growth / it's finally noticeable).

   나무가 눈에 보일 정도로 성장할 때까지 아무도 자신의 집 앞에 나무가 자라고 있다는 것에 관심을 기울이지 않는다.

Economy

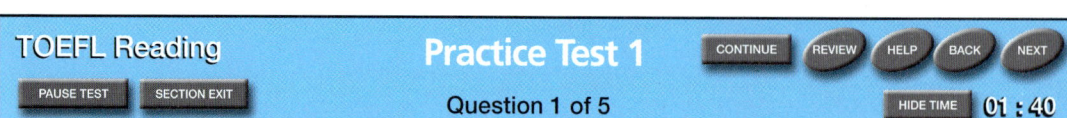

For a nation that has suffered poverty, disease, and a devastating earthquake, it is indeed good news that Haiti has a number of potentially lucrative gold, copper and silver mines. Ⓐ ■ Even more fortuitously, the Haitians stand to gain about half the profits from the foreign mining companies that plan to operate there, an unusually high amount. Ⓑ ■ History shows there are pitfalls a plenty for Haitii to avoid, however. Ⓒ ■ Open pit mines — the world's most common type — usually last for about 25 years, but leave **decimated** mountaintops, displaced communities, and environmental contamination. Ⓓ ■ When the resources are exhausted, usually after about 25 years, the pits can be refilled or converted into reservoirs. On the positive side, people like stone cutter Joseph Bernard, 47, are getting a paycheck and feeding their family. "I found a job, but many didn't," he says. "If more companies come, more people will work."

1. Look at the four squares [■] that indicate where the following sentence could be added to the passage.

They are potentially worth $ 20 billion, and the precious metal finds are already creating hundreds of jobs and new roads.

Where would the sentence best fit?
Click on a square [■] to add the sentence to the passage.

2. The word decimated in the passage is closest in meaning to

Ⓐ injured　　　　Ⓑ worsened　　　　Ⓒ downsized　　　　Ⓓ damaged

3. Directions: An introductory sentence for a brief summary of the passage is provided below. Complete the summary by selecting the THREE answer choices that express the most important ideas in the passage. Some sentences do not belong in the summary because they express ideas that are not presented in the passage or are minor ideas in the passage. **This question is worth 2 points**.

Drag your answer choices to the spaces where they belong. To remove an answer choice, click on it. To review the passage, click on **View Text**.

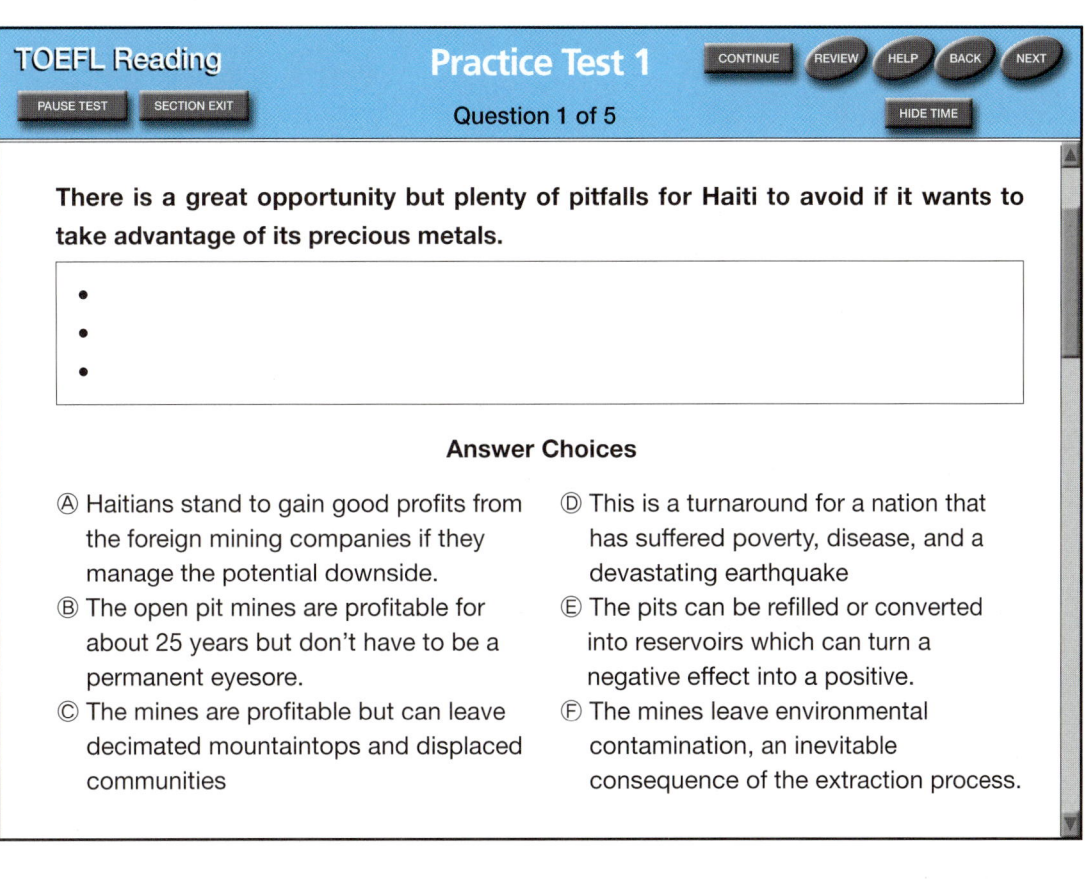

There is a great opportunity but plenty of pitfalls for Haiti to avoid if it wants to take advantage of its precious metals.

-
-
-

Answer Choices

Ⓐ Haitians stand to gain good profits from the foreign mining companies if they manage the potential downside.

Ⓑ The open pit mines are profitable for about 25 years but don't have to be a permanent eyesore.

Ⓒ The mines are profitable but can leave decimated mountaintops and displaced communities

Ⓓ This is a turnaround for a nation that has suffered poverty, disease, and a devastating earthquake

Ⓔ The pits can be refilled or converted into reservoirs which can turn a negative effect into a positive.

Ⓕ The mines leave environmental contamination, an inevitable consequence of the extraction process.

다음 문장을 ① 끊어 읽기 → 직독직해 ② 명사 [구, 절]에 대괄호 ③ 동사 [구]에 동그라미 ④ 세부정보에 소괄호를 한 후 핵심정보에 화살표로 연결하시오.

1. Even more fortuitously, the Haitians stand to gain about half the profits from the foreign mining companies that plan to operate there, an unusually high amount.

_____

_____

2. For a nation that has suffered poverty, disease, and a devastating earthquake, it is indeed good news that Haiti has a number of potentially lucrative gold, copper and silver mines.

_____

_____

American demand for goods grew with the growth of income and employment. But once the jobs started moving overseas through outsourcing the balance was upset. The country ended up with a large amount of structural unemployment. Thus the country had more people demanding goods and services than it had income and employment to pay for them. Imports grew, and the US balance of trade swung to negative, beginning almost thirty five years ago. **It** has not been positive since this time and factors such as international trade frictions, tariffs, duties, and product restrictions prevent the system from correcting itself in the short term. Workers who have lost their jobs have suffered economically from this structural change. Free market advocates say the system will correct itself over time, especially if trade barriers can be eliminated. That may indeed be true. **However, governments protect themselves and their politically sensitive interests, and therefore the prospect for anything like rapid change is limited.**

1. Which of the following can be inferred from the passage?

   Ⓐ The high level of structural unemployment will begin to change soon.

   Ⓑ Removing trade barriers could bring about the desired economic changes.

   Ⓒ The free market has a clear solution to bring about necessary change.

   Ⓓ The US economy could easily recover if the government was not politically sensitive.

2. The word It in the passage refers to

   Ⓐ Employment   Ⓑ Imports

   Ⓒ Demanding goods and services   Ⓓ The US balance of trade

3. Which of the sentences below best expresses the essential information in the highlighted sentence in the passage? Incorrect choices change the meaning in important ways or leave out essential information.

   Ⓐ There is some likelihood the situation can be corrected provided the government can protect itself.

   Ⓑ The government is not in any rush to correct things because it tends to put its own interests first.

   Ⓒ The situation is too politically sensitive for any change to be likely to occur.

   Ⓓ In order to protect themselves, governments need to bring only limited and gradual change.

다음 문장을 ① 끊어 읽기 → 직독직해 ② 명사 [구, 절]에 대괄호 ③ 동사 [구]에 동그라미 ④ 세부정보에 소괄호를 한 후 핵심정보에 화살표로 연결하시오.

1. Thus the country had more people demanding goods and services than it had income and employment to pay for them.

_____

_____

2. It has not been positive since this time and factors such as international trade frictions, tariffs, duties, and product restrictions prevent the system from correcting itself in the short term.

_____

_____

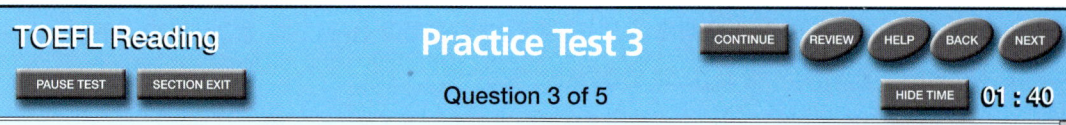
Skeptics once likened mining the deep to looking for riches on the moon. No more. Progress in marine geology, predictions of metal shortages in the decades ahead and improving access to the abyss are combining to make it real. Environmentalists have expressed growing alarm, saying too little research has been done on the risks of seabed mining. The industry has responded with studies, reassurance and upbeat conferences. The technological advances center on new robots, sensors and other equipment, some of it derived from the offshore oil and gas industry. Ships lower exploratory gear on long ropes and send down sharp drills that gnaw into the rocky seabed. All of this underwater machinery is making it more and more feasible to find, map and recover seabed riches. Industrial powers — including government-supported groups in China, Japan and South Korea — are hunting for sulfides in the Atlantic, Indian and Pacific Oceans. And private companies have made hundreds of deep assessments and claims in the volcanic zones around Pacific island nations: Fiji, Tonga, Vanuatu, New Zealand, the Solomon Islands and Papua New Guinea.

1. **Which of the following can be inferred from the highlighted sentence in the passage?**

   Ⓐ Mining the ocean deep was once thought to be extremely profitable.

   Ⓑ Nobody thought it would ever be possible to find riches on the moon.

   Ⓒ Skeptics were the first people to consider there was any possibility of mining the ocean bed.

   Ⓓ Anyone who believed it was possible to mine the ocean bed would probably have been considered crazy or foolhardy.

2. **According to the passage, how did the mining industry respond to environmentalists?**

   Ⓐ With growing alarm

   Ⓑ With new technological advances

   Ⓒ With too little research on the risks of seabed mining

   Ⓓ With studies and conferences

3. **Directions:** Select the appropriate phrases from the answer choices and match them to the group to which they relate. **This question is worth 3 points.**

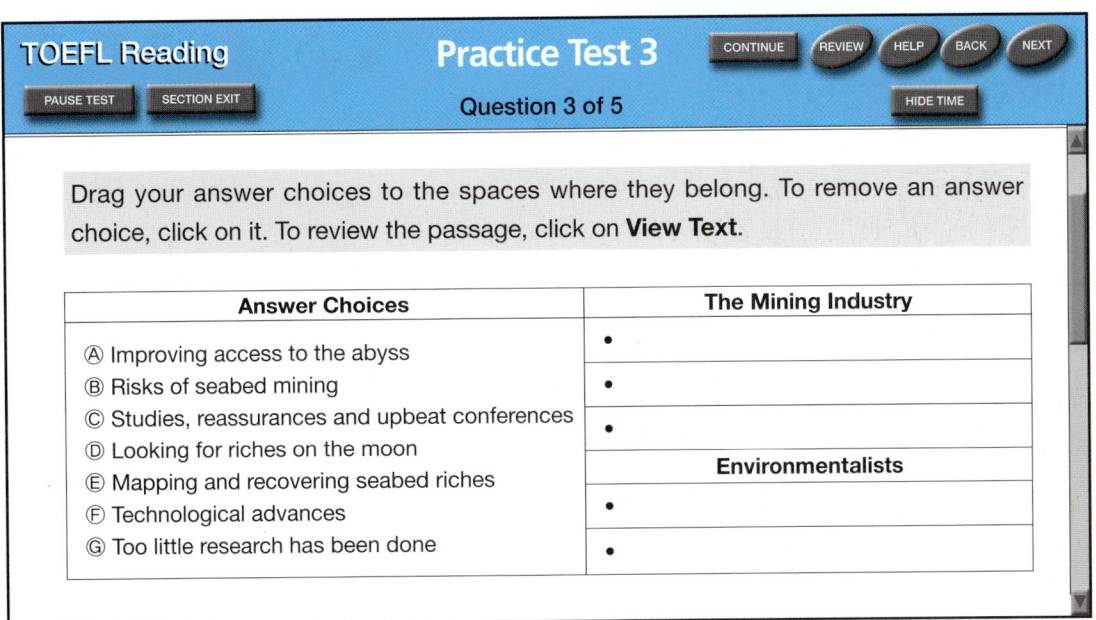

Drag your answer choices to the spaces where they belong. To remove an answer choice, click on it. To review the passage, click on **View Text**.

Answer Choices	The Mining Industry
ⒶImproving access to the abyss	•
ⒷRisks of seabed mining	•
ⒸStudies, reassurances and upbeat conferences	•
ⒹLooking for riches on the moon	**Environmentalists**
ⒺMapping and recovering seabed riches	•
ⒻTechnological advances	•
ⒼToo little research has been done	

다음 문장을 ① 끊어 읽기 → 직독직해 ② 명사 [구, 절]에 대괄호 ③ 동사 [구]에 동그라미 ④ 세부정보에 소괄호를 한 후 핵심정보에 화살표로 연결하시오.

1. Progress in marine geology, predictions of metal shortages in the decades ahead and improving access to the abyss are combining to make it real.

_____

_____

2. The technological advances center on new robots, sensors and other equipment, some of it derived from the offshore oil and gas industry.

_____

_____

TOEFL Reading

PAUSE TEST   SECTION EXIT

Practice Test 4

Question 4 of 5

CONTINUE   REVIEW   HELP   BACK   NEXT

HIDE TIME   01 : 40

Reference is made to the announcement (the "Announcement") of United Gene High-Tech Group Limited (the "Company") dated 25 June 2012 in relation to the proposed rights issue by the Company. Unless otherwise stated, **capitalized** terms used herein shall have the same meanings as those defined in the Announcement unless the context requires otherwise. In response to the Announcement made by the Company, on 26 June 2012, Best Champion notified the Company of **its** disposal of shares of the Company on 21 June 2012, reducing its shareholding in the Company to an aggregate of 5,437,980,000 shares. After further enquiries made by the Board on 27 June 2012, Best Champion notified the Company that, as at 25 June 2012, Best Champion beneficially owned, in aggregate 5,361,680,000 shares, representing approximately 44.08% of the issued share capital of the Company. Accordingly, the Company would like to make clarifications to the Announcement, as follows: The first paragraph under the section headed "Irrevocable Undertaking of the Undertaking Shareholder" on page 2 of the Announcement and the second and third paragraphs under the section headed "Background of the Undertaking Shareholder" on page 11 of the Announcement should be amended as follows: "As at 20 June 2012, being the date of signing of the Irrevocable Undertaking, Best Champion beneficially owned, in aggregate 5,591,020,000 shares, its **shares** representing approximately 45.96% of the issued share capital of the Company. Accordingly, the Undertaking Shareholder and its associates would be provisionally allotted 1,677,306,000 Right Shares pursuant to the Right Issue in respect of the shares."

1. The word **capitalized** in the passage is closest in meaning to

    Ⓐ profited from   Ⓑ provided with capital

    Ⓒ written or printed in capital letters   Ⓓ treated as assets

2. The word **its** in the passage refers to

    Ⓐ the Company   Ⓑ Best Champion

    Ⓒ the Board   Ⓓ United Gene High-Tech Group Limited

3. **Why does the author mention shares in the passage?**

    Ⓐ To inform shareholders how they will be affected by the sale of the company

    Ⓑ To urge shareholders not to sell their company shares

    Ⓒ To point out a mistake in the new share capital issue

    Ⓓ To notify Best Champion's entitlement in the issue of right shares

다음 문장을 ① 끊어 읽기 → 직독직해 ② 명사 [구, 절]에 대괄호 ③ 동사 [구]에 동그라미 ④ 세부정보에 소괄호를 한 후 핵심정보에 화살표로 연결하시오.

1. Reference is made to the announcement – the "Announcement" – of United Gene High-Tech Group Limited – the "Company" – dated 25 June 2012 in relation to the proposed rights issue by the Company.

_____

_____

_____

2. Unless otherwise stated, capitalized terms used herein shall have the same meanings as those defined in the Announcement unless the context requires otherwise.

_____

_____

3. After further enquiries made by the Board on 27 June 2012, Best Champion notified the Company that, as at 25 June 2012, Best Champion beneficially owned, in aggregate 5,361,680,000 Shares, representing approximately 44.08% of the issued share capital of the Company.

_____

_____

_____

4. The first paragraph under the section headed "Irrevocable Undertaking of the Undertaking Shareholder" on page 2 of the Announcement and the second and third paragraphs under the section headed "Background of the Undertaking Shareholder" on page 11 of the Announcement should be amended as follows:

_____

_____

_____

TOEFL Reading

PAUSE TEST   SECTION EXIT

Practice Test 5

Question 5 of 5

CONTINUE REVIEW HELP BACK NEXT

HIDE TIME 01 : 40

Despite an overall stagnation on the economy for nearly two decades, Japan's industries are still among the most highly advanced and innovative countries in the world. Japanese manufacturing products, particularly in electronics and automobiles, are the world leaders in both production and technological advancements in their respective fields. In 2010, this industry was responsible for 23 percent of Japan's GDP. Major industries in Japan include motor vehicles, electronic equipment, machine tools, steel and nonferrous metals, ships, chemicals, textiles, and processed foods. Japan's automobile industry produces the second largest amount of vehicles in the world behind China. However, Japanese automobile companies remain among the most valuable and technologically advanced in the world. Japan is home to six of the top twenty largest vehicle manufacturers in the world – Toyota(1st), Renault-Nissan(4th), Honda(8th), Suzuki(10th), Mazda(14th), Mitsubishi(16th). The automobile industry also managed to register a massive 10.5 percent growth in 2009, **in spite of** the global financial crisis. Japan is also the world's largest electronics manufacturer with prominent companies such as Sony, Casio, Mitsubishi Electric, Panasonic, Canon, Fujitsu, Nikon, and Yamaha. **Japanese electronic products are praised for their innovation and quality**. Backed by its high-tech industries and companies, Japan had the 8th highest industrial production growth rate in the world for 2010 at 15.5 percent. Simultaneously, Japan's industrial production growth rate was the highest among the G20 nations.

1. The phrase **in spite of** in the passage is closest in meaning to

    Ⓐ regardless of   Ⓑ because of

    Ⓒ unexpectedly   Ⓓ provoked by

2. **Which of the sentences below best expresses the essential information in the highlighted sentence in the passage? Incorrect choices change the meaning in important ways or leave out essential information.**

    Ⓐ Many cutting-edge technologies still come from Japan.

    Ⓑ The Japanese are proud of their companies.

    Ⓒ The Japanese are world-leaders but their companies are not well known.

    Ⓓ Japanese companies deserve credit for their outstanding standards.

3. **Directions:** An introductory sentence for a brief summary of the passage is provided below. Complete the summary by selecting the THREE answer choices that express the most important ideas in the passage. Some sentences do not belong in the summary because they express ideas that are not presented in the passage or are minor ideas in

TOEFL Reading

PAUSE TEST   SECTION EXIT

Practice Test 5

Question 5 of 5

CONTINUE   REVIEW   HELP   BACK   NEXT

HIDE TIME

the passage. **This question is worth 2 points**.

Drag your answer choices to the spaces where they belong. To remove an answer choice, click on it. To review the passage, click on **View Text**.

Many people think that Japanese products are superior to others.

-
-
-

Answer Choices

Ⓐ Japanese manufacturing products, particularly in electronics and automobiles, are the world leaders.

Ⓑ Major industries in Japan include many kinds of products.

Ⓒ Japanese automobile companies remain among the most valuable and technologically advanced in the world.

Ⓓ The automobile industry also managed to register a massive 10.5 percent growth in 2009, in spite of the global financial crisis.

Ⓔ Japanese electronic products are praised for their innovation and quality.

Ⓕ Japan's industrial production growth rate was the highest among the G20 nations.

다음 문장을 ① 끊어 읽기 → 직독직해 ② 명사 [구, 절]에 대괄호 ③ 동사 [구]에 동그라미 ④ 세부정보에 소괄호를 한 후 핵심정보에 화살표로 연결하시오.

1. Despite an overall stagnation on the economy for nearly two decades, Japan's industries are still among the most highly advanced and innovative countries in the world.

_____

_____

2. Japan is also the world's largest electronics manufacturer with prominent companies such as Sony, Casio, Mitsubishi Electric, Panasonic, Canon, Fujitsu, Nikon, and Yamaha.

_____

_____

Vocabulary & Paraphrasing

1. Write the word from the box that matches each meaning below.

grim	retreat	derive	skeptic	nuisance
menace	expedition	holistic	feasible	ecosystem

① to receive or obtain from a source or origin   _____

② an organized journey or voyage for a specific purpose   _____

③ an annoying person, thing, condition, practice, etc   _____

④ harsh or formidable in manner or appearance   _____

⑤ a community of living things and their environment   _____

⑥ of or relating to a doctrine of holism   _____

⑦ to withdraw, retire, or draw back   _____

⑧ to threaten with violence, danger, etc.   _____

⑨ able to be done or put into effect   _____

⑩ a person who mistrusts people, ideas, etc.   _____

Vocabulary & Paraphrasing

2. Translate the following questions into Korean and then paraphrase them according to the directions below.

① Although plankton makes up the bulk of the oceans' biomass, its biogeography and the structure of its ecosystems are an "almost virgin field for research." ➜ 접속사 바꿔 쓰기

_____

_____

② If the swarms of jellyfish menacing coastlines are left unchecked in the Mediterranean and elsewhere, they could make a grim vision of seas to come. ➜ 부정문, 쉬운 단어로 바꿔 쓰기

_____

_____

③ Environmentalists have expressed growing alarm, saying too little research has been done on the risks of seabed mining. ➜ 분사 구문 바꿔 쓰기

_____

_____

④ The continent is governed by the Antarctic Treaty System, a series of international agreements that regulates research and tourism. ➜ 문장의 태 바꿔 쓰기

_____

_____

Practice Test 1

1. Even more fortuitously, / the Haitians (stand) to gain / about half the **profits** / (from the foreign mining **companies)** / (that plan to operate there,) / an unusually high amount.

   더욱이 뜻밖에도 아이티 사람들은 그곳에서 작업할 예정인 외국 채광 회사로부터 대략 이익의 절반을 받을 수 있을 것으로 보이는데 이는 이례적으로 높은 비율이다.

2. For a **nation** / (that has suffered poverty, disease, / and a devastating earthquake,) / it (is) indeed good news / [that Haiti has a number of potentially lucrative gold, / copper and silver mines].

   빈곤, 질병 및 강진으로 고통을 겪은 나라로 잠재적으로 수익성이 높은 금, 구리 및 은 광산을 아이티가 많이 보유하고 있다는 것은 정말로 반가운 소식이다.

Practice Test 2

1. Thus / the country (had) more **people** / (demanding goods and services) / than it had **income and employment** / (to pay for them).

   따라서 미국에는 상품과 서비스를 구입할 만한 소득이 있고 일자리가 있는 사람보다 상품과 서비스를 요구하는 이들이 많아졌다.

2. It (has not been) positive since this time / and **factors** (such as international trade frictions, tariffs, duties, and product restrictions) / (prevent) the system (from **correcting** itself) / (in the short term).

   이때 이후로 그것이 흑자인 적은 없고 국제무역마찰, 관세, 세금과 상품규제 같은 요인들은 단기간 내에 무역 수지를 스스로 바로잡는 데에 방해가 된다.

Practice Test 3

1. [**Progress** (in marine geology,) **predictions** (of metal shortages in the decades ahead) / and improving **access** (to the abyss)] / (are combining) to make it real.

   해양 지질학의 발전, 수십 년 후 금속 부족에 대한 예측과 향상되고 있는 심연으로의 접근성은 해저 광산업을 현실화하기 위해 결합하고 있다.

2. [The technological advances] (center on) / [new robots, sensors and other equipment,] / some of it (derived from the offshore oil and gas industry).

   기술적인 발전은 새로운 로봇, 센서와 연안의 유류와 가스 산업으로부터 얻은 몇몇 다른 장비에 중점을 두고 있다.

Practice Test 4

1. Reference is made to **the announcement** – the "Announcement" – / (of United Gene High - Tech Group Limited – the "Company" –) / (dated 25 June 2012) / (in relation to the proposed rights **issue**) (by the Company).

   언급한 내용은 유나이티드 진 하이테크 그룹 회사의 제안된 권리의 사안에 관련한 2012년 6월 25일의 발표로 작성되었다.

2. Unless otherwise stated, / capitalized **terms** (used herein) / (shall have) the same **meanings** / (as those defined in the Announcement) / unless the context requires otherwise.

   달리 언급하거나 문맥에서 다르게 요구되지 않는 한 여기에 사용된 대문자로 쓰인 용어들은 발표에서 정의된 것과 같은 의미를 가질 것이다.

3. After further **enquiries** / (made by the Board on 27 June 2012,) / Best Champion (notified) the Company / [that, as at 25 June 2012, / Best Champion beneficially owned, / in aggregate 5,361,680,000 **Shares,**] / (representing approximately **44.08%**) / (of the issued share capital of the Company).

   2012년 6월 27일에 작성된 이사회의 추가 문의 이후에 베스트 챔피언은 2012년 6월 25일 날짜로 회사의 발행된 주식 자본의 약 44.08%에 해당하는 총 5,361,680,000주를 갖는다고 통보했다.

4. [The first **paragraph** / (under the section headed "Irrevocable Undertaking of the Undertaking Shareholder" / on page 2 of the Announcement) / and the second and third **paragraphs** / (under the section headed "Background of the Undertaking Shareholder" / on page 11 of the Announcement)] / (should be amended) as follows:

   발표의 2페이지 '회사 주주의 철회할 수 없는 동의'의 첫 번째 문단과 11페이지에 있는 '회사 주주의 배경'의 두 번째와 세 번째 문단은 다음과 같이 개정되어야 한다

Practice Test 5

1. Despite [an overall stagnation on the economy / for nearly two decades,] / Japan's industries (are) still / among [the most highly advanced / and innovative countries in the world].

   일본의 산업은 거의 20년 동안 전반적인 경기 침체에도 불구하고 아직까지 세계에서 가장 진보적이고 혁신적인 나라 중에 있다.

2. Japan (is) also / [the world's largest electronics **manufacturer**] / (with prominent **companies**) / (such as Sony, Casio, Mitsubishi Electric, Panasonic, Canon, Fujitsu, Nikon, and Yamaha).

   또한 일본은 소니, 카시오, 미쓰비시 전기, 파나소닉, 캐논, 후지쯔, 니콘, 야마하 같은 굴지의 회사들을 가지고 있는 세계 최대의 전자 제품 제조사이다.

Society

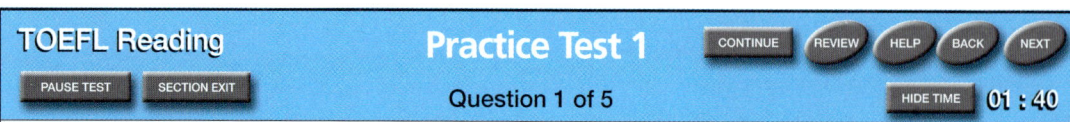

TOEFL Reading

Practice Test 1

CONTINUE   REVIEW   HELP   BACK   NEXT

PAUSE TEST   SECTION EXIT

Question 1 of 5

HIDE TIME   01 : 40

It is no understatement that social networking has enormously influenced and changed today's society. **Relationships, both social and in the workplace, have been re-defined and shaped so much that individuals can even share their everyday life with whomever they please with the simple click of a button**. Performed correctly, social networking is greatly productive in helping an individual and business grow and become successful. Social networking is about a configuration of individuals, brought together often by interpersonal means, such as friendship, common interests, or ideas. It can build strong foundations for relationships and create unity amongst people which in turn lessens the workload due to an enhanced productivity. However, as helpful as it is, when **reduced to** social networking through the internet, it can too quickly turn into a highly addictive procrastination tool that can lead to many hours of time wasting and at worst, create delusions about reality.

1. **Which of the sentences below best expresses the essential information in the highlighted sentence in the passage? Incorrect choices change the meaning in important ways or leave out essential information.**

   (A) Social networking has had a great and irrevocable impact on social life.
   (B) Without social networking we would not have such convenient ways of staying in touch with each other.
   (C) Social networking has profoundly altered our lives in ways that are both good and bad.
   (D) No one can deny the ease of use of social networking and how it has transformed our relationships.

2. **The phrase reduced to in the passage is closest in meaning to**

   (A) made lesser
   (B) failed to function
   (C) caused to collapse
   (D) divided into parts

3. **Directions:** Select the appropriate phrases from the answer choices and match them to the effect of social networking to which they relate. **This question is worth 3 points.**

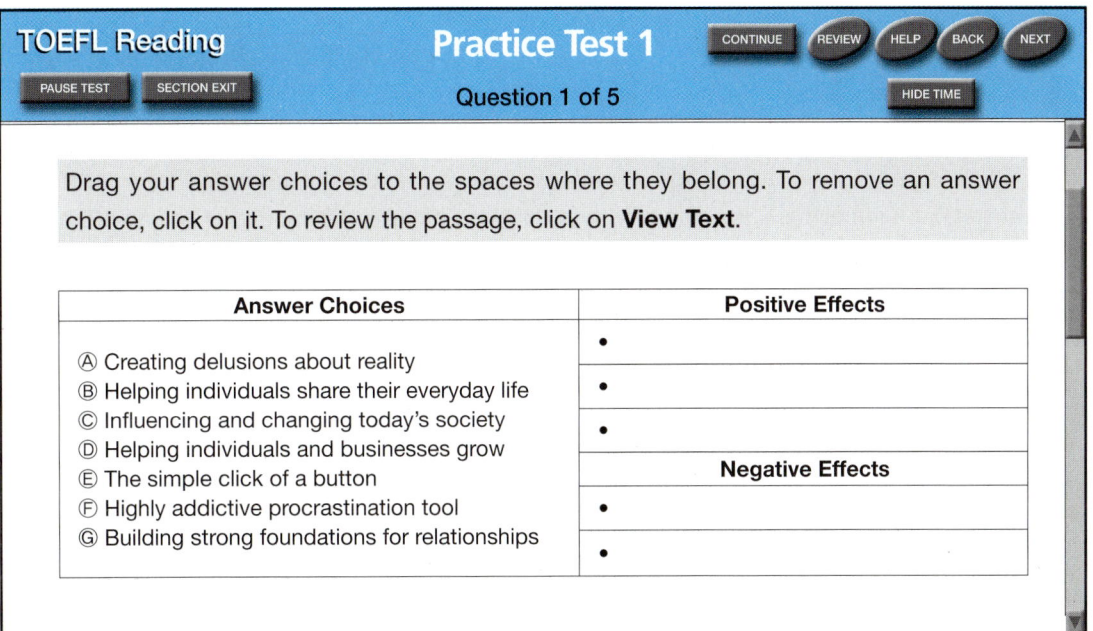

Drag your answer choices to the spaces where they belong. To remove an answer choice, click on it. To review the passage, click on **View Text**.

Answer Choices	Positive Effects
Ⓐ Creating delusions about reality	•
Ⓑ Helping individuals share their everyday life	•
Ⓒ Influencing and changing today's society	•
Ⓓ Helping individuals and businesses grow	**Negative Effects**
Ⓔ The simple click of a button	•
Ⓕ Highly addictive procrastination tool	•
Ⓖ Building strong foundations for relationships	

다음 문장을 ① 끊어 읽기 → 직독직해 ② 명사 [구, 절]에 대괄호 ③ 동사 [구]에 동그라미 ④ 세부정보에 소괄호를 한 후 핵심정보에 화살표로 연결하시오.

1. It can build strong foundations for relationships and create unity amongst people which in turn lessens the workload due to an enhanced productivity.

_____

_____

2. Relationships, both social and in the workplace, have been re-defined and shaped so much that individuals can even share their everyday life with whomever they please with the simple click of a button.

_____

_____

_____

TOEFL Reading

PAUSE TEST   SECTION EXIT

Practice Test 2

CONTINUE   REVIEW   HELP   BACK   NEXT

Question 2 of 5

HIDE TIME   01 : 40

WIA is a federal funded program designed to increase the occupational skills attainment, employment, job retention and earnings of participants, and to improve the quality of the workforce, reduce welfare dependency, and enhance the productivity and competitiveness of the nation. The State Dislocated Worker Program assists workers who lose their jobs because of layoff or plant closing. Ⓐ ■ MYP provides summer jobs and basic work skills training for youth age 14-21. Ⓑ ■ SCSEP provides part-time jobs for individuals age 55 and older. Ⓒ ■ DEED utilizes Wagner-Peyser funds to provide a labor exchange, connecting job seekers with potential employers. Ⓓ ■ DEED's Business Services efforts are meant to complement local efforts. The Business Outreach Plan connects these efforts in an integrated manner. The local outreach plan is incorporated with economic development, education and local entities identified by the Workforce Council.

1. Which of the following is NOT true according to the passage?

    Ⓐ There is little assistance for people who lose their jobs.

    Ⓑ Teenagers under 21 or people over 55 can get special assistance for jobs.

    Ⓒ There is a system for local businesses and DEED to work together.

    Ⓓ Part of WIA's goal is to keep people in jobs.

2. Look at the four squares [■] that indicate where the following sentence could be added to the passage.

Unemployment Insurance (UI), Veterans, Work Opportunities Tax Credit and Trade Adjustment Act programs are also accessed through DEED.

Where would the sentence best fit?
Click on a square [■] to add the sentence to the passage.

3. Directions: An introductory sentence for a brief summary of the passage is provided below. Complete the summary by selecting the THREE answer choices that express the most important ideas in the passage. Some sentences do not belong in the summary because they express ideas that are not presented in the passage or are minor ideas in the passage. **This question is worth 2 points**.

Drag your answer choices to the spaces where they belong. To remove an answer choice, click on it. To review the passage, click on **View Text**.

TOEFL Reading

PAUSE TEST   SECTION EXIT

Practice Test 2

Question 2 of 5

CONTINUE   REVIEW   HELP   BACK   NEXT

HIDE TIME

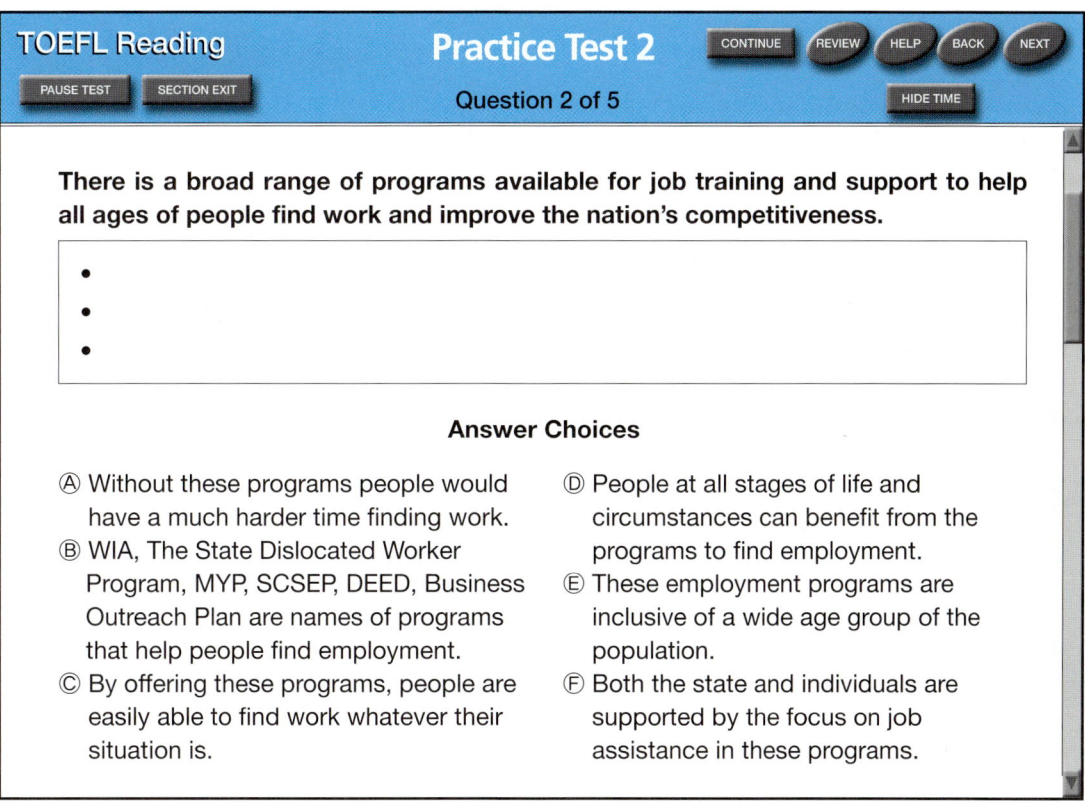

There is a broad range of programs available for job training and support to help all ages of people find work and improve the nation's competitiveness.

-
-
-

Answer Choices

Ⓐ Without these programs people would have a much harder time finding work.

Ⓑ WIA, The State Dislocated Worker Program, MYP, SCSEP, DEED, Business Outreach Plan are names of programs that help people find employment.

Ⓒ By offering these programs, people are easily able to find work whatever their situation is.

Ⓓ People at all stages of life and circumstances can benefit from the programs to find employment.

Ⓔ These employment programs are inclusive of a wide age group of the population.

Ⓕ Both the state and individuals are supported by the focus on job assistance in these programs.

다음 문장을 ① 끊어 읽기 → 직독직해 ② 명사 [구, 절]에 대괄호 ③ 동사 [구]에 동그라미 ④ 세부정보에 소괄호를 한 후 핵심정보에 화살표로 연결하시오.

1. WIA is a federal funded program designed to increase the occupational skills attainment, employment, job retention and earnings of participants, and to improve the quality of the workforce, reduce welfare dependency, and enhance the productivity and competitiveness of the nation.

_____

_____

_____

2. The local outreach plan is incorporated with economic development, education and local entities identified by the Workforce Council.

_____

_____

TOEFL Reading

PAUSE TEST   SECTION EXIT

Practice Test 3

Question 3 of 5

CONTINUE   REVIEW   HELP   BACK   NEXT

HIDE TIME   01 : 40

Two technological innovations profoundly changed daily life in the 19th century. They were both "motive powers:"steam and electricity. In a way, the development and application of steam engines and electricity to various tasks such as transportation and the telegraph affected human life by increasing and multiplying the mechanical power of human or animal strength or the power of simple tools. Those who lived through these technological changes felt them to be much more than technological innovations. **To them, these technologies seemed to erase the primeval boundaries of human experience, and to usher in a kind of Millennial Era, a New Age, in which humankind had definitively broken its chains and was able to annihilate time and space**. Even the inventions that were not simply applications of steam or electrical power, such as the recording technologies of **the photograph and the phonograph**, contributed to **this** by making the past available to the present and the present to the future.

1. **What does the author imply about the new technology in the highlighted sentence in the passage?**

    Ⓐ The technological innovations gave people a primeval experience.
    Ⓑ People felt overwhelmed by the new technology.
    Ⓒ The changes from the new technological innovations were unprecedented.
    Ⓓ A few people were interested in technology in the 19th century.

2. **Why does the author mention the photograph and the phonograph in the passage?**

    Ⓐ To argue that these inventions were not the same as applications of steam or electrical power
    Ⓑ To list more types of new technologies at that time
    Ⓒ To emphasize how all new technologies were part of this groundbreaking change
    Ⓓ To contrast them to the "motive power" technologies

3. **The word this in the passage refers to**

    Ⓐ the development of new technologies
    Ⓑ the ushering in of a new age
    Ⓒ human experience
    Ⓓ the annihilation of time and space

다음 문장을 ① 끊어 읽기 → 직독직해 ② 명사 [구, 절]에 대괄호 ③ 동사 [구]에 동그라미 ④ 세부정보에 소괄호를 한 후 핵심정보에 화살표로 연결하시오.

1. In a way, the development and application of steam engines and electricity to various tasks such as transportation and the telegraph affected human life by increasing and multiplying the mechanical power of human or animal strength or the power of simple tools.

---

2. To them, these technologies seemed to erase the primeval boundaries of human experience, and to usher in a kind of Millennial Era, a New Age, in which humankind had definitively broken its chains and was able to annihilate time and space.

TOEFL Reading

Practice Test 4

Question 4 of 5

CONTINUE   REVIEW   HELP   BACK   NEXT

PAUSE TEST   SECTION EXIT

HIDE TIME   01 : 40

Studies of the few remaining hunter-gatherer societies provide good examples of the "deprivation, crisis, experimentation" thesis. History shows that great changes have occurred not as a result of an abundance of materials, but the opposite, that is, as a result of existing resources being used up. What this means is that history is a reflection of The 2nd Law of Thermodynamics. Ⓐ ▪ The overall entropy process is always moving toward a maximum. Ⓑ ▪ With every single occurrence, some amount of energy is forever dissipated. Ⓒ ▪ In the course of history, critical watersheds are reached when all of the accumulated increase in entropy result in a change in the quality of the energy source of the environment itself. Ⓓ ▪ **The entropy of the environment becomes so high that a shift to a new energy environment occurs, along with the creation of new technology and the shaping of a new social, economic, and political institutions.**

1. According to the passage, which of the following is NOT true of the "deprivation, crisis, experimentation" thesis?

   Ⓐ Critical moments of change in history result from this process.
   Ⓑ It is the same as the history of the 2nd Law of Thermodynamics.
   Ⓒ The first stage of this is when resources are used up.
   Ⓓ The increase of entropy in the environment leads to a crisis.

2. Look at the four squares [▪] that indicate where the following sentence could be added to the passage.

   It is at these critical moments of change that the old way of doing things no longer works.

   Where would the sentence best fit?

   Click on a square [▪] to add the sentence to the passage.

TOEFL Reading

PAUSE TEST   SECTION EXIT

Practice Test 4

Question 4 of 5

CONTINUE   REVIEW   HELP   BACK   NEXT

HIDE TIME

3. **Which of the sentences below best expresses the essential information in the highlighted sentence in the passage? Incorrect choices change the meaning in important ways or leave out essential information.**

Ⓐ Social change is a function of the available energy in a society.

Ⓑ New technologies and societies are the result of the search for new sources of energy.

Ⓒ The imperative towards entropy precipitates sweeping social change.

Ⓓ As entropy increases so does the need for a new energy environment.

다음 문장을 ① 끊어 읽기 → 직독직해 ② 명사 [구, 절]에 대괄호 ③ 동사 [구]에 동그라미 ④ 세부정보에 소괄호를 한 후 핵심정보에 화살표로 연결하시오.

1. History shows that great changes have occurred not as a result of an abundance of materials, but the opposite, that is, as a result of existing resources being used up.

_____

_____

2. Studies of the few remaining hunter-gatherer societies provide good examples of the "deprivation, crisis, experimentation" thesis.

_____

_____

 TOEFL Reading

PAUSE TEST   SECTION EXIT

Practice Test 5

Question 5 of 5

    CONTINUE   REVIEW   HELP   BACK   NEXT

HIDE TIME   01 : 40

Are women and men equal in our society? Why or why not? Women's rights establish the same social and economic status for women as for men. Women's rights guarantee that women will not face discrimination on the basis of their sex. Until the second half of the 20th century, women in most societies were denied some of the legal and political rights according to men. Although women in much of the world have gained significant legal rights, many people believe that women still do not have equality with men. **This** is evident in the home, workplace, and society in general. **Look no further** than the home to see the first sign that men and women are not equal. The traditional role of man was to work and make the money which would be used by all in the household. The traditional role of the woman was to stay home, take care of the children, clean the house, and cook. Because society has always associated money with power, the person bringing home the money had the power. The man often makes the final decision on all household matters because he has the money. The workplace is another place where men and women are not equal. Men are often applauded for being assertive and giving orders. By giving orders, men are taking a leadership role. Demonstrating leadership ability is a quality that employers often look for.

1. According to the passage, which of the following is true of women's rights?

   Ⓐ Women's rights are not the same as political rights.

   Ⓑ Women have the same rights as men.

   Ⓒ Women lack equal rights as they still face discrimination in society and the home.

   Ⓓ Women should take the lead back from men to regain their rights.

2. The word **This** in the passage refers to

   Ⓐ Men and women are not equal

   Ⓑ Men and women's traditional roles have changed

   Ⓒ Women need to do more to become equal

   Ⓓ Women will never be equal to men

3. The phrase **Look no further** in the passage is closest in meaning to

   Ⓐ Don't go anywhere else

   Ⓑ This place is the best

   Ⓒ There's no need to go beyond this place

   Ⓓ The distance to reach the place is excessive

다음 문장을 ① 끊어 읽기 → 직독직해 ② 명사 [구, 절]에 대괄호 ③ 동사 [구]에 동그라미 ④ 세부정보에 소괄호를 한 후 핵심정보에 화살표로 연결하시오.

1. Because society has always associated money with power, the person bringing home the money had the power.

_____

_____

2. Look no further than the home to see the first sign that men and women are not equal.

_____

_____

3. The traditional role of man was to work and make the money which would be used by all in the household.

_____

_____

4. Demonstrating leadership ability is a quality that employers often look for.

_____

Vocabulary & Paraphrasing

1. Write the word from the box that matches each meaning below.

adverse	irrevocable	uncharacteristic	disseminate	attainment
amend	shareholder	incorporated	integrate	disposal

① to make or be made into a whole _____

② to change or rephrase by formal procedure _____

③ not able to be canceled or changed _____

④ hostile, unfavorable, or unfriendly _____

⑤ united or combined into a whole _____

⑥ not typical or usual _____

⑦ the owner of one or more shares in a company _____

⑧ to scatter or spread widely _____

⑨ the act or instance of getting rid of something _____

⑩ an achievement or the act of achieving _____

Vocabulary & Paraphrasing

2. Translate the following questions into Korean and then paraphrase them according to the directions below.

① Additionally, information will be distributed via email and will be available on RU-tv Channel 3 and via RU-info at 732-445-INFO (including 24-hour voice mail). → 쉬운 단어로 바꿔 쓰기

_____

_____

② WIA is a federal funded program designed to increase the occupational skills attainment, employment, job retention and earnings of participants in order to improve the quality of the workforce, reduce welfare dependency, and enhance the productivity and competitiveness of the nation. → 사물주어, 비교구문으로 바꿔 쓰기

_____

_____

_____

③ The lot number for the recalled product can be found on the side of the bottle label. → 사물주어로 바꿔 쓰기

_____

④ In response to the Announcement made by the Company, on 26 June 2012, Best Champion notified the Company of its disposal of Shares of the Company on 21 June 2012, reducing its shareholding in the Company to an aggregate of 5,437,980,000 Shares. → 접속사, 쉬운 단어로 바꿔 쓰기

_____

_____

_____

Practice Test 1

1. It can build strong **foundations** / (for relationships) / and create **unity** (amongst people) / which in turn **lessens** the workload / (due to an enhanced productivity).

이는 사람들의 관계를 형성하는 데 강한 기반을 만들 수 있고 그들 간에 화합을 조성하며 그로 인해 높아진 생산성의 향상으로 작업량을 줄여준다.

2. **Relationships**, / (both social and in the workplace,) / have been re-defined and shaped so much / that individuals can even **share** their everyday life / (with whomever they please) / (with the simple click of a button).

사회와 직장에서의 관계는 다시 정의될 만큼 아주 크게 형태가 바뀌어서 심지어 간단한 버튼 클릭으로 그들이 좋아하는 사람과 누구나 일상생활을 공유할 수 있다.

Practice Test 2

1. WIA is a federal funded **program** / (**designed**) / (to increase the occupational skills attainment, employment, job retention and earnings of participants,) / and (to improve the quality of the workforce, / reduce welfare dependency, / and enhance the productivity and competitiveness of the nation).

WIA는 복지 의존을 줄이고 근로자의 질을 향상시키며 국가의 경쟁성과 생산성을 강화하고자 참가자들의 직업적인 기술 성취도와 취업, 고용유지와 수입을 증진시키도록 디자인된 정부 지원 프로그램이다.

2. The local outreach plan is incorporated / with [economic development, education and local **entities**] / (identified by the Workforce Council).

지역적 봉사활동 계획은 경제적인 발전, 교육 그리고 노동자 의회에서 확인된 지역단체들과 함께 이루어진다.

Practice Test 3

1. In a way, / [**the development and application** / (of steam engines and electricity to various **tasks**) / (such as transportation and the telegraph)] / affected human life / (by increasing and multiplying the mechanical power / of human or animal strength / or the power of simple tools).

어떤 면에서 증기 엔진과 전기의 운송 및 전신 같은 다양한 업무로의 발전과 활용은 인간이나 동물 또는 단순한 도구의 원동력을 증가시키고 배가시킴으로써 인간의 삶에 영향을 미쳤다.

2. To them, / these technologies seemed to erase / [the primeval boundaries of human experience,] / and to usher in a kind of **Millennial Era**, / a New Age, / (in which humankind had definitively broken its chains / and was able to annihilate time and space).

그들에게 이 기술은 인간이 경험한 원시적 한계를 없애고 원시 시대와의 연결고리를 확실히 부수며 공간과 시간의 제약을 파괴할 수 있는 천년 시대, 신시대가 시작되게 하는 것으로 보였다.

Practice Test 4

1. History shows / [that great changes **have occurred**] / (not as a result of an abundance of materials,) / but the opposite, / that is, / (as a result of existing **resources** (being used up)).

역사는 큰 변화가 물질의 풍요에 따라 발생한 것이 아니라 그 반대로 기존의 자원을 완전히 소모한 결과로 발생해 왔다는 것을 보여준다.

2. [Studies of the few remaining hunter-gatherer societies] / provide good **examples** / (of the "deprivation, crisis, experimentation" thesis).

얼마 남지 않은 수렵, 채집사회에 대한 연구는 '결핍, 위기, 실험' 이론의 좋은 예를 제공한다.

Practice Test 5

1. Because society has always associated money with power, / **the person** (bringing home the money) / had the power.

사회는 항상 돈을 권력과 연관시켜 왔기 때문에 돈을 가정으로 가지고 오는 사람이 권력을 가졌다.

2. Look no further than the home / (to see the first sign) / [that men and women are not equal].

남성과 여성이 평등하지 않다는 첫 흔적은 다른 곳에서 찾지 말고 가정에서 찾아라.

3. [The traditional role of man] was / [to work and make **the money**] / (which would **be used**) / (by all in the household).

남성의 전통적인 역할은 일을 하고 가정에서 쓰일 모든 돈을 버는 것이었다.

4. [Demonstrating leadership ability] is / **a quality** (that employers often look for).

리더십 능력을 보여주는 것은 고용주가 흔히 찾는 자질이다.

Unit 05
Computer

The new TR940 and TR950 laptops are designed with everything a small or medium business needs. **For increased durability and strength without adding excess weight, the new T laptops are built using a unique fiberglass reinforced casing with a Honeycomb Rib structure, making them the ultimate road warrior laptops.** In addition, the laptops include a spill resistant keyboard, hard drive impact sensor and a sock absorbing design to ensure the laptops can take the stresses of the fast-paced business world. All models can be configured with 5th generation IC processors, **dedicated** Intel GMA HD 4000 graphics and generous storage, including a 4GB DDR3 main memory and up to a 500 GB hard disk drive. Weighing less than 5.3 pounds, measuring just one inch thin and available with 14.0-and 15.6-inch diagonal LED-back lit wide screen HD displays respectively, the TR940 and TR950 are not only durable, but also incredibly portable.

1. **Which of the sentences below best expresses the essential information in the highlighted sentence in the passage? Incorrect choices change the meaning in important ways or leave out essential information.**

   Ⓐ These laptops will become a best-selling product soon.

   Ⓑ They are extremely tough computers and will be able to withstand shocks.

   Ⓒ They will be excellent computers for playing all kinds of war and racing games.

   Ⓓ They are the lightest and the toughest screen laptops currently available.

2. **The word dedicated in the passage is closest in meaning to**

   Ⓐ made for multi purposes

   Ⓑ assigned or allocated to a particular project

   Ⓒ designed to fulfil one function

   Ⓓ set apart for a high purpose

3. **Which of the following can be concluded from the passage?**

   Ⓐ Only business people will like these computers.

   Ⓑ They will be easy to use for people who travel a lot.

   Ⓒ Users can expect the computers to give them a lot of stress.

   Ⓓ These computers will likely withstand a lot of punishment.

다음 문장을 ① 끊어 읽기 → 직독직해 ② 명사 [구, 절]에 대괄호 ③ 동사 [구]에 동그라미 ④ 세부정보에 소괄호를 한 후 핵심정보에 화살표로 연결하시오.

1. For increased durability and strength without adding excess weight, the new T laptops are built using a unique fiberglass reinforced casing with a Honeycomb Rib structure, making them the ultimate road warrior laptops.

_____

_____

_____

2. All models can be configured with 5th generation IC processors, dedicated Intel HD 4000 graphics and generous storage, including a 4GB DDR3 main memory and up to a 500 GB hard disk drive.

_____

_____

_____

Tracker is a small, square, waterproof device with embedded GPS and antennas that are in the form of flexible fins. You can mount it on any dog collar. In theory, you might also **attach it to your cat's collar**, but it looks a bit too bulky to be cat-friendly, unless you've got a pretty burly kitty — the Tracker website says it's designed for pets over 10 kilos. You then set a "Tracker Zone" that indicates the area surrounding your home where your pet is allowed to go. If the animal leaves the approved area, you get an e-mail and SMS alert —and can use the web or an iPhone or Android app to see its current location on a map. There's also a Trip mode that lets you temporarily shut off tracking when your dog is being walked or is otherwise away from home but under human supervision.

1. Directions: An introductory sentence for a brief summary of the passage is provided below. Complete the summary by selecting the THREE answer choices that express the most important ideas in the passage. Some sentences do not belong in the summary because they express ideas that are not presented in the passage or are minor ideas in the passage. **This question is worth 2 points**.

Drag your answer choices to the spaces where they belong. To remove an answer choice, click on it. To review the passage, click on **View Text**.

Tracker is a way for an owner to know where their pet is at all times.

-
-
-

Answer Choices

Ⓐ You can program the Tracker to keep your pet confined to a specific area.

Ⓑ It has embedded GPS and antennas that are in the form of flexible fins.

Ⓒ Tracker will alert you if your pet leaves the specified area.

Ⓓ The Trip mode allows you to over-ride the tracking function.

Ⓔ It even has an app so you can check where your pet is.

Ⓕ The Tracker can fit on any dog collar.

TOEFL Reading

PAUSE TEST   SECTION EXIT

Practice Test 2

Question 2 of 5

CONTINUE   REVIEW   HELP   BACK   NEXT

HIDE TIME

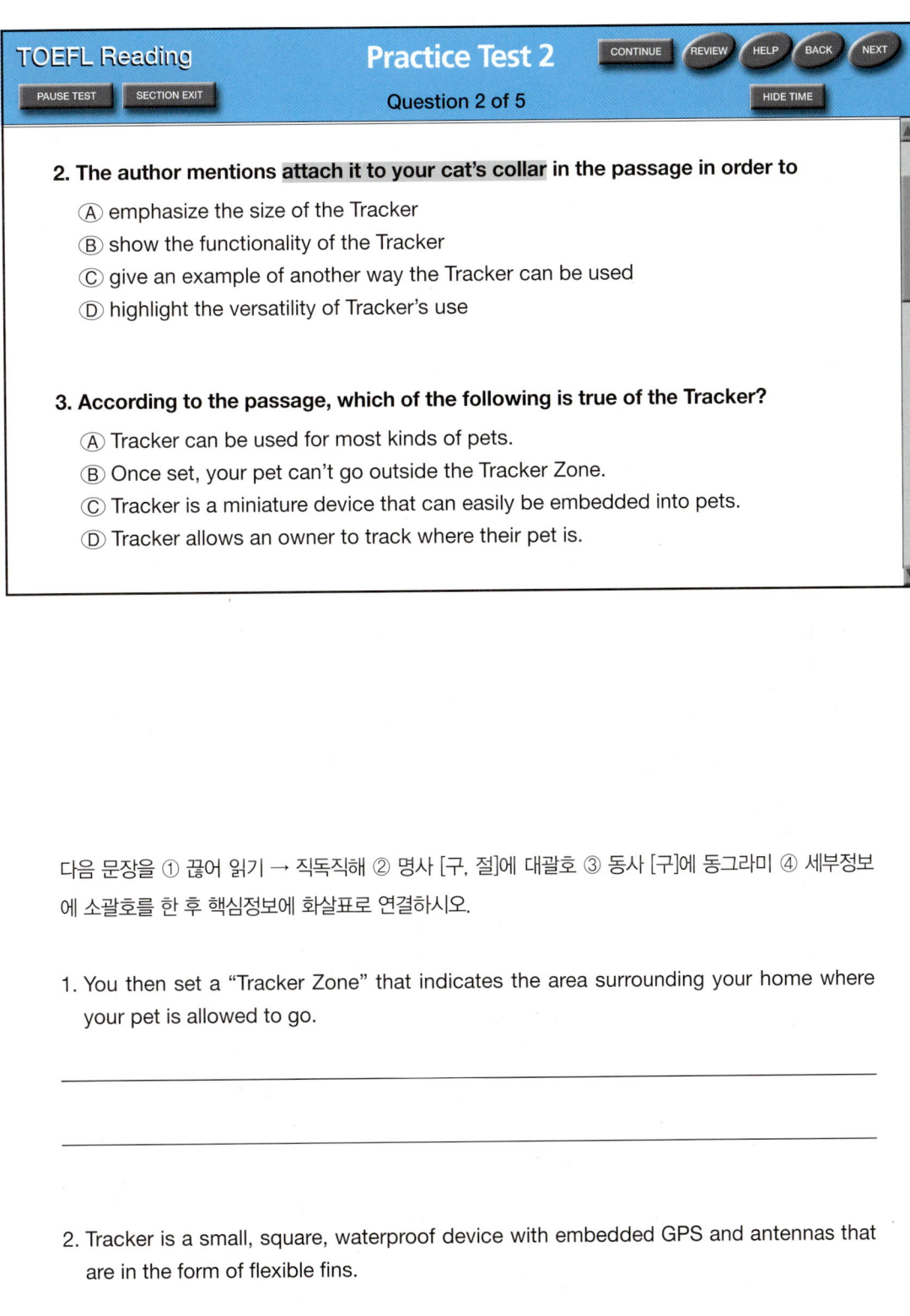

2. The author mentions attach it to your cat's collar in the passage in order to

   Ⓐ emphasize the size of the Tracker

   Ⓑ show the functionality of the Tracker

   Ⓒ give an example of another way the Tracker can be used

   Ⓓ highlight the versatility of Tracker's use

3. According to the passage, which of the following is true of the Tracker?

   Ⓐ Tracker can be used for most kinds of pets.

   Ⓑ Once set, your pet can't go outside the Tracker Zone.

   Ⓒ Tracker is a miniature device that can easily be embedded into pets.

   Ⓓ Tracker allows an owner to track where their pet is.

다음 문장을 ① 끊어 읽기 → 직독직해 ② 명사 [구, 절]에 대괄호 ③ 동사 [구]에 동그라미 ④ 세부정보
에 소괄호를 한 후 핵심정보에 화살표로 연결하시오.

1. You then set a "Tracker Zone" that indicates the area surrounding your home where
your pet is allowed to go.

_____

_____

2. Tracker is a small, square, waterproof device with embedded GPS and antennas that
are in the form of flexible fins.

_____

_____

235

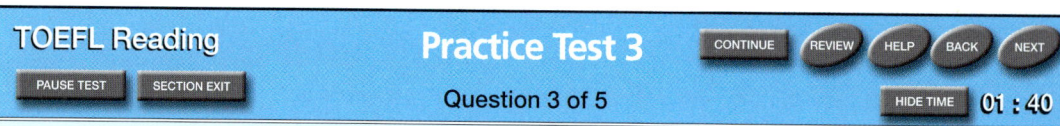
Computer crimes come in a variety of names and can include hate crimes, telemarketing and internet fraud, identity theft and credit card account theft. These are considered to be cyber crimes when the illegal activities are committed through the use of a computer and the internet. It is very difficult to gauge the amount of damage or financial loss that has resulted from computer crimes. Many times the victim does not even know that they have been targeted or even that they are a victim. Those that do realize that they are a victim of a computer crime many times do not report **it** to the authorities or have no way of knowing what caused them to be a victim in the first place. There is **a wide variety of computer crimes**, many ways in which they work and how they affect both the computers and the lives of the people they have targeted. The Department of Justice categorizes computer crime in three ways: the computer as a target, the computer as a weapon, and the computer as an accessory.

1. Directions: Select the appropriate phrases from the answer choices and match them to the category of cyber-crime to which they relate. Two of the answer choices will NOT be used. **This question is worth 3 points.**

Drag your answer choices to the spaces where they belong. To remove an answer choice, click on it. To review the passage, click on **View Text**.

Answer Choices	Types of Cyber-crime
Ⓐ Financial loss	•
Ⓑ Report it to the authorities	•
Ⓒ Credit card account theft	•
Ⓓ Hate crimes	**Effects of Cyber-crime**
Ⓔ Damage	•
Ⓕ The computer as an accessory	•
Ⓖ Internet fraud	

2. The word it in the passage refers to

    Ⓐ the victim   Ⓑ the victims' realization

    Ⓒ being targeted by the computer crime   Ⓓ the crime

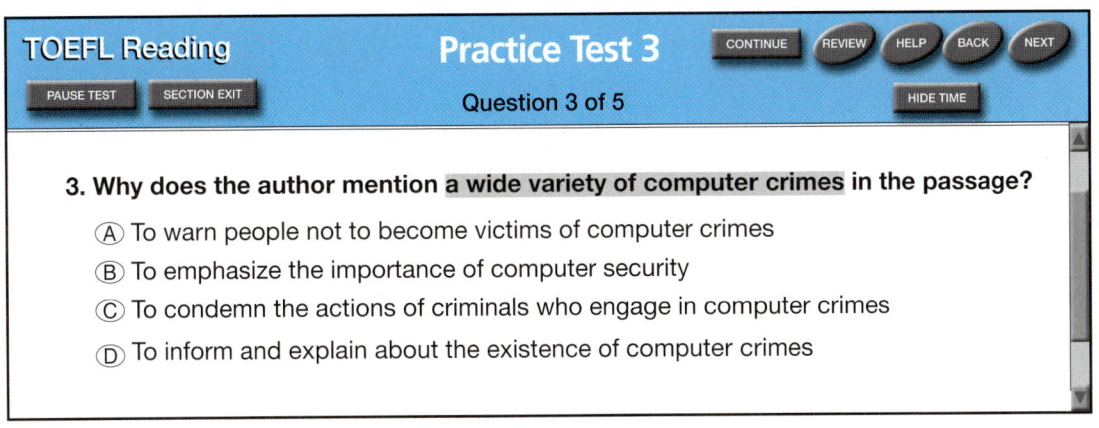

3. Why does the author mention a wide variety of computer crimes in the passage?

   Ⓐ To warn people not to become victims of computer crimes

   Ⓑ To emphasize the importance of computer security

   Ⓒ To condemn the actions of criminals who engage in computer crimes

   Ⓓ To inform and explain about the existence of computer crimes

다음 문장을 ① 끊어 읽기 → 직독직해 ② 명사 [구, 절]에 대괄호 ③ 동사 [구]에 동그라미 ④ 세부정보
에 소괄호를 한 후 핵심정보에 화살표로 연결하시오.

1. Many times the victim does not even know that they have been targeted or even that
   they are a victim.

_____

_____

2. Those that do realize that they are a victim of a computer crime many times do not
   report it to the authorities or have no way of knowing what caused them to be a victim
   in the first place.

_____

_____

_____

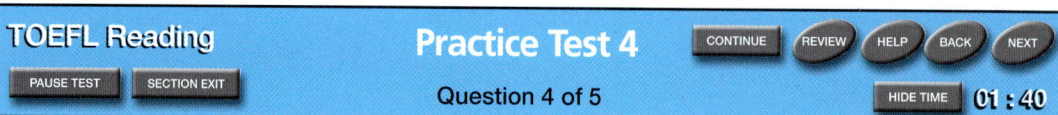
P's Storage Products Business Unit, a division of P America Electronic Components, Inc., and a committed technology leader, today announced the AL13SE series of 2.5-inch 6Gb/s SAS interface hard disk drives (HDDs), which offer enterprise-class performance in capacities ranging from 900GB to 300GB. Ⓐ ■ The AL13SE is the first 10,000RPM class model enterprise drive from P to achieve 900GB capacity and is also the first of P's 10,000RPM drives to employ a dual-stage head positioning actuator that provides additional performance gains, including a 32% increase in sustained transfer rate. Ⓑ ■ Designed for even the most demanding mission-critical applications, the AL13SE series features an operating reliability rating of 2,000,000 power-on hours, a 25% increase over prior-generation drives. Ⓒ ■ In keeping with P's leadership in power efficiency design, the AL13SE Series uses Supported Enhanced Power Condition State technology to reduce RPM idle speed. Ⓓ ■ "The AL13SE Series provides enterprise customers with capacities up to 900GB that support a broad range of enterprise applications," said the vice president of marketing at P's Storage Products Business Unit. "The increased performance and reliability of the AL13SE reflect our collaboration with our key partners to deliver small form-factor hard disk drives that address market requirements for **mission-critical** storage."

1. **The phrase mission-critical in the passage is closest in meaning to**
   Ⓐ leaving nothing to chance
   Ⓑ important
   Ⓒ whose failure will result in the failure of operation
   Ⓓ being uninterrupted

2. **Which of the following is true according to the passage?**
   Ⓐ With their increased capacity, the new drives have the same sustained transfer rate as previous drives.
   Ⓑ These drives have a 32% improvement in reliability.
   Ⓒ The company worked independently to develop the new model.
   Ⓓ The company prides itself on the energy efficiency of its products.

3. **Look at the four squares [■] that indicate where the following sentence could be added to the passage.**

   Besides the advanced technology, system compatibility is assured through usage of the industry-standard 512 byte sector size.

   Where would the sentence best fit?

   Click on a square [■] to add the sentence to the passage.

다음 문장을 ① 끊어 읽기 → 직독직해 ② 명사 [구, 절]에 대괄호 ③ 동사 [구]에 동그라미 ④ 세부정보에 소괄호를 한 후 핵심정보에 화살표로 연결하시오.

1. P's Storage Products Business Unit, a division of P America Electronic Components, Inc., and a committed technology leader, today announced the AL13SE series of 2.5-inch 6Gb/s SAS interface hard disk drives (HDDs) which offer enterprise-class performance in capacities ranging from 900GB to 300GB.

_____

_____

_____

2. In keeping with P's leadership in power efficiency design, the AL13SE Series uses Supported Enhanced Power Condition State technology to increase RPM idle speed.

_____

_____

3. "The AL13SE Series provides enterprise customers with capacities up to 900GB that support a broad range of enterprise applications," said the vice president of marketing at P's Storage Products Business Unit.

_____

_____

_____

4. "The increased performance and reliability of the AL13SE reflect our collaboration with our key partners to deliver small form-factor hard disk drives that address market requirements for mission-critical storage."

_____

_____

_____

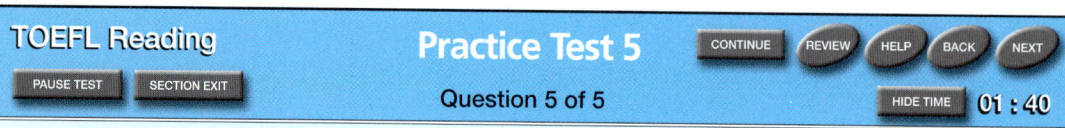

So let's take a look out where we came out performance-per-watt. If you take a look at the G4 chip that we have in the Powerbooks today, it's got a 0.27 performance per watt. **Now to put a G5 in which has got a lot higher performance, we needed a higher performance-per-watt too, so that the power didn't go up with that performance.** Well it turned out that the G5 was even worse than the G4 in terms of performance-per-watt, which is what kept us from doing what we wanted to. But the Core Duo was designed for this from the start. Look at that, and so it is 4 times better than the G4 and four and a half times better than the G5. And so today we are introducing a new notebook computer that we are calling the MacBook Pro. It's a new name, it's a new name because we're kind of done with Power and because we want Mac in the name of our products, so MacBook Pro and this is **the new MacBook Pro**.

1. **Which of the sentences below best expresses the essential information in the highlighted sentence in the passage? Incorrect choices change the meaning in important ways or leave out essential information.**

  Ⓐ With better performance-per-watt, the G5 would consume more power and lose performance.

  Ⓑ Along with high performance, the G5 gives a boost to power but it is worse than G4 in its performance.

  Ⓒ The G5 has higher performance but contrary to expectation, the G5 doesn't increase energy consumption.

  Ⓓ They had to improve efficiency to make the G5 workable.

2. **Why does the author mention the new MacBook Pro in the passage?**

  Ⓐ To explain about the new product.

  Ⓑ To detail specifications required to use a new product.

  Ⓒ To emphasize the name of a new notebook.

  Ⓓ To warn about the problems associated with the G5 chip.

3. **Directions:** An introductory sentence for a brief summary of the passage is provided below. Complete the summary by selecting the THREE answer choices that express the most important ideas in the passage. Some sentences do not belong in the summary because they express ideas that are not presented in the passage or are minor ideas in the passage. **This question is worth 2 points.**

TOEFL Reading

PAUSE TEST   SECTION EXIT

Practice Test 5

Question 5 of 5

CONTINUE   REVIEW   HELP   BACK   NEXT

HIDE TIME

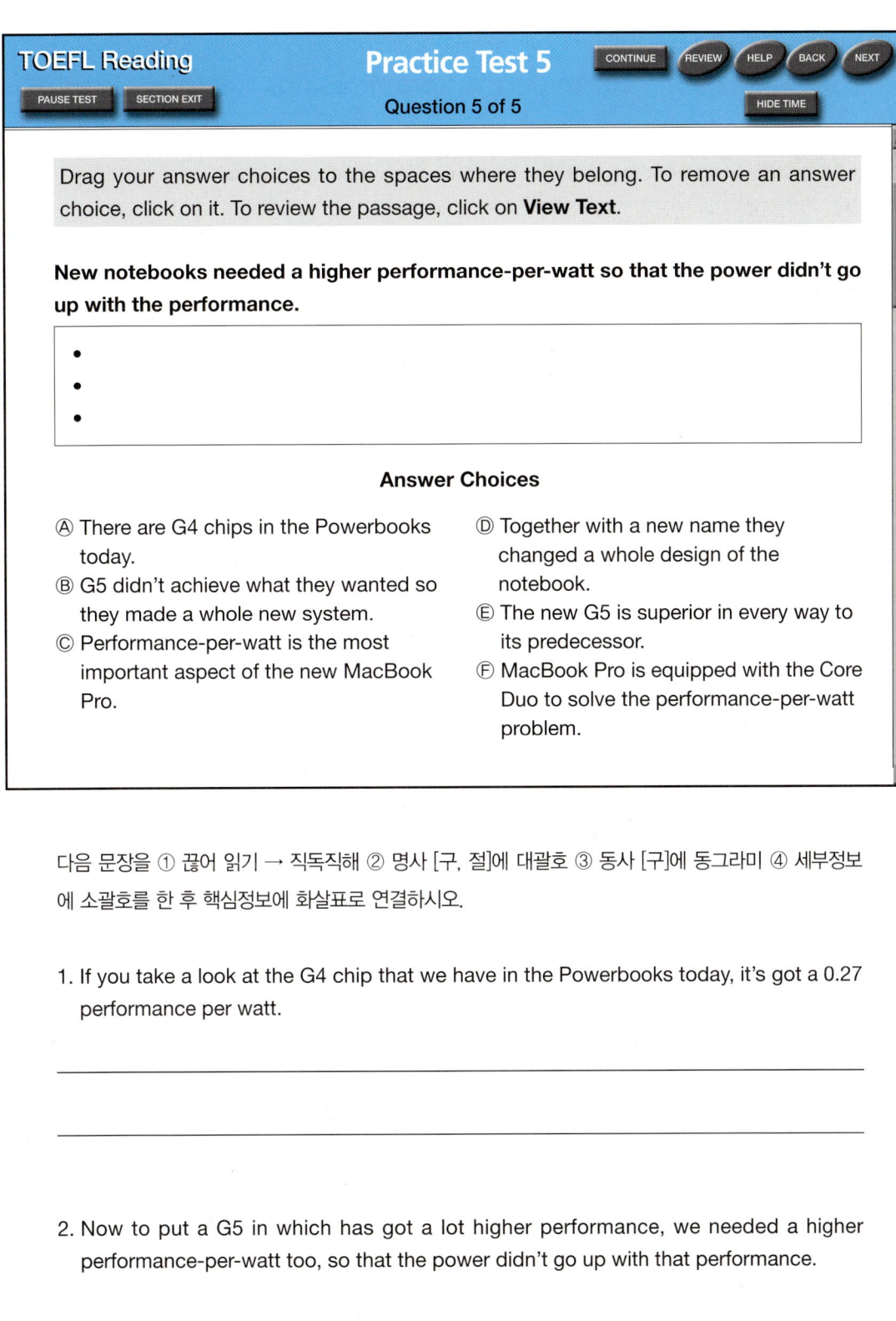

Drag your answer choices to the spaces where they belong. To remove an answer choice, click on it. To review the passage, click on **View Text**.

New notebooks needed a higher performance-per-watt so that the power didn't go up with the performance.

-
-
-

Answer Choices

Ⓐ There are G4 chips in the Powerbooks today.

Ⓑ G5 didn't achieve what they wanted so they made a whole new system.

Ⓒ Performance-per-watt is the most important aspect of the new MacBook Pro.

Ⓓ Together with a new name they changed a whole design of the notebook.

Ⓔ The new G5 is superior in every way to its predecessor.

Ⓕ MacBook Pro is equipped with the Core Duo to solve the performance-per-watt problem.

다음 문장을 ① 끊어 읽기 → 직독직해 ② 명사 [구, 절]에 대괄호 ③ 동사 [구]에 동그라미 ④ 세부정보에 소괄호를 한 후 핵심정보에 화살표로 연결하시오.

1. If you take a look at the G4 chip that we have in the Powerbooks today, it's got a 0.27 performance per watt.

_____

_____

2. Now to put a G5 in which has got a lot higher performance, we needed a higher performance-per-watt too, so that the power didn't go up with that performance.

_____

_____

241

Vocabulary & Paraphrasing

1. Write the word from the box that matches each meaning below.

compatability	reinforce	surgical	respectively	enhance
performance	configure	durable	collaboration	backlit

① to raise to a higher degree

_____

② used in surgery

_____

③ to give added strength or support to

_____

④ the act of working with others on a joint project

_____

⑤ separately in the order given

_____

⑥ capacity of being run on another computer without change

_____

⑦ illuminated from behind

_____

⑧ able to resist wear or decay well

_____

⑨ to set up as required

_____

⑩ the execution or accomplishment of work

_____

Vocabulary & Paraphrasing

2. Translate the following questions into Korean and then paraphrase them according to the directions below.

① Weighing less than 5.3 pounds, measuring just one inch thin and available with 14.0- and 15.6-inch diagonal LED-back lit wide screen HD displays respectively, the TR940 and TR950 are not only durable, but also incredibly portable. ➜ 분사구문, 접속사 바꿔 쓰기

_____

_____

_____

② Well it turned out that the G5 was even worse than the G4 in terms of performance-per-watt, which is what kept us from doing what we wanted to. ➜ 비교급, 동의어 바꿔 쓰기

_____

_____

③ Already showing tremendous advantages for surgeons in other parts of the world, the new S OLED monitor will now enhance surgical viewing in the U.S., and become the 'must have' medical display. ➜ 분사구문, 동의어 바꿔 쓰기

_____

_____

_____

④ The increased performance and reliability of the AL13SE reflect our collaboration with our key partners to deliver small form-fact of hard disk drives that address market requirements for mission-critical storage. ➜ 관계사, 쉬운 단어로 바꿔 쓰기

_____

_____

_____

Practice Test 1

1. For **increased** durability and strength / (without adding excess weight,) / the new T laptops (are built) / (using a unique fiberglass reinforced casing / with a Honeycomb Rib structure,) / making them / the ultimate road warrior laptops.

   새로운 T 노트북은 과도한 무게를 더하지 않고 내구성과 강함을 증가시키기 위해 허니콤 립 구조의 특수한 섬유 유리로 강화한 케이스로 만들어져서 외근이나 출장이 잦은 사원에게 최고의 노트북이 될 것이다.

2. All models can be configured / with [5th generation IC processors, / dedicated Intel HD 4000 graphics and generous **storage**,] / (including a 4GB DDR3 main memory / and up to a 500 GB hard disk drive).

   모든 모델은 5세대 IC 프로세서, 인텔 GMA HD 4000전용의 그래픽카드, 그리고 4GB DDR3 주기억장치와 500GB 하드디스크 드라이브를 포함한 넉넉한 저장 공간으로 환경설정되어 있다.

Practice Test 2

1. You then (set) a "Tracker Zone" / (that indicates **the area**) / (surrounding your home) / (where your pet is allowed to go).

   다음으로 애완동물이 돌아다녀도 되는 여러분의 집 주변 지역을 나타내는 '트래커 구역'을 설정하면 된다.

2. Tracker (is) a small, square, waterproof de**vice** / (with embedded **GPS and antennas**) / (that are in the form of flexible fins).

   트래커는 내장형 GPS와 유연한 지느러미 형태의 안테나가 장착된 작은 사각의 방수 장치이다.

Practice Test 3

1. Many times / the victim (does not even know) / [that they have been targeted] / or even [that they are a victim].

   대부분의 경우 피해자는 그들이 목표가 되었다든지 심지어 범죄의 피해자라는 것조차 모른다.

2. **Those** (that do realize / [that they are a victim of a computer crime many times]) / (do not report) it to the authorities / or (have) no way of knowing / [what caused them to be a victim in the first place].

   컴퓨터 범죄의 피해자가 되었음을 알게 된 사람들은 대부분 당국에 그것을 보고하지 않거나 무엇이 처음에 그들을 피해자로 만들었는지 알 방법이 없다.

Practice Test 4

1. [P's Storage Products Business Unit,] / [a division of P America Electronic Components, Inc.,] / and [a committed technology leader,] / today (announced) [the AL13SE **series** / (of 2.5-inch 6Gb/s SAS interface hard disk drives (**HDDs**))] / (which offer enterprise-class performance in **capacities**) (ranging from 900GB to 300GB).

   P 미국 전자부품 제조사의 한 부서인 P사의 스토리지 제품 사업부와 열성적인 기술 선도자는 오늘 900GB – 300GB 용량의 범위에 이르는 기업용 성능을 제공하는 2.5인치 6Gb/s SAS 인터페이스 하드 디스크 드라이브 (HDD)의 AL13SE 시리즈를 발표하였다.

2. In keeping with P's **leadership** (in power efficiency design,) / the AL13SE Series (uses) / [Supported Enhanced Power Condition State technology] (to increase RPM idle speed).

   P사의 전력 사용 효율성 설계 우월성을 지키며, AL13SE 시리즈는 RPM 공회전 속도를 증가시키기 위해 지원 개선 전력 조건 주립 기술을 사용한다.

3. "The AL13SE Series provides / enterprise customers with **capacities** up to 900GB / (that support a broad range of enterprise applications,") / (said) [**the vice president** of marketing] / (at P's Storage Products Business Unit).

   'AL13SE 시리즈는 기업 고객들에게 기업의 광범위한 응용 프로그램을 지원하는 최고 900GB의 용량을 제공한다.'고 P사의 저장매체 상품 사업부의 마케팅 부사장이 말했다.

4. ["The increased performance and reliability of the AL13SE] / (reflect) [our **collaboration** with our key partners] / (to deliver small form-factor hard disk **drives**) / (that address market requirements / for mission-critical storage.")

   'AL13SE의 향상된 성능과 신뢰성은 핵심 임무의 저장매체에 대한 시장의 요구를 다룬 소형 인수 하드 디스크 드라이브를 제공하기 위해 우리와 주요 파트너 업체들과의 협업을 반영한다.'

Practice Test 5

1. If you take a look at **the G4 chip** / (that we have in the Powerbooks today,) / it's got a 0.27 performance per watt.

   오늘날 파워북에 내장되어 있는 G4칩을 살펴보면 0.27 와트당 성능을 갖고 있다.

2. Now to put **a G5** in / (which has got a lot higher performance,) / we (needed) a higher performance-per-watt too, / (so that the power didn't go up / with that performance).

   그리고 훨씬 성능이 좋은 G5를 탑재하기 위해서는 더 높은 와트당 성능이 필요했다, 그래서 전력이 성능에 비례하여 증가하지 않았다

Nature

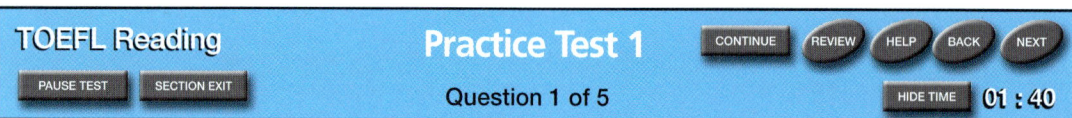
Monster-size squid that glow in the dark have been filmed for the first time in the wild. Ⓐ ■ The creatures were videotaped in the North Pacific Ocean off southeastern Japan. Ⓑ ■ The squid which can grow as big as humans uses bright, flashing lights on their arms to dazzle and catch prey. Ⓒ ■ Instead, scientists think, the deep-sea squid traps its victims using light-producing organs on the ends of two of its arms, stunning them with blinding flashes. Ⓓ ■ These organs, about the size of lemons, are called photophores. They are the largest photophores found in the animal kingdom and can be opened and closed like eyes. The octopus squid also glowed when it wasn't hunting. Researchers think these glows are used for communication, such as to warn other squid of danger or for attracting a mate. **Experts say the new video footage backs up what scientists previously thought about the way this glowing squid behaves.** The footage also shows the Dana octopus squid is a powerful and agile hunter. "Some people have said all deepwater squid are pretty sluggish because their muscles are not real firm when you catch them," said one scientist. "But this particular family has got very muscular fins, and that's what it's using for swimming."

1. **Which of the sentences below best expresses the essential information in the highlighted sentence in the passage? Incorrect choices change the meaning in important ways or leave out essential information.**

   Ⓐ Scientists had suspected it would be the case but this evidence surprised them.
   Ⓑ Without this confirmation, scientists would have had no way to know the truth about the squid.
   Ⓒ Scientists were ecstatic to find verification of what they had long suspected.
   Ⓓ Scientists had thought it was the case but now had proof.

2. **Look at the four squares [■] that indicate where the following sentence could be added to the passage.**

   This eight-armed species has catlike claws on its suckers but lacks the two long feeding tentacles that other big squid use to grab prey.

   Where would the sentence best fit?
   Click on a square [■] to add the sentence to the passage.

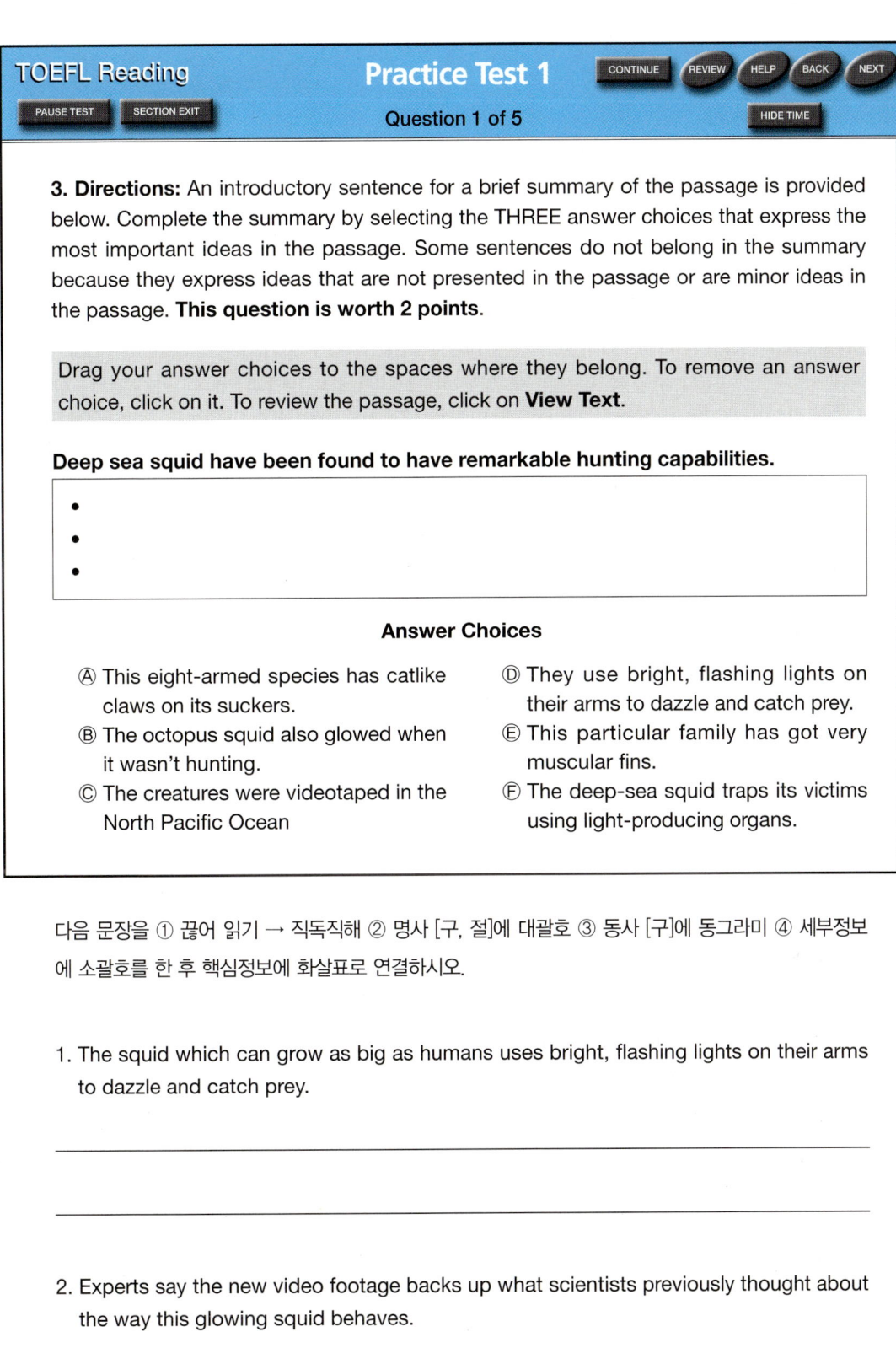

TOEFL Reading

PAUSE TEST   SECTION EXIT

Practice Test 1

Question 1 of 5

CONTINUE   REVIEW   HELP   BACK   NEXT

HIDE TIME

3. Directions: An introductory sentence for a brief summary of the passage is provided below. Complete the summary by selecting the THREE answer choices that express the most important ideas in the passage. Some sentences do not belong in the summary because they express ideas that are not presented in the passage or are minor ideas in the passage. **This question is worth 2 points**.

Drag your answer choices to the spaces where they belong. To remove an answer choice, click on it. To review the passage, click on **View Text**.

Deep sea squid have been found to have remarkable hunting capabilities.

-
-
-

Answer Choices

Ⓐ This eight-armed species has catlike claws on its suckers.

Ⓑ The octopus squid also glowed when it wasn't hunting.

Ⓒ The creatures were videotaped in the North Pacific Ocean

Ⓓ They use bright, flashing lights on their arms to dazzle and catch prey.

Ⓔ This particular family has got very muscular fins.

Ⓕ The deep-sea squid traps its victims using light-producing organs.

다음 문장을 ① 끊어 읽기 → 직독직해 ② 명사 [구, 절]에 대괄호 ③ 동사 [구]에 동그라미 ④ 세부정보에 소괄호를 한 후 핵심정보에 화살표로 연결하시오.

1. The squid which can grow as big as humans uses bright, flashing lights on their arms to dazzle and catch prey.

_____

_____

2. Experts say the new video footage backs up what scientists previously thought about the way this glowing squid behaves.

_____

_____

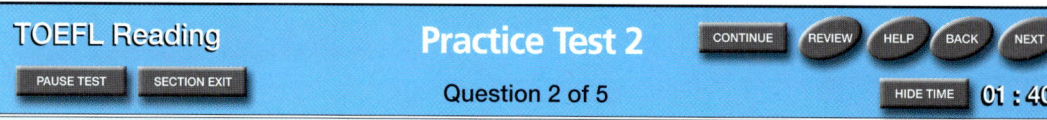

TOEFL Reading

PAUSE TEST   SECTION EXIT

Practice Test 2

Question 2 of 5

CONTINUE   REVIEW   HELP   BACK   NEXT

HIDE TIME   01 : 40

A surprising fact to many people is that landslides can occur virtually anywhere in the world. The traditional viewpoint that landslides are restricted to extremely steep slopes and inhospitable terrain does not accurately reflect the real nature of the problem. Most countries in the world have been affected in some manner by landslides. The reason for such wide geographic coverage has much to do with the many different **triggering mechanisms** for landslides. Excessive precipitation, earthquakes, volcanoes, forest fires and other mechanisms, and more recently, certain dangerous human activities are just some of the key causes that can trigger landslides. Similarly, landslides are known to occur both on land and under water; they can occur in bedrock or on soils; cultivated land, barren slopes and natural forests are all subject to landslides. Both extremely dry areas and very humid areas can be affected by slope failures, and most important, steep slopes are not a necessary prerequisite for landslides to occur. In some cases, gentle slopes as shallow as 1–2 degrees have been observed to fail.

1. The phrase triggering mechanisms in the passage is closest in meaning to

Ⓐ the lever pressed to fire a gun

Ⓑ device used to activate a mechanism

Ⓒ an event that sets a course of action in motion

Ⓓ fire or explosion

2. Directions: Select the appropriate phrases from the answer choices and match them to the landslides to which they relate. Two of the answer choices will NOT be used. **This question is worth 3 points**.

Drag your answer choices to the spaces where they belong. To remove an answer choice, click on it. To review the passage, click on **View Text**.

Answer Choices	Real Nature of the Problem
Ⓐ Gentle slopes observed to fail Ⓑ Only occurs in inhospitable terrain Ⓒ Natural forests subject to landslides Ⓓ Restricted to extremely steep slopes Ⓔ Excessive precipitation Ⓕ Dangerous human activities Ⓖ Both on land and under water	•
	•
	•
	Traditional Viewpoint
	•
	•

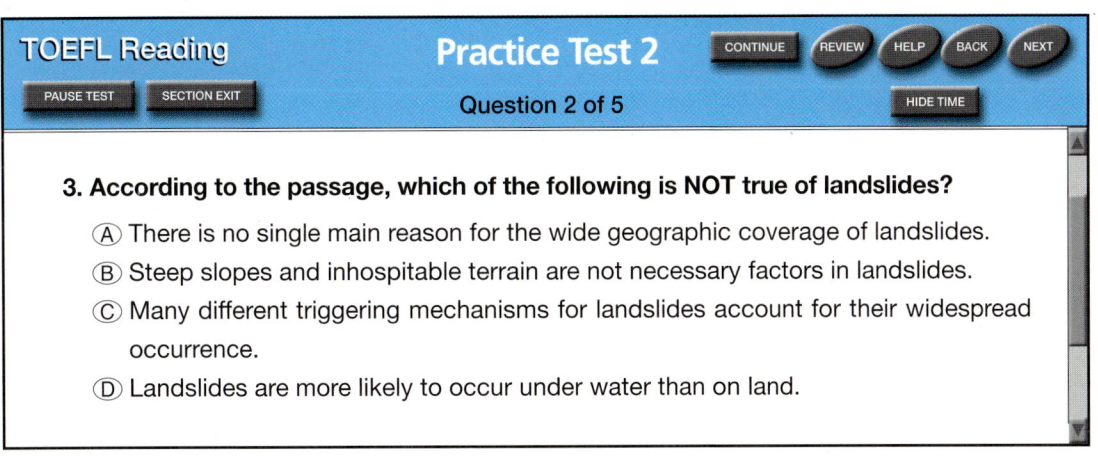

3. According to the passage, which of the following is NOT true of landslides?

Ⓐ There is no single main reason for the wide geographic coverage of landslides.

Ⓑ Steep slopes and inhospitable terrain are not necessary factors in landslides.

Ⓒ Many different triggering mechanisms for landslides account for their widespread occurrence.

Ⓓ Landslides are more likely to occur under water than on land.

다음 문장에 끊어 읽기, 긴 명사(주어나 목적어 보어로 사용되는 명사구, 명사절)에 대괄호, 핵심정보를 뒤에서 설명하는 세부정보(긴 수식어)에 소괄호와 화살표, 핵심정보(주절의 동사) 동사구에 동그라미 치고 직독직해 하시오.

1. The traditional viewpoint that landslides are restricted to extremely steep slopes and inhospitable terrain does not accurately reflect the real nature of the problem.

_____

_____

2. Excessive precipitation, earthquakes, volcanoes, forest fires and other mechanisms, and more recently, certain dangerous human activities are just some of the key causes that can trigger landslides.

_____

_____

A scientific sailing trip around the world has shed new light on the vast biodiversity in the world's oceans. The expedition has yielded about 1.5 million different plankton taxa, based on an initial preliminary analysis of samples. Scientists will spend years analyzing the catch. A 36-meter-tall research schooner returned to Lorient, France, on 31 March after a 362-day trip. Its mission was to help understand the evolution and ecology of plankton, roughly defined as anything that's small and floating in the ocean — including viruses, bacteria, protists, metazoans, and even fish larvae. Even though plankton makes up the bulk of the oceans biomass, **its** biogeography and the structure of its ecosystems are an "**almost virgin field**." The project which brings together physical oceanographers, marine biologists, imaging specialists, molecular biologists, bioinformaticists and modelers uses what it calls a "holistic" and "study it all" approach. It analyzes many species at once using a variety of methods, many of them automated. The team took samples in 153 different spots around the world, from the Mediterranean Sea and the Red Sea to the Pacific Ocean and the Antarctic region.

1. The word its in the passage refers to

   Ⓐ the oceans' biomass

   Ⓑ plankton

   Ⓒ the project

   Ⓓ fish larvae

2. The author mentions almost virgin field in the passage in order to

   Ⓐ explain why plankton have not been well studied up to the present

   Ⓑ identify what information has been missing from plankton studies so far

   Ⓒ contrast the information scientists have about plankton with what they know about other species

   Ⓓ emphasize the disparity between what is known about plankton and its distribution in the oceans

3. According to the passage, which of the following is NOT true of plankton?

   Ⓐ The study of plankton is a relatively new area of research.

   Ⓑ Plankton types make up most of the living matter in the ocean.

   Ⓒ Viruses and bacteria are types of plankton.

   Ⓓ The mission has so far failed to find anything new about plankton.

다음 문장을 ① 끊어 읽기 → 직독직해 ② 명사 [구, 절]에 대괄호 ③ 동사 [구]에 동그라미 ④ 세부정보에 소괄호를 한 후 핵심정보에 화살표로 연결하시오.

1. Its mission was to help understand the evolution and ecology of plankton, roughly defined as anything that's small and floating in the ocean — including viruses, bacteria, protists, metazoans, and even fish larvae.

_____

_____

_____

2. The project which brings together physical oceanographers, marine biologists, imaging specialists, molecular biologists, bioinformaticists and modelers uses what it calls a "holistic" and "study it all" approach.

_____

_____

_____

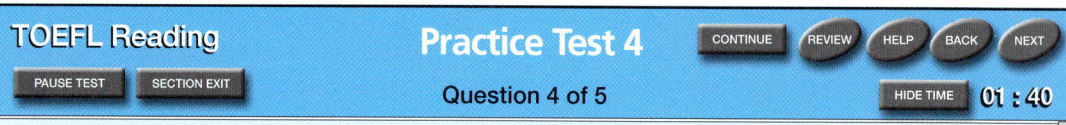
Some picturesque wilderness areas — including several U.S. national parks — will be in the 190-mile-wide (300-kilometer-wide) path of the full annular eclipse. Viewers in a broader track stretching for thousands of miles across northeastern Asia and the western two-thirds of the U.S. and Canada will see a **striking** partial eclipse instead. Unlike a total eclipse, in which the sun is entirely covered and the sky therefore gets dark, it never gets dark during an annular eclipse. **So the only loss in view from being off to the side of the zone of totality is that you won't see a complete ring and things won't appear symmetric, but you will still be able to see a partial eclipse of the sun.** Sunspots of various sizes will be covered by the advancing limb of the moon, then later uncovered as the moon retreats from the sun's face. Radio telescopes close to the path of annularity will make observations as the moon passes over sunspots and other sources of radio disturbances on the sun. Sunspots are linked to eruptions of intense electromagnetic radiation called solar flares, which can cause disturbances to radio communications on Earth and also hinder radio astronomers' views of the universe. Also, precise timing of the onset of annularity can provide data on possible changes in the diameter of the sun when compared with historical measurements.

1. The word **striking** in the passage is closest in meaning to

   Ⓐ coming into physical contact   Ⓑ shocking
   Ⓒ impressive   Ⓓ accidental

2. **What does the author imply about the view of the eclipse in the highlighted sentence?**

   Ⓐ The partial eclipse may not be as impressive as a total eclipse but will still be worth seeing.
   Ⓑ There is difference between this partial eclipse and a total eclipse.
   Ⓒ People should try to go to a vantage point in a wilderness area with a view of the full eclipse.
   Ⓓ It will be too bright to see the eclipse clearly.

3. **According to the passage, which of the following is NOT true of the eclipse?**

   Ⓐ More people will be able to see the partial eclipse than the annular eclipse.
   Ⓑ People outside some wilderness areas will still see the partial eclipse.
   Ⓒ Sunspots will cover the moon during the annular eclipse.
   Ⓓ Sunspots will not be visible for some time during the total eclipse.

다음 문장을 ① 끊어 읽기 → 직독직해 ② 명사 [구, 절]에 대괄호 ③ 동사 [구]에 동그라미 ④ 세부정보에 소괄호를 한 후 핵심정보에 화살표로 연결하시오.

1. Viewers in a broader track stretching for thousands of miles across northeastern Asia and the western two-thirds of the U.S. and Canada will see a striking partial eclipse instead.

_____

_____

_____

2. So the only loss in view from being off to the side of the zone of totality is that you won't see a complete ring and things won't appear symmetric, but you will still be able to see a partial eclipse of the sun.

_____

_____

_____

TOEFL Reading

PAUSE TEST   SECTION EXIT

Practice Test 5

Question 5 of 5

CONTINUE   REVIEW   HELP   BACK   NEXT

HIDE TIME   01 : 40

Nature does not always have a positive effect on us. Sometimes it can be quite negative, such as in the movie, The Beach. Although I didn't care for the movie as a whole, I was greatly impressed with the beauty of the beach portrayed. The goal of every character in the movie is to get in touch with nature via the beach. They clearly view nature the same way Emerson did when he said "It is the great organ through which the universal spirit speaks to the individual, and strives to lead the individual back to it." The characters seek out this perfect island in order to leave behind all the confusion and business of the world. The island that contains a flawless beach is described by more than one character as "an absolute perfect paradise." The camera work in this movie really highlights the beach as a major character in the film. The contrast between the pure white sand and the crystal clear blue water is remarkable. **The absolute beauty of the beach makes the characters completely understand the motivation to inhabit this island and never leave**.

1. According to the passage, which of the following is true of the beach?

   Ⓐ It was portrayed negatively in the movie.
   Ⓑ It was important to Emerson.
   Ⓒ It could be considered a character in the movie.
   Ⓓ The characters completely understood it.

2. Which of the sentences below best expresses the essential information in the highlighted sentence in the passage? Incorrect choices change the meaning in important ways or leave out essential information.

   Ⓐ The characters are enchanted by the beauty of the beach.
   Ⓑ There is an overwhelming motivation to stay there.
   Ⓒ The island exerts a calming effect on anyone who visits.
   Ⓓ It is impossible to resist the beauty of the tempting beach.

3. **Directions:** An introductory sentence for a brief summary of the passage is provided below. Complete the summary by selecting the THREE answer choices that express the most important ideas in the passage. Some sentences do not belong in the summary because they express ideas that are not presented in the passage or are minor ideas in the passage. **This question is worth 2 points**.

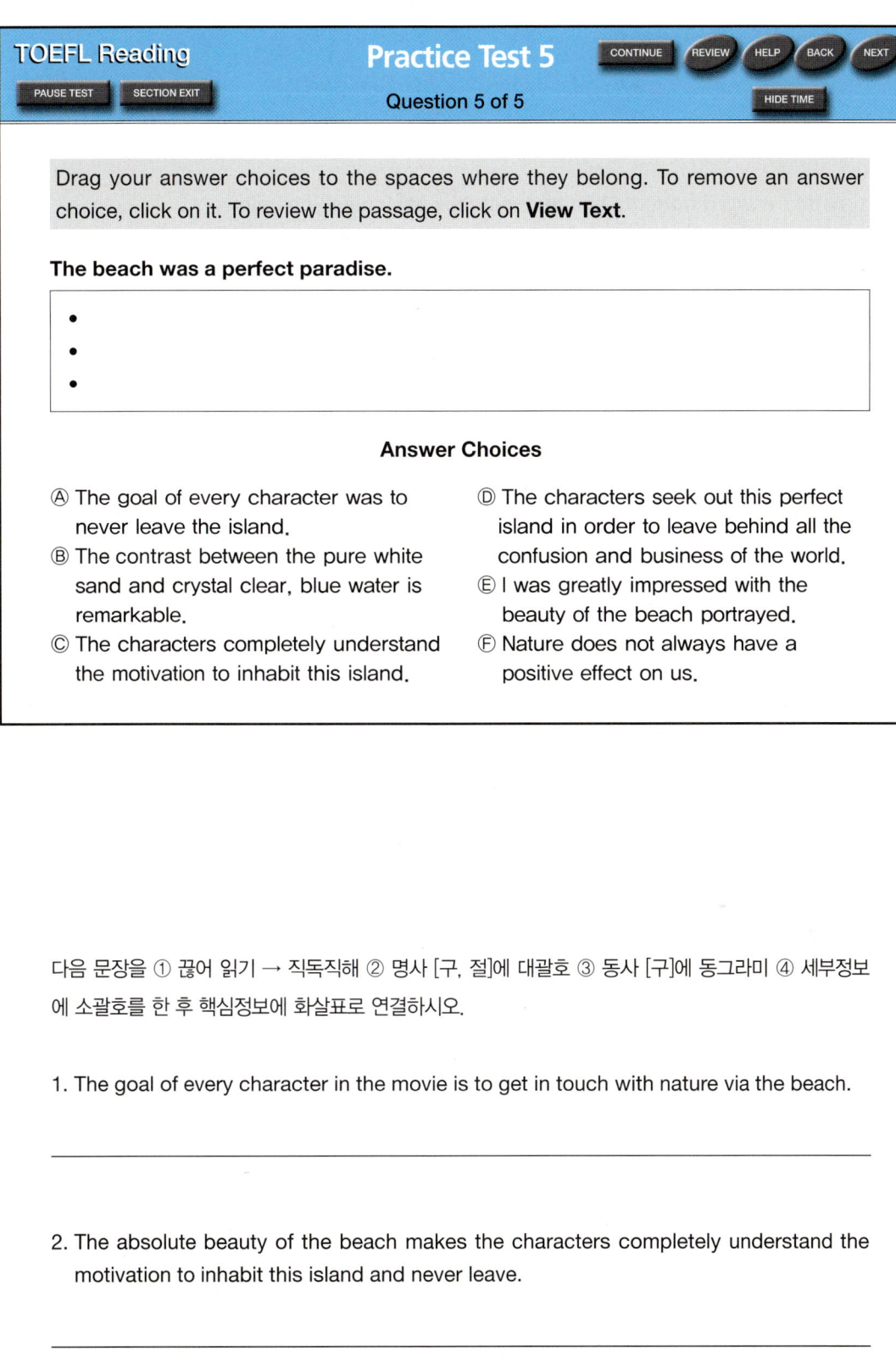

Drag your answer choices to the spaces where they belong. To remove an answer choice, click on it. To review the passage, click on **View Text**.

The beach was a perfect paradise.

-
-
-

Answer Choices

Ⓐ The goal of every character was to never leave the island.

Ⓑ The contrast between the pure white sand and crystal clear, blue water is remarkable.

Ⓒ The characters completely understand the motivation to inhabit this island.

Ⓓ The characters seek out this perfect island in order to leave behind all the confusion and business of the world.

Ⓔ I was greatly impressed with the beauty of the beach portrayed.

Ⓕ Nature does not always have a positive effect on us.

다음 문장을 ① 끊어 읽기 → 직독직해 ② 명사 [구, 절]에 대괄호 ③ 동사 [구]에 동그라미 ④ 세부정보에 소괄호를 한 후 핵심정보에 화살표로 연결하시오.

1. The goal of every character in the movie is to get in touch with nature via the beach.

_____

2. The absolute beauty of the beach makes the characters completely understand the motivation to inhabit this island and never leave.

_____

_____

255

Vocabulary & Paraphrasing

1. Write the word from the box that matches each meaning below.

photophore	symmetric	prerequisite	flare	expedition
precipitation	inhospitable	agile	ecology	tentacle

① the relationships of organisms with their environment   _____

② an organized journey or voyage for a specific purpose   _____

③ the amount of rain, snow, sleet, and dew   _____

④ quick in movement   _____

⑤ a slender flexible organ that serves as feeler in animals   _____

⑥ a sudden blaze or burst of flame   _____

⑦ well-proportioned or balanced   _____

⑧ something required as a prior condition   _____

⑨ not offering favorable conditions   _____

⑩ a luminous organ found in certain fishes   _____

Vocabulary & Paraphrasing

2. Translate the following questions into Korean and then paraphrase them according to the directions below.

① This eight-armed species has catlike claws on its suckers but lacks the two long feeding tentacles that other big squid use to grab prey. ➜ 동의어 바꿔 쓰기

_____

_____

② The traditional viewpoint that landslides are restricted to extremely steep slopes and inhospitable terrain does not accurately reflect the real nature of the problem.
➜ 접속사 바꿔 쓰기

_____

_____

③ The project which brings together physical oceanographers, marine biologists, imaging specialists, molecular biologists, bioinformaticists and modelers uses what it calls a "holistic" and "study it all" approach. ➜ 주어, 분사구문 바꿔 쓰기

_____

_____

_____

④ Sunspots of various sizes will be covered by the advancing limb of the moon, then later uncovered as the moon retreats from the sun's face. ➜ 수동태, 접속사 바꿔 쓰기

_____

_____

Practice Test 1

1. **The squid** / (which can grow as big as humans) / (uses) bright, flashing **lights** / (on their arms) / (to dazzle and catch prey).

발견된 오징어는 사람 크기만큼 자랄 수 있고 먹이를 눈부시게 하여 잡기 위해 앞다리의 번쩍이는 빛을 사용한다.

2. Experts (say) / [the new video footage backs up / [what scientists previously thought about **the way**] / (this glowing squid behaves)].

전문가들은 비디오의 장면이 과학자들이 이 빛을 내는 오징어의 행동양식에 대해 이전에 생각했던 방식을 뒷받침해준다고 말한다.

Practice Test 2

1. The traditional viewpoint / [that landslides are restricted / to extremely steep slopes / and inhospitable terrain] / (does not accurately reflect) the real nature of the problem.

산사태가 상당히 가파른 경사지와 황량한 지대에만 일어난다는 전통적인 견해는 문제의 본질을 정확히 반영하지 못한다.

2. [Excessive precipitation, earthquakes, volcanoes, forest fires / and other mechanisms, / and more recently, / certain dangerous human activities] / (are) just some of the **key causes** / (that can trigger landslides).

지나친 강수량, 지진, 화산, 산불 및 기타 요소들, 그리고 최근의 특정한 인간의 위험한 활동들도 산사태를 유발할 수 있는 주요한 원인들의 일부가 된다.

Practice Test 3

1. Its mission (was) [to help / understand the evolution and ecology of **plankton,**] / (roughly defined as **anything**) (that's small and floating in the ocean /— including viruses, bacteria, protists, metazoans, and even fish larvae).

그 배의 임무는 바이러스, 박테리아, 원생 생물, 후생 동물 그리고 해조류 유충을 포함한 작고 바다에 떠있는 대략 모든 것으로 규정지어진 플랑크톤의 진화와 생태계의 이해를 돕는 것이었다.

2. **The project** / (which brings together / physical oceanographers, marine biologists, imaging specialists, molecular biologists, bioinformaticists and modelers) / (uses) [what it calls a "holistic" / and "study it all" approach].

물리적 해양 탐사대, 해양 생물학자, 촬영 전문가, 분자 생물학자, 생물 정보학자와 모형 제작자가 모두 한자리에 모여서 하는 프로젝트는 '전체론적' 그리고 '협력 연구'라고 불리는 접근법을 사용한다.

Practice Test 4

1. **Viewers** (in a broader **track**) / (stretching for thousands of miles across northeastern Asia / and the western two-thirds of the U.S. and Canada) / (will see) [a striking partial eclipse] instead.

야생 보호구역 대신 북동쪽 아시아와 미국의 3분의 2인 서부와 캐나다를 가로질러 수천 마일이 확장된 넓어진 궤도에서 사람들은 인상적인 부분 일식을 볼 수 있을 것이다.

2. So [the only loss in **view**] / (from being off to the side of the zone of totality) / (is) [that you won't see a complete ring / and things won't appear symmetric,] / but you (will still be able to see) / [a partial eclipse of the sun].

그래서 개기 일식대로부터 떨어진 곳에서 볼 때 유일한 손해는 완전한 고리를 볼 수 없다는 것과 대칭으로 나타나지 않는다는 것이지만 여전히 해의 부분 일식은 볼 수 있을 것이다.

Practice Test 5

1. **The goal** (of every character in the movie) / (is) [to **get in touch** with nature] / (via the beach).

이 영화의 모든 출연자들의 목표는 그 해변을 통해 자연과 소통을 하려는 것이다.

2. [The absolute beauty of the beach] (makes) / **the characters** (completely understand **the motivation**) / (to inhabit this island / and never leave).

해변의 완벽한 아름다움은 출연자들이 섬에 거주하며 절대로 떠나지 않는 동기를 완전히 이해하게 해준다.

Education

With **the emphasis on standardized testing**, on attempting to constantly monitor, measure, and quantifying what students learn, teachers spend more of the school day engaged in direct instruction, substantially reducing or eliminating the opportunities children have for exploring, interacting, and learning on their own. Recess in many districts has vanished from the schedule entirely. After school, parents shuttle their kids from activity to activity, depriving them of unstructured time alone or with friends. That matters, according to researchers, not just because play reduces stress and makes children more socially competent. **It** matters also because play supposedly improves working memory and self-regulation; in other words, it makes kids sharper and better behaved. Ironically, by short-changing them on play in favor of academics, we may actually be inhibiting their development.

1. **The author mentions the emphasis on standardized testing in order to**

   Ⓐ inform about its value

   Ⓑ explain why researchers want to improve academics in schools

   Ⓒ advocate the need for kids to have more time for play

   Ⓓ warn about the consequences of kids having unstructured time alone

2. **The word It in the passage refers to**

   Ⓐ depriving children of play

   Ⓑ parents shuttling their kids from activity to activity

   Ⓒ making children more socially competent

   Ⓓ reducing stress through play

3. **Directions:** Select the appropriate phrases from the answer choices and match them to the type of activity to which they relate. **This question is worth 3 points.**

Drag your answer choices to the spaces where they belong. To remove an answer choice, click on it. To review the passage, click on **View Text**.

Answer Choices	Standardized Testing
Ⓐ Inhibiting their development	•
Ⓑ Improving working memory	•
Ⓒ After school	•
Ⓓ No unstructured time alone	**Play**
Ⓔ Being proven by researchers	•
Ⓕ Reducing stress	•
Ⓖ Reduced opportunities for exploring	

다음 문장을 ① 끊어 읽기 → 직독직해 ② 명사 [구, 절]에 대괄호 ③ 동사 [구]에 동그라미 ④ 세부정보에 소괄호를 한 후 핵심정보에 화살표로 연결하시오.

1. With the emphasis on standardized testing, on attempting to constantly monitor, measure, and quantify what students learn, teachers spend more of the school day engaged in direct instruction, substantially reducing or eliminating the opportunities children have for exploring, interacting, and learning on their own.

_____

_____

_____

_____

2. Ironically, by short-changing them on play in favor of academics, we may actually be inhibiting their development.

_____

_____

Popularization of science is nothing else than an endeavor to imagine scientific ideas in such a way that everyone, especially non-scientists, can grasp the fundamental concepts and have an idea of what science in essence is. Of course, no one really knows what 'science' is, not even the scientists themselves. Philosophers trying to describe what the scientific method could be and others trying to **state** what the scientific method should be found out that there is nothing like the 'one and only' scientific approach spending a lot of time. Therefore the impossibility to give a distinct and unique definition follows. Nevertheless, the phenomenon 'science' and its results do exist. Although nobody can tell exactly what 'science' is all about, everyone should have an idea anyway. The question at stake here is whether **this** is possible and, if so, to what extent.

1. Which of the following can be concluded from the passage?

Ⓐ The popularization of science is necessary for scientists.

Ⓑ It's impossible to define exactly what science is.

Ⓒ It is possible to clearly define what science is.

Ⓓ It is not only difficult to define what science is but also unclear if it is even possible.

2. The word state in the passage is closest in meaning to

Ⓐ declare

Ⓑ research

Ⓒ exhibit publicly

Ⓓ attribute

3. The word this in the passage refers to

Ⓐ people determine what science is all about

Ⓑ everyone has an idea what science is all about

Ⓒ the phenomena science and its results do exist

Ⓓ nobody can tell what science is all about

다음 문장을 ① 끊어 읽기 → 직독직해 ② 명사 [구, 절]에 대괄호 ③ 동사 [구]에 동그라미 ④ 세부정보에 소괄호를 한 후 핵심정보에 화살표로 연결하시오.

1. Although nobody can tell exactly what 'science' is all about, everyone should have an idea anyway.

_____

_____

2. Popularization of science is nothing else than an endeavor to image scientific ideas in such a way that everyone, especially non-scientists, can grasp the fundamental concepts and have an idea of what science in essence is.

_____

_____

_____

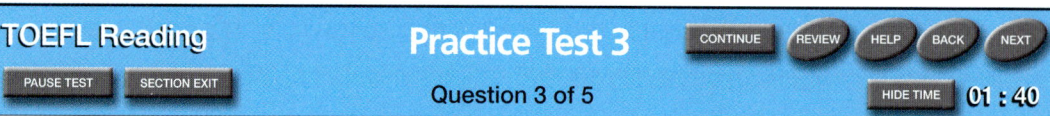

Obesity rates among children have nearly tripled in the last 30 years, prompting the American Medical Association to support legislation that would require obesity education in American schools. Classes that teach the causes of obesity, as well as the associated health risks involved, would begin for students in first grade and continue all the way until 12th grade. Prevention techniques would also be part of the curriculum and include tips on maintaining a healthy diet, exercise and staying active. Doctors would be encouraged to volunteer their time to teach these courses, according to the AMA. For schools already offering health education classes, the classes on obesity could simply be a new component of what they are already doing. The AMA has also adopted a policy that supports the taxation of sugar-sweetened beverages. The tax revenue would be used to fund obesity education for consumers.

1. Which of the sentences below best expresses the essential information in the highlighted sentence in the passage? Incorrect choices change the meaning in important ways or leave out essential information.

    (A) Doctors have decided to do whatever they can to deal with this issue.

    (B) Obesity rates will continue to rise in America unless the AMA treats obesity.

    (C) Doctors believe that education can help solve the problem of obesity.

    (D) Doctors are responsible for the increase in the obesity rate.

2. According to the passage, which of the following is true of the classes on obesity?

    (A) They will focus on the 30% of children who are obese.

    (B) They will become a part of the school curriculum.

    (C) Doctors have questioned whether they will be effective.

    (E) The current health education classes already cover much of the content of the proposed courses.

3. **Directions:** An introductory sentence for a brief summary of the passage is provided below. Complete the summary by selecting the THREE answer choices that express the most important ideas in the passage. Some sentences do not belong in the summary because they express ideas that are not presented in the passage or are minor ideas in the passage. **This question is worth 2 points**.

Drag your answer choices to the spaces where they belong. To remove an answer choice, click on it. To review the passage, click on **View Text**.

TOEFL Reading

PAUSE TEST   SECTION EXIT

Practice Test 3

Question 3 of 5

CONTINUE   REVIEW   HELP   BACK   NEXT

HIDE TIME

Concern about rising obesity levels has prompted efforts to make obesity education required in all schools.

-
-
-

Answer Choices

Ⓐ Obesity classes will be a component of the current health education curriculum.

Ⓑ Taxation of sugar-sweetened beverages will help to fund the new programs.

Ⓒ Information about the causes and the associated health risks will be included.

Ⓓ Legislation to make obesity education required is needed to overcome this problem.

Ⓔ It is hoped that doctors will take an active role in this education initiative.

Ⓕ Courses will include tips on prevention techniques, how to maintain a healthy diet, exercise and staying active.

다음 문장을 ① 끊어 읽기 → 직독직해 ② 명사 [구, 절]에 대괄호 ③ 동사 [구]에 동그라미 ④ 세부정보에 소괄호를 한 후 핵심정보에 화살표로 연결하시오.

1. Obesity rates among children have nearly tripled in the last 30 years, prompting the American Medical Association to support legislation that would require obesity education in American schools.

---

2. Classes that teach the causes of obesity, as well as the associated health risks involved, would begin for students in first grade and continue all the way until 12th grade.

Humans are complex beings. They adapt, learn, have intelligence and free will, can reason, feel emotions, and have a conscience. Although such qualities and attributes raise humans above the rest of other life forms, it is questionable as to where the idea of a conscience and emotions come from. Ⓐ ■ What exactly is it that stimulates our responses to certain situations and problems? The answer lies in human nature. What we as humans feel is right or wrong is somehow dictated by something beyond merely the individual. Ⓑ ■ In more specific terms, the question is whether or not our morality and our adherence to a moral code is something fixed and constant throughout humanity itself. **Francis Bacon stated that nature must first be obeyed before it can be put to use, and the same concept applies to humans**. Ⓒ ■ Before any judgment can be made about people, groups, ideas, or beliefs, one must first have a standard to compare this behavior to. Ⓓ ■ If there is no real Law of Nature, then no standard is set, and one thing cannot be compared to another because the standard is only set by opinion, not by fact. In reality, the Law of Nature is a reality which is independent of man-made ideas, although the way in which humans think is definitely influenced by the environment.

1. **Look at the four squares [■] that indicate where the following sentence could be added to the passage.**

The underlying question, therefore, becomes what that outside influence is: nature, our inherent human qualities themselves, or some man-made composite of other people and experiences?

Where would the sentence best fit?
Click on a square [■] to add the sentence to the passage.

2. **What does the author imply about nature in the highlighted sentence in the passage?**
   Ⓐ Humans are slaves to nature.
   Ⓑ Humans cannot ignore their own nature.
   Ⓒ Humans cannot act appropriately if they don't follow nature.
   Ⓓ Most people are unable to obey nature.

3. **Directions:** Select the appropriate phrases from the answer choices and match them to the Law of Nature to which they relate. **This question is worth 3 points.**

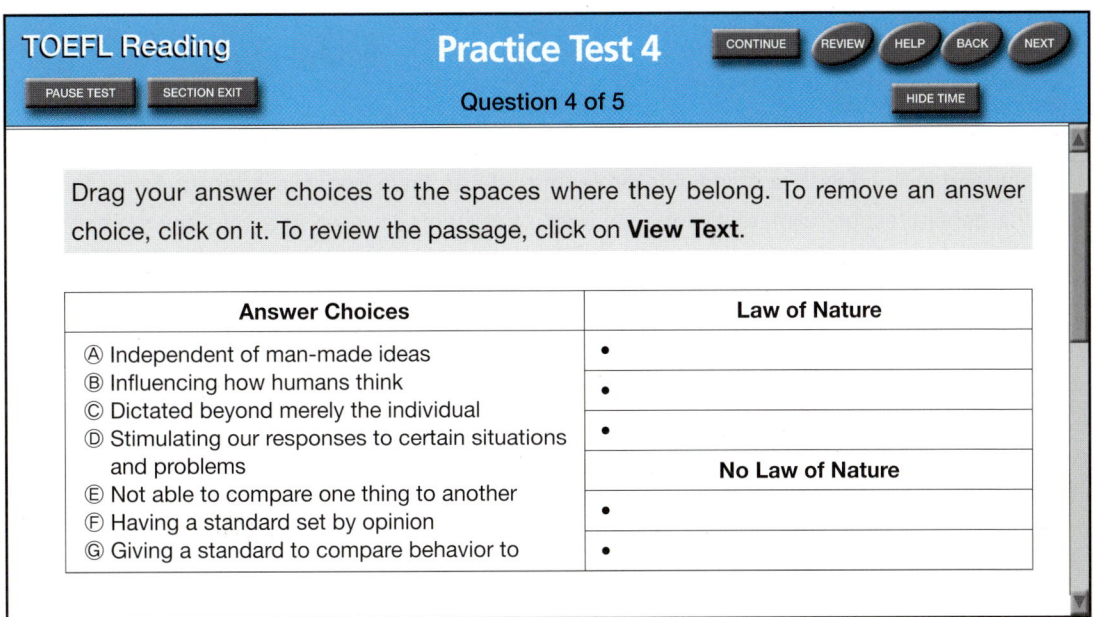

Drag your answer choices to the spaces where they belong. To remove an answer choice, click on it. To review the passage, click on **View Text**.

Answer Choices	Law of Nature
Ⓐ Independent of man-made ideas	•
Ⓑ Influencing how humans think	•
Ⓒ Dictated beyond merely the individual	•
Ⓓ Stimulating our responses to certain situations and problems	
	No Law of Nature
Ⓔ Not able to compare one thing to another	•
Ⓕ Having a standard set by opinion	•
Ⓖ Giving a standard to compare behavior to	

다음 문장을 ① 끊어 읽기 → 직독직해 ② 명사 [구, 절]에 대괄호 ③ 동사 [구]에 동그라미 ④ 세부정보에 소괄호를 한 후 핵심정보에 화살표로 연결하시오.

1. What we as humans feel is right or wrong is somehow dictated by something beyond merely the individual.

_____

_____

2. Francis Bacon stated that nature must first be obeyed before it can be put to use, and the same concept applies to humans.

_____

_____

3. In reality, the Law of Nature is a reality which is independent of man-made ideas, although the way in which humans think is definitely influenced by the environment.

_____

_____

Bullying in schools is a worldwide problem that can have negative consequences for the general school climate and for the right of students to learn in a safe environment without fear. **Bullying can also have negative lifelong effects on both the students who bully and their victims**. Bullying involves direct behavior such as teasing, taunting, threatening, hitting, and stealing that are initiated by one or more students against a victim. In addition to direct attacks, bullying may also be more indirect by causing a student to be socially isolated through intentional exclusion. While boys typically engage in direct attacks, girls who bully are more apt to use subtle indirect strategies, such as spreading rumors and enforcing social isolation. Whether the bullying is direct or indirect, the key component of bullying is that the intimidation happens repeatedly over time to create a pattern of harassment and abuse.

1. The author explains indirect bullying in the passage by

   Ⓐ describing how bullying by girls is different from that by boys
   Ⓑ explaining the effects of bullying
   Ⓒ giving evidence for different forms of bullying
   Ⓓ listing examples of bullying by one or more students

2. Which of the sentences below best expresses the essential information in the highlighted sentence in the passage? Incorrect choices change the meaning in important ways or leave out essential information.

   Ⓐ Bullies scar their victims for life.
   Ⓑ There may be long-term detrimental consequences of bullying for both parties.
   Ⓒ No one is safe from being bullied.
   Ⓓ Once a bully, always a bully.

3. Directions: An introductory sentence for a brief summary of the passage is provided below. Complete the summary by selecting the THREE answer choices that express the most important ideas in the passage. Some sentences do not belong in the summary because they express ideas that are not presented in the passage or are minor ideas in the passage. **This question is worth 2 points**.

Drag your answer choices to the spaces where they belong. To remove an answer choice, click on it. To review the passage, click on **View Text**.

TOEFL Reading

PAUSE TEST   SECTION EXIT

Practice Test 5

Question 5 of 5

CONTINUE   REVIEW   HELP   BACK   NEXT

HIDE TIME

The key point is that bullying occurs repeatedly over time.

-
-
-

Answer Choices

Ⓐ Bullying involves both direct and indirect behavior.

Ⓑ Its repetition is the most significant aspect of bullying.

Ⓒ Bullying by boys is more devastating than by girls.

Ⓓ Bullying usually shows a pattern of abuse.

Ⓔ Bullying can have negative lifelong effects.

Ⓕ Harassment has been planned and made.

다음 문장을 ① 끊어 읽기 → 직독직해 ② 명사 [구, 절]에 대괄호 ③ 동사 [구]에 동그라미 ④ 세부정보에 소괄호를 한 후 핵심정보에 화살표로 연결하시오.

1. Bullying in schools is a worldwide problem that can have negative consequences for the general school climate and for the right of students to learn in a safe environment without fear.

_____

_____

_____

2. Bullying involves direct behavior such as teasing, taunting, threatening, hitting, and stealing that are initiated by one or more students against a victim.

_____

_____

Vocabulary & Paraphrasing

1. Write the word from the box that matches each meaning below.

recess	revenue	adherence	obesity	vanish
fundamental	competent	prompt	morality	grasp

① temporary withdrawal   _____

② properly qualified   _____

③ hold firmly   _____

④ being an essential part of   _____

⑤ to move or induce to action   _____

⑥ the belief that some behaviour is right   _____

⑦ to disappear from sight quickly   _____

⑧ the income of a government from duties   _____

⑨ steady devotion or support   _____

⑩ the condition of being very fat   _____

Vocabulary & Paraphrasing

2. Translate the following questions into Korean and then paraphrase them according to the directions below.

① With the emphasis on standardized testing, on attempting to constantly monitor, measure, and quantifying what students learn, teachers spend more of the school day engaged in direct instruction, substantially reducing or eliminating the opportunities children have for exploring, interacting, and learning on their own. ➡ 관계대명사, 분사구문 바꿔 쓰기

_____

_____

_____

_____

② Popularization of science is nothing else than an endeavor to image scientific ideas in such a way that everyone, especially non-scientists, can grasp the fundamental concepts and have an idea of what science in essence is. ➡ 비교구문 바꿔 쓰기

_____

_____

_____

③ Classes that teach the causes of obesity, as well as the associated health risks involved, would begin for students in first grade and continue all the way until 12th grade. ➡ 주어 바꿔 쓰기

_____

_____

Practice Test 1

1. With **the emphasis** (on standardized testing,) / on attempting to constantly monitor, measure, and quantify [what students learn,] / teachers (spend) more of the school day / (engaged in direct instruction,) / (substantially reducing or eliminating the **opportunities**)(children have) / (for exploring, interacting, and learning on their own).

선생님들은 표준에 맞는 테스트에 중점을 두면서 학생들이 무엇을 배우는지 끊임없이 관찰하고 측정하며, 학생들이 배운 것을 수치화하고, 아이들이 탐험하고 상호작용하며 그들 스스로 배우는 기회를 많이 줄이거나 없애는 데 직접 지도 관여하며 학교에서 하루에 더 많은 시간을 보낸다.

2. Ironically, / by [**short-changing** them on play (in favor of academics),] / we (may actually be inhibiting) their development.

얄궂게도 학업에 편중하여 아이들을 놀지 못하게 하고 부당하게 다룸으로써 우리는 사실 그들의 발전을 억제하고 있는지 모른다.

Practice Test 2

1. Although nobody can tell / exactly [what 'science' is all about,] / everyone (should have) an idea anyway.

비록 아무도 '과학'이 정확하게 무엇에 관한 것인지 말할 수는 없지만 여하튼 모두들 어떤 것인지 알고 있어야 한다.

2. Popularization of science / (is) nothing else than **an endeavor** / (to image scientific ideas in such a way) / (that everyone, especially non-scientists, can grasp the fundamental concepts / and have an idea of / [what science in essence is]).

과학의 대중화란 단지 모든 사람들 특히 비과학자들이 기본 개념을 파악하고 과학이 본질적으로 무엇인지에 대한 생각을 갖게 하는 방식으로 과학적 생각을 이미지화하려는 노력에 불과하다.

Practice Test 3

1. [Obesity rates among children] / (have nearly tripled) in the last 30 years, / prompting the American Medical Association / to support **legislation** / (that would require / obesity education in American schools).

아동 비만율이 지난 30년간 거의 3배로 증가하게 되자 미국 의학 협회는 미국 내 학교에서 비만 교육을 필요로 하는 입법안을 지지하게 되었다.

2. **Classes** (that teach the causes of obesity,) / as well as [the associated health risks involved,] (would) (begin) for students in first grade / and (continue) all the way until 12th grade.

비만과 관련된 건강상의 위험뿐 아니라 비만의 원인을 가르치는 수업이 1학년을 대상으로 시작하여 12학년까지 계속될 것으로 보인다.

Practice Test 4

1. [What we (as humans) feel is right or wrong] / (is somehow dictated) (by **something**) / (beyond merely the individual).

인간으로서 우리가 옳고 그르다고 느끼는 것은 어떻게든 단순히 개개인을 뛰어넘는 그 무엇인가에 의해 좌우된다.

2. Francis Bacon (stated) / [that nature **must first be obeyed** / (before it can be put to use),] / and the same concept (applies to) humans.

프랜시스 베이컨은 자연을 지휘하려면 먼저 자연에 순응해야 한다고 말했고 그 같은 원리는 인간에게도 적용된다.

3. In reality, / [the Law of Nature] (is) **a reality** / (which is independent of man-made ideas,) / although **the way** (in which humans think) / **is definitely influenced** (by the environment).

비록 인간이 생각하는 방식은 분명히 환경의 영향을 받지만 실제로 자연의 법칙은 인간이 만들어낸 생각에서 독립적인 현실이다.

Practice Test 5

1. [Bullying in schools] is a worldwide **problem** / (that can have negative **consequences**) / (for the general school climate) / and (for **the right** of students) / (to learn in a safe environment / without fear).

학교에서의 왕따는 학교 전체적인 분위기와 학생들이 두려움 없는 안전한 환경에서 배울 수 있는 권리를 해할 수 있는 전 세계적인 문제이다.

2. Bullying (involves) direct **behavior** / (such as teasing, / taunting, / threatening, / hitting, and stealing) / (that **are initiated** by one or more students) / (against a victim).

왕따는 괴롭힘을 당하는 학생을 대상으로 한 명이나 그 이상의 학생들이 시작하는 놀리기, 비아냥거리기, 협박하기, 때리기 그리고 훔치기 같은 직접적인 행동들을 포함한다.

Culture

TOEFL Reading

Practice Test 1

CONTINUE   REVIEW   HELP   BACK   NEXT

PAUSE TEST   SECTION EXIT

Question 1 of 5

HIDE TIME   01 : 40

At the head of the divine hierarchy was Zeus, the spiritual father of gods and men. His wife was Hera, queen of heaven and guardian of the sanctity of marriage. Associated with them as the chief divinities of heaven were Hephaestus, god of fire and the patron of metalworkers; Athena, the virgin goddess of wisdom and war, preeminent as a civic goddess; Apollo, deity of light, poetry, and music, and his sister Artemis, goddess of wildlife and, later, of the moon; Ares, god of war, and his consort, Aphrodite, goddess of love; Hermes, the divine messenger, later, god of science and invention; and Hestia, goddess of the hearth and home. **Around these greater gods and goddesses were grouped a host of lesser deities, some of whom enjoyed a particular distinction in certain localities.** Among them were Helios, the sun; Selene, the moon (before Artemis came into existence); the attendants of the Olympians, such as the Graces; the Muses; Iris, goddess of the rainbow; Hebe, goddess of youth and cupbearer of the gods; and Ganymede, the male counterpart of Hebe. Poseidon, the worship of whom was often accompanied by worship of his wife, Amphitrite, ruled the sea. The Nereids, Tritons, and other minor sea deities were attending **them**.

1. **Which of the following is NOT true about the gods?**

   Ⓐ There were many less important gods.
   Ⓑ Apollo was one of the greater gods.
   Ⓒ Nereids were not minor deities.
   Ⓓ There were goddesses among the greater gods.

2. **Which of the sentences below best expresses the essential information in the highlighted sentence in the passage? Incorrect choices change the meaning in important ways or leave out essential information.**

   Ⓐ Another level of lower-ranking gods ruled over each of the elements.
   Ⓑ Other junior gods were assigned their own region of influence.
   Ⓒ Other gods and goddesses had different areas of specialization.
   Ⓓ Within certain regions, other gods achieved great distinction.

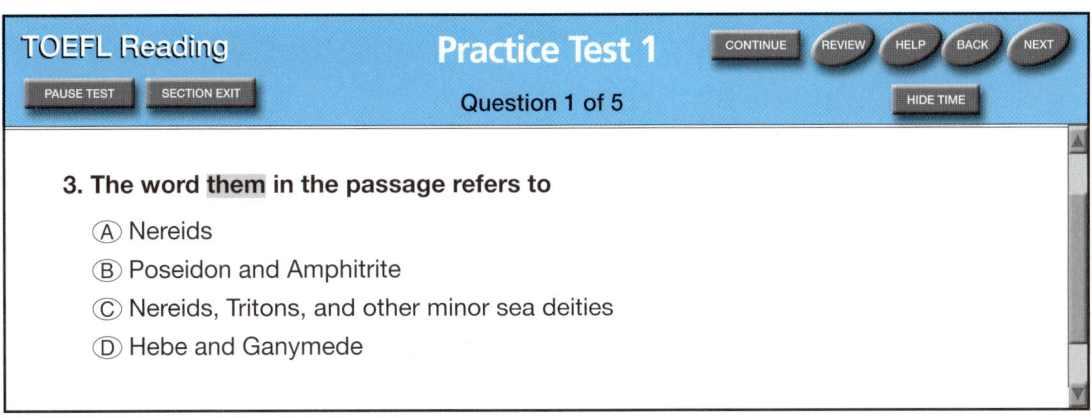

3. The word them in the passage refers to

Ⓐ Nereids

Ⓑ Poseidon and Amphitrite

Ⓒ Nereids, Tritons, and other minor sea deities

Ⓓ Hebe and Ganymede

다음 문장을 ① 끊어 읽기 → 직독직해 ② 명사 [구, 절]에 대괄호 ③ 동사 [구]에 동그라미 ④ 세부정보에 소괄호를 한 후 핵심정보에 화살표로 연결하시오.

1. Around these greater gods and goddesses were grouped a host of lesser deities, some of whom enjoyed particular distinction in certain localities.

_____

_____

2. Associated with them as the chief divinities of heaven were Hephaestus, god of fire and the patron of metalworkers; Athena, the virgin goddess of wisdom and war, preeminent as a civic goddess; Apollo, deity of light, poetry, and music, and his sister Artemis, goddess of wildlife and, later, of the moon; Ares, god of war, and his consort, Aphrodite, goddess of love; Hermes, the divine messenger, later, god of science and invention; and Hestia, goddess of the hearth and home.

_____

_____

_____

_____

_____

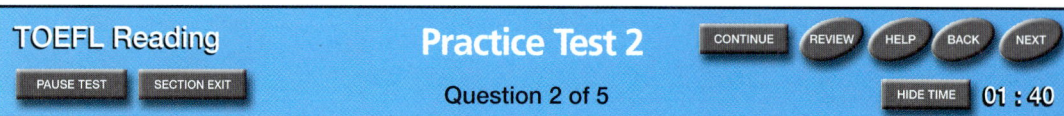

The first time I ever flew into JFK was during a flight back to NYC from Los Angeles. I hadn't gone to bed until the sun came up earlier that day, was running on just a couple of hours' sleep, and I was ready to get home and collapse onto my bed. So when faced with the decision to wait in the long taxi line or take up some guy on his car service option, my foggy brain decided the latter was a sound decision. I followed the guy to his "taxi" which was a rusty old pick-up truck, but thankfully had enough sense to stop, say "Absolutely not," and turn back around to deal with the line for a legit cab. Of course, now I know never to agree to an overzealous car service offer at the airport. Not only is it illegal, but it could very well be a scam. City cabs have a strict payment policy that can't be **fudged**. The illegal drivers just pull a number out of the air. My reason for telling this story which makes me look like a novice traveler is as a reminder to be aware of the many scams travelers can be presented with while on the road.

1. According to the passage, the writer initially decided to take the car service because

   (A) he wanted to go in a pick-up truck

   (B) he was tired and not thinking clearly

   (C) he thought it could be a scam

   (D) he thought it would be legal to take the car service

2. The word fudged in the passage is closest in meaning to

   (A) annoyed

   (B) randomly decided

   (C) aggressively chosen

   (D) faked

3. Directions: An introductory sentence for a brief summary of the passage is provided below. Complete the summary by selecting the THREE answer choices that express the most important ideas in the passage. Some sentences do not belong in the summary because they express ideas that are not presented in the passage or are minor ideas in the passage. **This question is worth 2 points**.

Drag your answer choices to the spaces where they belong. To remove an answer choice, click on it. To review the passage, click on **View Text**.

TOEFL Reading

PAUSE TEST   SECTION EXIT

Practice Test 2
Question 2 of 5

CONTINUE   REVIEW   HELP   BACK   NEXT

HIDE TIME

An overzealous car service offer at the airport should be a warning.

-
-
-

Answer Choices

Ⓐ There are many scams that can trick unwitting travelers.

Ⓑ The pick-up truck alerted him to the danger.

Ⓒ Even if waiting for a taxi was going to take a long time, they don't fudge the numbers.

Ⓓ Because his brain was foggy, the car service seemed like a good option.

Ⓔ Something that is illegal is a sign of a possible problem.

Ⓕ It's better to wait in line for a legitimate taxi.

다음 문장을 ① 끊어 읽기 → 직독직해 ② 명사 [구, 절]에 대괄호 ③ 동사 [구]에 동그라미 ④ 세부정보에 소괄호를 한 후 핵심정보에 화살표로 연결하시오.

1. I followed the guy to his "taxi" which was a rusty old pick-up truck, but thankfully had enough sense to stop, say "Absolutely not," and turn back around to deal with the line for a legit cab.

_____

_____

_____

2. My reason for telling this story which makes me look like a novice traveler is as a reminder to be aware of the many scams travelers can be presented with while on the road.

_____

_____

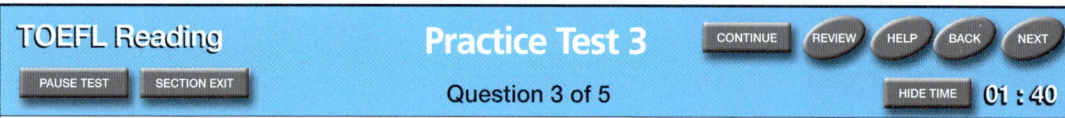

It's the state of Florida that has the greatest number of congested beaches in the US with two coastlines which offer seemingly endless stretches of sand, from Miami's party scene to secluded Caladesi Island. But it's California that is famous for surfing culture which claims the unquestionable honor of America's No.1 most crowded beach: Venice Beach, to be precise, which swarms with 16 million sunbathers, fortune-tellers, street performers, and people-watchers. Arriving at that estimate isn't an exact science as beach crowds are fluid and dynamic. To crunch the numbers, we relied on the United States Life saving Association which keeps attendance statistics for more than 200 beaches. When unavailable, we turned to government organizations like the New York City Parks Department. Not only did Coney Island make our list with 11 million annual visitors, but so did Rockaway Beach, along time destination for city-dwelling surfers that's recently become a hipster favorite. It's worth braving the crowds both on the sand and in line at the Rockaway Taco food truck. **Though not everyone may be convinced.** Once New York and other local authorities have the stats, they might like to boast about how many visitors their beaches receive. But if they proclaim those numbers too loudly, they might scare people away. As the great Yogi Berra put it, "Nobody goes there anymore, it's too crowded." If you do follow the wisdom of crowds, try to time it right by skipping the weekends or going early in the morning — so that you can appreciate the combination of natural beauty and boardwalk amusements that made these beaches popular in the first place. And if you just can't **take** the crowds, seek out one of the world's secret beaches instead.

1. What can be inferred from the highlighted statement?

Ⓐ Some people would prefer to go to a less crowded beach.

Ⓑ Some people don't believe the numbers from the New York City Parks Department.

Ⓒ The Rockaway Taco food truck isn't as great as they suggest.

Ⓓ You can only enjoy the beach if you go early in the morning or on weekdays.

2. The word take in the passage is closest in meaning to

Ⓐ choose   Ⓑ obtain   Ⓒ accept   Ⓓ tolerate

3. Directions: Select the appropriate phrases from the answer choices and match them to the response to the place to which they relate. Two of the answer choices will NOT be used. **This question is worth 3 points**.

TOEFL Reading

PAUSE TEST   SECTION EXIT

Practice Test 3

Question 3 of 5

CONTINUE   REVIEW   HELP   BACK   NEXT

HIDE TIME

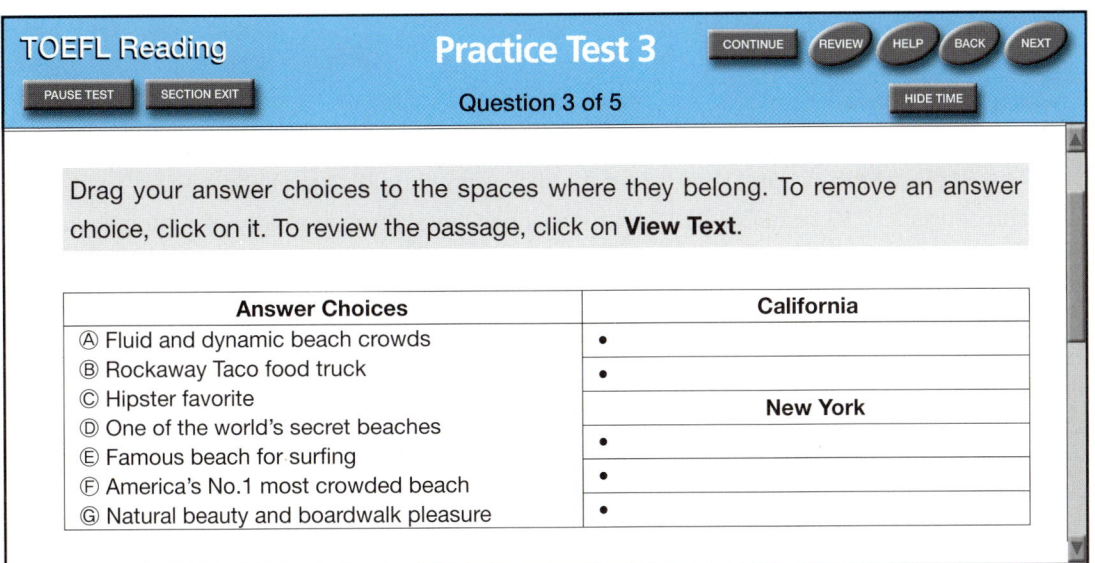

Drag your answer choices to the spaces where they belong. To remove an answer choice, click on it. To review the passage, click on **View Text**.

Answer Choices	California
Ⓐ Fluid and dynamic beach crowds	•
Ⓑ Rockaway Taco food truck	•
Ⓒ Hipster favorite	**New York**
Ⓓ One of the world's secret beaches	•
Ⓔ Famous beach for surfing	•
Ⓕ America's No.1 most crowded beach	•
Ⓖ Natural beauty and boardwalk pleasure	

다음 문장을 ① 끊어 읽기 → 직독직해 ② 명사 [구, 절]에 대괄호 ③ 동사 [구]에 동그라미 ④ 세부정보에 소괄호를 한 후 핵심정보에 화살표로 연결하시오.

1. It's the state of Florida that has the greatest number of congested beaches in the US with two coastlines which offer seemingly endless stretches of sand, from Miami's party scene to secluded Caladesi Island.

_____

_____

_____

2. But it's California that is famous for surfing culture which claims the unquestionable honor of America's No.1 most crowded beach: Venice Beach, to be precise, which swarms with 16million sunbathers, fortune-tellers, street performers, and people-watchers.

_____

_____

_____

TOEFL Reading

PAUSE TEST   SECTION EXIT

Practice Test 4

Question 4 of 5

CONTINUE   REVIEW   HELP   BACK   NEXT

HIDE TIME   01 : 40

The Shared Path project weaves for 10 kilometers through the Humber River Valley and consists of 13 historical nodes that describe Canada's early history as it happened along the banks of the Humber River. Ⓐ ■ Cultural heritage and Humber River history recognize the historic presence of First Nations on the Humber, who were later followed by the French and the British. La Societe d'histoire de Toronto initiated the project undertaken in partnership with Toronto and Region Conservation Authority (TRCA) and the City of Toronto. Ⓑ ■ Last month, more than 100 people gathered on the east bank of the Humber River in Etienne Brule Park for the official unveiling of the First Nations' Shared Path. Ⓒ ■ Plaques include text written in First Nations' languages. **The project dealt with concerns around recognition that these people were there, too; recognizing that there were three founding nations on the Humber River – First Nations, French and English settlers.** Ⓓ ■ First Nations' people have had their spaces lost and taken over by earlier settlers. This project is in a public park and the entire trail is accessible. Anyone can go there. Toronto's newest Discovery Walk honors the extensive history of First Nations on the Humber River.

1. **Why does the author write about The Shared Path project in the passage?**

   Ⓐ To recognize the cultural heritage of the First Nations of Canada
   Ⓑ To urge Canadians to acknowledge the heritage of the three founding nations of Canada
   Ⓒ To condemn the fact that First Nations' people have had their spaces taken over by earlier settlers
   Ⓓ To celebrate a major historical development

2. **What can be inferred from the highlighted statement?**

   Ⓐ The ruins of First Nations as well as French and English settlers were found along the Humber River.
   Ⓑ The Humber River was an important part of Canada's early history.
   Ⓒ There were many wars in the Humber river region amongst the three founding nations.
   Ⓓ The place of the First Nations has not been adequately acknowledged in Canadian history.

TOEFL Reading

PAUSE TEST   SECTION EXIT

Practice Test 4

Question 4 of 5

CONTINUE   REVIEW   HELP   BACK   NEXT

HIDE TIME

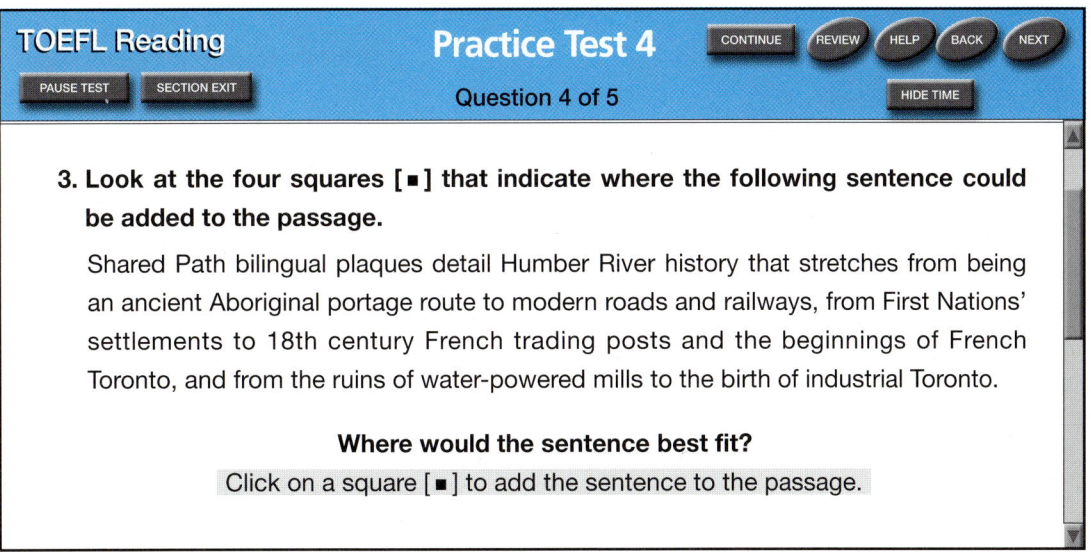

3. Look at the four squares [■] that indicate where the following sentence could be added to the passage.

Shared Path bilingual plaques detail Humber River history that stretches from being an ancient Aboriginal portage route to modern roads and railways, from First Nations' settlements to 18th century French trading posts and the beginnings of French Toronto, and from the ruins of water-powered mills to the birth of industrial Toronto.

Where would the sentence best fit?

Click on a square [■] to add the sentence to the passage.

다음 문장을 ① 끊어 읽기 → 직독직해 ② 명사 [구, 절]에 대괄호 ③ 동사 [구]에 동그라미 ④ 세부정보에 소괄호를 한 후 핵심정보에 화살표로 연결하시오.

1. The Shared Path project weaves for 10 kilometers through the Humber River Valley and consists of 13 historical nodes that describe Canada's early history as it happened along the banks of the Humber River.

2. First Nations' people have had their spaces lost and taken over by earlier settlers.

3. La Societe d'histoire de Toronto initiated the project undertaken in partnership with Toronto and Region Conservation Authority (TRCA) and the City of Toronto.

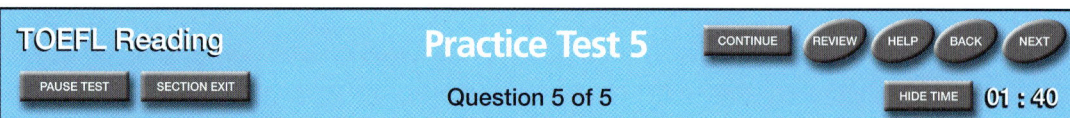

TOEFL Reading
PAUSE TEST   SECTION EXIT

Practice Test 5

CONTINUE   REVIEW   HELP   BACK   NEXT

Question 5 of 5

HIDE TIME   01 : 40

It's true that everyone comes to Paris to eat, and that can be equally inspiring and exhilarating. The complex rituals of the marketplace, the multiple facets of wine (and determining where best to drink it), how to know a place is good even if you've never heard of it — it takes time to **crack such codes**. A guide will help you do just that, while showing you the often secret haunts that you may not discover otherwise. Lyn has just spent the past few hours leading me around the Left Bank, sampling everything from lemon-curd pastry to donkey-meat salami as we go. Now we're about to finish the official tour portion of the day over some Japanese-style fried chicken and a glass of 2010 Morgon, the very first magnum of which the manager has held aside for Lyn. I love it here, and I want to help people experience the city like I do. To that end, Lyn offers a small number of private food tours for up to four people, all of which are full of tips based on the quirks of Parisian traditions and focused on food-centric neighborhoods such as Les Halles and St.-Germain. Here, she shares her little black book, from earthy bistros and category-defying markets to shops loaded with goods that you can't get anywhere but here. Paris at your fingertips? Look no further.

1. The phrase crack such codes in the passage is closest in meaning to

   (A) strike them out   (B) break them out

   (C) make them out   (D) translate them

2. In the passage, the author explains Lyn's role by saying that

   (A) she can show you great places to eat in Paris

   (B) the markets in Paris are frightening for people who go without her

   (C) it is impossible to eat in Paris without Lyn's guided tour

   (D) she has many shops loaded with goods

3. Directions: Select the appropriate phrases from the answer choices and match them to the tour style to which they relate. Two of the answer choices will NOT be used. **This question is worth 3 points**.

Drag your answer choices to the spaces where they belong. To remove an answer choice, click on it. To review the passage, click on **View Text**.

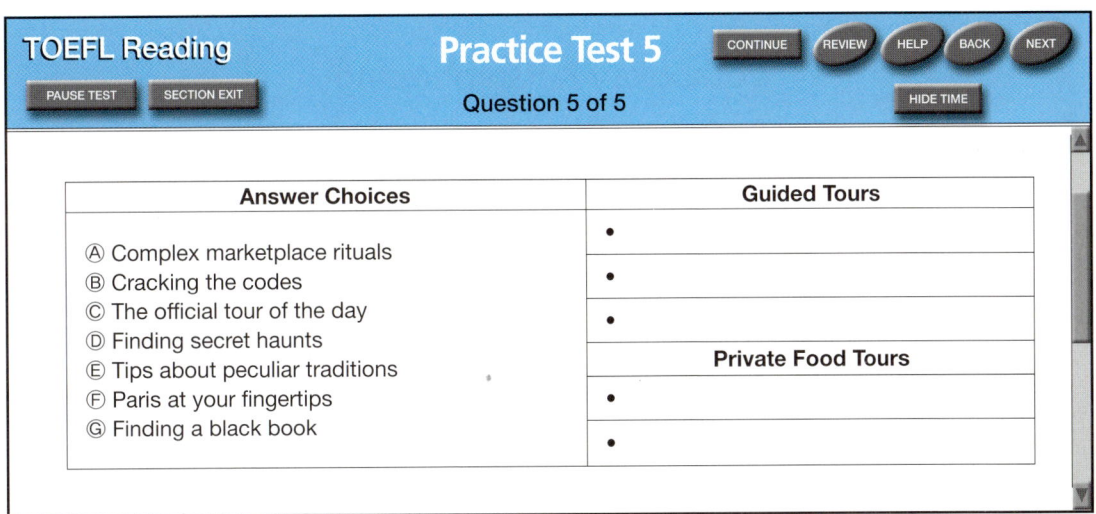

Answer Choices	Guided Tours
Ⓐ Complex marketplace rituals	•
Ⓑ Cracking the codes	•
Ⓒ The official tour of the day	•
Ⓓ Finding secret haunts	**Private Food Tours**
Ⓔ Tips about peculiar traditions	•
Ⓕ Paris at your fingertips	•
Ⓖ Finding a black book	

다음 문장을 ① 끊어 읽기 → 직독직해 ② 명사 [구, 절]에 대괄호 ③ 동사 [구]에 동그라미 ④ 세부정보에 소괄호를 한 후 핵심정보에 화살표로 연결하시오.

1. Now we're about to finish the official tour portion of the day over some Japanese-style fried chicken and a glass of 2010 Morgon, the very first magnum of which the manager has held aside for Lyn.

_____

_____

_____

2. Here, she shares her little black book, from earthy bistros and category-defying markets to shops loaded with goods that you can't get anywhere but here.

_____

_____

Vocabulary & Paraphrasing

1. Write the word from the box that matches each meaning below.

weave	deity	boardwalk	consort	swarm
plaque	novice	scam	congest	divine

① of or pertaining to a god _____

② a god or goddess _____

③ a husband or wife _____

④ to cheat by means of a trick _____

⑤ a person who is new to the work _____

⑥ to fill to excess _____

⑦ to move along in great numbers _____

⑧ any walk made of boards _____

⑨ to form by interlacing _____

⑩ a thin, flat plate or tablet _____

Vocabulary & Paraphrasing

2. Translate the following questions into Korean and then paraphrase them according to the directions below.

① Around these greater gods and goddesses were grouped a host of lesser deities, some of whom enjoyed a particular distinction in certain localities.
→ 도치구문, 쉬운 단어로 바꿔 쓰기

_____

_____

② I followed the guy to his "taxi" which was a rusty old pick-up truck, but thankfully had enough sense to stop, say "Absolutely not," and turn back around to deal with the line for a legit cab. → 분사구문 바꿔 쓰기

_____

_____

③ It's the state of Florida that has the greatest number of congested beaches in the US with two coastlines which offer seemingly endless stretches of sand, from Miami's party scene to secluded Caladesi Island. → 강조, 도치구문 바꿔 쓰기

_____

_____

_____

④ Shared Path bilingual plaques detail Humber River history that stretches from being an ancient Aboriginal portage route to modern roads and railways, from First Nations' settlements to 18th century French trading posts and the beginnings of French Toronto, and from the ruins of water-powered mills to the birth of industrial Toronto.
→ 관계대명사, 쉬운 말로 바꿔 쓰기

_____

_____

_____

Practice Test 1

1. Around these greater gods and goddesses / were grouped [a host of lesser deities,] / some of whom enjoyed a particular distinction / (in certain localities).

이런 위대한 신과 여신들 주위에는 하위 신들이 모여 있었으며 그중 몇몇은 정해진 위치에서 특정한 명성을 누렸다.

2. Associated with them / (as the chief divinities of heaven) were / [Hephaestus, god of fire and the patron of metalworkers; / Athena, the virgin goddess of wisdom and war, / preeminent (as a civic goddess;) / Apollo, deity of light, poetry, and music, / and his sister Artemis, goddess of wildlife / and, later, of the moon; / Ares, god of war, / and his consort, Aphrodite, / goddess of love; / Hermes, the divine messenger, / later, god of science and invention; / and Hestia, goddess of the hearth and home].

하늘의 최고 신들로서 이들과 관련된 불과 금속공의 후원자인 헤파이스토스, 지혜와 전쟁의 처녀 여신이며 도시의 여신으로서 뛰어난 아테나, 빛, 시 그리고 음악의 신인 아폴로, 그의 여동생이며 야생의 신으로 후에 달의 여신이 된 아르테미스, 전쟁의 신인 아레스, 그의 배우자이며 사랑의 여신인 아프로디테, 신성한 메신저이며 후에 과학과 발명의 신이 된 헤르메스, 건강과 가정의 여신인 헤스티아가 있었다.

Practice Test 2

1. I followed the guy to his "taxi" / (which was a rusty old pick-up truck,) / but thankfully had enough sense / (to stop, say "Absolutely not," and turn back around) / (to deal with the line for a legit cab).

나는 그 남자를 따라 낡고 녹이 슨 픽업 트럭인 그의 '택시'로 갔다. 그러나 고맙게도 멈추고 '절대 안 돼'라고 말하고 합법적인 택시를 타는 행렬로 다시 돌아갈 정도로 정신이 들었다.

2. [My reason for telling this story] / (which makes me look like a novice traveler) / is as a reminder / (to be aware of the many scams) (travelers can be presented with) / (while on the road).

내가 마치 초보 여행자같이 보일 수도 있는 이런 이야기를 하는 이유는 여행 중에 여행객들에게 다가오는 사기꾼들이 많다는 것을 알려 주고자 하는 것이다.

Practice Test 3

1. It's the state of Florida / (that has the greatest number of congested beaches in the US) / with two coastlines (which offer seemingly endless stretches of sand,) (from Miami's party scene to secluded Caladesi Island).

두 개의 해안을 따라 마이애미 파티 장면에서 저 멀리 한적한 캘러데시 섬까지 끊임없이 펼쳐져 있는 모래사장이 있고 많은 사람들이 모이는 혼잡한 해변을 미국에서 가장 많이 갖고 있는 주는 바로 플로리다이다.

2. But it's California / (that is famous for surfing culture) / (which claims the unquestionable honor) / (of America's No.1 most crowded beach: Venice Beach,) / to be precise, / (which swarms with [16million sunbathers, fortune-tellers, street performers, and people-watchers]).

하지만 파도타기 문화로 유명하고 미국 사람들이 가장 많이 찾는 제1의 해변은 캘리포니아이다. 더 정확히 말하면 1,600만 명의 일광욕을 즐기는 사람들, 점을 보는 사람, 거리 공연가, 사람 구경을 하는 사람들로 붐비는 두말할 것 없는 명성을 보여주는 베니스 해변이다.

Practice Test 4

1. The Shared Path project weaves / for 10 kilometers (through the Humber River Valley) / and consists of 13 historical nodes / (that describe Canada's early history) / (as it happened along the banks of the Humber River).

공동 산책로 프로젝트는 험버 강 계곡을 따라 10km를 누비며 험버 강둑을 따라 캐나다 초기 역사를 발생한 대로 보여 주는 13개의 역사적인 접점으로 구성되어 있다.

2. First Nations' people have had / their spaces (lost and taken over) / (by earlier settlers).

원주민들은 자신들의 거주지를 잃고 초기 정착민들에 의해 쫓겨나게 되었다.

3. [La Societe d'histoire de Toronto] / initiated the project / (undertaken in partnership with [Toronto and Region Conservation Authority (TRCA) / and the City of Toronto]).

토론토 역사 협회(La Societe d'histoire de Toronto)는 토론토 지역보존기관(TRCA)과 토론토 시와 협력하여 착수한 프로젝트를 추진하였다.

Practice Test 5

1. Now we're about to finish / [the official tour portion of the day] / (over some Japanese-style fried chicken / and a glass of 2010 Morgon,) [the very first magnum] / (of which the manager has held aside for Lyn).

이제 우리는 일본식 닭튀김과 린을 위해 매니저가 남겨두었던 올해 첫 포도주인 모르건 2010을 한잔하며 오늘의 공식적인 관광을 막 끝내려 한다.

2. Here, / she shares [her little black book,] / from [earthy bistros and category-defying markets] / to shops (loaded with goods) / (that you can't get anywhere but here).

이제 그녀는 소박한 작은 식당과 범주에 맞춰 분류하기 힘든 시장에서부터 다른 곳이 아닌 여기서만 얻을 수 있는 물건들로 북적이는 가게들까지 있는 비밀 기록부를 함께 나눌 것이다.

Science & Technology

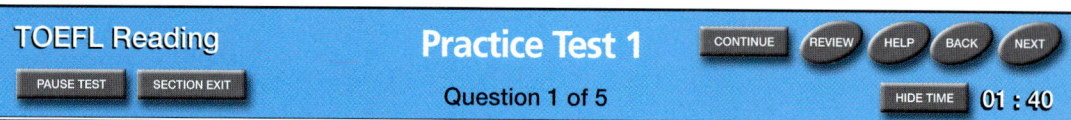
Scientists often use different species in the laboratory for research into human organ development. Zebra fish and mice have been used in this research. Both have internal organs that function in a manner similar to human organs. Genetic engineering can be used to produce zebra fish and mice that have genes which result in problems with development. Ⓐ ■ In order to analyze the genes involved in the formation of different organs, scientists would need to use thousands of mice over many years of study. Ⓑ ■ Scientists began to use zebra fish in the laboratory because they have several advantages over mice. Ⓒ ■ They develop into adults in about 90 days and produce hundreds of offspring from one mating. The embryo is transparent and develops outside the body of the female. Ⓓ ■ Scientists can actually see organs developing.

1. Which of the following is NOT true?

    Ⓐ Large numbers of mice need to be used for human organ development research.

    Ⓑ Zebra fish and mice used in the research have dominant genes.

    Ⓒ It is impractical to watch the development of organs in the mice's embryos.

    Ⓓ Zebra fish have more offspring than mice at a time.

2. Look at the four squares [■] that indicate where the following sentence could be added to the passage.

It would also be difficult to watch the development of organs in the embryos of mice since this development takes place in the mother's uterus.

Where would the sentence best fit?
Click on a square [■] to add the sentence to the passage.

3. Directions: Select the appropriate phrases from the answer choices and match them to the species to which they relate. Two of the answer choices will NOT be used. **This question is worth 3 points**.

Drag your answer choices to the spaces where they belong. To remove an answer choice, click on it. To review the passage, click on **View Text**.

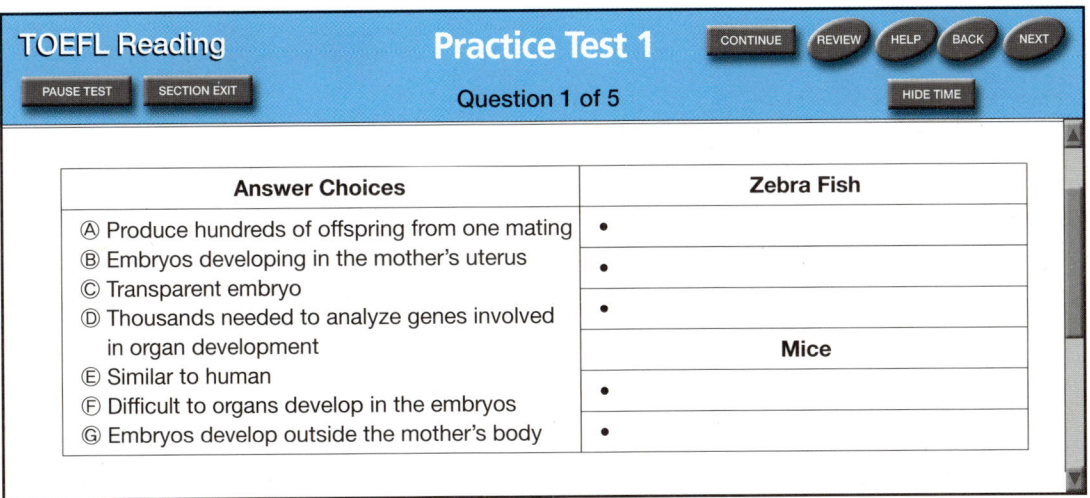

Answer Choices	Zebra Fish
Ⓐ Produce hundreds of offspring from one mating	•
Ⓑ Embryos developing in the mother's uterus	•
Ⓒ Transparent embryo	•
Ⓓ Thousands needed to analyze genes involved in organ development	**Mice**
Ⓔ Similar to human	•
Ⓕ Difficult to organs develop in the embryos	•
Ⓖ Embryos develop outside the mother's body	

다음 문장을 ① 끊어 읽기 → 직독직해 ② 명사 [구, 절]에 대괄호 ③ 동사 [구]에 동그라미 ④ 세부정보에 소괄호를 한 후 핵심정보에 화살표로 연결하시오.

1. Scientists often use different species in the laboratory for research into human organ development.

_____

_____

2. Genetic engineering can be used to produce zebra fish and mice that have genes which result in problems with development.

_____

_____

3. In order to analyze the genes involved in the formation of different organs, scientists would need to use thousands of mice over many years of study.

_____

_____

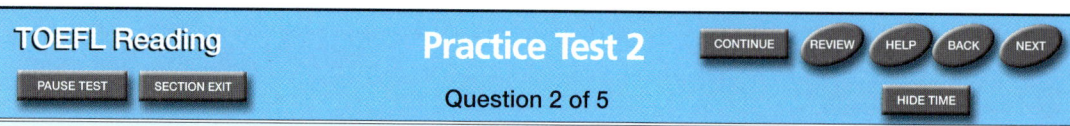
Despite the inherent differences between life on Earth and that aboard a colonial "worldship," much can be done to ensure that life aboard is as similar to terrestrial life as possible. **Design practices refined on Earth over the course of centuries can serve as valuable tools for the design of a sustainable space colony accommodating as many as 10,000 permanent colonists.** Presently, images often associated with space travel and its inhabitation bring a very utilitarian designed framework, clothes in lightweight metals and sterile fabrics, with bits of daily equipment floating aimlessly about. While space station predecessors such as SkyLab, Mir, and the International Space Station (ISS) may have employed such practical, **bare-bones** design solutions, attempting to imitate these habitats with the goal of providing any likeness of a permanent 'home' for colonists would be futile. While such methods may be relatively economic, the development and implementation of a perpetual worldship with permanent colonists requires the establishment of an entirely new design criterion, much more closely aligned with architectural and spatial design practices found here on earth.

1. **Which of the sentences below best expresses the essential information in the highlighted sentence in the passage? Incorrect choices change the meaning in important ways or leave out essential information.**

   A Existing space station designs would not be viable for long-term space colonies.

   B There would be no use trying to replicate space station conditions for space colonies.

   C Space stations were built for practical purposes but a space colony would need a new concept.

   D Without the example of space stations, scientists would not know the best conditions for a long-term space colony.

2. **The word bare-bones in the passage is closest in meaning to**

   A utilitarian   B basic

   C frugal   D modern

3. **Directions:** An introductory sentence for a brief summary of the passage is provided below. Complete the summary by selecting the THREE answer choices that express the most important ideas in the passage. Some sentences do not belong in the summary because they express ideas that are not presented in the passage or are minor ideas in the passage. **This question is worth 2 points.**

Drag your answer choices to the spaces where they belong. To remove an answer choice, click on it. To review the passage, click on **View Text**.

A worldship with permanent colonists requires an entirely new design criterion than that of the current space stations.

-
-
-

Answer Choices

Ⓐ The Earth provides the best model for the design of a potential space colony.

Ⓑ Future space colonies will be very different from life on Earth.

Ⓒ Design criteria for space stations will largely depend on economic factors.

Ⓓ Utilitarian requirements have to be considered to design space stations based on a model of the earth.

Ⓔ Life on a long-term space colony needs to be made to emulate that on earth.

Ⓕ New space colonies will need to be sustainable as well as inhabitable.

Ⓖ The present construction model of space stations is inadequate for a space colony.

다음 문장을 ① 끊어 읽기 → 직독직해 ② 명사 [구, 절]에 대괄호 ③ 동사 [구]에 동그라미 ④ 세부정보에 소괄호를 한 후 핵심정보에 화살표로 연결하시오.

1. Despite the inherent differences between life on Earth and that aboard a colonial "worldship," much can be done to ensure that life abroad is as similar to terrestrial life as possible.

_____

_____

2. Design practices refined on Earth over the course of centuries can serve as valuable tools for the design of a sustainable space colony, accommodating as many as 10,000 permanent colonists.

_____

_____

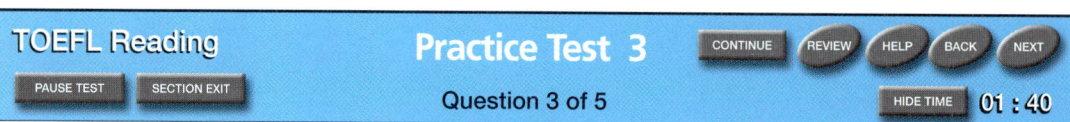
The sun plays two conflicting roles for life on our earth. On the one hand it warms the earth to temperatures in which we can survive and thrive; on the other it sends out life-threatening UV radiation and electrically charged particles. This flow of particles, called solar wind, blows through the planetary system at speeds of several million kilometers per hour and consists primarily of hydrogen and helium ions. Twenty-five years ago, **abrupt disturbances in the solar wind** were discovered which were due to eruptions on the sun's surface; their frequency varies over an 11-year cycle – from several per day to one every two weeks. These eruptions hurl an enormous mass of gas into interplanetary space. **These** occasionally reach the earth, particularly during periods of maximum solar activity. The bombardment of particles exposes astronauts in space to an increased dose of radiation for several hours and can destroy the electronic systems in telecommunications and television satellites.

1. **Why does the author mention abrupt disturbances in the solar wind in the passage?**

   Ⓐ To emphasize that the sun can be a threat to the earth
   Ⓑ To classify one of the types of threat the sun poses to the earth
   Ⓒ To give support to the argument that the sun threatens the earth
   Ⓓ To contradict the idea that the sun can threaten the earth

2. **The word These in the passage refers to**

   Ⓐ Disturbances in the solar wind
   Ⓑ Eruptions on the sun's surface
   Ⓒ Enormous masses of gas
   Ⓓ Interplanetary spaces

3. **Why would some electronic devices not work properly?**

   Ⓐ Because solar flares reach the earth with tons of particles
   Ⓑ Because nothing can be protected from the full force of the sun's heat
   Ⓒ Because strong winds create gas to disturb electronic systems
   Ⓓ Because solar eruptions overload the electrical system by generating massive energy

다음 문장을 ① 끊어 읽기 → 직독직해 ② 명사 [구, 절]에 대괄호 ③ 동사 [구]에 동그라미 ④ 세부정보에 소괄호를 한 후 핵심정보에 화살표로 연결하시오.

1. On the one hand it warms the earth to temperatures in which we can survive and thrive; on the other it sends out life-threatening UV radiation and electrically charged particles.

_____

_____

_____

2. Twenty-five years ago, abrupt disturbances in the solar wind were discovered which were due to eruptions on the sun's surface; their frequency varies over an 11-year cycle -- from several per day to one every two weeks.

_____

_____

_____

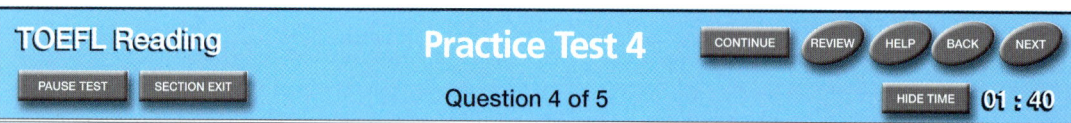
Much of NASA's current strategy is now about supporting the role of the private sector in human space flight operations by developing space flight – in the hope that access to low Earth orbit can be managed more cheaply and efficiently by commercial providers. In theory, that would free up NASA to advance with exploration beyond the Earth's orbit and make advances in technology. In this strategy, however, there is no clearly defined destination: the Moon, Mars or even a near-Earth asteroid are all listed as potential objectives. **This**, on the face of it, lacks the clarity of vision associated with specific goals – such as, say, a return to the Moon or a mission to Mars. **And the criticism that there is no mission to drive technological development or direct operational activities is fair, to a degree**. NASA works best when it is goal-orientated and going somewhere specific. Institutionally, it has an engineering culture mobilized by tightly defined requirements derived from those mission goals. And yet, NASA's strategy of embracing the private providers is no less bold than shooting for the Moon or Mars. In a sense, its sights are set on a destination: the future – one in which human space exploration can continue in an economically sustainable fashion. At the end of this month, Space X – a commercial outfit founded and run by a dotcom billionaire – hopes to launch an unmanned Dragon Capsule aboard one of its Falcon 9 launchers, and rendezvous that with the International Space Station. The Dragon capsule is capable of supporting a human crew of up to seven astronauts; if the tests are successful, Space X looks set to play a sizeable role in the future of human space flight.

1. Which of the following is NOT true according to the passage?

  Ⓐ NASA doesn't appear to have a clearly defined goal in its current strategy.

  Ⓑ NASA is taking the lead in human space flight operations.

  Ⓒ NASA supports commercial providers in developing space flight.

  Ⓓ In the future human space exploration may be economically sustainable.

2. The word This in the passage refers to

  Ⓐ A near-Earth asteroid

  Ⓑ Gaining access to low Earth orbit

  Ⓒ Exploration beyond the Earth's orbit

  Ⓓ Having no clearly defined destination

TOEFL Reading

PAUSE TEST   SECTION EXIT

Practice Test 4

Question 4 of 5

CONTINUE   REVIEW   HELP   BACK   NEXT

HIDE TIME

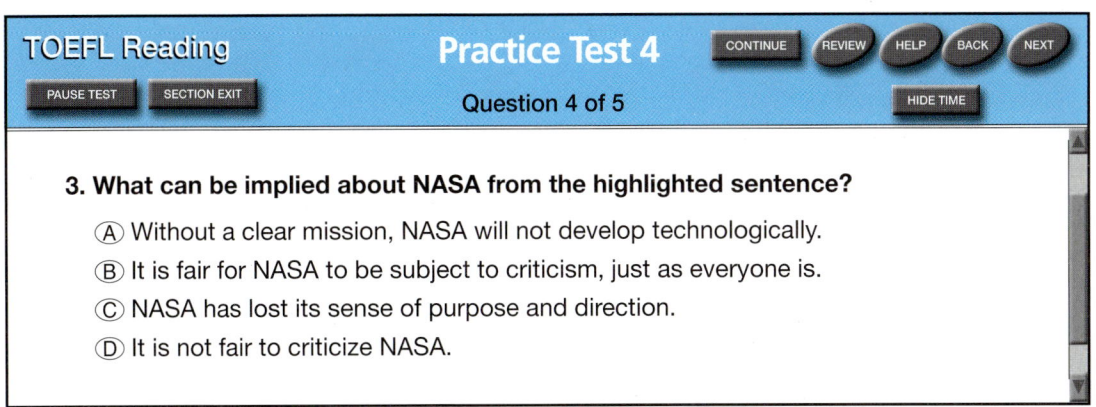

3. What can be implied about NASA from the highlighted sentence?

Ⓐ Without a clear mission, NASA will not develop technologically.

Ⓑ It is fair for NASA to be subject to criticism, just as everyone is.

Ⓒ NASA has lost its sense of purpose and direction.

Ⓓ It is not fair to criticize NASA.

다음 문장을 ① 끊어 읽기 → 직독직해 ② 명사 [구, 절]에 대괄호 ③ 동사 [구]에 동그라미 ④ 세부정보에 소괄호를 한 후 핵심정보에 화살표로 연결하시오.

1. Much of NASA's current strategy is now about supporting the role of the private sector in human space flight operations by developing space flight – in the hope that access to low Earth orbit can be managed more cheaply and efficiently by commercial providers.

_____

_____

_____

_____

2. At the end of this month, Space X – a commercial outfit founded and run by a dotcom billionaire – hopes to launch an unmanned Dragon Capsule aboard one of its Falcon 9 launchers, and rendezvous that with the International Space Station.

_____

_____

_____

TOEFL Reading

PAUSE TEST   SECTION EXIT

Practice Test 5

Question 5 of 5

CONTINUE   REVIEW   HELP   BACK   NEXT

HIDE TIME   01 : 40

Fuel cells are inefficient because the catalyst most commonly used to convert chemical energy to electricity is made of the wrong material. Rather than continue the futile effort to revise that material – platinum – to make **it** work better, we should start anew. Using platinum is like putting a resistor in the system. If we can find a catalyst that will do this more efficiently, it would reach closer to the limiting potential and get more energy out of the fuel cell. Even in the best of circumstances, the chemical reaction that produces energy in a fuel cell like those being tested by some car companies ends up wasting a quarter of the energy that could be transformed into electricity. This point is well-recognized in the scientific community, but to date efforts to address the problem have proved fruitless. The failure can be blamed on the reason for the energy loss. The most widely accepted theory says that impurities are binding to the platinum surface of the cathode and blocking the desired reaction. Data derived from oxygen-reduction experiments can be used to calculate the optimal bonding strengths between platinum and intermediate molecules formed during the oxygen-reduction reaction. The reaction takes place at the platinum-coated cathode. It has been found that the intermediate molecules bond too tightly or too loosely to the cathode surface, slowing the reaction and causing a drop in voltage. The result is the fuel cell produces about. 93 volts instead of the potential maximum of 1.23 volts. To eliminate the loss, according to our calculations, the catalyst should have bonding strengths tailored so that all reactions taking place during oxygen reduction occur at or as near to 1.23 volts as possible.

1. Which of the following can be concluded from the passage?

Ⓐ Scientists need to look for a new process instead of trying to improve the efficiency of fuel cells.

Ⓑ The inefficiency of fuel cells is out of the question for scientists.

Ⓒ A new catalyst is needed to improve the efficiency of fuel cells.

Ⓓ There are many problems to be overcome before electric cars can be efficient.

2. The word it in the passage refers to

Ⓐ the catalyst

Ⓑ the energy use

Ⓒ platinum

Ⓓ the system

TOEFL Reading

PAUSE TEST   SECTION EXIT

Practice Test 5

Question 5 of 5

CONTINUE   REVIEW   HELP   BACK   NEXT

HIDE TIME

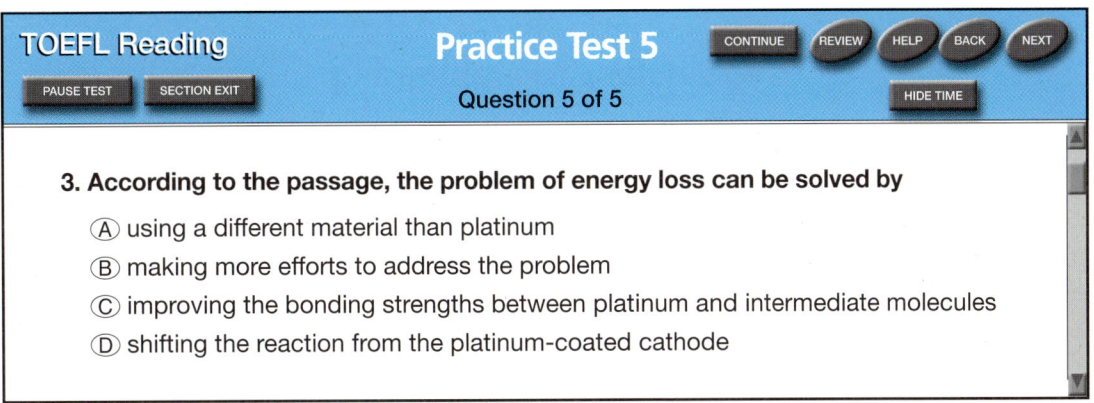

3. According to the passage, the problem of energy loss can be solved by

Ⓐ using a different material than platinum

Ⓑ making more efforts to address the problem

Ⓒ improving the bonding strengths between platinum and intermediate molecules

Ⓓ shifting the reaction from the platinum-coated cathode

다음 문장을 ① 끊어 읽기 → 직독직해 ② 명사 [구, 절]에 대괄호 ③ 동사 [구]에 동그라미 ④ 세부정보에 소괄호를 한 후 핵심정보에 화살표로 연결하시오.

1. Fuel cells are inefficient because the catalyst most commonly used to convert chemical energy to electricity is made of the wrong material.

_____

_____

2. If we can find a catalyst that will do this more efficiently, it would reach closer to the limiting potential and get more energy out of the fuel cell.

_____

_____

3. Data derived from oxygen-reduction experiments can be used to calculate the optimal bonding strengths between platinum and intermediate molecules formed during the oxygen-reduction reaction.

_____

_____

_____

Vocabulary & Paraphrasing

1. Write the word from the box that matches each meaning below.

utilitarian	sustainability	embracing	genetic	demise
dwarf	inherent	mitigation	rendezvous	perpetual

① taking or receiving gladly _____

② an animal or plant much below its average _____

③ going on for a long time _____

④ the act of becoming less severe _____

⑤ existing as an inseparable part _____

⑥ the quality of not being harmful to the environment _____

⑦ of genes _____

⑧ death or decease _____

⑨ designed for use rather than beauty _____

⑩ to assemble at an agreed time and place _____

Vocabulary & Paraphrasing

2. Translate the following questions into Korean and then paraphrase them according to the directions below.

① Despite the inherent differences between life on Earth and that aboard a colonial "worldship," much can be done to ensure that life abroad is as similar to terrestrial life as possible. ➜ 전치사 바꿔 쓰기

_____

_____

② The discovery was made using the Hubble space telescope to observe Pluto before the scheduled arrival of a NASA spacecraft in 2015. ➜ 문장의 태 바꿔 쓰기

_____

_____

③ It will impact regulations regarding substances such as hydrazine, which is used widely as a propellant in space programs and the development of Green Propulsion with propellants that have a reduced toxicity. ➜ 관계대명사, 동의어 바꿔 쓰기

_____

_____

_____

④ The Dragon capsule is capable of supporting a human crew of up to seven astronauts; if the tests are successful, Space X looks set to play a sizeable role in the future of human space flight. ➜ 문장의 태, 쉬운 단어로 바꿔 쓰기

_____

_____

_____

Practice Test 1

1. Scientists often (use) / different species (in the laboratory) / for **research** (into human organ development).

   과학자들은 종종 인간 장기의 성장 연구를 위해 실험실에서 다른 종의 생물을 사용한다.

2. Genetic engineering (can be used) / (to produce **zebra fish and mice**) / (that have **genes**) / (which result in **problems**) (with development).

   유전 공학은 장기 성장에 문제가 있는 유전자를 가진 제브라피시와 쥐들을 생산하는 데 사용될 수 있다.

3. In order to analyze **the genes** / (involved in the formation of different organs,) / scientists (would need) to use / thousands of mice (over many years of study).

   서로 다른 장기의 형성에 관련된 유전자를 분석하기 위해서 과학자들은 수년 넘는 연구에 수천 마리의 쥐를 필요로 할 것이다.

Practice Test 2

1. Despite [the inherent **differences**] / (between life on Earth and that aboard) / a colonial "worldship," / much (can be done) to ensure / [that life aboard is as similar / to terrestrial life as possible].

   지구에서의 삶과 정착지인 '세계 함정'에서의 삶이 근본적으로 차이가 있음에도 불구하고 승선한 삶을 최대한 지상의 삶과 유사하게 만드는 데 도움이 되도록 많은 일들이 이루어질 것이다.

2. Design **practices (refined** on Earth) (over the course of centuries) / (can serve) as valuable tools / for [the design of a sustainable space **colony,**] / (accommodating as many as 10,000 permanent colonists).

   지구에서 수 세기에 걸쳐 개발한 설계 제도는 최대 10,000명의 영구 정착민을 수용할 수 있는 지속 가능한 우주 식민지를 설계함에 있어 필요한 귀중한 도구의 역할을 할 수 있을 것이다.

Practice Test 3

1. On the one hand / it (warms) the earth to **temperatures** / (in which we can survive and thrive;) / on the other / it (sends out) / [life-threatening UV radiation / and electrically charged particles].

   한편으로 태양은 우리가 생존하고 번성할 수 있도록 지구의 온도를 올리고 다른 한편으로는 삶을 위협하는 자외선 방사와 전기로 충전된 입자들을 내보낸다.

2. Twenty-five years ago, / [abrupt **disturbances** (in the solar wind)] / (were discovered) (which were due to eruptions / on the sun's surface;) / their frequency (varies) / over an 11-year cycle / – from several per day / to one every two weeks.

   25년 전에 태양 표면의 폭발로 인해 태양풍의 돌연한 폐해가 밝혀졌다; 태양 폭발의 빈도는 하루에 여러 번에서 2주에 한 번까지 11년 주기로 다양하다.

Practice Test 4

1. Much of NASA's current strategy (is) now / about [**supporting** the role of the private sector / in human space flight operations] / (by developing space flight) / – in the hope / that [access to low Earth orbit] **can be managed** / more cheaply and efficiently / (by commercial providers).

   현재 NASA(미항공우주국)의 전략 중 많은 부분은 우주 비행을 발전시켜 인간의 우주 비행 작전에 참여하는 민간 부분의 역할을 지원하는 것이다 – 상업 서비스 제공자들로 인해 더 저렴하고 더 효율적으로 지구의 저궤도에 접근할 수 있다는 희망으로.

2. At the end of this month, / Space X – a commercial **outfit** / (founded and run by a dotcom billionaire) / – (hopes) to launch [an unmanned Dragon Capsule] / aboard [one of its Falcon 9 launchers,] / and **rendezvous** that / (with the International Space Station).

   이달 말에 우주선 X – 닷컴 회사의 억만장자가 자금을 마련하고 운영하는 상업팀 – 는 팰콘의 아홉 개 발사 장치 중의 하나로 무인 드래곤 캡슐을 발사하여 국제 우주 정거장과 랑데부할 것을 기대하고 있다.

Practice Test 5

1. Fuel cells (are) inefficient / because **the catalyst** (most commonly **used**) / (to convert chemical energy to electricity) / is made of the wrong material.

   연료 전지들은 화학적 에너지를 전기로 바꾸는 데 사용되는 가장 흔한 촉매가 잘못된 재료로 만들어지기 때문에 비효율적이다.

2. If we can find **a catalyst** / (that will do this more efficiently,) / it (would reach) closer to the limiting potential / and (get) more energy out of the fuel cell.

   만약 우리가 이것을 더욱 효율적으로 할 촉매를 발견할 수 있다면, 한계 가능성에 가까워지고 연료 전지로부터 더 많은 에너지를 얻게 될 것이다.

3. **Data** (derived from oxygen-reduction experiments) / (can be used) / (to calculate the optimal bonding **strengths**) / (between platinum and **intermediate molecules**) / (formed during the oxygen-reduction reaction).

   산소 증감 실험으로 인해 얻어진 자료는 백금과 산소 감소 반응 동안에 형성된 중간 분자 사이에 시각적인 결합력을 계산하기 위하여 사용될 수 있다.

Art & Literature

Medieval literature provides modern readers with clues to life in the Middle Ages. Take, for example, this line from a fourteenth-century work where the king has ordered his Roman guests to be given the finest accommodations available: They changed in chambers with chimneys. At this time all the people in the castle slept in the main hall to be near the fire, so individual rooms with heat were signs of great wealth. Further in the poem we can find what was considered fine food: peacocks and plovers in platters of gold / piglets and porcupines; and great swans on silver platters / Tarts of Turkey... The poem goes on to describe a magnificent feast and the finest tableware, all of which impressed the Romans greatly. Another reason to study them is their likely popularity. Before they were written down these tales were told by hundreds of minstrels in court after court and castle after castle. Half of Europe knew them. **Compare "that" to the place in our lives of popular books and it becomes clear that each story is more than a single thread in the fabric of medieval life.** How, then, can we ignore these literary pieces when seeking the truth of history?

1. Which of the following can be concluded from the passage?

    (A) We should read medieval literature to understand life at that time.

    (B) Medieval literature deals with all aspects of people's lives.

    (C) Literature can help us to understand the period in which it was written.

    (D) Literature is a valuable aid to understanding the Middle Ages.

2. The word that in the passage refers to

    (A) the tale being told by hundreds of minstrels

    (B) the story written down

    (C) half of Europe knowing the tales

    (D) a poem about a sumptuous feast and the finest tableware

3. Which of the sentences below best expresses the essential information in the highlighted sentence in the passage?

    (A) Medieval poetry had the same place in its society as popular books do in ours.

    (B) The whole of Medieval life was made up of stories, like ours is today.

    (C) The most important story in Medieval life was with an influence like our popular books.

    (D) There can be no comparison between the influence of poetry in Medieval times and our own time.

다음 문장을 ① 끊어 읽기 → 직독직해 ② 명사 [구, 절]에 대괄호 ③ 동사 [구]에 동그라미 ④ 세부정보에 소괄호를 한 후 핵심정보에 화살표로 연결하시오.

1. Take, for example, this line from a fourteenth-century work where the king has ordered his Roman guests to be given the finest accommodations available: They changed in chambers with chimneys.

_____

_____

2. Compare "that" to the place in our lives of popular books and it becomes clear that each story is more than a single thread in the fabric of medieval life.

_____

_____

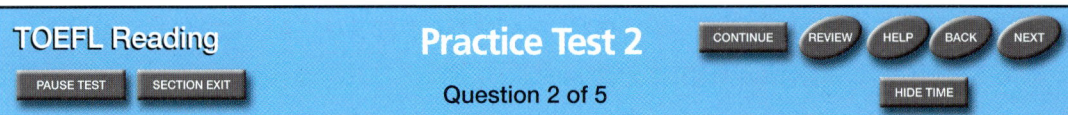

TOEFL Reading

Practice Test 2

CONTINUE   REVIEW   HELP   BACK   NEXT

PAUSE TEST   SECTION EXIT

Question 2 of 5

HIDE TIME

One significant body of landscape painting from the early Joseon period comprises works illustrating scenery or places in China of literary fame and with nostalgic associations — for example, the Xiao and Xiang rivers in the modern province of Hunan, a region historically identified with exile and lament. Though known and adapted during the Goryeo dynasty (918–1392), the theme reached a new height of popularity in the fifteenth and sixteenth centuries, with most extant paintings dating to the latter. Meanwhile, in contemporary Ming-dynasty China, the number and reputation of paintings on this subject dwindled, compared to the earlier Song period. The early Joseon scrolls and screens illustrating the Eight Views represent Korean transformations of this classic theme and of landscapes more broadly. Many landscapes from this period, chief among them the Eight Views, are painted in the An Gyeon style — coined after the most celebrated and influential landscapist of the early Joseon who was active around the mid-fifteenth century. Some notable features of the An Gyeon style include the cloudlike mountain forms and the pine trees; the dramatic interpenetration of solids and voids; the effective contrast between light and dark ink tones; and the powerful command of brushstrokes and modeling ink washes.

1. Which of the following can be concluded from the passage?

    (A) It shows how Chinese literary influenced Korean arts during the early Joseon period.

    (B) It describes the characteristics of landscape painting in the early Joseon dynasty.

    (C) It introduces some notable features of the An Gyeon style.

    (D) It compares the transformations of the arts between Goryeo dynasty and Joseon dynasty.

2. According to the passage, which of the following is NOT true of landscape painting from the early Joseon period?

    (A) Its scenes of places in China were popular in this period.

    (B) The An Gyeon style was used extensively in this period.

    (C) Contemporary Ming-dynasty Chinese painters started to lose interest in these scenes.

    (D) The early Joseon scrolls and screens illustrating the Eight Views imitated the Chinese style.

3. Directions: Select the appropriate phrases from the answer choices and match them to the era to which they relate. **This question is worth 3 points.**

TOEFL Reading

PAUSE TEST   SECTION EXIT

Practice Test 2

Question 2 of 5

CONTINUE   REVIEW   HELP   BACK   NEXT

HIDE TIME

Drag your answer choices to the spaces where they belong. To remove an answer choice, click on it. To review the passage, click on **View Text**.

Answer Choices	Early Joseon
Ⓐ Painted in the An Gyeon style	•
Ⓑ Loss of interest in scenes like the Xiao and Xiang rivers	•
Ⓒ Classic themes	•
Ⓓ Illustrating scenery or places in China of literary fame and with nostalgic associations	**Ming-dynasty China**
Ⓔ Extant paintings	•
Ⓕ Powerful command of brushstrokes and modeling ink washes	•
Ⓖ Identified with exile and lament	

다음 문장을 ① 끊어 읽기 → 직독직해 ② 명사 [구, 절]에 대괄호 ③ 동사 [구]에 동그라미 ④ 세부정보에 소괄호를 한 후 핵심정보에 화살표로 연결하시오.

1. Some notable features of the An Gyeon style include the cloudlike mountain forms and the pine trees; the dramatic interpenetration of solids and voids; the effective contrast between light and dark ink tones; and the powerful command of brushstrokes and modeling ink washes.

---

2. One significant body of landscape painting from the early Joseon period comprises works illustrating scenery or places in China of literary fame and with nostalgic associations — for example, the Xiao and Xiang rivers in the modern province of Hunan, a region historically identified with exile and lament.

The photographer's images of **the West Bank** look beyond the noisy commotion of one of the world's **intractable** accords, past what he terms "the theater of war" and the almost "ritualized" scenes of violence that seem to shape the outsider's view of the Middle East. The photos are "vignettes of an experience." They are bathed in a painterly glow, dwelling over terrain that is at once stark and desolate but suffused with centuries of accrued history and memory. In one, three foreign journalists stand atop the stony earth, at the center of the narrative they seek to tell. In another, an Israeli "Center for Tolerance and Human Dignity" — built despite local protests and appeals — emerges from what is the site of a 7th century Muslim cemetery. A twisted tree rises out of the fore ground, its leafless branches pointing limply at the new construction. A photo poised on a kitchen counter shows three men whose ties date back to this land well before 1948. **It's a mixture of nostalgia and also a proof of life. Here we have "a portrait of a family, a sense of roots, and a sense of place."** That idea of place and of a moment interests the photographer, who hopes to expand his work with field recordings and other media.

1. **What does the author imply about the West Bank in the highlighted sentences in the passage?**

   Ⓐ People long to return to an earlier, peaceful time.
   Ⓑ The people in the photograph are no longer alive.
   Ⓒ It is a sign that people are attached to the past and have hope for the future.
   Ⓓ Everything in the history repeats.

2. **The word intractable in the passage is closest in meaning to**

   Ⓐ liberal
   Ⓑ stubborn
   Ⓒ awkward
   Ⓓ uncooperative

3. **Directions:** An introductory sentence for a brief summary of the passage is provided below. Complete the summary by selecting the THREE answer choices that express the most important ideas in the passage. Some sentences do not belong in the summary because they express ideas that are not presented in the passage or are minor ideas in the passage. **This question is worth 2 points**.

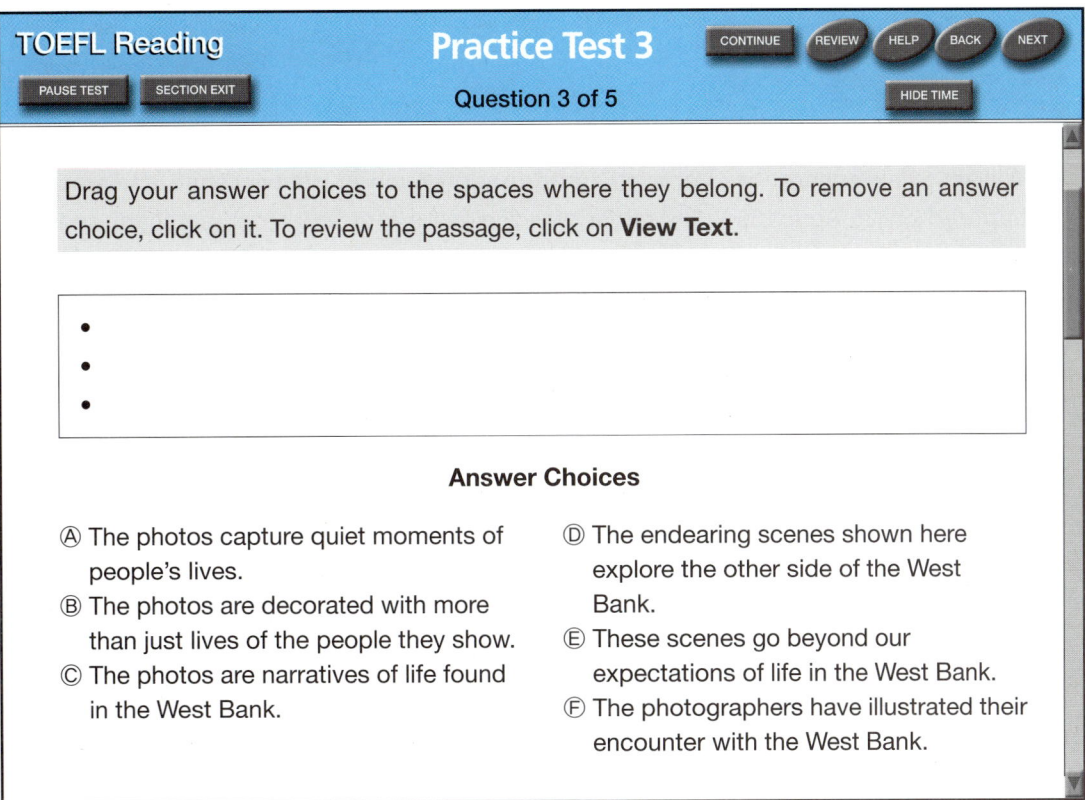

Drag your answer choices to the spaces where they belong. To remove an answer choice, click on it. To review the passage, click on **View Text**.

-
-
-

Answer Choices

Ⓐ The photos capture quiet moments of people's lives.

Ⓑ The photos are decorated with more than just lives of the people they show.

Ⓒ The photos are narratives of life found in the West Bank.

Ⓓ The endearing scenes shown here explore the other side of the West Bank.

Ⓔ These scenes go beyond our expectations of life in the West Bank.

Ⓕ The photographers have illustrated their encounter with the West Bank.

다음 문장을 ① 끊어 읽기 → 직독직해 ② 명사 [구, 절]에 대괄호 ③ 동사 [구]에 동그라미 ④ 세부정보에 소괄호를 한 후 핵심정보에 화살표로 연결하시오.

1. They are bathed in a painterly glow, dwelling over terrain that is at once stark and desolate but suffused with centuries of accrued history and memory.

_____

_____

2. A photo poised on a kitchen counter shows three men whose ties date back to this land well before 1948.

_____

_____

TOEFL Reading

PAUSE TEST SECTION EXIT

Practice Test 4

Question 4 of 5

CONTINUE REVIEW  HELP BACK NEXT

HIDE TIME 01 : 40

William Shakespeare was born in Stratford-upon-Avon in Warwickshire and was baptized on 26 April 1564. His father was a glove maker and wool merchant and his mother, Mary Arden, the daughter of a well-to-do local landowner. Shakespeare was probably educated in Stratford's grammar school. The next documented event in Shakespeare's life is his marriage in 1582 to Anne Hathaway, the daughter of a farmer. The couple had a daughter the following year and twins in 1585. There is now another gap, referred to by some scholars as "the lost years," with Shakespeare only reappearing in London in 1592, when he was already working in the theatre. Ⓐ ■ Shakespeare's acting career was spent with the Lord Chamberlain's Company, which was renamed the King's Company in 1603 when James succeeded to the throne. Ⓑ ■ Among the actors in the group was the famous Richard Burbage. The partnership acquired interests in two theatres in the Southwark area of London, near the banks of the Thames - the Globe and the Blackfriars. Shakespeare's poetry was published before his plays, with two poems appearing in 1593 and 1594, dedicated to his patron Henry Wriothesley, Earl of Southampton. Ⓒ ■ Records of Shakespeare's plays begin to appear in 1594, and he produced roughly two a year until around 1611. His earliest plays include "Henry VI" and "Titus Andronicus." "A Midsummer Night's Dream," "The Merchant of Venice" and "Richard II" all date from the mid to late 1590s. Some of his most famous tragedies were written in the early 1600s including "Hamlet," "Othello," "King Lear" and "Macbeth." His late plays, often known as the Romances, date from 1608 onwards and include "The Tempest." Ⓓ ■ The first collected edition of his works was published in 1623 and is known as "the First Folio."

1. **Look at the four squares [■] that indicate where the following sentence could be added to the passage.**

Most of Shakespeare's sonnets were probably written at this time as well.

Where would the sentence best fit?
Click on a square [■] to add the sentence to the passage.

2. **Why does the author mention Shakespeare's plays in the passage?**

Ⓐ To emphasize Shakespeare's great writing output
Ⓑ To persuade people to read Shakespeare's plays and poems
Ⓒ To praise the genius of Shakespeare, the writer and actor
Ⓓ To inform about Shakespeare's life and achievements

TOEFL Reading

PAUSE TEST   SECTION EXIT

Practice Test 4

Question 4 of 5

CONTINUE   REVIEW   HELP   BACK   NEXT

HIDE TIME

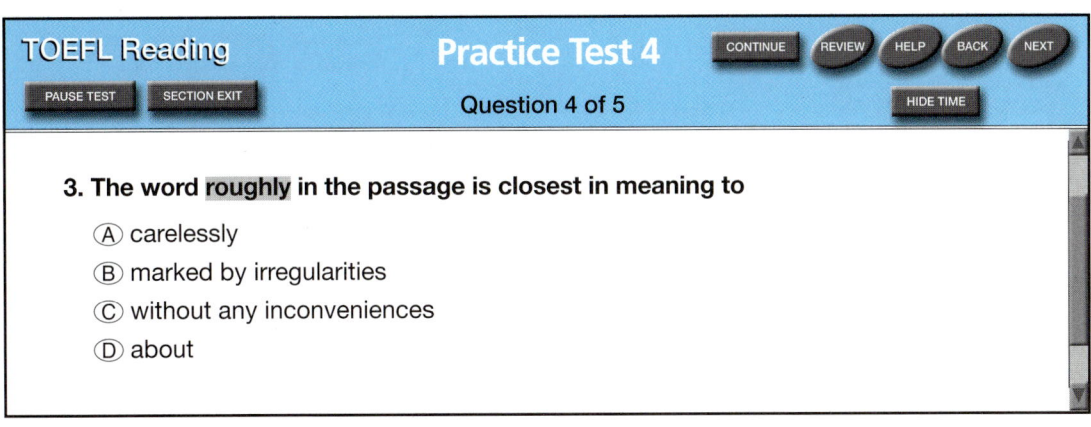

3. The word roughly in the passage is closest in meaning to

Ⓐ carelessly

Ⓑ marked by irregularities

Ⓒ without any inconveniences

Ⓓ about

다음 문장을 ① 끊어 읽기 → 직독직해 ② 명사 [구, 절]에 대괄호 ③ 동사 [구]에 동그라미 ④ 세부정보에 소괄호를 한 후 핵심정보에 화살표로 연결하시오.

1. Shakespeare's poetry was published before his plays, with two poems appearing in 1593 and 1594, dedicated to his patron Henry Wriothesley, Earl of Southampton.

_____

_____

2. His late plays, often known as the Romances, date from 1608 onwards and include "The Tempest."

_____

_____

3. The next documented event in Shakespeare's life is his marriage in 1582 to Anne Hathaway, the daughter of a farmer.

_____

_____

4. Some of his most famous tragedies were written in the early 1600s including "Hamlet," "Othello," "King Lear" and "Macbeth."

_____

_____

309

Britain has not always been pro-modern art. The papers used to sneer while the public would jeer. "Call that art" was the general refrain. Now the reverse is true, we don't seem to be able to get enough of the stuff. Why? Well, one reason is that all these modern art galleries have helped introduce the subject to a much wider audience, often in a way and within an environment that is friendly and welcoming. The idea that artists have spent the past 100 years hood-winking us has dissipated, to be replaced by an intellectual engagement with their work that many find rewarding. And because modern art is an ongoing story, with each new chapter bringing fresh ideas as well as adding historical context to the past, I think our involvement with the subject will increase, not decrease.

1. Which of the following would the author most likely support about modern art?

Ⓐ People in Britain will never like modern art.

Ⓑ People have started to show more interest in modern art.

Ⓒ People cannot be pro-modern art without going to art galleries.

Ⓓ There will continue to be more discussion about what modern art is.

2. Which of the following can be concluded from the highlighted sentence in the passage?

Ⓐ People didn't think it was art.

Ⓑ People wanted to have more art.

Ⓒ People didn't understand what modern artists were saying.

Ⓓ People thought the titles of the works reflected their artistry.

3. Directions: Select the appropriate phrases from the answer choices and match them to the response to modern art to which they relate. Two of the answer choices will NOT be used. **This question is worth 3 points.**

Drag your answer choices to the spaces where they belong. To remove an answer choice, click on it. To review the passage, click on **View Text**.

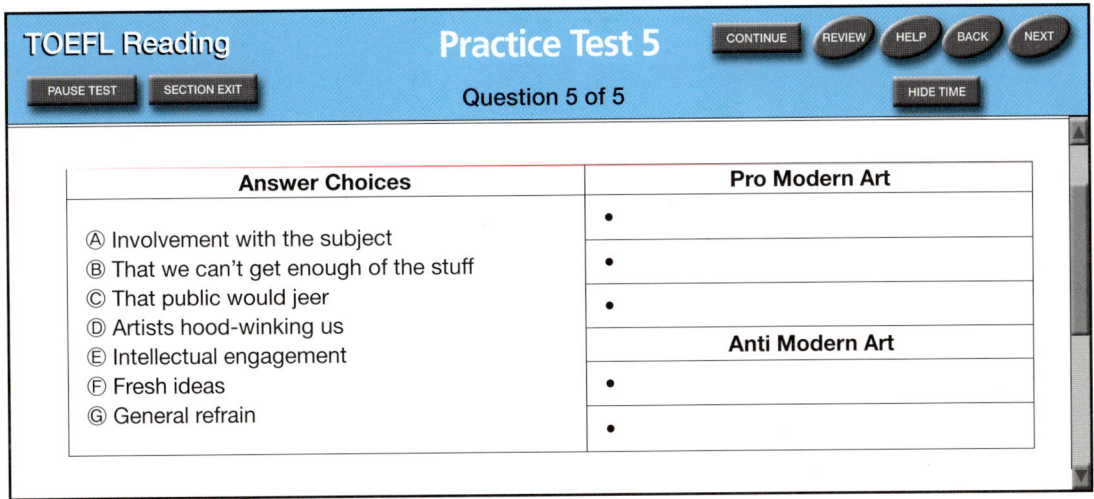

Answer Choices	Pro Modern Art
Ⓐ Involvement with the subject	•
Ⓑ That we can't get enough of the stuff	•
Ⓒ That public would jeer	•
Ⓓ Artists hood-winking us	**Anti Modern Art**
Ⓔ Intellectual engagement	•
Ⓕ Fresh ideas	•
Ⓖ General refrain	

다음 문장을 ① 끊어 읽기 → 직독직해 ② 명사 [구, 절]에 대괄호 ③ 동사 [구]에 동그라미 ④ 세부정보에 소괄호를 한 후 핵심정보에 화살표로 연결하시오.

1. Well, one reason is that all these modern art galleries have helped introduce the subject to a much wider audience, often in a way and within an environment that is friendly and welcoming.

_____

_____

_____

2. The idea that artists have spent the past 100 years hood-winking us has dissipated, to be replaced by an intellectual engagement with their work that many find rewarding.

_____

_____

311

Vocabulary & Paraphrasing

1. Write the word from the box that matches each meaning below.

roughly	patron	poacher	critical	refrain
stumble	top-notch	baffling	mythological	platter

① outstanding, excellent   _____

② of a body of myths   _____

③ to walk or go unsteadily   _____

④ a person who sponsors or aids artists and charities   _____

⑤ confusing or perplexing   _____

⑥ close to   _____

⑦ a person who catches fish or animals illegally   _____

⑧ large, shallow dish for serving food   _____

⑨ very important   _____

⑩ repeated lines of a song   _____

Vocabulary & Paraphrasing

2. Translate the following questions into Korean and then paraphrase them according to the directions below.

① I played in garage bands while he went to college; taught exotic martial arts while he made a grown-up income in suits and ties. ➜ 접속사, 분사 구문 바꿔 쓰기

_____

_____

② Having destroyed a great number of wild animals, human beings take particular pride in "saving" the ones still left. ➜ 분사구문 바꿔 쓰기

_____

_____

③ Whatever critical paradigm we use to discuss and analyze literature, there is still an artistic quality to the works. ➜ 양보구문 바꿔 쓰기

_____

_____

④ Some of his most famous tragedies were written in the early 1600s including "Hamlet," "Othello," "King Lear" and "Macbeth." ➜ 문장의 태, 전치사 바꿔 쓰기

_____

_____

Practice Test 1

1. Take, for example, this line / (from a fourteenth-century work) / (where the king has ordered his Roman guests / to be given the finest accommodations available:) / They changed / in chambers with chimneys.
예를 들어 14세기의 작품 중에 왕이 로마의 손님들에게 최고의 숙소를 제공받도록 지시한 한 글귀가 있다: 그들의 숙소는 굴뚝이 있는 방으로 변경되었다.

2. Compare that to the place / (in our lives of popular books) / and it becomes clear / [that each story is / more than a single thread / (in the fabric of medieval life)].
현대를 사는 우리 시대에 인기 있는 책들이 차지하는 위치와 비교해 볼 때 중세 시대의 각 이야기는 중세 시대의 삶을 수놓은 하나의 실낱 이상이라는 것이 분명해진다.

Practice Test 2

1. [Some notable features of the An Gyeon style] / include [the cloudlike mountain forms and the pine trees;] / [the dramatic interpenetration of solids and voids;] / [the effective contrast between light and dark ink tones;] / and [the powerful command of brushstrokes and modeling ink washes].
안견 스타일의 몇 가지 주목할 만한 기법은 채움과 비움의 극적인 투시, 명암과 잉크 색조 사이의 효과적인 대조 그리고 힘 있는 붓질과 수묵화의 입체감 표현법을 갖는 소나무와 구름 같은 산의 형태를 포함한다.

2. [One significant body of landscape painting] (from the early Joseon period) / comprises works (illustrating scenery or places in China / (of literary fame and with nostalgic associations)) / — for example, / the Xiao and Xiang rivers (in the modern province of Hunan,) / a region (historically identified with exile and lament).
조선 시대 초기 풍경화의 한 가지 중요한 부분은 예를 들어 망명과 애통으로 알려져 있는 역사적인 지역이며 지금의 후난 지역인 소상강같이 문학의 명성과 향수를 갖는 중국의 풍경이나 장소들을 보여주는 작업으로 구성되어 있다.

Practice Test 3

1. They are bathed in a painterly glow, / (dwelling over terrain) / (that is at once stark and desolate / but suffused with centuries / of accrued history and memory).
그것들은 삭막하고 동시에 황량하지만 쌓여 온 역사와 기억이 수백 년에 걸쳐 퍼져 있는 지역에 살고 있는 그림 같은 열정에 휩싸여 있다.

2. A photo (poised on a kitchen counter) shows / three men (whose ties date back to this land well / before 1948).
부엌 카운터에 아슬아슬하게 놓여 있는 사진 한 장은 1948년 전에 이 지역과 관련있는 세 명의 남자들을 잘 보여 준다.

Practice Test 4

1. Shakespeare's poetry was published before his plays, / (with two poems appearing in 1593 and 1594,)/ (dedicated to his patron Henry Wriothesley, / Earl of Southampton).
셰익스피어의 시는 사우샘프턴 백작이었던 그의 후원자 헨리 라이어스리에게 바치는 두 편의 시가 1593년과 1594년에 나타나면서 그의 연극 전에 출판되었다.

2. His late plays, / (often known as the Romances,) / date from 1608 onwards / and include "The Tempest."
종종 로맨스라고 불리는 그의 말기 연극들은 1608년도부터 시작되고 『폭풍우』를 포함한다.

3. [The next documented event (in Shakespeare's life)] / is his marriage (in 1582) (to Anne Hathaway,) / [the daughter of a farmer].
셰익스피어의 삶에 관해 다음으로 기록된 사건은 1582년에 농부의 딸이었던 앤 해서웨이와의 결혼이다.

4. [Some of his most famous tragedies] / were written in the early 1600s / (including "Hamlet," "Othello," "King Lear" and "Macbeth.")
그의 가장 유명한 비극 작품들은 1600년대 초기에 『햄릿』, 『오셀로』, 『리어왕』 그리고 『맥베스』를 포함하여 쓰여졌다.

Practice Test 5

1. Well, one reason is / [that all these modern art galleries / have helped introduce the subject / to a much wider audience,] / (often in a way and within an environment) / (that is friendly and welcoming).
한 가지 이유는 모든 현대 미술 갤러리가 종종 친숙하고 반기는 환경과 방식으로 훨씬 폭넓은 청중들에게 그 주제에 대해 소개하도록 도와 왔다는 것이다.

2. The idea [that artists have spent / the past 100 years hood-winking us] / has dissipated, / to be replaced (by an intellectual engagement / with their work) (that many find rewarding).
예술가들이 지난 100년 동안 우리를 눈가림해왔다는 생각은 많은 예술가들이 그들의 일이 보상을 얻는 지적 작업이라는 생각으로 바뀌면서 사라지게 되었다.

반석

TOEFL
급상승

Reading 스타트

[정답 및 해설]

Section 01 Powerful Reading Skills

Unit 01 끊어읽기

1. 주어파트가 길 때는 동사 앞에서 끊어읽기_ P. 12

Exercise

1. The art form of the opera / was first developed in Italy.
오페라의 예술 형태는 이탈리아에서 처음으로 발달했다.

2. Hundreds of children in African villages / are infected by malaria each day.
아프리카 마을의 수백 명의 아이들이 매일 말라리아에 감염된다.

3. The instabilities in the Earth's magnetic field / are caused by solar wind.
지구 자기장의 불안정성은 태양풍에 의해 발생한다.

4. The best way to improve your performance / is always to practice.
너의 연기를 향상시킬 수 있는 최선의 방법은 한결같은 연습이다.

5. A child that always receives sympathy / often cries over little troubles.
항상 동정을 받은 아이는 조그마한 어려움에도 자주 운다.

6. Finding financing partners to defray the expense / is very important for some studios.
비용 분담을 위해 재정 파트너를 찾는 일은 일부 영화사들에게 매우 중요하다.

7. Steve Jobs' most important contribution to American IT business / was his introduction of the iPhone.
스티브잡스가 미국 IT산업에 한 가장 커다란 기여는 아이팟의 소개이다.

8. The increasing importance of the media / is particularly observed in election campaigns.
미디어의 중요성은 선거운동에서 특히 보여 진다.

9. The collapse of Soviet Union in the 1990s / provided an important lesson for communist China.
1990년대 소련의 붕괴는 공산국가 중국에 중요한 교훈을 주었다.

10. The idea of the death penalty in that situation / doesn't make sense to me at all.
그 상황에서 사형을 시킨다는 발상은 내게 전혀 납득이 가지 않는다.

11. One way of satisfying this curiosity / is through travel.
이 호기심을 만족시키는 하나의 방법은 여행을 통해서이다.

12. People all around the world / spend an average of 1.1 hours on the road each day.
전 세계 사람들은 하루에 평균 1시간 10분정도를 도로상에서 보낸다.

13. The instabilities in the Earth's ozone layer / are being caused by global warming.
지구 오존층의 불안정은 지구온난화에 의해 발생되고 있다.

14. The number of hunting accidents / has increased sharply these days.
사냥 중의 사고 건수가 요즘 급격히 늘고 있다.

15. Ignoring other people and their advice / has eventually made me more popular.
다른 이들과 그들이 조언을 무시한 것이 나를 더욱 유명하게 만들었다.

16. People who ask you for money / will ask for more if you do them a favor.
당신에게 돈을 빌려 달라는 사람은 부탁을 들어주면 더 많이 요구할 것이다.

17. The student who finishes the test last / often receives a perfect grade.
마지막으로 시험을 마치는 학생이 종종 완벽한 점수를 받는다.

18. The deeply philosophical question of "why God created us" / was put to some students.
'신이 왜 우리를 만들었는가'라는 매우 철학적인 질문이 몇몇 학생들에게 던져졌다.

19. Bill Gates' most precious contribution to mankind / is his development of the Windows platform.
빌게이츠의 인류 역사상 가장 소중한 기여는 윈도우 플랫폼을 개발한 것이다.

20. The jobs that most companies provide in information and technology today / would have not been available several decades ago.
대부분의 회사들에게 정보와 기술을 제공하는 업무는 수십 년 전에는 이용이 가능하지 않았을 것이다.

21. Much of the scholarship of early women's studies / went into documenting the invidious nature of sexual differences.
초기 여성학 분야의 많은 연구들이 성별 차이의 부당한 점을 문헌화하는 방향으로 흘러갔다.

22. A list of authorized service depots / is packaged with the appliance.
지정 서비스 점의 명단은 제품과 함께 포장되어 있다.

23. Significant numbers of youngsters / are growing up in poverty.
상당히 많은 아이들이 빈곤 속에서 성장하고 있다.

24. The rights of the individual / are the most important rights in a free society.
개인의 권리는 자유사회에서 가장 중요한 권리이다.

25. The quick recognition of disease / is important to identify effective treatment.
병에 대한 빠른 인지가 효과적인 치료를 실시하는 데 중요하다.

26. The first indication of an anomaly / occurred three minutes before the plane crash.
첫 번째 이상 현상 신호가 여객기 추락 3분 전에 발생했다.

27. The first semester of freshman year / was the hardest year in dealing with organizations.
신입생으로 들어온 후의 첫 학기는 단체를 이끌기에 가장 힘든 시간이었다.

28. Accurate oven temperature and baking times / are critical.
정확한 오븐 온도와 조리시간은 중요하다.

29. Her hesitation about signing the contract / was based on financial concerns.
그녀가 계약서에 서명하는 것을 망설이는 것은 재정적인 염려 때문이었다.

30. A company representative from the oil company / talked about the oil spill.
그 석유회사의 대표는 그 석유 유출에 대해 얘기했다.

2. 긴 목적어나 보어 앞에서 끊어읽기_ P. 17

Exercise

1. Some people don't believe / that well begun is half done.
어떤 이들은 시작이 반이라고 생각하지 않는다.

2. Vincent refused / to accept my invitation to the garden party tonight.
빈센트는 오늘밤 나의 가든파티 초대에 응하는 것을 거절했다.

3. You see now / how foolish you are to say so.
네가 그렇게 말하는 게 얼마나 바보스러운지 이제 알겠지.

4. The desire for profit motivates / employers to operate their shops efficiently.
이득창출의 욕구가 고용인이 효율적으로 가게를 관리하게끔 동기를 부여한다.

5. The speaker showed / his knowledge of the subject by his excellent lecture.
강사는 주제에 대한 그의 지식을 훌륭한 강의로 보여줬다.

6. Our staff members are / people who take pride in their work and support each other.
우리 직원들은 자신의 일에 자부심을 가지며 서로 도와가는 사람들이다.

7. The US government has decided / to make a shift in its Asia-conscious foreign policy.
미국 정부는 아시아를 의식하는 외교정책을 바꾸기로 결정했다.

8. My father has / a miscellaneous collection of coins, stamps, and many other things.
우리 아버지는 잡다한 동전, 우표, 그리고 다른 많은 소장품들을 갖고 있다.

9. Some of the neutral countries tried / to get the warlike nations to discuss the terms of peace.
일부 중립국들은 교전국들이 싸움을 중지하고 화해조건을 논의하도록 노력했다.

10. The President of the United States found out / that maintaining security on the Korean Peninsular is not an easy task.
미국 대통령은 한반도의 안전을 유지하기가 쉬운 일이 아니라는 것을 알게 되었다.

11. That is / why I appreciate coming across poetry in everyday life.
이것이 내가 일상생활에서 시 감상을 즐기는 이유이다.

12. Columbia is / one of the most dangerous countries in the world for journalists.
콜롬비아는 세계에서 저널리스트에게 가장 위험한 나라 중의 하나이다.

13. Few people are aware / that our government is suffering from budget shortages.
우리 정부가 예산부족으로 어려움을 겪고 있다는 사실을 아는 사람은 거의 없다.

14. The essential role of hand gestures is / to mark the points of emphasis in our speech.
손동작의 중요한 역할은 연설 중에 강조할 부분을 표시하는 것이다.

15. The most important issue facing these Muslim countries is / understanding the differences among cultures.
이 이슬람 국가들을 대하는 가장 중요한 문제는 문화차이를 이해하는 것이다.

16. The best policy in the present situation is / that we should be honest enough to tell the truth.
현재 상황에서 최선의 방법은 우리가 진실을 말할 수 있을 정도로 정직해야 한다는 것이다.

17. The two Koreas should learn / the lesson of peaceful reunification from East and West Germany.
남한과 북한은 동독과 서독으로부터 평화통일의 교훈을 배워야 한다.

18. The American Revolution was / a war between England and the American colonies of England.
미국독립혁명은 영국과 미국의 영국식민지 간의 전쟁이었다.

19. Some hand gestures are used / when we want to express ourselves with great emphasis.
손동작의 일부는 우리가 표현하는 것을 크게 강조할 때 사용된다.

20. One of the most challenging experiences in my life was / climbing to the top of Mount Everest in Nepal last summer.
내 일생에 가장 도전적인 경험 중 하나는 작년 여름 네팔의 에베레스트 산을 오른 것이었다.

21. I think / the key thing is that both of the parties work together.
나는 중요한 것은 양당이 협력하는 것이라고 생각한다.

22. These giant jigsaws contain / air-filled cavities not easily penetrated by sound.
이 거대한 조각들은 소리가 쉽게 통과하지 않는 공기로 채워진 빈 공간이 포함되어 있다.

23. People don't know / much about the history of the Vatican.
사람들은 가톨릭교회의 역사에 대해서는 잘 모른다.

24. The computer is / one of the most widely used scientific tools.
컴퓨터는 가장 널리 사용되는 과학기기 중 하나이다.

25. They insist / that the rights of animals be acknowledged and respected.
그들은 동물의 권리도 인정받고 존중 받아야 한다고 주장한다.

26. The Renaissance was / a rebirth of ideas and morality.
르네상스는 사상과 도덕성의 부활이었다.

27. The good news is / that most cases are not serious and can be easily treated with medicine.
좋은 소식은 대부분의 병세가 그리 심각하지 않고 쉽게 약으로 치료될 수 있다는 점이다.

28. The research shows / that pre-school children are capable of thinking in abstract terms.
그 연구는 취학 이전의 아동들이 추상적인 용어로 생각할 수 있다는 것을 보여주고 있다.

29. She commended / the steadfast courage of families caring for handicapped children.
그녀는 장애아동을 돌보는 가정들의 확고한 용기를 칭찬했다.

30. The Mayan civilization is / one of the best-known civilizations that existed in the Americas.
마야 문명은 아메리카 대륙에 존재했던 가장 잘 알려진 문명 가운데 하나이다.

3. 전치사나 to부정사 앞에서 끊어읽기_ P. 22

Exercise

1. We had to go to the airport by taxi / in order not to miss the flight to Vancouver.
우리는 밴쿠버로 가는 비행기를 놓치지 않기 위해 택시로 공항에 가야했다.

2. He inspired people / to make peaceful protests and disobey the British laws.
그는 평화적으로 저항을 하면서 영국 법에 불복종하도록 사람들을 고무시켰다.

3. We are looking for opportunities / to improve organizational and operational efficiencies.
우리는 조직과 운영의 효율성을 더욱 향상시키기 위한 기회를 찾고 있다.

4. The authors are to be congratulated / on producing such a clear and authoritative work.
저자들은 그처럼 명료하고 권위 있는 저작물을 펴낸 데에 대해 축하를 받아 마땅하다.

5. The earth was entirely covered / by a warm water ocean, and pelted by ceaseless rain.
지구는 계속되는 폭우로 따뜻한 바닷물 속에 푹 잠겨 있었다.

6. Most American voters are divided / into two camps, Republicans and Democrats.
대부분의 미국 투표자들은 공화당과 민주당의 양 진영으로 나뉜다.

7. Major changes in tax and spending policies are / in the offing for the first time in 11 years.
11년 안에 처음으로 조세 및 지출정책에 변화가 머지않아 일어날 것이다.

8. We should carefully think about the reason for someone's behavior / to avoid coming to a hasty conclusion about it.
우리는 어떤 사람이 왜 그러한 행동을 했는지에 대해서 성급한 결론을 내리는 것을 피하기 위해 조심스럽게 생각해야 한다.

9. The federal government had control / over the states, industry, trade and slavery.
연방정부는 주, 산업, 무역과 노예제도를 관장했다.

10. The fireman rescued the baby / within a measurable distance of the building collapse.
소방관은 빌딩이 무너지기 직전에 아기를 구조했다.

11. I had a hard time convincing him / to turn himself in to the police.
나는 그가 경찰에 자수하도록 설득하느라 애먹었다.

12. A large dose of poison was detected / in the dead man's stomach.
죽은 사람의 위장에서 다량의 독약이 발견되었다.

13. Plenty of exercise is the best way / to lose weight without any side effects.
충분한 운동이 부작용 없이 살을 빼는 가장 좋은 방법이다.

14. Mexican immigration to the U.S. has increased greatly / in recent decades.
미국으로의 멕시코인의 이주는 최근 수십 년 동안 크게 증가해왔다.

15. Most Americans make it a rule / to make an appointment before their visit.
대부분의 미국인들은 방문하기 전에 약속 정하는 것을 규칙으로 삼고 있다.

16. It was not that easy for Monica / to forget the past and make a fresh start.
모니카에게 과거를 잊고 새로운 출발을 한다는 것이 그렇게 쉬운 일은 아니었다.

17. You must be out of your mind / to believe such nonsense and act in that way.
네가 그런 허튼소리를 믿고 그렇게 행동하다니 제정신이 아니구나.

18. The depression in the United States lasted / until the beginning of the Second World War.
미국의 불경기는 제 2차 세계대전 초까지 계속되었다.

19. The spider-monkey's tail can be used / to pick up fruit or grab the branches of trees.
거미원숭이의 꼬리는 물체를 집어 올리거나 나뭇가지를 붙드는 데 사용될 수 있다.

20. The commuting time is usually longer / for suburban residents than for those living in the city.
출퇴근 시간은 보통 도시 근교 거주자가 도시 거주자 보다 더 걸린다.

21. The personal computer was first developed / by Steve Jobs in the United States.
개인용 컴퓨터는 미국의 스티브 잡스에 의해 처음 개발되었다.

22. You must always work hard / in anything and everything to survive to the end.
무슨 일이든 끝까지 살아남기 위해서는 항상 열심히 일을 해야 한다.

23. The media plays a very important role / in election campaigns across the world.
대중매체는 전 세계에 걸쳐 선거운동에서 중요한 역할을 한다.

24. Don't come up with the evil intention / of using the Internet during the exams.
시험 중에 인터넷을 사용하겠다는 나쁜 생각을 갖지 마라.

25. I'd like to congratulate you / on your remarkable achievements in college.
나는 대학에서 이룬 너의 탁월한 성과에 대해 축하하고 싶다.

26. A father wanted to show his son / how to farm without agricultural chemicals.
아빠는 그의 아들에게 무농약 재배법을 보여주길 원했다.

27. The senator is accused of accepting bribes / in exchange for using his political influence.
그 상원의원은 그의 정치적 영향력을 사용하는 대가로 뇌물을 받은 혐의로 기소되어 있다.

28. A recent survey shows that there is a gap between the labor supply and demand / in the e-business industry.

최근의 조사는 전자 상거래 산업에서 노동공급과 수요사이에 차이가 있다는 것을 보여 준다.

29. It is vital to find investment partners / to pay for the cost of film production.

영화 제작비를 충당하기 위해서 투자가를 찾는 것은 매우 중요하다.

30. His articles are thoroughly enjoyable / for readers.

그의 기사들은 독자들에게 완전히 흥미롭다.

4. 접속사나 관계사 앞 끊어읽기_ P. 27

Exercise

1. Choosing a career is a matter / which calls for reflection.

직업을 선택하는 일은 신중을 요하는 문제이다.

2. I know in my bones / that I will never break up with Monica.

나는 모니카랑 절대 헤어지지 않으리란 걸 직감한다.

3. Mike called his girlfriend / whose hobby is going to the movies.

마이크는 취미가 영화감상인 여자친구에게 전화했다.

4. We started with an argument, / but our talks ended with an agreement.

우리는 논쟁으로 시작했지만 합의로 이야기를 마쳤다.

5. She felt very strongly / that I should be adopted by college graduates.

그녀는 내가 대학교 졸업자에게 입양되기를 굳게 마음먹었다.

6. The number of alligators / which they caught each time went down sharply.

그들이 매번 잡았던 악어의 숫자가 급격히 줄어들었다.

7. Amusement parks are packed with people / when the weather is nice.

놀이공원은 날씨가 좋을 때 사람들로 꽉 찬다.

8. The stock market had reached 2700 points / but nose-dived to 1900 points in a week.

주식시장은 2700포인트에 이르렀지만 1주일 만에 1900포인트까지 급격히 떨어졌다.

9. Rumor says / that there is a special chemical / which prevents cancer in this liquid.

소문에 의하면 이 액체에 암을 예방하는 특별한 화학물질이 있다.

10. Some of the students arrived early / and gathered near the main entrance, / even though they were not supposed to stay there.

비록 그들이 거기에 있기로 하진 않았지만 몇몇 학생들이 일찍 와서 정문 가까이에 모여 있었다.

11. The bank acknowledged its error / but refused to compensate the customers for their losses.

그 은행은 과실을 인정했지만 고객이 입은 손해에 대해서는 보상하기를 거절했다.

12. People have lost interest in modern arts / and have turned to sports stars / and other popular figures to find their role models.

사람들은 현대 예술에 대한 관심을 잃었고 그들의 롤모델을 찾기 위해 스포츠 스타와 다른 유명 인사들에게 의존하게 되었다.

13. His lecture made me focus on / what is more important in life.

그의 강의는 삶에서 보다 중요한 것에 중점을 두게 했다.

14. Advertisers change people's thinking by using language / which appeals to emotions.
광고주들은 감정에 호소하는 언어를 사용함으로써 사람들의 생각을 바꾼다.

15. Our store has a wide selection of cameras at reasonable prices, / so you don't have to shop around.
우리 가게에는 저렴한 가격의 다양한 종류의 카메라가 있다. 그래서 여러 상점을 돌아다니며 물건을 볼 필요가 없다.

16. A meteorologist is a person / who studies the earth's atmosphere to predict weather conditions.
기상학자는 기상 상태를 예측하기 위해 지구의 대기를 연구하는 사람이다.

17. The software filters out Internet sites / whose content is not suitable for children.
그 소프트웨어는 아이들에게 적절하지 않은 내용을 담고 있는 인터넷 사이트를 차단한다.

18. The child had suffered / what has become known as "battered baby syndrome."
그 아이는 '피학대아 증후군'으로 알려진 것에 의해 고통을 받았다.

19. At Taiji in Central Japan, they force the dolphins into a small inlet, / where the water turns red with their blood.
일본 중부지방인 Taiji에서, 사람들은 돌고래를 그들의 피로 붉게 물든 작은 입구로 몰아간다.

20. The whole team has autographed the football, / which will be used as a prize.
그 팀의 전체 선수들이 상으로 사용될 그 축구공에 사인을 했다.

21. They deserve your attention and care, / even if all you do is smile and say hello.
그들은 당신이 하는 일이 미소와 인사뿐이라 해도 당신의 주의와 관심을 받을 자격이 있다.

22. African slaves began to have the right to claim suffrage and citizenship / after the Civil War ended in 1866.
아프리카 노예들은 1866년 미국의 남북전쟁이 끝났을 때 참정권과 시민권을 갖게 되었다.

23. Audiences rarely find the speaker interesting / and don't try to listen carefully to what he says.
발표자에게 흥미를 느끼는 청중은 드물며 그의 얘기를 관심 있게 잘 들으려하지 않는다.

24. There is also a quantity discount, / which is offered to individuals / who order large quantities of a product.
다량 할인이 있다. 그것은 많은 양의 제품을 주문하는 개인에게 제공된다.

25. It's quite important for businessmen / who are engaged in international trade to learn about different cultures and to learn languages.
국제무역과 관련되는 사업가들에게는 다른문화와 언어를 배우는 게 꽤 중요하다.

26. We were amazed at a magical sunrise, / which made me understand / why Korea is often called "Land of the Morning Calm."
우리는 왜 한국이 종종 '고요한 아침의 나라'라고 불리는지를 우리에게 알게 해 준 황홀한 일출에 감탄했다.

27. All I ask in return is / that you take good enough care of yourself / so that someday you can do the same thing for someone else.
내가 바라는 것은 네가 언젠가 다른 이에게 같은 일을 하기 위해 자신을 충분히 잘 돌보는 것이다.

28. Most foreign workers are being taught by Korean coworkers or volunteers / who have no or little teaching experience.
대부분의 외국인 노동자들은 가르친 경험이 전혀 또는 거의 없는 한국인 직장동료나 자원봉사자들에게 교육을 받고 있다.

29. James II soon changed his mind / when he found out how attractive the game was, / and it immediately became popular again.
제임스 2세는 골프게임이 얼마나 매력적인지 깨닫고 마음을 바꾸었다. 그리고 그것은 바로 다시 인기를 끌게 되었다.

30. Place your watch on the table in front of you / or keep your eyes on the clock in the back of the room / if you don't want to go over the allotted time.

당신에게 주어진 시간을 넘기지 않길 원하면 당신 앞에 있는 테이블 위에다 시계를 두거나 방 뒤쪽에 있는 시계를 주시하라.

5. 쉼표, 콜론, 세미콜론 뒤, 삽입구 사이 끊어읽기_ P. 32

Exercise

1. The tango, / the traditional Argentine dance, / has a fascinating history.

아르헨티나의 전통 춤인 탱고는 대단히 흥미로운 역사를 갖고 있다.

2. When the civil war ended in 1866, / blacks could receive citizenship and the right to vote.

1866년 미국의 남북전쟁이 끝났을 때 흑인들은 시민권과 참정권을 갖게 되었다.

3. I remember the story of the child, / who was adopted and raised by a chimpanzee.

나는 침팬지에게 입양되어 키워진 아이의 이야기를 기억한다.

4. As a result, / the responsibilities and the discretion of the police have changed.

결과적으로, 경찰의 책임과 재량권이 바뀌었다.

5. Snake bites, / bee stings, / and hedgehog spines / give their victims a sharp pain.

뱀에 물림, 벌의 침, 고슴도치의 가시는 공격자에게 심한 통증을 준다.

6. After you hear a question, / read the four choices on your test paper, / and decide which one is correct.

질문을 들은 후에, 시험지에 있는 네 개의 선택지를 읽고 어느 것이 맞는지 결정하시오.

7. Five young women in the Chinese village, / who were waiting for the matchmaker to look them over, / were gathered together.

중국 마을에 그들을 알아보러 오는 중매쟁이를 기다리고 있는 젊은 여자 다섯 명이 함께 모여 있었다.

8. It's extremely important to learn different languages and learn about different cultures, / especially for those who are in the student exchange programs.

특히 교환학생 프로그램에 참여한 학생들에게는 다른 언어와 문화를 배우는 것이 극히 중요하다.

9. Many animals adjust to changes in their environment; / in ways of finding food, / protecting themselves from their enemies, / and reproducing.

많은 동물들은 그들의 환경의 변화에 적응한다; 예를 들어 먹이를 찾는 방법, 적으로부터 그들을 보호하거나 번식하는 등등.

10. Each year, / Brazilians all over the country celebrate Carnival, / a month long holiday, / with dancing, / parades, / extravagant costumes, / and traditional food.

매년 브라질 사람들은 전국에서 한 달 내내 춤과 퍼레이드, 화려한 의상, 전통음식과 함께하는 축제를 연다.

11. I say / follow your bliss and don't be afraid, / and doors will open when you don't expect them to.

나는 말한다, 당신이 행복을 느끼는 일을 추구하고 두려워하지 말라, 그러면 당신이 전혀 기대하지도 않았던 때 문이 열릴 것이다.

12. Alberto Giacometti, / known as a sculptor of tall, / haunting, / stick-like figures, / was born in 1901 in Borgonovo.

조각가로 알려진 키가 크고, 유령처럼 보이며, 막대기처럼 생긴 알베르토 자코메티는 1901년 보고노보에서 태어났다.

13. The consonant 'C' was left off; / but I realized that the tears that flowed with Tiffany's declaration made me the wealthiest woman in the world.

자음 c가 빠졌지만 나는 티파니의 고백과 함께 흐르는 그 눈물이 나를 세상에서 가장 부유한 여자로 만들었다는 것을 깨달았다.

14. Sir Francis Drake, / who was an English explorer, / privateer, / and pirate, / was the first English man to sail around the world.

프랜시스 드레이크경은 영국의 탐험가이자 선장이며 해적이었으며, 전 세계를 항해한 최초의 영국 사람이었다.

15. Buying packs of cigarettes everyday costs a lot of money in the long run; / moreover, smoking causes various diseases including cancer.

매일 담배를 몇 갑씩 사는 것은 길게 보면 돈이 많이 든다. 게다가 흡연은 암을 비롯한 여러 병의 원인이 된다.

16. A rich man once asked a friend, / "Why am I criticized for being miserly?"

한 부자가 친구에게 물었다. '나는 왜 구두쇠라고 비난을 받는 거지?'

17. The issues that were brought up included air pollution, / ozone depletion, / and global warming.

제기된 문제점은 대기오염, 오존층 파괴와 지구온난화를 포함한다.

18. He kept persuading juries, / under disadvantages, / and finally proved his innocence.

그는 불리한 상황에서도 계속 배심원을 설득했고, 결국 그의 무죄를 입증했다.

19. Grayson Bank is expected to announce, / as early as tomorrow, / that it is pulling its merger offer.

그레이슨 은행은 빠르면 내일 합병 제안의 수락을 발표할 예정이다.

20. Warning: / You are about to change your Internet settings. If you wish to continue click "OK," / otherwise click "Cancel."

경고: 인터넷 설정을 변경하려고 한다. 계속하려면 '확인'을, 취소하려면 '취소'를 누르시오.

21. Having watched the news on TV, / I know about the suicide bombing in Iraq.

TV에서 뉴스를 보았기 때문에, 나는 이라크에서의 그 자살 폭탄 테러에 대해 안다.

22. I used to be very active when I was in college / – going hiking, horseback riding, canoeing – / but I haven't done any of those things in years.

대학 다닐 때에는 매우 활동적이었다 –하이킹도 가고, 승마도 하고, 카누도 타고– 하지만 몇 년 동안 그 어떤 것도 못했다.

23. The Great Depression, / which started in 1929 in the United States, / was a severe economic crisis.

1929년에 시작된 대공황은 미국의 심각한 경제위기였다.

24. If you have finished selecting a topic for your assignment, / please begin the research project with your group members.

연구 과제의 주제를 정했으면, 조원들과 프로젝트에 대한 자료조사를 시작하시오.

25. The work of the housewife is varied; / she cleans, / washes, / cooks, / and takes care of the children.

전업주부의 일은 다양하다; 청소하고, 설거지와 빨래를 하고, 요리하고, 아이들을 돌본다.

26. The purpose of our business is to sell products, / to offer the best follow-up service, / and to make profits.

우리 사업의 목적은 물건을 파는 것, 사후 관리에 최선을 다하는 것, 그리고 수익을 올리는 것이다.

27. After you fill out a brief online subscription form, / your free publications will start arriving at your door.

간단한 온라인 구독 신청서를 작성한 후에, 무료 출판물이 당신 집으로 배달되기 시작할 것이다.

28. While he was in Mongolia, / the archaeologist found fossils, / which turned out to be dinosaur fossils.

몽고에 있는 동안, 고고학자는 화석을 발견했다. 그러나 그것들은 공룡화석으로 밝혀졌다.

29. I had easily answered all the questions until I read the last one: / "What is the name of the woman who manages the school?"

나는 마지막 문제를 읽을 때까지 모든 질문에 쉽게 답했다 : '학교를 운영하는 여자의 이름은 무엇인가?'

30. Over 10 million people all over the world enjoy celebrating the Rio Carnival every year, / which is also called the Samba Festival, / a month long holiday of dancing Samba.

매년 전세계 천만이 넘는 사람들이 리오 카니발을 즐긴다. 그것은 삼바 페스티발이라고도 부르며 삼바춤을 즐기는 한 달간의 휴가이다.

Unit 02 그려 읽기

1. 본동사구에 동그라미_ P. 38

Exercise

01. Any question (seems) easier after you get your paper back.

치른 시험지를 돌려받고 난 뒤에는 어떤 시험문제도 모두 쉬워 보인다.

02. In situations like this, I (used to lose) my temper when I was much younger.

이런 상황에서, 훨씬 어렸을 적에 나는 화를 내곤 했다.

03. When my two daughters went to visit their grandparents, I (could be absorbed in) reading.

두 딸이 조부모 댁에 놀러갔을 때, 나는 독서삼매경에 빠질 수 있었다.

04. Animals ultimately (depend on) other living things, a supply of plants, to live.

동물은 다른 살아있는 생명체에, 궁극적으로는 식물에 공급을 의존할 수밖에 없다.

05. Scientists (have found) a way to extend the life of the fruit fly by as much as one month.

과학자들은 초파리의 수명을 한 달정도 연장할 수 있는 방법을 발견했다.

06. This discovery (might someday help) humans' live longer and without disease.

이러한 발견이 언젠가는 인간이 무병장수하는데 도움이 될지도 모른다.

07. As a consultant, I (was supposed to spend) about an hour with the department heads discussing their thoughts.

자문위원으로서 나는 부서장들과 그들의 생각을 상의하는데 한 시간쯤 보내기로 예정되어 있었다.

08. Poetry (provides) us with what is missing in our own lives — the experience of imaginative pleasure.

시는 우리자신의 삶에서 상상의 즐거운 경험과 같은 뭔가 부족한 것을 우리에게 제공한다.

09. My teacher (said) that the United States was a colony of Great Britain for about 170 years from the beginning of the 17th century.

선생님께서 미국이 17세기 초부터 약 170년간 영국 식민지였다고 말씀하셨다.

10. Microsoft chairman Bill Gates (has promised) to donate $ 200 million to help libraries in low-income areas throughout America.

마이크로소프트 회장 빌게이츠는 미국 전역의 저소득 지역도서관에 200만 불을 기부하겠다고 약속해 왔다.

11. Many people (form) their first impression according to how you look.

많은 사람들은 그들 자신이 어떻게 보이냐에 따라 첫 인상을 좌우한다.

12. The official unemployment rate (has declined) modestly over the past year.

작년 한 해 걸쳐 공식적인 실업률은 완만히 감소해 왔다.

13. The leading candidate for President (said) that America was born in the 18th century out of the bold conviction that we are all created equal.

가장 유력한 대통령 후보는 미국이 18세기에 우리 모두 평등하게 창조됐다는 확고한 신념 아래 태어났다고 말했다.

14. In a study conducted at the university laboratory, the growth of some plants (was affected) by playing music to them.

그 대학 실험실에서 연구한 조사에서 몇몇 식물은 성장하는 데 음악을 틀어주는 것에 영향을 받았다.

15. Developing connections between commerce and culture (gives) us a chance to lift the fortunes and spirit of people all over the world.

나날이 증가하는 통상과 문화교류는 우리에게 세계 곳곳의 사람들의 부와 사기를 향상시키는 기회를 제공하고 있다.

16. A clear introduction (should be made), therefore, if you want to build good social relationships with others.

당신이 다른 사람과 좋은 사회적 관계를 만들기 원하면 확실한 소개를 받아야 할 것이다.

17. Nigeria, a former British colony, (is) one of the world's largest oil producers, but the oil industry (has produced) unwanted side effects.

이전 영국식민지였던 나이지리아는 세계에서 가장 큰 산유국 중 하나이지만 석유산업은 원치 않는 부작용을 낳았다.

18. It (seems) that English-speaking people are pretty good at inventing new words by clipping the longer forms or by putting the initials of some words together.

영어를 쓰는 사람들은 긴 서식을 짧게 줄이거나 머리글자를 여러 개 합쳐 새로운 단어를 잘 만들어 내는 것처럼 보인다.

19. Veterans from other countries who had fought in the Korean War (were impressed) by the Seoul World Cup Stadium and the panoramic views of Seoul from the 63 Building.

외국에서 온 한국전 참전용사들은 서울 월드컵경기장과 63빌딩에서 바라본 서울의 전경에 꽤 감동 받았다.

20. For many years men (caught and killed) the blue whales in huge factory ships, so that the number of blue whales decreased from hundreds of thousands to fewer than one thousand.

수년간 사람들은 흰긴수염고래를 잡아 거대한 가공설비를 갖춘 배에서 죽였다. 그래서 흰긴수염고래는 수십만 마리에서 천 마리 이하로 수가 감소하였다.

21. They (involve) physical skill, strength and endurance.

그것은 신체적 기술, 힘, 지구력을 포함한다.

22. This art and craft with a difference (inspires) me with a new idea.

이 색다른 미술용품은 나에게 새로운 아이디어를 불어 넣는다.

23. She (realized) that her youth and inexperience were being exploited.

그녀는 자신의 젊음과 경험 미숙이 이용당하고 있다는 것을 깨달았다.

24. The programs (would provide) workers with information about the risk of injuries.

이 프로그램은 근로자들에게 부상의 위험성에 대한 정보를 제공할 것이다.

25. (Do not experiment) with wild flowers unless you are certain they are edible.

그것들이 식용 가능하다는 것이 확실치 않으면 야생화로 실험하지 마라.

26. Sam (wanted) to stop watching the movie because he found it very boring.

Sam은 그 영화가 지루하다는 것을 알고 보는 것을 중단하고 싶었다.

27. They (estimate) that the trip from downtown to the airport will take less than half an hour.

그들은 시내에서 공항까지 가는 데 30분도 채 안 걸릴 것으로 어림잡고 있다.

28. Some cars on the KTX (are designated) as no smoking areas.

고속철도의 몇몇 칸은 금연 구역으로 지정되어 있다.

29. I fully (acknowledge) that there is more than one way to approach an issue.

나는 주제에 접근하는데 뭔가 다른 방법이 있다는 것을 완전히 인정한다.

30. It (was) so dark that I couldn't distinguish the faces of people right in front of me.

너무 어두워서 바로 앞에 있는 사람들의 얼굴을 식별할 수 없었다.

2. 명사 뒤에서 수식하는 긴 형용사 [구와 절]에 소괄호 치고 화살표_ P. 43

Exercise

01. The butterflies (which the entomologist found in Africa) turned out to be bats.

그 곤충학자가 아프리카에서 발견한 나비는 박쥐로 밝혀졌다.

02. The first emotions (surging in Ann's mind) were curiosity and jealousy.

Ann의 마음속에 용솟음치는 최초의 감정은 호기심과 질투심이었다.

03. My father took us to see a naughty bear (that caught our attention).

아버지는 관심을 끄는 장난꾸러기 곰을 보여주려고 우리를 데려갔다.

04. The number of deaths (caused by traffic accidents) has sharply increased since last year.

교통사고로 인한 사망자의 숫자가 작년 이후 급격히 증가하였다.

05. His airplane (which was expected to fly across the Atlantic ocean to New York) made an emergency landing on a deserted island.

대서양 건너 뉴욕으로 갈 예정이던 그의 비행기는 무인도에 비상착륙을 했다.

06. The jobs (that most companies are doing with information these days) were not available.

요즘 대부분의 회사들이 정보와 관련되어 수행하는 업무들이 가능하지 않았다.

07. In a laboratory study (conducted at the university,) some changes in plant growth patterns were brought about by playing music to the plants.

그 대학에서 행해진 실험실 연구에서 식물에 음악을 틀어줌에 따라 식물성장에 대한 몇몇 변화가 일어났다.

08. The women (wearing black and white uniforms) are walking down the main street.

검정과 하얀색 제복을 입고 있는 여자들이 중심가를 걷고 있다.

09. The importance (of chocolate as a food) is overshadowed by its universal use (as a snack).

식품으로서의 초콜릿의 중요성은 간식으로서의 일반적인 사용 때문에 가려졌다.

10. One of the best ways (to lose weight without side effects) is a balanced diet (with enough exercise).

부작용 없이 살을 빼는 가장 좋은 방법 중 하나는 충분한 운동과 함께하는 균형 잡힌 식이요법이다.

11. I have a boy (who watches commercials on television and then tries to get me to buy every item (he has seen)).

나에게는 TV광고를 보고 광고에서 본 모든 제품을 사달라고 조르는 아들이 있다.

12. I learned later that we had hit a car (coming from the other direction).

나는 나중에 우리가 반대편에서 오는 차와 부딪쳤다는 것을 알았다.

13. He doesn't seem like the kind of person (that would do something like that).

그는 그런 일을 할 사람 같지는 않다.

14. Growing as a person is to travel to places (where there are new challenges).

한 사람으로 성장한다는 것은 새로운 도전이 있는 장소로 여행하는 것이다.

15. People (walking down the street) are wearing leather jackets (as if they just arrived in a time machine).

길 아래로 걸어 내려가는 사람들은 마치 방금 타임머신에서 도착한 것 처럼 가죽재킷을 입고 있었다.

16. Peter Thompson, (with whom I have a close working relationship,) mentioned your name to me and strongly suggested I contact you.

나와 일을 주로 같이하는 피터 톰슨이 당신의 이름을 나에게 알려주고 만나봐야 한다고 강력히 추천해주었다.

17. The odd thing (about our communication) is we're more likely to talk about something (that is nothing).

우리의 의사소통에서 이상한 점은 당신이 무엇인가 특별한 것을 별것 아닌 것처럼 말하곤 하는 것이다.

18. We conducted a survey of the people (who lived near the airport and had complained for years about the noise).

우리는 공항 근처에 살며 소음에 대해 몇 년간 항의해 오고 있는 사람들을 설문조사 했다.

19. I was able for the first time in my life to say the exact thing (I wanted to say) at the exact moment (I wanted to say it).

나는 난생 처음으로 내가 말하고 싶은 바로 그것을 내가 그것을 말하고 싶은 바로 그 시간에 말할 수 있었다.

20. The astronauts will meet the rest of the other Russian crew (who have been working at the International Space Station since mid May).

우주 비행사들은 5월 중순부터 국제우주정거장에서 작업을 해 온 다른 러시아 승무원들과 만나게 될 것이다.

21. Their launch was watched by their families from an observation platform in the cosmodrome (located in the steppes of the central Asian country).

중앙아시아의 대초원에 위치한 우주발사기지의 관찰 전망대에서 가족들이 발사 장면을 지켜봤다.

22. The information (conveyed in this high-tech manner) somehow adds authority to what is conveyed, when in fact the Internet is a global conveyer of unfiltered, unedited, untreated information.

이런 첨단 기술방식으로 전달되어지는 정보는 사실은 인터넷이 여과되지 않고, 편집되지 않고, 처리되지 않은 정보를 전달하는 전 세계적인 매체임에도 불구하고 전달되는 내용에 권위를 더해준다.

23. One reason (most dogs are much happier than most people) is that dogs aren't affected by external circumstances the way (we are).

대부분의 개들이 대부분의 사람들보다 훨씬 더 행복한 한 가지 이유는 개가 우리(인간)처럼 외부 환경의 영향을 받지 않는 것이다.

24. This asymmetry means females (who warn close kin by emitting alarm calls,) while males generally do not emit calls.

이러한 불균형은 경고음을 냄으로써 가까운 친족에게 경고하는 암컷들이 되게 하며, 반면 수컷들은 대개 경고음을 내지 않는다.

25. Recent evidence suggests that the common ancestor (of Neanderthals and modern people,) (living about 350,000 years ago,) may have already been using pretty sophisticated language.

최근의 증거는 약 35만년 전에 살았던 네안데르탈인과 현대인의 공통 조상이 아주 세련된 언어를 이미 사용하고 있었을지도 모른다는 점을 시사한다.

26. The number of cars (exported in 2012) is greater than in 2011, but the average price is not much higher.

2012년에 수출된 차량의 수는 2011년보다 더 많지만 평균 가격은 크게 높지 않다.

27. Gregorio Dati was a successful merchant of Florence, (who entered into many profitable partnerships dealing in wool, silk, and other merchandise).

그레고리오 다티는 이문이 남는 많은 협력관계를 맺고 양털, 비단, 그리고 다른 상품 장사를 한 플로렌스의 성공한 상인이었다.

28. This is particularly true among people (who might not themselves have access to the Internet but hear a piece of news or gossip from the people around them who do have access).

이것은 스스로는 인터넷에 접근할 수 없지만, 인터넷에 접속하는 주위 사람들로부터 소식이나 소문을 들을 수 있는 사람들에게 특히 그러하다.

29. It appears that measures (that protect drivers from the consequences of bad driving) encourage bad driving.

운전자들을 잘못된 운전의 결과로부터 보호하는 수단들이 바람직하지 않은 운전을 조장하는 것처럼 보인다.

30. Fast muscle fibers are cells (that can contract more quickly and powerfully than slow muscle fibers but fatigue much more easily); they function best for short bursts of intense activity, like weight lifting or sprinting.

빠른 근섬유는 느린 근섬유보다 더 빠르고 강력하게 수축할 수 있지만, 훨씬 더 쉽게 피로해지는 세포이며; 그것은 역도나 단거리 경주와 같은 짧고 폭발적인 격렬한 활동에서 가장 잘 작용한다.

3. 동사(준동사) 뒤에서 수식하는 긴 부사 [구와 절]에 소괄호 치고 화살표_ **P. 49**

Exercise

01. It is generally accepted that people are motivated (by success).

사람들은 대체로 성공에 의해 동기부여 받는다는 것을 일반적으로 받아들인다.

02. You should keep eating fresh fruit and vegetables (to prevent diabetes).

당뇨병을 예방하려면 신선한 과일과 채소를 계속 먹어야 한다.

03. Employers run their businesses efficiently (to get more profits).

고용주들은 더 많은 이득을 얻으려고 사업을 효율적으로 운영한다.

04. He spent the whole weekend studying (in order to do well on his mid-term exam).

그는 중간고사를 잘 보기 위해 공부하느라 주말을 다 보냈다.

05. They spoke (in Korean) (in the interview) after the concert although the team members conducted the concert in Japanese.

비록 팀 구성원들이 일본어로 공연을 진행했지만 공연 후의 인터뷰에서는 한국어로 말을 했다.

06. The Korean government has spent a lot of money and time recently (trying to increase the birth rate).

한국정부는 출생률을 높이기 위해 최근에 많은 돈과 시간을 써 왔다.

07. The amusement parks in America were always crowded with tourists from Korea (when I visited there in 2012).

2012년에 내가 미국의 놀이공원을 방문했을 때는 언제나 한국에서 온 관광객들로 붐볐다.

08. Many housewives feel stressed (whenever they think of the upcoming holidays).

많은 주부들은 다가오는 명절만 생각하면 스트레스를 받는다.

09. All the new buildings were built in a modern style (so as to accommodate the airport around them).

주변의 공항에 어울리도록 새로운 건물은 현대식으로 지어졌다.

10. The Vietnamese found themselves continuously fighting against corruption and poverty (at the turn of the century).

베트남 사람들은 세기가 바뀔무렵 지속적으로 부패와 가난에 맞서 싸우고 있는 자신의 모습을 발견했다.

11. Alex liked sports and loud music a lot (like most other kids).

알렉스는 대부분의 다른 아이들처럼 스포츠와 시끄러운 음악을 아주 좋아했다.

12. I called him several times last night (to borrow some money from him).

나는 그에게 돈을 빌리려고 어젯밤에 여러 번 전화를 걸었다.

13. I started teaching English in China (as soon as I graduated from university in 1997).

1997년에 대학을 졸업하자마자 나는 중국에서 영어를 가르치기 시작했다.

14. King Harold was killed (at the Battle of Hastings) and his Anglo-Saxon army was defeated.

헤롤드왕이 헤이스팅즈 전투에서 전사하였고, 그의 앵글로–색슨족 군대는 패배하였다.

15. The farmer should change the cow's food slowly (so that the cow can adapt to the new food).

농부는 젖소가 새로운 먹이에 적응할 수 있도록 젖소의 먹이를 천천히 바꿔야 한다.

16. He could become a major league player quickly (as he is determined to create a role for himself and practices very hard).

그는 자신을 위한 역할을 만들어 내기로 다짐하고 아주 열심히 연습해서 빠르게 메이저리그 선수가 될 수 있었다.

17. England has not been isolated from Europe throughout its history (although it was an island nation).

섬나라임에도 불구하고, 영국은 역사 전반에 걸쳐 유럽으로부터 고립된 적이 없었다.

18. Many animals adapt to their surroundings (by scavenging for food, reproducing, and protecting themselves from predators).

많은 동물들은 음식을 찾고 번식하며 적으로부터 그들을 보호하므로 그들의 환경의 변화에 적응한다.

19. The pedestrian was lying (in the back of the ambulance) (in agony) (after a hit-and- run driver knocked him down and drove away).

보행자는 뺑소니 운전자가 그를 치고 도주한 후에 구급차량 뒤 좌석에서 고통을 느끼며 누워있었다.

20. Jeffrey Newell, president of Hartley Hotels, will come this week (to speak to local business people) (about ways to develop international tourism).

하틀리 호텔 회장인 제프리 뉴웰이 이번 주에 지역 경영인들에게 국제 관광 발전을 위한 방법에 대해 연설을 하러 올 것이다.

21. Elementary biology textbooks help to produce a misleading impression of what perception entails (by likening the eye to a camera).

기초 생물학 교과서는 눈을 카메라에 비유함으로써 인식이 수반하는 것에 대한 잘못된 인상을 만들어 내는데 기여하고 있다.

22. Drivers feel less vulnerable and tend to take more chances (as safety features are added to vehicles and roads).

운전자들은 안전장치들을 차량이나 도로에 추가할수록 위기의식을 덜 느끼게 되고 더 많은 모험을 하는 경향이 있다.

23. Scientists can lessen bias (by running as many trials as possible) and (by keeping accurate notes of each observation made).

과학자들은 가능한 한 많은 실험을 하고, 관찰한 것을 정확히 기록함으로써 편견을 줄일 수 있다.

24. According to recent studies, although praise may encourage children to continue an activity while an adult is watching, they are less likely to continue the activity (when the adult leaves) or to repeat the activity (in the future).

최근의 연구에 따르면 칭찬은 어른이 지켜보는 동안에는 아이들이 어떤 행동을 계속하도록 만들어 줄지는 모르지만 그 어른이 떠나게 되면 그 행동을 계속하거나 이후에 그 행동을 반복할 가능성은 낮다.

25. However, the disadvantage is shared (among all the cattle-owners using the pasture,) so that the individual owner suffers only a fraction of the disadvantage.

하지만 그 불이익은 목초지를 사용하는 모든 가축 소유주들 사이에 나누어져 개별 소유주는 불이익의 극히 일부만을 받게 된다.

26. Children who wear protective gear (during their games) have a tendency to take more physical risks.

게임을 하는 동안 보호 장구를 착용한 어린이들은 더 많은 신체적인 위험을 무릅쓰는 경향이 있다.

27. A black and white cat was sitting (in silence) (at the top of the steps) as soon as I opened the front door to look outside.

내가 밖을 내다보기 위해 현관문을 연 순간 검고 흰 고양이 한 마리가 계단 맨 위에 조용히 앉아있었다.

28. We stood back there (in order to see what was going on in the ice cube).

우리는 얼음조각안에서 무슨 일이 진행되는지 보기 위해 그 뒤에 서 있었다.

29. Body weight is usually normal or low (although people may perceive themselves as being overweight).

사람들은 자신들이 뚱뚱하다고 생각하지만 보통 그들의 몸무게는 정상이거나 저체중이다.

30. Henry was convicted of murder and sentenced to life in prison at Ken Wood Court (at the beginning of the month).

헨리는 이달 초에 캔우드 법정에서 살인죄가 인정되어 무기징역을 선고 받았다.

4. 긴 명사 [구와 절]에 대괄호 치기_ P. 54

Exercise

01. [What makes the neuron so special] is its ability to communicate.

뉴런을 특별하게 만드는 것은 전달 능력이다.

02. [Restrictions on trade with a country] influences its political development.

무역에 대한 제한은 그 나라의 정치 발전에 영향을 끼친다.

03. Many people make it a rule [not to call on others without an appointment].

많은 사람들은 약속 없이 다른 사람들을 방문하지 않는 것을 규칙으로 삼고 있다.

04. It's essential for an exchange student [to learn different languages and learn about other cultures].

교환학생이 다른 나라의 언어와 문화를 배우는 것은 중요하다.

05. You must find [what you think is right] and do something to achieve it.

당신이 맞다 생각하는 것은 찾고 그것을 성취하기 위해 뭔가를 해야 한다.

06. It is certainly true [that the sculpture is grotesque and doesn't match well with the buildings on the street].

그 조각상이 괴기스럽고 길가의 다른 건물들과 어울리지 않는다는 것은 분명한 사실이다.

07. Isn't it interesting [that the Industrial Revolution relied on the ability to transport materials and goods]?

산업 혁명이 재료와 상품을 수송하는 능력에 의존했다는 것이 흥미롭지 않은가?

08. When you open a bank account here, you will get [what is called a "student account" with special concessions for students].

여기서 은행계좌를 개설하면. 학생들에게 특별한 혜택을 주는 '학생계좌'라는 것을 얻게 될 것이다.

09. [The power struggle between the rich and the poor] has increased in strength or become more violent since the beginning of the 21st century.

21세기 초부터 빈부간의 권력다툼은 정도가 심해지거나 폭력적이 되어왔다.

10. [Describing the dimensions of a "typical" neuron] is not easy at all because these cells come in hundreds of different shapes and sizes - depending on their specific function.

이런 뉴런 세포들은 특정 기능에 따라 수백 가지의 다른 모양과 크기로 나타나기 때문에 전형적인 뉴런의 수치를 말한다는 것은 정말 쉽지 않은 일이다.

11. [Giving up bad habits] is not easy, especially when people get older.

나쁜 습관을 버리는 것은 사람이 나이를 먹을수록 쉽지 않다.

12. It seemed obvious until the 15th century [that the earth must be flat].

지구가 평평하다는 것은 15세기까지 명백해 보였다.

13. Many office workers complain [that they don't have enough time for their family].

많은 직장인들은 그들의 가족을 위해 보낼 시간이 부족하다고 불평한다.

14. [Fifteen minutes in warm water before going to bed] helps those who suffer from sleeplessness.

자러가기 전 따뜻한 물속에 15분 있는 것은 불면증으로 고통 받는 사람들에게 도움이 된다.

15. Maria didn't know [how to express her feelings] because it was the first time she had taken the top spot since her debut.

마리아는 데뷔 이래 처음으로 1위를 했기 때문에 어떻게 감정을 표현해야 할지 몰랐다.

16. Some teenagers earn money by working themselves instead of [waiting for an allowance from their parents].

어떤 십대들은 부모님으로부터 용돈을 기다리는 것 대신 스스로 일을 해서 돈을 번다.

17. [The increasing amount of information available to children] is hastening [the beginning of adulthood for many children these days].

아이들에게 이용 가능한 정보의 양이 늘어나는 것은 요즘 많은 아이들의 성인기의 시작을 촉진하고 있다.

18. [Providing up-to-date information about your products] will increase [your chances of doing better business] as more people will visit your site.

상품에 관한 최신정보의 제공은 더 많은 사람들을 당신의 웹사이트에 방문하게 하여 사업이 더 잘 되게 할 확률을 늘릴 것이다.

19. U.N. Secretary-General Ban Ki-moon realized [that encouraging developing countries to join international efforts to fight global warming is not easy].

반기문 UN사무총장은 개발도상국이 지구온난화 방지를 위한 국제적인 노력에 참여를 권하는 것이 쉽지 않다는 것을 깨달았다.

20. [Being with her] is as refreshing as [a colorful rainbow, a fresh box of crayons or a cool shower on a hot day].

그녀와 함께 하는 것은 색색의 무지개나, 새로 산 크레용상자, 또는 무더운 날의 시원한 소나기의 상쾌함처럼 아름답다.

21. [Making a good impression during the first meeting] is very important.

첫 만남에서 좋은 인상을 주는 것은 매우 중요하다.

22. Of course [one reason for the decline in newspaper readership] is due to the fact [we are doing more of our newspaper reading online].

물론 신문 읽기가 이처럼 감소하는 몇몇 이유는 우리들이 신문 읽기를 온라인으로 더 많이 하고 있기 때문이다.

23. China's state-owned media report that the new law, "Law on Penalties for Offenses against Public Order," provides guidelines on [how to punish violators for 128 different offenses].

새로 발효되는 '공공질서 위반처벌법'은 어떻게 128가지 위반행위에 대해 처벌할 것인가에 관한 지침을 제공하고 있다고 중국 관영통신은 보도했다.

24. [Using a computer for long periods] can also cause damage to our neck.

장시간 컴퓨터를 사용하는 것은 우리의 목에 무리를 줄 수 있다.

25. [Making better decisions when picking out jars of jam or bottles of wine] is best done with the emotional brain, which generates its verdict automatically.

잼이나 와인을 고를 때의 더 나은 결정은 무의식적으로 결정을 내리는 감정적 두뇌를 사용할 때 가장 잘 이루어진다.

26. The advantage is [that the cattle-owner receives all of the profit from the sale of the additional animal].

장점은 가축 소유주가 추가되는 가축의 판매에서 나오는 전체 이익을 갖는다는 것이다.

27. [The appeal to a genetic change driving evolution] gets gene-culture co-evolution backwards.

진화를 이끄는 유전적인 변화에의 호소는 유전과 문화의 공동 진화에 역행한다.

28. In [a complex, intellectually demanding and high-pressure task such as that of air traffic controllers,] for example, [having chronically high anxiety] is an almost sure predictor [that a person will eventually fail in training or in the field].

예를 들어, 항공교통 관제사와 같이 복잡하고 지적으로 힘들고 압박이 심한 업무에서 만성적으로 많은 걱정을 하는 것은 그 사람이 결국 훈련이나 실전에서 실패한다는 것을 거의 정확히 예언한다.

5. 연결어에 세모 치기_ P. 59

Exercise

01. The result is a wide range of regulations for maintaining the Thames as a public amenity. For example, Transport for London plays a role in regulating river use and river users.

결과는 템스 강을 공공 편의시설로 유지하기 위한 광범위한 규정들이다. 예를 들어 런던 교통부는 강의 사용과 사용자들을 규제하는 역할을 한다.

02. By 1857, Elizabeth opened a new hospital with her sister who is also a doctor. In addition to this, she also founded the first medical school for women.

1857년에 이르러 엘리자베스와 역시 의사인 그녀의 여동생은 새 병원을 개업했다. 이밖에도 그녀는 여성들을 위한 최초의 의과대학을 설립했다.

03. According to marketing research, there will be 138 million smart TV sets in use in 2015 , taking up 47 percent of the TV market. Nevertheless, some analysts point out that there exist hurdles for the penetration of smart TVs.

시장조사에 따르면 TV시장의 47%를 차지하는 1억 3천 8백만 대의 스마트 TV가 2015년에 사용될 것이라고 한다. 그럼에도 불구하고 전문가들은 스마트 TV의 진입에는 장애물들이 있다고 지적한다.

04. The Industrial Revolution relied on the ability to transport materials and goods. Hence, the story of the Industrial Revolution is also the story of a revolution in transportation.

산업혁명은 재료와 상품을 수송하는 능력에 의존했다. 그러므로 산업혁명의 역사는 수송에 있어서의 혁명에 대한 이야기이기도 하다.

05. A recent consumer report said that heavy metals were found in herbal medicines in markets. As a result, sales of herbal medicines have declined for the last three quarters since 2010.

최근 소비자보고서는 중금속이 한약에서 발견되었다고 밝혔다. 그래서 한약의 매출은 2010년 이후 지난 3분기 동안 감소해왔다.

06. No written records were made in prehistoric times by definition. However, we can get some insight into how the world and its mechanisms were understood or interpreted by prehistoric men by direct and indirect evidence.

정의상 선사시대에는 문서로 남은 기록이 없었다. 하지만 직접적인 증거와 간접적인 증거를 통해 선사시대 사람들이 어떻게 세상과 그 구조를 이해하고 해석했는지 식견을 얻을 수 있다.

07. The Fisheries Department has reported that the river has again become home to plenty of species of fish including sea bass, flounder, and salmon. Despite the good news, things were not always rosy.

수산부는 강이 농어, 넙치, 연어를 포함한 풍부한 어종의 서식지가 다시 되어졌다고 보고했다. 기쁜 소식임에도 불구하고 실상은 항상 밝지만은 않았다.

08. Clinton saw Gore's election as ratification of his own leadership. For this reason, he did more to help his protege's political fortunes than any president since Theodore Roosevelt.

클린턴은 고어의 당선을 자신의 지도력을 확인하는 것으로 보았다. 이런 이유로 그는 데어도르 루즈벨트 이후로 어떤 대통령보다 자신의 심복을 돕는 데 더 많이 애써 왔다.

09. Germany's national humiliation after the loss of World War I and the economic depression of the 1930s has received most of the blame for Hitler's popularity. Yet it is more alarming that he polled more voters in a free election than any other German before him.

제1차 세계대전에서의 패전 후 독일이 겪은 국가적 수모와 1930년대의 경제공황이 히틀러가 인기를 끌게 한 비난의 주 대상이다. 하지만 그가 자유선거에서 이전의 어떤 독일인보다 더 많은 표를 얻은 것은 더욱 경악스럽다.

10. Popular belief holds that a rattle snake's age can be told by counting its rings, but this is a fallacy. Actually, the snake may lose its old skin as often as four times a year.

사람들은 일반적으로 방울뱀의 나이를 고리의 수를 세어 알 수 있다고 믿고 있지만 이것은 그릇된 것이다. 사실 뱀은 일 년에 네 번씩 허물을 벗을 수도 있다.

11. The company is currently being challenged by the disqualification of the CEO. On top of the CEO's criminal charges, the company is facing a couple of law suits pending against it.

그 회사는 최근에 최고 관리자의 자격상실로 어려움을 겪고 있다. 최고 관리자의 범죄혐의 외에 회사는 몇 가지 미결 중인 소송에 직면해 있다.

12. The health plans in turn raise premiums to cover the more expensive costs. In short, the problem with the health insurance structure is that it is too market oriented.

의료보험은 더 비싼 비용을 덮기 위해서 대신 보험료를 올린다. 다시 말해 의료보험의 구조적 문제는 너무 시장 논리로 되어 있다는 것이다.

13. According to psychologists, your physical appearance makes up 55% of a first impression. The physical appearance includes facial expression, eye contact, and general appearance.

심리학자들에 의하면, 신체적인 외모가 첫인상의 55%를 형성한다. 신체적인 외모는 얼굴표정, 눈 맞춤, 그리고 전체적인 모습을 포함한다.

14. Regarding their marriages, you should know that the only way to have a wife there is to purchase her. For this reason, the girls are often mature when they are married, for the parents always keep them until they sell them.

그들의 결혼에 관해서 이야기하자면, 거기서 아내를 얻는 유일한 방법은 여자를 돈주고 사는 것이라는 사실을 당신은 알아야 한다. 그런 이유로, 소녀들은 그들의 부모가 그녀들을 팔 때까지 항상 보살피기 때문에, 결혼할 때 종종 성숙해져 있다.

15. Health care premiums are generally too expensive because of the potential for expensive treatments. On the other hand we are forced to pay all the medical insurance premiums the government has set.

의료보험료는 잠재적인 비싼 치료비 때문에 일반적으로 너무 비싸다. 반면에 우리는 정부가 정한 모든 의료보험료를 어쩔 수 없이 지불해야 한다.

16. Primitive man did not know what time meant. For instance, he kept no records of birthdays or wedding anniversaries or the hour of death. He had no idea of days or weeks or even years either.

원시인은 시간의 의미를 몰랐다. 예를 들어 그는 생일이나 결혼기념일, 또는 죽음의 시간에 대해 기록하지 않았다. 하루 또는 주나 년에 대해서도 전혀 알지 못했다.

17. I can't learn how to use a computer just by reading an instruction manual. However many people seem to learn how to use a computer just by reading the manual. Therefore people learn things in different ways.

나는 사용설명서를 읽는 것만으로는 컴퓨터 사용법을 배울 수 없다. 하지만 많은 사람들은 설명서를 읽는 것만으로도 컴퓨터를 배우는 것 같다. 따라서 사람들은 각자 다른 방식으로 배운다.

18. Some parents only control how long their kids watch television or play computer games while other parents decide what entertainment is appropriate for their children in the age of video cassettes, DVD's, computer games and cable television.

어떤 부모들은 비디오, DVD, 컴퓨터 게임, 케이블 TV의 시대에 자녀들에게 적합한 오락물을 골라주는 반면에 어떤 부모들은 자녀가 TV를 보거나 컴퓨터게임을 하는 시간만 통제한다.

19. Books, clothing, and buildings are some examples of material culture. We have a shared understanding of their purposes and meanings. In contrast, nonmaterial culture consists of human creations that are not physical. Examples of nonmaterial culture are values and customs.

책이나 의류, 건물은 물질 문화의 몇몇 예이다. 우리는 그 목적과 의미에 공통적인 이해를 갖는다. 반대로 비물질 문화는 물리적이 아닌 인간의 창작으로 이루어진다. 비물질 문화의 예는 가치와 관습이다.

20. In recent years, Colombia has not received much money from its exports. Its major export crop is coffee. But the demand for coffee in the world has dropped. Also, other countries have begun to export more coffee, so the price has fallen. Finally, the Colombian government has encouraged the farmers to produce more food so that the country can become self-sufficient in food; as a result, the farmers have produced less coffee. Because of these factors, Colombia now gets much less cash from its coffee exports than it did ten years ago.

최근에 콜롬비아는 수출로 많은 돈을 벌지 못했다. 콜롬비아의 주요 수출 작물은 커피이다. 하지만 세계의 커피 수요가 줄었다. 또한 다른 나라들이 더 많은 커피를 수출하기 시작해서 가격이 떨어졌다. 마침내 콜롬비아 정부는 농부들에게 국내에서 자급자족할 수 있도록 식량을 더 많이 생산할 것을 장려했다. 결과적으로 농부들은 커피를 덜 생산했다. 이러한 요인들 때문에 콜롬비아는 이제 10년 전보다 커피 수출로는 더 적은 외화를 벌어들인다.

21. His career, however, especially early on, knew the vicissitudes characteristic of Renaissance business. For example, while he was en route to Spain as his enterprise's traveling partner, a role typical for young men, pirates robbed him of all his goods, including a consignment of pearls, and of his own clothes.

그러나 그의 일은 특히 초기부터 르네상스시대의 사업특징인 우여곡절을 경험했다. 예를 들어 그가 젊은 사람들이 전형적으로 하던 역할인, 그의 사업의 여행 파트너로서 스페인으로 가는 길에, 해적들에게 진주 위탁판매품을 포함한 그의 모든 물건과 그의 옷을 약탈당했다.

22. Getting on a radio playlist was difficult, but once a song was in heavy rotation on the radio, it had a high probability of selling. Then, in the 1980s, came MTV, which became the second way to create a hit.

노래가 라디오 방송 예정 녹음 리스트에 올라가는 것이 어렵기는 했지만, 일단 라디오에서 자주 들리면, 그것은 팔릴 가능성이 아주 높았다. 그러다가 1980년대에 MTV가 등장했는데, 그것은 인기 앨범을 만드는 버금가는 길이 됐다.

23. Each person has his or her own truth, and there is distortion on both sides. Therefore, to apologize sincerely we must first listen attentively to how the other person really feels about what happened, not simply assert what we think happened.

각 사람은 그들만의 진실을 가지고 있고 양쪽 모두에 왜곡이 있다. 따라서 진정으로 사과하기 위해서는, 우리가 일어났다고 생각하는 것을 단순히 주장할 것이 아니라 일어난 일에 대해서 상대방이 정말로 어떻게 느끼는지에 대해 우선적으로 주의 깊게 들어야 한다.

24. There is, however, a limit to their benefit. Until recently, even "successful" agriculture failed to guarantee unlimited animal products to the masses. But industrial agriculture changed that, and since 1950, almost anyone in a developed country who could afford a car could also afford to eat meat, dairy products and / or eggs as often as he or she liked.

하지만, 유익성에는 한계가 있다. 최근까지는 '성공적인' 영농방식을 통해서도 서민들에게 동물성 식품을 무제한으로 공급하는 것을 보장해 주지 못했다. 하지만 산업형 영농방식으로 인해 그러한 상황이 바뀌었고, 1950년부터는 자동차를 구매할 경제적 형편이 되는 선진국의 거의 모든 사람이 육류나 유제품이나 계란을 원할 때마다 먹을 수 있는 형편이 되었다.

25. In the mid-1980s, the total aid flow to Egypt from the United States was equivalent to about seven percent of Egypt's economy. Today, it's about point-seven percent. So it's a 10-fold drop as compared to the size of the Egyptian economy. Thus, you don't get much leverage when you're looking at aid flows of point-seven percent the size of the Egyptian economy.

1980년대 중반, 이집트에 대한 미국의 원조 공급은 이집트 경제의 약 7%에 달했었다. 오늘날, 이 수치는 약 0.7% 수준이다. 결국 이집트 경제 규모와 비교했을 때 10배나 감소한 것이다. 따라서 이집트 경제의 0.7% 수준의 원조 공급을 볼 때, 많은 영향력을 얻을 수 없는 것이다.

26. A summer of drought in the United States and Russia has reduced expectations of corn and wheat supplies. As a result, the measure of food prices by the UN Food and Agriculture Organization rose six percent in July. But FAO economist Conception Calpe says the expected reductions did not get any worse in August.

미국과 러시아의 여름 가뭄으로 인해 옥수수와 밀의 공급량이 줄었다. 이에 따라 UN 식량농업기구가 집계한 식품 가격은 7월에 6% 상승을 보였다. 그러나 FAO의 경제학자인 컨셉션 카르페 씨는 예상된 공급량의 감소가 8월에 악영향을 주지는 않았다고 밝혔다.

27. The Study has raised new questions about "body mass index", or BMI. Namely, this is a measurement of body fat as a ratio of height to weight. BMI guidelines were used as a basis for the study. Recently, many public health experts have promoted BMI as a way to predict the risk of health problems. However, a person's BMI can be misleading in some cases.

이번 연구는 '체질량지수'에 대한 새로운 의문들을 불러 일으켰다. 즉, BMI는 키와 몸무게의 비율로 체지방을 측정하는 것이다. BMI의 지침들은 이번 연구의 기반으로 사용되었다. 최근 많은 공공 보건 전문가들이 BMI를 건강상의 문제가 발생할 위험을 예측하는 도구로서 사용할 것을 촉진해왔다. 하지만 특정한 경우에는 BMI가 오도될 수 있다.

28. Children with parents who didn't read to them were somewhat slow to learn at preschools. Conversely, preschoolers whose parents read to them were better prepared to begin school and performed at higher rates than those not exposed to reading.

부모가 책을 읽어주지 않은 아이들은 유치원에서 배우는 게 약간 느렸다. 반대로, 부모가 글을 읽어주는 취학 전 아동들은 독서에 노출되지 않은 아이들보다 더 높은 비율로 학업을 수행했고 학교를 시작하는 데 더 잘 준비가 되어 있었다.

29. Nonetheless, some observers say China needs to take steps before it can become the world's biggest economy. Also Patrick believes that several things could affect the country's economic growth. Therefore, China's growth is extremely resource dependent and those resources are becoming scarcer and scarcer. In particular, in northern China, there is a growing scarcity of water which, along with other resource constraints might limit China's prospects of going forward.

그럼에도 불구하고, 일부 관측자들은 중국이 세계 최대 경제 대국이 되기 위해서는 몇 가지 절차가 남아 있다고 주장한다. 또한 패트릭은 여러 가지 요소들이 중국의 경제 성장에 영향을 끼칠 수 있다고 생각한다. 그러므로, '중국의 성장은 자원에 극도로 의존하고 있고 이 같은 자원들은 점점 고갈되어 가고 있다. 특히, 중국 북부 수자원의 경우, 물 자원 부족 현상이 심해지고 있으며 다른 자원들과 함께 중국의 경제 발전 가능성을 제한할 수 있다.

30. Some consequences of this unconscious assumption that "good-looking equals good" scare me. For example, a study of the 1974 Canadian federal elections found that attractive candidates received more than two and a half times as many votes as unattractive candidates. Despite such evidence of favoritism toward handsome politicians, follow-up research demonstrated that voters did not realize their bias. In fact, 73 percent of Canadian voters surveyed denied in the strongest possible terms that their votes had been influenced by physical appearance; only 14 percent even allowed for the possibility of such an influence.

'잘생긴 것이 좋은 것이다.'라는 이러한 무의식적인 가정의 일부 영향력들이 나를 두렵게 한다. 예를 들어, 1974년 캐나다 연방 선거에 대한 연구에서는 매력적인 후보자들이 매력적이지 않은 후보자들보다 두 배 반 이상의 득표를 했다는 것을 보여주었다. 잘생긴 정치인들을 향한 치우친 애정에 대한 그와 같은 증거에도 불구하고, 후속 연구는 유권자들이 자신들의 편견을 깨닫지 못했다는 것을 보여주었다. 사실, 조사에 참여한 캐나다 유권자들 중 73%가 자신들의 투표가 신체적인 외모에 영향을 받았다는 것을 가능한 한 가장 강력한 어조로 부인했으며; 14% 만이 그러한 영향의 가능성을 인정할 정도였다.

Exercise 01

주제문: The worst thing about society silencing the expression of an opinion is that it is robbing the human race.

글의 구조: T(Topic sentence) ➡ S(Supporting sentences)

어떤 의견의 표현을 억누르는 사회의 가장 나쁜 점은 그것이 인간을 유린한다는 사실이다. 이는 현재의 세대뿐 아니라 미래의 사람들에게도 해를 끼친다. 또한 그 의견을 신봉하는 사람들 뿐 아니라 반대하는 사람들에게도 해가 된다. 만약 그 의견이 옳다면 우리는 모두 진실을 알게 될 기회를 놓치게 된다. 그 의견이 옳지 않다면, 그 생각에 대해 논의함으로써 배울 수 있는 진실에 대한 더 나은 의견을 얻을 수 없기 때문에 우리 모두 잃게 되는 것이다.

Exercise 02

주제문: Thus, there is no such thing as "material" progress in the sense of accumulating a "permanent" store of usable goods.

글의 구조: G(General statement) ➡ S(Supporting sentences) ➡ T(Topic sentence)

경제학자들은 영구적이고 무한한 물질적 진보라는 패러다임을 믿기 때문에 인간의 노동과 기계가 오직 가치만을 창출할 것이라는 생각에 집착한다. 그러나 우리는 어떤 종류의 에너지라도 가치 있는 어떤 것을 만들기 위해 사용될 때, 항상 더 큰 혼란과 폐기물을 생성의 대가로 치른다는 것을 열역학 제2법칙을 통해 알고 있다. 또한 우리가 만들어 낸 가치 있는 것들조차 마지막에는 폐기물이나 소모된 에너지가 된다는 것을 알고 있다. 따라서 사용 가능한 재화를 영원히 축적한다는 의미에서의 물질적 진보는 있을 수 없다. 왜냐하면 우리가 이 세상에서 만드는 모든 것들은 결국 바람속의 먼지처럼 사라져 버리기 때문이다.

Exercise 03

주제문: It was chiefly in the eighteenth century that a very different conception of history grew up. / This change by the historians in the eighteenth century contributed to developing the welfare of the society in their states.

글의 구조: T(Topic sentence) ➡ S(Supporting sentences) ➡ T(Topic sentence)

역사에 대한 새로운 개념이 성장한 시기는 주로 18세기였다. 역사가들은 자신들의 할 일이 상황설명이 아니라 국가의 성장, 번영, 역경의 연속적인 단계를 설명하거나 실례를 보여주어 문제를 해결하는 것이라고 믿게 되었다. 도덕, 산업, 지성, 예술의 역사, 태도와 신념의 변화, 시대를 지배했던 사상, 정치 조직의 흥망성쇠와 변화 등 다시 말해 국가의 복지와 관련된 개념이 역사가들의 주제가 되었다. 그들은 왕의 역사가 아니라 국민의 역사를 기록하려고 하였다. 그들이 특히 초점을 맞춘 부분은 인과관계의 사슬이었다. 이런 18세기의 역사가들에 의한 변화는 국가의 사회복지를 발전시키는 원인이 되었다.

Exercise 04

주제문: A technology revolution is fast replacing human beings with machines in virtually every sector and industry in the global economy.

글의 구조: T(Topic sentence) ➡ S(Supporting sentences)

기술혁명은 세계경제의 거의 모든 영역과 산업에서 인간을 기계로 빠르게 바꾸고 있다. 이미 수백만 근로자들이 경제와 관련된 공정에서 영구히 퇴출되었고, 전체적인 일과 직업의 목록은 줄고 재구성되거나 사라져 버렸다. 세계적 실업률은 1930년대 대공황이래로 가장 높은 단계에 이르렀다. 8억이 넘는 세계의 사람들이 현재 실업에 있거나 불완전 고용상태에 있다. 노동시장에 새로 진입하는 수백만이 일자리가 없다는 것을 알게 될 때 지금과 신세기 사이에 그 수치는 급격히 증가할 것이다.

주제문: the sole purpose of its founders was to realize the dream of spaceflight for the general public.

글의 구조: G(General statement) ➡ S(Supporting sentences) ➡ T(Topic sentence)

우주는 인류가 수년 동안 정복하고자 애써 온 개척지이지만, 현재까지 모두는 아니더라도 분별 있는 대부분의 사람들에게 자신의 생애 중에 우주 모험을 해보는 생각을 품고 있는 사람이 있다면 진지하게 받아들여지지 않았다. 하지만, 지난 몇 달 사이에 몇 가지 사건이 일어났는데 이는 이성적인 사람들로 하여금 민간인 유료 우주여행에 대한 자신들의 입장을 다시 생각해 보게 만들었다. 이런 모든 것이 현재 가능한 것은 공통 목표를 지닌 소수의 사람들이 모여 인류에 혜택을 줄 수 있는 대의명분을 발전시키기로 결심했기 때문이다. 우주 여행 분야에서 민간 기업가의 발전을 고취시키고자 하는 교육적 비영리 단체로써 엑스 프라이즈 재단이 1994년에 설립되었고, 재단 설립자들의 유일한 목적은 일반대중을 위한 우주 여행의 꿈을 실현하는 것이었다. 이런 사람들이 보다 많아진다면 세상은 정말 멋진 곳이 될 것이다.

주제문: We should further reduce our excessive reliance on prisons by making extensive use of alternatives to imprisonment

글의 구조: T(Topic sentence) ➡ S(Supporting sentences)

우리는 벌금, 배상이나 집행유예 같은 다른 광범위한 대안을 사용하여 징역에 대한 과도한 의존도를 더 많이 줄여야한다. 그것은 적어도 법률상의 제재를 위한 사회적 요구를 효과적으로 충족시켜 줄 수 있을 것이다. 하지만 그런 대안들은 출옥방법을 구입할 수 있는 부자의 수단이 되지 않도록 비슷한 범행을 저지른 모든 이들이 이용할 수 있어야 한다. 그리고 수감이 필요한 곳에서는 사회복지 훈련 시설, 복지관, 대용 수용시설이나 지역사회 안에 범죄자를 두는 다른 방법이 투옥보다 선호되어야 한다.

Exercise 01

지문의 내용과 일치하는 것은?

ⓐ 멘델스존의 영국여행의 첫 방문지는 런던이었다.

ⓑ 스코틀랜드의 휴가는 그의 성공과 관련이 적었다.

ⓒ 멘델스존의 스코틀랜드에서의 휴가는 지루했다.

ⓓ 멘델스존은 필하모니 음악회의 곡을 작곡했다.

[질문의 핵심어] 일치하는 것, where(스코틀랜드), how(즐거운), what(지휘)

[핵심어 & 핵심문장] But except for that, the trip didn't mean much to him in his career.

1829년에 멘델스존은 영국을 처음으로 방문했다. 그해 여름에 스코틀랜드에서 휴가를 보냈다. 에든버러를 방문하고 하이랜드를 거쳐 여행은 3주가 채 안 걸렸다. 에든버러를 방문했을 때 멘델스존은 작곡가 존 톰슨을 만났다. 그의 편지와 그가 그린 몇 폭의 풍경화에서 입증되었듯이 그 여행은 분명히 즐거운 추억을 많이 만들었다. 하지만 그밖에 그 여행은 그의 성공에 의미가 적은 것이었다. 그의 영국에서의 성공과 관련하여 가장 성공적인 사건 중 하나는 1844년 여름의 여덟 번째 방문이었다. 멘델스존은 런던에서 필하모니 음악회를 다섯 차례에 걸쳐 지휘했다.

Exercise 02

지문의 내용과 일치하지 않는 것은?

ⓐ 컴퓨터는 2진수를 사용한다.

ⓑ 2진수는 버트란, C++ 또는 포트란과 같은 모든 컴퓨터 언어의 가장 기본적인 형식이다.

ⓒ byte라는 단어는 binary의 B와 digit의 it에서 왔다.

ⓓ 테라바이트는 기가바이트보다 천 배 정도 크다.

[질문의 핵심어] 일치하지 않는 것, 2진수, 형식, byte, 테라바이트

[핵심어 & 핵심문장] Binary, forms, byte, terabyte. The word bit comes from the combination of 'B' from binary and 'it' from digit.

컴퓨터는 2진수라고 불리는 언어를 이용해서 컴퓨터의 부분에서 부분으로 정보를 전달한다. 2진법은 '네'와 '아니오' 같은 정보를 1이나 0의 연속으로 전환하는 부호체계이다. 2진수는 버트란, C++ 또는 포트란과 같은 모든 컴퓨터 언어의 가장 기본적인 형식이다. 하나의 1이나 0을 '비트'라고 하는데 가장 작은 정보 단위를 나타낸다. 비트라는 단어는 binary의 B와 digit의 it에서 왔다. 8비트가 연결되면 1바이트이다. 1000바이트는 1킬로바이트, 백만 바이트는 1메가바이트, 십억 바이트는 1기가바이트이다. 그리고 천 기가바이트에 달하는 정보단위를 테라바이트라고 한다.

Exercise 03

지문에서 밑줄 친 대상이 나머지 셋과 다른 것은?

[질문의 핵심어] 다른 것, 글의 등장인물 구분(필자의 아내와 교통경찰의 아내)

[핵심어 & 핵심문장] In her job as a beautician, my wife is a Sunday driver. The next day when ① she answered the phone, ~

직업이 미용사인 내 아내는 초보 운전자이다. 어느 날 그녀는 뒤쪽에서 고속도로 순찰차의 빨간 사이렌을 보고 깜짝 놀랐다. 이내 젊은 경찰관과 마주쳤고 속도위반 딱지를 뗐다. 다음날 ① 그녀가 전화를 받자 어떤 여자가 머뭇거리는 목소리로 어제 파크 가에서 과속 운전으로 딱지를 뗐었느냐고 물었다. 그렇다고 하자 전화를 건 ② 여자는 그 교통 경찰관의 아내이고 남편이 딱지를 뗀 부인이 이제까지 맡아 본 가장 향이 좋은 향수를 뿌리고 있었다고 여러 번 말했다고 고백했다. 그래서 ③ 그녀는 그 향수가 무엇인지 알아내기로 맘먹었다고 했다. ④ 그녀는 현재 내 아내의 최우수 고객 중의 한 명이며, 그래서 속도위반 딱지를 뗀 비용은 몇 배로 보상되었다.

지문의 내용과 일치하는 것은?

ⓐ 미국은 우주 무기의 개발에 제한을 두어야 한다.

ⓑ 미국은 전술 장치를 우주에 보유하고 있다.

ⓒ 미국은 대량 파괴 무기를 보유하고 있지 않다.

ⓓ 지구 어디에서나 일기 예보가 가능한 것은 아니다.

질문의 핵심어 내용과 같은 것 (선택지 ⓒ에서는 <u>우주에</u> 가 빠짐)

핵심어 & 핵심문장 The United States does have tactical devices in space. Currently the United States does not have weapons of mass destruction <u>in space</u>.

미국은 우주 무기의 개발에 제한을 두어야 할까? 우주 무기의 범주에는 어떤 것이 속해야 할까? 우주 무기의 개발에는 어떤 도전이 따를까? 이러한 개발이 우주여행을 위한 기술발달과 어떤 관련이 있을까? 이러한 발전이 이곳 지구에서의 생활에 어떤 영향을 미칠까? 현재 미국은 우주에 대량 파괴 무기를 보유하고 있지 않다. 미국은 이곳 지구에서 발생하는 군사 작전들을 지지하고 방어할 수 있는 전술 장치를 우주에 보유하고 있다. 미국은 항공기나 특수 작전 부대를 보유한 적국의 위성 관제소를 작동하지 못하게 하거나 파괴할 수 있다. 미군은 정찰 위성을 사용해서 자신들에게 확실한 전술적 이점을 제공해주는 가장 최신의 정보를 유용하게 활용할 수 있다. 지구 어디에서나 일기 예보는 언제든 이용 가능하다. 논리적으로 생각해 볼 때, 우주의 무기화는 미군이 앞으로 취할 다음 단계의 합리적인 목표일 것이다.

지문의 내용과 일치하지 않는 것은?

ⓐ 핸즈프리 기능이 있지만 일부 캔은 절단하는 동안에 붙잡고 있어야 한다.

ⓑ 알루미늄 캔은 이 캔오프너에 부적절하다.

ⓒ 이 오프너는 테두리가 있는 캔만 열 수 있다.

ⓓ 이 오프너는 날카로운 가장자리에 손이 베이는 것을 자동으로 막아준다.

질문의 핵심어 내용과 다른 것(자동으로 작동된다)

핵심어 & 핵심문장 however, handle with caution and always handle the cut lid with caution(however 뒤의 예외적인 내용에 주목)

이 캔오프너를 사용하여 깡통을 따는 방법이다. 아래 순서를 따르도록 한다.

1. 뚫는 레버를 들어 올린다.

2. 캔의 가장자리가 오프너에 위치하는 기둥아래에 오도록 기울이고, 절단기 날이 캔의 테두리 안쪽에 위치해 있는 걸 확인하면서 뚫는 레버를 누른다.

   이용정보: 핸즈프리(손을 사용할 필요 없는) 기능으로 인해, 절단하는 동안에 레버를 내리거나 캔을 잡고 있을 필요가 없다. 하지만, 길이가 길거나 무거운 캔이라면 받치고 있어야 한다.

3. 캔을 딸 때에는, 한 쪽 손으로는 캔을 잡고 다른 한 쪽 손으로는 레버를 들어 올린다.

   주의: 캔이나 뚜껑의 절단면에 닿지 않도록 조심한다. — 날카롭다. 캔을 여는 과정에서, 가장자리가 날카롭게 되는 것을 방지하기 위해 캔 오프너는 캔의 테두리를 둥글게 감을 것이다; 하지만, 가장자리가 둥글게 감겨있지 않을 때에는 조심해서 다루고 항상 주의해서 절단된 뚜껑을 취급한다.

4. 자석으로부터 뚜껑을 조심스럽게 폐기한다.

   중요 정보: • 잡아당겨 따는 손잡이가 있거나, 떼어서 쓰는 포일 밀봉, 또는 돌려 감아 따는 키가 부착되었거나 테두리가 없는 캔을 열 경우에는 이 캔 오프너를 사용하지 않는다.

   • 일반 캔 속의 주스나 음식이 얼어 있을 때, 냉동고에서 바로 꺼내 얼어있는 주스나 음식을 개봉하는데 사용 않는다.

   • 알루미늄 뚜껑은 자석에 붙지 않는다.

지문에서 밑줄 친 대상이 나머지 셋과 다른 것은?

핵심어 다른 것, 글의 지칭 구분(이식되는 세포와 이식하는 방법)

핵심어 & 핵심문장 One of ② them(앞 문장의 different ways) is engrafting or multiplying cells in the affected area.

배아 줄기 세포 이식은 신체의 특정 기능과 시스템을 맡고 있는 세포와 관련된 과정이다. 이식 과정에 사용되는 세포는 태아의 간, 흉선, 골수, 비장, 뇌 및 췌장에서 추출되어 '저온 보존된 현탁액'에 보관된다. 신체에 ① 그것들을 이식하는 것은 여러 가지 방법으로 행해질 수 있다.

② 그것들 중 하나는 환부에 세포를 접붙이거나 확대하는 것이다.

(A) 그러면 신경 성장 인자, 종양 괴사 인자, 인터류킨 등과 같은 상당한 양의 생물학적 활성 물질부터 생성이 시작될 것이다.

(B) 그런 다음 이러한 세포는 사라지거나 줄어든 세포를 보완하게 될 것이고 신체의 사라진 기능을 대신 [수리]할 것이다.

(C) ③ 그것들이 이식되면, 이들은 이동하여 세포 간에 연결을 만들고 다양한 효과를 나타낼 수 있다. 하지만, 인간의 신체에 이식이 제대로 되지 못한다면, ④ 그것들은 다 자란 세포보다 더 약한 면역 반응을 야기할 수 있다.

Unit 05 패러프레이징(Paraphrasing)

1. 동의어 찾기_ P. 82

Exercise

1. depend on / rely on / rest on

2. be accountable for / be to blame for / take charge of

3. supply A with B (A= 사람, B= 사물) / provide A with B / present A with B

4. about / regarding / concerning

5. immediately / right away / in no time

6. be patient with / tolerate / endure

7. accomplish / achieve / perform

8. give oneself to / devote oneself to / commit oneself to

9. be likely to / tend to / be apt to

10. neglect / ignore / overlook

11. practically / no better than / virtually

12. be worried about / be uneasy about / be concerned about

13. generally / usually / on the whole

14. be confused / be perplexed / be bewildered

15. be responsible for / be in charge of / answer for

16. run away / go away abruptly / escape

17. agree to / be faithful to / keep

18. be good at / be well informed in / be familiar with

19. clumsy / awkward / not skilled

20. no more than / only / just

2. 쉬운 단어로 바꿔 쓰기_ P. 83

Exercise

1. make / ugly   잘 맞지 않는 신발은 발을 기형으로 만들 수 있다.

2. informal / expression / used / conversation   '두드'는 일상적 구어로 '녀석'이란 뜻이다.

3. is / good / speaking   모니카의 주장은 항상 설득력을 갖기 때문에 그녀는 달변가이다.

4. useless   상식이 없는 지식은 쓸모없다.

5. best   한국 축구 선수 중에서는 박지성이 최고다.

6. twice / year   그 평화협상은 2001년 이래 여러 장소에서 1년에 두 번씩 열려왔으나 합의를 이끌어내는 데는 종종 실패했다.

7. have / never   너를 뉴욕에서 보리라고는 상상도 못했다.

8. goes / to   나는 콜로라도 덴버행 버스를 타야 한다.

3. 부정문 바꿔 쓰기_ P. 85

Exercise

1. hardly / ever   나의 노트북은 전에 보다 훨씬 느려서 몇 달째 거의 사용을 안 하고 있다.

2. when   나는 지하철에서 내릴 때까지 노트북을 기차에 두고 왔다는 사실을 알지 못했다.

3. was / only / confused   많은 종교와 그에 관련된 역사적 사건들에 관해 조사하면서 나는 성경이 유일한 신과 진리만 있다고 하는 것에 혼란에 빠질 수밖에 없었다.

4. always / gotten   마이크는 어떤 영어시험에서도 90점 이상의 점수를 받는 데 실패해 본 적이 없다.

5. only / with   백인 인종 차별주의자 정권 아래서 흑인들은 허락 없이 백인 지역을 지나쳐 가는 것이 허용되지 않았다.

6. Without / your / spending   전화 통화를 하고, 편지를 쓰고, 함께 있는 등 상당한 시간을 함께 보내지 않으면 우정은 사라질 것이다.

7. Anyone / should / not   어떤 사람도 과거의 잘못이 자신의 현재를 파괴하도록 하거나 미래를 어둡게 하도록 내버려두어서는 안 된다.

8. didn't / often   토론으로 그의 마음을 바꾸지는 못했으며, 다른 의견을 참지 못했다.

4. 문장의 태 바꿔 쓰기_ P. 87

Exercise

1. predicted   결승전에서 우리의 패배는 전 게임에서 우리의 스타플레이어인 제이슨의 부상으로 예견되었다.

2. was / told / to   지도 교수님은 그린박사님이 국제정치의 전문가이기 때문에 내게 그의 강의를 들으라고 했다.

3. has / never / been / solved / anyone   NASA 과학자들이 기대했던 것보다 문제가 쉽지 않았기 때문에 아무도 우주왕복선의 정확한 문제점을 아직 정확히 해결하지 못했다.

4. had / been / defeated   아버지는 그 여행에서 목적을 전혀 이루지 못했다.

5. should / be / encouraged   선생님은 학생들이 상상력을 개발하도록 격려해야 한다.

6. changed   규칙은, 그 경기가 얼마나 위험한 지 알렉스가 깨달았을 때 그에 의해 곧 바뀌었다.

7. should / be / made   당신이 다른 사람들과 좋은 사회적 관계를 만들려고 한다면 분명한 소개를 해야 할 것이다.

8. are / teaching   대부분의 외국인 노동자들은 가르친 경험이 전혀 또는 거의 없는 한국인 직장동료나 자원봉사자들에게 교육을 받고 있다.

5. 비교구문 바꿔 쓰기_ P. 89

1. not / any / longer   명왕성이 왜 행성으로 간주되지 않는지 생각해보자.
2. not / as / serious / as   홉킨스 의과대학 보고서에 따르면 카페인으로 야기되는 건강상의 문제가 대개 우리가 아는 것보다 심각한 건 아니라고 한다
3. when / more / higher   우리는 무선 이동 통신 기기의 총비용을 확인해 본 결과 기기의 기능이 많을수록 비용이 더 많이 들게 된다는 사실을 알게 되었다.
4. not / as / fast / as   오늘날 우주선은 광속의 1%의 속도도 내지 못한다.
5. the / worst / thing   그가 학업을 포기해야 했으므로 아버지가 갑자기 돌아가신 것은 최악의 상황이었다.

6. less / formally   우리가 글을 쓸 때보다 더 격식에 얽매이지 않고 말하기 때문에 이 프로그램은 말하기 목적으로 사용되는 좋은 안내서일 수 있다.
7. only   종래의 MP3플레이어는 듣기 기능만 되는 기기에 불과했다.
8. More / than   10% 미만의 구독자들이 그 일간신문의 구독연장을 안하기로 했다.

6. 강조 [도치]구문 바꿔 쓰기_ P. 91

1. never   대법관은 결코 권력에 영향을 받지 않을 사람으로 알려져 있다.
2. only / when / they / are / gone / and / we / never / see / them   오직 그들이 가고, 그들을 보지 못할 때에야 우리는 그들과 불가분의 관계라는 것을 깨닫는다.
3. Even / if / what   우리의 목표가 무엇이든 목표를 이루는 데 방해가 되는 장애물은 항상 있다.
4. None / of   알렉스와 가장 숙련된 시스템 기사 중 어느 누구도 암호를 복구할 수 없었다.
5. did / dream   나는 UN사무총장처럼 세계에서 영향력 있는 사람이 되리라고 꿈에도 생각하지 않았다.

6. always   예를 들어, 유명한 골프선수 잭 니클라우스는 골프를 칠 때마다 반드시 먼저 칠 것을 생각하고 상상 속에서 연습해 보았다.
7. could / no / longer / see   더이상 울창하게 나무가 우거진 해안도 없고, 어떤 야생도 볼 수 없었다.
8. coalition / cabinet / could / created   연립내각은 유럽대륙 국가에서 왕정을 전복시킨 후 가까스로 생길 수 있었다.

7. 전치사, 접속사 바꿔 쓰기_ P. 93

1. because / of   중국은 제대로 된 산업구조를 갖추지 않고 있어서 국내에서 가까운 장래에 충분한 바이오디젤을 생산하기는 어려울 것이다.
2. Although / he / has   심한 신체장애에도 불구하고 스티븐호킹은 이미 우주의 기원에 대한 매우 중요한 발견을 해냈다.
3. harshly / criticized   시민 단체들은 대규모 간척의 사례 조사 연구를 근거로 정부의 환경정책에 대한 비판의 목소리를 높였다.
4. Owing / to   애플과의 심한 경쟁으로 우리는 우리 제품을 최대한 빨리 시장에 내놓기를 바란다.
5. No / sooner / than   대통령이 의회에서 연설을 마치자마자 의원들은 기립 박수를 보냈다.

6. In / spite / of   그는 비록 많은 아름다운 곡들을 썼지만 옷을 허름하게 입었고 청소도 하지 않았다.
7. because   증가한 인구는 더 많은 식량 수요를 가져와서 더 많은 돈이 농업에 투자되었다.
8. as / well / as   상담사는 회사가 직면한 기회와 위기뿐만 아니라 회사의 강점과 약점도 더 객관적으로 분석할 수 있어야 한다.

8. 주어 바꿔 쓰기_ P. 95

Exercise

1. because / of / his / laziness   그는 게을러서 회사에 다닐 수 없었다.

2. Although / they / practiced / hard   열심히 연습했으나 그들의 공연은 어설프게 끝났다.

3. Thanks / to / the / Internet   인터넷은 우리가 지구 반대편에서 무슨 일이 일어나고 있는지 즉시 알고, 그곳의 문제를 이해하고, 스스로 평화를 촉진하게 확신시켜서 악인과 싸울 수 있게 해준다.

4. We   나쁜 날씨 때문에 우리는 여행을 계속하지 못했다.

5. careful / comparison / these / items   이 물건들을 자세히 비교해 보면 그 차이를 쉽게 구분하게 될 것이다.

6. She   고된 훈련과 의지로 그녀는 프로 배구팀에 입단하게 되었다.

7. He   그는 젊기 때문에 일을 할 수 있었다.

8. Lincoln   링컨은 변함없는 사랑과 유머로 그가 속한 모든 단체에서 지도자가 되었다.

9. 분사구문 바꿔 쓰기_ P. 97

Exercise

1. As / he / had / kept   그가 암으로 죽을 때까지 40년간 비밀을 간직함으로써 그 사건은 한국 근대사에서 풀리지 않은 미스터리 중 하나로 남게 되었다.

2. While / they / were / suffering   알츠하이머병을 앓으면서, 대략 400만이 넘는 미국인들이 기억을 상실하고 몸조차 돌보기 힘들게 되었다.

3. Having / known   많은 사람들을 알고 지내지만 교제나 유익한 대화, 지력, 사람의 마음을 움직이는 능력에 있어서 나는 그를 어떤 기업체의 중역이나 우리나라의 유명 인사보다 높게 평가하고 싶다.

4. Having   나는 새로운 프로젝트로 할 일이 많아서 사무실에서 밤을 새야 했다.

5. After / many / hospitals / recognized   유머의 치유능력을 인지한 후에, 많은 병원들은 웃음문제를 심각하게 받아들이기 시작했다.

6. When / Galileo / looked / through   갈릴레오가 그의 망원경을 통해 태양을 보았을 때 놀라운 것을 발견했지만 그것이 무엇인지 결코 설명할 수 없었다.

7. Playing / cards   우리는 카드 게임을 하고 있는 중에 누군가 방문을 노크하는 것을 들었다.

8. Not / knowing   그의 환자들은 최면상태에서 내내 그들의 몸에 무슨 일이 일어나는지 몰랐지만 대부분의 환자는 종종 치료되었다.

10. 관계사 구문 바꿔 쓰기_ P. 99

Exercise

1. that / doesn't   예외 없는 법칙은 세상에 하나도 없다는 것을 우리는 안다.

2. no / matter / who   나는 누구든 권력이 있으면 정치적 자살로 망치게 될 것이라 생각한다.

3. They   많은 고대 국가에서 나라의 안정은 땅을 소유하고 소중히 여기며 경작을 잘하는 농부에게서 나왔다.

4. No / matter / what   부모님이 뭐라고 하시든 나는 그녀와 결혼하기로 한 결정을 바꾸지 않겠다.

5. which   대부분의 강사가 가장 당황스럽게 느끼는 것 중 하나는 청중이 그들의 시계를 보는 것이다.

6. It   토요일로 계획되었던 야구 경기는 호우로 취소되었다.

7. them   내가 어렸을 때 즐겨 읽었던 그런 책들이 나에게 더이상 흥미를 주지 못하지만 몇몇 책은 아직 유익해 보인다.

▶ **Practice Test**

1.   P. 107

스파르타는 펠로폰네소스전쟁(BC 431-404)에서 경쟁 도시 국가인 아테네를 패배시킨 후에 파워의 절정에 도달한 고대 그리스의 한 전사 사회였다. 스파르타 문화는 그 국가와 병역의 충성심에 중심을 두고 있다. 7세의 나이에 스파르타 남자아이들은 엄격하며 국가가 후원하는 교육인 군대 훈련과 사회화 프로그램에 입학했다. 아고게로 알려진 그 시스템은 의무, 훈련 그리고 참을성을 강조했다. 스파르타 여자들은 군대에서 활동적이지는 않았지만 그들은 다른 그리스 여성들보다 교육을 받았고 더 많은 지위와 자유를 즐겼다. 스파르타 남자들은 전문적인 군인이었기 때문에 모든 육체노동은 노예 계급인 헬로트에 의해 이루어졌다. 그들의 용맹에도 불구하고 스파르타의 지배는 단명하였다: BC 371년에 그들은 레욱트라 전투에서 테베에 의해 패배했으며 그들의 제국은 오랫동안 쇠퇴해 갔다.

1. ⓑ

지문의 엄격한이라는 어휘와 의미가 가장 가까운 것은?

Ⓐ 정확한   ⓑ 가혹한

Ⓒ 관대한   Ⓓ 자극적인

해설_ rigorous는 '엄격한, 가혹한, 철저한'이라는 의미를 가지고 있다. 유의어로 strict, hard, tough, rough, severe, stern 등이 있다.

2. Ⓓ

아래 문장 중 어떤 것이 지문의 음영 처리된 문장의 핵심정보를 가장 잘 표현하고 있는가?

Ⓐ 테베가 없었다면 스파르타가 더 오래 군사적 지배를 누렸을 것이다.

ⓑ 스파르타인들은 군사적 기술이 부족하여 테베에 패했다.

Ⓒ 테베는 스파르타의 군사력에 제지당하지 않았고 유리한 방법으로 그들의 공격을 제압했다.

Ⓓ 막강한 군사력은 스파르타인들이 군사적 지배력을 오래 유지하기에 충분하지 않았다.

해설_ 주어진 지문에서 핵심은 '그들의 용감성에도 불구하고 스파르타의 지배는 단명하였다'는 구절이며 이어지는 테베의 승리는 스파르타의 단명을 설명한 예이므로 정답은 Ⓓ이다. 지문의 military bravery가 military power로 was short-lived가 not enough to maintain for long으로 바꿔 쓰였다.

3. Ⓐ

지문에 따르면 다음 중에 어느 것이 사실인가?

Ⓐ 스파르타 여자들은 다른 그리스 여자들이 얻지 못한 혜택을 누렸다.

ⓑ 스파르타의 군사력은 오랜 지배력을 의미한다.

Ⓒ 군대에 들어갈 집안 형편이 안되는 남자아이들은 노예나 육체노동을 해야 했다.

Ⓓ 전사 사회는 여성의 지위를 통해 규율을 잡았다.

해설_ 지문에서 스파르타 여자들이 군대에서 활동하지는 않았지만 다른 그리스 여성들보다 교육을 받았고 더 많은 지위와 자유를 즐겼다고 하였으므로 Ⓐ가 정답이다.

2.   P. 108

율리시스 그랜트(1822-1885)는 미국 남북전쟁(1861-1865) 동안에 승리한 북부군을 지휘하였으며, 1869년부터 1877년까지 18대 미국 대통령을 지냈다. 오하이오 태생이며 웨스트포인트를 졸업하고 멕시코-미국 전쟁(1846-1848)에서 싸웠다. 미국 남북전쟁 동안에 공격적이고 단호한 리더였던 그랜트는 모든 미국 부대의 지휘권을 쥐었다. 전쟁 후에 그는 국가 영웅이 되었고 1868년에 대통령으로 임명되었다. 그랜트 정부의 주된 초점은 개혁이었으며 또한 새로 풀려난 흑인 노예들의 시민권을 보호하려고 시도하는 동안 남북을 화해시키기 위해 일하였다. 그랜트가 개인적으로 정직한 반면에 그의 동료 몇몇은 부패되고 그의 정부는 여러 스캔들로 변색되었다. 퇴직 후에 그랜트는 그가 모은 모든 돈을 파산한 중개업 회사에 투자하였다. 그는 그의 마지막 날들을 그가 죽은 해에 출판된 그의 회고록을 쓰면서 보냈고 그 회고록은 비평가의 그리고 재정적인 성공을 입증하였다.

1. Ⓓ

아래 문장 중 어떤 것이 지문 속의 음영된 문장의 핵심정보를 가장 잘 표현하고 있는가?

Ⓐ 그랜트가 (남북전쟁 이후) 재건 기간 동안 흑인과 백인의 화해를 시킨 것은 중요했다.

ⓑ 재건 기간 동안 새로 풀려난 흑인 노예의 권리를 보호하는 것이 필요했다.

Ⓒ 남북 간의 화해에 집중하면서 흑인의 권리를 확보하는 것이 가능했다.

Ⓓ 그랜트 정부는 화해를 시키고 불공평과 계급을 타파하고자 노력했다.

해설_ 지문에서 '그랜트 정부의 주된 초점이 개혁이었으며 새로 풀

려난 흑인 노예들의 시민권을 보호하려고 시도하며 남북을 화해시키기 위해 일하였다.'고 하였으므로 ⓓ가 정답이다. 나머지 선택지는 초점을 벗어나거나 일부 사실만 언급하므로 오답이다.

2. ⓑ

작가는 지문에서 왜 율리시스 그랜트의 동료들이 부패했다고 언급하고 있는가?

ⓐ 율리시스 그랜트의 정직함과 강직함을 동료들의 성품과 대조하기 위해

ⓑ 그들이 그랜트 정부를 변색시키는 스캔들에 책임이 있다는 것을 보여주기 위해

ⓒ 정부를 통제하는 것이 얼마나 어려운지 예를 들기 위해

ⓓ 그 당시 정부의 도덕성 결여를 강조하기 위해

해설_ 지문에서 '그랜트가 개인적으로 정직한 반면에 그의 동료의 몇몇은 부패되고 그의 정부는 여러 스캔들로 퇴색되었다.'고 정부가 퇴색된 책임을 설명하고 있으므로 ⓑ가 정답이다.

3. ⓒ

지문의 비판적이라는 어휘와 의미가 가장 가까운 것은?

ⓐ 호의적이 아닌   ⓑ 필수적인

ⓒ 평가하는   ⓓ 심각한

해설_ 문맥에서 critical은 그랜트의 회고록에 관한 언급이다. 회고록이 비평가(평론가)에게 성공을 입증한 것이므로 평론가의 평가와 관련 있는 ⓒ evaluative(평가하는)가 정답이다.

Unit 02 **Fact & Negative Fact**

Practice Test

1.   P. 114

화상은 감염을 일으키고 상처를 남기며 암에 잘 걸릴 수 있게 하기 때문에 잘 관리하는 것이 중요하다. 1도 화상은 모든 화상들 중 정도가 가장 가볍다. 1도 화상은 화상 부위가 깊지 않은 편이어서 피부 아래 깊숙이 가지 않는다. 1도 화상은 대개 분홍이나 붉은색이며 아주 따갑다. 1도 화상은 압박을 가하면 종종 하얗게 변한다. 사람에 따라 1도 화상은 약간 부어오르기도 한다. 이런 가벼운 화상은 대개 3일에서 6일 내에 치료된다. 흔히 화상을 입은 피부 껍질은 새 건강한 피부를 만들어내며 1~2일 안에 벗겨진다. 사고가 일어난 후 즉시 화상 부위를 차가운 물에 담가 상처 부위의 온도를 낮춘다. 따끔거리는 통증이 줄어들기 시작할 때 화상 부위에 알로에 베라 또는 항생제 연고 같은 치료젤을 발라준다. 화상 부위를 마른 거즈 밴드로 덮고 통증을 덜하기 위한 조치를 취한다.

1. ⓒ

지문에 따르면 다음 중 어느 것이 1도 화상에 관해 추론될 수 있는가?

ⓐ 1도 화상은 사람들이 생각하는 것보다 심각하다.

ⓑ 1도 화상은 효과적으로 치료하기 어렵다.

ⓒ 1도 화상은 입원을 필요로 하지 않는다.

ⓓ 1도 화상은 가장 흔한 종류의 화상이다.

해설_ 작가는 1도 화상이 가볍고 3일에서 6일 내에 치료된다고 하였으므로 입원을 필요로 하지 않는다는 것을 추론할 수 있다. 따라서 ⓒ가 답이며 나머지 선택지는 지문과 다른 내용이거나 지문에 언급되어 있지 않으므로 잘못된 추론이다.

2. ⓑ

작가는 지문에서 왜 새 건강한 피부를 언급하고 있는가?

ⓐ 화상이 일시적이라는 것을 강조하기 위해

ⓑ 피부가 스스로 회복된다는 것을 보여주기 위해

ⓒ 분홍이나 붉은색을 띠는 화상과의 차이점을 비교하기 위해

ⓓ 1도 화상이 경미하다는 증거를 제시하기 위해

해설_ 새 피부가 만들어진다는 것은 스스로 회복된다는 의미이므로 답은 ⓑ이다.

3. ⓒ

지문에 따르면 다음 중에 어느 것이 사실인가?

ⓐ 1도 화상은 3일에서 6일간 만져서는 안 된다.

ⓑ 화상은 붓기가 사라질 때까지 건조한 상태를 유지해야 한다.

ⓒ 피부 층 아래의 화상은 1도 화상이 아니다.

ⓓ 피부가 하얗게 되면 압력을 가하는 것이 중요하다.

해설_ 세 번째 문장에서 '1도 화상은 화상 부위가 깊지 않은 편이어서 피부 아래 깊숙이 가지 않는다.'고 언급했으므로 ⓒ가 정답이다. 나머지 선택지는 문장의 일부를 바꾸거나 인과 관계가 바르지 않으므로 오답이다.

2.   P. 115

히터는 공기를 따뜻하게 하기 위해 엔진 냉각수를 사용한다. 만약 엔진이 차가운 상태라면 이런 시스템에서 오는 공기가 따뜻하다고 느껴지기까지는 몇 분이 걸릴 것이다. 온도를 최대치로 설정하라. 에어컨(A/C)이 꺼져 있는지 확인하라. 신선한 공기 모드를 선택하라. 원하는 속도로 팬을 설정하라. 이 버튼을 누르면 운전석 쪽과 조수석 쪽을 분리하여 온도와 모드를 설정할 수 있다. 듀얼 버튼의 표시등이 꺼져 있다면 운전석 쪽의 온도 조절 버튼과 모드 조절 버튼으로 양쪽을 동일한 온도와 모드로 조정할 수 있다. 듀얼 버튼을 누르면 운전석 쪽의 모드와 조수석 쪽의 모드를 분리하여 설정할 수 있다. 하지만 운전석 쪽에서 모드를 선

택한다면 조수석 쪽에서 모드를 선택하는 것은 불가능하다. 환기 장치를 통한 흐름은 외부 공기를 유입하고 내부에서 순환을 거쳐 뒤 창문 근처의 환기구로 배출한다.

1. Ⓐ

지문의 이 버튼이 가리키는 것은 ~이다.

Ⓐ 팬 속도 조절 버튼   Ⓑ 온도 조절 버튼

Ⓒ 운전석의 버튼   Ⓓ 조수석의 버튼

해설_ this button은 앞 문장 Set the fan to the desired speed(원하는 속도로 팬을 설정하라)에서 팬 속도 조절을 하는 버튼이므로 정답은 Ⓐ이다.

2. Ⓑ

지문의 배출하다라는 어휘와 의미가 가장 가까운 것은?

Ⓐ 지치다   Ⓑ 내보내다

Ⓒ 빼앗다   Ⓓ 파괴하다

해설_ 지문에서 exhaust는 환기구를 통해 들어온 공기에 관한 내용이므로 Ⓑ let out(내보내다)가 정답이다. 자주 쓰이는 exhaust의 일반적 의미의 Ⓐ wear out(지치다)은 문맥에 맞지 않으므로 오답이다.

3. Ⓓ

지문에 따르면 듀얼 버튼이 켜져 있을 때 어느 것이 사실이 아닌가?

Ⓐ 운전자가 조수석보다 모드 선택을 조절할 때 우선 순위를 갖는다.

Ⓑ 조수석의 온도와 운전석의 온도를 다르게 설정할 수 있다.

Ⓒ 조수석의 모드 선택이 가능하다.

Ⓓ 운전자가 (운전석과 조수석의) 양쪽을 동일한 온도와 모드로 조절할 수 없다.

해설_ 8번째(아래에서 5번째) 문장에서 듀얼 버튼을 눌러도 운전석 쪽에서 모드 선택이 가능하다고 하였으므로 답은 Ⓓ이다.

Unit 03 Vocabulary

Practice Test

1.   **P. 121**

인도의 챤드라얀 1호 위성은 2009년 9월, 달에 물의 존재 여부에 대해 확인하였으며 다른 행성으로 가던 다른 탐사선을 이용하여 관측소를 설립하였다. 달의 표면이 아직 지구의 건조한 사막보다 더 건조하지만 물이 있다는 증거가 있으며, 태양풍과 달 표면간의 상호 작용으로 인해 물과 수산성 분자가 있을 가

능성이 있다. 이 말은 넓은 호수와 넓은 바다가 있다는 의미는 아니지만 미래의 달 식민지 개척자들은 달 표면에서 물의 흔적을 찾아 추출해서 정화하여 마시고 음식물을 경작하고 산소와 연료를 만들어 낼 수도 있다. 아니면 달 식민지 개척자들은 달의 극지방으로 가서 가장 깊은 분화구에서 물을 캘 수도 있다. 2009년 10월 9일, NASA는 수명이 다한 로켓을 분화구에 떨어뜨려 100피트 넓이의 구멍을 만들었다. 이들은 거기에서도 물을 찾아냈다. 그 로켓으로 인해 생긴 먼지 기둥을 분석하여 먼지 기둥 속에 최소한 25갤런의 물이 얼어서 생긴 얼음을 발견하였다.

1. Ⓓ

지문의 경작이라는 단어와 의미가 가장 가까운 것은?

Ⓐ 정화   Ⓑ 생산

Ⓒ 발전   Ⓓ 재배

해설_ cultivation은 '경작'의 의미를 가지므로 선택지 Ⓓ growing(재배)이 정답이다. Ⓑ의 production은 제품의 생산을 가리킬 때 주로 사용되므로 Ⓓ growing이 더 가까운 의미를 갖는다.

2. Ⓒ

지문의 식민지 개척자라는 단어와 의미가 가장 가까운 것은?

Ⓐ 사기꾼   Ⓑ 거주자

Ⓒ 정착민   Ⓓ 노동자

해설_ colonist는 식민지로 이주하여 정착한 사람이므로 Ⓒ settlers가 정답이다. Ⓑ inhabitant는 이주해왔다는 의미가 없이 단순히 거주하는 사람을 가리키므로 오답이다.

3. Ⓓ

지문에 따르면 다음 중 어느 것이 달에 관해 추론될 수 있는가?

Ⓐ 태양풍이 없다면 아마 달에 물이 없을 것이다.

Ⓑ 달 식민지 개척자들은 물을 쉽게 추출할 수 있을 것이다.

Ⓒ 먼지의 존재는 달이 건조하다는 것을 확인시켰다.

Ⓓ 미래에 달에서 물을 얻는 여러 방법이 생길 것이다.

해설_ 지문 전체에서 태양풍과 달 표면간의 상호작용이나 분화구에서 물을 캘 수도 있다고 하였으므로 Ⓓ가 정답이다. Ⓐ는 지문의 내용만으로 추론할 수 없으므로 오답이다.

2.   **P. 122**

나는 우리 반에게 이 원칙을 가르쳐 주신 고등학교 시절 사진 선생님을 아직 기억한다. 그는 여러 주 동안 그 원칙을 우리에게 주입시켰고 그 이후로 약 20년 동안 인물 사진을 찍기 위해 카메라를 들 때마다 거의 매번 그의 말이 내 귓가에 계속 울렸

다. 그 원칙은 성의 있고 유익한 조언이었다. 그 당시 반 친구들과 내가 돌려받았던 인물 사진들을 돌이켜 생각해보면 대부분은 좀 더 사진틀을 채운 사진의 대상이 있었으면 더 좋았을 만한 것들이었다. 초창기 시절 내가 찍은 대부분의 사진들은 렌즈로부터 너무 뒤쪽에서 대상을 찍은 나머지 사진틀의 대상이 너무 작아서 세부 묘사가 **부족하고** 이미지가 희미하다. 대상으로 사진틀을 채우게 되면 해당 이미지를 보는 사람들이 방해를 받지 않은 상태에서 어디를 봐야 할지 알 수 있고 대부분 찍는 사람에게 **친근하면서도** 인상이 강렬한 인물 사진을 남겨줄 것이다.

1. Ⓐ
지문의 **부족한**이라는 단어와 의미가 가장 가까운 것은?
Ⓐ 결핍된　　　　　　Ⓑ 불안감을 주는
Ⓒ 강조하는　　　　　Ⓓ 효율적인
해설 lacking은 '부족한'의 의미를 가지므로 Ⓐ deficient(결핍된)가 정답이다. lacking이 포함된 문장에서 대상이 너무 작다고 하였으므로 세부 묘사가 부족하다는 것을 알 수 있다.

2. Ⓒ
지문의 **친근한**이라는 단어의 의미가 가장 가까운 것은?
Ⓐ 은밀한　　　　　　Ⓑ 특별한
Ⓒ 편안한　　　　　　Ⓓ 당면한
해설 intimate는 '친근한'이라는 의미로 Ⓒ cozy(편안한)가 정답이다. Ⓓ immediate는 발음이 비슷하지만 의미가 다른 오답이다.

3. Ⓑ
지문에 따르면 다음 중 어느 것이 사실인가?
Ⓐ 작가의 고등학교 선생님은 드럼 연주자였다.
Ⓑ 작가의 초기 인물 사진에서 대상이 너무 멀리 있었다.
Ⓒ 대상이 너무 크면 친근한 사진이 될 수 없다.
Ⓓ 성의 없이는 훌륭한 조언을 할 수 없다.
해설 지문의 네 번째 문장에서 작가가 초창기에 사진을 너무 뒤에서 찍었다고 하였으므로 Ⓑ가 정답이다. 지문에서 drum은 선생님의 말씀이 귀에 울렸다는 뜻이지 악기가 아니므로 Ⓐ는 오답이다.

4. Ⓓ
지문에 따르면 다음 중 어느 것이 작가의 고등학교 사진 선생님에 관해 추론될 수 있는가?
Ⓐ 그는 체계적이고 짜임새 있게 가르쳤다.
Ⓑ 그의 인물 사진은 많은 수상을 했다.
Ⓒ 일부 학생들은 수업이 지겨워서 그가 가르치는 것을 좋아하

지 않았다.
Ⓓ 그는 특정한 규칙을 고집했고 강경했다.
해설 지문의 두 번째 문장에서 선생님이 여러 주 동안 원칙을 주입시켰다고 하였으므로 Ⓓ가 정답이다. 추론을 할 때에는 지문에 언급된 사실만을 근거로 하여 답을 선택하고 논리의 비약을 하지 말아야 한다.

<table><tr><td>Unit
04</td><td>Reference</td></tr></table>

Practice Test

1.　　　　　　　　　　　　　　　　　　**P. 128**
만약 이 기술이 재현 가능하고 인간의 세포에서도 적용할 수 있다면 암 치료에도 가능성이 있다. **이것**은 암세포가 이미 현저하게 산성을 띠고 있으며 암 가소성을 유발할 수 있는 산성 미세 환경을 생성하기 때문에 약산성 PH 재구성을 기반으로 한다. 이 기술은 또한 아직 논란의 대상이며 확실한 정의가 힘든 VSELs와 MUSE세포가 생체 내에서 가소성과 관련이 있을 가능성도 있다. 만약 **'그것들'**이 STAP 줄기세포로 변한다 할지라도 스트레스로 거의 죽은 세포가 STAP에 잔류 손상을 남겨서 후에 나타날 수 있다는 우려 또한 제기되고 있다. STAP 세포의 핵형이 정상이라고 보고되고 있으나 필자는 세포의 핵이나 다른 곳에 더 작지만 여전히 중대한 손상이 이후에 심층 분석을 통해 나타날 수도 있지 않을까 한다. **결론**은 이 기술이 줄기 세포를 연구하는 이들에게는 놀라움과 흥분 그리고 회의적인 태도를 동시에 불러 일으킨 놀라운 개발로 남아 있다는 것이다.

1. Ⓓ
지문의 단어 **이것**이 가리키는 것은?
Ⓐ 재현 가능하고 인간의 세포에서도 적용할 수 있는 기술
Ⓑ 재현 가능한 기술
Ⓒ 인간의 세포에 적용할 수 있는 기술
Ⓓ 암 치료에 가능성이 있는 기술
해설 앞 문장에서 기술이 암 치료에도 적용가능성이 있다고 하였으므로 Ⓓ가 정답이다. 기술이 재현 가능하고 인간의 세포에서도 적용할 수 있다는 것은 기술에 대한 세부 설명이지 암 치료에 가능성이 있다는 핵심 설명은 아니다.

2. Ⓓ
단어 **그것들**이 가리키는 것은?
Ⓐ 핵형　　　　　　　Ⓑ 우려
Ⓒ 스트레스　　　　　Ⓓ 세포

해설_ they는 앞의 주절에 나오는 '스트레스로 거의 죽은 세포'를 가리키므로 정답은 ⓓ이다.

3. ⓑ
아래 문장 중 지문에 음영 처리되어 있는 문장의 핵심정보를 가장 잘 표현하고 있는 것은?
ⓐ 세포에 스트레스를 주는 것은 세포를 STAP 세포로 바꾸지만 손상을 남긴다.
ⓑ 스트레스로 만들어진 STAP 세포는 손상될 가능성이 있다.
ⓒ 스트레스가 없으면 세포는 STAP 세포로 변하지만 손상되지 않을 것이다.
ⓓ STAP 세포에 잔류 스트레스가 나중에 나타난다면 염려가 된다.

해설_ 음영 처리되어 있는 문장을 요약하면 스트레스를 받아 죽어가는 세포는 STAP 줄기세포로 변하더라도 손상이 나타날 가능성이 있다는 내용이므로 ⓑ가 정답이다. 나머지 선택지는 인과 관계 또는 접속사를 다르게 해석하여 의미를 현저히 바꾸거나 핵심정보를 생략하였으므로 오답이다.

4. ⓐ
지문의 결론이라는 구와 가장 가까운 것은?
ⓐ 요점   ⓑ 장점
ⓒ 이익   ⓓ 순손실

해설_ bottom line은 요점을 의미하며 암 치료 가능성이 있는 기술에 대한 설명 후에 요약을 하고 있으므로 ⓐ가 정답이다.

2.   P. 129
멕시코는 텍사스의 미국 합병 즉시 1845년 3월에 미국과의 관계를 끊었다. 9월에 제임스 케이 포크 대통령은 존 슬라이델을 멕시코시티에 밀사로 보내 국경 분쟁 지대에 관해 협상하고 멕시코에 불리한 미국 요구에 합의하고 3천만 달러에 뉴멕시코와 캘리포니아를 매입하도록 했다. 멕시코 대통령인 조세 호아킨 헤레라는 그의 나라를 분할하려는 슬라이델의 의도를 미리 인식하고 그를 받아들이는 것을 거절하였다. 1846년 5월 9일 포크는 미국의 요구와 슬라이델의 협상에 대한 그것의 거절을 구실로 적대 행위를 정당화하면서 의회에 전쟁의 메시지를 준비하기 시작하였다. 그날 저녁에 그는 4월 25일에 멕시코 군대가 리오그란데 강을 건너 테일러의 군대를 공격하여 16명을 죽이거나 부상을 입혔다는 전달을 받았다. 그의 빠르게 수정된 전쟁 메시지에서 – 5월 11일에 의회에 전달된 – 포크는 '멕시코가 우리의 영토를 침범하여 미국 사람의 피를 미국 땅에 흘리게 하였다.'라고 주장하였다.

1. ⓐ
지문의 분할이라는 단어와 가장 가까운 것은?
ⓐ 나누기   ⓑ 빼앗기
ⓒ 죽이기   ⓓ 설립하기

해설_ dismembering은 '분할'의 의미를 가지므로 유사어로서 ⓐ dividing이 정답이다. 문맥상 앞 문장에서 미국이 밀사를 보내 3천만 달러에 뉴멕시코와 캘리포니아를 매입하도록 했다고 하였으므로 ⓑ는 오답이다.

2. ⓑ
지문의 단어 그것의가 가리키는 것은?
ⓐ 의회의   ⓑ 멕시코의
ⓒ 미국의   ⓓ 포크의

해설_ its가 포함된 문장에서 미국의 요구와 슬라이델의 협상에 대한 거절을 한 쪽이 멕시코이므로 ⓑ가 정답이다. 지시하는 내용은 주로 지시어 바로 앞에 나온다.

3. ⓐ
지문에 따르면 다음 중 왜 포크는 의회에 전달된 전쟁 메시지를 수정하였는가?
ⓐ 전쟁을 하기 위한 더욱 강력한 타당한 이유를 가질 수 있어서
ⓑ 포크에 대한 모욕에 응답해야 해서
ⓒ 멕시코 대통령 조세 호아킨 헤레라가 나라를 분할하려고 해서
ⓓ 멕시코인들이 미국의 요구에 대한 지불을 거절해서

해설_ 전쟁 메시지의 수정이 멕시코 군대의 공격으로 미국인이 사망한 이후 이루어졌으므로 ⓐ가 정답이다. 나라를 분할하려고 한 것은 멕시코 대통령이 아니라 미국 대통령이므로 ⓒ는 오답이다.

Unit 05   Rhetorical Purpose

Practice Test

1.   P. 136
1940년대와 1950년대에 천문학자 루퍼월트는 지금도 폭넓게 받아들여지고 있는 목성의 사진을 얻기 위해 적용 가능한 모든 자료를 사용했다. 그는 대기의 낮은 총밀도와 관측된 고수소 화합물이 모두 태양과 별들의 대부분의 성분과 일치한다는 것에 주목했다. 이 '우주 구성 요소'의 가상 단순한 두 성분은 주로 수소와 헬륨이며 우주 물질의 거의 99%는 수소와 헬륨이 형성한다. 월트는 목성의 크기가 커서 우주 생성 때의 구성 요소들을 그대로 지니는 데 성공했다는 가설을 세웠다. 그는 또한 목

성이 대부분 액체나 가스로 되어 있다고 결론지으면서 내부 구조가 어떤지를 계산하기 위해 수소와 헬륨의 특성에 대한 그의 지식을 사용했다. 월트는 목성의 내부 깊은 곳에는 아마도 고체 물질의 핵이 있지만 목성의 대부분은 액체로 상당히 끈적거리고 관측이 가능한 대기의 깊은 아래쪽은 압축되어 있지만 아직 고체는 아니라고 했다. 위에서 보이는 목성의 대기권은 단지 수천 km 두께에 이르는 가스 바다의 얇은 최상위층이다.

1 Ⓓ
지문에서 작가는 ~을 강조하기 위해 고수소 화합물을 언급하고 있다.
Ⓐ 목성이 대부분 액체나 기체 상태라는 사실
Ⓑ 목성의 구성요소가 태양과 별의 구성요소들과 유사하지 않다는 것
Ⓒ 목성의 태고의 구성 요소들
Ⓓ 목성 대기의 우주 물질

해설_ 작가는 목성이 우주 생성 때의 구성 요소들을 그대로 갖고 있다는 가설을 세웠다. 그것을 증명하기 위해 목성 대기의 고수소 화합물(hydrogen-rich compounds)에 목성 대기의 우주 물질이 있다는 것을 언급하므로 Ⓓ가 정답이다. Ⓑ는 목성의 구성 요소가 태양과 별의 구성 요소들과 유사하므로 오답이다.

2 Ⓓ
지문에 따르면 어느 것이 사실인가?
Ⓐ 새로운 자료는 우리의 목성에 대한 이해를 크게 바꿔 놓았다.
Ⓑ 수소와 헬륨의 특성은 목성의 내부가 액체와 기체가 되는 것을 막는다.
Ⓒ 목성의 내부 구조에 관한 지식이 없었다면 월트는 다른 결론에 도달했을 것이다.
Ⓓ 태고의 구성 요소들을 보유하는 것은 목성 크기에 영향을 받는다.

해설_ 네 번째 문장에서 월트가 목성의 크기가 커서 태고의 구성 요소들을 지니는 데 성공했다고 하였으므로 Ⓓ가 정답이다. 나머지 선택지는 지문과 다른 내용이거나 언급되어 있지 않으므로 오답이다.

3 Ⓑ
지문의 가설을 세웠다라는 어휘와 의미가 가장 가까운 것은?
Ⓐ 받아들였다   Ⓑ 가정했다
Ⓒ 조사했다   Ⓓ 설명했다

해설_ hypothesized는 '가설을 세웠다'는 의미로 Ⓑ supposed(가정했다)가 유사한 어휘이다.

2.
P. 137
2013년 1월 22일 중국 펑윈 1C에서 나온 파편이 러시아의 블리츠 위성과 충돌했다. 펑윈 1C는 2007년 1월 11일에 위성 요격 미사일 시험에서 중국에 의해 파괴된 위성이다. 그 파편과의 충돌은 그것의 회전 속도, 비행 자세와 함께 러시아 위성의 궤도를 변경했다. 모스크바에 있는 정밀 기기 공학 연구소(IPIE)의 엔지니어가 블리츠 위성 궤도의 커다란 변화를 CSSI에게 보고한 2013년 2월 4일에서야 충돌 사실이 전해졌다. 블리츠는 국제 레이저 범위 서비스(ILRS)에 의해 정밀도로 추적되고 IPIE는 궤도의 장반경이 120m 급격히 감소하고 회전 속도와 비행자세의 변화를 감지했다. 이 사건을 주시하고 있는 팀은 위성의 데이터를 검토하고 어떤 우주 파편 조각이 블리츠 위성의 궤도 변화를 일으킬 정도로 큰지 결정하기 위해 마지막부터 거슬러 올라가며 일을 진행해야 했다. 그들은 펑윈 1C의 파편과 블리츠 위성이 밀접히 접근했음을 발견했다. 예측 거리로는 충돌을 배제할 것 같지만 그 근접이 궤도 추정 변경 10초 내에 발생했다는 사실은 펑윈 1C의 파편 조각이 실제로 블리츠와 충돌했다는 가능성이 높다는 것을 보여주었다.

1. Ⓑ
지문의 단어 그것의가 가리키는 것은?
Ⓐ IPIE   Ⓑ 블리츠
Ⓒ CSSI   Ⓓ 펑윈 1C

해설_ 지문에서 its 앞에 파편과 러시아 인공위성의 충돌이 있었다고 하였으므로 Ⓑ가 정답이다. 러시아 인공위성이 블리츠(BLITS)라는 것을 첫 문장에서 파악해야 한다.

2. Ⓓ
지문에서 작가는 ~를 위해 팀이 거슬러 올라가며 일을 진행해야 했다고 언급하고 있다.
Ⓐ 블리츠 위성이 궤도를 변경한 후 10초 내에 일어난 일을 발견하기
Ⓑ 위성의 움직임을 추적하는데 요구되는 고정 밀도를 측정하기
Ⓒ 충돌을 야기한 사건의 순서를 어떻게 정할지 찾기
Ⓓ 블리츠 위성이 궤도를 변경하게 한 파편이 어떤 것인지 결론내기

해설_ 지문에서 어떤 파편 조각이 블리츠 위성의 궤도 변화를 일으킬 정도로 큰지 결정하기 위해 거꾸로 일을 진행해야 했다고 하였으므로 Ⓓ가 정답이다. 조사팀은 블리츠 위성이 궤도를 변경하기 전 10초 내에 일어난 일을 찾는 것이지 이후가 아니므로 Ⓐ는 오답이다.

3. ⑩

지문에 따르면 다음 중 어느 것이 그 파편의 예측된 거리에 관해 추론될 수 있는가?

Ⓐ 충돌이 일어날 수 있다는 것을 나타내는 것 같았다.

Ⓑ 정확하지 않았다.

Ⓒ 무작위 요소를 고려하지 않았다.

Ⓓ 팀이 그들의 결론을 내리는 데 충분하지 않았다.

해설_ 예측된 거리는 충돌을 배제할 것 같지만 그렇지 않았다고 하였으므로 Ⓓ가 정답이다. 나머지 선택지는 지문에 없거나 다른 내용이므로 오답이다.

Unit 06 Inference

Practice Test

1.   P. 143

새로운 입자에 대한 첫 번째 증거 발표, 아마도 인류가 가장 오랫동안 기다려온 힉스 입자는 우리에게 많은 것을 가르쳐 줄 것이다 – 그리고 그 가르침은 모두 과학에 대한 내용만은 아닐 것이다. 힉스 입자가 탄생하는 데는 글로벌 공동체 차원의 납세자들이 자금을 지원한 국제적 팀이 있었다. 분명히 과학은 흥미가 넘치는 일임에 틀림없다. 힉스는 1960년대 처음 제안되었으며 모든 물체의 질량에 공통적으로 상호 작용하는 잔유물로 생각된다. 힉스라고 생각되는 몇백 개의 새로운 물체의 예를 생성하는 데에는 거대한 새로운 과학 장치, 즉 스위스 유럽 입자 물리 연구소 CERN의 LHC(강입자 충돌기)가 필요했다. 오랫동안 고대해 온 이 발견은 엄청난 지적 노력의 완성이고, 한편으로는 새로운 연구 분야의 시작이다. 그것은 또한 전 세계적 노력의 결과이다. 힉스는 넓은 의미에서 우리 모두가 만들어낸, 지구적 차원의 인류 공동체가 만들어낸 첫 번째 과학적 발견이라고 해도 과언이 아니다. 자연의 비밀이 우리 앞에 펼쳐져 있다고 말하는 것이 적합한 표현인 것 같다; 우리는 이 발견을 함께 소유하고 또 즐거워한다. 이것은 앞으로 다가올 많은 결과의 전주곡이 될 것이라고 희망한다.

정답_ Ⓓ

다음 중 어느 것이 지문의 내용으로부터 결론 내려질 수 있는가?

Ⓐ 힉스 입자는 과학자들 간의 세계적인 공동 작업 없이는 발견되지 못했을 것이다.

Ⓑ 작가는 이것이 발견되었다는 것을 믿을 수 없다.

Ⓒ 힉스 입자의 발견은 과학계의 대변혁을 일으킬 것이다.

Ⓓ 이 발견을 위해 수반된 노력의 규모는 매우 컸다.

해설_ 지문 전체에서 힉스 입자의 발견을 위해 자금, 과학 장치,

지적 노력 등 다방면에서 매우 큰 규모의 노력이 있었다고 하므로 Ⓓ가 정답이다.

2.   P. 144

허브의 얼굴이 굳어 나이 들고 의원답게 보였다. 나는 항상 관습에 얽매이지 않은 선택을 해왔었다: 그가 대학에 다니는 동안에 나는 작은 밴드에서 음악을 했고; 그가 양복과 넥타이를 입고 돈을 버는 동안 나는 외국 무술을 가르쳤다. 나의 부인인 캐롤라인과 나는 허브와 그의 부인이 똑똑한 두 남자아이를 가졌을 때 고양이 퍼레이드를 망쳤다. 나는 예술적이며 자유분방한 기질의 수도승과 유사했고; 그는 상냥하고 믿음직한 회사 간부였고 그리고 가정적인 남자였다. 그러나 우리가 어떻게 달랐든 간에 우리는 30년 우정을 통해 서로를 존경하며 자랐다. 우리는 여자친구 없는 사춘기의 이해할 수 없는 수치심, 고등학교에서 마리화나를 피는 저속한 부당한 짓들 그리고 데보와 엘비스 코스텔로와 같은 그 당시 새로운 음악의 발견을 경험했다. 20대에 우리는 철학에 대해 흥분하여 얘기하는 데 많은 시간을 보냈다 – 그때 내 친한 친구는 인도의 인습타파주의자 제이 크리슈나무르티였고 허브는 트라피스트회의 수도자인 토마스 머튼에 빠져 버렸다. 우린 각각의 결혼식에서 들러리였다(제인 오스틴에서 나온 것 같이 눈부시게 빛나는 그의 결혼식, 공원에 다수의 사람들이 있었던 나의 결혼식, 마치 비버리 힐빌리에서 나온 것처럼). 그리고 우리가 우리의 30대 후반에 비틀거리기 시작했을 때 우리는 중산층 중년 남자들에게 있는 평범한 존재에 관한 위기와 맞붙어 싸웠다. 이제 그 역사의 모든 것이 증발되어 버리는 것 같다.

정답_ Ⓑ

지문의 음영된 문장에서 무엇이 추론될 수 있는가?

Ⓐ 그들은 역사에 대한 관심을 잃었다.

Ⓑ 그들의 관계가 변한 것 같다.

Ⓒ 그들이 함께 했던 모든 일들을 더 이상 기억할 수 없었다.

Ⓓ 서로의 차이에도 불구하고 계속 가장 친한 친구로 남았다.

해설_ 지문 전체 글의 흐름에서 서로 달랐지만 친하게 보냈던 젊은 날을 회상했다. 하지만 마지막 문장에서 모든 것이 역사 속으로 사라진 것 같다고 하였으므로 Ⓑ가 정답이다.

Practice Test

1.   **P. 150**

노래하는 새들의 거의 대부분은 노래를 아비 또는 다른 수컷 같은 멘토로부터 배우거나 외운다. Ⓐ 그러나 흉내지빠귀는 대부분의 소리를 환경이나 가끔은 흉내지빠귀로부터 그리고 항상 다른 새의 발성대를 포함하여 배운다. Ⓑ 또한 흉내지빠귀의 노래는 포유류나 개구리 그리고 심지어는 자동차 알람이나 휴대 전화기 같은 전자 음향을 포함한다. 이 소리는 흉내지빠귀에게 익혀지고 외워져서 끝없이 확장되는 레퍼토리로 합쳐진다. Ⓒ 봄에서부터 다음 해 봄까지 한 마리의 수컷 흉내지빠귀는 동시에 더 많은 노래를 더하면서 그가 이전에 들었던 노래의 종류에 최소 35%에서 63%까지 반복을 한다. Ⓓ 그 결과 노년에 접어들었을 때 그의 목소리의 레퍼토리는 마침내 200개까지 늘어난다.

정답_ Ⓒ

다음 문장이 지문의 어느 곳에 추가될 수 있는지를 나타내는 네 개의 네모를 살펴보시오.

이 소리는 흉내지빠귀에게 익혀지고 외워져서 끝없이 확장되는 레퍼토리로 합쳐진다.

문장이 어느 곳에 가장 적합한가?

문장을 지문에 추가하도록 한 개의 네모 박스 [■]를 클릭하시오

해설_ 출제 문장의 지시어 these sounds가 가리키는 내용을 찾으면 Ⓒ가 정답이다. These sounds가 가리키는 흉내지빠귀의 노래가 확장되는 레퍼토리로 합쳐지므로 글의 흐름에도 적절하다.

2.   **P. 151**

일반적인 의료 서비스는 국가의 모든 시민을 위한 건강보험이다. 보편적인 건강보험의 조항이 개인의 인권을 침해하는가? Ⓐ 일부는 범용 시스템이 가난한 사람들을 지원하기 위해 부자로부터 일정 수준의 양도를 요구한다고 주장한다. Ⓑ 이러한 양도는 개인의 과세에 대한 자유를 침해한다. 다른 이들은 그것은 개인이 자유를 누릴 수 있게 하고 사회로서는(많은 군사 자금의 부담을 공유하거나 모두를 위한 교육을 제공하는 것처럼) 공동의 책임이라고 주장한다. Ⓒ 하지만 이러한 사회적 형평성과 개인의 자유가 반드시 충돌할 필요는 없다. Ⓓ 어느 순간에 논쟁은 오히려 실제보다 이념적이 되고 자주 개인의 자유를 지지하면서 보편적인 의료 서비스를 시도하는 대부분의 국가들은 일반적으로 건강한 사회에서 가치를 살핀다.

정답_ Ⓐ

다음 문장이 지문의 어느 곳에 추가될 수 있는지를 나타내는 네 개의 네모를 살펴보시오.

보편적인 건강보험의 조항이 개인의 인권을 침해하는가?

문장이 어느 곳에 가장 적합한가?

문장을 지문에 추가하도록 한 개의 네모 박스 [■]를 클릭하시오.

해설_ 출제 문장에서 건강보험 조항에 대한 개인 인권 침해 문제를 제시하고 있기 때문에 그에 대한 주장이 나오는 문장의 앞이 적절하다. 따라서 Ⓐ가 정답이다.

<table>
<tr><td>Unit
08</td><td>Summary</td></tr>
</table>

Practice Test

1.   **P. 160**

북미와 비교해 볼 때 페루에는 더 많은 역사가 있는 듯하다: 더 많은 콜롬비안 이전 시대, 더 많은 식민지 시대 그리고 최근까지 꽤 많은 역사를 갖고 있다. 페루에는 더 많은 새들이 있으며 이들의 화려한 날개에는 더 많은 색상이 있다. 그 어디에서보다도 페루에서 유래된 – 감자와 토마토를 포함하여 – 음식들이 더 많이 있다. 페루에는 비록 소수의 사람들이 사용하지만 더 많은 언어가 있다. 그곳의 기후는 더 다양하며 세계 생태계의 대부분이 이 길고도 얇게 펼쳐진 나라에서 공존하면서 서로 꼭 붙어 있다. 비가 오면 장대비가 내리고; 머리 위에 태양이 있을 때는 타는 듯이 뜨겁다. 강도 더 길고 넓고 빠르며 지진도 더 강하다. 페루에는 미 대륙에서 가장 깊은 협곡이 있으며 지구상에서 가장 건조한 사막이 있다. 페루에는 더 많은 종교가 있기 때문에 휴가도 분명히 더 많고, 달이 뜨지 않은 밤의 시골 들판에서 보는 하늘에는 더 많은 별들이 있는 듯하다.

정답_ Ⓓ, Ⓔ, Ⓕ

지시사항 지문을 간략하게 요약하기 위한 도입문장이 아래에 제시되어 있다. 지문에서 가장 중요한 정보를 담고 있는 3개의 선택지를 선택하여 요약을 완성한다. 지문에 제시되지 않은 정보나 세부정보를 담고 있는 일부문장은 요약에 들어가지 않는다. 이 문제는 2점이 주어진다.

선택지를 관련있는 곳으로 끌어당기시오. 끌어당긴 선택지를 삭제하려면 그 위에 대고 클릭하시오. 지문을 다시 보려면 **View Text** 아이콘을 클릭하시오.

페루는 극도로 치우치는 나라이다.

- Ⓓ
- Ⓔ
- Ⓕ

선택지

Ⓐ 아시아에 비해서 페루에는 더 많은 역사가 있는 듯하다.

Ⓑ 일부 언어는 소수의 사람들이 사용한다.

Ⓒ 세계 생태계의 대부분이 페루에서 서로 공존하면서 산다.

Ⓓ 비가 오면 장대비가 내린다.

Ⓔ 페루에는 미 대륙에서 가장 깊은 협곡이 있다.

Ⓕ 페루인들은 휴가가 더 많다.

해설_ 도입문장 '페루는 극도로 치우치는 나라이다'라는 주제를 지지할 수 있는 예를 고르면 Ⓓ, Ⓔ, Ⓕ가 정답이다. Ⓐ는 페루의 역사를 아시아가 아닌 북미와 비교하였고 Ⓑ, Ⓒ는 도입 문장인 페루의 극단적인 성격과 직접적인 관련이 없으므로 오답이다.

2. P. 161

신사실주의라 불리는 것의 가장 중요한 특성과 혁신은 이야기의 필요성이 단지 인간의 패배를 위장하는 무의식적인 방법이었다는 것과 그것과 관련된 상상의 유형이 존재하는 사회적 사실에 대해 더 이상 작동되지 않는 공식을 단순히 겹치기 한 기법이었다는 것을 인식하기 위함이다. 이제 현실은 그것을 직접 볼 수 있을 만큼 엄청나게 풍부하다고 인식되어졌다; 예술가들의 과제는 사람들을 은유적인 상황에 감동시키거나 분개하게 만드는 것이 아니고 그들과 다른 사람들이 행동하는 것, 현실적인 것들에 대해 정확히 있는 그대로 반영하도록 만드는 것이라고 인식되어졌다. 이는 이탈리아가 경험한 비판적이고 정치적인 의식의 서막을 의미했다. 이탈리아는 그때까지 역사가 없었고 나라로서 통일된 역사도 없었으며 단지 많은 분리된 소수 민족들, 분단된 작은 나라들 그리고 남쪽과 북쪽 간의 큰 격차의 역사를 가졌다.

정답_ Ⓐ, Ⓒ, Ⓓ

지시사항 지문을 간략하게 요약하기 위한 도입문장이 아래에 제시되어 있다. 지문에서 가장 중요한 정보를 담고 있는 3개의 선택지를 선택하여 요약을 완성한다. 지문에 제시되지 않은 정보나 세부정보를 담고 있는 일부문장은 요약에 들어가지 않는다. **이 문제는 2점이 주어진다.**

> 선택지를 관련있는 곳으로 끌어당기시오. 끌어당긴 선택지를 삭제하려면 그 위에 대고 클릭하시오. 지문을 다시 보려면 **View Text** 아이콘을 클릭하시오.

신사실주의와 이탈리아 역사는 이탈리아 예술가들의 시야에 비판적이고 정치적인 의식을 가져왔다.

- Ⓐ
- Ⓒ
- Ⓓ

선택지

Ⓐ 그들은 이야기를 단지 패배를 위장하는 무의식적인 방법이라고 여겼다.

Ⓑ 그들은 현존하는 사회적 사실에 단순한 기술을 덧붙였다.

Ⓒ 그들의 임무는 사람들이 사실에 관해 되돌아보게 하는 것이었다.

Ⓓ 그들은 그때까지 국가로서 통일된 역사가 없었다.

Ⓔ 이탈리아의 남쪽과 북쪽 간의 큰 격차가 있었다.

Ⓕ 이탈리아에는 분리된 소수 민족과 작은 나라들이 있었다.

해설_ 도입문장 '신사실주의는 이탈리아 예술가들의 시야에 비판적이고 정치적인 의식을 가져왔다.'와 관련된 중요정보를 고르면 Ⓐ, Ⓒ, Ⓓ이다. Ⓑ는 신사실주의가 비판한 대상이며 Ⓔ, Ⓕ는 신사실주의 등장시기의 이탈리아 역사에 관한 세부정보이므로 오답이다.

Unit 09 Category Chart

Practice Test

1. P. 170

여러 농부들에게 가축을 방목시킬 수 있는 땅이 가능한 상황에서는 땅이 남용되거나 땅의 질이 저하될 가능성이 있다. 마찬가지로 공동 어장 역시 남획할 우려가 있으며 어류들이 사라지는 지역도 있을 것이다. 공동 벌목 삼림 지대 역시 과도하게 채벌되고 황폐하게 될 수 있다. 이것은 경제학자들이 그것이 분명한 재산권의 문제라고 결정하였을 때 수세기 전 영국의 '인클로저 운동(개방 경지, 공유지, 황무지를 산울타리나 돌담으로 둘러놓고 사유지임을 명시한 운동)'을 추진하기 위해 사용했던 아주 오래된 문제이다. 아무도 공동 구역을 소유하지 않았기 때문에 아무도 그것을 관리하여 경제적 혜택을 갖지 않았다. 실로 각 개인이 다른 사람들이 사용하기 전에 그것의 안에 들어가 가능한 한 많이 가능한 한 빠르게 사용할 수 있는 혜택을 가지고 있었다. 그렇다면 실제로 모든 사람의 자산은 어느 누구의 자산도 아니었다 – 그리고 많은 경제학자들은 그 해결책은 공공 구역에 대한 개인 사유 재산을 허용하는 것이 분명하다고 생각하였다. 누구에게 할당할 것인가, 어떻게 할당할 것인가는 큰 문제가 아니었다. 문제는 일단 어떤 사람이 자산을 소유하면 그것을 관리하여 경제적 혜택을 갖게 되고 질이 떨어지는 것을 예방하게 되리라는 것이었다.

정답_ Common Areas – ⓒ, ⓕ, ⓖ / Private Property – ⓐ, ⓓ

지시사항 선택지에서 알맞은 구를 선택하여 그것과 관련된 토지 소유권에 맞게 연결하시오. **이 문제는 3점이 주어진다.**

선택지를 관련있는 곳으로 끌어당기시오. 끌어당긴 선택지를 삭제하려면 그 위에 대고 클릭하시오. 지문을 다시 보려면 **View Text** 아이콘을 클릭하시오.

선택지	공동 구역
ⓐ 질의 저하가 방지된	• ⓒ
ⓑ 인클로저 운동	• ⓕ
ⓒ 남용되거나 질이 저하된	• ⓖ
ⓓ 돌보아진	**사유 재산**
ⓔ 사유권의 문제	
ⓕ 관리에 대한 경제적 혜택 없음	• ⓐ
ⓖ 다른 사람보다 먼저 가능한 많이 사용하는	• ⓓ

해설_ 공동 구역에 관한 내용은 지문의 첫 번째(남용되거나 질이 저하된), 여섯 번째(다른 사람보다 먼저 가능한 많이 사용하는), 다섯 번째 문장(관리에 대한 경제적 혜택 없음)에 나와 있으므로 ⓒ, ⓕ, ⓖ를 찾을 수 있다. 지문의 마지막 문장에 공동 구역에 대한 장점(관리와 질이 떨어지는 것을 예방)이 나오므로 ⓐ와 ⓓ가 공동 구역에 관한 정답이다. ⓑ 인클로저 운동과 ⓔ 사유권의 문제는 공동 구역의 문제를 해결하기 위한 방안에 속하므로 오답이다.

2.
P. 171

인간이 만든 스트레스는 산호초에 큰 피해를 줄 수 있다. 농약과 토양 유출로 인한 오염으로 인해 캐리비안의 코스타리카 가장 자리에 위치한 작은 산호 구역을 질식시키고 있다. 인구 950만의 도시이자 인도네시아의 수도 자카르타 인근 산호가 미처리 폐수, 산호 채광과 토양 유출로 인해 사라지고 있다. 다이너마이트 어획이나 수족관 무역을 위한 대규모 불법 산호 채취 등으로 인해 필리핀을 둘러 싼 산호 구역이 황폐되었다. 심지어 생태 관광은 – 많은 사람들이 이 세계의 야생 지역을 구할 수 있기 희망하였으나 – 미숙한 다이버들이 그들이 소중히 여기는 바로 그 지역을 부주의하게 훼손시키고 있다. 단 한 번만 닿아도 민감한 산호 생성체에 치명적일 수 있다. '산호는 지

구상에서 가장 오래된 생태계입니다'라고 워싱턴 D.C의 스미스소니언 협회의 해양 생물학자가 말한다. '우리는 빠른 속도로 생태계를 파괴시키고 있으나 이제야 이것을 이해하기 시작했습니다.'

정답_ Pollution of Jakarta & Costa Rica – ⓐ, ⓑ, ⓕ / Pollution of the Philippines – ⓒ, ⓓ

지시사항 선택지에서 알맞은 구를 선택하여 그것과 관련된 오염원의 종류에 맞게 연결하시오. **이 문제는 3점이 주어진다.**

선택지를 관련있는 곳으로 끌어당기시오. 끌어당긴 선택지를 삭제하려면 그 위에 대고 클릭하시오. 지문을 다시 보려면 **View Text** 아이콘을 클릭하시오.

선택지	자카르타 & 코스타리카
ⓐ 농약으로 인한 오염	• ⓐ
ⓑ 미처리 폐수	• ⓑ
ⓒ 다이너마이트 어획	• ⓕ
ⓓ 불법 산호 채취	**필리핀**
ⓔ 능숙한 다이버들	
ⓕ 토양 유출	• ⓒ
ⓖ 민감한 산호 생성체	• ⓓ

해설 자카르타와 코스타리카의 산호 구역을 황폐화시키는 오염원은 지문의 두 번째(코스타리카) 세 번째(자카르타)에서 ⓐ 농약으로 인한 오염 ⓑ 미처리 폐수 ⓕ 토양 유출을 찾을 수 있다. 지문의 네 번째 문장에서 필리핀 근해의 ⓒ 다이너마이트 어획과 ⓓ 수족관 무역을 위한 불법 산호 채취를 고를 수 있다. 산호 채취는 자카르타와 코스타리카에서도 이루어지지만 불법인지 명확하지 않으므로 ⓓ는 필리핀에 속한다. ⓔ는 어느 나라인지 불문명하며 '능숙한(experienced)'이 아니라 미숙한(inexperienced) 다이버들이라고 하였으므로 지문의 내용과 일치하지 않는다. ⓖ 민감한 산호 생성체 또한 오염의 원인이 아니므로 오답이다.

Unit
01 History_ P. 175

01

긴 역사에도 불구하고 오늘날 존재하는 중국의 만리장성은 대부분 강력한 명나라 시대(1368-1644)에 건설되었다. **몽골**처럼 초창기 명나라 통치자들은 국경에 방어시설을 짓는 데 별 관심이 없었고 성벽 건설은 15세기 후반 이전까지 제한적이었다. 1421년 명의 황제 영락제는 '다두'라는 몽골 도시가 있던 자리를 베이징이라는 새로운 수도로 선언하였다. 명나라 통치자들의 강력한 영향력하에 중국 문화가 번성하였고 이 기간 동안 만리장성 이외에도 다리, 사원 및 탑을 포함하여 엄청나게 많은 건축물들이 세워졌다. 오늘날 알려져 있는 만리장성의 건설은 1474년 무렵 시작되었다. **초기 영토 확장 단계 이후에 명나라 통치자들은 매우 방어적인 자세를 취했고 만리장성의 개량과 증축이 이러한 전략의 핵심이었다.** 명나라 성벽은 랴오닝성 지방에 있는 압록강에서 간수 지방에 있는 타오라이 강의 동쪽 제방까지 확장되었고 오늘날의 랴오닝성, 허베이, 톈진, 베이징, 내몽골, 산시성, 섬서성, 린샤 및 간수를 가로질러 동쪽에서 서쪽으로 성벽길이 구불구불하게 나 있었다.

어휘_ the great wall of china 만리장성 Ming dynasty 명나라 시대. 명 왕조 fortifications 방어 시설. 요새화 proclaimed 선언 [선포]했다 flourished 번성했다 immense amount of 엄청난 양의 ~ territorial 영토의 expansion 확장. 팽창 from east to west 동서로

1. Ⓐ
작가는 지문에서 왜 **몽골**을 언급하고 있는가?
Ⓐ 당시 두 문화의 유사성을 비교하기 위해서
Ⓑ 중국이 몽골을 밀어냈다는 점을 강조하기 위해서
Ⓒ 초기 유사성에도 불구하고 중국이 몽골보다 우수하다는 사실을 보여주기 위해서
Ⓓ 비슷한 사고방식을 가진 또 다른 고대 문화의 사례를 제시하기 위해서

2. Ⓓ
아래 문장 중 어떤 것이 지문 속의 음영 처리된 문장의 핵심정보를 가장 잘 표현하고 있는가? 오답 선택지는 현저하게 의미를 바꾸거나 핵심정보를 생략한 것이다.
Ⓐ 명나라 통치자들에게 만리장성의 방어력만큼 중요한 것은 없다.
Ⓑ 명나라 통치자들은 즉시 공격에서 방어로 바꿀 수밖에 없었기 때문에 만리장성을 쌓기 시작했다.
Ⓒ 만리장성이 없었다면 명 통치자들은 계속해서 영토를 확장해야 했을 것이다.

Ⓓ 명나라 통치자들은 처음에는 새로운 지역으로 옮기고자 했으나 결국 가장 중요한 방어벽인 만리장성에 남게 되었다.

3. Ⓑ
지문에 따르면 다음 중 어느 것이 중국의 만리장성에 관해 사실이 아닌가?
Ⓐ 만리장성 건축은 명나라 통치자들의 중요한 방어 조치였다.
Ⓑ 만리장성은 제한된 공사 기간에 축조되었다.
Ⓒ 몽골은 자국의 국경 보호에 특별한 관심을 두지 않았다.
Ⓓ 베이징 시는 원래 몽골 시였다.

02

게르만족들이 서로마 제국에 입성했을 때 그들의 관습 및 전통을 함께 들여왔으며 그것들 중에는 사법 제도를 형성한 관습과 전통들도 있었다. 사회에서 **운용되는** 구성단위는 친족이나 씨족 또는 대가족이었다. 한 친족의 일원이 다른 친족의 일원을 해하거나 재산상의 해를 입혔을 때 피해자들의 친척들은 소위 피의 복수 또는 오래된 불화로 보복을 요구했다. 사람들이 운영한 그 집단적 성격 때문에 죄를 저지른 사람에게만이 아니라 그 자신이나 그 친족 일원에게도 보복이 요구된 것은 놀라운 일이 아니었다. 더불어 친족은 적들이 보복의 도를 넘어섰다고 여기고 응징의 적절한 균형 유지 수단으로써 그들만의 보복을 추구하고자 할 위험이 항상 있었다. 이런 '눈에는 눈, 이에는 이'의 보복게임들은 불평의 원인이 잊혀진 후에도 수년간 사람들이 살해되는 등 계속될 수 있었다.

어휘_ tribes 부족 comprised ~으로 구성되다 operative unit 운용되는 구성단위 kindred 일가친척이 됨 aggrieved 분개한 specifically 분명히. 명확하게 tit for tat 보복. 앙갚음

1. Ⓑ
지문의 **운용되는**이라는 단어와 의미가 가장 비슷한 것은?
Ⓐ 사용되는   Ⓑ 효과적으로 작동하는
Ⓒ 원하는 효과를 생산하는   Ⓓ 생산적인

해설_ 지문에서 씨족이 사회에서 운용되는(operative) 단위라는 것은 효과적으로 작동하는(functioning effectively) 단위라는 말이므로 Ⓑ가 정답이다.

2. Ⓒ
다음 중 어느 것이 지문의 내용으로부터 결론 내려질 수 있는가?
Ⓐ 게르만족의 기억력은 좋았다.
Ⓑ 이 종족은 자신이 입은 손해에 대하여 복수를 요구하지 않았다.
Ⓒ 잘못에 대해서 적절한 수준의 응징에 동의하기가 쉽지 않았다.
Ⓓ 종족들은 극심한 살기를 띠며 항상 다른 사람들을 공격할 기회를 엿보았다.

3. Ⓑ, Ⓒ, Ⓔ

지시사항 지문을 간략하게 요약하기 위한 도입문장이 아래에 제시되어 있다. 지문에서 가장 중요한 정보를 담고 있는 3개의 선택지를 선택하여 요약을 완성한다. 지문에 제시되지 않은 정보나 세부 정보를 담고 있는 일부 문장은 요약에 들어가지 않는다. **이 문제는 2점이 주어진다.**

선택지를 관련있는 곳으로 끌어당기시오. 끌어당긴 선택지를 삭제하려면 그 위에 대고 클릭하시오. 지문을 다시 보려면 **View Text** 아이콘을 클릭하시오.

집단사회에서 분쟁을 해결하는 방법들이 있었다.

> Ⓑ 피해자의 친척들은 복수나 불화의 상황에서 응징을 요구했다.
> Ⓒ 특별히 잘못한 개인만 응징하지 않았다.
> Ⓔ 보복 게임이 오랫동안 계속될 수 있었다.

선택지

Ⓐ 사회의 작용 단위는 친족이나 씨족 또는 대가족이었다.

Ⓑ 피해자의 친척들은 복수나 불화의 상황에서 응징을 요구했다.

Ⓒ 특별히 잘못한 개인만 응징하지 않았다.

Ⓓ 상대방들의 응징이 지나쳤다.

Ⓔ 보복 게임이 오랫동안 계속될 수 있었다.

Ⓕ 불평의 본래 기준이 잊혀졌다.

03

1945년 9월 2일 세계에서 가장 강대국인 두 나라가 냉전으로 알려진 자존심과 권력의 전쟁으로 치닫기 시작했다. 앞으로 다가올 시대에 얻게 될 명성을 위해 소련과 미국이 맹렬히 전투를 벌였다. 이 두 국가는 정치, 무기 및 과학 분야에서 세계 최고가 되고자 공격적으로 나아갔다. 이러한 행태는 우주 탐험에 대한 욕구를 크게 촉진했고 머지않아 역사를 영구적으로 바꾸어가는 것을 찾는 것을 부채질하게 되었다. **우주개발경쟁**은 경쟁을 지속시킬 만한 여러 동기와 상황을 갖고 있었다. 군사 안보가 주된 동기 중의 하나였다. 세계를 지배하는 힘을 갖기 위해 두 나라는 다른 나라보다 더 높이, 더 빨리, 그리고 더 멀리 갈 수 있는 미사일과 로켓을 만드는 게 필요했다. 이 라이벌들은 서로 우위를 차지하기 위해 우주에 눈을 돌려야 했다. 그들은 잠재적으로 우주 궤도에 무기 시스템을 지닐 수 있었고 적국의 통신을 가로채고 조사할 수 있었으며 달의 군사적 사용도 가능했다. **이러한 것들**이 군사적 분야의 우주개발에 자극이 되었다.

어휘_ the cold war 냉전체제 fiercely 사납게, 맹렬히 be venerated for ~에 대해 존경받다 aggressively 공격적으로, 정력적으로 need for ~을 필요로 하다 motivations 자극, 유도, 동기 dominance 우월, 지배 orbital weapon systems

궤도 무기 체계 intercept 가로채다, 가로막다

1. Ⓓ

작가는 지문에서 왜 **우주개발경쟁**을 언급하고 있는가?

Ⓐ 군무기 제조 규제를 촉구하기 위해서

Ⓑ 궤도무기(orbital weapon) 시스템의 능력과 가능성을 기념하기 위해서

Ⓒ 자존심으로 가득한 권력이 위험하게 확대되는 것을 비난하기 위해서

Ⓓ 발전으로 이어지는 근본 원인을 설명하기 위해서

2. Ⓐ

지문의 구문 **이러한 것들**이 가리키는 것은?

Ⓐ 궤도무기 시스템을 갖추고 적과의 통신을 차단 및 점검할 수 있으며 달에서 군 용도로 사용할 수도 있다.

Ⓑ 다른 나라보다 더 높이, 더 빨리, 더 멀리 날아가는 미사일과 로켓이 있다.

Ⓒ 서로에 대해 자신을 우세한 위치에 둔다.

Ⓓ 행동과 태도

3. Greatest in the World: Ⓓ, Ⓖ / Military Security: Ⓐ, Ⓔ, Ⓕ

지시사항 선택지에서 알맞은 구를 선택하여 그것과 관련된 경쟁의 동기에 맞게 연결하시오. **이 문제는 3점이 주어진다.**

선택지를 관련있는 곳으로 끌어당기시오. 끌어당긴 선택지를 삭제하려면 그 위에 대고 클릭하시오. 지문을 다시 보려면 **View Text** 아이콘을 클릭하시오.

선택지	세계 최고
Ⓐ 달에서 군 용도로 사용 Ⓑ 역사를 영원히 수정하기 Ⓒ 경쟁자 되기 Ⓓ 존경받는 명성 Ⓔ 궤도 무기 시스템 Ⓕ 빨라진 미사일과 로켓 Ⓖ 자존심과 권력	Ⓓ 존경받는 명성 Ⓖ 자존심과 권력
	군사 안보
	Ⓐ 달에서 군 용도로 사용
	Ⓔ 궤도 무기 시스템
	Ⓕ 빨라진 미사일과 로켓

04

최초의 유럽인 정착지는 16세기 초로 거슬러 올라가며, 플로리다와 캘리포니아에 있는 스페인 마을과 루이지애나에 있는 프랑스인들의 전초기지와 뉴잉글랜드의 영국인 임시거주지가 여기에 속했다. 영국이라는 나라와 식민지 엘리트 대표들로부터 독립을 원하던 영국 출신의 식민지 주민들은 1776년 미합중국의 독립을 선언하였다. Ⓐ■ 현재 이 나라의 사회계층, 인

종, 종족, 성의 관계는 식민지 시대부터 그 뿌리를 찾아 볼 수 있다. 영국 정착민들은 미 대륙 원주민을 노예로 만들고자 하는 노력이 실패하면서 남부에서 목화 농장에서 일을 시키거나 북부의 신흥 산업에서 일을 시키기 위해 백인들의 계약 하인으로 아프리카 노예를 수입하게 되었다. ⑧■ 영국의 세제는 가난한 백인 노동자들과 계약 하인들에게 불평등하게 부과되었다. **이 부분은 결국 미국혁명을 일으킨 시위와 영국제품 불매운동을 조장하는 데 주요한 원인이 되었다.** ⓒ■ 여성들은 전쟁 기간 동안 농장과 사업을 운영함으로써 혁명에 참여하였다. ⓓ■ **혁명의 평등주의 원칙은 노예들에게 적용되지 않았으며 독립 이후에도 모든 백인들에게 완전한 시민권이 주어진 것은 아니다.** 자산이 없는 남자와 여자에게는 참정권이 주어지지 않았다. 여성들에겐 20세기 초까지 참정권이 주어지지 않았다. 서부 애팔래치아 구역은 토지를 원하고 값싼 임금에서 자유롭고 싶은 가난한 백인이 정착하게 되었다.

어휘_ date from ~부터 시작되다 declared 선언했다 공표한 representatives 대표, 대표자 ethnic 민족의, 종족의 colonial period 식민지 시대 enslave 노예로 만들다 plantations 농장 (커피, 설탕, 고무 등) indentured servants 연한(年限) 계약 노동자 disproportionately 불균형적으로 the equalitarian rhetoric of the revolution 혁명의 평등주의 원칙 appalachians 애팔래치아 산맥 be settled by ~에 의해 장착되다 autonomy 자치권

1. ⓒ
다음의 문장이 지문에 추가될 수 있는 곳을 표시하는 네모 박스 [■]를 보시오.
이 부분은 결국 미국혁명을 일으킨 시위와 영국제품 불매운동을 조장하는 데 주요한 원인이 되었다.
문장이 어느 곳에 가장 적합한가?
문장을 지문에 추가하도록 한 개의 네모 박스 [■]를 클릭하시오.
해설_ 주어진 문장의 This sector(이 부문)가 가리키는 내용을 찾는다. 미국혁명을 일으킨 시위와 영국제품 불매운동을 조장하는 데 주요한 원인이 된 것은 British taxation(영국의 세제)이었으므로 ⓒ가 정답이다.

2. ⓐ
아래 문장 중 어떤 것이 지문 속의 음영 처리된 문장의 핵심정보를 가장 잘 표현하고 있는가? 오답 선택지는 현저하게 의미를 바꾸거나 핵심정보를 생략한 것이다.
ⓐ 평등권에 관한 혁명의 이상과 현실 사이에 괴리가 있었다.
ⓑ 혁명 지지자들은 불평이 있음에도 불구하고 자신들의 높은 이상을 실현할 수 있었다.
ⓒ 모두에게 평등권을 부여하기 위한 혁명의 노력이 좌절되었다.
ⓓ 혁명이 모두에게 평등권을 확대할 수 있으리라고 기대하는 것은 비현실적이었다.

3. ⓓ
지문에 따르면, 다음 중 어느 것이 혁명의 시작에 관해 추론될 수 있는가?
ⓐ 여성들은 전쟁 중에 여성 해방에서 급격한 진보를 할 수 있었다.
ⓑ 미국에서 온 사람들은 북미 원주민들을 노예로 삼고 싶지 않았다.
ⓒ 재산이 없는 사람들은 주로 정치적 이유로 애팔래치아 산맥의 서부로 이동했다.
ⓓ 가난한 백인 노동자들과 연기 계약 노동자들이 좀 더 공정하게 대우받았더라면 혁명이 일어나지 않았을 것이다.

05
왜 세계화, 민족주의, 맞물린 연합 및 다수 국가 간의 힘의 관계 이전이 특히 1914년에 전쟁이 발생하도록 결합하였을까? 이러한 요인들은 국가 간의 분쟁에 관해 **허용조건**이라고 생각될 수 있다: 그러한 요인들이 제1차 세계대전 발발의 길을 여는 데 기여했을지도 모르지만 어느 것도 단독으로 1914년 전쟁의 직접적인 원인이 된 것은 아니었다. 또한 그 운명의 해 이전에도 이러한 힘은 거의 확실히 유럽에 존재했다. 그럼 왜 그것들은 1908년에 오스트리아가 보스니아를 합병할 때 대 전쟁을 일으키기 위해 결합하지 않았을까? 왜 그들은 1912년과 1913년의 발칸 전쟁을 자극하지 않았으며 다음 글로벌 대화재를 낳지 않았을까? 우리가 여러 조건의 조합 중 하나의 특정 조합이 1914년에 제1차 세계대전을 일으켰다고 받아들인다면 왜 이러한 요인들이 더 일찍 또는 더 늦게 전쟁을 일으키지 못했는지 또는 그것들이 만연했음에도 불구하고 물리적 충돌을 왜 함께 피할 수 없었는지 또한 설명할 수 있어야 한다. 실제로 제1차 세계대전에 관한 풍부한 문헌에서 학자들은 이러한 중요한 사후가정을 분석하는 시도를 해왔다. 어떤 이들은 구조적인 조건이 실제로 유럽의 무력 충돌을 불가피하게 만들었다고 주장하고 있다 – 맞물린 연합, 영국과 독일 간의 전력 추이, 민족주의 및 기타 요인은 그 전쟁이 1914년에 일어나지 않았다면 1915년 또는 1916년에 발생하였을 것이라는 의미였다. 다른 분석가들은 세계대전이 오스트리아 대공 프란츠 페르디난트 암살의 직접적인 결과였다고 주장한다. 그가 1914년 6월 28일 사라예보에서 살해되지 않았거나 – 또는 총상을 입고 살아났다면 – 열강들은 그해뿐만 아니라 영구히 전쟁을 피할 수 있었을지 모른다. **하지만 대공의 암살과 같은 특이한 사건이 전쟁을 설명하는 열쇠라면 우리가 다른 근본적인 요인에 얼마나 많은 신빙성을 부여해야 할지 명확하지 않다.**

어휘_ interlocking alliances 맞물린 연합 pave the way 길을 닦다. 상황을 조성하다 prior to ~에 앞서 annexed 부가적 conflagration 큰불. 대화재 prevalence 널리 퍼짐 copious literature 풍부한 문학 inevitable 불가피한 assassination

암살 perpetuity 영속, 영존 idiosyncratic 특유한, 기이한 credence 신빙성 underlying factors 내재된 요소

1. Ⓐ

다음 중 어느 것이 지문의 내용으로부터 결론 내려질 수 있는가?

Ⓐ 학자들은 전쟁의 원인에 대해 결코 전적으로는 동의하지 않을 것이다.

Ⓑ 전쟁은 아무 때나 시작될 수는 없었을 것이다.

Ⓒ 시간은 전쟁을 하기에 무르익었고 하나의 작은 사건이 전쟁을 일으키기에 충분했다.

Ⓓ 전쟁은 과거에 피할 수 없었다.

해설_ 지문은 제1차 세계대전 발발 원인과 관련하여 학자들의 서로 다른 의견들을 다루므로 Ⓐ가 정답이다. 전쟁 발생에 관한 분석가들의 의견이 다르므로 나머지 보기 Ⓑ, Ⓒ, Ⓓ는 지문의 결론으로 부적절하다.

2. Ⓓ

지문의 허용조건이라는 구문과 의미가 가장 비슷한 것은?

Ⓐ 자유로운 조건   Ⓑ 제한된 조건

Ⓒ 선택적인 조건   Ⓓ 승인된 조건

해설_ conditions for permission은 허용된 조건이므로 Ⓓ conditions that are approved(승인된 조건)로 바꿔 말할 수 있다.

3. Ⓑ

아래 문장 중 어떤 것이 지문 속의 음영 처리된 문장의 핵심정보를 가장 잘 표현하고 있는가? 오답 보기는 현저하게 의미를 바꾸거나 핵심정보를 생략한 것이다.

Ⓐ 전쟁의 정확한 원인을 파악하는 것은 불가능하다.

Ⓑ 암살이 전쟁의 시작에 기여한 유일한 사건이라면 전쟁에 대한 다른 요인은 어떠한가?

Ⓒ 우리는 단지 하나의 고립된 사건에서 전쟁의 원인을 설명할 수 없다.

Ⓓ 근본적인 요인들은 전쟁의 원인에 암살만큼이나 중요하다.

해설_ 음영 처리된 문장은 특이한 사건이 전쟁을 설명할 때 중요하지만 전쟁에 대한 다른 요인도 살필 필요가 있다는 것이므로 Ⓑ가 정답이다. 특이한 사건이 전쟁을 일으키는 key(가장 중요한 이유)라고 하였으므로 보기 Ⓐ, Ⓒ, Ⓓ는 오답이다.

Vocabulary & Paraphrasing

1. 아래에 있는 각 뜻에 맞는 단어를 박스에서 찾아서 쓰시오.

① stagnation   ② unprecedented   ③ condemn

④ manifest   ⑤ indenture   ⑥ settlement

⑦ portage   ⑧ equalitarian   ⑨ undertake

⑩ disproportion

2. 다음 문장을 해석 후 아래 지시대로 paraphrasing(다른 말로 바꿔 표현하기)하세요.

① 인쇄 기술의 발명은 이러한 지식을 전례 없이 습득 가능하게 했다.

➡ 예시_ This knowledge was acquired in a completely new way through the invention of the printing press.

② 여성들에겐 20세기 초까지 참정권이 주어지지 않았다.

➡ 예시_ It wasn't until the early twentieth century that women were able to vote.

③ 일본의 산업은 거의 20년 동안의 전반적인 경기 침체에도 불구하고 아직까지 세계에서 가장 진보적이고 혁신적인 나라 중에 있다.

➡ 예시_ Japan's industries are still highly advanced and it is one of the world's most innovative countries even though its economy has been stagnating for almost twenty years.

④ 공동 산책로 프로젝트는 험버 강 계곡을 따라 10km를 누비며 험버 강둑을 따라 발생한 대로 캐나다 초기 역사를 보여 주는 13개의 역사적인 접점으로 구성되어 있다.

➡ 예시_ Canada's early history along the Humber River can be seen in 13 places along the Shared Path project as it leads 10 kilometers through the Humber River Valley

Unit 02 Environment_ P. 189

01

방대한 태평양을 건너, 힘이 센 다랑어는 일본의 손상된 핵발전소에서 새어 나온 방사능 오염을 6,000마일 떨어져 있는 미국 해안까지 옮겨 왔다. – 이동하는 거대한 물고기는 처음으로 방사능을 그런 거리까지 옮겨 왔다고 보인다. **방사능 세슘의 레벨은 작년에 캘리포니아 해안의 다랑어에서 측정된 양보다 10배가 높게 나타났다.** Ⓐ■ 하지만 그렇다 하더라도 그 물고기의 방사능 수치는 미국과 일본 정부에 의해 정해진 식용으로서의 안전 제한 기준보다 훨씬 낮다. Ⓑ■ 이전에 2011년 3월에 일어난 진도 9의 지진이 후쿠시마 다이치 원자로를 치명적으로 손상시킨 쓰나미를 일으킨 후에 더 작은 물고기와 플랑크톤에서 일본 바다의 방사능이 **상승한** 수준으로 나타났다. Ⓒ■ 그러나 거대한 물고기들은 대사 작용을 할 수 있고 방사능 물질을 저절로 흘려버릴 수 있기 때문에 세계를 항해한 큰 물고기에 핵 낙진이 남아 있을 것이라고 과학자들은 예상하지 않았다. 가장 크고 빠른 물고기인 태평양 다랑어는 10피트까지 자랄 수 있고 1,000파운드의 무게까지 나갈 수 있다. Ⓓ■ 그들은 일본 해안에 알을 낳고 무리지어 최고의 속도로 동쪽 캘리포니아 앞바다와 멕시코 바자 캘리포니아 끝까지 빠르게 수영한다. 후쿠시마 재난 다섯 달 후에 한 팀이 샌디에이고 해안에서 잡힌 태평양 다랑어를 테스트하기로 하였다.

놀랍게도 잡힌 열다섯 마리의 다랑어 모두의 조직 샘플은 이전에 포획된 것보다 더 높은 양의 두 가지 방사능 물질 – 세슘134와 세슘137 – 을 포함하고 있었다.

어휘_ mighty bluefin tuna 힘센 다랑어 radioactive contamination 방사능 오염 leaked from ~에서 누출된 migrating fish 이동하는 물고기 plankton 플랑크톤 radiation 방사선 magnitude-9 진도 9 tsunami 쓰나미 metabolize 대사작용을 하다 radioactive 방사능의 spawn 알을 낳다 breakneck 위험할 정도로 빠른 were caught off ~에 잡히다

1. Ⓐ

다음의 문장이 지문에 추가될 수 있는 곳을 표시하는 네모 박스 [■]를 보시오.

방사능 세슘의 레벨은 작년에 캘리포니아 해안의 다랑어에서 측정된 양보다 10배가 높게 나타났다.

문장이 어느 곳에 가장 적합한가?

문장을 지문에 추가하도록 한 개의 네모 박스 [■]를 클릭하시오.

해설_ 주어진 문장은 방사능 세슘의 레벨에 대한 설명이므로 앞에 방사능에 대한 일반적인 정보가 나와야 한다. 그리고 뒤에 방사능 수치가 높지만 식용 안전 제한 기준보다 훨씬 낮다는 내용이 적절하다. 따라서 Ⓐ가 정답이다.

2. Ⓑ

지문의 **상승한**이라는 단어와 의미가 가장 비슷한 것은?

Ⓐ 고상한   Ⓑ 증가한

Ⓒ 생산된   Ⓓ 지상의

해설_ 일본 바다의 방사능이 상승하였다는 문장에서 elevated(상승한)의 동의어는 increased(증가한)이므로 Ⓑ가 정답이다.

3. Ⓒ

지문에 따르면 과학자들은 잡힌 참치의 조직 샘플에서 높은 수준의 방사능 물질이 검출된 것 때문에 놀랐다. 왜냐하면

Ⓐ 세계를 헤엄쳐 다니는 대형 물고기여서

Ⓑ 물고기들은 일본 해변에서 산란하고 맹렬한 속도로 동쪽으로 헤엄쳐 가서

Ⓒ 물고기가 물질 대사를 하고 방사능 물질을 방출할 수 있어서

Ⓓ 예전에 일본 바다에 분포한 작은 물고기와 플랑크톤에서 높은 수준의 방사선이 발견되어서

02

아무것도 없던 땅에 나무를 심거나 부지를 만드는 조림 사업을 실시하면서 생기는 수분 고갈은 널리 시행되고 있는 연방 정책에 따른 의도하지 않은 결과이다. 수천 년 동안 번개나 인디언에 의해서 발생한 불로 나무의 수가 대략 1에이커당 수십 그루 정도로 줄었다. 1910년 발생한 산불은 산불과의 전쟁으로 이어졌고 이로 인해 경비 감시탑, 선전, 공중 투하 폭탄 및

색깔별 위험 경보가 생겨났다. 적과도 같은 불길을 잡기 위해 엘리트 팀이 훈련을 받았다. 매년 의회가 이러한 산불과의 전쟁으로 인한 활동에 자금을 지원해 왔지만 수십 년 동안 산불에 맞서 거둔 영웅적인 승리가 더 커진 전쟁에서 점차 패배로 바뀌고 있다. 연료가 증가하여 불이 났을 때, 더 뜨겁게, 더 빨리 그리고 더 크게 타오른다. 새로 심어진 더 많은 나무들은 적은 햇볕과 희박한 토양 영양분 그리고 희박한 수자원을 놓고 경쟁을 벌인다. 토종 야생 동물은 고통을 겪고 있다. 벌레와 질병이 더 빨리 퍼지고 있다. 공공 보조금으로 나무를 심어서 황무지와 도시 사이 접점 지역의 사유 재산을 보호한다. 습한 동부 주에서는 침식을 막고 하류로 배가 다닐 수 있는 강을 확보하기 위한 이런 조치가 적합했지만 **그것**은 비가 거의 오지 않는 서부에서는 역효과를 낳았다.

어휘_ depletion 고갈, 소모 afforestation 조림 federal policy 연방 대책 led to ~로 이어지다 watchtower 감시탑, 망루 propaganda 선전 ignite 불이 붙다. 불을 붙이다 nutrient 영양소 erosion 부식, 침식 navigable 가항의, 배가 다닐 수 있는 semiarid 강우량이 적고 증발이 심한

1. Ⓑ

다음 중 어느 것이 지문의 내용으로부터 결론 내려질 수 있는가?

Ⓐ 산불과의 전쟁은 결국 승리했다.

Ⓑ 조림과정에서 의도하지 않은 부작용이 나타났다.

Ⓒ 조림에 의해 산림 재고가 성공적으로 개선되었다.

Ⓓ 산불과의 전쟁은 결국 서부로 번졌다.

2. Ⓒ

지문의 단어 **그것**이 가리키는 것은?

Ⓐ 나무를 보호하는 것

Ⓑ 강을 배가 다닐 수 있게 하는 것

Ⓒ 나무를 심는 것

Ⓓ 침식을 막는 것

해설_ 지문에서 그것이 가리키는 것은 서부에서 역효과를 낳은 원인이다. 침식을 막고 하류로 배가 다닐 수 있는 강을 확보하기 위해 나무를 심었으므로 Ⓒ가 정답이다.

3. Ⓑ, Ⓓ, Ⓕ

지시사항 지문을 간략하게 요약하기 위한 도입문장이 아래에 제시되어 있다. 지문에서 가장 중요한 정보를 담고 있는 3개의 선택지를 선택하여 요약을 완성한다. 지문에 제시되지 않은 정보나 세부 정보를 담고 있는 일부문장은 요약에 들어가지 않는다. **이 문제는 2점이 주어진다.**

선택지를 관련있는 곳으로 끌어당기시오. 끌어당긴 선택지를 삭제하려면 그 위에 대고 클릭하시오. 지문을 다시 보려면 **View Text** 아이콘을 클릭하시오.

1910년 발생한 산불은 산불과의 전쟁으로 이어졌다.

Ⓑ 의회는 매년 전쟁 활동에 자금을 조달했다.

Ⓓ 정부는 화재 경보 시설에 대한 우려를 나타냈다.

Ⓕ 정예 팀은 적의 화염을 진화하도록 훈련받았다.

선택지

Ⓐ 부식을 예방하고 하류의 가항 하천을 확보하기 위한 조치는 반건조성 서부 지역에서 효과를 나타냈다.

Ⓑ 의회는 매년 전쟁 활동에 자금을 조달했다.

Ⓒ 토종 야생 동물이 고통받고 있다.

Ⓓ 정부는 화재 경보 시설에 대한 우려를 나타냈다.

Ⓔ 번개나 북미 원주민에 의해 발생한 화재는 산림 재고를 대략 에이커당 수십 그루의 나무로 제한하게 되었다.

Ⓕ 정예 팀은 적의 화염을 진화하도록 훈련받았다.

03

청정 우주의 목적은 우리가 처음 우주를 발견하였을 때처럼 깨끗한 환경을 다음 세대에 전해주는 것이다. 이 목적은 우주 프로그램에서 추진체로 널리 사용되는 **히드라진**과 같은 물질과, 독성이 감소된 추진체를 사용하는 녹색 추진 정책의 개발에 관한 규정에 영향을 미칠 것이다. 환경 친화성과 지속 가능성은 효율성 증가를 의미하며 산업에 경쟁력을 불어넣을 것을 기대하고, 따라서 에너지는 적게 사용하고 쓰레기는 더 적게 생성해서 비용을 감축시키는 기술을 살피고 있다. 마지막으로 통제적 및 비통제적 재반입 행사와 수동적인 지구 반입 시스템 및 적극적인 궤도 이탈 및 재궤도 돌입 시스템을 사용하여 우주 환경과 지구의 쓰레기에 미치는 영향을 최소화시킬 수 있도록 우주 파편을 감소시키는 일을 전망하고 있다. 25년 이내에 저궤도 밖으로 폐기된 위성을 다시 끌어와 묶거나 항행하는 것을 고려하고 있다. 새로운 '종말 디자인' 개념은 생존하고 있는 위성 무더기가 지상으로 재진입하여 충돌하는 것을 예방할 것으로 기대한다. 위성을 수리하거나 궤도에서 이탈시켜 지구로 돌아오게 하는 로봇 임무를 포함하여 기존의 쓰레기를 적극적으로 제거하는 것이 필요하다.

어휘_ pristine 완전 새 것 같은 hydrazine 히드라진 propellant 압축가스 green propulsion 녹색 추진력 toxicity 유독성 debris mitigation 잔해 완화 tether 묶다 chunk 덩어리

1. Ⓑ
지문에서 작가는 ~ 위해 **히드라진**을 언급하고 있다.

Ⓐ 환경 친화적 추진체의 필요성을 강조하기

Ⓑ 독성 추진체에 대한 예를 들기

Ⓒ 어떤 물질이 조절될 것인지 나열하기

Ⓓ 독성을 줄인 독성물질을 분류하기

2. Ⓑ
지문에 따르면 다음 중 어느 것이 사실인가?

Ⓐ 환경 친화적 기술은 효율적이지만 비용이 더 든다.

Ⓑ 로봇은 클린 스페이스 프로그램에서 역할을 맡을 것이다.

Ⓒ 25년 후, 저궤도에서 위성들이 사라질 리 없다.

Ⓓ 추진체가 우주 독성의 주요 원인이다.

**3. Environmental Sustainability – Ⓑ, Ⓓ, Ⓖ /
  Debris Mitigation – Ⓐ, Ⓒ**

지시사항 선택지에서 알맞은 구를 선택하여 그것과 관련된 오염 물질의 대응에 맞게 연결하시오. 각 항목은 정답으로 중복 선택되지 않는다. **이 문제는 3점이 주어진다.**

선택지를 관련있는 곳으로 끌어당기시오. 끌어당긴 선택지를 삭제하려면 그 위에 대고 클릭하시오. 지문을 다시 보려면 **View Text** 아이콘을 클릭하시오.

선택지	환경 지속 가능성
Ⓐ 수동식 궤도 이탈 시스템	Ⓑ 폐기물을 덜 발생시킴
Ⓑ 폐기물을 덜 발생시킴	Ⓓ 에너지 소모를 줄인 기술
Ⓒ 위성을 수리 또는 궤도 이탈 시키기 위한 로봇 임무	Ⓖ 경쟁 우위
Ⓓ 에너지 소모를 줄인 기술	**우주파편 감소**
Ⓔ 우주 프로그램에서 추진체로 널리 사용되는 히드라진	Ⓐ 수동식 궤도 이탈 시스템
Ⓕ 지구상의 쓰레기 자취	Ⓒ 위성을 수리 또는 궤도 이탈 시키기 위한 로봇 임무
Ⓖ 경쟁 우위	

04

과학자들은 남극과 그 주변의 바다가 그 지역을 이미 변화시키고 있는 다양한 물리적 영향력의 압력을 받고 있다고 경고한다. Ⓐ▪ 가장 당면한 위협은 지역의 온난화, 해양 산성화 그리고 해빙의 감소이며 이 모든 것이 지구의 이산화탄소의 정도와 관련되어 있다. 새로운 연구에 따르면 그 대륙이나 가까이 살고 있는 사실상 모든 동물들의 생존에 중요한 해빙 덮개는 이미 온난화로 줄어들고 있다. Ⓑ▪ 남극의 먹이 사슬에 중요한 요소인 크릴새우 같은 동물들의 포획이 남극에 위협을 주는 것처럼 관광객, 연구원들 그리고 다른 사람들의 방문 또한 남극 변화에 위협이 된다. Ⓒ▪ 남극 대륙은 연구와 관광을 규제하는 국제법인 남극 조약 체제에 의해 관리되고 있다. 지금까지 남극 조약은 남극의 환경과 자원을 보호하는 데 바람직한 역할을 해왔다. Ⓓ▪ **하지만 변화가 매우 빨라서 그것들은 각별한 주의를 필요로 한다.** 남미로부터 항해에 며칠 걸리지 않는 남극 반도는 특히 빨리 변화하고 있다. 반도의 파머기지를 둘러싸고 있는 지역은 지구 어느 지역보다 가장 빠른 겨울 온난화

를 경험하고 있으며 땅과 이어진 87%의 빙하도 줄어들고 있다. 남극해의 어떤 지역에서는 해빙이 지난 수십 년 전보다 3개월 넘게 없다. 생태계의 기반이 녹아 없어지고 있다. 예를 들어 해빙의 손실은 빙하 위에 살고 있는 아델리펭귄에게 피해를 주어왔다; **그것의** 개체 수는 1975년 이래로 80%가 줄어왔다. 이 지역의 크릴 새우(아델리펭귄의 주요한 먹이 자원이 되는) 또한 1991년 이래로 80%까지 줄어들고 있다.

어휘_ antarctica 남극대륙 acidification 산성화 carbon dioxide 이산화탄소 has been reduced by ~에 의해 감소되다 krill 크릴 antarctic treaty system 남극 조약 체제 glacier 빙하

1. ©
지문의 단어 **그것의**가 가리키는 것은?
Ⓐ 해빙　　　　　　　　Ⓑ 생태계의 기반
© 아델리펭귄　　　　　Ⓓ 땅과 이어진 빙하
해설_ 지문의 단어가 있는 문장에서 개체수가 줄어든 것은 아델리펭귄이므로 ©가 정답이다. its(그것의)바로 앞의 which lives on the ice(빙하위에 살고 있는)는 아델리펭귄에 대한 세부 설명이므로 Ⓐ, Ⓓ는 오답이다.

2. ©
다음 중 어느 것이 지문의 내용으로부터 결론 내려질 수 있는가?
Ⓐ 관광은 남극 대륙에 해롭기보다 오히려 득이 된다.
Ⓑ 남극 조약 체제는 재검토되어야 한다.
© 남극 대륙은 예전만큼 춥지 않다.
Ⓓ 해빙 커버는 결국 완전히 사라질 것이다.

3. Ⓓ
다음의 문장이 지문에 추가될 수 있는 곳을 표시하는 네모 박스 [■]를 보시오.
하지만 변화가 매우 빨라서 그것들은 각별한 주의를 필요로 한다.
문장이 어느 곳에 가장 적합한가?
문장을 지문에 추가하도록 한 개의 네모 박스 [■]를 클릭하시오.
해설_ 주어진 문장은 남극 조약이 남극의 환경과 자원을 보호하는 데 바람직한 역할을 해왔다는 앞의 내용과 대조된다. 그리고 뒤에 change(변화)에 대한 세부 설명이 나오는 게 자연스러우므로 Ⓓ가 정답이다.

05
종이를 만들거나 주택을 짓는 계획에 매년 수백만 그루의 나무가 파괴된다. 파괴된 나무를 심기 위해 새로운 프로그램들이 시작되고 있다. 자연을 해쳤을 때 얼마나 많은 손해가 발생될지 사람들은 거의 알지 못한다. 이러한 주택을 짓는 계획은 시원한 바람이 나뭇잎 사이로 통과할 수 있도록 두면서 아름다운 나무들이 있는 곳에 만들어진다. 현재 재활용 재단은 어

머니와 같은 지구를 구하기 위해서 어린아이들이 그들의 주변에 나무를 심을 수 있도록 하는 프로그램을 시작했다. 나무들이 거의 모든 거리 곳곳에 심어지고 있다. 아이들은 무슨 일이 일어날지 알지 못하지만 그들이 자신의 지역사회를 위해서 좋은 일을 하고 있다고 생각한다. 나무는 마을 곳곳의 보도 아래에서 뻗어 나온다. 나무가 눈에 보일 정도로 성장할 때까지 아무도 자신의 집 앞에 나무가 자라고 있다는 것에 관심을 기울이지 않는다. **미국의 대부분의 사람들은 그들이 모르는 사실이 그들을 다치게 할 수 있다고 생각하지 않는다.** 하지만 해가 될 수 있다. 나무는 많은 인명 피해를 가져왔다. 나무는 집 위로 자라거나 강한 뇌우로 인해 그것을 그것의 뿌리가 뽑힌 채 집 위로 날린다. 작년에 내가 살고 있는 마을 근처에 한 아버지가 아이들을 학교에 데려다주고 있었다. 그날 바람이 너무 세서 뿌리째 나무가 뽑혔고 지프차 바로 앞에 그 나무가 떨어져 뒤의 좌석에 있던 아이 셋이 모두 사망했다. 채널 7의 통계에 따르면 나무로 인해 작년 뉴저지의 사망률이 가장 높았다.

어휘_ millions of trees 수백만 그루의 나무 recycling foundation 재활용재단 creep up 기어오르다 blew off ~을 날렸다 statistics 통계

1. ©
아래 문장 중 어떤 것이 지문 속의 음영 처리된 문장의 핵심정보를 가장 잘 표현하고 있는가? 오답 선택지는 현저하게 의미를 바꾸거나 핵심정보를 생략한 것이다.
Ⓐ 당신은 항상 무슨 일이 일어날지 알 수 없다.
Ⓑ 그들이 그것에 대해 모른다면 아무것도 그들을 다치게 하지 않을 것이다.
© 사람들이 어떤 것을 인식하지 못하더라도 그것은 그들의 생명에 영향을 미칠 수 있다.
Ⓓ 무언가가 당신을 다치게 하지 않으면 당신은 그것에 대해 모른다.
해설_ 음영 처리된 문장에서 자신들이 모르는 사실들이 그들을 다치게 할 수 있다고 하였으므로 ©가 답이다.

2. Ⓓ
동네에 나무 심는 것에 관해서 작가는 다음 중 어느 것을 가장 지지할 것 같은가?
Ⓐ 중지되어야 한다.
Ⓑ 계속 나무를 심어야 한다.
© 더 많은 관심을 보여야 한다.
Ⓓ 더 신중하게 생각해야 한다.
해설_ 작가는 처음에 나무 심기에 대한 필요성과 사례를 언급하지만 중간부터 나무가 이웃에 주는 피해를 강조한다. 지문 전체에서 작가는 나무 심기에 대한 신중한 태도를 보이고 있으므로 Ⓓ가 정답이다.

3. Ⓓ, Ⓔ, Ⓕ
지시사항 지문을 간략하게 요약하기 위한 도입문장이 아래에 제시

되어 있다. 지문에서 가장 중요한 정보를 담고 있는 3개의 보기를 선택하여 요약을 완성한다. 지문에 제시되지 않은 정보나 세부정보를 담고 있는 일부 문장은 요약에 들어가지 않는다. **이 문제는 2점이 주어진다.**

선택지를 관련있는 곳으로 끌어당기시오. 끌어당긴 선택지를 삭제하려면 그 위에 대고 클릭하시오. 지문을 다시 보려면 **View Text** 아이콘을 클릭하시오.

나무는 이웃에 혜택을 줄 뿐만 아니라 해가 될 수도 있다.

Ⓓ 나무는 많은 사람들에게 인명 피해를 입혀 왔다.
Ⓔ 나무는 마을 곳곳의 보도 아래에서 뻗어 나온다.
Ⓕ 어린이들이 지역 사회를 위해 좋은 일을 하고 있다고 생각한다.

선택지

Ⓐ 시원한 바람이 잎을 통해 분다.
Ⓑ 나무가 모든 거리 모퉁이에 심어져 있다.
Ⓒ 아무도 자신의 집 앞에서 자라는 나무에 관심을 두지 않는다.
Ⓓ 나무는 많은 사람들에게 인명 피해를 입혀왔다.
Ⓔ 나무는 마을 곳곳의 보도 아래에서 뻗어 나온다.
Ⓕ 어린이들이 지역 사회를 위해 좋은 일을 하고 있다고 생각한다.

해설_ 도입문장은 대개 지문의 주제와 관련된다. 나무가 이웃에 주는 혜택으로 Kids think they are doing good for their community(어린이들이 지역 사회를 위해 좋은 일을 하고 있다고 생각한다). 피해로서 Trees have cost many people their lives(나무는 많은 인명 피해를 가져왔다). Trees creep up underneath the sidewalk all over town(나무는 마을 곳곳의 보도 아래에서 뻗어 나온다)가 중요한 정보가 될 수 있으므로 Ⓓ, Ⓔ, Ⓕ가 정답이다. Ⓐ, Ⓑ, Ⓒ는 도입문장(나무가 주는 혜택과 피해)의 중심내용이 아니거나 관련이 없으므로 오답이다.

Vocabulary & Paraphrasing

1. 아래에 있는 각 뜻에 맞는 단어를 박스에서 찾아서 쓰시오.

① magnitude ② annular ③ futile
④ forage ⑤ picturesque ⑥ catalyst
⑦ gauge ⑧ symmetric ⑨ spawn
⑩ tweak

2. 다음 문장을 해석 후 아래 지시대로 **paraphrasing**(다른 말로 바꿔 표현하기)하세요.

① 그러나 거대한 물고기들은 대사작용을 할 수 있고 방사능 물질을 저절로 흘려버릴 수 있기 때문에 세계를 항해한 큰 물고기에 핵낙진이 남아 있을 것이라고 과학자들은 기대하지 않았다.

➡ 예시_ Large fish that sail the world can process and eliminate radioactive substances so scientists thought they would not retain the nuclear fallout.

② 태양의 흑점들은 지구에서 무선 통신의 방해를 초래하고 또한 우주의 전파 천문학자들의 시야를 저해하는 태양 표면의 폭발이라

불리는 강렬한 전자기 방사선의 분출과 연관이 있다.

➡ 예시_ Disruptions to radio communications on Earth and obstructions to radio astronomers' views of the universe can be caused by sunspots which are connected to eruptions of intense electromagnetic radiation called solar flares.

③ 적절한 몸무게와 먹이 수집의 경험을 실험하기 위해서 연구자들은 핀의 머리보다 작은 전자 태그를 개미들 위에 얹고 누가 떠날 수 있는지를 통제하기 위해 미니 자동문을 개미집단 소굴에 설치하였다.

➡ 예시_ Researchers put tiny electronic tags smaller than a pinhead onto ants and set up a mini automatic door in the nest of the colony so they could to control who could leave in order to assess the connection between body weight and experience in searching for food.

④ 중간 분자들이 음극에 너무 빽빽하거나 너무 헐렁하게 결합하게 되면 반응을 감속시키고 전압을 떨어뜨린다는 사실이 발견되었다.

➡ 예시_ Voltage drops from the slowed reaction as a result of the intermediate molecules bonding too strongly or too weakly to the cathode surface.

Unit 03 Economy_ P. 203

01

빈곤, 질병 및 강진으로 고통을 겪은 나라로 아이티가 잠재적으로 수익성이 높은 금, 구리 및 은 광산을 많이 보유하고 있다는 것은 정말로 반가운 소식이다. **아이티의 광산들은 잠재적으로 200억 달러의 가치가 있으며 발견된 귀중한 금속들로 인해 벌써 수많은 일자리와 새로운 도로가 만들어지고 있다.** Ⓐ■ 더욱이 뜻밖에도 아이티 사람들은 그곳에서 작업할 예정인 외국 채광 회사로부터 이익의 대략 절반을 받을 수 있을 것으로 보이는데 이는 이례적으로 높은 비율이다. Ⓑ■ 하지만 역사를 통해 볼 때 아이티에는 피해야 할 위험이 많이 있다. Ⓒ ■ 세계적으로 가장 흔한 유형인 노천광은 대략 25년 동안 사용할 수 있지만 심하게 훼손된 산꼭대기와 주민들의 이주 그리고 환경 오염을 남긴다. Ⓓ■ 대체로 25년이 지나 자원이 고갈되면 채취장은 다시 채워지거나 저장소로 바뀔 수 있다. 긍정적인 측면을 살펴보자면 47세의 석공인 조셉 버나드 같은 사람들이 급료를 받아 가족을 부양하고 있다. '나는 직업이 있지만 대부분은 그렇지 못하다. 만약 더 많은 회사가 있다면 더 많은 사람들이 일을 할 것이다.'라고 그가 말했다.

어휘_ devastating 대단히 파괴적인 a number of ~의 수 lucrative 수익성이 좋은 fortuitously 우발적으로 pitfalls 위험, 곤란 reservoirs 저수지, 급수장

1. Ⓐ

다음의 문장이 지문에 추가될 수 있는 곳을 표시하는 네모 박스 [■]를 보시오.

아이티의 광산들은 잠재적으로 200억 달러의 가치가 있으며 발견된 귀중한 금속들로 인해 벌써 수많은 일자리와 새로운 도로가 만들어지고 있다.

문장이 어느 곳에 가장 적합한가?

문장을 지문에 추가하도록 한 개의 네모 박스 [■]를 클릭하시오.

해설_ 주어진 문장은 일반적인 사실에 뒤에서 나오는 세부설명이고 추가 정보가 이어서 나오므로 Ⓐ가 정답이다.

2. Ⓓ

지문의 심하게 훼손된이라는 단어와 의미가 가장 비슷한 것은?

Ⓐ 부상당한   Ⓑ 악화된

Ⓒ 축소된   Ⓓ 손상 입은

해설_ decimated(심하게 훼손된)를 설명한 선택지는 damaged(손상 입은)이므로 Ⓓ가 정답이다. 지문의 단어가 있는 문장은 노천광의 부작용을 설명하고 있으므로 산꼭대기가 훼손되었다고 추론해 볼 수 있다. Ⓐ injured는 신체의 부상을 의미하므로 오답이다.

3. Ⓐ, Ⓒ, Ⓔ

지시사항 지문을 간략하게 요약하기 위한 도입문장이 아래에 제시되어 있다. 지문에서 가장 중요한 정보를 담고 있는 3개의 선택지를 선택하여 요약을 완성한다. 지문에 제시되지 않은 정보나 세부 정보를 담고 있는 일부 문장은 요약에 들어가지 않는다. **이 문제는 2점이 주어진다.**

> 선택지를 관련있는 곳으로 끌어당기시오. 끌어당긴 선택지를 삭제하려면 그 위에 대고 클릭하시오. 지문을 다시 보려면 **View Text** 아이콘을 클릭하시오.

아이티가 귀금속의 활용을 원하면 좋은 기회가 있지만 피해야 할 위험도 도사리고 있다.

> Ⓐ 잠정적인 단점을 관리할 경우 아이티는 외국의 광업 회사에서 수익을 올리게 될 것이다.
> Ⓒ 광산은 수익성이 있으나 산봉우리를 훼손하고 주민을 추방시킨다.
> Ⓔ 갱은 다시 메워지거나 저장소로 변환되어 부정적인 효과를 긍정적인 효과로 돌릴 수 있다.

선택지

Ⓐ 잠정적인 단점을 관리할 경우 아이티는 외국의 광업 회사에서 수익을 올리게 될 것이다.

Ⓑ 노천광은 약 25년간 수익을 내지만, 영구적인 흉물이 될 필요는 없다.

Ⓒ 광산은 수익성이 있으나 산봉우리를 훼손하고 주민을 추방시킨다.

Ⓓ 이것은 가난, 질병, 파괴적 지진으로 고통받는 나라를 위한 정책의 전환이다.

Ⓔ 갱은 다시 메워지거나 저장소로 변환되어 부정적인 효과를 긍

정적인 효과로 돌릴 수 있다.

Ⓕ 광산은 환경 오염과 추출법이라는 필연적인 결과를 남긴다.

02

미국인의 상품에 대한 수요는 소득과 고용과 함께 성장했다. 하지만 일자리가 아웃소싱을 통해 해외로 떠나기 시작하자 균형이 깨졌다. 미국은 결국 거대한 구조적 실업을 떠안게 되었다. 따라서 미국에는 상품과 서비스를 구입할 만한 소득이 있고 일자리가 있는 사람보다 상품과 서비스를 요구하는 이들이 많아졌다. 수입은 늘어나고 미국의 무역 수지는 거의 35년 전부터 적자가 되기 시작했다. 이때 이후로 **그것**이 흑자인 적은 없고 국제무역마찰, 관세, 세금과 상품규제 같은 요인들은 단기간 내에 무역 수지를 스스로 바로잡는 데에 방해가 된다. 일자리를 잃은 근로자들은 이런 구조적 변화로 인해 경제적인 고통을 겪었다. 자유 시장주의자들은 특히 무역 장벽이 제거되면 시간이 흐르면서 제도가 스스로를 바로 잡는다고 주장한다. 아마 그것은 실제로 맞을 것이다. **하지만 정부는 그들과 그들의 민감한 정치적 이득을 보호하고 따라서 급격한 변화 등이 일어날 가능성은 크지 않다.**

어휘_ demand for ~에 대한 요구 end up 결국 ~이 되다 swung 흔들렸다 advocate 지지하다

1. Ⓑ

지문에 따르면 다음 중 어느 것이 추론될 수 있는가?

Ⓐ 높은 구조적 실업률이 곧 바뀌기 시작할 것이다.

Ⓑ 무역 장벽 제거는 바람직한 경제 변화를 초래할 수 있다.

Ⓒ 자유 시장은 필요한 변화를 가져올 수 있는 명쾌한 해결책이 있다.

Ⓓ 정부가 정치적으로 민감하지 않을 경우 미국 경제는 쉽게 회복될 수 있다.

2. Ⓓ

지문의 단어 **그것**이 가리키는 것은?

Ⓐ 고용   Ⓑ 수입

Ⓒ 상품과 서비스 수요   Ⓓ 미국의 무역 수지

해설_ it(그것)이 있는 문장에서 흑자인 적이 없는 것은 the balance of trade(무역 수지)가 적절하며 앞 문장에 무역 수지가 언급되어 있으므로 Ⓓ가 정답이다.

3. Ⓑ

아래 문장 중 어떤 것이 지문 속의 음영 처리된 문장의 핵심정보를 가장 잘 표현하고 있는가? 오답 선택지는 현저하게 의미를 바꾸거나 핵심정보를 생략한 것이다.

Ⓐ 정부가 스스로 보호할 수 있을 경우 상황이 정정될 가능성이 있다.

Ⓑ 정부가 자신의 관심을 가장 우선시하려 하기 때문에 서둘러 상황을 정정하지 않는다.

© 상황이 정치적으로 너무 민감해서 아무런 변화가 없을 것 같다.
Ⓓ 정부는 스스로를 보호하기 위해서 제한적이고 점진적인 변화를 가져와야 한다.

03

회의론자들은 한때 해저 광산업을 달에서 부를 찾는 것에 비유했었다. 하지만 더 이상 그렇지 않다. 해양 지질학의 발전, 수십 년 후 금속 부족에 대한 예측과 향상되고 있는 심연으로의 접근성은 해저 광산업을 현실화하기 위해 결합하고 있다. 환경 운동가들은 해저 광물의 위험에 대해 조사가 거의 되어 있지 않다고 말하면서 불안감을 더 크게 표현하고 있다. 그 산업은 연구와 확신 그리고 낙관적인 협의의 반응을 보여 왔다. 기술적인 발전은 새로운 로봇, 센서와 연안의 유류와 가스 산업으로부터 얻은 몇몇 다른 장비에 중점을 두고 있다. 선박들은 긴 밧줄에 탐험 장비를 내리고 암석 해저 속을 갉아대는 뾰족한 드릴을 내려 보낸다. 이 모든 수중 기계는 해저 재물을 찾고 지도를 만들고 인양하는 것을 점점 더 가능하게 해주고 있다. 산업강국들은 - 중국, 일본 그리고 한국에 정부가 지원하는 그룹들을 포함하여 - 대서양, 인도양 그리고 태평양에 있는 황화물을 찾고 있다. 그리고 비공개 기업들은 태평양 섬나라들: 피지, 통가, 바누아투, 뉴질랜드, 솔로몬 섬들과 파푸아 뉴기니 주위의 화산 지역에 대한 수백 개의 심층 평가와 소유권 주장을 하고 있다.

어휘_ skeptic 회의론자, 의심이 많은 사람 abyss 심연 environmentalist 환경운동가 seabed mining 해저자원개발 derived from ~에서 나오다 exploratory 탐사의 tether 묶다 gnaw 갉아먹다 feasible 실현 가능한 sulfide 황화물

1. Ⓓ
지문에 따르면 다음 중 어느 것이 음영 처리된 문장에 관해 추론될 수 있는가?
Ⓐ 심해저 채광은 한때 수익성이 매우 높을 것으로 생각되었다.
Ⓑ 달에서 부를 찾을 것이라고 아무도 생각하지 않았다.
© 회의론자들은 최초로 해저 채광이 가능할 것으로 생각했다.
Ⓓ 해저 채광이 가능하다고 믿었던 사람들은 비정상이거나 무모하다고 생각되었다.

2. Ⓓ
지문에 따르면 광산업은 환경 운동가들에게 어떻게 반응해 왔는가?
Ⓐ 불안해하면서
Ⓑ 신기술이 진보하면서
© 해저 채광의 위험에 대한 조사를 거의 하지 않고
Ⓓ 연구하고 협의하여

3. The Mining Industry: ©, Ⓔ, Ⓕ / Environmentalists: Ⓑ, Ⓖ

지시사항 선택지에서 알맞은 구를 선택하여 그것과 관련된 단체에 맞게 연결하시오. **이 문제는 3점이 주어진다.**

선택지를 관련있는 곳으로 끌어당기시오. 끌어당긴 선택지를 삭제하려면 그 위에 대고 클릭하시오. 지문을 다시 보려면 **View Text** 아이콘을 클릭하시오.

선택지	광산업
Ⓐ 심해 접근의 개선	© 연구, 재확신, 긍정적 협의
Ⓑ 심해 채광의 위험	Ⓔ 해저 재물의 지도를 만들고 인양
© 연구, 재확신, 긍정적 협의	Ⓕ 기술 발전
Ⓓ 달에서 부를 찾아	**환경운동가**
Ⓔ 해저 재물의 지도를 만들고 인양	Ⓑ 심해 채광의 위험
Ⓕ 기술 발전	Ⓖ 연구가 거의 수행되지 않음
Ⓖ 연구가 거의 수행되지 않음	

04

언급한 내용은 유나이티드 진 하이테크 그룹 회사의 제안된 권리의 사안에 관련한 2012년 6월 25일의 발표로 작성되었다. 달리 언급하거나 문맥에서 다르게 요구되지 않는 한 여기에 사용된 **대문자로 쓰인** 용어들은 발표에서 정의된 것과 같은 의미를 가질 것이다. 2012년 6월 26일에 그 회사에서 작성된 발표에 따라 베스트 챔피언은 2012년 6월 21일에 **그것의** 주식 보유량을 총 5,437,980,000주로 줄이면서 그것의 주식 처분을 회사에 통보했다. 2012년 6월 27일에 작성된 이사회의 추가 문의 이후에 베스트 챔피언은 2012년 6월 25일 날짜로 회사의 발행된 주식 자본의 약 44.08%에 해당하는 총 5,361,680,000주를 갖는다고 통보했다. 따라서 회사는 다음과 같이 그 발표 내용을 명확히 하고자 한다. 발표의 2페이지 '회사 주주의 철회할 수 없는 동의'의 첫 번째 문단과 11페이지에 있는 '회사 주주의 배경'의 두 번째와 세 번째 문단은 다음과 같이 개정되어야 한다: '철회할 수 없는 동의에 서명을 한 날짜인 2012년 6월 20일에 베스트 챔피언은 총 5,591,020,000주를 수익으로 소유하였으며 그것의 **주식은** 약 그 회사의 발행된 주식 자본의 45.96%에 해당한다. 그런 이유로 동의하는 주주와 그것의 협력자들은 주식에 대한 수당으로 주주 할당 발행에 따라 권리사안에 의해 1,677,306,000 주주 지분권을 일시적으로 할당받게 된다.'

어휘_ in relation to ~에 관하여 herein 여기에 disposal 처리, 처분 shareholding 주식 보유량 aggregate 합계 clarification 정화 irrevocable 변경할 수 없는 allotted 할당된 pursuant ~에 따른

365

1. ©

지문의 대문자로 쓰인이라는 단어와 의미가 가장 비슷한 것은?

Ⓐ 이익을 얻는
Ⓑ 자본으로 제공받는
© 대문자로 쓰이거나 인쇄된
Ⓓ 자산으로 처리된

해설_ capitalized terms(대문자로 쓰인 용어)에서 capitalized 는 written or printed in capital letters(대문자로 쓰이거나 인 쇄된)이므로 ©가 정답이다. Ⓑ provided with capital(자본으로 제공받는)은 문맥에 맞지 않아 오답이다.

2. Ⓑ

지문의 단어 그것의가 가리키는 것은?

Ⓐ 회사
Ⓑ 베스트 챔피언
© 이사회
Ⓓ 유나이티드 진 하이테크 그룹 회사

해설_ its(그것의)가 있는 문장에서 주식 보유량을 줄이면서 주식 처분을 회사에 통보한 측은 베스트 챔피언이므로 Ⓑ가 정답이다.

3. Ⓓ

작가는 지문에서 왜 주식을 언급하고 있는가?

Ⓐ 주주들이 회사의 매출에 어떻게 영향을 받을지에 대하여 알려주 기 위해서
Ⓑ 주주들이 회사 지분을 팔지 않게 설득하기 위해서
© 신주 공모 자본에서의 오류를 지적하기 위해서
Ⓓ 주권 발행 사안에서 베스트 챔피언의 자격을 알려주기 위해서

05

일본의 산업은 거의 20년 동안의 전반적인 경기 침체에도 불 구하고 아직까지 세계에서 가장 진보적이고 혁신적인 나라 중 에 있다. 일본의 제조 상품, 특히 전자 제품과 자동차는, 관련 분야의 생산과 기술의 진보라는 측면에서 세계적인 리더의 위 상을 갖추고 있다. 2010년 이 산업은 일본 GDP의 23%를 차지하였다. 일본 산업의 대부분은 자동차, 전자 장비, 기계 공 구, 철강과 비철 금속, 선박, 화학, 섬유 및 가공 식품 등이 차 지하였다. 일본의 자동차 산업은 세계에서 중국 다음으로 두 번째 규모의 자동차 생산국이다. 그러나 일본의 자동차 회사 들은 가장 가치가 높고 뛰어난 선진 기술을 자랑하고 있다. 전 세계 상위권 20위에 해당하는 차량 제작사 중에 6개 회사가 일본 회사이다 – 도요타(1위), 르노 닛산(4위), 혼다(8위), 스 즈키(10위), 마쓰다(14위), 미쓰비시(16위). 자동차 산업은 2009년 글로벌 금융 위기에도 불구하고 10.5%라는 대단한 성장률을 기록할 수 있었다. 또한 일본은 소니, 카시오, 미쓰비 시 전기, 파나소닉, 캐논, 후지쯔, 니콘, 야마하 같은 굴지의 회 사들을 가지고 있는 세계 최대의 전자 제품 제조사이다. 일본 의 전자 제품은 혁신과 품질로 칭송을 받고 있다. 첨단 산업과 회사들을 든든히 등에 지고 일본은 2010년 산업 생산 성장률

15.5%를 기록하여 전 세계 8위를 기록하였으며 동시에 일본 은 G20 국가 중 가장 높은 산업 성장률을 기록하였다.

어휘_ stagnation 침체 respective 각각의 nonferrous 비 철합금 massive 거대한 the global financial crisis 국제금 융위기 are praised for ~에 대해 칭찬하다 simultaneously 동시에, 일제히

1. Ⓐ

지문의 불구하고라는 어휘와 의미가 가장 비슷한 것은?

Ⓐ 상관없이
Ⓑ 때문에
© 뜻밖에
Ⓓ 화가 난

해설_ '일본의 자동차 산업이 글로벌 금융 위기에도 불구하고 성 장을 했다'에서 in spite of(불구하고)는 regardless of(상관없이) 로 바꾸어 쓸 수 있으므로 Ⓐ가 정답이다.

2. Ⓓ

아래 문장 중 어떤 것이 지문 속의 음영 처리된 문장의 핵심정보를 가장 잘 표현하고 있는가? 오답 선택지는 현저하게 의미를 바꾸거 나 핵심정보를 생략한 것이다.

Ⓐ 많은 첨단 기술은 여전히 일본에서 온다.
Ⓑ 일본인은 자신의 회사를 자랑스럽게 생각한다.
© 일본인은 세계를 이끌지만 회사는 잘 알려져 있지 않다.
Ⓓ 일본 회사는 그들의 뛰어난 표준에 대해 칭찬받을 자격이 있다.

해설_ 음영 처리된 문장 Japanese electronic products are praised for their innovation and quality(일본의 전자 제품 은 혁신과 품질로 칭송을 받고 있다)를 Japanese companies deserve credit for their outstanding standards(일본 회사 는 그들의 뛰어난 표준에 대해 칭찬받을 자격이 있다)로 가장 잘 바꿔 표현할 수 있으므로 Ⓓ가 정답이다.

3. Ⓐ, ©, Ⓔ

지문을 간략하게 요약하기 위한 도입문장이 아래에 제시되어 있다. 지문에서 가장 중요한 정보를 담고 있는 3개의 선택지를 선택하여 요약을 완성한다. 지문에 제시되지 않은 정보나 세부정보를 담고 있 는 일부문장은 요약에 들어가지 않는다. 이 문제는 2점이 주어진다.

선택지를 관련있는 곳으로 끌어당기시오. 끌어당긴 선택지를 삭 제하려면 그 위에 대고 클릭하시오. 지문을 다시 보려면 View Text 아이콘을 클릭하시오.

많은 사람들이 일본 제품을 다른 제품보다 우수하다고 생각한다.

Ⓐ 일본의 제조품은 특히 전자제품과 자동차에서 세계적 리더 이다.
© 일본의 자동차 회사는 세계에서 가장 가치 있고 기술적으로 진보된 상태로 남아 있다.
Ⓔ 일본의 전자 제품들은 혁신과 품질에 대한 칭찬을 받는다.

Ⓐ 일본의 제조품은 특히 전자제품과 자동차에서 세계적 리더이다.

Ⓑ 일본의 주요 산업은 많은 종류의 제품을 포함한다.

Ⓒ 일본의 자동차 회사는 세계에서 가장 가치 있고 기술적으로 진보된 상태로 남아 있다.

Ⓓ 자동차 산업은 글로벌 금융 위기에도 불구하고 2009년에 높은 10.5% 성장을 이루어 낼 수 있었다.

Ⓔ 일본의 전자 제품들은 혁신과 품질에 대한 칭찬을 받는다.

Ⓕ 일본의 산업 생산 증가율은 G20 국가 중 가장 높았다.

해설_ 도입문장에서 많은 사람들이 일본 제품을 다른 제품보다 우수하다고 생각한다고 하였으므로 관련된 문장은 일본 제품이 세계적인 리더이고 기술적으로 진보되었으며 품질에 대한 칭찬을 받는 것이다. 따라서 Ⓐ, Ⓒ, Ⓔ가 정답이다. Ⓑ, Ⓓ, Ⓕ는 도입문장의 핵심이 되는 일본 제품의 우수성에서 벗어나므로 오답이다.

Vocabulary & Paraphrasing

1. 아래에 있는 각 뜻에 맞는 단어를 박스에서 찾아서 쓰시오.

① derive　　② expedition　　③ nuisance
④ grim　　⑤ ecosystem　　⑥ holistic
⑦ retreat　　⑧ menace　　⑨ feasible
⑩ skeptic

2. 다음 문장을 해석 후 아래 지시대로 **paraphrasing**(다른 말로 바꿔 표현하기)하세요.

① 비록 플랑크톤이 해양 생물량의 대부분을 구성하고 있지만 플랑크톤의 생물 지리학과 생태계 시스템의 구조는 '거의 연구의 처녀지'이다.

➡ 예시_ The biomass of the ocean is predominantly made of plankton, but its biogeography and the way its ecosystems are organized is virtually new territory for research.

② 만약 지중해와 다른 곳에 해안을 위협하는 해파리의 무리를 손대지 않고 내버려두면 그것들은 바다의 앞날에 암울함을 드리울 것이다.

➡ 예시_ If nothing is done about the mass of jellyfish threatening coastlines in the Mediterranean and other places, the seas could be terrible to behold in the future.

③ 환경 운동가들은 해저 광물의 위험에 대해 조사가 거의 되어 있지 않다고 말하면서 불안감을 더 크게 표현하고 있다.

➡ 예시_ Environmentalists have become more and more concerned as they claim there has not been enough research into the effects of seabed mining.

④ 그 대륙은 연구와 관광을 규제하는 국제법인 남극조약 체제에 의해 관리되고 있다.

➡ 예시_ The Antarctic Treaty System, a group of international agreements to control research and tourism, governs the continent.

01

소셜 네트워킹이 오늘날의 사회에 엄청난 영향과 변화를 주었다는 것은 억제된 표현이 아니다. **사회와 직장에서의 관계는 다시 정의될 만큼 아주 크게 형태가 바뀌어서 심지어 간단한 버튼 클릭으로 그들이 좋아하는 사람과 누구나 일상생활을 공유할 수 있다.** 바르게 행해질 때 소셜 네트워킹은 개인과 사업을 성장시키고 성공하도록 돕는 데 굉장히 생산적이다. 소셜 네트워킹은 우정, 공통점이나 생각 같은 대인관계 수단에 의해 종종 함께 형성된 개개인의 형태에 대한 것이다. 이는 사람들의 관계를 형성하는 데 강한 기반을 만들 수 있고 그들 간에 화합을 조성하며 그로 인해 높아진 생산성의 향상으로 작업량을 줄여준다. 그러나 그렇게 유용한 만큼 인터넷을 통한 소셜 네트워킹으로 **줄어든** 경우 소셜 네트워킹은 많은 시간을 낭비시키는 중독성이 강한 미루는 도구로 빠르게 전락하거나 최악으로는 현실에 대한 망상을 일으키게 할 수 있다.

어휘_ enormously 엄청나게 configuration 배열, 배치 procrastination 지연, 연기 delusion 망상

1. Ⓓ

아래 문장 중 어떤 것이 지문 속의 음영 처리된 문장의 핵심정보를 가장 잘 표현하고 있는가? 오답 선택지는 현저하게 의미를 바꾸거나 핵심정보를 생략한 것이다.

Ⓐ 소셜 네트워킹은 사회생활에 돌이킬 수 없는 큰 영향을 미쳤다.

Ⓑ 소셜 네트워킹이 없었다면 우리는 이렇게 편리하게 연락을 주고받을 수 없었을 것이다.

Ⓒ 소셜 네트워킹은 우리 생활을 좋은 쪽으로 또는 안 좋은 쪽으로 크게 바꾸었다.

Ⓓ 소셜 네트워킹이 얼마나 사용하기 쉬운지, 우리의 관계를 얼마나 바꾸었는지를 거의 아무도 부인할 수 없다.

2. Ⓐ

지문의 줄어든이라는 구와 의미가 가장 비슷한 것은?

Ⓐ 축소되는　　　　　　　Ⓑ 기능하는 데 실패한

Ⓒ 붕괴의 원인이 되는　　Ⓓ 부분으로 나누어진

해설_ 지문에서 소셜 네트워킹이 인터넷을 통한 소셜 네트워킹으로 reduced to(줄어든)라고 하였으므로 가장 비슷한 단어는 Ⓐ made lesser(축소되는)이다.

3. Positive Effects: ⓑ, ⓓ, ⓖ / Negative Effects: ⓐ, ⓕ
지시사항 선택지에서 알맞은 구를 선택하여 그것과 관련된 소셜 네트워킹의 영향에 맞게 연결하시오. **이 문제는 3점이 주어진다.**

선택지를 관련있는 곳으로 끌어당기시오. 끌어당긴 선택지를 삭제하려면 그 위에 대고 클릭하시오. 지문을 다시 보려면 **View Text** 아이콘을 클릭하시오.

선택지	긍정적 영향
ⓐ 현실에 대한 오해를 생산함	ⓑ 각 개인의 일상생활을 공유하도록 도와줌
ⓑ 각 개인의 일상생활을 공유하도록 도와줌	ⓓ 개인과 사업의 성장 지원
ⓒ 오늘날의 사회를 변화시키거나 영향을 줌	ⓖ 관계를 위한 견고한 토대 마련
ⓓ 개인과 사업의 성장 지원	부정적 영향
ⓔ 간단히 버튼을 클릭함	ⓐ 현실에 대한 오해를 생산함
ⓕ 중독성이 강한 지연 도구	ⓕ 중독성이 강한 지연 도구
ⓖ 관계를 위한 견고한 토대 마련	

02

WIA는 복지 의존을 줄이고 근로자의 질을 향상시키며 국가의 경쟁성과 생산성을 강화하고자 참가자들의 직업적인 기술 성취도와 취업, 고용유지와 수입을 증진시키도록 디자인된 정부 지원 프로그램이다. 주 정부의 실직자 프로그램은 해고나 회사 폐쇄로 인하여 그들의 일자리를 잃은 사람들을 도와준다. ⓐ■ MYP는 14살에서 21살의 청소년들을 위해 기본적인 직업 기술 훈련과 여름 분기 직업을 제공한다. ⓑ■ SCSEP는 55살 이상의 개인들을 위해 파트타임 직업을 제공한다. ⓒ■ DEED는 잠재적인 고용주와 직업을 찾는 사람들을 연결하는 노동 교환을 제공하기 위해 와그너 페이서 기금을 사용한다. **실업자 보험 (UI), 전문가, 취업 지원 세금 공제와 무역 조정법 프로그램 또한 DEED를 통하여 연결될 수 있다.** ⓓ■ DEED의 사업 서비스 노력은 지역적 노력을 보완하는 것을 말한다. 사업의 봉사활동 계획은 이런 노력을 통합적인 방식으로 연결시킨다. 지역적 봉사활동 계획은 경제적인 발전, 교육 그리고 노동자 의회에서 확인된 지역단체들과 함께 이루어진다.

어휘_ retention 보유 dislocated worker program 실직자 프로그램 are meant to ~을 의미하다 in an integrated manner 통합적인 방식으로 is incorporated with ~와 통합되다 identified 확인된 the workforce council 노동 위원회

1. ⓐ
지문에 따르면 다음 중 어느 것이 사실이 아닌가?
ⓐ 실직한 사람들을 위한 지원이 거의 없다.

ⓑ 21세 미만의 10대 또는 55세 이상인 사람들은 구직에 대한 특별 지원을 받을 수 있다.
ⓒ 지역 사업과 DEED의 협업에 대한 시스템이 있다.
ⓓ WIA의 목표 중 하나는 사람들이 계속 일할 수 있게 하는 것이다.

2. ⓓ
다음의 문장이 지문에 추가될 수 있는 곳을 표시하는 네모 박스 [■]를 보시오.

실업자 보험 (UI), 전문가, 취업 지원 세금 공제와 무역 조정법 프로그램 또한 DEED를 통하여 연결될 수 있다.

문장이 어느 곳에 가장 적합한가?
문장을 지문에 추가하도록 한 개의 네모 박스 [■]를 클릭하시오.
해설_ 주어진 문장의 also로 보아 앞 문장에 DEED와 관련한 설명이 나옴을 알 수 있다. 그리고 뒤에 DEED에 대한 정보요약이 자연스러우므로 ⓓ가 정답이다.

3. ⓓ, ⓔ, ⓕ
지시사항 지문을 간략하게 요약하기 위한 도입문장이 아래에 제시되어 있다. 지문에서 가장 중요한 정보를 담고 있는 3개의 선택지를 선택하여 요약을 완성한다. 지문에 제시되지 않은 정보나 세부 정보를 담고 있는 일부 문장은 요약에 들어가지 않는다. **이 문제는 2점이 주어진다.**

선택지를 관련있는 곳으로 끌어당기시오. 끌어당긴 선택지를 삭제하려면 그 위에 대고 클릭하시오. 지문을 다시 보려면 **View Text** 아이콘을 클릭하시오.

모든 연령대의 사람들이 일자리를 찾는 데 도움을 주고 국가의 경쟁력을 향상시킬 수 있는 직업 훈련 및 지원이 가능한 다양하고 폭넓은 프로그램이 있다.

ⓓ 모든 인생 단계와 환경에 놓인 사람들은 프로그램의 도움을 받아 일자리를 얻을 수 있다.
ⓔ 이러한 고용 프로그램은 폭넓은 연령층을 포함한다.
ⓕ 나라와 개인 모두 이러한 프로그램의 취업 지원에 주력함으로써 도움을 받는다.

선택지
ⓐ 이 프로그램이 없다면, 사람들은 훨씬 더 힘들게 일자리를 구할 것이다.
ⓑ WIA, 정부 실직자 프로그램, MYP, SCSEP, DEED, 사업의 봉사활동 계획 등은 사람들의 구직 활동을 지원하는 프로그램의 이름이다.
ⓒ 이러한 프로그램을 제공함으로써 사람들은 어떠한 상황에서든 쉽게 일자리를 구할 수 있다.
ⓓ 모든 인생 단계와 환경에 놓인 사람들은 프로그램의 도움을 받아 일자리를 얻을 수 있다.
ⓔ 이러한 고용 프로그램은 폭넓은 연령층을 포함한다.
ⓕ 나라와 개인 모두 이러한 프로그램의 취업 지원에 주력함으로써 도움을 받는다.

03

두 가지의 기술 혁신이 19세기의 일상생활을 획기적으로 변화시켰다. 그것은 증기와 전기의 두 동력이다. 어떤 면에서 증기 엔진과 전기의 운송 및 전신 같은 다양한 업무로의 발전과 활용은 인간이나 동물 또는 단순한 도구의 원동력을 증가시키고 배가시킴으로써 인간의 삶에 영향을 미쳤다. 이런 기술적 변화를 겪으며 산 사람들은 기술이 기술적 혁신 이상의 것이 될 것이라 생각했다. **그들에게 이 기술은 인간이 경험한 원시적 한계를 없애고 원시 시대와의 연결고리를 확실히 부수며 공간과 시간의 제약을 파괴할 수 있는 천년 시대, 신시대가 시작되게 하는 것으로 보였다.** **사진과 축음기**의 기록하는 기술처럼 단순히 증기와 전력이 적용되지 않은 발명품들조차도 과거를 현재에 그리고 현재를 미래에 적용 가능하게 함으로써 **이것**에 기여했다.

어휘_ multiplying 중복하는 primeval 태고의 usher 안내원 annihilate 전멸시키다 phonograph 축음기

1. ©
작가는 지문 속의 음영 처리된 문장에서 새로운 기술에 관해 무엇을 암시하고 있는가?
Ⓐ 기술 혁신은 사람들에게 원시적 경험을 제공하였다.
Ⓑ 사람들은 신기술에 압도당했다.
© 신기술 혁신으로부터의 변화는 이례적이었다.
Ⓓ 19세기에는 소수 몇 사람만 기술에 관심이 있었다.

2. ©
작가는 지문에서 왜 사진과 축음기를 언급하고 있는가?
Ⓐ 이러한 발명이 증기력이나 전기력과 같지 않음을 주장하기 위해서
Ⓑ 당시의 더 많은 신기술을 열거하기 위해서
© 모든 신기술이 어떻게 이런 획기적 변화의 일부가 되었는지 강조하기 위해서
Ⓓ 그것들과 '원동력' 기술과 대조하기 위해서

3. Ⓑ
지문의 단어 이것이 가리키는 것은?
Ⓐ 신기술의 개발　　Ⓑ 신시대의 시작
© 인간 경험　　Ⓓ 시간과 공간의 소멸
해설_ this가 있는 문장에서 과거를 현재에 그리고 현재를 미래에 적용 가능하게 한 것은 앞 문장의 신시대의 시작(to usher in a kind of Millennial Era, a New Age)을 가리킨다. 따라서 Ⓑ가 정답이다.

04

얼마 남지 않은 수렵, 채집사회에 대한 연구는 '결핍, 위기, 실험' 이론의 좋은 예를 제공한다. 역사는 큰 변화가 물질의 풍요에 따라 일어나는 것이 아니라 그 반대로 기존의 자원을 완전히 소모한 결과로 일어난다는 것을 보여준다. 이것은 역사가 열역학 제2법칙을 반영한다는 의미이다. Ⓐ■ 전체적인 엔트로피 과정은 항상 최대치를 향해 움직인다. Ⓑ■ 매번 일이 발생할 때마다 일정량의 에너지가 영원히 소모된다. ©■ 역사의 흐름에서 중대한 전환기는 축적된 엔트로피 증가량의 합이 환경 자체 에너지의 질적 변화를 일으킬 때 찾아온다. **이런 중대한 변화의 순간에는 이전의 방식들이 더 이상 통하지 않는다.** Ⓓ■ 환경 엔트로피가 높아지면 새로운 기술과 사회, 경제, 정치 제도의 형성과 함께 새로운 에너지 환경으로의 이동이 일어난다.

어휘_ deprivation 박탈 use up 다 써버리다 reflection 반사, 반향 the 2nd law of thermodynamics 열역학 2법칙 entropy 엔트로피 dissipated 방탕한

1. Ⓑ
지문에 따르면 다음 중 어느 것이 '결핍, 위기, 실험' 이론에 관해 사실이 아닌가?
Ⓐ 역사에서 중요한 변화의 순간들은 이러한 과정에 기인한다.
Ⓑ 그것은 열역학 제2법칙의 역사와 같다.
© 이것의 첫 번째 단계는 자원을 완전히 사용하는 것이다.
Ⓓ 주변의 엔트로피 증가는 위기를 야기한다.
해설_ '결핍, 위기, 실험' 이론이 역사에서 제2법칙을 반영하였다고 했지만 그 이론이 제2법칙의 역사는 아니므로 Ⓑ가 정답이다.

2. Ⓓ
다음의 문장이 지문에 추가될 수 있는 곳을 표시하는 네모 박스 [■]를 보시오.
이런 중대한 변화의 순간에는 이전의 방식들이 더 이상 통하지 않는다.
문장이 어느 곳에 가장 적합한가?
문장을 지문에 추가하도록 한 개의 네모 박스 [■]를 클릭하시오.
해설_ 주어진 문장에 변화의 순간이 있고 그 앞에 변화에 대한 언급이 있어야 하므로 Ⓓ가 정답이다. 주어진 문장은 앞의 질적 변화에 대한 추가 설명이다.

3. ©
아래 문장 중 어떤 것이 지문 속의 음영 처리된 문장의 핵심정보를 가장 잘 표현하고 있는가? 오답 선택지는 현저하게 의미를 바꾸거나 핵심정보를 생략한 것이다.
Ⓐ 사회 변화는 사회의 가용 에너지에 대한 함수이다.
Ⓑ 신기술 및 신사회는 신 에너지원을 탐색한 결과다.
© 엔트로피를 향한 필연성은 전면적인 사회 변화를 촉발한다.
Ⓓ 엔트로피가 증가함에 따라 새로운 에너지 환경에 대한 필요성도 증가한다.

05

우리 사회에서 남성과 여성이 평등한가? 왜 그런가? 아니면 왜 그렇지 않은가? 여성의 권리는 여성들을 위해 남성과 같은 사회적 경제적 지위를 갖는다. 여성의 권리는 여성들이 그들의 성별을 기반으로 차별에 직면하지 않을 것을 보장한다. 20세기의 후반까지 대부분의 사회에서 여성들은 남성들에 의해 법적 그리고 정치적 권리의 일부가 부정되었다. 비록 세계의 대부분에 있는 여성들이 중요한 법적 권리를 얻게 되었다고 하더라도 많은 사람들은 여성들이 아직도 남성과 같은 평등을 갖고 있지 않다고 믿는다. **이것**은 일반적으로 집에서 직장에서 그리고 사회에서 분명해 보인다. 남성과 여성이 평등하지 않다는 첫 흔적은 **다른 곳에서 찾지 말고** 가정에서 찾아라. 남성의 전통적인 역할은 일을 하고 가정에서 쓰일 모든 돈을 버는 것이었다. 여성의 전통적인 역할은 집에 머물고 아이들을 돌보며 집을 청소하고 요리를 하는 것이었다. 사회는 항상 돈을 권력과 연관시켜 왔기 때문에 돈을 가정으로 가지고 오는 사람이 권력을 가졌다. 남성들이 돈을 가지고 있기 때문에 가정사에 대한 모든 최종 결정을 남성들이 자주 한다. 직장은 남성과 여성이 평등하지 않은 또 다른 장소이다. 남성들은 적극적이고 지시하는 것에 박수를 받는다. 지시를 함으로써 남성들은 리더 역할을 하고 있다. 리더십 능력을 보여주는 것은 고용주가 흔히 찾는 자질이다.

어휘_ guarantee 굳은 약속 discrimination 차별 according to ~에 따라서 take care of ~을 돌보다 applauded 박수를 쳤다 assertive 적극적인

1. ©
지문에 따르면 어느 것이 여성의 권리에 관해 사실인가?
Ⓐ 여성의 권리는 정치적 권리와 다르다.
Ⓑ 여성은 남성과 동일한 권한을 갖는다.
© 여성은 여전히 가정과 사회에서 차별당하므로 동등한 권리가 부족하다.
Ⓓ 여성은 자신의 권리를 회복하기 위해 남성으로부터 제자리를 찾아야 한다.
해설_ 지문의 여섯 번째 문장에서 많은 사람들이 여성들과 남성들이 평등하지 않다고 믿는다고 하였으므로 ©가 정답이다. Ⓐ, Ⓑ, Ⓓ는 지문과 다르거나 없는 내용이므로 오답이다.

2. Ⓐ
지문의 단어 **이것**이 가리키는 것은?
Ⓐ 남성과 여성은 평등하지 않다.
Ⓑ 남성과 여성의 전통적인 역할이 변했다.
© 여성은 동등하게 되기 위해 더 많은 일을 할 필요가 있다.
Ⓓ 여성은 결코 남성과 평등할 수 없다.
해설_ This(이것)가 있는 문장의 앞에서 many people believe that women still do not have equality with men(많은 사

람들은 여성들이 아직도 남성들과 같은 평등을 갖고 있지 않다고 믿는다)이라고 하고 이것이 집에서 직장에서 그리고 사회에서 분명해 보인다고 하였으므로 Ⓐ가 정답이다.

3. ©
지문의 **다른 곳에서 찾지 말고**라는 구와 가장 비슷한 것은?
Ⓐ 다른 어떤 곳에도 가지 마라
Ⓑ 여기가 최고이다
© 이곳을 벗어날 필요가 없다
Ⓓ 그곳에 이르는 거리가 지나치게 멀다
해설_ Look no further(다른 곳에서 찾지 말고)는 There's no need to go beyond this place(이곳을 벗어날 필요가 없다)로 가장 잘 바꿔 표현할 수 있다. 따라서 ©가 정답이다.

Vocabulary & Paraphrasing

1. 아래에 있는 각 뜻에 맞는 단어를 박스에서 찾아서 쓰시오.

① integrate ② amend ③ irrevocable
④ adverse ⑤ incorporated ⑥ uncharacteristic
⑦ shareholder ⑧ disseminate ⑨ disposal
⑩ attainment

2. 다음 문장을 해석 후 아래 지시대로 paraphrasing(다른 말로 바꿔 표현하기)하세요.
① 추가적으로 정보는 이메일을 통해 배포되거나 RU 텔레비전 채널 3과 732-445-인포의 RU-인포(24시간 음성 메일도 포함하여)로 얻을 수 있을 것이다.

➡ **예시_** You can also find information sent by email on RU-tv Channel 3 and by RU-info at 732-445-INFO (including 24-hour voice mail).
② WIA는 복지 의존을 줄이고 근로자의 질을 향상시키며 국가의 경쟁성과 생산성을 강화하고자 참가자들의 직업적인 기술 성취도와 취업, 고용 유지와 수입을 증진시키도록 디자인된 정부 지원 프로그램이다.

➡ **예시_** The federal government funds WIA to help improve people's job skills, their ability to keep their jobs, and their ability to earn more money so that workers are better trained, people are less dependent on welfare, and the nation is more productive and competitive.
③ 수거된 제품의 제품 번호는 병 라벨의 옆면에서 볼 수 있다.

➡ **예시_** The side of the bottle label has the lot number for the recalled product.
④ 그 회사에서 작성된 발표에 따라 베스트 챔피언은 2012년 6월 21일에 회사 내의 주식 보유량을 총 5,437,980,000주로 줄이면서 주식 처분을 회사에 통보했다.

➡ **예시_** On 26 June 2012, in response to the Company's directive, Best Champion informed the Company it had sold its Shares of the Company on that date, so that its total shareholding was now 5,437,980,000 Shares.

Unit 05 Computer_ P. 231

01

새로운 TR940과 TR950 노트북은 소규모나 중간 크기의 사업에 필요한 모든 것을 갖게 디자인되어 있다. **새로운 T 노트북은 과도한 무게를 더하지 않고 내구성과 강함을 증가시키기 위해 허니콤 립 구조의 특수한 섬유 유리로 강화한 케이스로 만들어져서 외근이나 출장이 잦은 사원에게 최고의 노트북이 될 것이다.** 게다가 T 노트북은 흘림 방지 키보드, 하드 드라이브 충격 센서와 빠르게 진행되는 비즈니스 세계의 압박을 확실히 받아들일 수 있도록 충격 흡수 디자인을 갖고 있다. 모든 모델은 5세대 IC 프로세서, 인텔 GMA HD 4000 **전용의** 그래픽카드, 그리고 4GB DDR3 주기억장치와 500GB 하드디스크 드라이브를 포함한 넉넉한 저장 공간으로 환경설정되어 있다. 각각 5.3파운드보다 가벼운 무게로, 1인치 얇고 14.0과 15.6인치 사선 LED 와이드 스크린 디스플레이를 갖고 있어서 TR940과 TR950은 내구성뿐만 아니라 믿을 수 없을 정도로 휴대가 간편하다.

어휘_ durability 내구성, 내구력 fiberglass 섬유 유리 honeycomb rib structure 벌집형 늑골 구조 spill 엎지르다 the fast-paced 빨리 진행되는 incredibly 믿을 수 없을 정도로

1. ⓑ

아래 문장 중 어떤 것이 지문 속의 음영 처리된 문장의 핵심정보를 가장 잘 표현하고 있는가? 오답 선택지는 현저하게 의미를 바꾸거나 핵심정보를 생략한 것이다.

ⓐ 이 노트북은 조만간 가장 잘 팔리는 제품이 될 것이다.
ⓑ 그 컴퓨터는 매우 견고해서 충격에도 거뜬할 것이다.
ⓒ 그 컴퓨터의 품질은 매우 우수해서 모든 종류의 전쟁이나 레이싱 게임을 즐길 수 있다.
ⓓ 이 노트북은 유통되는 제품들 중에서 가장 가볍고 견고한 화면을 갖추었다.

2. ⓒ

지문의 전용의라는 단어와 의미가 가장 비슷한 것은?

ⓐ 다목적용으로 만들어진
ⓑ 특정 프로젝트에 할당되거나 배정된
ⓒ 한 가지 기능을 수행하도록 설계된
ⓓ 고도의 목적을 위해서 따로 둔

해설_ dedicated는 문맥에서 '전용의'라는 뜻으로 쓰였으므로 designed to fulfil one function(하나의 기능을 수행하도록 설계된)과 의미가 가장 비슷하다.

3. ⓓ

다음 중 어느 것이 지문의 내용으로부터 결론 내려질 수 있는가?

ⓐ 사업가들만 이 컴퓨터를 좋아할 것이다.
ⓑ 제품은 여행을 많이 하는 사람들이 사용하기 쉬울 것이다.
ⓒ 사용자들은 그 컴퓨터가 스트레스를 많이 줄 것으로 예상할 수 있다.
ⓓ 이 컴퓨터는 여러 차례 충격이 있어도 괜찮을 것이다.

02

트래커는 내장형 GPS와 유연한 지느러미 형태의 안테나가 장착된 작은 사각의 방수 장치이다. 어떤 개 목걸이에도 트래커를 고정시킬 수 있다. 원래는 **고양이의 목걸이에도 그것을 부착할 수 있지만** 꽤 덩치가 큰 고양이가 아니라면 트래커의 부피가 커서 약간 부담스러워 보일 수 있다. 트래커 웹사이트에는 10kg 이상의 애완동물에게 적합하다고 쓰여 있다. 다음으로 애완동물이 돌아다녀도 되는 여러분의 집 주변 지역을 나타내는 '트래커 구역'을 설정하면 된다. 만약 애완동물이 승인된 지역을 벗어나게 되면 이메일과 SMS 경고를 받게 되고 웹이나 아이폰 및 안드로이드 어플을 사용해서 지도에서 현위치를 찾을 수 있다. 여러분의 개가 사람의 감독하에 산책 중이거나 집에서 멀리 떨어져 있을 때 일시적으로 추적을 멈출 수 있는 여행 모드도 있다.

어휘_ embedded 내장형 dog collar 개목걸이 tracker zone 추적 구역 alert 경계하는 경보를 발하다

1. ⓐ, ⓒ, ⓔ

지시사항 지문을 간략하게 요약하기 위한 도입문장이 아래에 제시되어 있다. 지문에서 가장 중요한 정보를 담고 있는 3개의 선택지를 선택하여 요약을 완성한다. 지문에 제시되지 않은 정보나 세부정보를 담고 있는 일부 문장은 요약에 들어가지 않는다. **이 문제는 2점이 주어진다.**

> 선택지를 관련있는 곳으로 끌어당기시오. 끌어당긴 선택지를 삭제하려면 그 위에 대고 클릭하시오. 지문을 다시 보려면 **View Text** 아이콘을 클릭하시오.

트래커는 애완동물이 어디 있는지 주인이 언제든지 알 수 있는 방법이다.

> ⓐ 애완동물을 특정 지역에 두기 위해서 트래커를 프로그래밍할 수 있다.
> ⓒ 애완동물이 특정 지역을 벗어날 경우 트래커는 경보음을 발생시킬 것이다.
> ⓔ 앱도 갖추고 있어서 애완동물이 어디에 있는지 확인할 수 있다.

선택지

ⓐ 애완동물을 특정 지역에 두기 위해서 트래커를 프로그래밍할 수 있다.

Ⓑ 구부러지는 지느러미 형태를 띤 안테나와 GPS를 끼워 넣었다.

Ⓒ 애완동물이 특정 지역을 벗어날 경우 트래커는 경보음을 발생시킬 것이다.

Ⓓ 여행 모드를 사용하면 추적 기능을 무효로 할 수 있다.

Ⓔ 앱도 갖추고 있어서 애완동물이 어디에 있는지 확인할 수 있다.

Ⓕ 트래커는 어떤 개목걸이에도 잘 맞는다.

2. Ⓓ
지문에서 작가는 ~ 위해 고양이의 목걸이에도 그것을 부착한다를 언급하고 있다.

Ⓐ 트래커의 크기를 강조하기

Ⓑ 트래커의 기능을 보이기

Ⓒ 트래커가 다르게 사용되는 예를 들기

Ⓓ 트래커 사용의 다양한 용도를 강조하기

3. Ⓓ
지문에 따르면 다음 중 어느 것이 트래커에 관해 사실인가?

Ⓐ 트래커는 대부분의 애완동물에 사용될 수 있다.

Ⓑ 일단 설정되고 나면 애완동물은 트래커 영역 밖으로 갈 수 없다.

Ⓒ 트래커는 애완동물에 쉽게 삽입되는 소형 장치다.

Ⓓ 트래커를 달면 주인은 애완동물이 어디에 있는지 추적할 수 있다.

03

컴퓨터 범죄는 여러 가지의 이름으로 발생하며 증오 범죄, 텔레마케팅, 그리고 인터넷 사기, 신원 도용과 신용카드 계좌 도용을 포함할 수 있다. 불법적인 활동이 컴퓨터와 인터넷 사용을 통해 행해질 때 이들은 사이버 범죄로 간주된다. 컴퓨터 범죄로부터 발생하는 손해나 재정적인 손실의 양을 측정하기는 매우 어렵다. 대부분의 경우 피해자는 그들이 목표가 되었다든지 심지어 범죄의 피해자라는 것조차 모른다. 컴퓨터 범죄의 피해자가 되었음을 알게 된 사람들은 대부분 당국에 **그것**을 보고하지 않거나 무엇이 처음에 그들을 피해자로 만들었는지 알 방법이 없다. 범죄자들은 여러 방법으로 작업하며 그들이 목표로 한 컴퓨터와 사람들의 삶에 영향을 끼치는 **광범위한 컴퓨터 범죄**가 있다. 사법부는 컴퓨터 범죄를 세 가지로 구분한다: 컴퓨터가 목표로, 컴퓨터가 무기로, 컴퓨터가 방조자로 사용된 경우이다.

어휘_ fraud 사기, 사기꾼 gauge 게이지, 측정기 authorities 당국, 관계자 in the first place 우선, 첫째로

1. Types of Cyber-crime: Ⓒ, Ⓓ, Ⓖ /
   Effects of Cyber-crime: Ⓐ, Ⓔ

지시사항 선택지에서 알맞은 구를 선택하여 그것과 관련된 컴퓨터 범죄의 범주에 맞게 연결하시오. 각 항목은 정답으로 중복 선택되지 않는다. **이 문제는 3점이 주어진다.**

선택지를 관련있는 곳으로 끌어당기시오. 끌어당긴 선택지를 삭제하려면 그 위에 대고 클릭하시오. 지문을 다시 보려면 **View Text** 아이콘을 클릭하시오.

선택지	컴퓨터 범죄의 유형
Ⓐ 재정 손실	Ⓒ 신용카드 계좌 도난
Ⓑ 당국에 보고	Ⓓ 증오 범죄
Ⓒ 신용카드 계좌 도난	Ⓖ 인터넷 사기
Ⓓ 증오 범죄	컴퓨터 범죄의 영향
Ⓔ 손해	Ⓐ 재정 손실
Ⓕ 부속품으로서의 컴퓨터	Ⓔ 손해
Ⓖ 인터넷 사기	

2. Ⓓ
지문의 단어 그것이 가리키는 것은?

Ⓐ 피해자   Ⓑ 피해자의 인식

Ⓒ 컴퓨터 범죄의 목표가 됨   Ⓓ 범죄

해설_ 대부분의 피해자가 당국에 보고하지 않는 것은 문장의 앞부분에 나오는 a computer crime(컴퓨터 범죄)이므로 Ⓓ가 정답이다.

3. Ⓓ
작가는 왜 지문에서 광범위한 컴퓨터 범죄에 관해 언급하고 있는가?

Ⓐ 사람들이 컴퓨터 범죄의 희생자가 되지 않도록 경고하기 위해서

Ⓑ 컴퓨터 보안의 중요성을 강조하기 위해서

Ⓒ 컴퓨터 범죄에 관여하는 범죄자들의 행동을 비난하기 위해서

Ⓓ 컴퓨터 범죄의 존재를 알리고 설명하기 위해서

04

P 미국 전자부품 제조사의 한 부서인 P사의 스토리지 제품 사업부와 열성적인 기술 선도자는 오늘 900GB – 300GB 용량의 범위에 이르는 기업용 성능을 제공하는 2.5인치 6Gb/s SAS 인터페이스 하드 디스크 드라이브 (HDD)의 AL13SE 시리즈를 발표하였다. Ⓐ■ AL13SE는 P사에서 개발한 첫 1만 RPM급 모델 기업형 드라이브로서 용량이 900GB에 달하며 동시에 기존의 지속 전송률에서 32% 증가된 것은 물론 추가 성능 이점을 제공하는 듀얼 스테이지 헤드 위치 작동 장치를 구축할 수 있는 P사의 첫 1만 RPM 드라이브이기도 하다. Ⓑ■ AL13SE 시리즈는 요구도가 가장 높은 핵심 임무 응용 프로그램용으로 실계되었으며 운영 신뢰성이 200만 작동 시간으로, 이전 세대 드라이브 대비 25% 증가한 것이 그 특징이다. Ⓒ■ P사의 전력 사용 효율성 설계 우월성을 지키며, AL13SE 시리즈는 RPM 공회전 속도를 증가시키기 위해 지원 개선 전력 조건 주립 기술을 사용한다. **첨단 기술 외**

에도, 시스템 적합성은 산업 표준 512바이트 섹터 사이즈를 사용하여 보장된다. Ⓓ▪ 'AL13SE 시리즈는 기업 고객들에게 기업의 광범위한 응용 프로그램을 지원하는 최고 900GB의 용량을 제공한다.'고 P사의 저장매체 상품 사업부의 마케팅 부사장이 말했다. 'AL13SE의 향상된 성능과 신뢰성은 **핵심 임무의** 저장매체에 대한 시장의 요구를 다룬 소형 인수 하드 디스크 드라이브를 제공하기 위해 우리와 주요 파트너 업체들과의 협업을 반영한다.'

어휘_ enterprise-class 기업등급 actuator 작동기 collaboration 공동작업 mission-critical 임무수행에 필수적인 storage 창고, 보관소

1. Ⓒ
지문의 **핵심 임무의**라는 구와 의미가 가장 비슷한 것은?
Ⓐ 무슨 일이든 운에 맡기지 않는
Ⓑ 중요한
Ⓒ 임무가 실패하면 작동이 멈추게 되는
Ⓓ 방해받지 않는

해설_ '핵심 임무의'라는 말은 '임무가 실패하면 작동이 멈추게 되는' 것을 말하므로 Ⓒ가 정답이다. Ⓑ는 Ⓒ에 비해 약한 표현으로 가장 근접한 의미가 아니다.

2. Ⓓ
지문에 따르면 다음 중 어느 것이 사실인가?
Ⓐ 용량이 늘어난 새 드라이브는 이전의 드라이브와 같은 안정된 전송률을 보인다.
Ⓑ 이 드라이브는 신뢰성이 32% 향상되었다.
Ⓒ 회사는 새로운 모델을 개발하기 위해서 독립적으로 작업했다.
Ⓓ 회사는 자사 제품의 에너지 효율성에 자부심을 가진다.

해설_ 지문 전반에 걸쳐 새로 출시되는 제품의 에너지 효율성에 대해 강조하므로 Ⓓ가 정답이다. Ⓑ는 32%가 지속 전송률이며 25%가 신뢰성이므로 오답이다.

3. Ⓓ
다음의 문장이 지문에 추가될 수 있는 곳을 표시하는 네모박스 [▪]를 보시오.
첨단기술 외에도, 시스템 적합성은 산업 표준 512바이트 섹터 사이즈를 사용하여 보장된다.
문장이 어느 곳에 가장 적합한가?
문장을 지문에 추가하도록 한 개의 네모 박스 [▪]를 클릭하시오.
해설_ 주어진 문장의 첨단기술은 앞 문장의 Supported Enhanced Power Condition State technology(지원 개선 전력 조건 주립 기술)를 가리킨다.

05
자, 그럼 와트당 성능의 아이디어가 어디서 나왔는지 살펴보자. 오늘날 파워북에 내장되어 있는 G4칩을 살펴보면 0.27 와트당 성능을 갖고 있다. **그리고 훨씬 성능이 좋은 G5를 탑재하기 위해서는 전력이 성능에 비례하여 증가하지 않도록 더 높은 와트당 성능이 필요했다.** 하지만 G5가 G4에 비해 와트당 성능 면에서 더 좋지 않다는 것이 바로 우리가 해결하지 못했던 과제였다는 것이 밝혀졌다. 하지만 코어 듀오는 바로 이런 문제를 해결하기 위해 디자인되었다. 보면 이 제품은 G4에 비해 네 배 이상의 성능을 그리고 G5에 비해 네 배 반 이상의 성능을 자랑한다. 그래서 오늘 우리는 맥북프로라는 노트북을 소개하게 되었다. 새롭게 이름을 붙였다. 우리는 파워가 들어가는 제품을 끝내고 이름에 맥이 들어가기를 희망하기 때문에 이 이름을 짓게 되었다. 그래서 이 제품은 맥북프로, **새로운 맥북프로**이다.

어휘_ performance-per-watt 와트당 성능 was designed for ~을 위해 설계되었다

1. Ⓓ
아래 문장 중 지문에 음영 처리된 문장의 핵심정보를 가장 잘 표현하고 있는 것은? 오답 선택지는 현저하게 의미를 바꾸거나 핵심정보를 생략한 것이다.
Ⓐ 더 나은 와트당 성능을 가진 G5는 더 많은 전력을 소비하고 성능을 잃게 될 것이다.
Ⓑ 높은 성능과 함께 G5는 전력 향상을 제공하지만 성능에서 G4보다 더 안 좋다.
Ⓒ G5는 고성능이지만 예상과 반대로 에너지 소비를 증가시키지 않는다.
Ⓓ 그들은 G5가 작동될 수 있도록 효율성을 개선해야 했다.

해설_ 음영 처리된 문장을 간단히 하면 'G5를 탑재하기 위해서 더 높은 와트당 성능이 필요했다'는 것이므로 Ⓓ They had to improve efficiency to make the G5 workable(그들은 G5가 작동될 수 있도록 효율성을 개선해야 했다)이 정답이다.

2. Ⓐ
작가는 지문에서 왜 **새로운 맥북프로**를 언급하고 있는가?
Ⓐ 새로운 제품에 대해 설명하기 위해
Ⓑ 새 제품을 사용하는 데 필요한 것들의 세부 설명을 위해
Ⓒ 새 노트북의 이름을 강조하기 위해
Ⓓ G5칩과 관련된 문제에 대해 경고하기 위해

해설_ 지문의 뒤 부분에서 맥북프로를 새로운 제품이라고 소개하였으므로 Ⓐ가 정답이다. 이름의 강조보다 새로운 제품의 출시가 내용의 핵심이므로 Ⓒ는 오답이다.

3. Ⓑ, Ⓒ, Ⓕ

지시사항 지문을 간략하게 요약하기 위한 도입문장이 아래에 제시되어 있다. 지문에서 가장 중요한 정보를 담고 있는 3개의 선택지를 선택하여 요약을 완성한다. 지문에 제시되지 않은 정보나 세부 정보를 담고 있는 일부 문장은 요약에 들어가지 않는다. **이 문제는 2점이 주어진다.**

> 선택지를 관련있는 곳으로 끌어당기시오. 끌어당긴 선택지를 삭제하려면 그 위에 대고 클릭하시오. 지문을 다시 보려면 **View Text** 아이콘을 클릭하시오.

새 노트북은 전력이 성능에 비례하여 증가하지 않도록 더 높은 와트당 성능이 필요했다.

> Ⓑ G5가 그들이 원했던 바를 이루지 못해서 완전히 새로운 시스템을 만들었다.
> Ⓒ 와트당 성능은 새로운 맥북프로의 가장 중요한 측면이다.
> Ⓕ 맥북프로는 와트당 성능 문제를 해결하기 위해 코어 듀오가 장착되어 있다.

선택지

Ⓐ 오늘날 파워북에는 G4칩이 있다.
Ⓑ G5가 그들이 원했던 바를 이루지 못해서 완전히 새로운 시스템을 만들었다.
Ⓒ 와트당 성능은 새로운 맥북프로의 가장 중요한 측면이다.
Ⓓ 새 이름과 함께 그들은 노트북의 전체 디자인을 변경했다.
Ⓔ 새로운 G5는 그 이전의 제품보다 모든 면에서 우수하다.
Ⓕ 맥북프로는 와트당 성능 문제를 해결하기 위해 코어 듀오가 장착되어 있다.

해설_ 더 높은 와트당 성능이 필요했다는 도입문장과 관련하여 가장 중요한 정보는 G5로는 새로운 시스템을 만들기에 부족했고 와트당 성능이 새로운 맥북프로의 가장 중요한 측면이며 와트당 성능 문제를 해결하기 위해 코어 듀오가 장착되어 있다는 것이다. 따라서 Ⓑ, Ⓒ, Ⓕ가 정답이다. Ⓐ, Ⓓ, Ⓔ는 도입문장과 관련한 중심 정보를 포함하지 않으므로 오답이다.

Vocabulary & Paraphrasing

1. 아래에 있는 각 뜻에 맞는 단어를 박스에서 찾아서 쓰시오.

① enhance	② surgical	③ reinforce
④ collaboration	⑤ respectively	⑥ compatability
⑦ backlit	⑧ durable	⑨ configure
⑩ performance		

2. 다음 문장을 해석 후 아래 지시대로 paraphrasing(다른 말로 바꿔 표현하기)하세요.

① 각각 5.3파운드보다 가벼운 무게로, 1인치 얇고 14.0과 15.6인치 사선 LED 와이드 스크린 디스플레이를 갖고 있어서 TR940과 TR950은 내구성뿐만 아니라 믿을 수 없을 정도로 휴

대가 간편하다.

➡ **예시_** The incredible portability and durability of the TR940 and TR950 are due to their weighing less than 5.3 pounds, measuring just one inch thick and being available with 14.0-and 15.6-inch diagonal LED-back lit wide screen HD displays respectively.

② 하지만 G5가 G4에 비해 와트당 성능 면에서 더 좋지 않다는 것이 바로 우리가 해결하지 못했던 과제였다는 것이 밝혀졌다.

➡ **예시_** We couldn't do what we wanted to because it was proved that the performance-per-watt of the G4 was even better than the G5.

③ 이미 다른 나라에서 외과 의사들에게 막대한 이점을 보이면서 새로운 S OLED 모니터는 이제 미국에서 수술 시야를 향상시키고 꼭 가져야 하는 의료 디스플레이가 될 것이다.

➡ **예시_** The new S OLED monitor already shows great benefits for surgeons in other parts of the world, and will now improve surgical viewing in the U.S., becoming the essential medical display for doctors.

④ AL13SE의 향상된 성능과 신뢰성은 핵심 임무의 저장매체에 대한 시장의 요구를 다룬 소형 인수 하드 디스크 드라이브를 제공하기 위해 우리와 주요 파트너 업체들과의 협업을 반영한다.

➡ **예시_** We have worked together with our main partners to provide small form-fact of hard disk drives that fulfill market crucial storage needs, which is reflected in the improved performance and reliability of the AL13SE.

Unit 06 Nature_ P. 245

01

어둠에 빛나는 괴물 크기의 오징어가 야생에서 처음으로 촬영되었다. Ⓐ■ 그 생물은 일본 남동부에서 떨어진 북태평양에서 비디오로 녹화되었다. Ⓑ■ 발견된 오징어는 사람 크기만큼 자랄 수 있고 먹이를 눈부시게 하여 잡기 위해 앞다리의 번쩍이는 빛을 사용한다. **이 여덟 개의 다리를 갖고 있는 생물은 흡입판에 고양이 발톱 같은 것이 있지만 다른 거대한 오징어가 먹이를 잡기 위해 사용하는 두 개의 기다란 급수용 촉수가 부족하다.** Ⓒ■ 대신 과학자들은 심해 오징어가 두 개의 앞다리 끝에 있는 발광 기관에서 나오는 섬광으로 기절시켜 먹이를 잡는다고 생각한다. Ⓓ■ 이 기관은 레몬만 한 크기로 발광기라고 한다. 심해 오징어의 발광기는 동물의 왕국에서 발견되는 것 중에서 가장 크며 눈처럼 열고 닫힐 수 있다. 먹이를 사냥하지 않을 때 문어 오징어도 빛을 낸다. 과학자들은 문어 오징어의 발광이 다른 오징어에게 위험을 경고하거나 짝을 유인하는 것 같은 의사소통을 위해 사용된다고 믿는다. **전문가**

들은 비디오의 장면이 과학자들이 이 빛을 내는 오징어의 행동양식에 대해 이전에 생각했던 방식을 뒷받침해준다고 말한다. 또한 화면에는 다나오징어가 힘세고 날렵한 사냥꾼이라는 것을 보여준다. '몇몇 사람들은 심해 오징어가 잡혔을 때 근육이 실제로 딱딱하지 않기 때문에 모든 심해 오징어가 아주 느리게 움직인다고 말해왔다. 하지만 이 특별한 어족은 잘 발달된 근육 지느러미를 갖고 있고 그래서 그 지느러미를 수영할 때 사용한다.'고 과학자가 말했다.

어휘_ squid 오징어 glow 빛나다 flashing 반짝이는 organ 장기, 기관 photophore 발광기 agile 날렵한 sluggish 느릿느릿 움직이는

1. Ⓓ

아래 문장 중 어떤 것이 지문 속의 음영 처리된 문장의 핵심정보를 가장 잘 표현하고 있는가? 오답 선택지는 현저하게 의미를 바꾸거나 핵심정보를 생략한 것이다.

Ⓐ 과학자들은 그것이 사실임을 의심했지만 이 증거를 보고 놀랐다.

Ⓑ 이러한 확인이 없었다면 과학자들은 오징어에 대한 진실을 알 방법이 없었을 것이다.

Ⓒ 과학자들은 오랫동안 의심했던 사실에 대한 증거를 발견하고 열광했다.

Ⓓ 과학자들은 그것이 사실이라고 생각했는데 이제 증거를 확보했다.

2. Ⓒ

다음의 문장이 지문에 추가될 수 있는 곳을 표시하는 네모 박스 [▪]를 보시오.

이 여덟 개의 다리를 갖고 있는 생물은 흡입판에 고양이 발톱 같은 것이 있지만 다른 거대한 오징어가 먹이를 잡기 위해 사용하는 두 개의 기다란 급수용 촉수가 부족하다.

문장이 어느 곳에 가장 적합한가?

문장을 지문에 추가하도록 한 개의 네모 박스 [▪]를 클릭하시오.

해설_ 주어진 문장은 심해 오징어가 사냥할 때의 약점을 말한다. 뒤에 약점을 보강하기 위한 대안의 내용이 적절하므로 Ⓒ가 정답이다. 뒤 문장의 instead(대신에)에 주목한다.

3. Ⓐ, Ⓓ, Ⓕ

지시사항 지문을 간략하게 요약하기 위한 도입문장이 아래에 제시되어 있다. 지문에서 가장 중요한 정보를 담고 있는 3개의 선택지를 선택하여 요약을 완성한다. 지문에 제시되지 않은 정보나 세부 정보를 담고 있는 일부 문장은 요약에 들어가지 않는다. **이 문제는 2점이 주어진다.**

> 선택지를 관련있는 곳으로 끌어당기시오. 끌어당긴 선택지를 삭제하려면 그 위에 대고 클릭하시오. 지문을 다시 보려면 **View Text** 아이콘을 클릭하시오.

심해 오징어는 뛰어난 사냥 능력을 갖는 것으로 밝혀졌다.

> Ⓐ 다리가 여덟 개인 종은 빨판에 고양이 같은 발톱을 가지고 있다.
> Ⓓ 문어나 오징어는 사냥감을 눈부시게 하여 포획하기 위해서 다리에 있는 밝고 반짝이는 불빛을 사용한다.
> Ⓕ 심해 오징어는 발광 기관을 사용하여 먹잇감을 잡는다.

선택지

Ⓐ 다리가 여덟 개인 종은 빨판에 고양이 같은 발톱을 가지고 있다.

Ⓑ 문어나 오징어는 사냥하지 않을 때에도 빛을 냈다.

Ⓒ 생물들은 북태평양에서 촬영되었다.

Ⓓ 문어나 오징어는 사냥감을 눈부시게 하여 포획하기 위해서 다리에 있는 밝고 반짝이는 불빛을 사용한다.

Ⓔ 이렇게 특이한 어족은 근육이 매우 발달한 지느러미를 갖고 있다.

Ⓕ 심해 오징어는 발광 기관을 사용하여 먹잇감을 잡는다.

해설_ 지문의 앞부분에 오징어가 먹이를 잡는 기능에 대해 서술되어 있다. 사냥 능력과 연관된 핵심어(key word) cat-like claws on its suckers, dazzle and catch prey, traps its victims를 찾으면 Ⓐ, Ⓓ, Ⓕ가 정답이다.

02

많은 사람들이 놀랄 만한 사실은 산사태가 세계 어디에서나 발생할 수 있다는 사실이다. 산사태가 상당히 가파른 경사지와 황량한 지대에만 일어난다는 전통적인 견해는 문제의 본질을 정확히 반영하지 못한다. 세계 많은 나라들이 어떤 식으로든 산사태의 영향을 받아왔다. 지리적 범위가 이렇게 넓게 나타나는 이유는 많은 다른 산사태를 유발하는 요소들과 관계가 있다. 지나친 강수량, 지진, 화산, 산불 및 기타 요소들, 그리고 최근의 특정한 인간의 위험한 활동들도 산사태를 유발할 수 있는 주요한 원인들의 일부가 된다. 마찬가지로 산사태는 땅과 물속에서 일어나는 것으로 알려져 있다. 산사태는 암반이나 토양에서 발생할 수 있다. 경지나 메마른 경사지, 자연림 모두에서 산사태가 일어날 수 있다. 심하게 건조하거나 매우 습한 지역들 모두 경사면 붕괴에 의해 영향을 받을 수 있으며 가장 중요한 것은 산사태가 발생하는 데에 가파른 경사가 필수 조건은 아니라는 사실이다. 어떤 경우에는 1~2도의 평평하고 부드러운 경사면이 무너지는 게 관측된 적이 있다.

어휘_ landslide 산사태 inhospitable 불친절한, 사람이 지내기 힘듦 triggering 촉발, 촉발시키다 are known to ~에 알려지다 bedrock 기반, 기반암 are all subject to ~에 전적으로 따르다 prerequisite 전제조건

1. Ⓒ

지문의 유발하는 요소라는 구와 의미가 가장 비슷한 것은?

Ⓐ 총을 쏘기 위해 눌러진 레버

Ⓑ 메커니즘 활성화에 사용되는 장치

ⓒ 행동 방향을 유발하는 사건

ⓓ 화재 또는 폭발

2. Real Nature of the Problem: ⓐ, ⓒ, ⓖ / Traditional Viewpoint: ⓑ, ⓓ

지시사항 선택지에서 알맞은 구를 선택하여 그것과 관련된 산사태 항목에 맞게 연결하시오. 각 항목은 정답으로 중복 선택되지 않는다. **이 문제는 3점이 주어진다.**

선택지를 관련있는 곳으로 끌어당기시오. 끌어당긴 선택지를 삭제하려면 그 위에 대고 클릭하시오. 지문을 다시 보려면 **View Text** 아이콘을 클릭하시오.

선택지	문제의 본질
ⓐ 실패로 관측된 완만한 경사	ⓐ 실패로 관측된 완만한 경사
ⓑ 황량한 지형에서만 발생함	ⓒ 산사태를 겪는 천연 조림
ⓒ 산사태를 겪는 천연 조림	ⓖ 육지와 수중 모두
ⓓ 급경사에 제한된	**전통적인 견해**
ⓔ 과잉 강수	ⓑ 황량한 지형에서만 발생함
ⓕ 위험한 인간 활동	ⓓ 급경사에 제한된
ⓖ 육지와 수중 모두	

해설_ 지문의 후반부에 전통적인 견해와 문제의 본질에 대한 설명이 나오며 문제의 본질은 ⓐ, ⓒ, ⓖ 전통적인 견해는 ⓑ, ⓓ가 정답이다. 선택지의 Excessive precipitation(심한 강수량)과 Dangerous human activities(인간의 위험한 활동)는 산사태의 원인이며 견해와 관련이 없으므로 제외한다.

3. ⓓ

지문에 따르면 다음 중 어느 것이 산사태에 관해 사실이 아닌가?

ⓐ 지리적으로 광범위한 산사태 범위에 대한 주요 원인은 간단하지 않다.

ⓑ 급경사 또는 황량한 지형은 산사태에 필요한 요인이 아니다.

ⓒ 산사태에 대한 다양한 유발 메커니즘이 광범위한 산사태 발생을 설명해준다.

ⓓ 산사태는 육지보다 수중에서 더 빈번하게 발생한다.

해설_ 끝에서 세 번째 문장에 산사태가 땅과 물속에서 일어난다고 하였지만 어디에서 더 자주 발생하는지는 나와 있지 않다. 따라서 ⓓ가 정답이다.

03

과학을 목적으로 항해를 하며 세계 일주를 하는 것은 세계 해양의 방대한 생물의 다양성에 새로운 불빛을 비추었다. 탐험은 샘플의 초기 예비 분석을 바탕으로 하여 약 1,500만 개의 다른 플랑크톤 생물군을 산출해 냈다. 과학자들은 채집을 분석하는 데 여러 해를 보낼 것이다. 36m 크기의 연구 범선은 362일 동안의 여행 후에 3월 31일에 프랑스의 로리앙에 돌아왔다. 그 배의 임무는 바이러스, 박테리아, 원생 생물, 후

생 동물 그리고 해조류 유충을 포함한 작고 바다에 떠 있는 대략 모든 것으로 규정지어진 플랑크톤의 진화와 생태계의 이해를 돕는 것이었다. 비록 플랑크톤이 해양 생물량의 대부분을 구성하고 있지만 **그것의** 생물 지리학과 생태계 시스템의 구조는 '**대부분 연구의 처녀지**'이다. 물리적 해양 탐사대, 해양 생물학자, 촬영 전문가, 분자 생물학자, 생물 정보학자와 모형 제작자가 모두 한자리에 모여서 하는 프로젝트는 '전체론적' 그리고 '협력 연구'라고 불리는 접근법을 사용한다. 프로젝트는 대부분이 자동화되어 있고 다양한 방법으로 많은 종류를 즉시 분석한다. 프로젝트 팀은 전 세계에서 지중해와 적해에서부터 태평양 그리고 남극구까지 153개의 다른 지점에서 샘플을 가지고 왔다.

어휘_ biodiversity 생물의 다양성 expedition 탐험 taxa 분류군 (TAXON의 복수형) schooner 스쿠너 archaea 고세균류 protists 원생생물 metazoan 후생생물 larvae 유충 (larva의 복수형) ecosystems 생태계 molecular 분자의 bioinformaticist 생물정보학자 holistic 전체론의

1. ⓑ

지문의 단어 **그것의**가 가리키는 것은?

ⓐ 바다의 생물량   ⓑ 플랑크톤

ⓒ 프로젝트   ⓓ 해조류 유충

해설_ its가 있는 문장에서 해양 생물량의 대부분을 구성하고 있지만 생물 지리학과 생태계 시스템의 구조가 알려지지 않는 것은 plankton(플랑크톤)이다.

2. ⓓ

지문에서 작가는 ~ 위해 **대부분 연구의 처녀지**를 언급하고 있다.

ⓐ 플랑크톤이 현재까지 충분히 연구되지 않은 이유를 설명하기

ⓑ 지금까지 플랑크톤 연구에서 어떤 정보가 누락되었는지 확인하기

ⓒ 과학자들이 플랑크톤에 대해서 확보한 정보와 다른 종에 관한 정보를 대조하기

ⓓ 대양에서 플랑크톤에 관하여 알려진 것과 그 분포 간의 차이를 강조하기

해설_ almost virgin field(대부분 연구의 처녀지)가 있는 문장 앞부분에 Even though plankton makes up the bulk of the oceans biomass(비록 플랑크톤이 해양 생물량의 대부분을 구성하고 있지만)이라는 대조되는 개념이 있다. 따라서 플랑크톤의 분포에 비해 알려진 정보가 적다는 차이를 강조한 ⓓ가 정답이다.

3. ⓓ

지문에 따르면 다음 중 어느 것이 플랑크톤에 관해 사실이 아닌가?

ⓐ 플랑크톤 연구는 비교적 새로운 연구분야다.

ⓑ 플랑크톤 종류는 대부분의 바다 생물체를 구성한다.

ⓒ 바이러스와 박테리아는 플랑크톤의 종류다.

ⓓ 조사단은 지금껏 플랑크톤에 대해서 새로운 것을 발견하지 못했다.

04

몇몇의 그림 같은 야생 보호구역은 – 몇몇 미국 국립 공원을 포함하여 – 너비 190마일(300km 너비)의 완벽한 고리 모양의 일식의 경로에 놓이게 될 것이다. 야생 보호구역 대신 북동쪽 아시아와 미국의 3분의 2인 서부와 캐나다를 가로질러 수천 마일이 확장된 넓어진 궤도에서 사람들은 **인상적인** 부분 일식을 볼 수 있을 것이다. 해가 완전하게 가려지고 그래서 하늘이 어두워지는 완전한 일식과는 달리 부분 일식 동안에는 하늘이 전혀 어두워지지 않는다. **그래서 개기 일식대로부터 떨어진 곳에서 볼 때 유일한 손해는 완전한 고리를 볼 수 없다는 것과 대칭으로 나타나지 않는다는 것이지만 여전히 해의 부분 일식은 볼 수 있을 것이다.** 다양한 사이즈의 태양의 흑점들이 달의 상승하는 가장자리에 의해 덮이고 후에 달이 해의 표면으로부터 후퇴하면서 보일 것이다. 고리 모양의 경로에 가까이 있는 전파 망원경은 달이 태양의 흑점들과 전파 방해의 다른 원천들을 지날 때 관찰할 것이다. 태양의 흑점들은 지구에서 무선 통신의 방해를 초래하고 또한 우주의 전파 천문학자들의 시야를 저해하는 태양 표면의 폭발이라고 불리는 강렬한 전자기 방사선의 분출과 연관이 있다. 또한 고리 시작의 정확한 타이밍은 역사적인 계측과 비교할 때 태양 지름의 가능한 변화에 대한 자료를 제공할 수 있다.

어휘_ picturesque 그림같은 the full annular eclipse 전체 금환식(金環蝕) partial eclipse 부분식 symmetric 대칭적인 limb 가장자리, 둘레 radio disturbance 전파교란 are linked to ~에 연결되다 solar flare 태양의 폭발 astronomer 천문학자 diameter 지름, 배율

1. ©
지문의 인상적인이라는 단어와 의미가 가장 비슷한 것은?

Ⓐ 물리적으로 접촉하는 　　　　Ⓑ 충격적인

© 인상 깊은 　　　　　　　　Ⓓ 우연한

해설_ striking이 있는 문장에서 striking partial eclipse(인상적인 부분 일식)는 '인상적인'이라는 의미이므로 © impressive(인상 깊은)가 정답이다.

2. Ⓐ
작가는 지문 속의 음영 처리된 문장에서 일식에 관해 무엇을 암시하고 있는가?

Ⓐ 부분 일식은 개기 일식만큼 인상적이지 않을 수 있지만 여전히 볼만할 것이다.

Ⓑ 부분 일식과 개기 일식 사이에는 차이가 있다.

© 개기 일식을 보려면 벌판의 전망 좋은 장소에 가야 한다.

Ⓓ 너무 환해서 일식을 명확히 볼 수 없을 것이다.

3. ©
지문에 따르면 다음 중 어느 것이 일식에 관해 사실이 아닌가?

Ⓐ 사람들은 완전한 일식보다는 부분 일식을 더 많이 볼 수 있을 것이다.

Ⓑ 몇몇 야생 보호 구역을 벗어나더라도 부분 일식이 보일 것이다.

© 완전한 일식 도중 태양 흑점이 달을 가릴 것이다.

Ⓓ 개기 일식 도중 태양 흑점이 한동안 보이지 않을 것이다.

05

자연이 항상 우리에게 긍정적인 영향을 주지는 않는다. 때때로 영화 '더 비치'에서처럼 꽤 부정적일 수 있다. 비록 그 영화를 전체적으로 좋아하지는 않지만 나는 영화에 나온 해변의 아름다움에 크게 감명을 받았다. 이 영화의 모든 출연자들의 목표는 그 해변을 통해 자연과 소통을 하려는 것이다. 그들은 에머슨이 '이는 보편적인 영이 인간과 소통을 하며 인간을 다시 자연으로 이끌기 위해 애쓰는 오르간의 건반이다.'라고 말했을 때와 같은 식으로 자연을 분명히 바라본다. 출연진들은 세상의 모든 일들과 혼란을 떠나기 위하여 이 완벽한 섬을 찾는다. 흠이 없는 해변을 갖고 있는 섬은 '완벽한 파라다이스'로 여러 출연자들에 의해 묘사된다. 이 영화의 카메라 작업은 해변을 영화의 주요 등장인물로 확실히 강조한다. 깨끗한 흰 모래와 투명하고 깨끗한 파란 물의 대조는 주목할 만하다. **해변의 완벽한 아름다움은 출연자들이 섬에 거주하며 절대로 떠나지 않는 동기를 완전히 이해하게 해준다.**

어휘_ care for ~을 보살피다 as a whole 전체로서 seek out ~을 찾아내다 flawless 흠 하나 없는 inhabit 거주하다

1. ©
지문에 따르면 다음 중 어느 것이 해변에 관해 사실인가?

Ⓐ 영화에서 부정적으로 묘사되었다.

Ⓑ 에머슨에게 중요했다.

© 영화의 등장인물로 간주될 수 있다.

Ⓓ 출연자들이 해변을 완전히 이해했다.

해설_ 지문의 끝에서 세 번째 문장에 카메라 작업이 해변을 영화의 주요 등장인물로 강조한다고 하였으므로 ©가 답이다.

2. Ⓐ
아래 문장 중 어떤 것이 지문 속의 음영 처리된 문장의 핵심정보를 가장 잘 표현하고 있는가? 오답 선택지는 현저하게 의미를 바꾸거나 핵심정보를 생략한 것이다.

Ⓐ 출연자들은 해변의 아름다움에 넋을 잃는다.

Ⓑ 거기에 머물 압도적인 동기 부여가 있다.

© 섬은 방문하는 사람을 진정시키는 효과를 발휘한다.

Ⓓ 매력적인 해변의 아름다움에 저항하는 것은 불가능하다.

음영 처리된 문장의 핵심정보는 해변의 아름다움에 출연자들이 감동받은 것이므로 정답은 Ⓐ이다. 섬에 머물 동기 부여는 해변의 아름다움을 설명하기 위한 세부정보이므로 Ⓑ는 오답이다.

3. Ⓐ, Ⓒ, Ⓓ

지시사항 지문을 간략하게 요약하기 위한 도입문장이 아래에 제시되어 있다. 지문에서 가장 중요한 정보를 담고 있는 3개의 보기를 선택하여 요약을 완성한다. 지문에 제시되지 않은 정보나 세부정보를 담고 있는 일부 문장은 요약에 들어가지 않는다. **이 문제는 2점이 주어진다.**

> 선택지를 관련있는 곳으로 끌어당기시오. 끌어당긴 선택지를 삭제하려면 그 위에 대고 클릭하시오. 지문을 다시 보려면 **View Text** 아이콘을 클릭하시오.

해변은 완벽한 파라다이스였다.

> Ⓐ 모든 등장인물의 목표는 그 섬을 결코 떠나지 않는 것이었다.
> Ⓒ 등장인물들은 이 섬에 거주하는 동기를 완전히 이해한다.
> Ⓓ 등장인물들은 모든 혼란과 세상의 비즈니스를 뒤로 남기기 위해 완벽한 섬을 찾는다.

선택지

Ⓐ 모든 등장인물의 목표는 그 섬을 결코 떠나지 않는 것이었다.

Ⓑ 새하얀 모래와 맑은 푸른 물의 대비는 놀랍다.

Ⓒ 등장인물들은 이 섬에 거주하는 동기를 완전히 이해한다.

Ⓓ 등장인물들은 모든 혼란과 세상의 비즈니스를 뒤로 남기기 위해 완벽한 섬을 찾는다.

Ⓔ 나는 묘사된 해변의 아름다움에 크게 감동했다.

Ⓕ 자연이 우리에게 항상 긍정적인 영향을 미치지는 않는다.

해설_ 도입문장 '해변은 완벽한 파라다이스였다.'를 설명하기 위한 중심정보가 되는 것은 등장인물의 목표와 동기가 세상일과 혼란을 뒤로 하고 섬에 거주하기 원하는 것이므로 Ⓐ, Ⓒ, Ⓓ가 정답이다. Ⓑ, Ⓔ는 아름다움만 묘사된 파라다이스의 세부정보이며 Ⓕ는 관계없는 정보이므로 오답이다.

Vocabulary & Paraphrasing

1. 아래에 있는 각 뜻에 맞는 단어를 박스에서 찾아서 쓰시오.

① ecology	② expedition	③ precipitation
④ agile	⑤ tentacle	⑥ flare
⑦ symmetric	⑧ prerequisite	⑨ inhospitable
⑩ photophore		

2. 다음 문장을 해석 후 아래 지시대로 paraphrasing(다른 말로 바꿔 표현하기)하세요.

① 이 여덟 개의 다리를 갖고 있는 생물은 흡입판에 고양이 발톱 같은 것이 있지만 다른 거대한 오징어가 먹이를 잡기 위해 사용하는 두 개의 기다란 급수용 촉수가 부족하다.

➡ **예시_** This eight-legged creatures have claws like a cat on the suction plate, but they fall short of two long tentacles to supply food which other giant squid use to catch prey.

② 산사태가 상당히 가파른 경사지와 황량한 지대에만 일어난다는 전통적인 견해는 문제의 본질을 정확히 반영하지 못한다.

➡ **예시_** The traditional view is that landslides take place only in the quite steep zone where it is hard for people to live, but it does not accurately reflect the nature of the problem.

③ 물리적 해양 탐사대, 해양 생물학자, 촬영 전문가, 분자 생물학자, 생물 정보학자와 모형 제작자가 모두 한자리에 모여서 하는 프로젝트는 '전체론적' 그리고 '협력 연구'이라고 불리는 접근법을 사용한다.

➡ **예시_** Marine expeditions, marine biologists, shooting experts, molecular biologists, and biological information scholars, and modelers gather in one place for the project using an approach called "overall" and "joint research."

④ 다양한 사이즈의 태양의 흑점들이 달의 상승하는 가장자리에 의해 덮이고 후에 달이 해의 표면으로부터 후퇴하면서 보일 것이다.

➡ **예시_** The rising edge of the moon will cover various sized sunspots and uncover them while the moon is retreating from the surface of the sun.

Unit 07 Education_ P. 259

01

선생님들은 **표준에 맞는 테스트에 중점**을 두면서 학생들이 무엇을 배우는지 끊임없이 관찰하고 측정하며, 학생들이 배운 것을 수치화하고, 아이들이 탐험하고 상호작용하며 그들 스스로 배우는 기회를 많이 줄이거나 없애는 데 직접 지도 관여하며 학교에서 하루에 더 많은 시간을 보낸다. 휴식 시간은 많은 지역에서 완전히 사라지고 있다. 방과 후에 부모들은 아이들이 혼자 또는 친구들과 보내는 계획이 짜여져 있지 않은 시간들을 박탈하면서 아이들을 과외활동에서 다른 과외활동으로 실어 나른다. 연구원들에 따르면 놀이가 그저 스트레스를 줄이고 아이들이 사회적으로 능숙하게 해주기 때문에 그것이 문제가 되는 것은 아니다. **그것**은 놀이가 또한 작업 기억력과 자기 통제를 향상시킨다고 추정되기 때문에 문제가 된다. 다시 말해 놀이는 아이들이 더 똑똑하게 그리고 바르게 행동하게 만든다. 얄궂게도 학업에 편중하여 아이들을 놀지 못하게 하고 부당하게 다룸으로써 우리는 사실 그들의 발전을 억제하고 있는지 모른다.

어휘_ put emphasis on ~을 강조하다 be engaged in ~에 관여하다 recess 휴회기간 vanished 사라졌다 self-regulation 자기관리 in favor of ~에 찬성하여 inhibiting 억제

1. ©

지문에서 작가는 ~ 위해 표준에 맞는 테스트에 중점을 언급하고 있다.

Ⓐ 그 가치를 알리기
Ⓑ 연구원들이 왜 학교 교육을 개선하고 싶어 하는지 설명하기
© 어린이들이 더 많은 놀이 시간을 가져야 할 필요성을 옹호하기
Ⓓ 어린이들이 혼자 계획이 짜여 있지 않은 시간을 가져야 하는 데 대한 중요성을 경고하기

2. Ⓐ

지문의 단어 그것이 가리키는 것은?

Ⓐ 아이들의 놀이 빼앗기
Ⓑ 활동마다 부모들의 자녀 실어 나르기
© 어린이들의 사회적 경쟁력 향상시키기
Ⓓ 놀이를 통한 스트레스 줄이기

해설_ it은 문장에서 아이들이 놀이를 못함으로써 발생하는 문제점을 가리키므로 아이들에게서 놀이를 박탈하는 것이 된다.

3. Standardized testing: Ⓐ, Ⓓ, Ⓖ / Play: Ⓑ, Ⓕ

지시사항 선택지에서 알맞은 구를 선택하여 그것과 관련된 활동의 유형에 맞게 연결하시오. **이 문제는 3점이 주어진다.**

> 선택지를 관련있는 곳으로 끌어당기시오. 끌어당긴 선택지를 삭제하려면 그 위에 대고 클릭하시오. 지문을 다시 보려면 **View Text** 아이콘을 클릭하시오.

선택지	표준에 맞는 테스트
Ⓐ 그들의 발전을 저해함	Ⓐ 그들의 발전을 저해함
Ⓑ 작동 기억을 향상시킴	Ⓓ 계획이 짜여 있지 않은 시간이 따로 없음
© 방과 후	Ⓖ 감소된 탐색 기회
Ⓓ 계획이 짜여 있지 않은 시간이 따로 없음	**놀이**
Ⓔ 연구원들에 증명됨	Ⓑ 작동 기억을 향상시킴
Ⓕ 스트레스를 줄임	Ⓕ 스트레스를 줄임
Ⓖ 감소된 탐색 기회	

02

과학의 대중화란 단지 모든 사람들 특히 비과학자들이 기본 개념을 파악하고 과학이 본질적으로 무엇인지에 대한 생각을 갖게 하는 방식으로 과학적 생각을 상상하는 노력에 불과하다. 물론 정말로 '과학'이 무엇인지는 아무도 알지 못하며 심지어 과학자들도 알지 못한다. 과학적 방법이 무엇인지 기술하고자 한 철학자들과 과학적 방법이란 어떤 것이어야 하는지 언급한 사람들은 오랜 시간을 보내며 '하나의 유일한' 과학적 접근법은 없다는 것을 알아냈다. 따라서 명확한 고유의 정의를 내리지 못하게 되었다. 그럼에도 불구하고 '과학' 현상과 그

결과는 존재한다. 비록 아무도 '과학'이 정확하게 무엇에 관한 것인지 말할 수는 없지만 여하튼 모두들 어떤 것인지 알고 있어야 한다. 여기에서 중요한 질문은 이것이 가능한지 가능하다면 어느 정도까지 가능한 것인지의 여부이다.

어휘_ nothing else ~을 빼고는 다른 아무것도 one and only 유일한. 오직 at stake 성패가 달려 있는. 위태로운

1. Ⓓ

다음 중 어느 것이 지문의 내용으로부터 결론 내려질 수 있는가?

Ⓐ 과학의 대중화는 과학자들에게 필요하다.
Ⓑ 과학이 무엇인지 정확하게 정의하는 것은 불가능하다.
© 과학이 무엇인지 분명하게 정의하는 것은 가능하다.
Ⓓ 과학이 무엇인지 정의하는 것은 비록 가능하더라도 어려울 뿐만 아니라 분명하지 않다.

2. Ⓐ

지문의 언급하다라는 단어와 의미가 가장 비슷한 것은?

Ⓐ 분명히 말하다   Ⓑ 연구하다
© 공개적으로 전시하다   Ⓓ 결과로 보다

해설_ 언급하다(state)와 동의어는 Ⓐ declare(분명히 말하다)이다.

3. Ⓑ

지문의 단어 이것이 가리키는 것은?

Ⓐ 사람들이 과학이란 정확히 무엇인지 밝힌다.
Ⓑ 모든 사람들이 과학이 무엇인가에 대한 견해를 가진다.
© 현상 과학과 그 결과가 존재한다.
Ⓓ 과학이 정확히 무엇인가에 대해 말할 수 있는 사람은 아무도 없다.

해설_ this가 있는 문장 앞에서 모두들 과학이 어떤 것인지 알고 있어야 한다고 하였으므로 Ⓑ가 정답이다. 과학이 정확하게 무엇에 관한 것인지는 알 수 없다고 하였으므로 Ⓐ는 오답이다.

03

아동 비만율이 지난 30년간 거의 3배로 증가하게 되자 미국 의학 협회는 미국 내 학교에서 비만 교육을 필요로 하는 입법안을 지지하게 되었다. 비만과 관련된 건강상의 위험뿐 아니라 비만의 원인을 가르치는 수업이 1학년을 대상으로 시작하여 12학년까지 계속될 것으로 보인다. 건강한 식습관, 운동 그리고 활동력 유지에 관한 간단한 조언과 더불어 예방 기술 또한 커리큘럼의 일부가 될 것이다. 미국 의학 협회에 따르면 의사들이 시간을 내어 자발적으로 이러한 수업에서 강의하도록 권장하고 있다. 건강 교육을 이미 실시하고 있는 학교들은 비만 수업은 이미 실행하고 있는 수업의 새로운 일부에 불과하게 될 것이라고 하였다. 미국 의학 협회는 또한 설탕 첨가 음료에 대한 과세 정책을 지지하기로 하였다. 세입액은 소비자들을 위한 비만 교육의 자금 지원을 위해 사용될 것이다.

어휘_ obesity 비만 legislation 제정법, 입법 be part of ~의 일부가 되다 be encouraged to ~하도록 장려되다 taxation 조세

1. ⓒ

아래 문장 중 지문에 음영 처리된 문장의 핵심정보를 가장 잘 표현하고 있는 것은? 오답 선택지는 현저하게 의미를 바꾸거나 핵심정보를 생략한 것이다.

Ⓐ 의사들은 이 문제를 처리하기 위해 가능한 한 무엇이든 하기로 결정했다.

Ⓑ 미국 의학 협회가 비만을 처리하지 않을 경우 미국에서 비만율은 계속 증가할 것이다.

ⓒ 의사들은 교육이 비만 문제를 해결하는 데 도움이 될 수 있다고 생각한다.

Ⓓ 의사들은 비만율 증가에 책임이 있다.

2. Ⓑ

지문에 따르면 어느 것이 비만 수업에 관해 사실인가?

Ⓐ 그들은 비만 어린이의 30%에 초점을 맞출 것이다.

Ⓑ 이는 학교 교육과정의 일부가 될 것이다.

ⓒ 의사들은 이들이 효과적일지에 대한 의문을 가져왔다.

Ⓓ 현재의 건강 교육 수업은 제안된 강좌 내용의 대부분을 이미 다루고 있다.

3. Ⓐ, ⓒ, Ⓕ

지시사항 지문을 간략하게 요약하기 위한 도입문장이 아래에 제시되어 있다. 지문에서 가장 중요한 정보를 담고 있는 3개의 선택지를 선택하여 요약을 완성한다. 지문에 제시되지 않은 정보나 세부 정보를 담고 있는 일부 문장은 요약에 들어가지 않는다. **이 문제는 2점이 주어진다.**

> 선택지를 관련있는 곳으로 끌어당기시오. 끌어당긴 선택지를 삭제하려면 그 위에 대고 클릭하시오. 지문을 다시 보려면 **View Text** 아이콘을 클릭하시오.

증가하는 비만 수준에 대한 우려는 모든 학교에서 필요한 비만 교육을 실시하려는 노력을 하게 하고 있다.

> Ⓐ 비만 수업은 현재의 건강 교육 과정의 요소가 될 것이다.
> ⓒ 원인 및 관련된 건강상의 위험에 대한 정보가 포함될 것이다.
> Ⓕ 강좌에는 예방 기법, 건강식과 운동, 활동적인 생활을 유지하는 방법에 대한 조언이 포함될 것이다.

선택지

Ⓐ 비만 수업은 현재의 건강교육 과정의 요소가 될 것이다.

Ⓑ 설탕이 함유된 음료에 대한 과세가 새 프로그램의 기금을 마련하는 데 도움이 될 것이다.

ⓒ 원인 및 관련된 건강상의 위험에 대한 정보가 포함될 것이다.

Ⓓ 이 문제를 극복하기 위해서 비만 교육을 필수로 하는 법률 제정이 필요하다.

Ⓔ 이러한 교육 정책에 있어서 의사들이 적극적인 역할을 할 것으로 기대된다.

Ⓕ 강좌에는 예방 기법, 건강식과 운동, 활동적인 생활을 유지하는 방법에 대한 조언이 포함될 것이다.

04

인간은 복잡한 존재이다. 그들은 적응하면서 배우고 지능과 자유 의지를 지니고 있으며 합리적으로 판단할 수 있고 감정을 느끼며 양심이 있는 존재이다. 비록 이러한 자질과 특성으로 인해 인간이 다른 생명체보다 우월하긴 하지만 양심과 감정이 어디에서 오는 것인지에 관해서는 의심스럽다. Ⓐ▪ 정확하게 무엇이 특정 상황과 문제에 대해 우리가 반응하도록 자극하는 것일까? 해답은 인간 본성에 있다. 인간으로서 우리가 옳고 그르다고 느끼는 것은 어떻게든 단순히 개개인을 뛰어넘는 그 무엇인가에 의해 좌우된다. **따라서 근본적인 질문은 외부적으로 영향을 주는 것이 무엇인지가 된다: 그것은 본성, 타고난 인간의 자질 아니면 다른 사람들과 경험의 인위적인 혼합일까?** Ⓑ▪ 좀 더 구체적으로 말해서 우리의 도덕성과 도덕 규범의 준수가 인간성 그 자체를 통해서 정해지고 변함 없는 것인지 아닌지가 질문 사항이다. **프랜시스 베이컨은 자연을 지휘하려면 먼저 자연에 순응해야 한다고 말했고 그 같은 원리는 인간에게도 적용된다.** ⓒ▪ 사람들, 단체, 생각 및 믿음에 대해서 판단하기 전에 먼저 그 판단을 비교할 만한 기준을 지니고 있어야 한다. Ⓓ▪ 만약 실질적인 자연의 법칙이 존재하지 않는다면 기준이 없는 것이고 따라서 사실에 의거해서가 아니라 의견에 따라 기준이 세워지기 때문에 무언가를 다른 것과 비교하는 것이 불가능해진다. 비록 인간이 생각하는 방식은 분명히 환경의 영향을 받지만 실제로 자연의 법칙은 인간이 만들어낸 생각에서 독립적인 현실이다.

어휘_ complex beings 복잡한 존재 morality 도덕, 도덕률 adherence 고수 law of nature 자연법 be compared to ~에 비유되다

1. Ⓑ

다음의 문장이 지문에 추가될 수 있는 곳을 표시하는 네모 박스 [▪]를 보시오.

따라서 근본적인 질문은 외부적으로 영향을 주는 것이 무엇인지가 된다: 그것은 본성, 타고난 인간의 자질, 아니면 다른 사람들과 경험의 인위적인 혼합일까?

문장이 어느 곳에 가장 적합한가?

문장을 지문에 추가하도록 한 개의 네모 박스 [▪]를 클릭하시오.

해설_ 주어진 문장은 인간의 본성에 끼치는 영향에 대한 질문이다. 따라서 그 질문(the question)에 대해 구체적인 설명을 한(In more specific terms) 문장 앞 Ⓑ가 정답이다.

2. Ⓑ

작가는 지문 속의 음영 처리된 문장에서 자연에 관해 무엇을 암시하고 있는가?

Ⓐ 인간은 자연의 노예이다.

Ⓑ 인간은 자신의 본성을 무시할 수 없다.

Ⓒ 인간이 자연을 따르지 않을 경우 적절하게 행동할 수 없다.

Ⓓ 대부분의 사람들은 자연에 순종할 수 없다.

3. Law of Nature: Ⓐ, Ⓒ, Ⓖ /
   No Law of Nature: Ⓔ, Ⓕ

지시사항 선택지에서 알맞은 구를 선택하여 그것과 관련된 자연의 법칙에 맞게 연결하시오. **이 문제는 3점이 주어진다.**

선택지를 관련있는 곳으로 끌어당기시오. 끌어당긴 선택지를 삭제하려면 그 위에 대고 클릭하시오. 지문을 다시 보려면 **View Text** 아이콘을 클릭하시오.

선택지	자연의 법칙
Ⓐ 인간의 생각과는 따로 떨어짐	Ⓐ 인간의 생각과는 따로 떨어짐
Ⓑ 인간이 어떻게 생각하는지에 영향을 줌	Ⓒ 단순히 개인을 넘어 좌우됨
Ⓒ 단순히 개인을 넘어 좌우됨	Ⓖ 행동을 비교할 기준을 제시함
Ⓓ 특정한 상황과 문제에 대한 우리의 반응을 자극함	자연의 법칙 아님
Ⓔ 어떤 것을 다른 것과 비교할 수 없음	Ⓔ 어떤 것을 다른 것과 비교할 수 없음
Ⓕ 의견에 따라 설정된 기준을 가짐	Ⓕ 의견에 따라 설정된 기준을 가짐
Ⓖ 행동을 비교할 기준을 제시함	

05

학교에서의 왕따는 학교 전체적인 분위기와 학생들이 두려움 없는 안전한 환경에서 배울 수 있는 권리를 해할 수 있는 전 세계적인 문제이다. **왕따는 또한 괴롭힘을 행한 학생과 희생자 모두에게 평생 부정적인 영향을 줄 수 있다.** 왕따는 괴롭힘을 당하는 학생을 대상으로 한 명이나 그 이상의 학생들이 시작하는 놀리기, 비아냥거리기, 협박하기, 때리기 그리고 훔치기 같은 직접적인 행동들을 포함한다. 직접적인 가해뿐만 아니라 왕따는 한 학생을 의도적인 따돌림으로써 집단적으로 고립시키는 더욱 간접적 방법으로 이루어질 수 있다. 남자아이들은 전형적으로 직접적인 공격을 하는 반면에 왕따를 가하는 여자아이들은 루머를 퍼뜨린다든가 어울리지 못하게 강요하는 등으로 미묘하며 간접적인 방법을 사용하는 경향이 있다. 왕따가 직접적이든 간접적이든 왕따의 핵심 요소는 협박이 괴롭힘과 학대의 패턴이 만들어지도록 시간이 흐르며 반복적으로 일

어난다는 것이다.

어휘_ bullying 왕따 teasing 괴롭히는 taunting 조롱하는 key component 기준 성분 intimidation 협박 harassment 괴롭힘

1. Ⓐ

작가는 지문에서 ~으로써 간접적인 왕따에 대해 설명하고 있다.

Ⓐ 여자아이들에 의한 왕따가 남자아이들의 왕따와 다르다는 것을 기술함

Ⓑ 왕따의 결과를 설명함

Ⓒ 왕따의 다른 형태에 대한 증거를 제공함

Ⓓ 한 명 또는 그보다 많은 학생에 의한 왕따의 사례를 나열함

해설_ 작가는 지문의 중간 부분에서 남자아이들과 여자아이들의 왕따 방법이 다르며 간접적인 왕따가 주로 여자아이들 간에 사용된다고 설명하고 있다. 따라서 Ⓐ가 정답이다.

2. Ⓑ

아래 문장 중 지문에 음영 처리된 문장의 핵심정보를 가장 잘 표현하고 있는 것은? 오답 선택지는 현저하게 의미를 바꾸거나 핵심정보를 생략한 것이다.

Ⓐ 괴롭히는 사람은 피해자에게 평생 상처를 남긴다.

Ⓑ 양쪽 모두에게 왕따의 장기적 부정적 결과가 나타날 수 있다.

Ⓒ 왕따로부터 누구도 안전하지 않다.

Ⓓ 한 번 괴롭히는 사람은 영원히 괴롭힌다.

해설_ 음영 처리된 문장의 핵심정보는 왕따의 가해자와 피해자가 모두 장기적으로 부정적 영향을 받을 수 있다는 것이므로 Ⓑ가 정답이다.

3. Ⓑ, Ⓓ, Ⓕ

지시사항 지문을 간략하게 요약하기 위한 도입문장이 아래에 제시되어 있다. 지문에서 가장 중요한 정보를 담고 있는 3개의 보기를 선택하여 요약을 완성한다. 지문에 제시되지 않은 정보나 세부정보를 담고 있는 일부 문장은 요약에 들어가지 않는다. **이 문제는 2점이 주어진다.**

선택지를 관련있는 곳으로 끌어당기시오. 끌어당긴 선택지를 삭제하려면 그 위에 대고 클릭하시오. 지문을 다시 보려면 **View Text** 아이콘을 클릭하시오.

중요한 점은 왕따가 시간이 지남에 따라 반복적으로 발생한다는 것이다.

Ⓑ 반복은 왕따의 가장 중요한 측면이다.

Ⓓ 왕따는 일반적으로 학대의 패턴을 보여준다.

Ⓕ 괴롭힘이 계획되고 만들어져 왔다.

선택지

Ⓐ 왕따는 직접 및 간접 행동을 모두 포함한다.

Ⓑ 반복은 왕따의 가장 중요한 측면이다.

Ⓒ 소년에 의한 왕따는 소녀에 의한 것보다 더 파괴적이다.

381

ⓓ 왕따는 일반적으로 학대의 패턴을 보여준다.

ⓔ 왕따는 평생 부정적인 영향을 미칠 수 있다.

ⓕ 괴롭힘이 계획되고 만들어져 왔다.

해설_ 왕따가 지속적으로 반복하여 발생한다는 도입문장을 설명하는 중심정보는 반복이 왕따의 가장 중요한 측면이고 학대의 패턴을 보이며 괴롭힘이 계획되고 만들어졌다는 것이므로 ⓑ, ⓓ, ⓕ가 정답이다. 나머지는 왕따의 반복과 관련이 없다.

Vocabulary & Paraphrasing

1. 아래에 있는 각 뜻에 맞는 단어를 박스에서 찾아서 쓰시오.

① recess   ② competent   ③ grasp
④ fundamental   ⑤ prompt   ⑥ morality
⑦ vanish   ⑧ revenue   ⑨ adherence
⑩ obesity

2. 다음 문장을 해석 후 아래 지시대로 **paraphrasing**(다른 말로 바꿔 표현하기)하세요.

① 선생님들은 표준에 맞는 테스트에 중점을 두면서 학생들이 무엇을 배우는지 끊임없이 관찰하고 측정하며, 학생들이 배운 것을 수치화하고, 아이들이 탐험하고 상호 작용하며 그들 스스로 배우는 기회를 많이 줄이거나 없애는 데 직접 지도 관여하며 학교에서 하루에 더 많은 시간을 보낸다.

➡ **예시**_ While involved in direct instruction during the day at school, teachers spend a lot of time focusing on standardized testing, and trying to constantly observe and measure what students learn, which reduces or eliminates a lot of opportunities for children to explore, interact, or learn themselves.

② 과학의 대중화란 단지 모든 사람들 특히 비과학자들이 기본 개념을 파악하고 과학이 본질적으로 무엇인지에 대한 생각을 갖게 하는 방식으로 과학적 생각을 이미지화하려는 노력에 불과하다.

➡ **예시**_ The popularization of science is nothing but an endeavor to imagine scientific ideas in a way that all people, particularly non-scientists, can understand the basic concepts and have an idea of what science essentially is.

③ 비만과 관련된 건강상의 위험뿐 아니라 비만의 원인을 가르치는 수업이 1학년을 대상으로 시작하여 12학년까지 계속될 것으로 보인다.

➡ **예시**_ It is believed that classes teaching the cause of obesity and the health risks associated with it should start in the first grade, and continue until 12th grade.

Unit 08 Culture_ P. 273

01

신의 계급에서 수반은 신과 인간들의 영적 아버지인 제우스이다. 그의 아내는 하늘의 여왕이며 결혼의 성스러움의 수호자인 헤라였다. 하늘의 최고 신들로서 이들과 관련된 불과 금속 공의 후원자인 헤파이스토스, 지혜와 전쟁의 처녀 여신이며 도시의 여신으로서 뛰어난 아테나, 빛, 시 그리고 음악의 신인 아폴로, 그의 여동생이며 야생의 신으로 후에 달의 여신이 된 아르테미스, 전쟁의 신인 아레스, 그의 배우자이며 사랑의 여신인 아프로디테, 신성한 메신저이며 후에 과학과 발명의 신이 된 헤르메스, 건강과 가정의 여신인 헤스티아가 있었다. **이런 위대한 신과 여신들 주위에는 하위 신들이 모여 있었으며 그중 몇몇은 정해진 위치에서 특정한 명성을 누렸다.** 그들 중에는 태양의 헬리오스, (아르테미스가 존재하기 이전) 달의 셀레네, 신들의 수행원인 그레이스 자매들, 뮤즈들, 무지개의 여신인 아이리스, 청춘의 여신이며 신들의 술을 따르는 헤베, 그리고 헤베에 대응되는 남자 가니메데가 있었다. 포세이돈은 종종 그의 아내인 암피트리테의 숭배를 함께하며 바다를 다스렸다. 네레이스들, 트리톤들, 그리고 바다의 다른 작은 신들이 **그들**을 수행하였다.

어휘_ hierarchy 계급, 계층 sanctity 신성함 consort 배우자, 어울리다 cupbearer 술 따르는 사람 be accompanied by ~을 동반하다 deities 신

1. ⓒ

지문에 따르면 다음 중 어느 것이 신들에 관해 사실이 아닌가?

ⓐ 많은 하위 신들이 있었다.

ⓑ 아폴로는 최고의 신 중 하나였다.

ⓒ 네레이스는 작은 신이 아니었다.

ⓓ 최고의 신 중에는 여신이 있었다.

2. ⓐ

아래 문장 중 지문에 음영 처리된 문장의 핵심정보를 가장 잘 표현하고 있는 것은? 오답 선택지는 현저하게 의미를 바꾸거나 핵심정보를 생략한 것이다.

ⓐ 또 다른 단계의 하위 신들이 각 요소를 지배했다.

ⓑ 다른 하위 신들은 그들이 영향을 끼칠 수 있는 지역이 정해져 있었다.

ⓒ 다른 신들과 여신들은 다른 전문적인 영역을 가지고 있었다.

ⓓ 특정 지역에서 다른 신들은 출중했다.

3. ⓑ

지문의 단어 **그들**이 가리키는 것은?

ⓐ 네레이스들

ⓑ 포세이돈과 암피트리테

ⓒ 네레이스들, 트리톤들, 그리고 바다의 다른 작은 신
ⓓ 헤베와 가니메데

02

내가 처음으로 비행기를 타고 JFK공항으로 간 것은 로스앤젤레스에서 NYC공항으로 돌아가는 비행기를 탈 때였다. 그날 나는 해가 일찍 떠오를 때까지 잠을 청할 수가 없어서 겨우 두 시간밖에 잠을 잘 수 없었다. 그래서 집으로 돌아가서 침대에 쓰러지고 싶었다. 그래서 택시를 타기 위해 긴 행렬 속에서 기다릴 것인가 또는 자기 차를 가지고 손님을 태워 주는 남자를 따라갈 것인가를 결정해야 했다. 나의 혼미한 뇌는 후자를 택하는 것이 현명한 처사라고 결정하였다. 나는 그 남자를 따라 낡고 녹이 슨 픽업 트럭인 그의 '택시'로 갔다. 그러나 고맙게도 멈추고 '절대 안 돼'라고 말하고 합법적인 택시를 타는 행렬로 다시 돌아갈 정도로 정신이 들었다. 물론 나는 공항에서 지나치게 열성적인 차량 서비스를 절대로 이용하지 말아야 한다는 것을 알고 있었다. 불법일 뿐만 아니라 바가지일 가능성도 있다. 시에서 운영하는 택시는 매우 엄격한 요금 정책을 따르기 때문에 **바가지를 당하는** 일이 없게 되어 있다. 불법 기사들은 아무 데나 돌아다닌다. 내가 마치 초보 여행자같이 보일 수도 있는 이런 이야기를 하는 이유는 여행 중에 여행객들에게 다가오는 사기꾼들이 많다는 것을 알려 주고자 하는 것이다.

어휘_ a couple hours 2시간 legit 합법적인 overzealous 지나치게 열성적인 not only A but also B A뿐 아니라 B 역시 scam 신용사기 fudged 날조했다 novice 초보자

1. ⓑ
지문에 따르면 작가는 처음에 ~ 때문에 차량 서비스를 이용하기로 결정했다.
ⓐ 픽업 트럭으로 가기를 원했기
ⓑ 피곤하고 혼미했기
ⓒ 사기일 수 있다고 생각했기
ⓓ 차량 서비스 이용이 합법적일 것이라고 생각했기

2. ⓓ
지문의 **바가지를 당하는**이라는 어휘와 의미가 가장 비슷한 것은?
ⓐ 짜증나는   ⓑ 무작위로 결정되는
ⓒ 적극적으로 선택되는   ⓓ 속는

3. ⓐ, ⓑ, ⓔ
지시사항 지문을 간략하게 요약하기 위한 도입문장이 아래에 제시되어 있다. 지문에서 가장 중요한 정보를 담고 있는 3개의 선택지를 선택하여 요약을 완성한다. 지문에 제시되지 않은 정보나 세부 정보를 담고 있는 일부 문장은 요약에 들어가지 않는다. **이 문제는 2점이 주어진다.**

선택지를 관련있는 곳으로 끌어당기시오. 끌어당긴 선택지를 삭제하려면 그 위에 대고 클릭하시오. 지문을 다시 보려면 **View Text** 아이콘을 클릭하시오.

공항에서 과열된 차량 제공 서비스는 경고를 받아야 한다.

ⓐ 관광객들이 의식을 못 하게 속이는 많은 사기가 있다.
ⓑ 픽업 트럭은 그에게 위험을 경고해 줬다.
ⓔ 뭔가 불법인 것은 생길 수 있는 문제의 징조이다.

선택지
ⓐ 관광객들이 의식을 못 하게 속이는 많은 사기가 있다.
ⓑ 픽업 트럭은 그에게 위험을 경고해 줬다.
ⓒ 택시를 기다리는 데 시간이 오래 걸리지만 택시는 요금을 속이지 않는다.
ⓓ 그는 혼미했기 때문에 차량 서비스가 좋은 선택으로 보였다.
ⓔ 뭔가 불법인 것은 생길 수 있는 문제의 징조이다.
ⓕ 합법적인 택시를 줄서서 기다리는 것이 낫다.

03

두 개의 해안을 따라 마이애미 파티 장면에서 저 멀리 한적한 캘러데시 섬까지 끊임없이 펼쳐져 있는 모래사장이 있고 많은 사람들이 모이는 혼잡한 해변을 미국에서 가장 많이 갖고 있는 주는 바로 플로리다이다. 하지만 파도타기 문화로 유명하고 미국 사람들이 가장 많이 찾는 제1의 해변은 캘리포니아이다. 더 정확히 말하면 1,600만 명의 일광욕을 즐기는 사람들, 점을 보는 사람, 거리 공연가, 사람 구경을 하는 사람들로 붐비는 두말할 것 없는 명성을 보여주는 베니스 해변이다. 이러한 예상치는 해변의 사람들이 유동적이고 역동적이기 때문에 정확한 과학적 숫자는 아니다. 수를 알아내기 위해 우리는 200여 개의 해변을 찾은 사람들의 통계를 가지고 있는 미국 구조대 연합회의 도움을 받았다. 여기에서 통계를 알 수 없을 때는 뉴욕 시 공원 부서와 같은 정부 기관에 도움을 호소하였다. 우리의 목록에는 1,100만 명의 사람들이 방문한 코니 섬도 있었을 뿐만 아니라 도시에 거주하는 파도타기하는 사람들의 여행지로 최근 유행을 쫓는 사람들이 가장 좋아하는 로커웨이 해변도 포함되어 있었다. 해변에 있는 사람들이나 로커웨이 타코 음식 트럭에 줄 서 있는 많은 사람들을 용기를 내서 대해 볼 만하다. **모든 사람이 동의하지는 않겠지만,** 뉴욕과 다른 지방 당국의 통계가 있기 때문에 이 해변에 얼마나 많은 방문객들이 찾아오는지 자랑할 수도 있을 것이다. 하지만 그들이 이러한 숫자를 지나치게 알리면 사람들이 안 오는 일이 생길 수도 있다. 위대한 요기 베라가 '이젠 아무도 거기 가지 않아, 그곳에는 너무 사람이 많아.'라고 말한 것처럼 말이다. 사람들의 지혜를 따른다면 이 해변을 가장 많이 찾게 만든 브로드 워크

(해변이나 물가에 판자를 깔아 만든 길)를 걷는 즐거움과 자연의 아름다움의 조화를 감상하기 위해서는 아침 일찍 가거나 주말은 피하여 시간을 맞추는 게 좋다. 사람들이 붐비는 것을 **견디기** 힘들면 대신 세계적으로 숨겨진 해변 중의 하나인 곳을 찾는 것도 좋다.

어휘_ congested 붐비는, 혼잡한 seemingly 외견상으로는, 겉보기에는 sunbathers 일광욕 crunch 고속으로 처리하다 rely on ~을 의지하다 city-dwelling 도시 주거, 주택 hipster 최신 정보통 stats 통계 boardwalk 판자를 깔아서 만든 길

1. Ⓐ
음영 처리된 문장에 따르면 다음 중 어느 것이 추론될 수 있는가?
Ⓐ 몇몇 사람들은 덜 붐비는 해변에 가는 것을 선호할 것이다.
Ⓑ 몇몇 사람들은 뉴욕 공원 부서에서 밝힌 숫자를 믿지 않는다.
Ⓒ 로커웨이 타코 음식 트럭은 제안하는 것처럼 좋지 않다.
Ⓓ 아침 일찍 또는 평일에 해변에 간다면 당신은 해변을 즐길 수 있다.

2. Ⓓ
지문의 **견디다**라는 어휘와 의미가 가장 비슷한 것은?
Ⓐ 선택하다   Ⓑ 얻다
Ⓒ 받아들이다   Ⓓ 참다

3. California: Ⓔ, Ⓕ / New York: Ⓑ, Ⓒ, Ⓖ
지시사항 선택지에서 알맞은 구를 선택하여 그것과 관련된 장소에 맞게 연결하시오. **이 문제는 3점이 주어진다.**

선택지를 관련있는 곳으로 끌어당기시오. 끌어당긴 선택지를 삭제하려면 그 위에 대고 클릭하시오. 지문을 다시 보려면 **View Text** 아이콘을 클릭하시오.

선택지	캘리포니아
Ⓐ 유동적이고 역동적인 해변의 사람들	Ⓔ 파도타기로 유명한 해변
Ⓑ 로커웨이 음식 트럭	Ⓕ 미국에서 가장 붐비는 해변
Ⓒ 유행을 쫓는 사람들이 좋아하는	**뉴욕**
Ⓓ 세계적으로 숨겨진 해변 중의 하나	Ⓑ 로커웨이 음식 트럭
Ⓔ 파도타기로 유명한 해변	Ⓒ 유행을 쫓는 사람들이 좋아하는
Ⓕ 미국에서 가장 붐비는 해변	Ⓖ 자연의 아름다움과 산책로 즐거움
Ⓖ 자연의 아름다움과 산책로 즐거움	

04
공동 산책로 프로젝트는 험버 강 계곡을 따라 10km를 누비며 험버 강둑을 따라 캐나다 초기 역사를 발생한 대로 보여 주는 13개의 역사적인 접점으로 구성되어 있다. Ⓐ▪ 문화유산

과 험버 강 역사는 험버 강에서 원주민들이 역사적으로 존재하였다는 것을 보여 주며, 이들은 후에 프랑스인들과 영국인들에게 쫓겨나게 되었다. 토론토 역사 협회(La Societe d'histoire de Toronto)는 토론토 지역보존기관(TRCA)과 토론토 시와 협력하여 착수한 프로젝트를 추진하였다. Ⓑ▪ 지난달 100여 명의 사람들이 원주민들의 공동 산책로를 공식적으로 공개하기 위해 에티엔 브룰레이 공원의 험버 강 동편 강둑에 모였다. **공동 산책로의 명판은 험버 강의 역사를 고대 원주민 육로인 현대의 도로와 철로까지, 첫 원주민 초기 시대에서 18세기 프랑스 무역 중심지와 프랑스 토론토의 출발까지, 물방아의 유적에서부터 산업시대 토론토의 탄생까지 두 언어로 상세히 소개한다.** Ⓒ▪ 명판의 내용은 원주민의 언어를 포함한다. **프로젝트는 이 사람들도 이 지역에 살았다는 것을 인식하고자 하였다; 즉 험버 강은 3개국(원주민, 프랑스인과 영국의 정착민)이 나라의 기반을 삼은 곳이었다.** Ⓓ▪ 원주민들은 자신들의 거주지를 잃고 초기 정착민들에 의해 쫓겨나게 되었다. 이 프로젝트는 국립공원 안에 있으며 전체 산책로를 모두 가 볼 수 있다. 누구나 그곳에 갈 수 있다. 토론토의 최근 디스커버리 워크는 험버 강에서 시작된 광범위한 원주민 역사를 기념한다.

어휘_ consist of ~로 구성되다 node 마디, 매듭 cultural heritage 문화유산 unveiling 제막식, 덮개를 벗기다 plaque 명판, 플라그 entire trail 등산로 전체, 전체 흔적

1. Ⓐ
작가는 지문에서 **공동 산책로 프로젝트**를 왜 언급하고 있는가?
Ⓐ 캐나다 원주민의 문화유산을 인식하기 위해
Ⓑ 캐나다인이 캐나다를 설립한 세 국가의 유산을 인정하도록 촉구하기 위해
Ⓒ 원주민이 초기 정착민에게 그들의 거주지를 빼앗겼다는 사실을 비난하기 위해
Ⓓ 주요한 역사적 발전을 축하하기 위해

2. Ⓓ
음영 처리된 문장에 따르면 다음 중 어느 것이 추론될 수 있는가?
Ⓐ 프랑스와 영국 정착민뿐만 아니라 원주민의 유적들도 험버 강을 따라 발견되었다.
Ⓑ 험버 강은 캐나다 초기 역사의 중요한 부분이었다.
Ⓒ 캐나다를 설립한 3개국 간의 많은 전쟁이 험버 강 지역에서 있었다.
Ⓓ 원주민의 거주지는 캐나다 역사에서 충분히 인정되지 않아왔다.

3. Ⓒ
다음의 문장이 지문에 추가될 수 있는 곳을 표시하는 네모 박스 [▪]를 보시오.

공동 산책로의 명판은 험버 강의 역사를 고대 원주민 육로인 현대의 도로와 철로까지, 첫 원주민 초기 시대에서 18세기 프랑스 무역 중심지와 프랑스 토론토의 출발까지, 물방아의 유적에서부터 산업시대 토론토의 탄생까지 두 언어로 상세히 소개한다.

문장이 어느 곳에 가장 적합한가?
문장을 지문에 추가하도록 한 개의 네모 박스 [■]를 클릭하시오.

05

모든 사람들이 파리에 먹으러 간다는 것은 사실이고 그 또한 영감을 주고 기분을 들뜨게 하는 일일 것이다. 시장의 복잡한 관습, 와인의 복합적인 양상(그리고 어디서 마시는 것이 가장 좋은지 결정하는 것), 심지어 당신이 그곳에 대해 들어 본 적이 없는데 어떻게 장소가 좋은지 아는 것 – **이런 암호를 깨는** 데는 시간이 걸린다. 가이드는 반대로 당신이 발견할 수 없는 숨어 있는 곳들을 종종 보여주면서 당신이 그것을 할 수 있도록 도와줄 것이다. 린은 레프트 뱅크 주변으로 우리를 데려가서 레몬 커드 패스트리에서부터 당나귀 고기 살라미까지 모든 것을 시식하며 지난 몇 시간을 보냈다. 이제 우리는 일본식 닭튀김에 린을 위해 매니저가 남겨두었던 올해 첫 포도주인 모르건 2010을 한잔하며 오늘의 공식적인 관광을 막 끝내려 한다. 난 정말 여기가 좋고 나처럼 사람들이 이 도시를 체험할 수 있도록 돕고 싶다. 끝으로 린은 레스 할레스와 세인트 저르메인 같은 음식이 유명한 동네를 중심으로 페르시안 전통의 특이함을 바탕으로 한 정보로 가득 찬 4인까지의 소그룹을 위해 개인별 음식관광을 제안한다. 이제 그녀는 소박한 작은 식당과 범주에 맞춰 분류하기 힘든 시장에서부터 다른 곳이 아닌 여기서만 얻을 수 있는 물건들로 북적이는 가게들까지 있는 비밀 기록부를 함께 나눌 것이다. 직접 느낄 수 있는 파리? 멀리서 찾지 마라.

어휘_ exhilarating 아주 신나는 rituals 의례, 의식 절차 facet 측면, 양상 haunts 나타나다, 출몰하다 magnum 매그넘(포도주 등을 담는 1.5리터짜리 병), 역작 quirk 기이한 일, 기벽 category-defying 분류를 거부하는

1. ©

지문의 **이런 암호를 깨다**라는 구문과 의미가 가장 비슷한 것은?
Ⓐ 독립하다　　　　　　　Ⓑ 발생하다
© 이해하다　　　　　　　Ⓓ 번역하다

해설_ 지문에서 crack such codes(이런 암호를 깨다)는 들어 본 적이 없는 장소가 왜 좋은지 알게 되는 것이므로 문맥상 '이해하다'가 적절하다. 따라서 ©가 정답이다. Ⓓ는 문맥상 번역하는 게 아니므로 적절하지 않다.

2. Ⓐ

지문에서 작가는 ~고 말하므로써 린의 역할을 설명하고 있다.
Ⓐ 당신에게 파리에서 식사할 좋은 장소를 안내할 수 있다
Ⓑ 그녀 없이 가는 사람들에게 파리의 시장은 무섭다
© 린의 가이드 관광 없이 파리에서 식사하는 것은 불가능하다
Ⓓ 상품을 구비한 많은 상점을 갖고 있다

해설_ 지문에서 린은 관광객을 안내하며 여러 음식을 시식하게 해주었고 개인별 음식관광을 제안하고 있으므로 정답은 Ⓐ이다.

3. Guided Tours: Ⓐ, ©, Ⓓ /
Private Food Tours: Ⓔ, Ⓕ

지시사항 보기에서 알맞은 구를 선택하여 그것과 관련된 관광에 맞게 연결하시오. 각 항목은 정답으로 중복 선택되지 않는다. **이 문제는 3점이 주어진다.**

> 선택지를 관련있는 곳으로 끌어당기시오. 끌어당긴 선택지를 삭제하려면 그 위에 대고 클릭하시오. 지문을 다시 보려면 **View Text** 아이콘을 클릭하시오.

보기	가이드 관광
Ⓐ 시장의 복잡한 관습	Ⓐ 시장의 복잡한 관습
Ⓑ 암호를 깨는 것	© 하루의 공식적인 관광
© 하루의 공식적인 관광	Ⓓ 숨어 있는 곳들 찾기
Ⓓ 숨어 있는 곳들 찾기	**개별 음식 관광**
Ⓔ 독특한 전통에 대한 조언	Ⓔ 독특한 전통에 대한 조언
Ⓕ 파리를 직접 느낌	Ⓕ 파리를 직접 느낌
Ⓖ 비밀 기록부 찾기	

해설_ 지문의 앞과 중간 부분에서 시장의 복잡한 관습과 공식적인 관광, 숨어 있는 곳들을 찾기는 가이드 관광에 대한 설명이다. 뒤 부분에서 개별 음식관광이 페르시안 전통정보를 바탕으로 구성되고 파리를 직접 느낄 수 있다고 하였으므로 Guided Tours: Ⓐ, ©, Ⓓ / Private Food Tours: Ⓔ, Ⓕ가 정답이다. Ⓑ, Ⓖ는 관광을 설명하기 위한 비유로 등장한 표현이므로 오답이다.

Vocabulary & Paraphrasing

1. 아래에 있는 각 뜻에 맞는 단어를 박스에서 찾아서 쓰시오.

① divine	② deity	③ consort
④ scam	⑤ novice	⑥ congest
⑦ swam	⑧ boardwalk	⑨ weave
⑩ plaque		

2. 다음 문장을 해석 후 아래 지시대로 paraphrasing(다른 말로 바꿔 표현하기)하세요.

① 이런 위대한 신과 여신들 주위에는 하위 신들이 모여 있었으며 그중 몇몇은 정해진 위치에서 특정한 명성을 누렸다.

➡ 예시_ Sub-gods gathered around these great gods and goddesses, and a few of them enjoyed a certain reputation in a fixed position.

② 나는 그 남자를 따라 낡고 녹이 슨 픽업 트럭인 그의 '택시'로 갔다. 그러나 고맙게도 멈추고 '절대 안 돼'라고 말하고 합법적인 택시를 타는 행렬로 다시 돌아갈 정도로 정신이 들었다.

➡ 예시_ I followed the man to his old rusty pickup truck, "taxi", but thankfully stopped, saying "No, never," regaining my senses to return to the line for a legitimate taxi.

③ 두 개의 해안을 따라 마이애미 파티 장면에서 저 멀리 한적한 캘러데시 섬까지 끊임없이 펼쳐져 있는 모래사장이 있고 많은 사람들이 모이는 혼잡한 해변을 미국에서 가장 많이 갖고 있는 주는 바로 플로리다이다.

➡ 예시_ Along the coast of the United States where sand constantly stretches away from Miami's party scene to the secluded Caladesi Island, the state of Florida has the greatest number of crowded beaches in the US.

④ 공동 산책로의 명판은 험버 강의 역사를 고대 원주민 육로인 현대의 도로와 철로까지 첫 원주민 초기 시대에서 18세기 프랑스 무역 중심지와 프랑스 토론토의 출발지까지, 물방아의 유적에서부터 산업시대 토론토의 탄생까지 두 언어로 상세히 소개한다.

➡ 예시_ Shared Path nameplates describe Humber River history in two languages. The history lies from being an ancient native American transport route to modern roads and railways, from First Nations' settlements to 18th century French trading posts and the beginnings of French Toronto, and from the ruins of water mills to the birth of industrial Toronto.

Unit 09 Science and Technology_ P. 287

01

과학자들은 종종 인간 장기의 성장 연구를 위해 실험실에서 다른 종의 생물을 사용한다. 제브라피시와 쥐들이 이런 연구에 사용되어 왔다. 둘 다 인간 장기와 비슷한 역할을 하는 내부 장기를 가지고 있다. 유전 공학은 장기 성장에 문제가 있는 유전자를 가진 제브라피시와 쥐들을 생산하는 데 사용될 수 있다. Ⓐ■ 서로 다른 장기의 형성에 관련된 유전자를 분석하기 위해서 과학자들은 수년 넘는 연구에 수천 마리의 쥐를 필요로 할 것이다. **게다가 장기 형성은 어미의 자궁에서 발생하기 때문에 쥐의 배아의 장기 형성을 관찰하는 것은 어려울 수 있다.** Ⓑ■ 과학자들은 제브라피시가 쥐에 비해 몇몇 장점이 있기 때문에 실험실에서 제브라피시를 사용하기 시작했다. Ⓒ■ 그들은 90일 안에 다 자라고 한 번의 짝짓기로 수백 마리의 새끼를 낳는다. 그 배아는 투명하고 암컷의 몸 밖에서 성장한다.

Ⓓ■ 과학자는 실질적으로 장기가 성장하는 것을 볼 수 있다.

어휘_ internal organs 내부기관, 내장 genetic engineering 유전공학 offspring 자식, 자손 mating 짝짓기 embryo 배아

1. Ⓑ
지문에 따르면 다음 중 어느 것이 사실이 아닌가?
Ⓐ 많은 쥐가 인간 장기 개발 성장 연구에 쓰일 필요가 있다.
Ⓑ 연구에 사용되는 제브라피시와 쥐는 우성 유전자를 갖는다.
Ⓒ 생쥐의 배아 장기의 성장을 살피는 게 거의 힘들다.
Ⓓ 제브라피시는 한 번에 쥐보다 더 많은 새끼를 갖는다.

2. Ⓑ
다음의 문장이 지문에 추가될 수 있는 곳을 표시하는 네모 박스 [■]를 보시오.
게다가 장기 형성은 어미의 자궁에서 발생하기 때문에 쥐의 배아의 장기 형성을 지켜보는 것은 어려울 수 있다.
문장이 어느 곳에 가장 적합한가?
문장을 지문에 추가하도록 한 개의 네모 박스 [■]를 클릭하시오.

3. Zebra Fish: Ⓐ, Ⓒ, Ⓖ / Mice: Ⓑ, Ⓓ
지시사항 선택지에서 알맞은 구를 선택하여 그것과 관련된 생물 종에 맞게 연결하시오. 각 항목은 정답으로 중복 선택되지 않는다.
이 문제는 3점이 주어진다.

선택지를 관련있는 곳으로 끌어당기시오. 끌어당긴 선택지를 삭제하려면 그 위에 대고 클릭하시오. 지문을 다시 보려면 **View Text** 아이콘을 클릭하시오.

선택지	제브라피시
Ⓐ 한 번의 짝짓기에서 수백 마리의 새끼를 생산	Ⓐ 한 번의 짝짓기에서 수백 마리의 새끼를 생산
Ⓑ 어미의 자궁에서 성장하는 배아	Ⓒ 투명한 배아
Ⓒ 투명한 배아	Ⓖ 배아가 엄마의 몸 밖에서 성장
Ⓓ 장기 성장에 관여하는 유전자를 분석하는 데 필요한 수천 마리	쥐
Ⓔ 인간 장기와 비슷한	Ⓑ 어미의 자궁에서 성장하는 배아
Ⓕ 배아의 장기 성장이 어려운	Ⓓ 장기 성장에 관여하는 유전자를 분석하는 데 필요한 수천 마리
Ⓖ 배아가 엄마의 몸 밖에서 성장	

해설_ Ⓕ는 배아의 장기 성장이 아니라 성장을 관찰하는 것이 어려우므로 오답이다.

02

지구에서의 삶과 정착지인 '세계 함정'에서의 삶이 근본적으로 차이가 있음에도 불구하고 승선한 삶을 최대한 지상의 삶과 유사하게 만드는 데 도움이 되도록 많은 일들이 이루어질 것이다. **지구에서 수 세기에 걸쳐 개발한 설계 제도는 최대**

10,000명의 영구 정착민을 수용할 수 있는 지속 가능한 우주 식민지를 설계함에 있어 필요한 귀중한 도구의 역할을 할 수 있을 것이다. 현재 우주 여행과 우주에서의 삶과 관련된 이미지들은 종종 매우 실용적인 차원에서 설계된 틀, 경량 금속으로 된 피복, 무균 섬유, 방향 없이 둥둥 떠다니는 약간의 장비 등을 떠올리게 한다. 이전의 스카이랩, 미르 같은 우주 정거장과 국제 우주 정거장(ISS)은 그러한 실용적이고 기본만 있는 설계 솔루션만을 구축한 반면 영구적인 '집'과 같은 거주지를 새 정착민들에게 비슷하게 하려는 시도들이 성공할 가능성도 있다. 그러한 방안들이 다소 경제적이라면 정착민들이 영구적으로 살 수 있는 영구적인 '세계 함정'을 개발하기 위해서는 전체적으로 새로운 설계 기준의 구축과 여기 지구에 있는 건축학적, 공간적 디자인 관례를 훨씬 더 밀접하게 조정할 필요가 있다.

어휘_ is similar to ~와 비슷하다 inhabitation 주거, 주소 conjure 마술을 하다 clad ~을 입은 sterile 불임의, 메마른 emulate 모방하다 semblance 외관, 겉모습 perpetual 끊임없이 계속되는

1. Ⓐ
아래 문장 중 지문에 음영 처리된 문장의 핵심정보를 가장 잘 표현하고 있는 것은? 오답 선택지는 현저하게 의미를 바꾸거나 핵심정보를 생략한 것이다.
Ⓐ 기존 우주 정거장의 설계는 장기적인 우주 식민지 실행에 가능하지 않을 것이다.
Ⓑ 우주 식민지를 위해 우주 정거장을 위한 조건을 복제하려고 하여도 아무 소용이 없을 것이다.
Ⓒ 우주 정거장은 실용적인 목적을 위해 만들어졌지만 우주 식민지는 새로운 개념이 필요할 것이다.
Ⓓ 우주 정거장의 실례가 없다면 과학자들이 장기적인 우주 식민지에 대한 최상의 조건을 모를 것이다.

2. Ⓑ
지문의 기본만 있는이라는 어휘와 의미가 가장 비슷한 것은?
Ⓐ 실용적인   Ⓑ 기본적인
Ⓒ 검소한   Ⓓ 현대적인

3. Ⓐ, Ⓔ, Ⓖ
지시사항 지문을 간략하게 요약하기 위한 도입문장이 아래에 제시되어 있다. 지문에서 가장 중요한 정보를 담고 있는 3개의 선택지를 선택하여 요약을 완성한다. 지문에 제시되지 않은 정보나 세부정보를 담고 있는 일부 문장은 요약에 들어가지 않는다. 이 문제는 2점이 주어진다.

선택지를 관련있는 곳으로 끌어당기시오. 끌어당긴 선택지를 삭제하려면 그 위에 대고 클릭하시오. 지문을 다시 보려면 View Text 아이콘을 클릭하시오.

영구적인 식민지로서의 세계 함정은 현재의 우주 정거장에 비해 완전히 새로운 설계 기준을 필요로 한다.

Ⓐ 지구는 잠재적인 우주 식민지 디자인에 가장 적합한 모델을 제공한다.
Ⓔ 장기적 우주 식민지에서의 삶은 지구의 삶을 모방하도록 만들어질 필요가 있다.
Ⓖ 우주 정거장의 현재 건설 모델은 우주 식민지에 불충분하다.

선택지
Ⓐ 지구는 잠재적인 우주 식민지 디자인에 가장 적합한 모델을 제공한다.
Ⓑ 미래의 우주 식민지는 지구의 생활과 크게 다를 것이다.
Ⓒ 우주 정거장에 대한 설계 기준은 주로 경제적 요인에 따라 달라질 것이다.
Ⓓ 실용적인 요구는 지구 모델에 기초하여 우주 정거장을 설계하도록 고려되어야 한다.
Ⓔ 장기적 우주 식민지에서의 삶은 지구의 삶을 모방하도록 만들어질 필요가 있다.
Ⓕ 새로운 우주 식민지는 거주뿐 아니라 지속 가능해야 한다.
Ⓖ 우주 정거장의 현재 건설 모델은 우주 식민지에 불충분하다.

03
태양은 지구의 생물에게 두 가지 상충되는 역할을 한다. 한편으로 태양은 우리가 생존하고 번성할 수 있도록 지구의 온도를 올리고 다른 한편으로는 삶을 위협하는 자외선 방사와 전기로 충전된 입자들을 내보낸다. 태양풍이라고 불리는 이 입자들의 흐름은 시속 수백만km로 행성계를 통해 불며 주로 수소와 헬륨이온으로 이루어져 있다. 25년 전에 태양 표면의 폭발로 인해 태양풍의 돌연한 폐해가 밝혀졌다; 태양 폭발의 빈도는 하루에 여러 번에서 2주에 한 번까지 11년 주기로 다양하다. 이런 폭발은 거대한 가스 덩어리를 행성 간의 우주 공간에 퍼붓는다. 이것들은 특히 태양 활동이 최고조로 달하는 기간에 간헐적으로 지구에 도달한다. 그 가스 덩어리 입자들의 폭격은 우주에서 활동 중인 우주 비행사를 몇 시간 동안 증가한 양의 방사선에 노출되게 하고 원거리 통신과 텔레비전 위성 장치의 전자 시스템을 파괴할 수 있다.

어휘_ radiation 방사선 particle 입자, 조각 hydrogen 수소 helium 헬륨 abrupt 갑작스러운 eruption 폭발, 분화 hurl 던지다 bombardment 포격, 폭격 astronaut 우주 비행사

1. Ⓒ
작가는 왜 지문에서 태양풍의 돌연한 폐해를 언급하고 있는가?
Ⓐ 태양이 지구에 위협이 될 수 있다는 것을 강조하기 위해
Ⓑ 태양이 지구에 취하는 위협의 유형 중 하나를 분류하기 위해
Ⓒ 태양이 지구를 위협한다는 주장을 지원하기 위해
Ⓓ 태양이 지구를 위협할 수 있다는 아이디어를 부정하기 위해

2. ©

지문의 단어 이것들이 가리키는 것은?

Ⓐ 태양풍 폐해
Ⓑ 태양 표면의 폭발
© 가스의 거대한 질량
Ⓓ 행성 간의 우주 공간

3. Ⓐ

왜 몇몇 전자 기기가 제대로 작동하지 않을 수 있는가?

Ⓐ 태양 표면의 폭발이 많은 양의 입자와 함께 지구에 도달하기 때문에
Ⓑ 아무것도 태양열의 파괴력으로부터 보호될 수 없기 때문에
© 강한 바람이 전자 시스템을 방해하는 가스를 만들기 때문에
Ⓓ 태양 폭발은 엄청난 에너지를 발생시켜 전기 시스템에 과부하를 주기 때문에

04

현재 NASA(미항공우주국)의 전략 중 많은 부분은 우주 비행을 발전시켜 인간의 우주 비행 작전에 참여하는 민간 부분의 역할을 지원하는 것이다 – 상업 서비스 제공자들로 인해 더 저렴하고 더 효율적으로 지구의 저궤도에 접근할 수 있다는 희망으로. 이론적으로 이 전략은 지구의 궤도 너머의 탐험이 진전되고 기술이 발전하도록 NASA에 날개를 달아 줄 것이다. 하지만 이 전략에서 분명하게 정의한 목적은 없다: 달, 화성 또는 지구와 가까운 소행성 모두 목적지가 될 수 있다. 표면적으로 볼 때 이것은 예를 들어 달로의 귀환이나 화성으로 미션과 같은 특별한 목적이 결부된 분명한 비전이 결여되어 있다. **그리고 기술 개발이나 직접적인 작전 활동을 추진할 임무가 없다는 비판은 어느 정도 일리가 있다.** NASA는 목표 지향적이고 무엇인가 구체적일 때 가장 왕성한 활동을 해왔다. 제도적으로 NASA는 임무의 목표에서 얻어진 정확히 규정된 요구 사항에 따라 움직이는 엔지니어링 문화를 가지고 있다. 그리고 아직까지 민간 사업자를 도입하려는 NASA의 전략은 달이나 화성에 대고 총을 쏘는 것만큼이나 대담한 일이다. 어떤 면에서 이것은 미래라는 목적지를 설정한 것이다: 인간의 우주 탐험은 경제적으로 지속 가능한 방법으로 계속될 것이다. 이달 말에 우주선 X – 닷컴 회사의 억만장자가 자금을 마련하고 운영하는 상업팀 – 는 팰컨의 아홉 개 발사 장치 중의 하나로 무인 드래곤 캡슐을 발사하여 국제 우주 정거장과 랑데부할 것을 기대하고 있다. 드래곤 캡슐은 최고 7명의 우주인까지 인간 승무원을 지원할 수 있다; 이 시험이 성공한다면 우주선 X는 미래 인간의 우주 여행에 중대한 역할을 하게 될 것으로 보인다.

어휘_ in the hope that ~을 희망하여, 희망을 갖고 orbit 궤도 institutionally 제도적으로 be derived from ~에서 나오다, 파생하다 embracing 껴안은 outfit 옷, 장비 rendezvous 만남, 만나다

1. Ⓑ

지문에 따르면 다음 중 어느 것이 사실이 아닌가?

Ⓐ NASA는 현재의 전략이 명확하게 정의된 목표를 가지고 있지 않아 보인다.
Ⓑ NASA는 인간의 우주 비행 운영에 앞장서고 있다.
© NASA는 우주선 개발에 민간 사업 공급자를 지원하고 있다.
Ⓓ 인간의 우주 탐사는 미래에 경제적으로 지속될 수 있을 것이다.

2. Ⓓ

지문의 단어 이것이 가리키는 것은?

Ⓐ 지구 근접 소행성
Ⓑ 낮은 지구 궤도로의 접근 확보
© 지구 궤도를 넘어선 탐험
Ⓓ 더 명확하게 정의된 목적지의 부재

3. Ⓐ

작가는 지문 속의 음영 처리된 문장에서 NASA에 관해 무엇을 암시하고 있는가?

Ⓐ 명확한 임무 없이는 NASA가 기술적으로 발전하지 않을 것이다.
Ⓑ 단지 누구나처럼 NASA가 비판의 대상이 되는 것은 타당하다.
© NASA는 목적과 방향의 감각을 잃었다.
Ⓓ NASA를 비난하는 것은 타당하지 않다.

05

연료 전지들은 화학적 에너지를 전기로 바꾸는 데 사용되는 가장 흔한 촉매가 잘못된 재료로 만들어지기 때문에 비효율적이다. 우리는 **그것**이 보다 역할을 잘하게 하기 위해 재료 – 백금 – 를 더욱 효율적으로 만들고 고치려는 무모한 노력을 계속하기보다는 새로운 출발을 해야 한다. 백금을 사용하는 것은 시스템에 저항기를 놓는 것과 같다. 만약 우리가 이것을 더욱 효율적으로 할 촉매를 발견할 수 있다면, 한계 가능성에 가까워지고 연료 전지로부터 더 많은 에너지를 얻게 될 것이다. 심지어 최상의 환경에서도 몇몇의 자동차 회사들에 의해 테스트된 연료 전지의 에너지를 생산하는 화학적 반응은 전기로 변화할 수 있는 에너지의 4분의 1을 낭비한다. 이러한 점은 과학 분야 사회에서 잘 인식되어 있지만 지금까지 그 문제를 다루기 위한 노력은 성과가 없었다고 판명되었다. 실패는 에너지 손실의 이유에 책임을 둘 수 있다. 가장 널리 받아들여진 이론은 불순물들이 음극의 백금 표면에 붙어 있어 기대되는 반

응을 막고 있다는 것이다. 산소 증감 실험으로 인해 얻어진 자료는 백금과 산소 감소 반응 동안에 형성된 중간 분자 사이에 시각적인 결합력을 계산하기 위하여 사용될 수 있다. 그 반응은 백금이 입혀진 음극에서 발생된다. 중간 분자들이 음극에 너무 빽빽하거나 너무 헐렁하게 결합하게 되면 반응을 감속시키고 전압을 떨어뜨린다는 사실이 발견되었다. 그 결과는 연료 전지가 잠재적으로 최대 1.23볼트 대신에 0.93볼트 정도 생산한다는 것이다. 손실을 없애기 위해서는 우리의 계산에 따르면 산소 감소 동안 일어나는 모든 반응이 1.23볼트 아니면 가능한 1.23볼트에 가깝게 발생하도록 촉매가 결합력이 꼭 맞게 만들어져야 한다.

어휘_ fuel cell 연료전지, 연료전지 발진 inefficient 비효율적인 catalyst 촉매, 기폭제 is made of ~로 구성되다 anew 다시, 새로 fruitless 성과 없는 impurity 불순물 cathode 음극 platinum-coated cathode 백금 도금된 음극(캐소드) tailored 잘 맞도록 만든

1. ©
다음 중 어느 것이 지문의 내용으로부터 결론 내려질 수 있는가?
Ⓐ 과학자들은 연료 전지의 효율을 개선하기 위해 노력하는 대신에 새로운 절차를 찾을 필요가 있다.
Ⓑ 연료 전지의 효율성은 과학자들이 의논해 봐야 불가능하다.
© 신규 촉매는 연료 전지의 효율을 향상시키기 위해 필요하다.
Ⓓ 전기 자동차가 효율적이 되기까지는 극복해야 할 문제가 많다.
해설_ 지문의 주제는 '연료 전지의 효율성을 향상시키기 위해 새로운 촉매가 필요하다' 이며 주제를 따르는 세부설명이 뒤에 나오므로 ©가 정답이다.

2. Ⓐ
지문의 단어 그것이 가리키는 것은?
Ⓐ 촉매   Ⓑ 에너지 사용
© 백금   Ⓓ 시스템
해설_ it가 있는 문장에서 그것의 역할을 더 잘하기 위한 방법을 찾으므로 가리키는 대상은 앞 문장의 the catalyst(촉매)이다. 따라서 정답은 Ⓐ이다.

3. ©
지문에 따르면 에너지 손실의 문제는 ~으로써 해결될 수 있다.
Ⓐ 백금 이외의 다른 재료를 사용함
Ⓑ 문제점을 해결하기 위해 더 많은 노력을 기울임
© 백금과 중간 분자의 접합 강도를 향상시킴
Ⓓ 백금 코팅된 음극으로부터의 반응을 이동시킴
해설_ 지문의 후반부에서 백금이 입혀진 음극과 중간 분자들이 너무 빽빽하거나 헐렁하게 결합되면 에너지 손실이 발생한다고 하였으므로 정답은 ©이다.

Vocabulary & Paraphrasing

1. 아래에 있는 각 뜻에 맞는 단어를 박스에서 찾아서 쓰시오.

① embracing   ② dwarf   ③ perpetual
④ mitigation   ⑤ inherent   ⑥ sustainability
⑦ genetic   ⑧ demise   ⑨ utilitarian
⑩ rendezvous

2. 다음 문장을 해석 후 아래 지시대로 paraphrasing(다른 말로 바꿔 표현하기)하세요.

① 지구에서의 삶과 정착지인 '세계 함정'에서의 삶이 근본적으로 차이가 있음에도 불구하고 지구 저 너머의 삶을 최대한 지상의 삶과 유사하게 만드는 데 도움이 되도록 많은 일들이 이루어질 것이다.

➡ 예시_ There are clear differences between them but there are many ways that life on a colonial "worldship" can be made as close as possible to life on Earth.

② 그 발견은 2015년 NASA 우주선이 예정대로 도착하기 전에 명왕성을 관찰하기 위해 허블 우주 망원경을 사용하던 중에 이루어졌다.

➡ 예시_ Scientists made the discovery with the Hubble space telescope when they were observing Pluto before a NASA spacecraft was due to arrive there in 2015.

③ 그것은 우주 프로그램에서 추진제로 널리 사용되는 히드라진과 같은 물질과 독성이 감소된 추진제와 함께 녹색 추진 정책의 개발에 관한 규정에 영향을 미칠 것이다.

➡ 예시_ There will be an effect on the rules for substances like hydrazine, used as a propellant in space programs, and the development of Green Propulsion with propellants containing less toxicity.

④ 드래곤 캡슐은 최고 7명의 우주인까지 인간 승무원을 지원할 수 있다; 이 시험이 성공한다면 우주선 X는 미래 인간의 우주여행에 중대한 역할을 하게 될 것으로 보인다.

➡ 예시_ Up to seven astronauts can be supported by the Dragon capsule and Space X may play a significant role in future manned space flight if tests prove successful.

Unit 10 Art & Literature_ P. 301

01
중세 문학은 현대 독자들에게 중세 시대의 생활상을 엿볼 수 있는 기회를 제공한다. 예를 들어 14세기의 작품 중에 왕이 로마의 손님들에게 최고의 숙소를 제공받도록 지시한 한 글귀가 있다: 그들의 숙소는 굴뚝이 있는 방으로 변경되었다. 이 당시 성 안에 사는 모든 사람들은 벽난로 근처 중앙 홀에서 잠을 잤기 때문에 개인 방에 불이 있다는 것은 대단한 부의 상징이

었다. 또한 시를 통해서 고급 음식이 어떤 것인지 알 수 있다. 금 접시에 담은 공작과 물떼새 / 새끼돼지와 고슴도치; 그리고 은 접시에 담아온 커다란 백조 / 터키 타르트…. 시는 로마 사람들에게 매우 깊은 인상을 남긴 호화로운 연회와 고급 식기들을 묘사하고 있다. 중세 문학을 연구하는 또 다른 이유는 이들의 대중적 인기이다. 이 이야기들은 글로 쓰이기 전에 이미 수많은 음유 시인들에 의해 궁궐에서 궁궐로, 성에서 성으로 이야기가 전해졌다. 유럽의 절반은 이 이야기들을 알고 있다. **'그것'을 현대를 사는 우리 시대에 인기 있는 책들이 차지하는 위치와 비교해 보면 각 이야기는 중세 시대의 삶을 수놓은 하나의 실낱 이상이라는 것이 분명해진다.** 그렇다면 우리는 역사의 진실을 연구하면서 어떻게 이러한 문학 작품들을 무시할 수 있을까?

어휘_ Medieval literature 중세 문학 the Middle Ages 중세시대 the finest accommodations 최고의 숙소 peacocks and plovers 공작과 물떼새 a sumptuous feast 호화스러운 연회 hundreds of minstrels 수많은 [수백의] 음유시인

1. ⓓ
다음 중 어느 것이 지문의 내용으로부터 결론 내려질 수 있는가?
Ⓐ 우리는 그 당시의 삶을 이해하는 중세 문학을 읽어야 한다.
Ⓑ 중세 문학은 사람들의 삶의 모든 측면을 다룬다.
Ⓒ 문학은 우리가 그것이 쓰인 기간을 이해하게 도와준다.
Ⓓ 문학은 중세 시대를 이해하는 데 귀중한 도움이 된다.

2. Ⓐ
지문의 단어 그것이 가리키는 것은?
Ⓐ 수백 명의 음유 시인들에 의해 들려지는 이야기
Ⓑ 쓰여 내려오는 이야기
Ⓒ 이야기를 아는 유럽의 절반
Ⓓ 화려한 진수성찬과 최고급 식기에 관한 시

3. Ⓐ
아래 문장 중 어떤 것이 지문 속의 음영된 문장의 핵심정보를 가장 잘 표현하고 있는가?
Ⓐ 중세의 시는 우리 시대에 인기 있는 책들이 있는 것처럼 그 사회에서 같은 위치를 지녔다.
Ⓑ 전체적인 중세의 삶은 오늘날 우리의 삶처럼 이야기로 구성되었다.
Ⓒ 중세에 가장 중요한 이야기는 우리의 인기 도서만큼 영향력을 가졌다.
Ⓓ 중세 시대와 우리 시대에 시가 끼치는 영향력은 비교할 수 없다.

02
조선 시대 초기 풍경화의 한 가지 중요한 부분은 예를 들어 망

명과 애통으로 알려져 있는 역사적인 지역이며 지금의 후난 지역인 소상강같이 문학의 명성과 향수를 갖는 중국의 풍경이나 장소들을 보여주는 작업으로 구성되어 있다. 그림의 주제는 고려 시대에(918~1392)에 알려지고 채택되었음에도 불구하고 15세기와 16세기에 이르러 후세에까지 대부분 현존하는 그림들과 함께 새로운 인기를 누렸다. 그러는 동안에 당시 중국의 명나라 왕조 때는 이를 주제로 한 그림의 수와 명성이 송나라 초기 시대에 비해 줄어들었다. 조선 초기의 팔경을 표현하는 족자와 가리개는 이런 고전적 주제와 풍경화의 한국적 변화를 더욱 넓게 대표한다. 팔경 중에 으뜸이 되는 이 시대의 많은 풍경화들은 15세기경에 활동했던 조선 초기의 가장 유명하고 영향력 있는 풍경화가 이후에 생긴 안견 스타일로 그려졌다. 안견 스타일의 몇 가지 주목할 만한 기법은 채움과 비움의 극적인 투시, 명암과 잉크 색조 사이의 효과적인 대조 그리고 힘 있는 붓질과 수묵화의 입체감 표현법을 갖는 소나무와 구름 같은 산의 형태를 포함한다.

어휘_ significant 중요한 with exile and lament 망명과 애통으로 dwindled 줄어들었다 notable feature 주목할 만한 기법 interpenetration 상호 침투, 상호 표현 brushstroke 붓질

1. Ⓑ
다음 중 어느 것이 지문의 내용으로부터 결론 내려질 수 있는가?
Ⓐ 그것은 조선 초기 동안 중국 문학이 어떻게 한국 미술에 영향을 미쳤는지 보여준다.
Ⓑ 그것은 조선 초기의 산수화의 특성을 설명한다.
Ⓒ 그것은 안견 스타일의 주목할 만한 기법을 소개한다.
Ⓓ 그것은 고려 시대와 조선 시대 간의 예술의 변화를 비교한다.

2. Ⓓ
지문에 따르면 다음 중 어느 것이 조선 시대 초기 풍경화에 관한 사실이 아닌가?
Ⓐ 중국에 있는 그 장소의 풍경은 이 시대에 인기가 있었다.
Ⓑ 안견 스타일이 이 시대에 광범위하게 사용되었다.
Ⓒ 당대 명나라 왕조 화가는 이 풍경에 흥미를 잃기 시작했다.
Ⓓ 팔경을 그린 조선 초기의 족자 및 가리개는 중국 스타일을 모방했다.

3. **Early Joseon: Ⓐ, Ⓓ, Ⓕ /**
Ming-dynasty China: Ⓑ, Ⓒ
지시사항 선택지에서 알맞은 구를 선택하여 시대와 관련된 칸에 맞게 연결하시오. **이 문제는 3점이 주어진다.**

선택지를 관련있는 곳으로 끌어당기시오. 끌어당긴 선택지를 삭제하려면 그 위에 대고 클릭하시오. 지문을 다시 보려면 **View Text** 아이콘을 클릭하시오.

선택지	조선 초기
Ⓐ 안견 스타일로 그려진	Ⓐ 안견 스타일로 그려진
Ⓑ 샤오와 시앙 강 같은 풍경에 흥미를 잃음	Ⓓ 명성과 향수를 갖는 중국의 풍경이나 장소들을 보여주는
Ⓒ 고전적 주제	Ⓕ 힘 있는 붓질과 수묵화의 입체감 표현법을 갖는
Ⓓ 명성과 향수를 갖는 중국의 풍경이나 장소들을 보여주는	**명 왕조**
Ⓔ 현존하는 그림	Ⓑ 샤오와 시앙 강 같은 풍경에 흥미를 잃음
Ⓕ 힘 있는 붓질과 수묵화의 입체감 표현법을 갖는	Ⓒ 고전적 주제
Ⓖ 망명과 애통으로 알려져 있는	

03

전에 그가 전쟁의 상영장이라 일컬었으며, 중동의 국외자의 시선을 형성할 것 같은 폭력의 거의 의례적인 장면들로 이뤄진, 사진가의 **웨스트 뱅크** 이미지들은 세계의 아주 **다루기 힘든** '화합'의 난리 법석 이상으로 보였다. 그 사진들은 '경험의 소품문(小品文)들'이었다. 그것들은 삭막하고 동시에 황량하지만 쌓여 온 역사와 기억이 수백 년에 걸쳐 퍼져 있는 지역에 살고 있는 그림 같은 열정에 휩싸여 있다. 한 사진에는 3명의 외국 저널리스트들이 그들이 말하기를 원하는 이야기의 중심인 돌이 많은 땅 맨 꼭대기에 서 있다. 다른 사진에는 지역의 항의와 항소에도 불구하고 세워진 이스라엘의 '관용과 인간 존엄성 센터'가 7세기 무슬림 공동묘지 지역에서 모습을 드러내고 있다. 비틀린 나무는 전경으로부터 솟아 있고 나뭇잎 없는 가지들은 새로운 건축지를 흐느적대며 가리키고 있다. 부엌 카운터에 아슬아슬하게 놓여 있는 사진 한 장은 1948년 전에 이 지역과 관련있는 세 명의 남자들을 잘 보여 준다. **이는 향수와 또한 삶의 증거와의 혼합이다. 여기 '한 뿌리와 그리고 장소의 의미를 갖는 한 가족의 초상화가 있다.'** 그 장소와 순간의 생각은 현지 녹화와 다른 매체와 함께 그의 작업을 확장할 수 있도록 희망하는 한 사진작가를 흥미롭게 한다.

어휘_ hurly burly 난리법석 the theater of war 전쟁의 상영장, 전쟁터 ritualized scene 의례적인 장면 vignette of an experience 경험의 소품문(비네트) A gnarled tree 비틀린 나무

1. Ⓒ
작가는 지문 속의 음영 처리된 문장에서 **웨스트 뱅크**에 관해 무엇을 암시하고 있는가?
Ⓐ 사람들은 이전의 평화로운 시간으로 돌아가기를 간절히 원한다.
Ⓑ 사진에 나오는 사람들은 더 이상 살아 있지 않다.
Ⓒ 그것은 사람들이 과거에 대한 애착과 미래에 대한 희망을 갖는다는 신호이다.
Ⓓ 역사의 모든 것은 반복된다.

2. Ⓑ
지문의 **다루기 힘든**이라는 어휘와 의미가 가장 비슷한 것은?
Ⓐ 진보적인
Ⓑ 완고한
Ⓒ 어색한
Ⓓ 비협조적인

3. Ⓒ, Ⓓ, Ⓕ
지시사항 지문을 간략하게 요약하기 위한 도입문장이 아래에 제시되어 있다. 지문에서 가장 중요한 정보를 담고 있는 3개의 선택지를 선택하여 요약을 완성한다. 지문에 제시되지 않은 정보나 세부 정보를 담고 있는 일부 문장은 요약에 들어가지 않는다. **이 문제는 2점이 주어진다.**

선택지를 관련있는 곳으로 끌어당기시오. 끌어당긴 선택지를 삭제하려면 그 위에 대고 클릭하시오. 지문을 다시 보려면 **View Text** 아이콘을 클릭하시오.

Ⓒ 사진은 웨스트 뱅크에 있는 삶의 이야기이다.
Ⓓ 여기에 표시된 사랑스러운 풍경은 웨스트 뱅크의 다른 쪽을 살펴보게 한다.
Ⓕ 사진작가는 웨스트 뱅크와의 만남을 설명해 왔다.

선택지
Ⓐ 사진은 사람들의 삶의 조용한 순간을 포착한다.
Ⓑ 사진은 그것들이 보여주는 사람들의 삶 이상의 것으로 장식되어 있다.
Ⓒ 사진은 웨스트 뱅크에 있는 삶의 이야기이다.
Ⓓ 여기에 표시된 사랑스러운 풍경은 웨스트 뱅크의 다른 쪽을 살펴보게 한다.
Ⓔ 이 풍경은 우리의 웨스트 뱅크 삶의 기대를 넘어선다.
Ⓕ 사진작가는 웨스트 뱅크와의 만남을 설명해 왔다.

04

윌리엄 셰익스피어는 워릭셔의 스트랫퍼드 어폰 에이번에서 태어났고 1564년 4월 26일에 세례를 받았다. 그의 아버지는 장갑을 만들고 모직을 파는 상인이었고 그의 어머니인 메리 아든은 잘사는 지역의 지주였다. 셰익스피어는 아마도 스트랫퍼드의 그래머 스쿨에서 교육을 받았을 것이다. 셰익스피어의 삶에 관해 다음으로 기록된 사건은 1582년에 농부의 딸이었던 앤 해서웨이와의 결혼이다. 셰익스피어 부부는 다음 해에 딸을 가지게 되었고 1585년에는 쌍둥이를 얻었다. 몇몇 학자들에 따르면 그가 연극계에서 이미 일을 하고 있었던 1592년 런던에서만 다시 나타난 것으로 보아 '잃어버린 세월'이라는 공백이 있었다고 한다. Ⓐ ■ 셰익스피어의 연기자로서의 커리어는 제임스가 왕위 계승에 성공한 1603년에 왕의 회사로 개명한 체임벌린 경의 회사와 함께했다. Ⓑ ■ 그 그룹의 연기자들 중 유명했던 사람은 리처드 버비지였다. 합작 회사는 런던의 서더크에 템스 강의 둑 근처에 있는 두 개의 극장인 더 글로

브와 블랙프라이어스에 관심을 가졌다. 셰익스피어의 시는 사우샘프턴 백작이었던 그의 후원자 헨리 라이어스리에게 바치는 두 편의 시가 1593년과 1594년에 나타나면서 그의 연극 전에 출판되었다. **셰익스피어 소네트의 대부분은 이때 작성되었을지 모른다.** ⓒ ■ **셰익스피어의 연극** 기록은 1594년에 나타나기 시작하며 그는 1611년까지 **대강** 1년에 두 편을 제작했다. 그의 가장 초창기 연극들은 『헨리 6세』와 『타이투스 안드로니카스』를 포함한다. 『한여름 밤의 꿈』, 『베니스의 상인』 그리고 『리처드 2세』는 모두 1590년 중반부터 후반까지의 작품들이다. 그의 가장 유명한 비극 작품들은 1600년대 초기에 『햄릿』, 『오셀로』, 『리어왕』 그리고 『맥베스』를 포함하여 쓰여졌다. 종종 로맨스라고 불리는 그의 말기 연극들은 1608년도부터 시작되고 『폭풍우』를 포함한다. ⓓ ■ 수집된 그의 작품의 초판은 1623년에 출판되었고 『더 퍼스트 폴리오』로 알려져 있다.

어휘_ well-to-do 잘사는. 부유한 the lost year 잃어버린 세월 *Henry VI* 「헨리 6세」 *Titus Andronicus* 「타이투스 안드로니카스」 *A Midsummer Night's Dream* 「한여름 밤의 꿈」 *The Merchant of Venice* 「베니스의 상인」 *Richard II* 「리처드 2세」 *Hamlet* 「햄릿」 *Othello* 「오셀로」 *King Lear* 「리어왕」 *Macbeth* 「맥베스」 *The Tempest* 「템페스트(폭풍우)」

1. ⓒ
다음의 문장이 지문에 추가될 수 있는 곳을 표시하는 네모 박스 [■]를 보시오.
셰익스피어 소네트의 대부분은 이때 작성되었을지 모른다.
문장이 어느 곳에 가장 적합한가?
문장을 지문에 추가하도록 한 개의 네모 박스[■]를 클릭하시오.

2. ⓓ
작가는 왜 지문에서 **셰익스피어의 연극**에 관해 언급했는가?
ⓐ 셰익스피어의 위대한 저술 작품을 강조하기 위해
ⓑ 사람들이 셰익스피어의 희곡과 시를 읽도록 설득하기 위해
ⓒ 작가이자 배우였던 셰익스피어의 천재성을 찬양하기 위해
ⓓ 셰익스피어의 삶과 업적에 대해 알리기 위해

3. ⓓ
지문의 **대강**이라는 어휘와 의미가 가장 비슷한 것은?
ⓐ 부주의하게   ⓑ 불규칙적으로 표시된
ⓒ 불편 없이   ⓓ 대략

05
영국이 현대 미술에 항상 호의적인 것은 아니었다. 대중이 야유하면서 신문도 비웃곤 했다. **'저런 것을 예술이라고 부르니'가 일반적인 평가였다.** 이제 그 반대가 사실이며 우리는 그 소

재를 충분히 얻지 못하는 것 같다. 왜 그런가? 한 가지 이유는 모든 현대 미술 갤러리가 종종 친숙하고 반기는 환경과 방식으로 훨씬 폭넓은 청중들에게 그 주제에 대해 소개하도록 도와 왔다는 것이다. 예술가들이 지난 100년 동안 우리를 눈가림해왔다는 생각은 많은 예술가들이 그들의 일이 보상을 얻는 지적 작업이라는 생각으로 바뀌면서 사라지게 되었다. 그리고 현대 미술은 과거에 역사적 문맥을 더할 뿐 아니라 신선한 발상을 불러오는 각각의 새로운 시기와 함께 계속되는 이야기이기 때문에 나는 그 주제에 관한 우리의 연관이 줄어들지 않고 늘어날 것이라 생각한다.

어휘_ pro-modern art 현대미술 sneer 비웃다. 조롱하다 jeer 야유하다 hood-winking 눈가림 dissipate 소멸하다. 사라지다 refrain 반복어구

1. ⓑ
현대 미술에 관해서 작가는 다음 중 어느 것을 가장 지지할 것 같은가?
ⓐ 영국에 있는 사람들은 현대 미술에 결코 호의적일 수 없다.
ⓑ 사람들이 현대 미술에 대한 관심을 표시하기 시작했다.
ⓒ 사람들이 미술관에 가지 않는다면 현대 미술을 좋아할 수가 없다.
ⓓ 현대 미술이 무엇인지에 대한 더 많은 논의가 진행될 것이다.
해설_ 지문의 내용은 이전에 천대받았던 현대 미술에 대한 사람들의 관심이 높아졌다는 것이므로 ⓑ가 정답이다.

2. ⓐ
다음 중 어느 것이 지문 속의 음영 처리된 문장으로부터 결론 내려질 수 있는가?
ⓐ 사람들은 그것을 예술이라고 생각하지 않았다.
ⓑ 사람들은 예술성을 더 갖고 싶었다.
ⓒ 사람들은 현대 미술 작가들이 뭐라고 했는지 이해하지 못했다.
ⓓ 사람들은 작품의 제목이 예술성을 반영한다고 생각했다.
해설_ "Call that art" was the general refrain.은 반어적 표현인 Do you call that art?(저런 것을 예술이라고 부르니?)가 refrain(반복어구)이었다는 뜻이므로 ⓐ가 정답이다.

3. **Pro Modern Art:** ⓑ, ⓔ, ⓕ /
   Anti Modern Art: ⓒ, ⓓ
선택지에서 알맞은 구를 선택하여 그것과 관련된 현대 예술에 대한 반응에 맞게 연결하시오. **이 문제는 3점이 주어진다.**

선택지를 관련있는 곳으로 끌어당기시오. 끌어당긴 선택지를 삭제하려면 그 위에 대고 클릭하시오. 지문을 다시 보려면 **View Text** 아이콘을 클릭하시오

선택지	현대 예술에 호의적	
Ⓐ 주제와 관련됨	Ⓑ 우리가 그것을 충분히 얻지 못함	
Ⓑ 우리가 그것을 충분히 얻지 못함	Ⓔ 지적 작업	
Ⓒ 대중이 야유를 함	Ⓕ 신선한 발상	
Ⓓ 우리를 눈가림하는 예술가들	현대 예술에 적대적	
Ⓔ 지적 작업	Ⓒ 대중이 야유를 함	
Ⓕ 신선한 발상	Ⓓ 우리를 눈가림하는 예술가들	
Ⓖ 일반적인 반복 어구		

해설_ 지문의 That we can't get enough of the stuff(우리가 그 소재를 충분히 얻지 못함)에서 the stuff는 pro-modern art 를 가리키므로 현대 예술에 호의적인 항목이다. 그리고 현대 예술 이 지적 작업이며 신선한 발상을 갖고 오는 새로운 시기의 이야기 라고 하였으므로 Pro Modern Art – Ⓑ, Ⓔ, Ⓕ / Anti Modern Art – Ⓒ, Ⓓ가 정답이다. 보기 Ⓖ는 일반적인 반복어구가 무슨내 용인지 빠져 있으므로 오답이다.

Vocabulary & Paraphrasing

1. 아래에 있는 각 뜻에 맞는 단어를 박스에서 찾아서 쓰시오.

① top-notch ② mythological ③ stumble
④ patron ⑤ baffling ⑥ roughly
⑦ poacher ⑧ platter ⑨ critical
⑩ refrain

2. 다음 문장을 해석 후 아래 지시대로 paraphrasing(다른 말 로 바꿔 표현하기)하세요.

① 그가 대학에 다니는 동안에 나는 작은 밴드에서 음악을 했고; 그가 양복과 넥타이를 입고 돈을 버는 동안 나는 외국 무술을 가르쳤다.

➡ 예시_ When he was in college, I played in garage bands; when he earned money making suits and ties, I was a martial arts teacher.

② 인간들은 많은 야생 동물들을 멸종시키면서 아직 남아 있는 동 물들을 '구하는' 특별한 자부심을 가지고 있다.

➡ 예시_ Humans have killed most wild animals, but now feel proud to "save" the ones that are left.

③ 우리가 문학을 의논하고 분석하는 데 어떤 중요한 전형적인 예 를 사용하건 간에 아직도 그 작품들에는 예술적인 특성이 있다.

➡ 예시_ There remains an artistic quality to literature, regardless of the critical paradigm we use to discuss and analyze it

④ 그의 가장 유명한 비극 작품들은 1600년대 초기에 햄릿」, 「오 셀로」, 「리어왕」 그리고 「맥베스」를 포함하여 쓰였다.

➡ 예시_ He wrote "Hamlet," "Othello," "King Lear" and "Macbeth" as well as some of his most famous tragedies in the early 1600s.

TOEFL iBT에 반드시 출제되는 영단어 완벽 마스터

TOEFL
필수영단어
5000

FL4U컨텐츠 저 / 128*188mm / 444쪽 / 15,000원

TOP 50 Greatest Speeches in America

미국 명연설문 베스트 ★ 50

First Inaugural Address; I Have a Dream; etc.,

김정우 저 / 170*220mm / 448쪽 / 15,000원(mp3 CD포함)

반석
TOEFL 급상한
Final Test 3

박세연, 크리스틴 한, 빅토리아 신, 최종훈 저

영단기 토플 **No.1** 최정예 강사진의
토플 최단기 완성, 최종 마무리테스트

- **박세연** Reading_ 최소단어로 독해력을 높이는 기적을 실현하다
- **크리스틴 한** Listening_ 문제 예측 스킬로 리스닝 정복을 앞당기다
- **빅토리아 신** Speaking_ 비밀 문장으로 정답을 막힘없이 토해내다
- **최종훈** Writing_ 만능 에세이로 라이팅 부담을 한방에 날리다

Bansok

박세연, 크리스틴 한, 빅토리아 신, 최종훈 저
188*258mm / 각 136, 136, 140쪽
각 10,000원(mp3 CD포함)